19.95

EDUCATION and CULTURAL PROCESS

Anthropological Approaches

Second Edition

EDUCATION
and CULTURAL
PROCESS

Anthropological Approaches
Second Edition

Edited by   **George Dearborn Spindler**
Stanford University

WAVELAND

PRESS, INC.

Prospect Heights, Illinois

For information about this book, write or call:

Waveland Press, Inc.
P.O. Box 400
Prospect Heights, Illinois 60070
(312) 634-0081

I claim the privilege, as editor, of dedicating this book to
The Women in My Life
Winifred
Corabelle
Louise
Sue
Vicki
Rebecca
Sarah

*To my father, Frank Nicholas Spindler, who taught psychology,
ethics and philosophy, and uncommon sense at Central State Teachers
College for many years,
and to students everywhere.*

George Spindler has been working on the relationship of Anthropology and Education since 1946, when he published his first article on the subject in the *Journal of Education.* Often cited as a "Father" of the field of educational anthropology, he has published, as editor and contributor, five major volumes on anthropological applications to the analysis of educational process. *Education and Cultural Process: Anthropological Approaches, Second Edition* is the sixth. These publications span more than three decades (1955-1987). He has taught both educational psychology and the social foundations of education at Stanford University, as well as introductory anthropology, cultural transmission, native North American cultures, and psychological anthropology. Recently he and Dr. Louise Spindler, his wife and collaborator, have developed new approaches to training in ethnographic methods applicable to the study of schooling and a new course in the anthropology of American culture. Together they have done field research among three American Indian communities, in Germany, and in schools in Wisconsin and California.

CONTENTS

Preface   *xvii*

Part I   Background

Preview   *2*

1 **Theory, Research and Application
   in Educational Anthropology**   **5**
   Elizabeth M. Eddy

   The Formative Years: 1925-1954   6
   The Ethnography of Childhood as
       Applied Anthropology   9
   The Stanford Conference, 1954   13
   Institutionalization and Specialization:
       1955 to the Present   15
   Educational Anthropology as
       Specialized Anthropology   17
   The Council on Anthropology
       and Education   20
   A Look Ahead   21
   References   22

2 **The Anthropology of Learning**   **26**
   Harry F. Wolcott

   Looking Back   27
   Why an "Anthropology of Learning"
       Just Now?   29
   The Anthropology of Learning:
       An Inventory   30
       Anthropology as a Resource on "Learning"   31
       Why Everyone Doesn't Learn Everything   32
       Things Learned versus the Learning Itself   32

Through Whose Efforts Does Culture Get
    Transmitted?   33
Language Acquisition as a Model for
    Cultural Acquisition   34
The Question of Innate Capacity   35
Learning "About" Versus Learning "To"   36
Intentionally in Learning   37
The Polyphasic Nature of Learning   39
The Importance of the Setting   39
The Importance of Intimacy or
    Social Distance   40
The Essential Continuity of Cultural
    Acquisition   42
The Anthropology of Learning: Some Next
    Steps and Some Cautions   42
Summary   48
References   49

3   Do Anthropologists Need Learning Theory?   **53**
George and Louise Spindler

Current Works in Anthropology   56
The Instrumental Model   57
Social Learning Theory   59
Critical Learning Periods   60
Theories of Teaching   64
Conclusion   66
References   67

4   Roots Revisited: Three Decades of Perspective   **70**
George D. Spindler

Concern Number One: The Search for a
    Rationale and Encompassing Philosophy   71
Concern Number Two: Sociocultural
    Contextualization   72
Concern Number Three: Education and
    the Life Cycle   74
Concern Number Four: Intercultural Learning
    and Understanding   75
Finale   76

5   Thirty-three Years as A Marginal Native   **78**
George D. Spindler

Biography   78
Analysis   82
Recommendations   84

Part II   Some Foundations of Primate Learning

Preview   86

6   **Community and Hominid Emergence**   89
    Solon T. Kimball

    References   95

7   **Primate Biology and Behavior:
    A Stimulus to Educational Thought and Policy**   97
    Marion Lundy Dobbert and Betty Cooke

    Introduction—Why Primates? 97
    Biology and Learning in Primates   99
    The Social Nature of Primates   102
    Peers and Older Playmates   104
    The Learning Process in Primates   106
    Summary and Conclusions   109
    References   113

Part III   Approaches to the Study of Schools

Preview   118

8   **The School and Its Community Context:
    The Methodology of a Field Study**   120
    Richard L. Warren

    Background for the Selection of a Site   121
    Selecting a Site   122
    Developing the Study of the School   123
    Developing the Study of the Community   128
    Questions of Procedure and Data Analysis   132
    Conclusions   134

9   **The Teacher as an Enemy**   136
    Harry F. Wolcott

    Antagonistic Acculturation   137
    Classroom Learning Kwakiutl Style—
        as Seen by the Teacher   138
    Classroom Learning Kwakiutl Style—
        as Seen by the Pupils   141
    The Teacher as an Enemy   144
    Conclusion   148
    References and Further Reading   149

10 **Ethnography: An Anthropological View**   151
    George and Louise Spindler

    What Do Ethnographers Study? 151
    In a Nutshell   153

What is Education   153
Good Ethnography   154
Concepts Precede Method   155

Part IV   **Education and Cultural Process in the United States**

Preview   158

11   **Why Have Minority Groups in North America Been Disadvantaged by Their Schools?**   **160**
George D. Spindler

Is Harlem School?   160
At Rosepoint?   163
In the Mopass Residential School?   165
Is There a Way Out of the Dilemma?   168
References   172

12   **Achieving School Failure: An Anthropological Approach to Illiteracy and Social Stratification**   **173**
Ray McDermott

Abstract   173
Introduction   173
The Ontogeny of Pariah Minorities   174
The Social Organization of Status and
      the Politics of Everyday Life   179
A Biobehavioral Ethnography of
      Reading Disabilities   184
Perception   190
Language Structure and Function   191
Attitudes   194
Ethnographic Summary   194
Biculturation and Acquisition of Pariah Status   195
Communicative Code Differences and the
      Inhibition of School Learning   197
Black-White Communicative Code Differences   199
Identity and Mobility   202
Summary   203
References   204

13   **Education and Communitarian Societies— The Old Order Amish and the Hutterian Brethren**   **210**
John A. Hostetler

World View and Social Structure   211
Similarities in World View   211
The Amish Community   212
The Hutterite Community   213

The Areas of Tension and Defensive Structuring   214
   Amish Education   215
   Amish Controls Over the Socialization Process   218
   Hutterite Education   219
   Hutterite Control Over the
      Socialization Process   222
Assimilation and Disruption Patterns   223
   Patterns of Mobility in Amish Society   224
   Patterns of Mobility in Hutterite Society   225
Conclusions   226
References   228

**14   Beth Ann—A Case Study of Culturally
Defined Adjustment and Teacher Perceptions   230**
George D. Spindler

The Classroom and Beth Anne's Place in It   231
The Evidence   232
   Observations   233
   Psychological Test Results   233
   Sociometric Results   236
   Home Visit and Parent Interview   237
   Teachers' Responses to the Evidence   240
   Interpretation   241
   Conclusion   243
   References   244

**15   The Elementary School Principal:
Notes from a Field Study   245**
Harry F. Wolcott

The Ethnographic Approach   246
Methods in Fieldwork   248
   Enumeration and Census Data   248
   Participant Observation   249
   Informant Interviewing   250
From the Field Notes: Proceedings of
   the Principal Selection Committee   252
   Mr. Seventh   255
   Mr. Fifth   256
   Mr. Fourth   260
   Mr. Third   261
   Mr. Second   262
   Mr. First   264
Discussion and Comments   266
   Lack of Professional Knowledge
      Associated With the Role   267
   An Esteem for Personal Feelings   268
   A Proclivity toward "Variety-
      Reducing" Behavior   269

Conclusion   270
References and Further Reading   272

16   Playing by the Rules   **274**
Margaret A. Gibson

The Punjabi Case   275
Conclusion   279
References   280

17   The Culture of Competition in American Schools   **282**
Shelley V. Goldman
Ray McDermott

The Use of Competition In American Schools   284
   The Competitive Life at Allwin School   286
Confronting Competitive Pressures in an
   Alternative Public School   290
The Promise of Looking To the
   Inner-City Community   291
Insuring Success Insures Success   295
   Exterminating Illiteracy   296
Conclusion   298
References   298

**Part V   Cultural Process in Education
                 Viewed Transculturally**   **301**

Preview   302

18   The Transmission of Culture   **303**
George D. Spindler

What Are Some of the Ways That
   Culture Is Transmitted?   303
This Is How It Is In Palau   304
How Is It Done In Ulithi?   306
What Is It Like To Be Initiated In Hano?   311
What Happens in Gopalpur?   315
And among the Eskimo?   316
In Sensuron?   318
How Goes It in Guadalcanal?   321
How Do They Listen in Demirciler?   324
What Does Cultural Transmission Do
   for the System?   326
Modernizing Cultures: What Is the
   Purpose of Education?   327
Conclusion   332
References and Further Reading   333

Contents   xiii

Preview—Part A: Traditional non-literate societies 335

19 **Instruction and Affect in Hopi Cultural Continuity**   337
    Dorothy Eggan

        References 355

20 **Contrasts between Prepubertal and
    Postpubertal Education**   359
    C.W.M. Hart

        Prepubertal and Postpubertal Education—
            How Do They Differ? 361
            Regulation 361
            Personnel 364
            Atmosphere 368
            Curriculum 369
        Conclusion 371
        References 377

21 **Some Discontinuities in the Enculturation
    of Mistassini Cree Children**   378
    Peter S. Sindell

        Self-reliance and Dependence 380
        Interpersonal Relations 381
        Cooperation and Competition 382
        Expression and Inhibition of Aggression 382
        Role Expectations for Children 383
        Conclusions 385
        References 386

Preview—Part B: Complex modern societies 387

22 **In Prospect for a Controlled Cross- Cultural
    Comparison of Schooling: Schoenhausen and Roseville**   389
    George and Louise Spindler

        Introduction 389
        Schoenhausen, Germany and Roseville, USA 390
        Methodology 392
            The Use of Film in Reflective
                Crosscultural Interviewing 393
            To Sum Up 396
            Work to be Done 397
        Final Comment 398
        Acknowledgements 399
        References 399

**23 Learning in Rural Communities:
Cognitive Development in Norway and Hungary   401**
Marida Hollos

Introduction   401
Cross-Cultural Findings on Rural-
    Urban Differences in Cognitive Growth   402
    Piagetian Research   402
    Linguistic Development   405
    Summary   405
    Logical Operations and Social Cognitions   406
Learning in Norway   408
    The farm child   409
Village and Town Children   415
    The Cognitive Tests   417
    Results   418
Cognitive Development in Three
    Hungarian Communities   421
Conclusion   426
References   428

**24 Social Typing at Hanseong Elementary:
A Transcultural Model of Social Bias Schooling   430**
James H. Robinson

The Cultural Contexts   430
Education and Society   431
Hanseong Elementary School   432
The Model of Social Typing   434
The Results of the Statistical Analyses   435
The Ethnographic Analysis   438
Teacher-Student Interactions   441
    Peer Interactions   445
    Education in Asia and American:
        toward a transcultural model   448
References   449

**25 Seishin Kyōiku in a Japanese Bank:
A Description of Methods and Consideration of
Some Underlying Concepts   451**
Thomas P. Rohlen

Roto   453
Endurance Walk   456
Some Considerations for the
    Anthropology of Education   458

Part VI   The Teaching of Anthropology

Preview   464

26   **Transcultural Sensitization**   **467**
     George D. Spindler

        The Technique and Its Results   468
        Conclusions   477
        Implications   479
        References   479

27   **An Experimental Ninth-Grade Anthropology Course**   **481**
     Paul Bohannan
     Merwyn S. Garbarino
     Earle W. Carlson

        First Quarter: Cultural and Social Anthropology   483
        Second Quarter: Human Origins and Prehistory   486
        Third Quarter: Comparative Civilizations   488
        The Following Two Years   490
        Conclusions   491
        References   494

28   **Teaching and Learning Anthropology:**
     The Case Study Approach   **496**
     George and Louise Spindler

        The Introductory Course in
            Sociocultural Anthropology   497
            Type 1   498
            Type 2   498
            Type 3   499
            Implementation   501
        To Summarize   503
        References   504

PREFACE

This volume really began with the publication of *Education and Anthroplogy in 1955* (Stanford University Press). That book was an edited version of a 4-day conference seminar in Carmel Valley, California supported by the Carnegie Foundation and organized by George and Louise Spindler. Twelve prominent anthropologists and as many prominent educators exchanged papers and views on topics that still concern us (see Chapter Four). One chapter from that volume, C.W.M. Hart's classic paper on prepubertal and postpuberal education survives in this book. Eight years later (1963) *Education and Culture: Anthropological Approaches* was published by Holt, Rinehart and Winston under G. Spindler's editorship. The first edition of *Education and Cultural Process* was published by Holt, Rinehart and Winston in 1974. The revision of that book, the present volume, contains fourteen new chapters. These new chapters represent significant recent developments and issues in our field. The fourteen chapters retained from the 1974 edition represent established areas in the anthropology of education.

Each of the six parts of this volume are arranged around certain themes. Part 1 presents both the history of our field and contemporary issues about education as cultural transmission and the learning of culture. Part 2 is about non-human primate antecedents to human culture and its acquisition. Part 3 includes three chapters that sample how anthropologists study education. Part 4 deals with education and cultural process in a wide variety of schools and their communities in the United States. Part 5 looks in depth at education as cultural transmission in nine different cultures and many more in the introductory discussion of cultural transmission. Part 6 attends to the teaching of anthropology at the high school and introductory college course level.

Anthropology is comprised of several major areas—biological, archeological, linguistic, and cultural—and many divisions of these. Some workers distinguish a social from a cultural anthropology, but for most American anthropologists the latter term covers both the social and cultural dimensions. In this book we are concerned with some of the significant ways in which the concepts, methods, and information subsumed by cultural anthropology can be applied to the analysis of educational process.

This diversity of interests, skills, and knowledge is one of the primary assets of anthropology and makes anthropological analyses different from those of psychology and sociology. Certainly no anthropologist controls the essen-

xvii

tial knowledge in all the major fields and topical areas. But most cultural anthropologists are *aware* of these fields and areas and of some of the significant ideas and findings in them. This awareness makes a difference in the way anthropologists study phenomena and what they make of their study. There is an eclecticism, an eagerness for new approaches, a willingness to borrow from other disciplines, and a manner of seeing relationships that are more often left unrelated and unseen, that seem less characteristic of other disciplines.

The transcultural perspective is also a special feature of anthropology. Every anthropologist reads about other ways of life both casually and professionally, often in great detail and breadth, and puts the information into a more or less systematic frame of reference, so the data are not mere curiosa. One's fieldwork is nearly always in a cultural context other than one's own, and usually in a language one has had to learn. The transcultural experience makes one view behavior differently—it may even make one a different kind of person. The transcultural context is one of the factors that makes the treatment of the topics covered here anthropological, for the topics themselves are not the exclusive domain of anthropology. The transcultural perspective is not always made explicit in data presentation and analysis. It is present, however, even when—perhaps particularly when—the anthropologist studies his or her own culture.

This book is intended as a text in the anthropology of education, for courses and seminars that utilize anthropological materials and perspectives in the analysis of educative processes. These courses and seminars are offered to both the upper-division undergraduate and the first- or second-year graduate student. Some are given in schools of education, others in departments of anthropology. Many are listed in both, as they are at Stanford. This book may also be used as a text or collateral reading in the cultural foundations of education, the sociology of education, in teacher-training and curricular courses, and in other foundational areas, such as philosophy, history, and psychology, as well as in applied anthropology and cultural dynamics courses that are in part concerned with education. It must therefore serve a wide range of interests and expertise in both anthropology and education. It is designed with this diverse audience in mind. Anthropology lends itself comfortably to this use.

G.D.S.
Calistoga, California
1986

PART I

Background

Preview
1. ELIZABETH EDDY   *Theory, Research, and Application in Educational Anthropology*
2. HARRY WOLCOTT   *The Anthropology of Learning*
3. GEORGE and LOUISE SPINDLER   *Do Anthropologists Need Learning Theory?*
4. GEORGE SPINDLER   *Roots Revisited: Three Decades of Perspective*
5. GEORGE SPINDLER   *Thirty-three Years as a Marginal Native*

PREVIEW

Educational Anthropology or the anthropology of education, (either one sounds awkward) has as long a history as anthropology itself. Our anthropological ancestors were interested in education and during the formative years of the 1920's and 1930's, most notable cultural anthropologists had something to say about education, and said it well. Elizabeth Eddy, in the first chapter of this section, outlines major stages in the history of our sub-discipline. It is important for us to know that educational anthropology is not an upstart field of recent interest without roots in the mainstream of anthropological inquiry and thought. Though there may be some tendency in contemporary work to detach educational anthropology from the rest of the discipline, the history of our sub-discipline is embedded in the history of anthropology, and if we have a future, it will continue to be so.

There is a tendency for fellow anthropologists to think of educational anthropology as applied anthropology. There is, it is true, a strong amelioration tionist orientation, as Ted Brameld would say it, in our field, but educational anthropology is, and must be, more than applied anthropology. I do not mean to suggest that an applied label is demeaning. Far from it. But to apply anthropological concepts, perspectives, methods of research, guiding models and paradigms, and interpretive principles to the process of education in our own society and abroad, requires that theory and practice be joined. We cannot be guided alone by the demands of our society for the solution of immediate educational problems. We must maintain a disciplinary posture and approach the study of problems in a disciplinary manner with appropriate tools. This first section provides background for how anthropologists talk about and study educational processes.

My presidential address for the Council of Anthropology and Education follows. Eddy describes the 1954 Stanford Conference as culminating previous developments in the field and inaugurating new developments. I extract four major concerns from the 1954 Conference and comment on the state of the art today in their light. My persuasion is more toward the development of a conceptual, some would say theoretical ordering, of the phenomena of education, and less toward applied.

In the next chapter Harry Wolcott takes up a long-standing argument always present, though often only implicitly, in our formulations of what we are studying when we study education. My position has consistently been that we are primarily concerned with cultural transmission. Wolcott feels that this position overlooks what takes place as individuals acquire their culture. There can be no argument that denies that individuals must learn as well as be taught their culture and I have assumed this to be the case. This assumption, however, leaves important work unfinished, and Wolcott shows us some of what we must do if we are to explore the terrain left unexplored.

My purpose as one of the founders of the field has been to give the anthropology of education a focus by defining our special area to be cultural transmission. I go further now in claiming that we are primarily concerned, as a discipline, with *intentional intervention* in the learning process. The reason why children don't learn everything, a question that Fred Gearing has raised, is that all societies intervene, literally *interfere,* with what children are learning at critical points throughout the entire developmental process. These interventions—from weaning and toilet training to kindergarten, to instruction in high school, occupational training, to the rituals of death—never teach what they are intended to teach—for human beings never learn only one thing at a time. Concomitant learning always takes place. In internally consistent cultural systems the concomitant and intended learning will be at least congruent. In internally inconsistent or disintegrating cultural systems the intended and concomitant will often be at odds. Wolcott's essay, and the next chapter by G. & L. Spindler, explore the complex relationship between cultural transmission and the learning of culture. If we are to attend to the learning of culture rather than, or in addition to the transmission of culture as a focus of an anthropology of education, as Wolcott suggests, we must appraise the models of learning that psychologists have developed, for psychology has a long history of attention to learning. Our chapter asks the question "do anthropologists need learning theory?". Are the models developed by the psychologists appropriate to our use? The answers we leave to the reader to discover.

In the last chapter in this section I allude to my own career biography as an anthropologist in a professional school of education. This is the milieu in which most of the anthropology of education is being done at present. Though there are a few anthropologists in departments of anthropology who study schools, and more who do research in the training of children and youth cross-culturally, the greatest share of education-relevant work and dissemination of findings will be done in the professional education contest. This creates some problems, for professional anthropologists are not trained to be professional educators, and professional educators are not trained in, or have often not even been exposed to anthropology. This chapter describes how it worked out for one anthropologist. Though my experience is to some degree unique, it exhibits several common elements with the experiences of others.

The five chapters of Part I cover critical issues of contemporary educational anthropology as well as an overview of the history of the field. It provides useful background for the rest of the book.

The Editor

ELIZABETH M. EDDY/*University of Florida*

1 Theory, Research, and Application in Educational Anthropology

Educational anthropology, usually referred to as anthropology and education, has developed within the context of the rise of anthropology as a profession. The transition of anthropology from an avocation pursued by the independently wealthy or those who made their living in other fields into a profession that provides a livelihood for its practitioners did not occur until the early years of this century. The process of professionalization required the establishment of the discipline within reputable universities, the anthropological training of students who subsequently would support themselves by work in this field, and the increased production of scientific research and publications that were sufficiently technical to be comprehensible primarily to fellow practitioners.[1]

Substantial growth in the number of professional anthropologists is a post-World War II phenomenon. In the United States, the postwar years were accompanied by unprecedented changes in the funding of anthropologists and their careers, intense expansion of specialization within the discipline, and a proliferation of professional associations and journals organized by and for specialized interest groups.

Educational anthropologists represent one of many interests groups but, unlike some specialists, their historical roots date from the late 19th century when anthropology emerges as a science. An important reason for the long history of anthropological interest in education is that the process of professionalization was intertwined inevitably with the promotion of the discipline as a legitimate and needed new area of scientific teaching within

---

[1]Langham (1981:245) recently has schematized the criteria for professionalism in science as follows: (1) rigorous training by compenent practitioners of the discipline; (2) earning a living on the basis of one's contributions to the subject; (3) the propagation of one's scientific contributions by training students who will earn their living from the subject; (4) the utilization or establishment of whatever institutions are necessary to fulfill the second and third criteria; (5) the production of scientific contributions that are sufficiently technical as to be understandable only to a group of fellow practitioners which therefore functions as the exclusive judge and audience for one's work.

institutions of higher education. Yet as early as the late 1800's, a few anthropologists were concerned with the practice of education outside the academy. It was then that the potential contributions of anthropology to pedagogy, the school curriculum, and an understanding of the culture of childhood were first recognized (Barnes and Barnes 1896; Chamberlain 1896; Fletcher 1888; Stevenson 1887; Vandewalker 1898). Prior to World War I the fullest and most widely known statement along these lines was that of Maria Montessori, whose *Pedagogical Anthropology* was published in the United States in 1913.

The early beginnings of educational anthropology are important, but contemporary educational anthropology is primarily the outgrowth of social and cultural anthropology as it developed during the 1920's. For this reason, the focus here is on signigicant relationships between the growth of professionalism in anthropology and the development of educational anthropology as an area of specialization within the discipline during the past 60 years. The historical trends in educational anthropology throughout this period will be divided into two time periods: the formative years, 1925-1954; the institutionalization and specialization years, 1955 to the present.

I argue below that the Conference on Anthropology and Education convened at Stanford in 1954 and the formal organization of the Council on Anthropology and Education in 1970 marked major turning points in the history of educational anthropology. Each event culminated previous developments and inaugurated new ones in the field. But these events also mirrored important shifts in professional anthropology as a whole. The changes represented more than the replacement of older theories and research methodologies with newer ones. In addition, they reflected important changes in the sources of economic support for anthropological work, modifications in the relationship of anthropology to applied problems, and more elaborated definitions of the meaning of professionalism.

The factual material and analysis presented here are preliminary at best. A history of educational anthropology has yet to be written, and the history of anthropology itself is only beginning to be documented adequately.[2] Thus the pages to follow provide but a sketch of a much longer story that requires extensive scholarly endeavor and documentation before it can be told fully.

The Formative Years: 1925-1954

An examination of the Roberts and Akinsanya chronological bibliographies on anthropological studies of childhood and anthropology and

---

[2]To the best of my knowledge, the most extensive work in the history of educational anthropology is being done by Joan I. Roberts, who is preparing a book on this topic. My article has benefitted from her unpublished manuscript titled "Anthropology and Education."

education reveals a remarkable array of anthropologists who engaged in research related to formalized systems of education and the enculturation of the child during the years between 1925 and 1954 (1976:375-412; see also Roberts, n.d.). The roster reads like a *Who's Who* of American and British founders of modern anthropology. Luminaries include Gregory Bateson, Ruth Benedict, Franz Boas, John Dollard, John Embree, E.E. Evans-Pritchard, Raymond Firth, Meyer Fortes, John Gillin, Alexander Goldenweiser, Felix Keesing, Melville Herskovits, H. Ian Hogbin, Ralph Linton, Bronislaw Malinowski, Margaret Mead, Siegfried Nadel, Morris Opler, Hortense Powdermaker, Paul Radin, Robert Redfield, Audrey Richards, Edward Sapir, Laura Thompson, W. Lloyd Warner, Mark Hanna Watkins, Camilla Wedgewood, John Whiting, Monica Wilson, and others.

With the exception of Boas and Malinowski, these notables began their careers after anthropology had broken with 19th century unilineal evolution and the extreme diffusionist theories of Grafton Elliot Smith, W. J. Perry, and Fritz Graebner. In England, the publication in 1922 of Malinowski's *Argonauts of the Western Pacific* and Radcliffe-Brown's *The Andaman Islanders* ushered in "practical" or "applied" anthropology, the terms subsequently used by Malinowski (1929) and Radcliffe-Brown (1930), respectively, to denote the emergence of social anthropology as a new branch of the discipline. For both Malinowski and Radcliffe-Brown, there was a close relationship between theoretical and practical applied anthropology. Oriented toward the study of human behavior and institutions in the contemporary world, they argued that the scientific knowledge produced by this type of study would be capable of application by those concerned with the practical problems of planning administrative and educational policies for native populations in the British colonies.

In the United States, Franz Boas' choice of the study of adolescence among a primitive people for Margaret Mead's fieldwork in 1925 marked a similar transition of the discipline into the study of a new set of problems related to the modern world. In *Coming of Age in Samoa* (1928), Mead argued the value of comparing American civilization with "simpler" societies in order to illuminate our own methods of education. By the mid-1930s the study of culture and personality was well established in American anthropology. Mead and other leaders in this field gave considerable attention to the practical relevance of their work to educational problems.

On both sides of the Atlantic, the internal intellectual developments that foreshadowed the florescence of modern social and cultural anthropology were influenced significantly by a transformation in the institutional framework within which the discipline developed after 1920. The major changes were modification in the economic base for funding anthropological research, the growth of an interdisciplinary movement in the social sciences, and the academic expansion of anthropology within universities (Stocking 1976:9-13). These changes were interrelated and greatly facilitated by the liberal funding provided by American foundations for the development of the social sciences, including British social anthropology and the redirection of cultural anthropology in the United States.

The Rockefeller Foundation played the major role by making the support of the social sciences the chief objective of the Laura Spelman Rockefeller Memorial Fund. These monies provided unprecedented funding for the creation of facilities for social science research both at home and abroad and the fellowship monies for the training of able persons working in the social sciences. Important roles also were played by the Carnegie, Phelps-Stokes, Julius Rosenwald, Macy, and other philanthropic agencies. The foundations were instrumental in bringing together anthropologists and other social scientists for the investigation of practical social problems related to topics such as race, immigration, the development of colonial peoples, the consequences of intercultural contact, and the impact of social change. They fostered the international exchange of scholars, which, in the case of anthropology, brought Malinowski, Radcliffe-Brown, and others to American universities as lecturers who diffused new ideas and perspectives into the American version of the discipline.[3]

Within American universities, the linkage of anthropology to the social sciences was expressed organizationally in the formation of new departments in combination with sociology during the 1930s — a common practice until well after World War II. In England, the London School of Economics was already a model of an interdisciplinary college devoted to teaching and research in the social sciences and had been so since its founding by Sydney and Beatrice Webb in 1895. It was there that Malinowski received his training in ethnology prior to World War I and conducted his world-renowned seminars during the 1920s and 1930s.

At this time, anthropology was a young science, and those who entered it typically came by a roundabout way after professional training and experience in other fields. Many of the leaders were the offspring of professionals in other disciplines. For some, interdisciplinary growth and development occurred as a consequence of marriage. For example, Malinowski was the son of an eminent linguist who had done work in Polish ethnography and folklore. Malinowski himself received a doctorate in physics and mathematics at the University of Cracow before beginning postgraduate work at the London School of Economics in 1910 (Firth 1981:101). Margaret Mead was the daughter of an economist father and sociologist mother and completed an M.A. in psychology before entering the graduate program in anthropology at

---

[3]Comments about the role of American foundations in the building of the social sciences are based on my own current, archival research on the history of applied anthropology in Britain, reading of secondary sources, and discussions with Lawrence Kelly. The impact of American foundations on anthropology at the London School of Economics is thoroughly presented by Fisher (1977).

Columbia. Her first husband, Luther Cressman, was a graduate student in sociology and an ordained Episcopal clergyman at the time of their marriage. Her second and third husbands, Reo Fortune and Gregory Bateson, were British-trained social anthropologists (Mead 1972:passim). Meyer Fortes, a native of South Africa, held a Ph.D. in psychology and had professional experience in the first Child Guidance Clinic established in England before undertaking postgraduate training in anthropology under Malinowski, Firth, and Seligman at the London School of Economics in the 1930s (Fortes 1978:2-3). Others in this period represented similar anticipatory socialization patterns that undoubtedly influenced their later professional contributions to anthropology as a social science and to work in interdisciplinary groups.

In summary, the formative years of educational anthropology occurred within the context of disciplinary developments in theory and research methodology that advanced anthropological studies of contemporary peoples in a rapidly changing world. A foundation-based economic support system gave high priority to the development of the social sciences because of their potential contribution to a scientific approach to the management of critical social problems. Within anthropology, the Rockefeller and other foundations were supportive especially of those who were leaders in the new social anthropology in Britain and the redirection of cultural anthropology in the United States. The foundations specifically fostered interdisciplinary relationships among social scientists and between them and those in other professions who were engaged in what a later generation would call the administration and delivery of human services. A major result of these trends was the definition of the social sciences as applied sciences. Thus, to be a modern social and cultural anthropologist during these years also was to be an applied anthropologist. Many who entered the profession at this time brought past experiences congruent with these trends, and a remarkable number of them gave attention to educational processes and problems.

The Ethnography of Childhood as Applied Anthropology

The application of anthropology to education during this period emphasized several themes. At the theoretical level, anthropologists challenged Freud, Piaget, Watson, and others who generalized about human development and behavior and ignored data about cross-cultural variations that anthropologists were beginning to assemble. During the 1920s and 1930s, the eugenics movement was strong and anthropologists actively refuted those who claimed that human behavior was determined biologically. These debates over theory were more than academic. At the time, they were major controversies over conceptions about the intellectual nature of the child and they had important implications for educational policy.

Between the mid-1920s and the mid-1950s, anthropological research related to child development increased rapidly, not only in then remote parts of the world such as Africa and Oceania, but also in the United States. During the 1930s, for example, American anthropologists participated in the work of several commissions established by the Progressive Education Association with the support of funds from the General Education Board (Rockefeller Foundation) and the Carnegie Corporation. Their activities included the development of proposals and materials for revising the social studies curriculum in secondary schools, and the initiation of intensive studies of adolescents, their school life, and the communities in which they lived. In addition, anthropologists participated in the 1934 Hanover Conference on Human Relations that carried forward inquiries into the enculturation and socialization of the child that began with the Seminar on the Impact of Culture on Personality in 1930 at Yale under the direction of Edward Sapir and John Dollard. The Hanover Conference formulated an unpublished outline that guided investigations and educational programs such as those of the Progressive Education Association (Frank 1955).

The application of fieldwork methodologies to the study of American communities began in the late 1920s and produced classic studies which revealed that within American society there are diversities of enculturation and participation in formal educational systems related to differences in race, ethnicity, and social class (Davis, Gardner, and Gardner 1941; Dollard 1937; Drake and Cayton 1945; Gillin 1948; Hollingshead 1949; Johnson 1941; Lynd and Lynd 1929,1937; Warner 1942; Warner and Lunt 1941; Warner, Havighurst, and Loeb 1944; West 1945). During the 1930s, a few American anthropologists also were involved with the educational problems of Native Americans. As employees of the Bureau of Indian Affairs, they wrote historical and ethnographic texts for use in Indian schools and developed orthographies for use in bilingual school texts (Kennard and MacGregor 1958:832-835).

Along with professionals trained in psychology, psychiatry, and medicine, anthropologists participated in a six-year cooperative social action research program on Indian personality, education, and administration. This program was initiated in 1941 by the United States Department of the Interior and Commissioner of Indian Affairs John Collier. It was established first in cooperation with the Committee on Human Development at the University of Chicago and later with the Society for Applied Anthropology. An inter-disciplinary study of 1,000 Indian children in 12 reservations representing 5 tribes, the project was oriented toward the collection of scientific data that later became the basis for preparing recommendations to improve federal policies in Indian administration and educational programs (Kennard and MacGregor 1953:835; Thompson 1951). After World War II, the application of ethnographic studies of children to federal policies continued to be a major concern among some anthropologists who joined with other social scientists and played an influential role in the 1954 U.S. Supreme Court *Brown v. Board of Education of Topeka* decision (Kluger 1976:passim).

The involvement of anthropologists with matters of public policy related to education was not confined to the United States. In England during the 1920s, intensive efforts of a small but extraordinarily influential group of leading missionaries, educators, members of Parliament, colonial officers, and others succeeded in attracting the active participation of the Phelps-Stokes Fund and the Carnegie Corporation in seeking better solutions to the problems of education in Africa.[4] These and other philanthropic organizations long had been engaged in attempts to improve schooling for Negroes in the South, and the British sought models based on this experience that might be relevant to African education in rural areas. Under the leadership of Thomas Jesse Jones, an American sociologist who had conducted a survey of Negro education in the South (Jones 1917) and was the educational director of the fund, the Phelps-Stokes Fund supported two major surveys of African education. The first Phelps-Stokes Commission visited West and South Africa in 1920-21; three years later, the second Commission went to East, Central, and South Africa (Jones 1922-1925).

In 1923 an Advisory Committee on Native Education in Tropical Africa was established in London by the Secretary of State for the Colonies. This committee was instrumental in fostering greater political concern with African education and supportive of developing innovative approaches based on scientific knowledge. One consequence of these activities was that in 1925 the Carnegie Foundation made the first of many grants to African education and provided funds to the Kenya Education Department for the development of a Jeanes school to train supervisors for village schools. (The name "Jeanes" was taken from the name attached to itinerant supervisors of rural Negro schools in the American South because initial monies used to support this program there had been provided by the privately endowed Jeanes Fund in the United States.)

Philanthropic American efforts in African education during the 1930s and 1940s were extensive and represented what was then considered to be the best thought on educating the "backward races" as well as an exportation to Africa of the philosophy of industrial and vocational education that had been instituted at Tuskeegee, the Hampton Institute, and other southern schools. Even at the time, the philosophy was controversial within American education, and later historical events demonstrated clearly that it appraised inadequately the educational needs and aspirations of both African and American blacks. Yet during the interwar years, the programs often were innovative and brought educational resources to Africa and to the South that otherwise would not have been forthcoming.

Those who were instrumental in turning British attention to the problem of education in Africa during the early 1920s later became key figures in the

---

[4]See Berman (1970) and Heyman (1970) for full accounts of the role of the Phelps-Stokes Fund and the Carnegie Corporation in African education at this time.

founding of the International Institute of African Languages and Cultures in 1926. Assisted by grants from the Laura Spelman Rockefeller Memorial Fund, and subsequently from the Rockefeller Foundation, the Institute was based in London, but represented an international effort on the part of missionaries, linguists, government officials, educators, and others to achieve a scientifically based understanding of Africa and its native peoples and institutions. From the beginning, both Seligman and Malinowski played an important role in the Institute, but it was the latter who became the more extensively involved in developing the Institute's anthropological research program by training the first generation of anthropologists to undertake modern ethnographic field studies in Africa. Nearly all the early studies on childhood development in African societies are a direct result of Malinowski's working relationships with the Institute and his training of anthropologists, missionaries, educators, and others in ethnographic field methods.[5]

Similar to developments in the United States, what began as ethnographies of childhood and the effects of culture and other environmental factors on children was applied to educational problems, especially those that resulted from culture contact. Malinowski himself traveled to South Africa in 1934 to address the New Education Fellowship, an international conference on progressive education attended by anthropologists, educators, and missionaries who were committed deeply to the need of Western educators to take indigenous native systems of education into account when formulating educational policies (Malinowski 1936). Further, upon his return to England, Malinowski became involved directly in the support of modifications in a particular school in South Africa so that changes could occur that would apply anthropological data to the formal educational system. The theme was echoed in the pages of *Africa*, the official journal of the Institute, by Malinowski's students and by others writing throughout the 1930s and 1940s.

During the same summer of 1934, while Malinowski was in Africa, Radcliffe-Brown was in New Haven giving lectures on comparative sociology. The occasion was a conference titled "Education and Culture Contacts" convened at Yale under the leadership of Charles Loram, who then chaired the Department of Culture Contacts and Race Relations in the Yale Institute of Human Relations. Funded by the Carnegie Corporation, the conference participants included directors of education, inspectors of schools, missionaries, government officials, social workers, and foundation representatives from the West Indies, India, the Philippines, Great Britain, China, and the United States. The major theme was the need to adapt education to individual and community needs rather than to transfer Western educational practices

---

[5]The importance of Malinowski in developing anthropology and education has been grossly overlooked in America. My statements about his contributions are based on archival materials at the London School of Economics that I only have begun to analyze.

wholesale (Heyman 1970: 126-129). Two years later, in 1936, Felix Keesing organized a five-week study conference at the University of Hawaii that brought together 66 educators and social scientists from 27 nations to examine problems of education and adjustment among peoples of the Pacific (Keesing 1937).

After the war, Margaret Mead helped organize a 1949 conference on "The Educational Problems of Special Cultural Groups" at Teachers College in New York. Sponsored by Teachers College, the Carnegie Corporation, and the General Education Board, this conference was attended by colonial educators from the British Africa territories and American educators from the South in order to discuss the education of Negros in the United States and Africa. In terms of Anglo-American relations, this conference represents a turning point. It marked the end of the era in which attempts were made to apply the experience of American Negro education in the South to the problems of African education (Heyman 1970: 135-148).

The Stanford Conference, 1954

This summary of selected highlights in the history of educational anthropology between the 1920s and the late 1940s is sufficient to reveal the primary trends in the field at this time. The major research focus was on studies of childhood and youth in a wide variety of societies including the United States. These data often, but not always, were gathered within the context of broadly based ethnographies or community studies in which data about children and educational processes were only a portion of the total data collected. In the United States, the rise of "culture and personality" as a widely recognized area of scientific inquiry promoted the growth of interest in cross-cultural studies of childhood. In Britain, the impetus came from those who foresaw the strategic importance of education in a rapidly changing empire. Both at home and abroad, American foundations and a few government officials were instrumental in nurturing an emphasis on interdisciplinary collaboration and the application of research to public policy in education.

Anthropological contributions to education during the 1930s and 1940s were impressive. However, as Margaret Mead later observed, the interplay between anthropology and education had been largely "dependent upon personalities rather than any on-going institutionalized process of any sort" (quoted in Spindler 1955:29). The occasion of her remark was the 1954 Stanford Conference on Education and Anthropology, which partially summarized prior developments in the field but also set new directions for the future. A recent retrospective article by Spindler summarizes four major concerns that were thematic throughout the conference: "the search for a philosophical as well as a theoretical articulation of education and anthropology; the necessity for sociocultural contextualization of the educative process; the relation of education to 'culturally phrased' phases of the life cycle; the nature of intercultural understanding and learning" (Spindler 1984:4).

Cast in an exploratory framework, the conference was designed explicitly to address the frontiers of the relationships between the two fields rather than to evaluate what had been done in the past. At the time of the conference, there was no such thing as "educational anthropology" and, as Spindler notes, the conference did not aim to create it (Spindler 1955:5). The status of the field was evident in the then recent compendium *Anthropology Today* (1953) edited by Kroeber, which did not include education in the index despite the attention given to the role of anthropologists in the educational programs of the Bureau of Indian Affairs (Kennard and MacGregor 1953:834-835) and UNESCO (Metraux 1953:886-890) and the inclusion of an article by Mary Hass titled "The Application of Linquistics to Language Teaching" (1953).

The Stanford Conference was funded by the Carnegie Corporation and coordinated by George Spindler, who had accepted a joint appointment as Associate Professor in the School of Education and in the Department of Sociology and Anthropology at Stanford after receiving his Ph.D. in anthropology, sociology, and psychology at UCLA in 1952. Half of the 22 participants were from Stanford. Anthropologists and educators were represented evenly, and the anthropologists included scholars long associated with the field such as John Gillin, Margaret Mead, and Felix Keesing and other comparative newcomers, such as Spindler himself, Bernard Siegel, C.W.M. Hart, Jules Henry, Dorothy Lee, Cora DuBois, and Solon Kimball, who in 1953 had accepted a position at Teachers College, Columbia, as Professor of Anthropology in the Department of Philosophy and the Social Sciences. Anthropological respectability was given to the conference by the presence of Alfred Kroeber, then Professor Emeritus at Berkeley. Moreover, the American Anthropological Association co-sponsored the conference, together with the Stanford School of Education and Department of Sociology and Anthropology.

In several respects, the Stanford conference foreshadowed the institutionalization of the relationship between anthropology and education that was to come in the years ahead. Early in the conference both Mead and Keesing commented on the need for institutionalization if the anthropological work of the past was not simply to return to mainstream anthropology. Mead's summary of the conference made the point forcefully:

> [T]his conference has raised the question rather seriously as to whether the communication is between *anthropology* and *education* as such. I mean, can someone defined as pure anthropologist who has no experience in education, who has not primarily studied education in primitive societies, who is not interested in teaching. . .engage in a very profitable form of communication except at the book-reading source material level? . . .So there's a possibility that the communication will have to proceed majorly

[sic] either from anthropologists who have taken an active interest in education—an acting professional interest—or educators who've taken an
active interest in anthropology. . . And educators should be very careful when they want an anthropologist to cooperate with them, either to
expose such anthropologists to a couple of years of internship in the situation where they want them to cooperate, or get anthropologists who have
really worked in a field that is relevant, and not order them from the super-
market. . . (quoted in Spindler 1955:272).

The issues raised by Mead and Keesing presaged the developments in the
professionalization of the field described in the remainder of this article.

Institutionalization and Specialization: 1955 to the Present

The institutionalization of the relationships between anthropology and
education may be seen best against the backdrop of the vast changes in
anthropology that occurred after World War II. American isolationism was
broken by the war, resulting in the expansion of American influence throughout the world. Educational subsidies provided to veterans made it possible for
large numbers of them to return to college and university campuses.
Unprecedented numbers of students began to take anthropology courses and
to enter graduate programs in the field. The numbers increased as the postwar
"baby-boom" generation entered colleges and universities in the 1960s. The
1950s and 1960s were times of intense educational activity and growth in the
discipline.

Nourished by rapidly growing student enrollments at all levels and profuse
public funding for higher education, anthropologists devoted primary
attention to the building of anthropology within the academy. Dozens of
departments were founded where none had existed before or an anthropology
severed joint departmental relationships with sociology. Major efforts were
made to initiate new graduate programs and to expand old ones so that
properly trained anthropologists could fill a demand for teachers of
anthropology that far exceeded the supply.

The importance given to teaching in the early 1960s was evident especially in
the Educational Resources in Anthropology (ERA) project at Berkeley.
Supported by the Course Content Improvement Section of the National
Science Foundation, the project sponsored a series of symposia throughout the
country on the teaching of anthropology in colleges and universities. In 1963
these papers and additional materials concerned with basic resources for
teaching anthropology were published in two volumes by the American
Anthropological Association (Mandelbaum, Lasker, and Albert 1963a,
1963b). The volume titled *The Teaching of Anthropology* covered topics
related to teaching in all major subfields, including applied anthropology.
Attention was given to the undergraduate and graduate curriculum and to
interdisplinary relations in teaching anthropology as part of the curriculum in

humanities, biological sciences, and social sciences, or in professional schools and colleges. The articles on this latter topic included one authored by Kimball on "Teaching Anthropology in Professional Education" (Mandelbaum, Lasker, and Albert 1963a:493-502).

The postwar years of academic expansion saw considerable change in the areal and theoretical interests of anthropologists. The earlier leaders of modern anthropology had pioneered anthropological research on a global scale. What had been done by a handful of innovators during the prewar years now became common as anthropologists in training went to foreign settings all over the world to experience fieldwork as a rite of passage into the profession. A changed institutional and economic framework now linked anthropology to interdisciplinary area centers backed by the Social Science Research Council, the Ford Foundation, and the newly established anthropology units of the Smithsonian Institute, National Science Foundation, and the National Institute of Mental Health. Funding from these and other sources, the rise of modern transportation, and the growth of graduate training made it possible for American anthropologists and their students to turn away from the study of cultural diversity at home in favor of study abroad.

Diversity in areal specialization was accompanied by diversity in theoretical interests. No longer dominated by the models of structural-functionalism introduced by Malinowski and Radcliffe-Brown and the culture-personality paradigms of Mead and others, contemporary sociocultural anthropology is noteworthy for theoretical diversity, eclecticism, and debate. Further, a wide variety of methodological tools currently are used to collect data and test theory in field settings. Concomitantly, increased specialization within the discipline is a major trend in professional training and in the professional activities of teaching, publication, and association.

The professionalization of anthropologists that occurred during the halcyon era after World War II was directed toward academic models of professional practice that gave little heed to the application of anthropology to political, economic, or social problems. The development of career roles outside the academy was neglected by a new generation of leaders who themselves had not experienced postdoctoral unemployment and assumed naively that academic expansion would continue indefinitely. The rise of new anthropological theory frequently was intertwined with overt and often unknowledgeable attacks on the motivations or political sympathies of those who earlier had done applied work in the complex settings of the modern world. For all of these reasons, applied anthropology was downgraded or discarded as an area of mainstream anthropological training and interest.

Today the situation is quite different than it was during the 1950s and 1960s. The dramatic postwar expansion of higher education has ended, and doctoral students in anthropology no longer assume that their professional careers will be spent within academe. Of necessity, there is renewed interest in applied anthropology and the practice of anthropology in nonacademic settings. New professional publications, networks, and associations are emerging that define nonacademic employment as a valid anthropological career line. Young anthropologists pioneering in this direction are gradually becoming visible within the profession of anthropology as a whole.[6]

In brief, the post-World War II history of educational anthropology has developed within the milieu of rapid expansion and diversification within the discipline. Although foundations continue to support anthropological research, the major funding comes from governmental sources at the federal and state levels. Anthropology is widely accepted as a discipline at nearly all major universities in the country. At the undergraduate level, the teaching of anthropology occurs in most junior colleges and four-year colleges and is an important basis of support for graduate programs within universities. Despite the successful expansion of anthropology in the academic world, the discipline has been slow to develop career opportunities for anthropolgists elsewhere. There are signs that new types of career lines may be emerging currently as one consequence of the end of the abnormal growth period in higher education during the decades after World War II.

Educational Anthropology as Specialized Anthropology

The growth of anthropology as a separate field within higher education was paralleled by its expansion into professional colleges of education. As noted, George Spindler and Solon Kimball were appointed to leading positions in colleges of education in the early 1950s. Although they were not the first anthropologists to teach anthropology to educators, their appointments signaled the beginning of concerted efforts to train graduate students who would be specialists in the field of educational anthropology. Specialized training currently exists at several universities, including Harvard, Stanford, Teachers College (Columbia), and the Universities of Florida, Georgia, Oregon, Minnesota, Pennsylvania, Pittsburgh, the State University of New York at Buffalo, and Michigan State.

During the 1950s and 1960s, the teaching of anthropology also increased at the precollegiate level. This was an era when a new social studies movement emerged in which the social sciences gained a larger share of the curriculum. Most social sciences obtained a foothold prior to the war, but anthropology

---

[6]These include the Society for Applied Anthropology publication *Practicing Anthropology;* in founding of the Society of Professional Anthropologists (SOPA) in Tucson, AZ in 1974; and the establishment of similar organizations in other major cities. A recent directory of practicing anthropologists (American Anthropological Association 1981) lists 353 names, but it is estimated that there are approximately 1,300 anthropologists in nonacademic employment (American Anthropological Association 1982:5). As part of the current reorganization of the American Anthropological Association, a Practicing Anthropology Unit is in the process of formation.

did not make its first appearance until the post-World War II period (Dynneson 1975). For this reason, several anthropologists became involved in presenting the case for anthropology at the precollegiate level, with special attention given to the social studies curriculum. John Chilcott, Solon Kimball, Dorothy Lee, Margaret Mead, and Robert Redfield are among the contributors to educational journals on this topic.[7]

As anthropology began to be taught more widely in professional colleges of education and schools, there were obvious needs for appropriate teaching materials. Anthropology received its first federal support for curriculum development and discipline-oriented teacher training in the early 1960s. Throughout that decade, curriculum development became a conspicuous activity of educational anthropologists.

In 1962 NSF extended support to the Anthropology Curriculum Study Project (ACSP) and at about the same time began to support the Education Development Center's anthropologically oriented curriculum development project, *Man: A Course of Study.* In 1964 the U.S. Office of Education initiated support for the University of Minnesota's Project Social Studies, which also was oriented strongly toward anthropology (Dynneson 1975).

In 1963, a curriculum development project of another type was initiated at Hunter College. Funded by the U.S. Office of Youth Development and Juvenile Delinquency, and known as the Teacher Resources in Urban Education Project (Project TRUE), this program employed several anthropologists and others to develop curricular materials for the training of teachers working in inner city schools. Many of the materials developed by anthropologists were based on data collected within the schools or from extended interviews with beginning teachers (Eddy 1967, 1969; Fuchs 1966, 1969; Moore 1967). Others were based on extensive reviews of the literature (Roberts 1967, 1971).

Additional curricular materials that could be used in the anthropological training of educators were developed in the late 1960s by George and Louise Spindler, who served as editors of a series of *Case Studies in Education and Culture* published by 'Holt, Rinehart and Winston, and by Solon Kimball, who edited the *Anthropology and Education Series* published by Teachers College Press.[8] Like many of the Project TRUE materials, the volumes in these series usually were based on field research. Finally, in 1963, George Spindler edited a collection of articles titled *Education and Culture,* which could be used as an introductory text, and in 1965 George Kneller published *Educational Anthropology*, which treated the basic concepts of culture and personality as well as problems of education in American public schools.

---

[7] See Dwyer-Schick (1976) for an annotated bibliography of publications related to the study and teaching of anthropology.

[8] Both series have been reviewed recently in the *Anthropology and Education Quarterly.* See Eddy 1983; Spindler and Spindler 1983.

In part, the curriculum development efforts of the 1960s were a response to renewed federal efforts to improve the teaching of science in a post-Sputnik age. But they were also an attempt to demonstrate the relevance of anthropology to contemporary educational problems. The 1960s were years of turmoil in American cities and the deprivation and poverty of millions of Americans in urban slums and encapsulated rural areas came to the forefront of national attention. In particular, the failure of formal schooling to meet the needs of Blacks, Hispanics, Native Americans, and other minorities became dramatically evident. There was a spate of attacks upon formal schooling, and it was within this context that curriculum development activities in anthropology and education occurred.

In the mid-1960s, the federal government began to encourage more widespread anthropological research within American schools. The Culture of Schools program was initiated in 1965 under Stanley Diamond at Syracuse University. Developed at the request of Francis A.J. Ianni, then Deputy Commissioner for Research in the United States Office of Education, the program was designed not merely to apply prior knowledge but to promote collaboration between experienced anthropologists and other behavioral scientists in order to develop the foundations for research in American mass education. After a year and a half, the program was transferred to the sponsorship of the American Anthropological Association, while maintaining the support of the Office of Education (Wax, Diamond, and Gearing 1971:x). The result was the Program in Anthropology and Education directed by Fred Gearing.

Under both programs, a series of conferences was organized through the years 1966-1968. At the time, only a small number of anthropologists had engaged in research and writing germane to the social organization and cultural role of formal schooling in America. However, there were others who had undertaken recent research in educational systems abroad or had participated actively in precollegiate curriculum development or the training of educators in colleges of education. Still others were beginning to examine the application of sociolinguistics to the problems of cross-cultural communication in schools. The conferences brought together representatives from all of these groups, several others whose research training and interests were in fields outside of anthropology, and a few who were involved directly in action programs oriented toward educational reform.

The Culture of Schools program and the Program in Anthropology and Education were instrumental in the establishment of national visibility for what rapidly was becoming the next generation of educational anthropoligists. By the end of the 1960s, the institutionalization of educational anthropology as a legitimate specialization within the discipline almost was complete. The field was established in schools of education, the journals of professional educators, federally-sponsored conferences, the social studies curriculum, funded research projects, and some of the professional anthropological journals and meetings. Those trained in this specialty were beginning to be accepted as fellows of the American Anthropological Association and as members of educational professional associations. The organizational expression of the professionalization process came in 1968 at the annual meeting of the American Anthropological Association in Seattle when, after a series of informal meetings, an ad hoc Group on Anthropology and Education was founded. The work of this group laid the groundwork for the formal organization of the Council on Anthropology and Education (CAE) in 1970.

The Council on Anthropology and Education

The emergence of CAE in 1970, the immediate initiation of a CAE *Newsletter,* and the subsequent evolution of the *Newsletter* into the journal *Anthropology and Education Quarterly* in 1977, culminated a long series of research and other activities that began in the 1920s and led to the formation of an area of professional specialization in the discipline (Chilcott 1984; Singleton 1984). As noted, the Culture of Schools program and the Program in Anthropology and Education played a vital role in the professionalization process. The first eight and two subsequent presidents of CAE and three of the four editors of the *Newsletter* and *Quarterly* also were active participants in at least one of the conferences sponsored by these programs.

Scientific and practical problems germane to education, which, in varying degrees, engaged nearly all of the leaders of modern anthropology during the 1930s and 1940s, are currently of interest to only a segment of those who pursue anthropological careers. Nevertheless, the most recent published bibliography in the field of anthropology and education (Rosenstiel 1977) lists 3,434 annotated entries; elsewhere, Robert (n.d.) has reported that more than half of the known publications have appeared since 1965. Moreover, the paid membership of CAE was 749 in March 1982 (American Anthropological Association 1982:5).

In several respects, CAE as an organization reflects a remarkable continuity with the leaders of modern anthropology who first drew attention to the importance of education in the contemporary world. First, there is the emphasis on anthropology as a discipline concerned with cross-cultural and comparative studies of contemporary peoples. Second, there is a reaffirmation of American society as a multicultural society and an important field of anthropological inquiry. Third, there is the reaffirmation of the view that anthropology should be concerned with child development and learning in all of the various ways and environments in which they occur. Fourth, there is the insistence that ethnographic studies of learning and teaching systems have implications for educational policy. Finally, there is the recognition that education today occurs within the context of sweeping cultural, social, political, economic, and technological change.

Just as the 1954 Stanford Conference had done, so also the 1970 founding of CAE foreshadowed important new developments during the years that followed. These include the noteworthy contributions of cognitive and sociolinguistic research to communication processes in classrooms and other educational settings, the gradual incorporation of ethnographic methods into educational research, the increased attention to education within developing countries, and the recent emergence of a nucleus of educational anthropologists who are working productively in nonacademic positions. It also may be that the council form of organizing diverse interest groups eventually will become a model for professional association within the discipline as a whole.

A Look Ahead

Our era is one in which able young people continue to want to become anthropologists, notwithstanding the paucity of academic career positions. In the 1930s and 1940s, these factors combined to produce a remarkably talented group of leaders who laid the foundation for a modern anthropology in which theory, research, and application were viewed as interrelated aspects of scientific development in the discipline. It was not until the late 1950s that anthropology became characterized widely as an exclusively academic endeavor by a rising new generation of leaders who failed to envision the temporary nature of academic expansion and lacked understanding of the contribution of applied research in the building of science.

The founders of contemporary social and cultural anthropology defined it as applied anthropology. Congruently, those who engaged in research related to education typically did so within a professional milieu that emphasized the application of their studies to major educational problems at home and abroad. Within both anthropology and educational anthropology, this professional orientation eroded during the postwar years, largely due to the disciplinary focus on the building of academic departments and careers. Applied anthropology continued to develop, but it was comprised primarily of activities that sometimes engaged anthropologists who were employed securely in academic positions.

The advent of diminished career opportunities within the academy and new federal research funding priorities and accountability have combined to create a situation during the 1980s that has fostered the revival of concerted efforts to integrate theory, research, and application. On the cutting edge of this revival are a young generation of anthropologists who are carrying anthropology forward into the corporations, government agencies, human services professions, and other institutions and organizations seeking anthropological contributions to the amelioration of nonacademic problems. These anthropologists define their work as *practicing anthropology,* and they are in the process of attempting to develop new types of anthropological careers. They represent still another stage in the development of anthropology as a profession.

If the past is prologue to the future, we may anticipate that educational anthropology will once again be at the forefront of the discipline by incorporating the research and activities of practicing educational anthropologists into the profession of anthropology. This renewal of the practice of anthropology in nonacademic settings is the opportunity of the present and the hope of the future if educational anthropology, and indeed the discipline itself, is to realize its full contribution to the 21st century.

References

American Anthropological Association, 1981, *Directory of Practicing Anthroplogists.* Washington, DC: American Anthropological Association.

_____, 1982, *Anthropology Newsletter* 23:5. Washington, DC: American Anthropological Association.

Barnes, Earl, and Mary S. Barnes, 1896, *Education Among the Aztecs.* Stanford, CA: Leland Standord Jr. University, Studies in Education 2:73-80.

Berman, Edward Henry, 1970, *Education in Africa and America: A History of the Phelps-Stokes Fund,* 1911-1945. Unpublished doctoral dissertation, Teachers College, Columbia University.

Chamberlain, Alexander, 1896, *Child and Childhood in Folk Thought.* New York: Macmillan.

Chilcott, John, 1984, *From Newsletter to Quarterly,* 1973-1976. Anthropology and Education Quarterly 15:67-69.

Davis, Allison, Burleigh B. Gartner, and Mary R. Gardner, 1941, *Deep South: A Social Anthropological Study of Caste and Class.* University of Chicago Press.

Dollard, John, 1937, *Caste and Class in a Southern Town.* New York: Harper and Brothers.

Drake, St. Clair, and Horace R. Cayton, 1945, *Black Metropolis: A Study of Negro Life in a Northern City.* New York: Harcourt Brace.

Dwyer-Schick, Susan, 1976, *The Study and Teaching of Anthropology: An Annotated Bibliography.* Athens, GA: Anthropology Curriculum Project, Publication No. 76-1.

Dynesson, Thomas, 1975, *Pre-collegiate Anthropology: Trends and Materials.* Athens, GA: Anthropology Curriculum Project, Publication No. 75-1.

Eddy, Elizabeth M., 1967, *Walk the White Line: A Profile of Urban Education.* Garden City, NY: Doubleday.

_____, 1969, *Becoming a Teacher: The Passage to Professional Status.* New York: Teachers College Press.

_____, 1983, Review Essay: *The Anthropology and Education Series,* Solon T. Kimball, General Editor. Anthropology and Education Quarterly 14:141-147.

Firth, Sir Raymond, 1981, Bronislaw Malinowski. *In Totems and Teachers: Perspectives on the History of Anthropology.* Sydel Silverman, ed. pp. 101-137. New York: Columbia University Press.

Fisher, Donald, 1977, *The Impact of American Foundations on the Development of British University Education,* 1900-1939. Unpublished doctoral dissertation, University of California, Berkeley.

Fletcher, Alice C., 1888, *Glimpses of Child-Life Among the Omaha Indians.* Journal *of American Folklore 1:115-123.*

Fortes, Meyer, 1978, "An Anthropologist's Apprenticeship." In *Annual Review of Anthropology.* Vol. 8. B.J. Siegel, A.R. Beals, and Stephen A. Tyler, eds. pp. 1-30. Palo Alto, CA: Annual Reviews, Inc.

Frank, Lawrence K., 1955, "Preface." In *Educatin and Anthropology,* G.D. Spindler, ed. pp. vii-xi. Stanford University Press.

Fuchs, Estelle S., 1966, *Pickets at the Gates. New York: Free Press.*

_____, 1969, *Teachers Talk: Views from Inside City Schools.* Garden City, NY: Doubleday.

Gillin, John P., 1948, "The Old Order Amish of Pennsylvania." In *The Ways of Men.* John P. Gillin, ed. pp. 209-220. New York: Appleton-Century-Crofts.

Haas, Mary R., 1953, "The Application of Linguistics to Teaching." In *Anthropology Today.* Alfred Kroeber, ed. pp. 807-818. University of Chicago Press.

Heyman, Richard D., 1970, *The Role of Carnegie Corporation in African Education,* 1925-1960. Unpublished doctoral dissertation, Teachers College, Columbia University.

Hollingshead, August B., 1949, *Elmtown's Youth.* New York: John Wiley.

Johnson, Charles S., 1941, *Growing Up in the Black Belt: Negro Youth in the Rural South.* Washington, DC: American Council on Education.

Jones, Thomas J., 1917, *Negro Education, A Survey of the Private and Higher Schools for Colored People in the United States.* 2 volumes. Washington, DC: Government Printing Office.

_____, 1922, *Education in Africa: A Study of West, South and Equatorial Africa by the African Education Commission.* New York: Phelps-Stokes Fund.

_____, *Education in East Africa: A Study of East, Central and South Africa by the Second African Education Commission.* Under the auspices of the Phelps-Stokes Fund, in cooperation with the International Education Board. London: Edinburgh House.

Keesing, Felix, 1937, *Education in Pacific Countries.* Kelley and Walsh.

Kennard, Edward A., and Gordon MacGregor, 1953, *Applied Anthropology in Government: United States."* In *Anthropology Today.* Alfred Kroeber, ed. pp. 832-840. University of Chicago Press.

Kimball, Solon T., 1963, "Teaching Anthropology in Professional Education." In *The Teaching of Anthropology.* D. Mandelbaum, G. Lasker, and E. Albert, eds. pp. 493-502. Washington, DC: American Anthropological Association.

Kluger, Richard, 1976, *Simple Justice: This History of Brown v. Board of Education and Black America's Struggle for Equality.* New York: Alfred Knopf.

Kneller, George F., 1965, *Educational Anthropology: An Introduction.* New York: John Wiley.

Kroeber, Alfred, ed., 1953, *Anthropology Today: An Encyclopedic Inventory.* University of Chicago Press.

Langham, Ian, 1981, *The Building of British Social Anthropology.* Boston, MA: D. Reidel.

Lynd, Robert S. and Helen Lynd, 1929, *Middletown.* New York: Harcourt Brace.

————, and ————, 1937, *Middletown in Transition.* New York: Harcourt Brace.

Malinowski, Bronislaw, 1922, reissued 1984, *Argonauts of the Western Pacific.* Prospect Heights, IL: Waveland Press.

————, 1929, *Practical Anthropology.* Africa 2:23-38.

————, 1936, *Native Education and Culture Contact. International Review of Missions* 25:480-517.

Mandelbaum, David G., Gabriel W. Lasker, and Ethel M. Albert, eds., 1963a, *The Teaching of Anthropology.* Washington, DC: American Anthropological Association.

————, 1963b *Resources for the Teaching of Anthropology.* Washington, DC: American Anthropological Association.

Mead, Margaret, 1928, *Coming of Age in Samoa.* New York: William Morrow.

————, 1972, *Blackberry Winter.* New York: William Morrow.

Metraux, Alfred, 1953, "Applied Anthropology in Government: United Nations." In *Anthropology Today,* Alfred Kroeber, ed. pp. 880-894. University of Chicago Press.

Montessori, Maria, 1913, *Pedagogical Anthropology.* New York: Frederick A. Stokes.

Moore, G. Alexander, 1967, *Realities of the Urban Classroom: Observations in Elementary Schools.* Garden City, NY: Doubleday.

Radcliffe-Brown, A.R., 1922, *The Andaman Islanders.* Cambridge: University Press.

————, 1930, "Applied Anthropology." In *Report of the Twentieth Meeting of the Australian and New Zealand Association for the Advancement of Science,* pp. 267-280. Reprinted in *Research in Economic Anthropology,* Vol. 3., 1980. G. Dalton, ed., pp. 123-134. Greenwich, CT: JAI Press.

Roberts, Joan I., 1967, *School Children in the Urban Slum.* New York: Free Press.

————, 1971, *The Scene of the Battle: Group Behavior and Urban Classrooms.* New York: Doubleday.

————, n.d., *Anthropology and Education.* Unpublished manuscript.

————, and Sherrie K. Akinsanya, 1976, *Educational Patterns and Cultural Configurations.* New York: David McKay.

Rosenstiel, Annette, 1977, *Educatin and Anthropology: An Annotated Bibliography.* New York: Garland.

Singleton, John, 1984, *Origins of the AEQ: Rituals, Myths, and Cultural Transmission. Anthropology and Education Quarterly* 15:11-16.

Spindler, George D., 1984, *Roots Revisited: Three Decades of Perspective. Anthropology and Education Quarterly* 15:3-10.

————, ed., 1955, *Education and Anthropology.* Stanford, CA: Stanford University Press.

————, 1963, *Education and Culture.* New York: Holt, Rinehart and Winston.

————, and Louise Spindler, 1983, *Review Essay: The Case Studies in Education and Culture From Cradle to Grave. Anthropology and Education Quarterly* 14:72-80.

Stevenson, Matilda C., 1887, *Religious Life of the Zuni Child.* Washington, DC: U.S. Bureau of American Ethnology, Fifth Annual Report, 1883-84.

Stocking, George W., Jr., 1976, "Ideas and Institutions in American Anthropology: Thoughts Toward a History of the Interwar Years." In Selected Papers from the American Anthropologist, 1921-1945. G.W. Stocking, Jr., ed. pp. 1-50. Washington, DC: American Anthropological Association.

Thompson, Laura, 1951, *Personality and Government: Findings and Recommendations of the Indian Administration Research.* Mexico, D.F.: Ediciones del Instituto Indigenista Interamericano.

Vandewalker, Nina, 1898, "Some Demands of Education Upon Anthropology." *American Journal of Sociology* 4(1):69-78.

Warner, William Lloyd, 1942, "Educative Effects of Social Status." In *Environment and Education: Symposium.* Ernest W. Burgess, W. Lloyd Warner, Franz Alexander, and Margaret Mead, eds. pp. 16-28. University of Chicago Press.

Warner, William Lloyd, and Paul Lunt, 1941, *The Social Life of a Modern Community.* New Haven: Yale University Press.

Warner, William Lloyd, Robert J. Havighurst, and Martin B. Loeb, 1944, *Who Shall Be Educated?* New York: Harper and Brothers.

Wax, Murray L., Stanley Diamond, and Fred O. Gearing, 1971, *Anthropological Perspectives on Education.* New York: Basic Books.

West, James, 1945, *Plainville, U.S.A.* New York: Columbia University Press.

HARRY F. WOLCOTT/*University of Oregon*

2   The Anthropology of Learning

For a number of years I have been wondering how "the anthropology of learning" might look if we were to make it a subject for systematic inquiry. How might anthropological research inform current thinking about learning and how might reawakened interest in the topic of learning inform anthropological research? Might an infusion of anthropological concern help human learning recapture the level of interest it deserves and once had?

I have always been skeptical of social scientists or educators who regard teaching and learning as one and the same. I have also been uncomfortable with anthropological nonchalance in seeming to equate the *transmitting* of culture—particularly with self-conscious efforts within a society to do so—with the *learning* of culture. Societies are often portrayed as both overbearing in their domination over the individuals who comprise them and overly successful in their efforts to produce, or *reproduce*, the very type of individual the society wants. If I once had to accept on faith that such complete and exquisite conformity existed in societies that I could only know through reading, I recognized that such uniformity was not present in societies I could observe firsthand.

That anthropologists have shown more interest in reporting what transmitters try to transmit than what learners are actually learning seems understandable. Self-conscious efforts to transmit culture capture our attention and give the fieldworker explicit behavior to observe and to describe. Before we can call this "enculturation," however, we need at least to include someone (in addition to the fieldworker) willing to heed the messages being transmitted. As to what is being made of the messages, the immediate results are hard to assess but the long-term results are apparent: enculturation works!

My years of teaching "anthropology and education" have provided excellent opportunity for drawing upon anthropological materials as resources for examining teaching and learning in noninstitutional settings. But only recently did I feel ready to pull together some ideas about the "anthropology of learning" as an area of collective academic interest and to invite colleagues to share their views on the topic. We first formalized our thoughts in a symposium on the Anthropology of Learning presented at the American Anthropological Association meetings in December 1980.

Although that event marked the beginning of a dialogue, our effort should be regarded as a renewed interest rather than a new one. A first task that faced each of us was to reflect upon the ways that earlier contributors in anthropology and related social sciences have brought us to where we are today.

In anthropological fashion, our papers show a tendency to link ideas rather closely to the elders with whom we associate them. But, also in anthropological fashion, there are numerous ideas, concepts and hypotheses floating about that have not been subjected to rigorous review. A curious characteristic of anthropology, comforting to those within its sphere and confounding to outsiders, is that hypotheses are conceived rather promiscuously and then abandoned to make it quite on their own. Our effort to talk about an anthropology of learning, no matter how loosely defined, provides an occasion to sift carefully through myriad possible explanations suggested by others. Perhaps academic ideas, like academicians themselves, should be subject periodically to "up or out" scrutiny. Literally and figuratively, which among a storehouse of anthropological ideas related to learning should we be promoting?

Looking Back

I would not dream of drawing attention to the anthropology of learning without acknowledging Margaret Mead's longtime interest in both teaching and learning. Although she was careful to distinguish between them (cf.1964), I think that, like most anthropologists, her attention was drawn more to processes of teaching than to learning per se. That interest is stated succinctly in *Culture and Commitment*:

> Man's most human characteristic is not his ability to learn, which he shares with many other species, but his ability to teach and store what others have developed and taught him. Learning, which is based on human dependency, is relatively simple (1970:72).

Mead once proposed a contrast between "learning cultures" and "teaching cultures" (Mead 1942, as noted in Gearing 1973). A "learning culture" refers to a small, homogenous group that shows little concern for transmitting culture because there is virtually no danger of anyone going astray. "Teaching culture" refers to societies that regard it as imperative that those who know inform and direct those who do not know. Mead's view of the contrast between learning and teaching is apparent in her observation in *Culture and Commitment* that "Learning, which is based on human dependency, is relatively simple. But human capacities for creating elaborate teachable systems . . . are very complex" (1970:72).

Mead was usually in the mainstream of ideas. Her cavalier dismissal of learning as "simple" is reflected in the writings of other anthropologists. Ethnographers have not customarily paid much attention to children other than to place them conveniently about so that they could "soak up" their culture, play at it, or help with appropriate tasks. Powdermaker's description of culture transmission in Lesu aptly characterizes how anthropologists have tended to portray children as ever-present but minimally engaged, patiently waiting for the onset of puberty before suddenly blossoming into adult roles: "We find the children always observers or minor participants of the adult society" (1971:100).

The work of Bateson, on the other hand, serves as reminder that some anthropologists have extended their interests to include a consideration of learning or have felt free to explore beyond customary anthropological bounds, although Bateson himself did ponder whether anthropologists had anything to offer on the topic of learning other than their questions:

> As is usual in anthropology, the data are not sufficiently precise to give us any clue as to the nature of the learning processes involved. Anthropology, at best, is only able to *raise* problems of this order. The next step must be left for laboratory experimentation (1972:115).

"Raising problems" was something that Bateson did extremely well, however, and he frequently turned his attention to raising problems about the nature of the learning process. At one time he wrote that "All species of behavioral scientists are concerned with 'learning' in one sense or another of that word" (1972:279). His legacy includes the contract first introduced in 1942 between what he called *proto-learning* (rote learning, or the "simple learning curve") amd *deutero learning*: progressive change in the rate of proto-learning, or "learning how to learn." (At one time he even extended the concept to "trito learning," but eventually he settled for deutero learning as adequate to account for meta-learning.) He also proposed a hierarchical classification of learning "levels" based upon the assumption that "all learning is in some degree stochastic (i.e., contains components of 'trial and error')" and thus that the *types of errors to be corrected* provide the basis for a classification of learning levels (1972:287ff).

Zero learning: learning not subject to correction by trial and error.

Learning I: revision of choice within an unchanged set of alternatives.

Learning II: revision of the set within which choice is made, thus the learning of contexts.

Learning III: learning of the contexts of contexts—a corrective change in the system of sets.

I could cite numerous scholars in addition to Bateson, Mead, and Powdermaker to illustrate how anthropologists have variously concerned themselves with, or ignored, the teaching and learning of culture. The topic of education has always received some anthropological attention; occasionally it has provided a major focus and major contribution (e.g., Benedict 1938; Fortes 1938; Gladwin 1970; Pettitt 1946). Recent and noteworthy high points in a modest but persistent interest in learning (as contrasted with the formal transmission of culture) include a symposium held in 1972 at the annual meeting of the American Ethnological Society and the set of papers from that symposium later published in a monograph edited by Kimball and Burnett, *Learning and Culture* (1973). The publication of Hansen's book, *Sociocultural Perspectives on Human Learning* (1979), which includes a 28-page bibliography, suggests that "anthropological contributions to the study of knowledge transmission" are not withering away.

Why an "Anthropology of Learning" Just Now?

These seem propitious times for expanding the dialogue between anthropologists and educators that has been gaining momentum for a quarter-century. In the 1970s, "things ethnographic" definitely caught the educator eye (cf. Wolcott 1982). Wide interest in ethnography provides us with an unusual opportunity to demonstrate that anthropology has more to offer to the field of education than simply a "fieldwork" approach to research. Perhaps anthropology can serve as a reminder to educational researchers that their preoccupation with method borders on making method an end in itself. Anthropological concern has never been with method per se. Its focus is in making sense of the lived-in world. As usual, Geertz has said it eloquently:

> Like all scientific propositions, anthropological interpretations must be tested against the material they are designed to interpret; it is not their origins that recommend them (1968:vii);
> The validity of both my empirical conclusions and my theoretical premises rests, in the end, on how effective they are in so making sense of data from which they were neither derived nor for which they were originally designed (p.viii).

Now that "ethnographic method" has caught educator attention, there is opportunity to get beyond ethnographic *technique* into the realm of the stuff with which ethnographic research deals, a realm that Geertz describes as cultural interpretation (1973).

To date, our ethnographic opportunities, both in schools and out, have focused largely on teachers and teaching. What can we now bring to the understanding of learners and learning? And, recognizing that psychologists and educational psychologists have attended to—one might even say usurped—the question of *learning in school*, what can we say about learning that is *not* school related?

To begin, we might ask how learning itself has become so uninteresting a topic? Edward Hall refers in *Beyond Culture* to the "miracle of learning"

(1976:173), but one gets little sense of awe or excitement in psychological treatises on the topic. For most students, "learning" is as dull and pedestrian a topic of study today as it was for me as an undergraduate almost 35 years ago; I still hear college students insist that all they need to know and all they want to know about learning is contained in the sterile definition, "a change in behavior." Learning has become synonymous with classroom performance for pupils, sophomoric performance for sophomores, and maze performance for mice. What undergraduate would ever think of comparing the learning drive to the sexual drive the way Hall does (although I must leave to him the methodological issues involved in this comparison):

> The sexual drive and the learning drive are, if one can measure the relative strength of such disparate urges, very close to each other in the power they exert over men's lives (1976:207).

For my part, I have pondered the salutary effect it might have on the teaching profession if teachers were to take "learning" as their central professional and intellectual concern, committed to knowing what is known about learning, conversant with and critical of competing theories, thoroughly up-to-date on current research, and intrigued with understanding how learning occurs not only among their students but among themselves as well. What a remarkable contribution anthropology could make to teaching if it could help teachers develop a proprietary interest in the natural (and very social) process of human learning and help educators shape a learning-centered rather than a teaching-centered profession.

The Anthropology of Learning: An Inventory

I have begun to identify a corpus of anthropological terms, labels, ideas, and questions related to the topic of learning. A bit of stock-taking seems in order as a starting place. What new light can we bring to these issues? Which concepts and ideas nest with others? Which of the multifarious terms and ideas introduced in recent years continue to warrant attention?

Since I will later take issue with the idea of "gradualness" in learning, let me note that, although I have been accumulating this corpus for years, I think I can trace back to the very moment when the idea of the anthropology of learning first flashed through my mind. The occasion was an informal session at the American Anthropological Association meetings in Washington, D.C., in November 1976, when Solon Kimball and George Spindler were invited to reminisce about the "evolution" of anthropology and education as an area of inquiry. Even as the two men spoke, I found myself reflecting on the different perspective and contribution each had made to the development of anthropology and education, including rather different emphases on teaching and learning.

George Spindler, my esteemed mentor, has always been keenly interested in the processes of cultural transmission and in identifying "cultural antecedents" of behavior. That interest is evident in much of his own writing. It is epitomized in his Burton Lecture on "The Transmission of American Culture" (Spindler 1959) and in his chapter "The Transmission of Culture" (Spindler 1973:207-245; 1974:279-310). Spindler's concern for processes of cultural transmission has itself been transmitted to his students and provides a theme in much of their work. He has interpreted cultural transmission very literally, focusing almost exclusively on what humans do, consciously and explicitly, to transmit culture. Spindler has pondered aloud—although I think not in public—whether anthropologists rightfully have any professional interest in learning processes at all. Many share what Goodenough describes as this "tempting" view that, since anthropologists are concerned with the patterns characterizing *groups*, they should confine themselves to phenomena at the group level of abstraction (Goodenough 1981:52).

Solon Kimball has also addressed the topic "The Transmission of Culture" in a paper that first appeared in 1965 and has been frequently reprinted, but his interests have often found him writing about the learning of culture as well. He has described his baptism to fieldwork as a process of "learning a culture" (1972). In organizing his own papers for publication in a single volume, he placed six of them, including his chapter on cultural transmission, in a section entitled "Culture and Learning" (1974).

It is hardly surprising that Spindler's comments during that session reflected his interest in processes related to the transmission of culture and that Kimball's comments touched as well upon aspects of learning. At some point during the dialogue, Kimball mentioned that, in his opinion, the literature of anthropology offers a rich resource for the study of human learning. That thought "struck home" as I realized what a fresh perspective anthropology might bring in rekindling interest in learning as a natural process rather than as an activity restricted to laboratories and schools. I believe Kimball stated rather boldly that anthropology has "even better materials on learning that psychology has." Ever since that day, I have been trying to get Kimball to elaborate on that sentence, and he has been trying to recall whether he actually said it. For me, the idea of the anthropology of learning was conceived at that moment. The event of the Kimball-Spindler dialogue provides a starting point for my review.

Point 1: Anthropology as a Resource on "Learning"

If anthropology is a rich resource on learning, it is a largely untapped one and its utility has not yet been demonstrated. To the best of both Kimball's and my knowledge, no one has prepared a bibliography dealing exclusively with anthropological contributions to the study of the learning process and anthropological sources rich with descriptions about learning, although many such references are cited in bibliographies in anthropology and education dealing with closely related topics (cf. Burnet 1974a; Hansen 1979; Harrington 1979).

A first step was to begin compiling such a bibliography. In a project initiated with the help of Barbara Harrison while she was a doctoral student in anthropology and education, I have begun to identify and annotate those references. Our starting point was with studies in language and culture acquisition in natural settings. It is hoped that our "working bibliography" will provide a test of the assertion that the materials are both valuable and interesting.

Point 2: Why Everyone Doesn't Learn Everything

In an open discussion immediately following the Kimball-Spindler dialogue, Fred Gearing posed two related questions that have since proved as provocative for my students as they did at that moment for me. "It's somewhat of a wonder," Gearing began, either in those words or in words to that effect, "that anyone ever learns anything. But, given that they do, then we can also ask why everybody doesn't learn everything?"

Gearing has a special talent for phrasing questions that invite involvement. His questions typically point as well to his own current interests, and so it is with these questions. Stated in what he describes as its more exact form, Gearing and his colleagues have been investigating the issue of "what constraints, necessarily noncognitive and nonmotor in nature, reduce the expectable randomness" that keeps almost everyone from learning almost everything (cf. Gearing and Sangree 1979:1).

Point 3: Things Learned versus the Learning Itself

As my previous point suggests, Fred Gearing is among the minority of anthropologists who have expressed long-term interest in the "receiving" as well as the transmitting of culture. In an earlier discussion dealing with the development of "anthropology and education," Gearing once posited a hypothetical juncture in the evolution of cultural anthropology, a juncture at which *processes* involved with the *transmission* of culture, rather than a preoccupation with the *content* of it, might have become the core of anthropological inquiry:

> If learned behavior is the subject matter, then things learned and the learning itself are opposite sides of the same coin. In the historical flip of that coin . . . culture fell up and cultural transmission down (1973:1225).

Had learning won out at the moment of Gearing's hypothetical coin toss, there would have been no need to develop a special subfield of anthropology and education. But with culture *content* serving as the core of the discipline, the question of how content is transmitted tends to be overshadowed by the endless task of description. The "road not taken" would have led to a more overriding concern for cultural process instead of a preoccupation with cultural content.

Point 4: Through Whose Efforts Does Culture Get Transmitted?

Given their preoccupation with cultural inventory, it is noteworthy that anthropologists have given at least passing attention to educational processes, particularly to child-training practices. Mead's characterization of some societies as "learning cultures," in which there seems so little likelihood of anyone failing to "catch" the cultural heritage that no self-conscious effort is made to transmit it, reminds us how easy it is to regard culture as virtually self-transmitting. Spindler has made the assertion in this regard that "It would be difficult for a child *not* to learn his culture" (Spindler 1973:225). In the broadest sense, of course, that statement is not only true but need not be made with any tentativeness. A comparable statement holds for learning the language(s) heard about us. We neither invent language and culture on our own nor have any options about learning them.

Those anthropologists interested in enculturation have attended almost exclusively to aspects of *transmission.* They follow a normal human propensity to be attracted by novelty and movement and a professional concern for *content* and the manner in which it is presented. Whether or not the children fall asleep while hearing a story or watching a dance, the culture content embedded in the words and actions of the transmitters is there to be recorded. More than that, the very process of transmitting culture is a time for defining it as well, as Pettitt aptly observed in *Primitive Education in North America* (1946):

> Primitive education was a community project in which all reputable elders participated at the instigation of individual families. The result was not merely to focus community attention on the child, but also to make the child's education a constant challenge to the elders to review, analyze, dramatize, and defend their cultural heritage.

Pettitt's oft-quoted words appear in discussions about the process of cultural transmission. I think they help explain why even those anthropologists not particularly intrigued with enculturation per se have nonetheless been attentive to the transmitters. What better source of data for the ethnographer than the self-conscious efforts of elders bent upon reviewing, analyzing, dramatizing, and defending their culture?

Our efforts on behalf of an anthropology of learning now invite careful attention to what it is that learners learn of their culture and to how and why learners attend to some things rather than others. Our starting point is to recognize that we all have to acquire some cultural knowledge in at least one major cultural system and no one, not even the anthropologist, is going to acquire all of it.

What I think we might now attend to, more than we have in the past, is the critical role that learners themselves play in the process of cultural transmission. If it is obvious that there must be a learner in order for cultural transmission to take place, we have not been as attentive to the fact that the learner holds the ultimate answer to the question of what has been transmitted. This idea is hardly a new one, but it has made remarkably little headway. Almost 50 years ago Sapir warned against the "convenient but dangerous metaphor that culture is a "neatly packed-up assemblage of forms of behavior handed over piece-meal . . . to the passively inquiring child." Culture is not something "given", Sapir wrote, but something to be "gradually and gropingly discovered" (1934:414).

More recently, Wallace has used the term "rediscover" to convey the magnitude of the task of transmitting culture and the impossibility for the transmitters to accomplish the process solely through their own efforts:

> In a radical sense, then, it would appear that much of every culture must be literally rediscovered in every generation because of the impossibility of describing, and therefore communicating (Wallace 1970:109).

Keesing takes a bolder step by suggesting that perhaps cultural learning "takes place not so much through the child rearing practices of a society as *in spite of them*" (1976:203). If Keesing's statement seems too extreme, how can we better convey our understanding of the nexus between culture as portrayed and culture as discovered, between culture as "taught" and culture as "caught"?

Our inquires will no doubt bring us back to fields once figuratively plowed by anthropologists of the old "Culture and Personality" school. This time, however, our attention will be, in Wallace's well-posed contrast, to the "organization of diversity" rather than to the "replication of uniformity" (1970:22ff.). If each of us must literally "rediscover" culture, then an anthropology of learning must attend not only to what societies insist that their neophytes know, but also to what those neophytes actually learn. We have to account for the inevitable diversity of each individual's experience, as well as for an incredible human capacity for discerning the patterned regularity that makes culture possible. For some insight into how the individual learner approaches this task, we can turn to colleagues who have been doing exciting things in a related area of natural learning: language acquisition.

Point 5: Language Acquisition as a Model for Cultural Acquisition

Studies in language acquisition seem to offer a promising direction for an anthropology of learning. Language acquisition is hardly a new field of inquiry, but I share with others a sense of its growing importance for understanding the processes of cultural acquisition (cf. Brukman 1973; Goodenough 1981; Schwartz 1981).

I recognize the long debate regarding the suitability of language acquisition processes as analog for cultural acquisition, including the problem that language must then double both as an aspect of cultural learning and as a model for it. I also recognize the problem of referring to a language acquisition "model" that implies that linguists are themselves in agreement about how the process occurs. Yet I am intrigued with the similarities of issues related to the biological basis for language and cultural learning, the utility of talking about each of them as the learning of a set of unwritten rules that guides the operation of appropriate (linguistic or cultural) behaviors, and the contrast linguists have made between *performance* (what one actually does) and *competence* (the totality of what one understands).

Surely one of the most exciting contributions from linguistics for the study of cultural acquisition is the conceptualization shared by many child language learning scholars of the language learner as an *active participant in the learning process,* an incipient but persistent "theory builder" constantly (though not often consciously) sifting and sorting and seeking regularity from a continuous, almost random bombardment of linguistic and cultural elements swirling about.[1] In essence, all human beings are confronted anew with rediscovering — figuring out for themselves — how their social environment "works." Until we figure out how those about us go about getting what they need and want, we cannot get the system to work, or to work predictably, on our own behalf. Each of us must "gropingly discover" the unexplicated rules of our language through deriving a grammar for at least one of the languages spoken around us. As well, each of us must work out a comparable "grammar" of what Geertz calls the "informal logic of actual life" (1973:17).

Psychometricians to the contrary, the tasks of discerning underlying pattern and regularity in that "blooming, buzzing confusion" are not behaviors in which half a population falls below some statistical midpoint. Every normally endowed, normally functioning human is engaged life-long in a constructive and effortful process to figure things out sufficiently well to develop a personal life-style and live out a unique life within some linguistically and culturally bounded system(s). Our ecological environment presents a certain range of possibilities, and biological needs create some urgencies and predispose us toward others. But we learn to cope with these exigencies, and to cope with our fellow "copers" as well, through figuring out underlying "grammars" and recognizing significant variation in the styles those about us use in behaving and in communicating. We are all figuring things out (and only more or less successfully) all the time. In our awe at the magnitude of this task as it confronts the newborn, we lose sight of the fact that for each of us the task of figuring things out continues to the moment we draw our last breath.

Point 6: The Question of Innate Capacity

Do we need to declare a moratorium while we await the answer to the debate

---

[1]Psychologists may insist that they have long touted this view. The importance they have assigned to the learner has varied considerably over the years, however. In a 1974 paper, educational psychologist Wittrock commended "the current welcomed shift" in cognitive psychology "toward reinstating the learner... as a primary determiner of learning with understanding and long-term memory" (1974:87).

on whether or to what extent we are "programmed to learn" (cf. Pulliam and Dunford 1980)? Chomsky's early hypothesis about the innateness of linguistic capacity, that humans are born preprogrammed with a Language Acquisition Device, might seem to offer a convenient wayside resting point for those who insist upon a final resolution of basic heredity-versus-environment issues. Does our analogy to language acquisition require some anthropologist to propose a comparable "Cultural Acquisition Device" to explain how humans are so adept at acquiring culture?

Once again, Bateson points a way out of the seeming morass of the heredity-environment issue. He urges us to attend to the extensive overlap where resolution is not the critical issue:

> The problem in regard to any behavior is clearly not "Is it learned or is it innate" but "Up to what logical level is learning effective and down to what level does genetics play a determinative or partly effective role"? (Bateson 1972:307)

Point 7: Learning "About" Versus Learning "To"

Thirty years ago analytical philosophers like Gilbert Ryle, the source of Geertz's notion of "thick description," were making what I find to be a useful distinction between *learning about* (or *learning that) versus learning to* (or *learning how*) (cf. Carroll 1968). If such simple and direct language is adequate for our purposes, I suggest we adopt it.

If we wish to build our taxonomies upon anthropological sources, Anthony Wallace has proposed a classification of learning according to the kinds of "matter" to be learned. He identifies three: *technic* ("how to" learning), *morality* (consideration for the welfare of the group), and *intellect* (a tradition and way of thinking) (Wallace 1961). Technic, as Wallace points out, is the most (conspicuous" matter of learning and has been subject to the most intensive analysis by psychologists and educators. That is hardly surprising in an era when a concern for measurements has been so central in scientific thinking.

Anthropologists, too, have been interested in "how to" learning, but I think their commitment to context finds them particularly suited to inquire into the learning of morality and intellect. I find Wallace's ideas about the learning of morality especially provocative, for he is describing the learning of human qualities that find their expression in placing the welfare of the group above one's own needs or interests. Morality, as Wallace uses the term, is "sharply distinguished from mere propriety, conformity, and respectablitity"; it is the sort of behavior most *conspicuously* exhibited in heroic action but most *commonly* practiced in the "humble endurance of discomfort, protracted over decades, by inconspicuous people in positions of authority" (p. 32). Such learning cannot be explained apart from a cultural context.

Point 8: Intentionality in Learning

How can we best describe and distinguish among the various ways that humans acquire their cultural knowledge? Two frequently heard terms are "observational learning" and "imitation." Neither term seems sufficiently precise. Can we find better words to convey our sense of the processes that are involved?

Personally, I recommend against using the term *imitation.* Although its broad definition includes the ideas of "modeling," I think modeling should be the preferred term when that describes how we believe learning to be occurring, if only because modeling is "less imprecise." I suspect that when my students use the term imitation they are really thinking "mimicking." To say, for example, that we learn any substantial part of language by mimicking (imitating) words and sentences—and I always find some students who insist that's how we do it—is quite absurd. We do not learn to speak by mimicking. If we did, we would be doomed to speak only those words or phrases we have heard before! That our speech resembles the speech of somebody rather than a generalized "everybody" implicates a process of modeling. Modeling seems critical for learning language and for learning culture as well.

The phrase "observational learning" seems to make "learning" synonymous with "watching" or even "seeing." Inadvertently, the phrase cloaks rather than reveals the very processes we are trying to understand. If we "learn" everything we observe, we are back to Gearing's question: Why then don't we all learn almost everyhing? When my students in Western Oregon insist that we learn what we see around us, I ask them why we do not all become Douglas fir trees, since that is what we see everywhere. And as they explain why we do *not* become Douglas firs, they recognize how observation must be joined to other mental processes before we can associate it with learning.

Both "imitation" and "observational learning" seem more helpful than Spindler's depiction of learning one's culture by a process of "osmosis" (Spindler 1973:225). Yet one can see how Spindler wanted to convey the pervasiveness of cultural influences. Other terms have also been suggested to account for cultural influence. Although they seem preferable to "osmosis," they fail to provide a distinction, if a careful examination of learning requires it, between what one invites into one's mind and what else either tags along or sneaks in uninvited. I am not sure of the origins or use among anthropologists of such related terms as *concomitant learning, incidental learning, unintended learning,* and *latent learning.*

Lawrence Frank may have been responsible for introducing the term "concomitant learning" to anthropologists. I first heard the term used by Spindler. When I subsequently organized a paper of my own around the concept of concomitant learning (Wolcott 1969), I linked that concept to "incidental" and to "unintended" learning and called attention to earlier use that both Jules Henry and George Spindler had made of contrasts between intended and unintended learning in the school setting (cf. Henry 1960; Spindler 1959).

"Latent learning" proves even more elusive, but joins company with such terms as "no-trial" learning and "vicarious" learning suggested by educational psychologists like Gage and Berliner (1975) and social learning theorists like Bandura (1977). Educational psychologist Wittrock reminds us that "People learn . . . sometimes without practice, without reinforcement, and without overt action" (1979:5. Ralph Peterson once recounted how his belated and sudden mastery of a skill required in building a log cabin in Idaho over a period of summers was identified by a neighbor as an example of "winter learning." Have we been sufficiently attentive to folk taxonomies in our examination of learning phenomena?

Such an array of terms provides tempting labels when we want to explain how a member of a society is suddenly able to perform a skill or enact a role that has not previously been mastered and may never have been practiced. Especially when we speak of learning "about," as, for example, in learning about how things were in the "good old days" or learning about experiences like drowning or starving to death, it is obvious that thought processes themselves, rather than practice or firsthand experience, may satisfy the condition that the learner be actively involved. Which of these terms best convey our present level of understanding?

I do not deny that something goes on in human cognition that can be called "observational learning" or even "learning by osmosis." But I hope we can find more precise ways to describe that learning. More importantly, can we find ways to distinguish circumstances when we have every reason to believe learning is taking place from other moments when we believe it might be taking place? Should we make a distinction between intentional learning— dare I introduce such a term? — and incidental learning, "second-order" stuff that *may or may not* be retrieved in some future intentional learning effort. Incidental learning, it seems to me, might include everything from miniscule details one may be asked to recall ("Do you remember seeing where I left my car keys?") to those "whole integrated patterns of behavior" we are said to acquire almost subconsciously. (As grandson, was I also learning the complementary social role of how to act as a grandfather?) And if even so vague a notion as incidental learning does not include all the experiences to which a learner is exposed, if learning is something different from the complete osmosis of everything within the range of one's senses, then what are the outer limits beyond which learning does not occur? In a practical, everyday sense, what are the boundaries for what any particular human should learn, might learn, and does learn (cf. Wallace 1961:38)?

Traditionally, anthropoligists have attended to the venerable old storytellers, dancers, and singers who go on hour after hour. But what happens if the children are distracted, inattentive, daydreaming, or, worst of all, asleep? When children focus attention on other children, instead of on the formally appointed transmitters, and children are remarkably attentive to other children, then what is *actually* being learned? It is time at least for us to ask.

Point 9: The Polyphasic Nature of Learning

I might have included Henry's idea of *polyphasic learning* among the terms just reviewed, since it, too, deals with peripheral learning. I treat it separately here, consistent with what I take to be Henry's intent in noting not simply that humans can learn more than one thing at a time, but that they are *incapable* of learning *only* one thing at a time (Henry 1955:196ff). Although this seems the kind of pronoucement one must take on faith, I have always felt that Henry's idea of polyphasic learning warrants more attention than it has received. Here is an opportunity to reexamine it.

Point 10: The Importance of the Setting

When anthropologists turn their attention to learning, they do not perforce think of schooling; they have customarily been careful to distinguish "learning done in schools" from learning in other settings. Wallace has proposed what he calls a "scale of generality" for describing human learning:

> It is convenient to arrange the circumstances of human learning in the form of a scale of generality, each category of which is contained in, and implied by, its succeeding category. If we take *schooling* as the initial category, it is followed by *education,* then *enculturation,* then *learning* itself (Wallace 1961:29).

In a somewhat similar vein, learning modes have been contrasted according to the formality of the setting, distinguishing *formal learning* done in schools, *nonformal* (i.e., noninstitutionalized) *learning* through sources like the media, and *informal learning,* the learning individuals engage in throughout their lives (cf. Wilbert 1976).

There are other ways to classify learning settings in addition to their formality. Whiting and child, for example, have noted how the tasks expected of young males in some societies (e.g., the daily herding of livestock) place them in learning environments dominated by male peers, while in the same society young girls might be expected to help with household chores in learning environments dominated by older females (1953). Poirier has noted a similar contrast among nonhuman primates (1973:29). Some years ago Barker and his associates were attempting to examine learning in terms of the "behavior settings" in which it occurred, another way to examine learning environments (cf. Barker 1968).

These various ways of looking at "learning settings" present some problems. For example, a preoccupation with settings rather than with the content of them invites confusion between quantity and quality. It may be that father's few words of praise or reprimand in the evening are of more consequence than the entire day's opportunities for diversion with other herdsboys. An underlying question is, "When, and in what ways, do learning settings make a difference?" And how, in turn, do elements within the different settings in which we interact (in space and time) serve subsequently as mnemonics to help us recall previously learned behaviors appropriate to them (cf. Harwood 1976)?

Point 11: The Importance of Intimacy or Social Distance

Closely allied with the consideration of settings are questions of who we learn from, the latter characteristically viewed by anthropologists in terms of generation, kinship, or social distance. For even if we adopt Keesing's proposition that cultural learning occurs *in spite of* rather than *because of* child-rearing practices, culture is learned nonetheless, and it is learned from those with whom one is in rather close proximity. Anthropological pronouncements on the influence of "significant others" in this process fare better when examined separately than when viewed collectively.

Little systematic attention has been given to considerations of "generation" in human learning. Anthropologists have raised some interesting questions, however. I can recall when it was vogue to quote (or at least be conversant with Bruner's "early learning hypothesis": that which is learned earliest (and thus from persons with whom one is close) is the most resistant to change; that which is learned later is most readily discarded, in conditions of culture contact (Bruner 1956a, 1956b). Yet Bruner informs me (personal communication, 1980) that although a literature "grew up around it" and influenced a great deal of his subsequent work, he does not believe that anyone has made a systematic attempt to test the hypothesis. Our stock-taking provides an opportunity to review this concept.

Similarly, Tax once suggested that we glean most of our cultural knowledge from those only slightly older and in turn convey to those only slightly younger most of what they will learn. Tax emphasized the point that "a chief way—not an incidental way, but a chief way—the traditional adult culture is transmitted in all or most societies is through the peer group" in the passage of information "from slightly older to slightly younger people" (1973:50).

Tax observes that it is probably "an illusion of our culture and other cultures that parents, teachers, learners and others teach anything to people 20 or 25 years their junior" (pp. 50-51). As a middle-aged adult, I continue to influence, and to be influenced by, those closest to me in age. On reflection, I am sure this has always been the case for me, and I assume it is largely true for others. Yet I think it erroneous to suggest that we are not influenced by those much older or that we exert no influence on those much younger. The question properly posed directs us to ask how and what we learn from people of various kinship designations and generations.

At the same time that I draw attention to this learn-then-teach cycle that Tax describes as the "short-jump percolation" of information, I must note that anthropologists have rightly called attention to the enculturative influence of every family member. They have made a particular effort to show how certain functions that mainstream American families assume to be the "normal" child-rearing responsibilities of (two) parents are often performed by others (e.g., older siblings, mother's brother, "equivalent" members of extended families) in different societies. But we need not cite exotic circumstances to bring attention to the influence of people in roles other than parents and peers. In our own society, for example, we have given rather slight attention to the role of grandparents in cultural acquisition. Margaret Mead often alluded to the educative influence of grandparents and wrote personally of her experience of grandmothering (Mead 1972:273-294). Ethnographic accounts sometimes mention grandparent-grandchild relationships, especially if they are characterized by special behavior such as the "joking relationship" and reciprocal forms of address noted among some American Indian tribes. Perhaps the anthropology of learning can draw attention to the influence that grandparents exert in our efforts to discover our culture and locate ourselves in it.

I wonder how parents and grandparents play different and complementary roles as models in our learning. Our parents attend to our everyday needs and daily deportment. Do grandparents convey a bigger sense of family and cultural heritage? Did I perchance learn *how* to behave from my parents and *why* I would want to behave that way from my grandparents? Is there any doubt that a grandfather who died years before I was born (hardly a coincidence that I bear his name) nevertheless exerted a benign grandfatherly influence over me whenever I was lauded for seeming to exhibit one of his fondly recalled traits?

Also unsorted is the cross-cultural examination of the circumstances by which persons charged with formal responsibilities as educators are to be regarded as strangers or friends. When the social distance between learner and teacher is great, Tax's hypothesis might suggest that efforts would be made to narrow the gap (e.g., assign teachers only slightly older than the students, or address teachers by kin terms). We often see "beginning" teachers try to effect this closeness, but my sense of the anthropological evidence is that teachers have traditionally been cast in the role of stranger. In the absence of real strangers to perform some formal ceremony or initiation, it has been pointed out that a group can *create* strangers with the use of masks (cf. Hart 1955, including the discussants' comments following his presentation). In our society (and certainly among professional educators), we virtually insist that didactic instruction be given by strangers. We do not want to be "lectured to" by friends. At the same time, we expect public school teachers to be friends, or at least friendly, particularly in the early years of schooling. What cross-cultural and comparative questions could sharpen our perspective?

Point 12: The Essential Continuity of Cultural Acquisition

Previous points dealt with settings and personnel. A related issue, raised but not resolved, is that of continuity in cultural acquisition. Years ago Benedict wrote a remarkable essay, "Continuities and Discontinuities in Cultural Conditioning," in which she noted that "from a comparative point of view, our culture goes to great extremes in emphasizing contrasts between the child and the adult" (Benedict 1938). Ethnographic attention has often been drawn to such contrasts, particularly if the ethnographer perceived a romantic period of carefree youth terminated abruptly at a formal transition into adult status. Hart's provocative paper "Contrasts between Prepubertal and Postpubertal Education," first published in 1955, makes splendid use of contrasts among preliterate societies that have formal "pre-initiation" education and post-initiation education. I do not believe we have addressed the issue of whether or not contrasts or inconsistencies in the process of cultural conditioning can reach such proportion as to constitute true "discontinuities."

From the point of view of a society intent on dramatizing the transition from a previous status to a new one, it seems appropriate to speak of efforts to *create* discontinuity. And to an outside observer like the anthropologist, such abrupt transitions might appear as discontinuities. From the point of view of the learner, however, the idea of discontinuity seems suspect. The drama of being inducted into "initiation school" or into the army, or being married to a stranger through prior family arrangement, may be intended to create discontinuity and may seem a discontinuity to the observer. To participants reared with the expectation that someday this would happen, no matter how traumatic and disorienting the event, it seems to me that it is entirely consistent with those expectations. It does not really matter if you cry yourself to sleep as long as you get up when the bugle blows; you knew this was how it would be.

The Anthropology of Learning: Some Next Steps and Some Cautions

There are already anthropologists whose careers are marked with notable contributions to understanding the enculturation process. If we can induce them to include more attention to the learning of culture as well as to the teaching of it, our efforts at "revitalizing" learning will be well rewarded. In addition, perhaps we can spark new interest and enlist a broader commitment to describing learning-related aspects of behavior among those whose major research interests lie elsewhere. To that end, some next steps and some cautions are outlined here.

One way to stimulate broader participation might be to call for more systematic anthropological attention to the learning of *particular* aspects of culture, such as Philip's examination of how lawyers acquire legal jargon (Philips 1982). In a study that must have seemed daring when reported three decades ago, sociologist Becker provides another model in "Becoming a Marihuana User" (Becker 1953). An opportunity to study urban African beer gardens prompted me to look at "Becoming a Drinker" (Wolcott 1974:205-215). I imagine that careful anthropological attention to the ways particular groups of people acquire particular skills and understandings related to social (and antisocial) behaviors, comparable to contemporary studies of drinking or drug use, could provide a valuable resource for administrators and policy makers who assume responsibility when any pattern of behavior becomes identified as a social issue or social problem. My hunch is that the teaching and learning involved in the acquisition of "antisocial" behaviors are often rapid, secluded, and highly personal, circumstances difficult to research but not beyond the ethnographic imagination. In fact, ethnographers are probably at those very scenes right now but are looking at cultural practice rather than cultural acquisition.

We might also invite more systematic attention to discerning the moment in individual life cycles when people learn particular facets of their culture. I remember reading an article in which Margaret Mead reported being questioned (was it during her doctoral oral?) about the point in its life when an infant actually *became* Kwakiutl or Hopi or a member of whatever society. The question proves provocative for turning attention to the continuous process of *becoming*, rather than focusing on a state of *being*. Mead's answer was, in effect, that a Kwakiutl infant of age one month is just that much of a Kwakiutl, a 10-year-old Hopi is just that Hopi, and so on.

It is understandable that anthropologists inquiring into a culture are drawn toward older informants who are, in one sense, the best source of cultural knowledge. But in our ethnographic determination to "get right to the source," we inadvertently gloss over the age-grading of knowledge. We lost track of the fact that even our oldest informants continue to learn. I recall a conversation with an old Kwakiutl man who was explaining something of the contemporary form of traditional Kwakiutl social organization. Having been struck by how uninformed my Kwakiutl pupils were about the ways of their people (and having thereby forfeited a golden opportunity to observe cultural acquisition in process), I was wondering about the circumstances under which my elderly informant had become so knowledgeable. I asked him when he had learned what he was now explaining to me, fully expecting him to say that his grandfather had passed this knowledge on to him while he was a young boy. Instead, to my disappointment, he confessed that only recently had he learned much of what he was telling me. I had become so intent on learning how it was to be Kwakiutl that I had failed to realize that my most informed informants were still "becoming" Kwakiutl as they assumed new roles as elders and guardians of their heritage (cf. Wolcott 1967).

The anthropological tenet that the informant is the teacher and the fieldworker is the learner has also kept us from systematic attention to what members of a society do *not* know, do not *yet* know, or may *never* be expected (or even allowed) to know because of their particular circumstances. As Robert Tonkinson has reminded me, informants have a tendency to behave as if they know everything; they feel an obligation to be fully informed. The difficulty of inquiring into what individuals do *not* know is thus complicated by creating the informant role in which an individual is supposed to be all-knowing. But informants do make errors, and the systematic analysis of those errors can lead to a clearer understanding of what informants themselves know or have yet to know (cf. Cancian 1963).

In our call for more anthropological attention to learning, I think attention should be focused on learning that occurs in natural settings rather than on learning done in schools. This is not to say that school learning is unimportant or that anthropologists have nothing to offer; rather, I think, school learning already receives adequate attention and anthropologists are contributing to that work. Of late, "anthropology and education" seems to have focused unduly on schools and given too little attention to education in broader cultural context. Schools should not dominate either our research or our perspective when schooling itself deals with such a narrow spectrum of the cultural repertoire. We should be bringing our anthropology to bear on classroom observations, not drawing our perspectives from them. Perhaps this is why Lave's work on the apprenticing of tailors in Liberia, viewed as an alternative *to* formal schooling rather than an alternative form *of* it, has struck such a note of interest in anthropology and education (cf. Lave 1977, n.d.; see also Lancy 1980).

To whatever extent learning one's language or culture of "orientation" differs from learning alternative forms of it (dialects, microcultures) or alternatives to it (second language, another "macro" or "national" culture), then the frequent and satisfying claim that the anthropologist in the field is "just like a child" also warrants critical review. Perhaps the very opposite of that assertion is true: nothing is more unnatural and unchildlike than the ethnographer learning a culture, since the ethnographer is trying quite self-consciously to learn "another" culture and to make that learning explicit. By contrast, "natural" learners ease into their first culture casually, effortlessly, and essentially unaware of the process. A closer examination of the analog between culture acquisition and ethnographic research could add to our understanding of both processes (cf. insightful comments in this regard in Burnett 1974b).

Some scholars interested in second-language learning make a distinction between language *acquisition* and language *learning*. They use the former, more inclusive term to refer to processes of interaction through which one acquires a feeling for a whole language system. Language "learning," on the other hand, refers to self-conscious processes involving error correction and the presentation of explicit rules (cf. Krashen 1981:2; see also Corder 1967; Lawler and Selinker 1971).

In this paper I have used the terms acquisition and learning interchangeably.

Until scholars interested in second-language learning began making a distinction between the terms, I think they were used interchangeably by most linguists and anthropologists.[2] I wonder now if a more self-conscious anthropology of learning might make better use of this distinction. Of course, "acquisition" may prove in the long run to be no more than a fancy synonym for "osmosis," acknowledging the presence of a complex process without in the least helping us to understand it. Nonetheless, our concern with identifying appropriate terms serves notice of our effort to distinguish broad, pervasive learning "contexts" from attempts to induce learning through purposeful engagement, error correction, and the explicit teaching of rules. Extending the distinction between acquisition and learning into the cultural sphere provides a perspective for understanding why anthropologists, for all their success at "learning" other cultures, seldom achieve the "good intuitions" or "deep understandings" to the degree that the natives have, even though the anthropologist may easily outperform the native in "explaining" a particular society.

What if we were to incorporate the *acquisition* versus *learning* contrast into our dialogues on cultural learning, henceforth restricting our use of the term "learning" to those circumstances where we can muster evidence not only that something has been learned but that there was also a self-conscious effort to accomplish that learning? Linguists already make splendid use of children's "rule-governed errors" in speech (e.g., "He goed") to infer processes in child language acquisition (cf. Corder 1967). We could be making better use of errors to infer processes in children's cultural acquisition as well (cf. Heider 1976 for an example of using errors to posit the sequence in which children come to understand a kinship system). Unless learner errors are subject to intentional efforts at correction and rule explication, however, they provide evidence of the broad and largely subconscious activity of acquiring language or culture rather than evidence of the self-conscious and focused activity of learning.

The distinguishing feature between acquisition and learning seems to be *intentionality*. The term learning, then, could be restricted to those things in the vast repertoire of stuff we carry about in our heads that we have consciously tried to make sense of or that someone has either succeeded in teaching us or has tried unsuccessfully to teach (thus accounting for things

---

[2]Cazden notes that, although the terms have not been used contrastively by scholars in the first-language field, the term that individual scholars choose usually reflects their theoretical perspective, the psycholinguists of Chomsky persuasion addressing themselves to the process of language acquisition, and behaviorists consistently employing "learning" as their preferred term (Cazden 1980, personal communication). Anthropologists seem not to have used the terms contrastively: compare Keesing's "Learning a Culture" (1976:201-203) and Schwartz's "Acquisition of Culture" (1981:4-17).

"not learned"). Presumably, we will continue to use "learning" in both its broad "acquisition" sense and in the more restricted sense suggested here. Even a clearer recognition of differing levels of consciousness and degrees of intentionality, however, might help lend precision to our efforts to understand the complex process of cultural acquisition.

The tendency to view learning as "problem solving" seems to me to present another potential problem, that of taking too restricted a view of how learning works. Unquestionably, problem solving creates opportunities for learning, but the idea that learning occurs *only* during problem solving is too restrictive. Years ago Lee pondered the topic in an essay on "Autonomous Motivation" (Lee 1961) in which she asked why humans engage in behavior for no apparent social reason, the kind of behavior reflected in Leigh-Mallory's alleged response about why one climbs mountains: because they are there. In fact, explanations of a social world founded entirely on the concept of "need reduction" seem strained if one looks at humans as *problem finders* as well as *problem seekers*. As Jacob Getzels notes,

> there seem to be as yet ill-defined neurogenic needs that are gratified by stimulation, needs for excitement, novelty, sensory variation, and perhaps above all for the challenge of the problematic . . . The learner is not only a problem-solving and stimulus reducing organism but also a problem-finding and stimulus seeking organism (Getzels 1974:536).

My hunch is that in attending to the "imponderabilia of actual life" anthropologists have probably observed far more "problem finding and stimulus seeking" behavior than they have reported. They have not made much of such behavior because they have tended to view it as idiosyncratic and individual. If we were to aggregate such behaviors, we might see patterns that reflect cultural influences in terms of the ordinary range of behaviors from which one may select alternatives or "do one's own thing." Do some societies foster problem finding more than others? Stated another way, in what ways do different societies accommodate problem-finding and stimulus-seeking behavior?

Just as we might reexamine whether we are viewing problem solving or problem seeking in our investigations into cultural acquisition, I think we should see what an anthropological perspective brings to the issue of *gradualness* versus *gestalts* (or "spurts") in learning. Gradualness is a compelling notion; clearly the life-long accumulation of knowledge is a gradual process. Neither languages nor cultures are acquired quickly. But the appropriateness of talking about the accumulation of knowledge as a long-term process may mask that, except on the most abstract of levels, learning seems to proceed in spurts, bursts, and flashes. Piaget has posited a number of learning stages for the young. Research on brain growth indicates that the developing brain, too, alternates between periods of rapid growth and periods of rest. (It is also characteristic of our level of understanding that there are arguments over whether growth spurts precede, accompany, or follow learning spurts.) What ethnographic evidence can we provide to illustrate what Beals refers to as "dramatic intuitive leaps" that humans are capable of making (Beals 1973:129)? What kind of evidence from ethnographic observation can we bring to support or refute Hall's observation in *Beyond Culture* that "People learn in gestalts—complete units—which are contexted in situations and can be recalled as wholes" (Hall 1976:130-131)?

Growing out of a reexamination of such comfortable but nonetheless questionable assumptions as learning being *only* problem solving or *always* gradual and continuous, it is probably wise to conclude this assessment of possible next steps by urging that we continue to work from our traditional "worm's eye view" in providing an anthropological dimension to the study of cultural acquisition. Anthropology's most vital contribution to the understanding of learning, for now at least would seem to be its traditional ethnographic concern for specificness, for details in context. Our task is not to provide a treatise on learning per se but to provide an accumulation of richly contextualized, culturally oriented, easily accessed accounts of learning to be or become *something* or *someone* in a *particular* place, time, and setting. For the anthropologist, the model must be more like Whiting's *Becoming a Kwoma* (1941) than Allport's *Becoming* (1955).

At the same time, and with the advantage of 40 years of hindsight, Whiting's monograph stands as reminder of the perils of laying out one's data on the Procrustean bed of currently popular theory or of using field research to prove rather than to probe. Whiting describes *Becoming a Kwoma* as a "pioneering attempt to apply learning theory to anthropological data" (1941:xix). He invested heavily in reinforcement ("the most basic of learning principles," p. 172), in a set of four "essential conditions for habit formation" comprised of *drive, response, cues,* and *reward* (p. 173), and in the concept of *imitation* ("one of the most important mechanisms by which culture is transmitted," p. 196). He tells us that

> A Kwoma child learns but a small part of his cultural habits by free trial and error, that is, without some member of his society guiding and direct- ing him. . . He is forced [and, later, "compelled"; cf. p. 200] to learn, not the habits which might be most rewarding to him alone, but the habits which are specified in the cul- ture as being best (p. 177).

Whiting also dismisses "free trial and error," referring to "learning which takes place without the guidance or interference of any other person" (p. 177n), as an important avenue for learning.

Whiting's confidence that all learning could be explained by the theories he was applying kept him from probing into some theory-shaking subtleties in what he himself observed and reported:

> The circumstances which determine when one should ask for food and when one may take it without asking were too subtly shaded for me to

appreciate. I can simply record that Kwoma culture contains both these customs and that children learn to distinguish between them (p. 42).

The Whitings and their students have, of course, continued to examine these topics throughout a lifetime of study on socialization practices. By 1975, their explanations had moved away from John Whiting's earlier emphasis on reward and deliberate instruction:

> It is in the assignment of tasks and the punishment of disobedience rather than in deliberate instruction or rewarding and punishing specific behaviors that [parents] have the greatest effect . . . Having been assigned a task, children are motivated to imitate the behavior of those who are competent. Their skills are more likely to come from observations than from instruction (Whiting and Whiting 1975:180).

The softening evident in this latter statement of the primacy Whiting once assigned to deliberate instruction is, I think, indicative of the growing interest being directed to what learners themselves are up to. The irony is that Whiting was at the brink of discovery years ago. With the benefit of hindsight, one wonders what would have happened had he set his "pioneering effort" in a different direction, to use anthropological data to ask what it is of human behavior for which learning theory must account. That same opportunity—and peril—exist today, for we are no less subject to the influence of current theory than was Whiting at the time of his Kwoma research. But the lesson is clear: Our explanations must work in the natural settings in which ethnographic research is conducted. And that stands to be the major contribution from the anthropological study of learning.

Summary

I view rather critically the tendency to equate what cultural transmitters are attempting to transmit with what cultural acquirers are necessarily acquiring. The call proposed here for an anthropology of learning is a call for increased attention to the processes through which individuals continue throughout their lives to "gropingly discover" what they need to know. An anthropology of learning can also serve as a reminder that learning remains an individual matter; culture is, at best, only imperfectly "shared." As Goodenough states, "People learn as individuals. Therefore, if culture is learned, its ultimate locus must be in individuals rather than in groups" (1981:54).

I have examined a number of learning-related terms and concepts that anthropologists have used or introduced. It is time for sifting and sorting. To the end of providing some structure for the anthropology of learning, I have attempted to identify central issues and have raised cautions, primarily with the intent of keeping our attention focused on what we have actually observed, rather than borrowing too heavily from psychological theory or working from popular anthropological assumptions that have not themselves been subjected to scrutiny.

I am quite taken with the generally accepted view among linguists that sees learning as a constructive and effortful process. In that view, learners are seen as active hypothesis makers or theory builders constantly discovering and refining a set of underlying principles that corresponds closely enough with the behavior of other humans around them to guide the conduct of their everyday lives. A distinction between *cultural acquisition* and *cultural learning,* comparable to the distinction second-language learning scholars are making between language acquisition and language learning, could prove helpful in accounting for the fact that learners accumulate a storehouse of data that far exceeds what they are actively attending to at any given moment.

To be able better to distinguish the learned from the learnable in all that stuff we carry about in our heads would help us with the dilemma of seeming at once to explain so much and so little when we observe that it would be "difficult" for children not to learn their culture. The signal contribution from a rekindled anthropological interest in learning may come not from the recognition of the inevitability of acquiring one's culture but from the reminder that human social learning is essentially a process of active rediscovery. For even as we display new facets of our own linguistic or cultural competence, we only succeed in proving that we have rediscovered, and now claim as our own, what our elders knew all the time.

References

Allport, Gordon W., 1955, *Becoming: Basic Considerations for a Psychology of Personality.* New Haven, Conn.: Yale University Press.

Bandura, Albert, 1977, *Social Learning Theory.* Englewood Cliffs, NJ: Prentice-Hall.

Barker, Roger G., 1968, *Ecological Psychology: Concepts and Methods for Studying the Environment of Human Behavior.* Standord, CA: Stanford University Press.

Bateson, Gregory, 1942, *"Social Planning and the Concept of Deutero-Learning."* In *Science, Philosophy and Religion, Second Symposium* by the Conference on Science, Philosophy and Religion. New York: Harper & Row.

_____, 1972, *Steps to an Ecology of Mind.* San Francisco, CA: Chandler.

Beals, Alan, 1973, *Culture in Process,* 2nd ed. New York: Holt, Rinehart and Winston.

Becker, Howard S., 1953, *Becoming a Marihuana User. American Journal of Sociology.* 59:235-242.

Benedict, Ruth, 1938, *Continuities and Discontinuities in Cultural Conditioning.* Psychiatry 1:161-67.

Brukman, Jan, 1973, "Language and Socialization: Child Culture and the Ethnographer's Task." In *Learning and Culture.* Solon T. Kimball and Jacquetta Burnett, eds., pp. 43-58. Seattle: University of Washington Press.

Bruner, Edward M., 1956a, *Cultural Transmission and Culture Change. Southwestern Journal of Anthropology* 12:191-199.

———, 1956b, Primary Group Experience and the Processes of Acculturation. *American Anthropologist* 58:605-623.

Burnett, Jacquetta Hill, 1974a *Anthropology and Education: An Annotated Bibliographic Guide.* New Haven, CT: Human Relations Area Files Press.

———, 1974b, *On the Analog between Culture Acquisition and Ethnographic Method.* [Council on] *Anthropology and Education Quarterly* 5(1):25-29.

Cancian, Frank, 1963, *Informant Error and Native Prestige Ranking in Zinacantan. American Anthropologist* 65:1068-1075.

Carroll, John B., 1968, *On Learning from Being Told. Educational Psychologist* 5(2):1-10.

Corder, S.P., 1967, *The Significance of Learner's Errors. International Review of Applied Linguistics in Language Teaching* 5:161-170.

Fortes, Meyer, 1938, *Social and Psychological Aspects of Education in Taleland.* Africa 11, No. 4 (Supplement).

Gage, N.L., and David Berliner, 1975, *Educational Psychology.* Chicago: Rand McNally.

Gearing, Frederick O., 1973, "Anthropology and Education." In *Handbook of Social and Cultural Anthropology.* John J. Honigmann, ed. Chicago: Rand McNally.

———, and Lucinda Sangree, eds., 1979, *Toward a Cultural Theory of Education and Schooling.* The Hague: Mouton Publishers.

Geertz, Clifford, 1968, *Islam Observed.* Chicago: University of Chicago Press.

———, 1973, "Thick Description." In *The Interpretation of Cultures.* New York: Basic Books.

Getzels, Jacob W., 1974, *Images of the Classroom and Visions of the Learner.* School Review 82(4):527-540.

Gladwin, Thomas, 1970, *East is a Big Bird.* Cambridge, MA: Harvard University Press.

Goodenough, Ward H., 1981, *Culture, Language and Society,* 2nd ed. Menlo Park, CA: Benjamin/Cummings Publishing Co.

Hall, E.T., 1976, *Beyond Culture.* Garden City, NY: Doubleday.

Hansen, Judith Friedman, 1979, *Sociocultural Perspectives on Human Learning: An Introduction to Educational Anthropology.* Englewood Cliffs, NJ: Prentice-Hall.

Harrington, Charles, 1979, *Psychological Anthropology and Education: A Delineation of a Field of Inquiry.* New York: AMS Press.

Hart, C.W.M., 1955, "Contrasts between Prepubertal and Postpubertal Education." In *Education and Anthropology.* George D. Spindler, ed. Stanford, CA: Stanford University Press.

Harwood, Frances, 1976, *Myth, Memory, and the Oral Tradition: Cicero in the Trobriands. American Anthropologist* 78:783-796.

Heider, Karl G., 1976, *Dani Children's Development of Competency in Social Structural Concepts. Ethnology* 15(3):47-62.

Henry, Jules, 1955, "Culture, Education, and Communication Theory." In *Education and Anthropology.* George D. Spindler, ed. Stanford, CA: Stanford University Press.

———, 1960, *A Cross-Cultural Outline of Education.* Current *Anthropology* 1:267-305.

Keesing, Roger M., 1976, *Cultural Anthropology: A Contemporary Perspective.* New York: Holt, Rinehart and Winston.

Kimball, Solon T., 1965, *The Transmission of Culture. Educational Horizons* 43(4):161-165.

————, 1972, "Learning a New Culture." In *Crossing Cultural Boundaries.* Solon T. Kimball and James B. Watson, eds. San Francisco: Chandler.

————, 1974, *Culture and the Educative Process.* New York: Teachers College Press.

————, and Jacquetta Hill-Burnett, eds., 1973, *Learning and Culture.* Seattle: University of Washington Press (for the American Ethnological Society).

Krashen, Stephen, 1981, *Second Language Acquisition and Second Language Learning.* Elmsford, NY: Pergamon Press.

Lancy, David F., 1980, *Becoming a Blacksmith in Gbarngasuakwelle. Anthropology and Education Quarterly* 11:266-274.

Lave, Jean, 1977, *Cognitive Consequences of Traditional Apprenticeship Training in West Africa. Anthropology and Education Quarterly* 8:177-180.

————, n.d., *Tailored Learning: Education and Cognitive Skills among Tribal Craftsmen in West Africa.* University of California, Irvine. Unpublished manuscript (1980).

Lawler, J., and L. Selinker, 1971, *On Paradox, Rules, and Research in Second Language Learning. Language Learning* 21:27-43.

Lee, Dorothy, 1961, "Autonomous Motivation." In *Anthropology and Education.* Frederick C. Gruber, ed. Philadelphia: University of Pennsylvania Press.

Mead, Margaret, 1942, "Educational Effects of Social Environment as Disclosed by Studies of Primitive Societies." In *Symposium on Environment and Education.* E. W. Burgess et al, eds. Chicago: University of Chicago Press.

————, 1964, *Continuities and Discontinuities in Cultural Evolution.* New Haven, CT: Yale University Press.

————, 1970, *Culture and Commitment.* Garden City, NY: Doubleday.

————, 1972, "On Being a Grandmother." In *Blackberry Winter,* New York: Morrow.

Pettitt, George, 1946, *Primitive Education in North America.* University of California Publications in *American Archaeology and Ethnology* 43(1).

Philips, Susan U., 1982, "The Language of Socialization of Lawyers: Acquiring the "Cant." In *Doing the Ethnography of Schooing.* George D. Spindler, ed. New York: Holt, Rinehart and Winston.

Poirier, Frank E., 1973, "Socialization and Learning among Nonhuman Primates." In *Learning and Culture.* Solon T. Kimball and Jacquetta Hill-Burnett, eds. Seattle: University of Washington Press (for the American Ethnological Society).

Powdermaker, Hortense, 1971, *Life in Lesu.* New York: W.W. Norton. [Originally Published in 1933]

Pulliam, H. Ronald, and Christopher Dunford, 1980, *Programmed to Learn: An Essay on the Evolution of Culture.* New York: Columbia University Press.

Sapir, Edward, 1934, "Emergence of a Concept of Personality in a Study of Cultures." *Journal of Social Psychology* 5:408-415.

Schwartz, Theodore, 1981, *The Acquisition of Culture.* Ethos 9(1):4-17.

Spindler, George D., 1959 *The Transmission of American Culture.* Cambridge, MA: Harvard University Press.

————, 1973, "Cultural Transmission." In *Culture in Process,* 2nd ed. Alan R. Beals, with George D. Spindler and Louise Spindler. New York: Holt, Rinehart and Winston.

————, 1974, "The Transmission of Culture." In *Education and Cultural Process.* George D. Spindler, ed. New York: Holt, Rinehart and Winston.

————, ed. 1978, *The Making of Psychological Anthropology.* Berkeley, CA: University of California Press.

Tax. Sol, 1973, "Self and Society." In *Reading in Education*. Malcolm P. Douglass, ed. Columbus, Ohio: Chas. E. Merrill.

Wallace, Anthony F.D., 1961, "Schools in Revolutionary and Conservative Societies." In *Anthropology and Education*. Frederick C. Gruber, ed. Philadelphia: University   University of Pennsylvania Press.

_____, 1970, *Culture and Personality,* 2nd ed. New York: Random House.

Whiting, Beatrice B., and John W.M. Whiting, 1975, *Children of Six Cultures: A Psycho-Cultural Analysis.* Cambridge, MA: Harvard University Press.

Whiting, John W.M., 1941, *Becoming a Kwoma: Teaching and Learning in a New Guinea Tribe.* New Haven, CT: Yale University Press.

_____, and Irving Child, 1953, *Child Training and Personality.* New Haven, CT: Yale University Press.

Wilbert, Johannes, ed., 1976, *Enculturation in Latin America: An Anthology.* UCLA Latin American Center Publications. University of California, Los Angeles.

Wittrock, M.C., 1974, "Learning as a Generative Process." *Educational Psychologist* 11(2):87-95.

_____, 1979, "The Cognitive Movement in Instruction." *Educational Researcher* 8(2):5-11.

Wolcott, Harry F., 1967, reissued 1984, *A Kwakiutl Village and School.* Prospect Heights, IL: Waveland Press.

_____, 1969, *Concomitant Learning: An Anthropological Perspective on the Utilization of Media.* In *Educational Media: Theory into Practice.* Raymond V. Wiman and Wesley C. Meierhenry, eds. Columbus, OH: Chas. E. Merrill.

_____, 1974, *The African Beer Gardens of Bulawayo: Integrated Drinking in a Segregated Society.* Rutgers Center of Alcohol Studies, Monograph No. 10.

_____, 1982, "Mirrors, Models, and Monitors: Educator Adaptations of the Ethnographic Innovation." In *Doing the Ethnography of Schooling.* George D. Spindler, ed. New York: Holt, Rinehart and Winston.

GEORGE and LOUISE SPINDLER/*Stanford University*

3   *Do Anthropologists Need Learning Theory?*[1]

We heard rather frequently about learning and learning theory in the 1940s and 1950s. There were what seemed to be clear indications that anthropologists, particularly those working on culture change, needed learning theory and were willing and able to go to psychologists to get it. Since then we have heard frequently about learning, but very little about explicit learning theories or models derived from work by psychologists. We read for this paper to find out what had happened and to see what we might be missing. We summarize some of our encounters as we traveled through psychological country. To reflect the exploratory nature of this trip, we will pose, and tentatively answer, several questions that emerged during our travels. We begin with a period now more than 40 years past and finish with some current trends. We make no claim that our comments are exhaustive. We think, however, that we have a fair sample of what is available and that this sample suggests that many of us anthropologists are overlooking valuable resources. We also auggest there are some problems in the use of psychological concepts. Our first question: *What explicit learning theories did anthropologists use in the 1940s and 1950s at the beginning of the modern era of anthropology?* Our memory of the early period, resulting particularly from our interest in the psychological aspects of culture change, served us rightly. A. Irving ("Pete") Hallowell and John Gillin, among others, used explicit learning theory in the analysis of culture change. Gillin's "Acquired Drives in Culture Contact (1942) is one of the best examples. He writes,

> Learning theory is of signigicance to anthropology because it provides a system of principles for the explanation and prediction of the acquisition and performance of learned behavior of individuals, provided the conditions of learning and performance can be specified. For human beings the most important set of such conditions are those established by the

[1]We wish to express our deep gratitude to Lee Shulman, Albert Bandura, Arthur Coladarci, and Gilbert Herdt for their generous help on various aspects of the materials and formulations represented in this paper.

Reprinted from the *Anthropology and Education Quarterly [13: 109-124] with permission.*

culture of the society in which the individuals live . . . The culture of a
society is manifested through customs, which are actually habits (learned
activities) common to the membership of a society or to categories of a
society . . .(p. 545).

He makes a case for analysis of culture change among the Flambeau Band
of Chippewa in Northern Wisconsin in learning theory terms derived largely
from the works of Clark Hull, as exemplified and developed by Mowrer
(1939), Miller and Dollard (1941), and Whiting (1941). His basic and enduring
point is that most of what a member of a subordinate minority can do in
interaction with the dominant society is punished. This leads to negativism,
which is described by laymen as laziness and apathy, and by anthropologists as
"social disorganization" and "cultural disintegration." Even when members
of the subordinate society attempt to emulate members of the dominant
society or do as they are taught in the schools managed by these members, they
are punished—put in their place. The results are not only apathy, anxiety, and
alcoholism, but also a turning away from the dominant society by physical
isolation and the reaffirmation of the traditional culture.

Although a reading of Gillin's article reminds us how our analytic models
have changed as well as how politicized we have become, the basic point made
still seems sound, as we understand matters from our own fieldwork with the
Menominee and our contacts with the Chippewa. Learning theory seemed to
help Gillin to focus on some useful relationships.

Hallowell likewise engaged problems of culture change with explicit learning
theory models in mind. As he said,

> It is hard to see how culture—an abstract summation of the mode of life of
> a people—can exert influence except as it is a definable constituent of the
> activities of human individuals in interaction with each other. In the last
> analysis it is individuals who respond to and influence one another
> (Hallowell 1945:174).

And further, "in order to learn something one must want something, notice
something, do something, and get something" (p. 185). Hallowell had some
problems in his applications of learning theory (though they were not made
explicit by him) in that he was firmly convinced that people are creators rather
than passive bearers of culture, but the learning theory of that time was
fundamentally behavioristic despite some moves toward cognition and
motivation.

Social learning theory in the 1940s developed out of Clark Hull's earlier
work and was expressed in most meaningful form in Neal Miller's and John
Dollard's *Social Learning and Imitation* (1941). These works in turn combined
and developed ideas from Pavlov, Terman, Thorndike, and other pioneers in
psychology. The formula was drive, cue, response, reward. As John Dollard
said, "The individual must be driven or excited in order to learn. He must hit
upon a response which is to be learned. This response must be made in the

presence of relevant environmental and somatic cues. The connection between cues and response must be cemented by reward" (Dollard 1945:442).

The key here is that the learner must "hit upon the response which is to be learned." As Albert Bandura once remarked, "If one had to learn to drive a car that way the results could be fatal."[2] The image of the learner perpetually trying out random responses "to be learned" has disappeared in the recent works of psychologists like Bandura. In his *Social Learning Theory* (1977) he moves decisively into a cognitive mode stressing self-regulation. But Hallowell did not have this kind of help, and he was never quite able to resolve the tension between his view of humans as creators of culture and a learning model that made them almost random experimenters with potentially fatal behaviors.

In contract, Homer Barnett, writing nearly a decade later than Hallowell, developed a theory of cultural innovation and diffusion that shifted responsibility from motivated happenstance to the perceiving and thinking individual (Barnett 1953). Barnett's innovator perceives and analyzes two or more existing cultural configurations, identifies similarities, and substitutes a new mental configuration combining elements in a novel way for the preexisting ideas. The potential acceptor of a cultural innovation goes through the same process as the innovator: analyzing, identifying, and combining. Barnett the anthropologist paralleled what some cognitive psychologists began to develop explicitly in the mid-1950s. The results of this work (by psychologists) appeared in the 1960s and 1970s as "central processing," "self-regulation," and "information processing." Although Barnett's formulations are widely known within anthropology, they have been underused, probably because anthropologists are, on the whole, deeply prejudiced against interpretations stressing the individual and using psychologically toned models.

In problem areas not primarily concerned with culture change, acculturation, or innovation, and utilizing explicit learning theory, Beatrice and John Whiting have for years dominated the scene. Were we even to begin to speak of their work, there would be nothing else in this paper. Those interested are urged to read their chapter in *The Making of Psychological Anthropology* (MOPA) (G. Spindler 1978) and a recent article in *Ethos* (B. Whiting 1980). Suffice it to say here that they were rescued early from any excesses of Pavlovian, or even Hullian, learning theory by inclusion of Lewinian field theory and Freudian concepts of projection and defense against anxiety.

Whether or not one agrees with the assumptions and procedures engendered

---

[2]Bandura, responding to an earlier draft of this paper, remarked "I cite this example in illustrating the limitations of a theory that assumes we can learn only by doing (M.R. Jones, ed., *Nebraska Symposium on Motivation*, 1962:260-261). The reinforcement theories of learning ignored the pervasive and powerful mode of learning by observation."

by the Whiting's dedication to hologeistic research one must credit them with some of the most innovative combinations of psychological and cultural theory yet produced by anthropologists or, for that matter, anyone else.

The only rival of comparable stature who made learning a primary focus in the earlier period is Margaret Mead, although she does not use learning theory in the specific sense that the Whitings do. Again, whole books have been and will be written about her, and we must pass by her mountain of works with a genuflection and an acknowledgment that she was one of the first anthropologists to be seriously interested in cognition as well as character formation and that she used almost every imaginable evocative device in her fieldwork. A reading of her chapter in MOPA (Mead 1978) will help to bring her work into focus.

Other anthropologists used explicit learning theory in the early period, but we must move to the next question: *Who uses learning theory now?*

Current Works in Anthropology

Many current works in psychological anthropology assume that learning is the basic process, but few apply explicit learning theory and even fewer cite learning theorists. We found a parallel to this situation in our 1963 review of the uses of psychology in the analysis of culture change (Spindler and Spindler 1963b). Anthropologists tend to be eclectic in their use of theories, models, paradigms, and methods. Citation of the original sources of ideas probably seems irrelevant to their current concerns. Furthermore, there is a generalized diffusion of concepts and models between psychology and anthropology (in both directions) that militates against precise designation of sources.

In Erika Bourguignon's text, *Psychological Anthropology* (1979), learning is a keystone. "One of the major discoveries of anthropology in the course of the last century has been precisely the importance of learning in the development of culture . . . We learn certain aspects of behavior without being aware of them . . . We pick them up through imitation and identification with models . . . (p. 7). Elsewhere she discusses language learning, primate learning, learning and socialization, cultural acquisition, and other aspects of learning, but few citations can be identified as references to explicit learning theories or models.

This situation is not very different from that displayed in MOPA. Although "learning" is indexed in various forms, and learning is basic to most of the work (their own) discussed by the 20 anthropologists contributing to this volume, there are only four pages indexed for learning theory. One of them refers to the "veterans" of the culture and personality movement represented in the book, whose theoretical position is "derived from neo-Freudianism, Gestalt, and social learning theory . . ." (G. Spindler 1978:2). An examination of the references cited in MOPA reveals bibliographic items representing learning theory cited in chapters by Michael Coie, Douglass Price-Williams, and Ted and Nancy Graves. Elsewhere learning as a process is taken for granted, but explicit learning theory is rarely used or cited.

A recent book by Judith Friedman Hansen (1979), *Sociocultural Perspectives on Human Learning: An Introduction to Educational Anthropology*, is concerned with social and cognitive learning, particularly the latter, within a basically cultural knowledge framework. There are discussions about social learning, cognitive styles in learning, and the psychobiological foundations of learning, as well as the learner's processing of information, the school as a kind of model environment for learning, and so forth. There is ample referencing of relevant research by anthropologists and psychologists. There are few citations of specific learning theories or learning theoreticians (Jerome Bruner and Jean Piaget are exceptions) and little on social learning theory. Richard Shweder's three-part analysis of what is wrong with "Culture and Personality," recently published in *Ethos* (Shweder 1979, 1980) is also characterized by sophisticated treatment of the psychological processes relevant to our concerns as anthropologists, but rarely refers to explicit learning theories or theoreticians in text or references. Hansen and Shweder may have been influenced by a shift in interests within psychology from learning theory to information processing, although interdisciplinary influences rarely diffuse so quickly.

We are not criticizing Bourguignon, the contributors to MOPA, Hansen, or Shweder. We are making a point that could be made with many other publications: anthropologists working in sectors of our discipline where psychologizing is done acknowledge the significance of learning and know something (in some cases a great deal) of its varieties, but rarely cite explicit learning theories or acknowledge explicit debts to learning theorists. Concepts of learning are usually applied in analyses that stay largely within a cultural, or language and culture, frame of reference. Perhaps this is exactly what we should be doing. Nevertheless, it may be worth our while to see what is available in psychology that might be useful.

Our next question: *What kinds of learning theory do anthropologists need?* We can, of course, touch upon only a few possible concerns and possible relevances.

The Instrumental Model

The answer to this question will depend upon what kind of anthropologist is engaged with what kind of problem. Quite naturally, we start with our kind of anthropologist with our kind of problem. Among the Blood and Mistassini Cree of Canada, and in urbanizing villages of the Rems valley near Stuttgart, Germany, we have used an eliciting instrument consisting of contextually accurate line drawings representing activities that are traditional, modern, and urban, in varying degrees (L. Spindler 1978; G. Spindler 1974a; G. and L. Spindler 1982), to elicit choices from respondents that they then must rationalize. With it we have elicited responses from several hundred children and their parents and teachers. The results of its use have been fed into a model of psychocultural process that we term instrumental. We cite it here to illustrate how a culture-relevant model can use learning theory profitably. It is not held up as an ideal model. It is an attempt to delineate some significant outcomes of cultural transmission and cultural acquisition in a manner that can be treated statistically to provide reliable statements of broad trends in these outcomes.

The central idea is that a sociocultural system provides instrumental behaviors (including occupations, sex roles, recreational activities, interpersonal skills, use of possessions, habitation, etc.) that lead to desired goals and states of being. The relationships between activities and end states are termed instrumental linkages. Members of a society must be enculturated to them. They must learn to perceive them, assign priorities to them, and maintain cognitive control over them in order to survive, and particularly to prosper, in their society. In a sociocultural system undergoing change there will be a number of alternatives in instrumental linkages and their supporting values.

The instrument, termed the Instrumental Activities Inventory (IAI), and its supporting model place the emphasis on the choosing, decision-making, self-justifying individual, who must not only make choices, assign priorities, and defend them, but must also maintain cognitive control, especially in a changing environment, over potentially conflicting means, ends, and supporting values. By doing these things individuals exhibit cultural competence. Cultural competences are learned in schools, among other places, and schools are in part organized to transmit them. We regard these instrumental means-ends relationships as one version of the primary material of cultural transmission. We have studied the manner in which the elementary school packages this material in the changing environment of an urbanizing area and the influence of this packaging on the children attending the school.

The IAI model makes possible some consistent attention to children's perceptions of the world into which they are enculturating, the culture they are acquiring, and the concepts held by their teachers and parents of these same relationships. Neither the model nor the instrument specifies the *processes* of cultural transmission or cultural acquisition. The instrument elicits responses that are, in part, the product of those processes. They can be treated analytically in various ways to provide a measurable parameter to define the surface level of the phenomena to be studied.

Although we were in contact with Albert Bandura at Stanford University during both his and our formative years, we did not realize how relevant his theoretical models of social learning theory were to our interests, as sketched above, until we read his recent synthesis (Bandura 1977) for this paper. We sample his theoretical position as an example of a kind of learning theory model useful to anthropologists.

Social Learning Theory

In social learning theory (SLT), as Bandura and associates conceive of it, there is "continuous *reciprocal interaction* between *cognitive, behavioral,* and *environmental* determinants" (Bandura 1977:194). People learn by *observing* the outcomes of their actions. They *develop hypotheses* about which responses are most appropriate in which settings. This *acquired* information acts as a *guide* for further action (p. 17). Behavior is *learned symbolically* through *central processing* of response information before it is performed. By observing a *model* of the *desired behavior*, an individual forms an idea of how response components must be *combined* and *sequenced* to produce new behavior. That observers learn *without performance* (therefore, without extrinsic reinforcement) is amply documented (p. 35). *Abstract modeling* is very important. By observing, people derive *principles* underlying specific performances for *generating behavior* that goes beyond what they have seen or heard. *Vicarious reinforcement*, where the observer has seen others reinforced for certain behaviors, actually results in faster learning than directly experienced reinforcement (p. 118). *Vicarious observation* of reinforced behaviors arouses expectations, therefore not only informing, but also *motivating. Context* is critically important. The same behavior can have markedly different consequences depending on the settings in which it is expressed, the person toward whom it is directed, and when it is performed (p. 125). *Inequitable reinforcement* occurs as social structure, status, and power differences become significant determinant factors in *modeling*.

As Bandura and associates have developed it through long-term experiments and controlled observation, SLT is a far cry from "hitting upon" a response that is reinforced and then added to the accumulation of similarly reinforced responses, as in the formulations of the 1940s (although we should remember that Miller and Dollard's *Social Learning and Imitation,* 1941, preceded by Clark Hull's work, is where SLT started).

The instrumental model and its field research implementation could use SLT to good advantage, as can any other theoretical construct that specifies the results of learning and requires attention to the processes of learning. SLT helps explain how instrumental behaviors are acquired, how instrumental linkages are formed, and how cognitive control is developed and maintained over them. Relationships among behaviors and goals and states of being are not discovered by contingent reinforcement alone. Observation of models, anticipation of reinforcement, vicarious observation, images of future outcomes serving as current motivations for behaviors, goal setting and self-regulated reinforcement are all helpful concepts that make both acquisition and maintenance of instrumental relationships by the individual learner more understandable. The role of the school in transmitting instrumental linkages and priorities is made more clear if we think of the school experience as presenting both explicit and implicit models, coding model events for memory representation, and reinforcing retention and appropriate performance. The school, classroom, and playground provide contexts within which these processes occur.[3]

Critical Learning Periods

What is not as adequately explained by the SLT model we have discussed is how learning occurs during *critical learning periods*, such as initiation.[4] There

---

[3]Readers should be aware that both the instrumental model and SLT depend upon a basic assumption that cultural transmission, cultural acquisition, and social learning subsume processes that eventuate in the development of cognitive organization, cultural competence, and sociopersonal identities. These end results can be termed psychocultural. We are interested in these results and the processes leading to them. A thoroughly situationist or context-oriented theoretical model would not attend to psychocultural results or cultural antecedents. Interaction and communication within bounded contexts would be the focus. Although in our ethnographic work in classrooms and schools, educational anthropologists attend to the minutiae of everyday behavior—the politics of interpersonal behavior—they are usually also concerned with the end products of these processes. These end results are often quite inexactly defined or only implicit.

In *Doing the Ethnography of Schooling* (DEOS) (G. Spindler 1982), of the 14 anthropologists contributing chapters describing some of their work, the majority appear to assume or explicitly state their concern with end results of a broadly psychocultural nature, as well as with apriori cultural patterning. A minority appear to work entirely within a bounded context, assuming no particular end result resident in persons, even as social actors. An analysis in depth might reveal hidden agendas, but we cannot make the claim that this is the case. There are issues here that we cannot resolve even if we had space in this article to do so. Readers may profit by examining the article by Funnel and Smith critiquing intrapsychic and interpsychic models (Funnel and Smith, 1982), the collection of colleaguial works in DEOS, and a recent paper by Schwartz (1981) that in interesting ways parallel our discussion.

[4]Although the statement made in text seems appropriate, given the present state of SLT and its recent history, Bandura provided an extension of his position in the following comment:

> In the social learning analysis, brief experiences can have profound effects on persons when they are inducted into a relatively closed milieu. A totalistic environment supplies a pervading new reality—new kinships, all-encompassing modes of conduct, few vestiges of individuality, and substantial rewarding and coercive power. The power of social influence is further enhanced by curtailing personal ties to exposure to one's close associates. I am currently writing a paper on "The Psychology of Life Paths" which is concerned with how certain experiences branch people into new trajectories of life (originally presented in a presidential address at the annual meeting of the Western Psychological Association, Los Angeles, 1981. G.S.).

is a substantial, if somewhat convoluted, anthropological literature on initiation rituals and their functions, but little of it addresses directly the question of what initiates learn as a result of being torn from their families, enjoined to avoid all contact with females, whipped, smoked, starved, circumcised, subincised, forced to act as partners to eager fellateds, and subjected to hours and days of esoteric symbols, unfathomable mysteries, and bull roaring.[5] It should be obvious that we are talking about initiation of males at puberty in societies where such initiations take particularly strenuous forms and involve insignificant hazing. Our subsequent remarks apply to these kinds of events but are applicable in some degree to many critical learning periods we have termed *cultural compressions* (G. Spindler 1974b). What we want to get some help on from psychology is how learning occurs under threat, under traumatic and heavy superordinate authority, and where abrupt discontinuity in social roles and culturally defined expectations is experienced. We particularly want to understand better why such educational management seems to be highly successful as measured by retention of what is learned and commitment to it.

Our preliminary search of the literature has not revealed as much relevant work by psychologists as we had hoped. We will mention briefly several promising leads, confining ourselves to learning-relevant models.

Leon Festinger's resolution of dissonance model (Festinger 1957) seems promising at first glance. Two elements are in a dissonant relation if, considering these two alone, the obverse of one element would follow from another. The resolution of the dissonant relationship leads to the exclusion of one element and the strengthening of the other. People are motivated to be consistent; therefore, they try to resolve these contradictions. The presence of dissonance is enough in itself (given certain conditions) to give rise to pressures (from within the individual) to reduce or eliminate it.

There are, for us, two problems with the resolution of dissonance model. The first is that it is difficult or impossible to reduce the dissonance in our critical learning period to contradiction in *elements*. The "contradictions" that initiates in societies like the Australian desert Arunta, Mardudjara, Walbiri, or the New Guinea highland Sambia must resolve is between being a boy and being a man, being part of the women's world and a part of the men's world, being irresponsible and being responsible (for ritual, theology, sacred

---

[5]A major exception to this statement is recent work by Gilbert Herdt (1981) and by him and his colleagues (Herdt 1982). Herdt's writings treat with certain aspects of male initiation among the Sambia of Papua New Guinea highlands involving prolonged ritual fellatio. These works utilize concepts and models from symbolic, ethnosemantic, semiotic anthropology and from psychoanalytic theory and analysis. Herdt's own analyses are heavily psychological and represent a creative union of semiotic and psychoanalytic thinking that will, we think, characterize much of the newly reemerging psychological anthropology.

and secular power), for being soft and being hard, being children and being warriors. It is also between going along with the drama of initiation as it unfolds and resisting it and its managers.

The second problem with the resolution of dissonance model, for our purposes, is that if people are socially compelled to undergo painful experience, they do not experience dissonance—according to the theory. It is only if they submit to such treatment with minimal inducement that they experience dissonance and seek gratification for their actions.

Initiation rituals violate both conditions, contradiction in elements and free-choice conditions. The initiation ritual is an intensive period of forced learning when the initiate has no real choice, and where, in the more dramatic initiations of the type alluded to, the initiate is usually fearful, perhaps disgusted and frustrated, and sometimes in traumatic shock (though we know far less about how initiates feel than we should). In the general sense of the term, the dissonance is profound, extending far beyond "two elements of which the obverse of one would follow from the other." In the specific and limited sense of the term, as used in Festinger's model, the concept is not applicable. Nevertheless, with appropriate modification the concept, if not the model, might be made useful.

The notion that dissonance, interpreted more broadly than Festinger's model allows, is resolved by excluding one element or complex of elements (roles, values, life-styles, etc.) and strengthening the other is appealing. It makes sense, given anthropological observations of religious, nativistic, reaffirmative, and revitalizing movements, as well as less dramatic forms of response to polarization of culturally phrased alternatives. Festinger's theory does not, however, permit this kind of analysis. It defines the conditions of its workability too narrowly. This is frequently the case with models that are constructed and honed to fit the conditions of credibility imposed by procedures of experimental verification in the laboratory. It is one of the significant barriers to the use, by anthropologists, of psychological theory, at least of the kind most acceptable to academic psychology.

Other work, like that of Schein, Schneier, and Barker (1961) on coercive persuasion, seems relevant. The use of anticipated reward in a context of fear seems to be a powerful teaching technique. The captive's or initiate's dependency on his mentors or captors (being cut off from all other reference groups and exposed to only one point of view) seems to produce a shift in identification, often radical, for prisoners of war, new members of religious cults, Sambia, Arunta, and Walbiri initiates, and victims of kidnap. For the Sambia, Arunta, and Walbiri, it is permanent.

Compliance theory in general seems to offer possibilities. One is reminded of Stanley Milgram's (1963, 1974) classic and controversial experiments in which subjects are ordered by a "prestigious" scientist in a laboratory setting to administer apparently painful, even lethal electric shocks to learners whenever they make errors on a learning task. Most people administering shocks quickly "learn" obedience, even when they know what they are commanded to do is wrong. Compliance theory has deep roots in Solomon Asch's experimental studies of the effects of group persuasion upon modification and distortion of judgments in group contexts. People comply to group judgments even when they "know" the group is in error (Asch 1958). Personal security and even self-esteem seem to be dependent upon the approval earned by compliance.

Latent learning is another area for possibly productive engagement. We have already touched upon a form of latent learning in the discussion of SLT. Social learning theory distinguishes between learning and performance. Many repertoires of behavior are learned observationally but are not performed until the appropriate circumstances arise. For example, children learn parental roles through observation but do not express what they have learned until they become parents. The extent of their observational learning can be shown through doll play enactments; they often enact the parental roles and specific mannerisms with considerable fidelity.

Learning without performance has been observed by anthropologists in the field, but most often in connection with tasks such as teaching, weaving, or making canoes. Rarely has latent learning with respect to ritual or to esoteric knowledge been recorded. And yet it is difficult to imagine young initiates acquiring all the cultural knowledge required of them as initiated men after a few days or weeks of ritual (through stages of initiation often extend over many months or even years), however harsh their perceptors may be and however compliant the initiates may be. This is especially unlikely in contexts such as the North American woodlands, where the initiate is isolated from all human contact until a spirit being appears to him or her in a vision experience. We hypothesize that much cultural knowledge, some in considerable detail, has been acquired, that can only be activated at the right time—one of those times being after initiation. Herbst Barry and Alice Schlegel have recently suggested something of this sort (1980), as Paul Spencer did somewhat earlier (Spencer 1965, 1970).

Psychologists have worked on latent learning for some time. Latent learning necessarily requires cognitive processing of observations that can be activated later when called for. The early work of people like Edward Tolman (1948) on cognitive maps in rats and man can be taken as a starting point. Neisser's recent studies on cognitive schemata (1976) are a modern statement of this processing. Latent learning is also central to social learning theory. The discrepancy between learning and performance is most marked in behavior that is socially disapproved of until it becomes permissible to express it (Bandura 1965). This is, of course, precisely the situation for preadolescent youngsters who enter the initiatory period (we hypothesize) with a great deal of knowledge they cannot express in behavior until they have been initiated.

We have not mentioned psychoanalytic theory as a source of learning models for us, although there are many points where it is relevant. For example, concepts of reaction formation and compensatory identification, as anxiety-reducing strategies that both motivate and fixate learning, are relevant to what we observe in initiations and cult movements, as well as to personal adaptation in culture-conflict situations. The resolution of "dissonance" model we have discussed begins, in fact, to look a little psychodynamic.

The work of the Piagetian school also provides useful models, although we tend to feel with Margaret Mead that Piaget's formulation of fixed sequences of cognitive maturation places us under severe constraints when applied cross-culturally. Even most Piagetians have abandoned the strong form of the theory with its invariant succession of distinct stages. (Mead's 1978 analysis is useful here.) Nevertheless, Piaget's thinking is at the base of much modern learning theory.

Our final question shifts the emphasis from learning to teaching, a shift that has occurred during the last two decades in educational psychology and that may be overdue for anthropologists interested in cultural *transmission*. Of course, teaching without learning is futile, so theories about teaching are also about learning, and particularly about environments for learning. Our questions is: *What theories about teaching are there that anthropologists can use?*

Theories of Teaching

We start with Jerome Bruner's formulation of "learning by discovery," a formulation that draws from both Piaget and Plato (Shulman 1970) and that can be termed cognitive. In this learning model, which is also a teaching model, learners manipulate materials, after becoming familiar with them, in response to a problem until they begin to perceive a pattern. In a style that can be called Socratic, the teacher poses leading questions but does not demonstrate or produce solutions. The learners continue to find patterns and eventually produce solutions that correspond with intuitive regularities they already understand.

There has been strong opposition to Bruner's models, particularly from B. F. Skinner, Robert M. Gagne, and David Ausubel. Their disagreements mirror deeper conflicts that have been present since psychology divorced from philosophy. Gagne and Ausubel in particular are proponents, in different ways, of an opposed teaching-learing model called "guided learning" (Shulman 1970:30). In this model, teaching begins with a task analysis: what is it you want the learner to be able to do? Their model(s) can be described as behavioristic, for they are stated specifically and behaviorally. The route to being "able to do it" is a hierarchy of tasks, each of which is prerequisite to the next. The stress, for Ausubel, is on meaningful verbal learning and systematically guided exposition. A careful sequencing of instructional experiences is required. Guided learning leads to programmed instruction.

Discovery learning leads to open classrooms and an emphasis on learning process rather than mastery of knowledge and specific skills.[6] (It is only fair to say, however, that Gagne and Ausubel differ on objectives, though not so much on method.) We find Lee Shulman's analysis of the oppositions and overlaps of these two opposing teaching-learning models and their relationships to antecedent concepts, including those of Piaget, very instructive (Shulman 1970).

We can identify both guided and discovery learning in traditional Menominee teaching (G. Spindler, 1963a; G. and L. Spindler 1971) and in the schools in Germany where we are presently working (G. Spindler 1974a; G. and L. Spindler 1982). The Menominee emphasize discovery learning and the Germans guided learning. Would a dissection of our observations along these lines in these two groups lead us to a better understanding of how culture is transmitted? It probably would if we could translate the teaching-learning models in cultural terms.

The most recent and influential theory of teaching-learning is information processing. This "new mainstream has emerged to replace the older battleground of behaviorism and cognitive psychology . . ." (Shulman 1977:3). This cognitive model is now dominant among most educational and learning psychologists. (Simon 1979. See Bandura 1978: 52, 56 for some comments on the limitations of information-processing models.) The history of information processing models is brief, going no father back that *A Study of Thinking* by Bruner, Goodnow, and Austin in 1956. Noam Chomsky contributed to it with his presentation of transformational grammar in 1957. Jean Piaget antidated the whole revolution. J. McVickers Hunt's *Intelligence and Experience* (1961) synthesizes Piagetian theory and information processing into a single perspective.

Information processing covers several different types of learning and, by implication, teaching. The core perspective is that of "the learner as a goal-seeking problem-solver whose ability to deal rationally with his environment is profoundly constrained by the intrinsic limitation of his capability for processing information" (Shulman 1977:8). Because the learner has

---

[6]The comment made by Bandura to the rough draft of this paper at this point is worth passing on.

> The appropriateness of a given teaching model depends on the nature of the activity. "Learning by discovery" would be most wasteful, if not disasterous in activities that require certain competencies and errors produce aversive consequences. One would not use "learning by discovery" in teaching brain surgery, flying, swimming, etc. Effective guided learning is usually the systematization of discovery learning. To teach problem solving through graded exposition someone had to discover the essential components of the problem solving process. The current "knowledge engineering" by computer scientists illustrates this process. The experience and judgments developed by experts (e.g. doctors) in years of practice are being reduced to programmatic form.

limitations in attention, short-term memory, and encoding for long-term storage and retrieval, he constructs a simplified model of real problems in order to cope with them. This is demonstrably true in the short run. It is a questionable assumption in the long run of cultural construction.

The information-processing model can tell us something about instruction in our own and other cultures. It can also tell us something about culture. Culture is a product of human information processing as well as a template for it. Many of the peculiarities of ritual and myth and some concepts of self versus environment can be seen as the products of intrinsic limitations on the human capability for processing information. And yet the fact that culture is cumulative, that it is the product of generations of goal-seeking information processors, makes culture transcendent of human limitations. Furthermore, culture incorporates and balances the rational, irrational, and nonrational. Culture is technology, fact, myth, cosmology, innuendo, symbol, and metaphor. Culture exceeds individual human capability but is produced by humans.

Herein lies the dilemma for anthropologists interested in learning. Our task, we believe, is to study the transmission and acquisition of culture, that which transcends human capacities and yet is created by humans. We have scarcely begun to understand how we may study this process. Attention to interaction and communication in social context is essential but will tell us only indirectly about cognitive processing. Studies of language acquisition are promising, but idiom goes only so far. Studies of the brain and its functioning will tell us some things we need to know, but the discoveries issuing from them must be translated into culture-relevant terms. Learning starts with the first eye blink, perhaps before, and goes to theories of relativity. As anthropologists, we are primarily concerned with the social meaning ascribed to both. Our total sociobiologic and cognitive-cultural evolution has produced and has been the consequence of relationships among culture, learning, the human organism, and social-life-in-environment that we strive to understand.

Conclusion

Our message is that there is much in the works of our psychologist colleagues that we might familiarize ourselves with if we are better to understand how culture is transmitted and acquired. The *answers* will not be where we look, but possible leads to illuminating perspectives may be discovered by those who look for them. Anthropologists have often gone along their own paths without realizing that others are traveling in the same direction, but on different paths. And yet we must remember that our immediate task is different than that of psychologists. They are interested in mechanisms through which social influences exert their effects on individuals, but they assume culture as a constant or as an irritating variation they must control. We are interested in how culture in its varieties in time and place is acquired and reshaped by each new generation. This requires a focus on individuals as social agents and complex symbolic processors and on culture as the sine qua non of human nature. Our task is complex and we can use all the help we can get.

References

Asch, Solomon E., 1958, "Effects of Group Pressure upon Modification and Distortion of Judgments." In *Readings in Social Psychology,* 3rd ed. E.E. Maccoby, T.M. Newcomb, and E.L. Hartley, eds. New York: Holt, Rinehart and Winston.

Bandura, Albert, 1965, *Influence of Models' Reinforcement Contingencies on the Acquisition of Imitation Responses. Journal of Personality and Social Psychology* 1:589-595.

————, 1977, *Social Learning Theory.* Englewood Cliffs, NJ: Prentice-Hall.

————, 1978, *The Self System in Reciprocal Determinism. American Psychologist* 33:344-358.

Barnett, Homer, 1953, *Innovation: The Basis of Cultural Change.* New York: McGraw-Hill.

Barry, Herbst, III, and Alice Schlegel, 1980, *Early Childhood Precursors in Adolescent Initiation Ceremonies. Ethos: Journal of the Society for Psychological Anthropology* 8:132-145.

Bourguignon, Erica, 1979, *Psychological Anthropology.* New York: Holt, Rinehart and Winston.

Bruner, Jerome, Jacqueline Goodnow, and G.A. Austin, 1956, *A Study of Thinking.* New York: Wiley.

Chomsky, Noam, 1957, *Syntactic Structures.* The Hague, Mouton.

Dollard, John, 1945, "Learning." In *The Science of Man in the World Crisis.* Ralph Linton, ed. New York: Columbia University Press.

Festinger, Leon, 1957, *A Theory of Cognitive Dissonance.* Stanford, CA: Stanford University Press.

Funnel, Robert, and Richard Smith, 1981, "Search for a Theory of Cultural Transmission in an Anthropology of Education: Notes on Spindler and Gearing." *Anthropology and Education Quarterly,* 12(4): 275-300.

Gillin, John, 1942, "Acquired Drives in Culture Contact." *American Anthropologist* 44:545-554.

Hallowell, A. Irving, 1945, "Sociopsychological Aspects of Acculturation." In *The Science of Man in the World Crisis.* Ralph Linton, ed. New York: Columbia University Press.

Hansen, Judith Friedman, 1979, *Sociocultural Perspectives on Human Learning: An Introduction to Educational Anthropology.* Englewood Cliffs, NJ: Prentice-Hall

Herdt, Gilbert H., 1981, *Guardian of the Flutes: Idioms of Masculinity: A Study of Ritualized Homosexual Behavior.* New York: McGraw-Hill.

————, ed., 1982, *Ordeals of Meaning.* Berkeley: University of California Press.

McVickers-Hunt, J., 1961 *Intelligence and Experience.* New York: Ronald Press.

Mead, Margaret, 1978, "The Evocation of Psychologically Relevant Responses in Ethnological Field Work." In *The Making of Psychological Anthropology.* G. Spindler, ed. Berkeldy: University of California Press.

Milgram, Stanley, 1963, "The Behavioral Study of Obedience." *Journal of Abnormal and Social Psychology* 67:371-378.

———, 1974, *Obedience to Authority, An Experimental View.* New York: Harper & Row.

Miller, Neal E., and John Dollard, 1941, *Social Learning and Imitation.* New Haven: CT: Yale University Press.

Mowrer, O.H., 1939, "Anxiety Reduction and Learning." *Journal of Experimental Psychology* 27:497-516.

Neisser, V., 1976, *Cognition and Reality: Principles and Implication of Cognitive Psychology.* San Francisco: W.H. Freeman.

Schein, E.H., I. Schneier, and C.H. Barker, 1961, *Coercive Persuasion.* New York: Norton.

Schwartz, Theodore, 1981, "The Acquisition of Culture." *Ethos: Journal of the Society for Psychological Anthropology* 9:4-17.

Shulman, Lee S. 1970, "Psychology and Mathematics Education." In *The Sixty-ninth Yearbook of the National Society for the Study of Education, Part 1.* Chicago: University of Chicago Press.

———, 1977, Psychology and Mathematics Education Revisited: Forschung Zum Prozess des Mathematiklernens, Reihe: Materialle und Studien, Band 2, Institut fur Didaktik der Mathematiks der Universitat, Bielefeld.

Shweder, Richard, 1979-80, "Rethinking Culture and Personality Theory, Part 1. *Ethos: Journal of the Society for Psychological Anthropology* 7:255-278; Part II, 7:279-312; Part III, 8:60-94.

Simon, Herbert A., 1979, *Information Processing Models of Cognition.* Annual Review of Psychology. pp. 363-396.

Spencer, Paul, 1965, *The Samburn: A Study of Gerontocracy in a Nomadic Tribe.* London: Routledge & Kegan Paul.

———, 1970, "The Function of Ritual in the Socialization of Samburn Moran." In *Socialization: The Approach from Social Anthropology.* Philip Mayer, ed. pp. 127-158. London: Tavistock.

Spindler, George, 1963a, "Personality, Sociocultural System and Education among the Menomini." In *Education and Culture: Anthropological Approaches.* G. Spindler, ed. pp. 351-399. New York: Holt, Rinehart and Winston.

———, 1974a "Schooling in Schonhausen: A Study of Cultural Transmission and Instrumental Adaptation in an Urbanizing German Village." In *Education and Cultural Process: Toward an Anthropology of Education.* New York: Holt, Rinehart and Winston.

———, 1974b "Cultural Transmission." In *Educational and Cultural Process.* New York: Holt, Rinehart and Winston.

Spindler, George D., ed., 1978, *The Making of Psychological Anthropology.* Berkeley: University of California Press.

———, 1982, *Doing the Ethnography of Schooling: Educational Anthropology in Action.* New York: Holt, Rinehart and Winston.

Spindler, Louise, 1978, "Researching the Psychology of Culture Change and Unbanization." In *The Making of Psychological Anthropology.* George Spindler, ed. Berkley: University of California Press.

Spindler, George, and Louise Spindler, 1963b, "Psychology in Anthropology: Applications to Culture Change." In *Psychology: A Study of a Science.* S. Koch, ed. New York: McGraw-Hill.

_____, and _____, 1971, reissued with changes 1984, *Dreamers with Power: The Menomini Indians.* Prospect Heights, IL: Waveland Press.

_____, and _____, 1982, "From the Familiar to the Strange and Back Again." Roger Harker and Schonhausen. In *Doing the Ethnography of Schooling: Educational Anthropology in Action.* G. Spindler, ed. New York: Holt, Rinehart and Winston.

Tolman, Edward C., 1948 *Cognitive Maps in Rats and Men. Psychological Review* 55:189-208.

Whiting, Beatrice, 1980, "Culture and Social Behavior." A Model for the Development of Social Behaviors. *Ethos: Journal of the Society for Psychological Anthropology* 8:95-116.

Whiting, John, 1941, *Becoming a Kwoma.* New Haven, CT: Yale University Press.

_____, and Beatrice Whiting, 1978, "A Strategy for Psychocultural Research." In *The Making of Psychological Anthropology.* G. Spindler, ed. Berkeley: University of California Press.

GEORGE D. SPINDLER/*Stanford University*

4   Roots Revisited: Three Decades of Perspective

Three decades ago, in the spring of 1954, twenty-two anthropologists and educationists met at Carmel Valley Ranch, California, for four days to present and discuss ten papers centering on how anthropology and education might be beneficial to each other. The proceedings were published with the title *Education and Anthropology* by the Stanford University Press under my editorship. The volume contains all ten papers and an edited, but quite complete, transcript of the discussion. Many seem to regard this conference as the beginning of educational anthropology. There were, of course, antecedents in the work of people like Jules Henry, Margaret Mead, the Whitings, Sol Kimball, and a few others, but the conference did take place in the formative period of our subdiscipline.

Preparation for the conference began in 1952 and involved many anthropologists and educationists not present at Carmel Valley. It was supported by the Carnegie Foundation and sponsored by the American Anthropological Association and the Department of Anthropology and School of Education at Stanford. Since fourteen of the twenty-two participants (eight anthropologists and six educators) are dead, we are fortunate to have the recorded transcript of the discussion as well as the papers stimulating the discussions; it is in these discussions that we can see the concerns of those present, representing both anthropology and education, expressed in their full and most dramatic form.

I hope to communicate some sense of our antecedents, our "roots" if you will, by selecting four concerns that were thematic throughout the discussions.

- The search for a philosophical as well as a theoretical articulation of education and anthropology;
- The necessity for sociocultural contextualization of the educative process;
- The relation of education to "culturally phrased" phases of the life cycle;
- The nature of intercultural understanding and learning.

Reprinted from the *Anthropology and Education Quarterly [15: 3-10, 1984] with permission.*

I do not intend a full and measured critique of current work in the light of the past and, in effect, will cite none of it. I will make a few general comments about some gains and losses.

Concern Number One: The Search for a Rationale and Encompassing Philosophy

As Alfred Kroeber pointed out during the conference, anthropology became a social science last of all. First it was one of the humanities and a positivistic natural science. In contrast to sociology, economics, and political science, all with a strong sense of utility from the beginning, the early anthropologists were not "ameliorationists." Kroeber observed that educators "see the jam they're in" and "naturally they tend to call in others who can perhaps help extricate them—anthropologists or such . . . The public seems to look upon them [educators] as put in control, and then expects their right answers to lead us all out of the woods" (p. 248).

Kroeber was reluctant to offer educators any advice but he did point out that anthropologists need not fear the educator's need for evaluation. "I hold a personal view," mused Kroeber "which may sound paradoxical: the biologist also deals with value, although he has been taught as a scientist and naturalist not to make value judgments. When the biologist says a seal is a good swimmer, but a poor walker. . ." he is "evaluating" what seals do compared with other animals (p. 248). Anthropologists always have been making value judgments, "whether they knew it or not." I infer that Kroeber would try to avoid personal biases and moral judgments but would agree that an analysis of the effectiveness of an educational program in the light of its declared goals and in comparison to alternative procedures would be acceptable anthropological behavior. This received wisdom does a lot, for me at least, to legitimize evaluative ethnography, if it is done carefully and objectively. There was a strong sense expressed at the conference, however, that anthropologists could study and report on educative process and systems, but they should refrain from advocating specific policy decisions, since these are essentially political and administrative domains. This is still a moot point in current discussions.

Ted Brameld, an educational philosopher then at New York University and much concerned with the articulation of educational and anthropological theory, took a consistent reconstructionist view. He was disturbed by what he regarded as two persistent and pernicious themes that kept surfacing in the comments by anthropologists. One was that of culture *sui generis,* as Malinowski, Lowie, and particularly Leslie White, conceived of it: a phenomenon "wholly of its own kind"—nothing impinges on it, it is autonomous and changes only through self-contained immanent forces; it is predestined and predetermined. (Kroeber said that he himself in the past probably had "certain inclinations in that direction which, however, I hope I have purged" [p. 251]). The other theme was that of implicit, tacit culture, the unconscious patterning of behavior by culture, as formulated by Sapir (and others since then). Brameld was disturbed by Sapir's explicit statements, reinforced by anthropologists in the discussion, that making certain aspects of the implicit explicit could dull the edge of reform and of social and political movements. Anthropologists, along with Sapir, were asking the question: How much self-consciousness of this "hidden dimension" (our current term) can an individual, group, or society stand? Brameld objected to these themes and their implications as "undemocratic," and as "disturbing arguments to anyone who takes a transformative view of culture"; he regarded them as "untenable in a democratic society" (p. 235).

It seems to me the issue that disturbed Brameld is still with us. Our phrasing of education as culture transmission in itself confronts educationists with the problem. Do cultures perpetuate themselves endlessly and change only with immanent forces over which we have no control? And if we do not even know what the implicit patterns of behavior are, how can planned, intentional innovation take place? Are the things we do as educators doomed to be "chiefly reflexive or reproductive" rather than "normatively creative and recreative" (p. 221)?

Jules Henry reassures Brameld that educators always have been innovative: "For example, as changes began to take place in the Middle Ages, as power began to shift from the nobility and the church to the bourgeoisie, you had the introduction of the teaching of bookkeeping, the teaching of the vulgar languages, and the teaching of law" (p. 254); similar changes occurred with the Industrial Revolution. However, even these changes, we could infer, were reflexive. They were responses to the changes in power structure and socioeconomic imperatives occurring in the milieux of the school, not so much a product of purposeful, normative design as immanent forms of social evolution.

Although our current understanding of implicit culture would affect Brameld's argument, and I think the culture sui generis argument is overdrawn (though you wouldn't think so if you reread Leslie White), I miss broad philosophic discussions of this kind. Are we concerned with broad philosophical implications of our findings that transcend specific issues of theory?

Concern Number Two: Sociocultural Contextualization

The second major concern is about the sociocultural contextualization of schooling. The anthropologists who were present, with strong reinforcement from the educators, focused on this relationship throughout the conference. Sol Kimball said that "understanding of the educative process can be gained only as we focus upon the child in his total habitat'' (p. 84). Bernard Siegel produced two models of the educative process in American communities, one of them interrelating acculturative factors affecting the transmission of cultural materials in the school system, the other a communications system model delineating channels through which explicit culture reaches the child. Both models placed schooling in a complex of institutions, power structures, peer groups, the home and family, ethnicity, and so forth.

Margaret Mead, as discussant for a brilliant and controversial paper by Dorothy Lee on discrepancies in the teaching of American culture in home economics programs, noted that the way anthropologists study any specialized form of education is to "look at who does it, where they come from, how they're trained, how they're selected, what their history is, what their value system is, and then what happens to them in the community" (p. 177). Lee herself analyzed the home economics programs as presenting work and leisure, duty and fun, the given and the chosen, the self and society, as dualisms of opposition. She described conflict areas in sibling and marital relationships expressed consistently in the home economics manuals, and the "work" of ordinary home life presented as being without value (p. 169). Work was something to be done efficiently so that one may have leisure time where pleasure and spontaneity are possible.

What Dorothy Lee did was to reveal through her analysis the basic assumptions about family, home, marriage, work, leisure, creativity, the given and the chosen, that are a part of mainstream American culture and that underlie the specific normative statements contained in the home economics manuals used to guide teachers in the conduct of these programs. Her analysis was related to the culture baseline of the manuals and classes in home economics (though this relationship was more explicit in the discussion than in her paper), rather than to the community as a social structure, which was the contextual connection of greatest importance for John Gillin and Sol Kimball.

Jules Henry, in "Culture, Education and Communications Theory," continued the dialogue on the cultural contextualization of schooling. He described "target-seeking and diffuse," "additive and spiraling," and "monophasic and polyphasic" learning. The specific forms of these dualisms are less important for our purposes than the fact that in all instances he related the forms of learning to culture contexts. Monophasic learning, for example, he linked with cultures where "tight, indissoluble associations" are required, such as in traditional China, and polyphasic learning with a culture such as that of upper middle-class American society where value is placed on speed, individuality, switching from one activity to another, flexibility, change, and recombination. Further, he saw teaching as including those procedures that made these styles of learning operative. Phrased more broadly, he saw cultural transmission as presenting, organizing, stimulating, and coercing in such a manner as to engender certain processes of cultural acquisition. Thus teaching and learning, and cultural transmission and acquisition, were perceived as enbedded in a cultural matrix and as an expression of it. Nor did he neglect relations to social structure, as indicated in his analysis of target-seeking and diffuse learning and teaching in Hopi society.

I miss discussions such as Henry's in the current educational anthropology literature. It is not entirely absent, to be sure, but the focus has been so exclusively on the classroom, or at least on the school, that the cultural contextualization, as well as the immediate community contextualization, is not developed in most published works. In our long-term project in the Schönhausen Grundschule (field research in 1968, 1977, and 1981), we have found that a cultural we well as community analysis is indispensable. We do not understand how this little school could resist effectively the massive efforts of the ministry of education to transform it, without understanding the elemental cultural assumptions and expectations that teachers carry with them into classrooms and that underlie all stylistic differences between teachers, however dramatic they may appear.

Beyond cultural contextualization, another feature of Henry's analysis, and one that appeared in many forms throughout the conference, was that education must be seen from a cross-cultural perspective if one is to escape the blinders imposed by one's own cultural experience. This would appear to be the *sine qua non* of an anthropological approach, yet I see very little explicit concern with cross-cultural reference points or comparisons in current work in our field. "Making the familiar strange," as Louise Spindler and I have pointed out in a chapter by that title in *Doing the Ethnography of Schooling* (Holt, Rinehart and Winston 1982), is a first step to understanding what is happening in a classroom.

Concern Number Three: Education and the Life Cycle

The third concern that I wish to select from those expressed in the Carmel conference involves the relation of teaching and learning to the life cycle. C.W.M. Hart, in what I regard as one of the most illuminating contributions to an anthropology of education ever written, placed the relationship of education to life cycle in dramatic perspective in his analysis of prepubertal training and postpubertal initiation among the Tiwi. His contention that early childhood experience was highly variable intraculturally, and therefore not a reliable antecedent variable interculturally, was hotly contested by Margaret Mead, Bill Martin, and most others at the conference who held a stake in current child development and early learning formulations. Hart's contention that education during adolescence, particularly in the form of dramatic initiation rituals, is especially significant in determining the relationship of the individual to the culture and social structure was, on the whole, strongly supported and expanded upon in the discussion. The particulars of his analysis must be left unstated. I hope you will find time to read or reread the article and perhaps even the discussions. I feel the paper to be so provocative that I have reprinted it three times.

In general terms, Hart analyzes education at adolescence as the most important period for the recruitment of new members for society and for the engendering of commitments to the culture's norms and values (though he does not use these terms). He shows how the curriculum, the instructors, the paraphernalia, and the atmosphere of the initiation experience regularize cultural transmission in contrast to the laissez faire and variety of early childhood experience.

Whether we accept Hart's null hypothesis on early childhood training or accept fully the implications of his analysis of education at adolescence, we have to acknowledge the importance of the life cycle as a framework within which education occurs. No educational system anywhere has failed to incorporate recognition of life stage differences into its philosophy and organization of resources and experience for education. Yet one does not see much explicit attention to this in our current literature in educational anthropology. We study elementary classrooms and teaching-learning experiences as though they not only were isolable socioculturally but as though they were somehow removable from the life cycle. And we have neglected secondary education grossly. We appear to have accepted child development, pediatric, and psychodynamic early-learning hypotheses too uncritically. For our purposes as students of cultural transmission, education in the years beyond childhood, particularly at adolescence, may be more important.

Concern Number Four: Intercultural Learning and Understanding

The fourth and final concern that I will touch upon is that of inter-cultural learning and understanding. Cora DuBois wrote the paper to which the conferees — particularly Larry Frank, known for his creative thinking in this area — responded. DuBois proposed that intercultural education must involve affective as well as cognitive learning. She also presented a theme recurrent in many of the discussions on other topics: "Education is both the deliberate inculcation of knowledge, attitudes, and values and the unconscious transmission of modes of preceiving the world" (p. 91). Frank expanded the themes DuBois presented, using the concepts of analogical and digital learning, the first being holistic, metaphoric, empathetic; the second being pieces of information, facts, numbers, names for things. It is interesting that this dualism anticipates recent work on left and right brain functions. Hilda Taba called attention to primary learning involving direct experience and secondary learning as involving symbols acquired vicariously. There was general agreement that we could learn to understand other cultures in ways resembling how we learned to understand our own.

DuBois' paper and the discussion of it remind me that we aren't doing much about teaching and learning intercultural understanding. Multicultural education programs abound, but anthropology is only weakly represented, if at all. If any discipline should be able to provide both the materials and the rationale for communicating such understanding, it is anthropology. Sadly, however, most anthropology appears to be taught digitally, linearly, and badly, by people who themselves were taught this way. The affective, analogical, metaphoric, primary aspects of communication are left to be communicated by chance and through concomitant learning, which always is uncontrolled. Professors of anthropology most often teach about specialized topics of particular interest to them as professionals, even in introductory courses. The concomitant lessons are that anthropology is only narrowly and incidentally concerned with the basic issues of human adaptation in a changing, challenging, self-created-as-well-as-natural environment, and that it is boring. Unless anthropology can separate academic concern for specialized topics of interest to professional cliques from the need to communicate broad understandings of the human condition to nonprofessionals, it never will manage to teach anyone any intercultural understanding. Nevertheless, the resources are there in films and ethnographies, concepts and models, and in fieldwork experience, and they can be organized effectively to stimulate the growth of that understanding.

In our little subdivision called educational anthropology, we appear, however, to have abandoned the cross-cultural, comparative stance that would make possible effective intercultural teaching. We have turned our attention almost exclusively to schooling in our society, and not to education or cultural transmission in the broader sense. Though this focus is important, and will continue to be one of our major preoccupations, we cannot afford to neglect one of the fundamental tenets of the anthropological perspective—that we come to understand our own culture by understanding, or at least attempting to understand, others.

Finale

I have selected these four major concerns out of a larger variety of possibilities expressed at the Carmel Valley conference of 1954. I have said little about the general agreement on the part of anthropologists and educationists alike that ethnographic studies of both formal and nonformal aspects of schooling were much needed. We now have arrived at the point where this need is being acted upon and the products of this action are being accepted by educators. Why it took almost three decades for this to happen is a topic in itself.

I have selected these concerns for attention because I believe them to be areas of potential contribution that have been relatively neglected, and progressively more so in the thirty years since the conference. We have made important gains in those decades, and I do not want my concern for neglected areas to distract from those gains. Thanks to classroom microstudies derived from sociolinguistic and interactionist paradigms and methods, we know much more about communication in small classroom groups and in dyadic relationships than anyone dreamed about in Carmel Valley in 1954. Recent work on culturalecological factors in relation to school performance shows what a macro-orientation can do. We also have managed to produce some fairly credible theoretical models of cultural transmission. No one but Jules Henry (in what became his "Cross-Cultural Outline for Education") had tried to do that by 1954, and even Henry's effort names things rather than explains relationships.

What I have attempted to do is call attention to the larger arena of legitimate concerns and purposes of an anthropology of education. Anthropology furnishes resources in information, insights, ideas, and methods that have been tapped only slightly in our work to date.

The anthropologists at the Carmel meeting, including Kroeber, DuBois, Gillin, Henry, Mead, Felix Keesing, Siegel, Kimball, Hart, Dorothy Lee, (and the organizers, George and Louise Spindler) were all experienced researchers with established reputations. But they were not narrow or cliquish in their concerns. They wanted to examine the corpus of anthropology to see what it might have to offer education. Though they could not anticipate some of the accomplishments and directions of development that would take place by 1984, they were able to provide a broad charter that I think we would do well to examine.

Anthropology, as a discipline and as an accumulation of experience and materials, has much to offer that is directly relevant to education and that is different from that offered by any sibling discipline. If we exploit that uniqueness, we can make a distinctive contribution to a better understanding of educational process and to the solution of some educational problems. If we do not exploit our heritage, both as a heritage and as a foundation for new and innovative development, we will become a poor copy of sociology or psychology or become incorporated in the vast menage of professional education as a culturally tinged way of talking about matters defined entirely in educationist terms.

GEORGE D. SPINDLER/*Stanford University*

5   *Thirty-Three Years as a Marginal Native*

Three themes interweave in my discussion of the role of anthropology in the school of education: the two subcultures (the School of Education and the Department of Anthropology) and adaptations one can make to them; the kinds of roles one can play in each, with emphasis on the infiltrator-helper role and the organizer-power role; and the attitudes of anthropological and educationist colleagues. This discussion is offered in two parts, one autobiographical and one briefly analytic. The latter is intelligible only with the foundations laid by the former

Biography

I grew up in an education-oriented milieu. My father was a professor of educational philosophy and psychology at a teachers' college in central Wisconsin, I spent most of my elementary and middle school years in the training school where eager young women and men practice taught, went through the process myself in the same school later on, and taught for two years in two different high schools in Wisconsin before World War II. During my three years of service I spent most of the time teaching until I went overseas in 1944 to help finish off the German Army in Italy. It never occurred to me that I wanted to be anything but a teacher, and by the time I was five I had my three dolls (boys often had dolls when I was a child) actively engaged in my play classroom. I mention this because it makes a difference. Teaching and learning have been my first concerns and a joint appointment in anthropology and education seemed as inevitable as Winter in Wisconsin.

I came to Stanford in 1950 as a member of a team researching classrooms and schools under the direction of Professor Robert Bush, an educator. He thought an anthropologist might bring a perspective not brought by the psychiatrist, sociologist and educationists already on the team. We did case studies of some eighty classrooms and schools and indeed there was plenty for

Presented at the invited session sponsored by the Council for Anthropology and Education at the 82nd annual meetings of the American Anthropological Association.

an anthropologist to do. I quickly learned how to do school ethnography, though at first I couldn't see anything interesting enough to include in my notes. Compared to my field work with the traditional Menominee in their Medicine Lodge or Dream Dance the school was an all too familiar place. But eventually I came to see the classroom and school as one of the strangest places imaginable.[1]

I learned something else of equal importance—that one had to give as well as take if one wanted to do field research. I had already learned something of that in my Menominee field work but the relationship was not formalized in any way. Dr. Bush created the research program as an aspect of the Stanford Consultation Service. Our purposes were two-fold. We would collect data from individual teachers and their classrooms, principals and their schools, and superintendents and their systems, but in return we would counsel with every participant in the program to "improve professional competence". This meant that we collected data and then sifted it through as a team to see how we could help the person(s) studied. In my assigned cases I did what I eventually came to term "cultural therapy" in which I worked through material with the teacher or principal studied that would sensitize them to the sources of cultural bias that appeared to be influencing their behavior as professionals. It is relevant that when we approached schools to explain our project and call for volunteers virtually every prospective candidate volunteered! We chose the "cases" we would work with out of a hat, literally. During the years that we worked in depth with these many teachers, special service people, and administrators, we never received even one complaint about anything we did.

This was a splendid initiation into relationships between anthropology and education and helps to account for a strong feeling on my part that they had a lot to offer each other. Shortly after my arrival at Stanford then Dean John Bartky asked me to teach the first level educational psychology and the educational sociology foundations courses. He wanted to see what an anthropologist would do with what he regarded as basic but rather sterile courses. I was dismayed when I saw the texts most often used in such courses and invented various procedures to elicit data from the students and use those data in extended analyses of probable cultural and psychological influences on classroom behavior. For the sociology course I elicited value-oriented responses to an open-ended sentence "values test." For the psychology course I had the hundred or so students in each class respond to selected pictures from the Murray Thematic Perception Test, then spent weeks analyzing ways in which revealed perceptions of interpersonal relationships would be carried into the classroom. This is not all that we did but it was a good running start into something interesting. I taught these courses into the sixties, along with the

---

[1]See George and Louise Spindler, 1982, From Roger Harker to Shoenhausen and Back Again: Making the Familiar Strange in G. Spindler, ed. *Doing the Ethnography of Schooling.* Holt, Rinehart and Winston, NY.

more conventional anthropology courses in the department program and another course for graduate students first called "The Individual, Culture, and Society", since I wanted to be sure to include everything that I could think of that might be relevant to a psychological as well as cultural view of teaching and learning. Eventually, after a stage called "Socialization and Enculturation of the Child" I settled on "Cultural Transmission", which it has been ever since. Some 4,000 graduate students, mostly in education with a notable few from anthropology, psychology, and sociology have taken the course, still being offered now at Stanford and Wisconsin. In some ways this course has been my most important contribution to the School of Education program. Since then I have also developed and taught, with Louise Spindler, a training seminar on the ethnography of schooling, and this may now be my most important contribution. At times I have also taught Comparative Education for the School of Education, and for some years had an annual seminar on special topics in cultural transmission, likewise for the School of Education.

Meanwhile, I was engaged with a full program of teaching for the Department of Anthropology, particularly in psychological anthropology (first called personality and culture), Peoples of North America, cultural change, and introductory sociocultural anthropology. Recently Louise and I have developed a course on the anthropology of American culture which has been particularly rewarding. All of my courses that originated within and for education have been cross-listed with anthropology. Few anthropology students have taken them. None of my courses and seminars in anthropology excepting the current ethnography training seminar are cross-listed in education, but they are offered with both lower and upper division numbers so that graduate students can take them for credit. Most of my classes in anthropology have a substantial representation of education graduate students.

While course offerings were being developed and implemented I was also advising doctoral students in both the School of Education and the Department of Anthropology. My first advisees in education were Harry Wolcott, Richard Warren, Richard King, and John Singleton, whom many of the readers of this volume will recognize immediately, and a number of education students less well known to anthropologists, such as Clarence Fishburn, Russell Sharp, Murray Shipnuck, and others. The first four did very substantial work in anthropology, the others did some work in anthropology and scattered courses in sociology. In both preparations there was much in professional education courses and seminars that overlapped with anthropological interests but was rarely labelled. We did not have a "program" in educational anthropology and didn't seem to need one. Wolcott, Warren, King, and Singleton all did their dissertation fieldwork in "other" cultures and their publications (and dissertations) were all first-rate anthropology and extraordinary educational anthropology. There were no students in the early period (to 1965) from the Department of Anthropology who did their fieldwork or got a degree within the framework of an educational anthropology.

I also found myself on many dissertation and advisement committees in the School of Education—whenever there was a cultural or social or "personality and culture" component in the formulations of intended analyses in the dissertation proposal. I was also an active member of the "hatchet" committee which was the gatekeeper for promotion to candidacy for the advanced degrees and for monitoring dissertation proposals. Since my own training had been conjointly in anthropology, sociology, and psychology, I found the role congenial as far as behavioral science coverage was concerned. My committee memberships extended throughout the structure of the School of Education—into administration, the foundations (psychology, sociology, philosophy, history), counseling and guidance, elementary education, secondary education, overseas education and development, and so forth. It is difficult for outsiders to understand how complex schools of education are. However complex they are, there is not a single division where a sociocultural, or psychocultural, anthropological competence is without relevance—though sometimes it takes some bending to make the potential relevance operational.

Eventually we formed a program in educational anthropology in the framework of a Social Area Committee that subsumed sociology, history, philosophy, and anthropology. I was joined in the development first by Robert Textor and more recently by Shirley Heath. I initially resisted the inaugeration of such a program. At present there is such a program at Stanford, it has students, and is rated as successful. Most of my recent education-based dissertators for the Ph.D. have been in this program and they have all found employment. They are well trained in anthropology and in various skill and competence categories within the School of Education. They write clearly anthropological dissertations; for example on the family culture of incest, social and educational adaptations of Vietnamese migrants, the politicization of ethnic identity in bilingual program legislative action, education as an instrumentality for the maintenance of ethnic identity in a Peruvian Japanese community, and the non-implementation of legislated bilingual program requirements at the local level. I honestly don't know how many dissertations in the School of Education I have chaired, and I certainly don't know how many I have been a committee member on. There have been many. With my advisees in the Department of Anthropology and those in education, I have always had a heavier than normal load of dissertation and graduate program advisement.

During the past decade there has been a growing interest from within the department of anthropology in education-related research and some interest in the course offerings of the School of Education. I have had several doctoral level advisees and chaired several dissertations on recognizable educational anthropology from within the department. Dissertations on the ethnography of a career apprentice program, inner city schools, and a half-way house for parolees, are examples.

While this has been going on I have also carried on my own research program, advised a normal load of anthropology graduate students, supervised a wide range of dissertations in anthropology, taught a full complement of anthropology courses and seminars, and chaired the department of anthropology for two short periods and one long (four year) period.

Though I took early retirement in 1978 to get out of some of what was becoming an increasing overload, I have continued in these same capacities to the present and probably will for some time. The early retirement did allow me to rearrange some time and I am grateful for both the opportunity to retire and the opportunity to continue, at Stanford, and since the fall of 1979, at Wisconsin. At present (1986) I am contemplating some one-quarter stands in the University of California system.

Analysis

I offer my own case history as background for a brief analysis of certain aspects of roles in the two contexts we are discussing.

One can see that there are various roles that are heuristic to the situation. I was an infiltrator in the sense that I did infiltrate dissertation and advisement committees from the start. In this infiltration I disseminated anthropological concepts, literature, perceptions and prejudices. In my role as "hatchet" man on the gatekeeping committee I had a golden opportunity to disseminate anthropology, but I believe I disseminated more behavioral science than anthropology. I could not, for example, actively promote ethnographic approaches. The research orientation at that time in the School of Education was so weak that I knew that ethnography would become a hobby horse for the weakest of the weak. Now that the School of Education at Stanford has a reputation as one of the strongest schools in North America, and much of this strength is in research, it is possible to promote ethnography as an approach to the study of educational problems that the hardware of the other behavioral sciences and particularly neo-experimental and correlational educational psychology have not been wholly successful with.

This infiltrator-helper role is one of the most important, perhaps the most important role that the anthropologist *cum* educationist can play. Without it most of professional education will go unaffected by anthropology. It is a role that psychology recognized immediately and long ago and now psychological paradigms, models, theories, and prejudices dominate the research side of education.

The infiltrator-helper-disseminator role is also developed through courses. If one can get the course or seminar in the required category so much the better. The material acquired in the course(s) by students keeps cropping up in unlikely contexts. The attention of educationist advisors is captured when student advisees start using words, referring to concepts and literature, that their advisors do not know. A very important part of the legitimacy of anthropology and its field arm, ethnography, can be secured with substantial course offerings within the schools of education, taught by anthropologists who have sincere and deep interests in the educative process.

The organizer-power role is seen when one becomes chair of dissertation committees. This role is quite different than the infiltrator role, for one has the decision-making capacity and can utilize university-wide resources, such as anthropologist colleagues, research opportunities and funding, to make the arrangement work. It is important to have a well worked out base in the school of education before this role is mounted. If courses and seminars, gatekeeping functions, and general legitimacy have not been secured, the chair role will be most uncomfortable, the committee won't work, and the student advisee will be seriously damaged.

The cultures of the two contexts are quire different. The School of Education is infinitely more complex than that of the department of anthropology. One must learn some organization-relevant techniques if one is to get along in it. Other aspects of the culture are important: the personal style of the educators may appear to the anthropologist to be much more conservative than that of anthropologist colleagues. The differences are often more apparent than real. At the personal and private level educators can be as unconservative as anyone. In the workplace the educator is likely to appear more conventionally dressed, groomed, and acceptable to the outside world. Though deviant behavior will be accepted to a certain extent, it behooves the infiltrator to learn how to recognize the boundaries between accepted, tolerated, and negatively sanctioned behavior.

There is an aspect of anthropological culture, however, that is more important than any of the above. That is, anthropologists tend to feel that only anthropology, in its more or less pure form, is worth doing. One's research may be in a barrio in Los Angeles, the inner city, in the Amazon basin, or in the highlands of New Guinea, but it will start and end with clear anthropological rules, jargon, concepts and credibility. Though this is laudable in some ways, it is an attitude that can be damaging in the education context if over-applied. All of us who have really worked in depth and have lasted in educationist contexts have learned to let a little judicious dilution, pollution, and taking of the other's views get into out formulations and what we expect our students to formulate. It is interesting that in prospect of fieldwork anthropologists are enjoined to learn to speak the language of the native as quickly and thoroughly as possible, and yet they balk at making adaptations to the language of the native in the professional context of the school of education.

More damaging to the anthropological educationist is the attitude, on the part of the colleagues in anthropology, that what one does in the school of education just doesn't count for much. There are no sour grapes in my fruit dish when I say this. I have "lucked out" for several reasons, among them that my research record in "pure" anthropology was strong enough to get me to tenure. But I doubt that most of my colleagues in anthropology have ever read anything I have ever written in educational anthropology or would want to if they were asked to read it. It is though I have had two quite separate careers.

This is not good for people—being judged in two contexts that never really communicate effectively with each other excepting in the role relationship of the person who bridges the gap. It creates strains, spoils identities, creates insecurity, reinforces hostility, and can result in low security, slow promotion, and non-recognition. I did not suffer these consequences personally in serious degree. I believe it is because I was a 100 percenter in both contexts, or at least a 95 percenter in anthropology and a 70 percenter in education and I had strong support for what I was going from both the Deans of the School of Education and the Chairmen of the Department of Anthropology. I have nearly worn myself out several times and as I look back I am not sure I would do it again, even though the rewards have been great within my own framework of understandings and self-evaluation and have been surprisingly good institutionally and professionally. And yet, when I think back over all the excitement and challenge, I'm not at all sure I would have been happy as a regular, academic anthropology professor.

Recommendations
The basic recommendation I want to make is that if you think you are interested in the application of anthropology to analysis of the educative processes and/or in improving teacher education, administrative practice, curriculum, counseling and guidance, you should make a career commitment to professional education, get a position in a school of education, and place your fate in the hands of your educationist colleagues. If you are a successful infiltrator and become a successful organizer-exploiter in that context they will appreciate you and will furnish you with life-long security and appropriate kudos. But if you do that, if you are a "real" anthropologist, you will look longingly across the chasm between your homestead and your adopted country and wish sometimes you could just be an anthropologist.

PART II

Some Foundations of Primate Learning

Preview
6. SOLON T. KIMBALL   *Community and Hominid Emergence*
7. MARION LUNDY DOBBERT and BETTY COOKE   *Primate Biology and Behavior: A Stimulus to Educational Thought and Policy*

PREVIEW

There was nothing in the first edition of this book (1974) on non-human primate learning. The presence of part II, devoted to the foundations of primate learning, attests to the increasing attention this topic has received over the past decade. Field and laboratory studies of many species of monkeys and apes have proliferated and we know much now that was only intimated a decade ago. In my course at Stanford University in cultural transmission, taught primarily for education students, I started including, about a decade ago, a week of non-human primate behavior and the origins of human social organization and culture, before getting on into human culture case analyses. I found this introduction to the process of learning and the nature/nurture interaction essential, so have I included it in the revision of this book.

What is most important is that primate learning occurs in the social context and is not simply a case of individual development — a kind of linear unfolding of genetically determined abilities and characteristics.

All primate societies, both human and non-human, are characterized by certain axes around which behavior is organized: dominance; sexual bonding; mother-infant bonding; age differentiated roles; and sex differentiated roles. Humans vastly complicate the relationships clustered and patterned around these axes through the use of symbols, language, history and myth, but the axes are still there. Understanding the continuity between us human primates and our near primate relatives is essential to understanding the elemental facts about how we acquire culture and become human.

There has been a recent shift towards biological explanation of human behavior. This is helpful insofar that it calls attention to the fact that we are indeed, biological, and that our behaviors have both a biological basis and biological consequences. This is unhelpful insofar as we are led to believe that we do not *learn* how to behave, that our social behaviors and cognitive processing are innate, and that our socialized selves are not products of social organization and culture. Such an orientation does not make sense, given our myriad of observations of both human and non-human primate social behavior, and it can have dangerous ideological consequences.

The two chapters of Part II call attention to the nature of primate learning by placing this learning where it must be—in the social context. Solon Kimball calls attention to the *community* in both human and non-human primate society. Marion Dobbert and Betty Cooke show how we may look into non-human primate learning and maturation for a better understanding of learning among humans.

In both chapters *learning* rather than *teaching* is the focus. This gives further support to Harry Wolcott's position, as developed in Chapter Two in Part I. Teaching, however, may be considered a largely human development, though as with most behaviors, there is no absolute division between humans and other primates in this respect. Both apes and monkeys, and in fact many other mammals, create learning situations for their young and may "teach" by example, but there is little evidence of intentional intervention in the learning process. The full development of intention in teaching, and intervention in learning, and the construction of complex learning environments such as initiation ceremonies and schools, are limited to humans. Human motivations and intentions are guided and shaped by culture. Human communication is dominated by language. Human purposes are explicitly as well as implicitly defined by culture. And human culture is played out in the human community.

Humans seem, in all societies, to be concerned with teaching their children their way of life. In this way they achieve a kind of immortality through the maintenance of beliefs, values, moral codes and world views through time. Not all human societies, however, start intervening in the learning process so earnestly and so early as we do in contemporary America and in all other western societies. Conventional schooling in the west starts very early and confines young children to small spaces and limits their experience and exploration to what adults judge to be important, including such fine and complex motor and cognitive skills as reading and writing.

We know that all primates, human and non-human, are unparalleled learners. Children, like young chimpanzees, learn very well without being taught. Children learn even something as complex and subtle as speech without being taught. Learning occurs through modeling, through adaptation to the environment, and through play. Our schools, with their confinement and separation from life seriously hamper each of these learning mediums.

An examination of primate learning, of both human early learning in other cultures and non-human primate learning, could lead us to question the extent and severity of our early intentional interference in learning. It could even lead us to a restructuring of our schools to make them safe environments, less removed from life, for exploratory learning.

These are the type of questions that Dobbert and Cooke raise in their chapter. Part II raises fundamental issues about learning, teaching, culture, and community that must be considered in a mature anthropology of education. The two chapters included here represent a vast and growing litera-ture. They are unique in that both are written by educational anthropologists who are not specialists in primatology or biological anthropology, but rather in cultural anthropology and education. They are therefore clearly focused on processes that are of acknowledged importance to the anthropology of education.

The Editor

SOLON T. KIMBALL/*University of Florida*

6   *Community and Hominid Emergence*[1]

In retrospect, the perspective of the protagonists of primate evolution equals that of the fossil record itself in shaping their discussions. New bones evoke widely contrasting inferences. For example, the controversy over the origin of hominids continues to boil. Among the paleoanthropologists we have heated disagreement between Richard Leakey and Donald Johanson (Leakey and Lewin 1978; Johanson and Edey 1981). Although both have equal access to the fossil record, there is wide divergence in their speculative conclusions.

Anthropologists are not bothered by this type of scientific quarrel. It is part of the process by which facts are interpreted and new conclusions reached. Furthermore, there is no challenge to the basic assumption that unites them all. It is agreed that the crucial separation between humans and apes is based on culture: the presence of language, symbols, and the ability to make tools. It was accepted that the definition of a true hominid would be determined by these characteristics.

The relative serenity of this scientific setting disappeared with the appearance of a challenging view in sociobiology (Wilson 1975). This new view no longer accepted *Homo sapiens* as a biological mix of learned and inherited traits. Instead, the biological factor became dominant. There is a resemblance between the two views in the agreement that the biological basis of behavior is highly significant, but otherwise they are poles apart in the significance attached to the influence of culture in human development.

Our problem is not to attempt a reconciliation or to argue the relative merits of the contrasting views. Instead, the cogency of the anthropological view seems to have been diminished, owing in part to its failure to give adequate attention to all the cultural variables, in particular, human organization as a cultural phenomenon. Specifically, community has been totally neglected as a

---

[1] I am grateful to my colleague, Dr. Linda Wolfe, and to Ms. Elizabeth Peters for their constructive comments about aspects of primate groups and learning mentioned in this paper.

---

variable in human evolution, although the interaction that arises from reproduction and nurturance have been given some attention. Arensberg (1981:569) has described how at the simplest level of community grouping the process of sharing evokes organizational regularities.

When we consider the consequences of the emergence of ordered cooperative relations among members of a favorably situated primate group, we can conclude that we have encountered an incipient form of community. Concurrently, technology, language, symbols, and probably institutional behavior beyond the bonding of reproduction or infant care find a favorable environment in which in develop. This is the thesis that I wish to explore in the context of the relation between the biological base and the accrued knowledge that hominids preserve in the organization of community. The evolutionary result has been the appearance of something new in the world-humanity. In this examination we must keep in mind that the psychologically based theories of learning that permeate anthropology have proved a detriment in understanding the importance of community.

The problem examined in this paper is the connection between community and human learning. I believe that the prevalent explanations of the phylogenetic origins of *Homo sapiens* as a large brained, bipedal, articulate, symbol using, tool maker derived from either a technologically based hand-eye-brain syndrome or from the organic-interactional mother-infant bonding, or both, are inadequate. These explanations fail to take into account the social context as a systemic variable. It is proposed here that an incipient human community, the band, was the organizational variable that shaped the human biogram. It was a group whose members provided the essentials of protection, food, and creature comforts for themselves and their offspring. Their organizational system included the division of labor based upon complementarity between males and females and age and status differences within a three-generational population (Arensberg 1961:241-264).

It is only in the environmental setting of community that nurturance is provided for humans during a prolonged infancy and where additional needs are met during an even longer period of dependency. In the meantime, physical maturation and cultural learning coincide to bring the individual to adulthood and through sharing keep alive the temporarily enfeebled and the old. The extensive cultural learning that hominids required from a repository of community life could have been acquired only if the brain was specifically structured at birth to receive, assimilate, and organize experiences from the specific environment of community. Thus the evolutionary process, operating within an environent of community, favored the appearance of species that joined organic development and cultural learning as essentials for adult maturation. Such plasticity, however, imposed one crucial limitation. Achieving humanity was possible only if the infant was reared in the human environment of culture and community.

With this perspective about the human animal, many of the problems of learning become clarified. In particular, the specification of community as the context within which the individual derives identity and personality viewed as the expression of the group-shared cultural heritage of world view, assist greatly in our interpretation of these dimensions.

Relatively few anthropologists have made contributions to an anthropologically oriented learning theory, even though culture transmission is acknowledged as a major area of concern. This deficiency may be attributed to a continued domination by a traditional anthropology that emphasizes descriptive ethnography, and to the theoretical biases of structuralism, materialism, or symbolism where culture transmission has not been considered significantly relevant. Furthermore, the overwhelming attention given to the findings of neurologists such as Pavlov, psychologists Thorndike and Skinner, or the assumptions of Freud and other psychoanalysts may have contributed to an acceptance that body and mind were the legitimate foci for studying learning.

The transmission of culture has always been a subdivision within the discipline of anthropology. The major emphasis in American anthropology, until the 1930s. was on invention, diffusion, and acculturation. Such a focus increased our knowledge of the prehistoric connections between peoples and gave some insight into the selective processes of origin, incorporation, and transformation of cultural traits (Dixon 1928). Until the advent of child-rearing studies, however, very little attention was paid to the processes of the transmission of culture between the generations. In such studies, ethnographic observation specifically focused on the formation of personality, recording the sequence and substance of what the infant learned, from whom, and in what circumstances. (Mead 1928, 1930, 1963). Gradually, other aspects of the learning process were included as attention turned to the formal and informal learning situations in schools and play groups.

The truth is that anthropology has produced, over the years, a rich body of data, and some theory, which entitles it to claim a major and oftentimes challenging posture, vis-a-vis psychology and other disciplines, regarding the process of learning and its programmatic application (Roberts and Akinsanya 1976; Kimball 1974:465-482).

In the assessment of the evidence that validates the significance of an anthropological contribution to learning theory, I will first enumerate some of the conventional wisdom from anthropology, following which I will discuss the relation between the phylogeny of *Homo sapiens* and the setting of community.

A controversy that has engaged both anthropologists and psychologists for several decades has been that of the relative importance of genetic inheritance contrasted with that of the influence of the environment on the development and behavior of the individual. Experimenters attempted to discover what behavior was innate or instinctive and what was learned or acquired. MacDougall, one of the fiercest contenders in this quarrel, chopped the tails off mice generation after generation to determine if the tailessness might not become embedded in the inheritance. The mice gave up not a centimeter of their rightful tailed inheritance. He and others also divided lists of human qualities into those that were instinctive and/or learned. There were the "hard data" studies of identical twins by Sir Cyril Burt, whose conclusions favored the advocates of genetic behavior. Unfortunately, his basic research has recently been exposed as a scientific hoax. The decipherment of the genetic code by biologists and subsequent achievement of cloning has stimulated the popular press to cultivate the impression that science can reproduce identical individuals. Such publicity fans once again the notion of the supremacy of the biological component in human behavior.

Anthropologists' embroilment in the nature-nurture controversy was always tempered by empirical observations that showed that infants born to parents of one culture and reared by foster parents in another culture reflected, as adults, the cultural setting of their upbringing and not that of their biological parents. However, when questions are raised about the relative capabilities of different races in respect to their intelligence, anthropologists join a shouting match that reflects cultural biases more than it does empirical evidence. I remind you of the widely held conventional view that all groups of humankind share capabilities that permit them to become fully human. Proof that any of the diversities reflected in summations of national character have any genetic basis has yet to be established.

We must turn now to the fascinating problem of the process by which the potentials of an individual become transformed into a human being. The reasoning and the assumptions inherent in such an explanation reveal why the nature versus nurture controversy was based upon a false question and why the anthropological perspective is far more inclusive than that of either the psychologist or the biologist.

There are a few anthropologists who either have or are at the verge of adding the essential variable in their speculations about the emergence of *Homo sapiens*. Decades ago Wood Jones proposed that a progessive ape descended from the trees, perfected a bipedal gait as he walked upright, converted his forelimbs to manipulative purposes, and retained the primitive flexibility of the hand as he began to manufacture tools (Jones 1916). In those days it was agreed that only a brainy fellow would have enough sense to come down to earth and begin to make tools. We believe differently today. Fossil evidence from the Olduvai gorge and the Ethiopian plateau prove that our putative ancestors, although characters of little brain, walked upright and also made tools. As the tools improved over time, so also did the size of the brain. Hence a temptation to deduce a causal connection between technology and evolving humanity. Additional speculation has centered on the capacity to evoke the past and anticipate the future through articulate speech and language (Krantz 1980:773-792).

Humanity, by definition, required a specific combination of physical, psychic, cultural, social, and perhaps spiritual attributes. Utilizing inference and extrapolation, I postulate a social unit that was, in effect, an aboriginal form of the human community, the band. The hierarchy of status and complementarity between the sexes was expressed in and reinforced through the external relations that arise from the use and protection of recources, from the division of labor within the domestic group, from the sharing and distribution of food and other goods, from stabilized consort relations between adult males and females, and from their joint parenting of dependent young.

We are all aware that maturation among humans requires a longer time span than that of any other primate. The prolonged nurturance in infancy and lengthened childhood provides the opportunity for acquisition of the learning necessary in a species much of whose behavior is a conditional blending of heredity and environment. The normal infant born into a human community possesses the capability to become human, but humanity is achieved only within a human environment; it is not an inevitable consequence.

If we recall some of the prevalent views in anthropology of a past that focused on the individual, we can appreciate why these views have contributed little to an evolutionary problem. There is a subtle but fundamental difference in conceptualization between the conventional wisdom of psychological anthropology and the implication of the view that humanity is a consequence of community. The former holds that "human character is built upon a biological base which is capable of enormous diversification in terms of social standards" (Mead 1939:x). The objection is to the assumption that the biological dimension is a fixed base. Instead, it is proposed here that the human organism must be viewed as a developmental variable (Davis, 1949). It reaches normal maturity in the context of and in conjunction with a favorable environment; human nurturance requires more than simple caretaking of physical and psychological needs. Primate phylogeny bestowed the progeny of *Home sapiens* with a neural plasticity capable of responding to the "enormous diversification" of cultural variables within the social setting of community. If the infant is born neurologically deficient, no infusion of environmental ingredients can produce a true human. The impairment of neural plasticity inhibits the genetically inherent potential from being realized. If, on the other hand, the environmental setting fails to structure the plasticity in a human direction, the potential of the biological base is destroyed or remains unrealized. In effect, we are dealing with a system in which all the variables are in a relationship of contingent consequences (Chapple 1970).

At birth all infants have been programmed to respond to stimuli that are either pleasurable or painful, regardless of whether they originate inside or are external to the organism. Repletion leads to sleep, flatulence to howls. Excessive heat, pressure, or noise produce stress and response, avoidance, or protest. The response of the infant to repetitive caretaking activities requires a minimum of learning, although there may be some imprinting. The neural modification we label learning appears when the individual begins to manipulate the world external to his psyche, which contrasts with the implanting of reflexes established by response to repetitive stimuli.

The infant of *Homo sapiens*, in order to survive and develop, required a lengthy period of nurturance and dependency preliminary to the achievement of organic, neural, and behavioral maturity. That such a precarious arrangement, as a necessary prelude to maturity, could have become phylogenetically established and perpetuated is indeed a miracle. Regardless of whether one attributes the resulting humanity to a carefully conceived plan of a master intelligence or the whimsical quirk of nature, nevertheless it worked.

The emergence of a species where the newborn arrives with a limited neural structuring, an organic immaturity requiring lengthy dependency, and with the human community as a necessary legacy and environment for maturity was a unique event in the cosmos. From this original precarious innovation eventually came an explosive growth of a radically new way (other than genetic encoding) for preserving and transmitting experience — the culture tradition. It was an arrangement where nature experimented, if not gambled, with the substitution of an infinitely variable and expandable cultural inheritance for one limited by the constraints of a genetic code. If we ponder the implication of such an arrangement for a moment, we cannot help but be astounded by its fragility as well as admire its ingeniousness.

The essential caretaking practices for infant survival are the same for all cultures, but their pattern, however, will be culturally specific. For example, Caudill conducted a comparative study of the nurturant behavior by middle-class Japanese and American parents on their first-born infants. He discovered that Japanese practices were influenced by the belief that the infant needed to be incorporated as a family member. In contrast, the American parents believed that at birth the infant was a family member and needed to be trained to be independently responsible. By three months the infants' behavioral patterns were already reflecting the implicit cultural assumptions of their respective parents (Caudill and Weinstein 1970). In consequence, infant initiations and responses have become patterned in the neural system by the cultural setting (Campion and Smith 1934). When Ruth Benedict contrasted the measured tread of the Apollonian Zuni, with the frenetic exuberance of the Dionysian Sioux, she called attention to the powerful influence of the cultural milieu in shaping national character (Benedict 1934). Implicit in this comparison of cultural extremes was the assumption that the differential organization of cultural experience reflected a learning process in each society that was also distinctive because culturally acquired. This line of reasoning leads us to the further conclusion that within the generalities of pan-human learning each of humankind's community — cultural systems utilizes a distinctive learning process.

The cosmic view of learning developed here extends backward into the misty reaches of *Homo sapiens'* phylogenetic past and forward to the culture-laden present. It posits that an early species of primates clustered in an aboriginal community where the members shared in mutual protection, subsistence, and nurturance, and in their mutuality and diversity of role provided an optimum environment for developing articulate speech, the use of symbols, and the skills of making and using tools. The consequence of these cultural innovations was to develop the potential for the transmission of this cultural heritage and to inhibit genetic specialization as an alternative to ensuring group perpetuity.

Among the great consequences that flowed from an inheritance of intermingled organic and cultural origins came the sense of self in the context of beginning and end, personality derived from participation with others, and the incorporation of a community-shared perception of reality. Such a formulation of interdependent phylogenetic origins and community-culture patterns furnishes an anthropological perspective of universal significance for specifying and programming the transmission of the cultural heritage.

References

Arensberg, Conrad M., 1961, "The Community as Object and as Sample." *American Anthropologist* 63(2):241-264.

_____, 1981, "Cultural Holism through Interactional Systems." *American Anthropologist* 83:3.

Benedict, Ruth, 1934, *Patterns of Culture.* Boston: Houghton Mifflin.

Campion, George and G. Elliott Smith, 1934, *The Neural Basis of Thought.* London: Harcourt, Brace, Co.

Caudill, William and Helen Weinstein, 1970, "Maternal Care and Infant Behavior in Japanese and American Urban Middle Class Families." In *Families in East and West: Socialization Process and Kinship Ties.* Reuben Hill and Rene Konig, eds. The Hague: Mouton.

Chapple, Eliot D., 1970, *Culture and Biological Man: Explorations in Behavioral Anthropology.* New York: Holt, Rinehart and Winston.

Davis, Kingsley, 1949, *Human Society.* New York: The MacMillan Co.

Dixon, Roland B., 1928, *The Building of Culture.* New York: Charles Scribner's Sons.

Johanson, Donald, and Maitland Edey, 1981, *Lucy: The Beginnings of Humankind.* New York: Simon & Schuster.

Jones, F. Wood, 1916, *Aboreal Man.* London: E. Arnold.

Kimball, Solon T., 1974, *Culture and the Educative Process: An Anthropological Perspective.* New York: Teachers College Press.

Krantz, Gouver S., 1980, "Sapienization and Speech." *Current Anthropology* 21(6): 773-792.

Leakey, Richard, and Roger Lewin, 1978, *People of the Lake: Mankind and Its Beginnings.* Garden City, NY: Doubleday.

Mead, Margaret, 1928, *Coming of Age in Samoa: A Psychological Study of Primitive Youth for Western Civilization.* New York: Morrow.

_____, 1930, *Growing Up in New Guinea: A Comparative Study of Primitive Education.* New York: Morrow.

_____, 1939, *From the South Seas: Studies of Adolescence and Sex in Primitive Societies.* New York: Morrow.

_____, 1963, *Socialization and Enculturation. Current Anthropology* 2:181-188.

Roberts, Joan I., and Sherrie K. Akinsanya, 1976, *Schooling in the Cultural Context: Anthropological Studies of Education.* Part IV:257-340. New York: David McKay.

Singh, J.A.L., and Ribert Zingg, 1942, *Wolf-Children and Feral Man.* New York: Harpers.

Wilson, E.O., 1975, *Sociobiology: The New Synthesis.* Cambridge, MA: Harvard University Press.

MARION LUNDY DOBBERT and BETTY COOKE/*University of Minnesota*

7   *Primate Biology and Behavior: A Stimulus to Educational Thought and Policy*

Introduction - Why Primates?

The study of primates has been found to be useful both in giving perspective to human behavior and in abstracting principles of behavior which can be assessed in light of their relevance to humans (Hinde, 1972, 1982). In this paper an alternative approach to thinking about human learning and its implications for educational theory and practice will be offered based on primate biological and behavioral research.

Western European society has long been intellectually biased against the use of animals as models for humans (see Walker, 1983, for a detailed discussion). Although other cultures, such as Native American ones, have found sources for ideals in animals and their traits, Westerners have separated themselves cognitively, ideologically, morally and affectively from a sympathetic vision of their animal brethren which could encourage learning from biological, ethological, and behavioral studies. It is most important that we recognize these culturally acquired biases because they serve as blocks to the scientific use and evaluation of an entire set of pertinent information.

The starting point for a scientifically well grounded theory of learning/education lies in the active incorporation of the principles of evolution into educational thought. Rozin and Kalat make a sound point:

> Given the constraints on adaptation produced by basic properties of the nervous system, the cost of evolving specializations, and the fact that most species face a common set of problems, we doubt that a separate learning mechanism would exist for every situation, or that there would be separate laws for each species. (Rozin & Kalat quoted in Johnston, 1981, p. 129)

One can come to precisely the same conclusion from a second starting point, that of comparative anatomy. The brains of non-human primates and humans are structured very similarly (Walker, 1983). Studies of primate intelligence also support this position. Primates have shown themselves capable of cross

Submitted for publication in *Education and Cultural Process, 2E* and printed by permission of the authors.

modal learning, give evidence of long term memory, exhibit transfer learning, and display innovative behavior (Rogers & Davenport, 1975; Rumbaugh, 1970, 1975). Studies of the use of natural, wild primate call or language systems (see, for example, Snowden, Brown, & Petersen, 1982) and of chimpanzees' use of various human-devised languages give increasingly strong evidence for the use of abstract, functional conceptual categorization by primates—whatever one may think about what these studies show about the "true" language abilities of the animals.[1] Additionally, intelligence of non-human primates has also been fairly extensively tested using human intelligence tests. Their scores generally resemble those of human toddlers in both total points gained and tasks completed (Chevalier-Skolnikoff, 1977; Gibson, 1977; Parker, 1977; Rumbaugh, 1975; Walker, 1983).

The capabilities of non-human primates are often underestimated for another reason, behavioral observation does not show them doing the kinds of things we humans do. Rumbaugh (1975) argues that this is misleading and that the non-human primates have many latent capacities. For example, squirrel monkeys do not actively mother as do humans, but if an abnormal infant is born that is very dependent and unable to cling, the mother will become pro-active. It is these latent capacities which provide evolutionary potential in a species and which, in primate evolution, lead to the development of culture in humans.

We are arguing here that we should *begin* formulating theories of learning, and therefore of education, with the basic study of primates. But we must add, to *begin* with a physiological, primate based theory is *not to end* there. Our own interests in primate research stem from humanistic educational concerns, a concern on one hand for more humane parenting and the development of improved parenting skills and on the other for moral education and the design of moral societies. If we want to establish scientifically sound approaches in our own fields, we must apprehend human nature correctly and precisely. It is for this reason that we have turned to primate research.[2]

---

[1]The extreme opposition, i.e., those who think chimps have shown no language ability whatsoever, such as Sebeok and Umiker-Sebeok, have attributed the findings of the human-contrived language experiments to the "clever Hans" phenomena. But Walker (1983) refutes this with evidence of responses in which trainers are not present. Further, such arguments are inconsistent with findings of communication and behavior studies in natural settings. In addition, even such distant relatives of homo sapiens as the Old World monkeys have the specific cerebral assymetries associated with language (Falk, 1980).

[2]Despite the similarities cited here and in the following sections of the paper, it is very important that one proceed cautiously. The biological and behavioral building blocks of human and monkey or ape daily living systems are similar, but in the different species they contribute to quite different overall systems. Some primates are troop dwelling, some solitary; with some sex is the basis of the primary social structure, with others it is dominance relations. It is usually thought that the best evidence for

We are not, of course, the first theorists to take a position which starts from primate research and use it to raise issues about human education (Blurton-Jones, 1972; Herzog, 1974; Kimball, 1982; Poirier & Hussey, 1982; Reynolds, 1976; Washburn, 1973; Wolcott, 1982). In the body of this paper we attempt to move toward a scientifically based theory of child rearing and education which is not limited by our human cultural biases and history. In organizing our findings, we have taken a position which arises from the literature reviewed: 1) humans must be seen first as biological beings who 2) must, by the fundamental nature of their biology, interact socially and 3) must therefore learn through processes that are socially oriented. The educational argument is developed in three subsections relating to the biological, social, and learning process data reviewed.

Biology and Learning in Primates

Forming the substrate for the characteristics and behavior of any order or species of living beings is its basic biology. Old world monkeys and hominoidea (apes and humans) share some 30 million years of evolutionary history since the rise of the earliest primates about 70 million years ago. This long shared history is the basis of a similarity so profound that some human blood factors (Rh,M,N,etc.) were first discovered in monkeys. Looking at this biological base from an educational perspective we note four aspects of it that have important educational implications: 1) the primate sensory system, 2) the patterns of periodic rhythms and hormone flows, 3) the generalized genetic design for learning, 4) the primate development pattern.

An understanding of the primate sensory system is of critical importance in developing a solidly based theory of learning. The most important sense in all primates is vision. It is so important that Chalmers (1980) says it is almost a defining characteristic of the order. The major brain connections that developed during primate and later specifically human evolution are those between manipulation, fine coordination, and vision (Walker, 1983). The early stages of the maturation of this circuit are easily seen in infant reaching and batting behaviors. However, although the obvious aspects of this behavior are submerged with growth, it does not disappear, as Piaget has noted in his discussion of the sensorimotor and concrete operations stages in humans.

---

factors that are strongly important in understanding humans will come from our phylogenetically closest relatives, but modern research has modified this dictum.

There is some evidence that measured intelligence in primates correlates better with a terrestrial life style than with evolutionary position (Rumbaugh, 1975). But, in any case, we must never make the mistake of thinking that similar processes in non-human primates and in humans are identical and we must avoid over-emphasizing single factors as have some of the prominent popular "ethological" texts.

Unfortunately, many of our formal and informal teaching strategies of lecturing and explaining seem to assume that hearing is our major and best developed sense.

A second aspect of human biology which is of great importance in educational design are the cycladic rhythms and hormonal outputs. Cycladic and hormonal patterns in humans are the equivalents of the fixed behavioral patterns we see in other orders of animals because all these fixed patterns are ultimately based in the rhythms of the biochemical, electrophysiological, and endocrine systems (Chapple, 1970). Infants begin to develop these rhythms at about six weeks of age, but child rhythms do not function as do adult rhythms even as late as the age of ten (Hellbruge cited in Chapple, 1970).

The neuro-hormonal outputs of the body also shape another fundamental characteristic of the individual, his/her temperament or emotional reactivity. Emotional responses are involuntary and result biologically from the trigger of some stimulus.[3] The triggered response differs from one individual to the next in readiness of the bodily system to respond to a stimulus, duration of response, and physiological strength of response.

The existence of these rhythms and hormonal states has important educational implications because they determine an individual's state of attention and readiness (Chance, 1978). In all animals, approach, which is essential to learning, is facilitated by a low level of arousal, while fear or apprehension suppress approach behaviors (Mason, 1965). Readiness and approach behaviors preparatory to learning can be enhanced by reducing fear and apprehension levels. In young children, as in other young primates, this can best be accomplished by permitting them to cling until arousal levels drop to the low levels which facilitate approach, play, and curiosity behaviors. It follows that attempts to teach children, or adults, to control or suppress emotions are misguided; one needs to treat emotions as existing, on-going biological processes and educate individuals to deal with them as such. Emotional education systems calling for the open identification and naming of interior states followed by a rational response make good biological sense. A biological viewpoint also suggests that individual self-paced teaching designs will be stronger than socially derived uniform schedules. Since the rhythms of activity-inactivity and hormonal flows vary in periodicity, amount, and duration from individual to individual, no two persons are necessarily in a state of readiness for learning at any particular time.

---

[3]Many object to a biological interpretation of emotion, feeling that it belittles human emotional experience, but Chapple offers three arguments for accepting the biological view in addition to the general evolutionary argument which he takes for granted: 1) Drugs and electrical stimulation produce predictable regular emotions in animals and humans. (The experiments with cats are well known.) 2) Emotion is experienced as interior. 3) There is an obvious physical involvement of the body in all strong emotions.

A third biological fact of extreme importance is the fact that humans and, to a lesser extent, all primates are genetically designed to learn, to learn easily, and to learn well. This fact has been carefully documented for primates in the familiar Japanese macaque films and for humans by Bloom (1964). This ability is apparently an adaptation to the complex and often surprising environments faced by primates, most of which are seriously outclassed in size and weight by both the predators and other foragers who share their environments. One way this learning is accomplished is through the "polyphasic" abilities of human learners (Henry, 1960), who learn simultaneously through many bodily senses and functions.

Human adults, however, when functioning as educators, cross-culturally fail to note the fact that human children are designed to learn (Henry, 1960), probably because as mature, skilled, fully enculturated members of society adults most easily see children's deficiencies. Therefore, they deliberately set out to teach the young of the one species which least requires teaching. The point we wish to make here is the biological one—juvenile primates, including humans, when left to their own devices, with just a bit of supervision to prevent harm, as are immature baboons and macaques and many children in non-Western cultures such as the Mbuti (Turnbull, 1978), will learn easily and well during all their pre-adult years to the point where they will be ready to step into and learn adult roles through practice when they reach that age.[4]

A fourth aspect of primate biology with important educational implications is that of the primate pattern of development. The growth cycle of young primates has been divided into four specific developmental stages by some primate researchers (Harlow & Harlow, 1966; Scott & Marston, 1950) during which experience and learning within the social group are of primary importance. These four periods include the neonatal period; the period of transition, when adult and infantile patterns overlap; the period of peer socialization; and the juvenile or subadult period. In relation to the overall notion of development through the life cycle, Poirier (1977) pointed out:

> At different times in the life cycle qualitatively and quantitatively different things occur, and unless we isolate behaviors at an early age, we may be unable to understand later social development .. By the same token, because we designate a behavior as important during one life stage, this doesn't necessarily imply that it will be important during another. (p. 12)

These same conclusions can be found in child development literature. Developmental biology and psychology and their learning implications have been widely studied and commented upon, and giant figures such as Gesell and

---

[4]The best proof of this in our own society comes from the fact that whatever it is that schools do do, when they teach reading, writing, geometry, civics and Spanish, they do not teach adult daily living roles—parenting, being a politician, bargaining, protesting, getting along on too little income, household scheduling, etc.

Piaget have done enormous service in focusing attention on the relationship between maturity, development and learning.

The Social Nature of Primates

The social environment provides the context within which most young primates learn and mature. The importance to learning of the social context and the geographic niche it occupies is emphasized extensively throughout the literature on primate learning and socialization (Chevalier-Skolnikoff, 1977; Dolhinow, 1972; Herzog, 1974; Kimball, 1982; Lancaster, 1975; Poirier, 1972; Poirier & Hussey, 1982). Because of the highly social nature of primates, both groups and individuals can be viewed as the adaptive units of the species. Within the group, both direct individual learning in interaction with the environment and the passing on of group traditions occur. The learning of traditions provided within the social group "is superior to individual learning if the new behavior is difficult to acquire individually in direct interaction with the environment" (Poirier & Hussey, 1982, p. 137). The social life in the group requires that an individual primate demonstrate both predictability in its behavior and the capability of flexibility in its responses under appropriate conditions. The individual behaviors of primates are controlled by a continual process of social learning resulting from group interactional patterns. The ability to learn to act in accordance with social modes is crucial since individuals whose behavioral traits do not conform sufficiently to group norms are less likely to reproduce biologically or to be reproductive socially and ideologically.

It is the long period of physical maturation in primates which provides the necessary opportunity for learning in a social context. As stated by Poirier and Hussey (1982), "There is a spiral of social dependency and intelligence; ever greater learning necessitates ever greater social dependency, and long dependency allows further learning" (p. 144). There must be at least one socializing agent to teach the growing youngster, and the earliest and most important socializing agent is usually the mother, although other individuals may substitute permanently or temporarily. The primate mother-infant relationship sets the foundation for all other relationships the primate will encounter throughout its life, and this relationship is, in turn, influenced by other relationships of the mother. The interactional pattern between the mother infant dyad derives its original form and later permutations not only from characteristics inherent in the pair itself, but also from the social and physical surroundings of which they are a part.

The infant-mother relation is the most intense known, and because of its nature the mother, by definition, stands initially for the whole world to a young primate. This is a *two-way relationship* based on her normal and affectional ties in which each member of the pair both gives and receives

(Montague provides an interesting discussion of this in *The Direction of the Human Development*, 1970). That this relationship is initially fragile and is vulnerable into the transition period has been established beyond any doubt by maternal deprivation studies in non-human primates, such as Harlow and Harlow's (1962), and in humans with studies of institutionalized infants and maternal absence and of abnormal mothers (Ainsworth, 1973; Bowlby, 1969, 1972; Henry, 1971; Spitz, 1945).

Humans and many other primates, particularly the ground-dwellers are social and *must* live socially to survive. Baboons and humans, for example, develop elaborate social systems as a major part of their ecological adaptation. In baboons this is seen in the dominance hierarchy, in grooming, and in feeding behavior; and in humans in the division of labor. These elaborate structures are founded upon the build-up of affectional ties beginning with the first two of the basic primate systems, the infant-mother system and the maternal system (Harlow & Harlow, 1965), which together form a single two-way system (Montague, 1970).

> One of the ways in which primates differ from other animals is in the strength, duration and diversity of their affectional systems, systems which bind together various individuals within a species in coordinated and constructive social relations. (Harlow & Harlow, 1965, p. 287)

The earliest social experience of a young primate, that of bonding with its mother, "represents the primary adaptive strategy of higher primates, so that it is not surprising that powerful emotional supports have evolved which lead the growing infant to form these bonds in the first place and to maintain them and form new ones during its life" (Lancaster, 1975, p. 21). The infant-mother system has its foundation in primate basic biology and depends initially upon the reflexes of clinging and sucking. With time and history of the satisfaction of basic needs, it develops and generalizes to a tie where contact, warmth, and protection are important. Of the greatest importance here is intimate physical contact, as opposed to mere nursing, because it is the foundation of the maternal bond of trust which itself is later generalized and serves as the foundation for broader social ties (Harlow & Harlow, 1965). From an educational viewpoint, we need to note here that the critical factor in the formation of the social tie is intimate *physical* contact. In non-human primates, when the social ties generalize to other individuals the mode continues to be based on physical contact.

The young primate learns by observation and practice in the context of these affectional bonds. Primates seem to not simply observe a new behavior pattern, recognize it as useful, and adopt the behavior. The proper emotional climate and interest that comes from the presence of a positive emotional bond is also needed in order for the observer/learner to really perceive the new behavior (Lancaster, 1975). The neonatal period of primate interaction with its mother provides the infant primate the opportunity to learn to develop these emotional attitudes and bonds. In consequence *all* early learning is closely linked with affectional ties.

Peers and Older Playmates

The single most important learning task of the transitional, peer socialization, and juvenile developmental periods is that of learning to live socially. Historians of childhood such as Aries have pointed out that childhood as we know it today was "invented" rather late in European history. Actually, this is not true. Childhood was "invented" some 30 or 40 million years ago by the primate order. Lancaster (1975) emphasizes the importance of this period.

> In many ways the single most important adaptation of the higher primates (Old World monkeys, apes, and humans) is a pronounced division of roles between adults and young. One might almost say that upon this all else depends. Clearly a characteristic of these primates is the very long time that it takes to grow up, especially when relative body size is considered. Obviously it takes years for an adult elephant weighing literally tons to grow, but it is surprising to find that it takes a three pound Talapoin monkey (the smallest of the Old World monkeys) three years to reach maturity. Growth here has to be in nervous tissue, the brain, and not in simply bone and muscle... This is the time for development of the brain through play and learning without which the special intelligence characteristic of the higher primates would be impossible. (p. 35)

How does social learning take place during childhood? Piaget, in considering this issue educationally, has correctly pointed out that human children do not think like adults. Perhaps more important is the fact that in all species young and juvenile primates do not behave like adults. Developmentally, childhood in all primates is characterized by peer play. What most educational researchers have failed to notice is that for these youthful primates, peer play is the appropriate method of learning, and perhaps the *only* efficient major method of learning for them at this stage of mental development. If we look at the behaviors of wild primates during this period, we find that they eat, sleep, groom, explore and play, with play making up 70% of the non-solitary behavior of young chimpanzees, for example (Mason, 1965).

In the transitional stage, infants begin coordinated movements away from their mothers toward both each other and objects via approach and withdrawal, rough and tumble play, or contact-manipulation. This initiates the development of the third affective system, the peer system, which is developed fully through constant peer social or interactive play. The fourth affectional system, the heterosexual, is also developed through physical play through acts including all the basic social behaviors of self-presentation, greeting, aggressive postures and gestures as well as reproductive behaviors (Harlow & Harlow, 1965). Physical contact and social experience form the cornerstones for the development of these two affectional systems, both of which are fostered in a protected atmosphere where adults of both sexes are strongly attracted to the young.

Pedagogically, western educators in recent periods have made a major mistake in assessing the relationship of the affectional systems to educational designs. Our modern culture seems to assume that the need for an emotional component underlying educational endeavors ends when a child reaches age six or seven. Looked at from the perspective of primate research, this assumption is clearly an error. During the third and fourth developmental periods, the peer play and juvenile periods, which are the equivalent of the older child and the teen period in humans, both the age-mate or peer and the sexual/heterosexual systems of affection are established (Harlow & Harlow, 1965). The link between affection and learning is not dropped; rather, it is maintained and expanded.

Beyond the mother-infant bond and specific peer relationships, the larger social structure and context also play a major role in the learning of a young primate. Because social living is a dominant factor in most primate lifestyles, each individual must adapt to life with other individuals, even if it means constant subjection to aggression or very low status in the group. There are usually "rules" to be learned related mainly to social roles and to what can and cannot be done. Most of these restrictions of social activity are learned early in life when the consequences of breaking them are minimal. The young primate's learning of group limits and dominance relationships begins through the relationship to its mother and is influenced by her status in the group and her relationships with others including her kin. In addition, Poirier (1972) pointed out:

> It has been suggested that the basis of the dominance hierarchy is established in the play group wherein youngsters compete for food, travel routes, and resting places. Within the play group youngsters may learn cooperation, group-positive behaviors, thus establishing close social bonds that will later help maintain group unity. Adjustments seem to appear during play that enable a young primate to function properly as an adult member of the species and to occupy a position within the social organization of the group. (p. 23)

Lancaster (1975) suggested that one of the aspects of a stable social structure is that it underlies what Chance and Jolly (1970) called an "attention structure."

> This term refers to the fact that subordinate individuals are usually very much aware of what dominant animals are doing when the subordinates may seem to be going about their business... In contrast, very dominant animals do not often pay attention to the behavior of subordinates unless it actively intrudes upon them. (Lancaster, 1975, p. 45)

Positive emotional bonds between individuals as well as the previously discussed state of optimal activity (Gard & Meier, 1977) seem to be necessary in order for this attention and interest to occur.

Another part of the social context that needs to be considered is the relationship between young primates and mature males. The males' socializing role is likely to be the most variable relationship experienced by the young primate in terms of the amount and kind of contact which it has with males during its early years. The adult male's role also varies according to age, dominance, specific social group, and individual idiosyncracies. The role most often assumed is a protective response toward youngsters, but this varies in pattern and extent.

Of the five basic primate affectional systems described by Harlow and Harlow (1965), the fifth and final system to develop is the paternal affectional system. The prototypical behavior for this system is the adult make performing *generalized* fathering behavior within the group—protecting the females and their offspring, guarding the troop as a whole, in some cases even adopting infants. It would seem that an emotional bond of some sort between males and primate young would be vital for the performance of whatever type of fathering behavior is observed in primates.

In addition, previous experience with infants is especially crucial for the expression of paternal behavior. Such previous experience appears to be a prerequisite for displaying adequate infant caregiving behavior for adult female primates as well. The data signal the importance of creating opportunities for children to interact with males, both older youth and adults, kin as well as non-kin, in order for both male and female children to learn about the male role and the contribution males make to social groups, including the family. The traditional school system which has exposed children mainly to female teachers does not allow ample opportunity for children to observe male role behavior.

The Learning Process in Primates

In the preceding sections we have described the way in which learning processes in human and non-human primates are founded upon their basic biology and rooted in their essentially social nature. It is within this context that we describe the four primary learning mechanisms common to all primates. The first of these is *observation and modeling* (Poirier, 1973) in which the young observe others doing things and try them out. Studies of wild primates reveal that the young observe intensively and try things themselves many times. This kind of learning is equally important in humans. Sylva, Bruner, and Genova (cited in Chalmers, 1980) conducted a study with six-year-olds in which they were asked to clamp sticks together to open a distant box. One group was given a small amount of instruction; a second the same amount of instruction plus they were permitted to manipulate, play with, the objects; a third group received just extensive oral instruction. The second group out-performed both non-manipulative groups.

The protected, leisure atmosphere of the stable primate group is critical for observational learning because it permits the focused attention and provides the emotionally relaxed atmosphere essential to readiness and approach. The group is also essential in this process for another reason because, as noted above, primate cognitive development and learning are intricately intertwined with and dependent upon affectional development, emotions, and community ties.

A second form of learning comes from *social experience*. Social, that is inter-individual, contact and interaction per se are the major building blocks of social structure. Mason (1978) found that social experience is critical to the building and maintenance of complex social structures. Groups formed from young rhesus macaques deprived of early social experience lived together peacefully enough but their social structure was simplified, dyadic, and linear. Further, any social contact, friendly or antagonistic, builds structure by definition because it reduces the time and attention available for other contact (Vaitl, 1978) and because it creates relationships which are then activated in other situations. For example, Seyforth, Chaney and Hinde (1978) showed that for old world monkeys grooming relations are structured differently for juvenile males and females and provide the social experience and contact necessary for their later roles as female members of a structured troop and as males who will need sexual access. Whiting and Whiting (1975) found that nurturant and responsible adult behavioral profiles were developed in societies where children had experience with child care and work tasks respectively. In interaction, the young work out an identity for themselves and with their peers, and they begin developing a social structure which is flexible, fluid and experimental, the experience which will guide them in their adult lives.

The third form of learning fostered by the protected group atmosphere is *social conflict learning.* Poirier (1973) quoting Berlyne points out that conflict

> is an inescapable accompaniment of the existence of all higher animals, because of endless diversity of the stimuli that act upon them and of the responses that they have the ability to perform. (p. 22)

He continues,

> In primate societies there is a continual interplay of friendly, sexual, aggressive, and fearful impulses, all of which must be individually balanced The balancing of these, rather than the actual experiences of punishment and reward, help maintain the social framework, and, when the balance is upset, permit relearning and modification by other means than aggression. (p. 22)

The key element in the social order constructed in part through such interaction is neither physical superiority nor aggression but social skill and experience (Chalmers, 1980; Van Lawick-Goodall, 1971; Lancaster, 1975; Symons, 1978; Voland, 1977). It appears that a balance of cooperation and social conflict and competition are necessary components of group interaction for young primates and lead to their learning of the social structure and their position within it because of the fact that "group integration is a complex process relying on mutually reciprocal patterns of naturalistic behavior modified and made specific by learning and conditions" (Poirier, 1972, p. 17).

The fourth form of learning protected and encouraged by primate social groups is *play*, which is estimated by many (e.g. Lancaster, 1975; Poirier, Bellisari & Haines, 1978) to be the most significant modality for learning. Poirier (1973) comments:

> The period of maximal nonhuman primate social play may correspond to the brief period of avian imprinting. During play an animal learns which species it belongs to. Far from being a "spare-time," superfluous act, play at certain crucial early life stages seems necessary for the occurrence and success of later social life... The longer the period of infant dependency the more vulnerable the infant is to influences and interactions adversely affecting its social development. Therefore, the more essential it is that there be a means of ensuring continuous corrective interactions with its species. Play might serve this function. (Loizos, 1968).

Further, in our own experience we have found that children and young adolescents express forcefully a need to play using words that suggest they feel an urge as physical and pressing as their urges to eat when hungry.

Play contains all the necessary elements for optimal learning—a slightly aroused but open emotional state, repetition, contact and manipulation, and the free combination of the physical, cognitive, and behavioral elements of adult life. These elements are picked up and tried out over and over again, in many sequences and combination, often in an exaggerated or magnified form and in a context where the performance failure has few negative outcomes and lacks serious consequences. Harlow's work was the first to highlight the importance of this seemingly trivial type of learning for general intelligence. It was he who realized that insight is actually founded upon previous trial and error learning with similar types of problems; or to put it another way, that insight is a result of learning set formation (see Schrier's, 1984, defense of Harlow). In other words, the more children play freely, the more experience they build up and the more likely they are to be able to solve complex problems in later life. Baldwin and Baldwin (1978) have documented the formal structural similarities between the creative process and the play process. From this point of view a good learning design would make available to children *all* the *real* elements of adult life, except perhaps the very dangerous, and would encourage any use or experimentation in an emotionally open but slightly aroused atmosphere. A poor learning design would limit elements to book, papers and pencils and rely primarily upon adult directed activity in an authoritarian, anxiety provoking atmosphere.

Summary and Conclusions

Before we draw our own conclusions, we would like to quote a statement from Washburn, a well-known primatologist, with which we agree:

> A view of traditional European educational practices from the vantage point of a primatologist suggests that the school system is based on a series of traditional mistakes... To the student of monkey behavior, schools seem grounded in ignorance of the kind of being they are trying to teach. The view of the human being as a particular kind of primate makes the school seem strange and leads to the conclusion that human customs are not necessarily efficient, necessary, or useful in the way that they are supposed to be. Educational institutions cannot be designed effectively without regard for the biology of human beings... Through a profound misunderstanding of the nature of primate biology, the schools reduce the most intelligent primate to a bored and alienated creature. (1973, p. 131)

In Western societies the general focus of educational planning has been on older children and young adults within a formal school context. The research reviewed here strongly suggests that both the age and institutional focus are misguided. Since the experiences of a developing primate from infancy through adolescence are extremely important to their learning throughout the life cycle, much more attention should be given to early experiences. From the crucial months of infancy throughout the adolescent years, high priority should be given to efforts which support and promote optimal social and physical *environments* for the young in order for them to learn and develop to their optimal biological potential. Supprt for those who care for and educate children and youth should also be high on the agenda of social and educational policies since these people are so important for what they provide in children's lives. In particular, the major socializing agent of young children, usually the mother, so critical in their early learning, needs to be recognized and supported by society. This can be done both informally through strengthened neighborhood or kin support for new mothers, for example, or formally through specific educational offerings for new parents in child development and appropriate caregiving skills.

But this is not enough. Modern societies should aim to increase the overall societal level of child raising and caregiving skills. Educational programs for children of various ages, adolescents, and young adults, both females and males, should include active daily interaction with infants and children and provide information about child development and cargiving. As a part of these programs, young people in our society will need to be helped to recognize the importance of the social group and to receive guidance in building skills for developing and maintaining social support throughout their lifetimes. Continuing education parenting programs would ideally offer emotional support and ideas and give aid in developing and strengthening social ties with others. Linking expectant or new parents to other parents who are experiencing or have experienced the same problems and concerns they would be dealing with could be a component of these programs. Direct caregiving help from social network members could contribute to the reduction of maternal stress due to the pressure of constant caregiving, allowing the mother time for other essential tasks and providing both the mother and infant with greater variety of stimulation. Whatever direction supports for new parents, especially mothers, may take, the evidence is clear that the rearing and education of children should not be done in social isolation but rather within complex group interactions within thoughtfully designed environments.

One of the most serious "mistakes" found in contemporary education is the failure of schools to recognize, plan for, and use the biologically based emotional, affectional, and hormonal systems of their students as a major component of the educational process. Earlier educators in the Western tradition did not necessarily make the error of ignoring the emotional component of education. A number of historical Western models, including the classical mentoring, the Greek dramaturgical, and the medieval maternal education models,[5] included a deliberate emotional component, but most post-industrial school models have an almost exclusive cognitive focus. Clearly, an educational design based on sound primate theory would deliberately foster the development of affectional ties between teachers and learners and would not expect learning to occur unless or until this had occurred. Further, opportunities to develop and use maternal and paternal types of caring behaviors should be a regular part of our educational pattern. Because of the biological base of the affection which we are trying to foster, all of these must include real physical contact, experimentation, and the opportunity for development of emotional ties.[6] This is not to say that such interaction should not be supervised, graded, and some limits placed upon it. What we are saying is that our society inhibits and disrupts affectinal development in many ways, to its own ultimate detriment by giving children too little, too late and ending what we do give too soon.

When we examine Western learning designs in light of the basic primate learning process, another basic error stands out. Teacher focused school

---

[5]Again we acknowledge our debt to Ayers Bagley, as well as to our colleague, Robert Beck, for this insight.

[6]Examples include Mbuti mixed age play groups (Turnbull, 1978), the restrained, responsible heterosexual experimentation permitted by the Ngoni (Reed, 1968), the way many American Blacks relate older to younger children (see for example Ward, 1971), the manner in which various non-Western societies nourish, protect and encourage the foundational mother-infant system by making the new mother and infant the center of attention. The mother is coddled with the best foods; she and the infant are visited; parties are held to celebrate every small advance in the child's growth or maturation; relatives come forward with advice and help. Too, in many societies birth of a child raises the parents' social status in a formal and definite manner.

designs and relatively isolated nuclear family dwellings eliminate a very great deal of peer learning experience. One important educational implication for human children that arises from research on young primates is the *vital* nature of experience within groups in which opportunities are available for children to learn to behave cooperatively as well as deal with conflict and competition in a relatively balanced manner. It is important that this group interaction should occur within familiar groups with whom children have regular, ongoing contact in order for them to learn the group organization and their place in it. From a primate theory perspective schools should be structured to encourage this kind of vital social and peer learning. This could be accomplished by designing schools as rich environments in which adults would work and *groups* of children would be free to roam about, select, and play with any of the elements of adult activity. In this setting children would be allowed to experiment and instruct each other; they would not be given instruction unless they specifically requested it. Because it is a *fundamental* form of primate learning, peer/social learning should also be extended in life into adult situations. In addition, many studies have indicated the effectiveness of peer based teaching-learning systems in humans (Cloward, 1976; Feldman, Shehan, & Allen, 1976; Hoopes, n.d.; Johnson & Johnson, 1975). Slightly older, more experienced peers appear to be the best teachers. There is also some evidence that for human children mixed age and sex groups are most effective in socializing for peaceful cooperative group living (Dobbert, 1981). The primate research does not, then, tell us anything novel here—what it does do is show us how much we underestimate the importance of peer learning.

Closely related to peer learning is play. The research indicates that primate play has complex multiple functions (Fagen, 1981; Poirier, Bellisary & Haines, 1978; Smith & Fraser, 1978). Among these are 1) the physical regulation of growth, 2) the development of motor and cognitive skills, 3) the generation of behavioral flexibility, and 4) the learning and cementing of social relations. With the exception of early childhood specialists, our society seems to vastly underestimate the importance of play in all four of these areas, especially for older children. We seem unaware that full growth is not achieved before the early twenties and the exaggerated, repetitive, high-energy qualities of play are probably essential until growth is completed. In wild primates rough and tumble play is performed by animals of the pre-teen/teen equivalent stage in humans. Further, social play provides, by definition, social learning opportunities in a social context requiring fairness, role reversal and de-emphasis upon dominance (Fagen, 1981) in order to engage and keep play partners. Through play the individual tries out various stragegies and develops into a functional group member, via trial and error and repetition. Most importantly, the young learn the limits of their self-assertiveness (Poirier, 1973). Thus, by limiting play we probably interfere with optimal social development and prevent self-corrective social skill learning.

The standard average classroom appears to be designed to reduce as much as possible the possibility of play and of social interaction between children so as to focus upon task accomplishment and upon adult direction. Educational theorists such as Montessori and Dewey, with his Darwinian social orientation, were on the right track but did not go far enough. Recently Harlen Hansen and his colleagues (Davis, Davis, Hansen, & Hansen, 1973) have developed the Playway system, where we can find the beginnings of ideas for reconciling schooling with the needs of our species. From a primate perspective, we need to take play, not the three R's, as the central metaphor for education.

As educators we feel there is an additional reason for attending to play and for fostering it in children, a reason which has not, to the best of our knowledge been discussed in the literature. Looking at human culture and human work in a comparative primate context, we have come to the conclusion that both are fundamentally elaborations of primate play and not so much elaborations of primate foraging, social, reproductive, and protective activity. Phylogenetically speaking, too, Huizinga's (1955) name *homo ludens* would seem to be as accurately descriptive as *homo sapiens*. Descriptions of work as play coming from artists, musicians, mathematicians, and theoretical physicists further support our contention that much arises from play because it is precisely these highly human activities which require superb emotional control, great empathy, and the highest rational faculties which characterize both *homo sapiens* and *homo ludens* and make one whole of the two halves.

In concluding our arguments we would like to take note of a major generalized factor relating to learning and teaching in primates, the fact that non-human primates do very little teaching, that is, there is almost *no direct instruction or demonstration* and very little correction. Yound wild primates spend enormous amounts of time just watching, as do young humans, and, like them, appear to be capable of learning without any other form of learning or any action taken place (Devore, n.d.). Throughout development, social behaviors and adult skills are learned gradually in the play and peer interaction context where they appear in forms *unlike* those of the actual adult activity (Chalmers, 1980). Because primates, especially humans are genetically designed to learn via their brain structure, their polyphasic sensibilities, and through their long development, young primates, including humans, do not need instruction. That this is true can be easily demonstrated from the cross-cultural (human) literature. Many societies, including the Mbuti, the !Kung, and the Dakota, do not assume children need instruction and give very little. Children are expected to look, learn, follow, and perhaps ask, and the children do grow into complete, acculturated adults.

How does it happen then that complex, stated-based societies, wherever they arose upon the globe, have assumed the opposite and have independently developed formal instruction based in schools? Some might think that complex societies by their natures require schools and schooled children for their perpetuation, and that "natural" primate methods will not do for any complex society. Historically, it may be true that schools were necessary in state formation and initial maintenance. Cohen (1975) has noted that they functioned cross-culturally to break down local ties, create a national identification through literature, religion, and a behavioral code, and develop loyalty by forming a national, identifiable elite to occupy critical positions in the governmental, church, economic, military, and diplomatic spheres. For the purpose of creating identification, schooling, through direct instruction in groups of similarly treated individuals, is a powerful tool. But for teaching life, culture, creativity, schools are extremely weak tools. Historically, the period of state formation is long past in our own part of the world, and contemporary schooling is an anachronism which ought to be treated as such. Whether schools are based upon a series of mistakes as Washburn opined or on past necessity, they no longer serve us or our children well in the modern world. We might wish to maintain school buildings and educational specialists, but what goes on in those buildings needs to be completely redesigned to enhance rather than inhibit learning.

References

Ainsworth, M. (1973). The development of infant-mother attachment. In B. Caldwell & H. Ricciuti (Eds.), *Review of Child Development Research* (Vol. 3, pp. 1-94). Chicago: University of Chicago Press.

Baldwin, J.D., & Baldwin, J.I. (1978). Reinforcement theories of play, creativity and psychosocial growth. In E.O.Smith (Ed.), *Social Play in Primates* (pp. 231-257). New York: Academic.

Bloom, B. (1964). *Stability and Change in Human Characteristics.* New York: Wiley.

Blurton-Jones, N. (1972). *Ethnological Studies of Child Behavior.* Cambridge: Cambridge University Press.

Bowlby, J. (1969). *Attachment and Loss: Vol. 1. Attchment.* New York: Basic Books.

———, (1972). *Attachment and Loss: Vol. 2. Separation.* New York: Basic Books.

Chalmers, N. (1980).*Social Behavior in Primates.* Baltimore: University Park Press.

Chance, M.R.A. (1978). Attention structure and social organization (Round table discussion). In D.J. Chivers & J. Herbert (Eds.), *Recent Advances in Primatology* (pp. 93-97). New York: Academic.

———. & Jolly, C.J. (1970). *Social Groups of Monkeys, Apes and Men.* London: Jonathan Cape.

Chapple, E. (1970). *Culture and Biological Man: Explorations in Behavioral Anthropology.* New York: Holt, Rinehart and Winston.

Chevalier-Skolnikoff, S., & Poirier, F.E. (Eds.). (1977). *Primate Bio-Social Development: Biological, Social and Ecological Determinants.* New York: Garland Publishing.

Cloward, R.D. (1976). Teenagers as tutors of academically low-achieving children. In V.L. Allen (Ed.), *Children as Teachers: Theory and Research on Tutoring* (pp. 219-229). New York: Academic.

Cohen, Y. (1975). The state system, schooling, & cognitive and motivational patterns. In N.K. Shimahara & A. Scrupski (Eds.), *Social Forces and Schooling* (pp. 103-104). New York: David McKay.

Davis, D., Davis, M., Hansen, H., & Hansen, R. (1973). *Playway: Education for Reality*. Minneapolis, MN: Winston Press.

Devore, I. (films, n.d.). Baboon development: The young infant-birth to four months and The older infant-four months to one year. Newton, MA: Education Development Center.

Dolhinow, P. (Ed.). (1972). *Primate Patterns*. New York: Holt, Rinehart, & Winston.

Dobbert, M.L. (1981, November). *Designing Peaceful Societies*. Paper presented at the Meeting of the American Anthroplogical Association, Los Angeles, CA.

Falk, D. (1980). Language, handedness, and primate brains: Did the Australopithecines sign? *American Anthropologist, 82*, 72-78.

Fagen, R. (1981). *Animal Play Behavior*. New York: Oxford University Press.

Feldman, R.S., Shehan, L., & Allen, V. (1976). Children tutoring children: A critical review of research. In V.L. Allen (Ed.), *Children as Teachers: Theory and Research on Tutoring*. New York: Academic.

Gibson, K. (1977). Brain structure and intelligence in macaques and human infants from a Piagetian perspective. In S. Chevalier-Skolnikoff & F.E. Poirier (Eds.), *Primate Bio-Social Development: Biological, Social, and Ecological Determinants* (p. 113-158). New York: Garland.

Harlow, H.F., & Harlow, M.K. (1962). Social deprivation in monkeys. *Scientific American, 207*, 136-146.

_____, & _____, (1965). The affectional systems. In A. Schrier, H. Harlow, & F. Stollnitz (Eds.), *Behavior of Nonhuman Primates: Modern Research Trends* (Vol. 2, pp. 287-334). New York: Academic.

_____, & _____, (1966). Learning to love. *American Scientist, 54*, 244-272.

Henry, J. (1960). A cross-cultural outline of education. *Current Anthropology, 1*, 267-305.

_____, (1971). *Pathways to Madness.* New York: Random House.

Herzog, J.D. (1974). The socialization of juveniles in primate and foraging societies: Implications for contemporary education. *Council on Anthropology and Education Quarterly, 5*, 12-17.

Hinde, R.A. (1972). *Social Behavior and Its Behavior in Subhuman Primates.* Eugene: Oregon State System of Higher Education.

_____, (1982). The uses and limitations of studies of nonhuman primates for the understanding of human social development. In L.W. Hoffman, R. Gandelman, & H.R. Schiffman (Eds.), *Parenting: Its Causes and Consequences* (pp. 5-17). Hillsdale, NJ: Lawrence Erlbaum.

Hoopes, M. (n.d.). A group discussion plan, Mimeo. University of Minnesota.

Huizinga, J. (1955). *Homoludens.* Boston: Beacon.

Johnson, D.W., & Johnson, R. (1975). *Learning Together and Alone: Cooperation, Competition and Individualization.* Englewood Cliffs, NJ: Prentice Hall.

Johnston, T.D. (1981). Contrasting approaches to a theory of learning. *The Behavioral and Brain Sciences, 4*, 125-173.

Kimball, S.T. (1975). Community and hominid emergence. *Anthropology and Education Quarterly, 13*, 125-131.

Lancaster, J.B. (1975). *Primate Behavior and the Emergence of Human Culture*. New York: Holt, Rinehart, & Winston.

Mason, W.A. (1965). Determinants of social behavior in young chimpanzees. In A. Schrier, H. Harlow, & F. Stollnitz (Eds.), *Behavior of Nonhuman Primates: Modern Research Trends* (Vol. 2, pp. 335-364). New York: Academic

_____, (1978). Ontogeny of social systems. In D.J. Chivers, & A. Jerbert (Eds.), *Recent Advances in Primatology* (pp. 5-14). New York: Academic.

Montagu, A. (1970). *The Direction of Human Development*. New York: Hawthorn.

Parker, S.T. (1977). Piaget's sensorimotor series in an infant macaque: A model for comparing unstereotyped behavior and intelligence in human and nonhuman primates. In S. Chevalier-Skolnikoff & F.E. Poirier (Eds.), *Primate Bio-Social Development: Biological, Social, and Ecological Determinants* (pp. 43-112). New York: Garland.

Poirier, F.E. (Ed.). (1972). *Primate Socialization*. New York: Random House.

_____, (1973). Socialization and learning among nonhuman primates. In S. Kimball & J. Burnett (Eds.), *Learning and Culture: Proceedings of the 1972 American Ethnological Society Symposium on Learning and Culture*. Seattle: University of Washington Press.

_____, (1977). Introduction. In S. Chevalier-Skolnikoff & F.E. Poirier (Eds.), *Primate Bio-Social Development: Biological, Social, and Ecological Determinants* (pp. 1-39). New York: Garland.

_____, Bellisari, A., & Haines, L. (1978). Functions of primate play. In E.O.Smith (Ed.), *Social Play in Primates* (pp. 143-168). New York: Academic.

_____, & Hussey, L.K. (1982). Nonhuman primate learning: The importance of learning from an evolutionary perspective. *Anthropology and Education Quarterly, 13,* 133-148.

Reed, M. (1968). *Children of Their Fathers*. New York: Holt, Rinehart & Winston.

Reynolds, V. (1976) *The Biology of Human Action*. San Francisco: W.H. Freeman.

Rogers, C.M., & Davenport, R.K. (1975). Capacities of nonhuman primates for perceptional integration across sensory modalities. In R.H. Tuttle (Ed.), *Socioecology and Psychology of Primates* (pp. 343-352). The Hague: Mouton.

Rumbaugh, D.M. (1970). Learning skills of primates. *Primate Behavior,* 1-70.

_____, (1975). The learning and symbolizing capacities of apes and monkeys. In R.H. Tuttle (Ed.), *Socioecology and Psychology of Primates* (pp. 353-368). The Hague: Mouton.

Schrier, A.M. (1984). Learning how to learn: The significance and current status of learning set formation., *Primates, 25,* 95-102.

Scott, J.P., & Marston, M. (1950). Critical periods affecting the development of normal and maladjustive social behavior of puppies. *Journal Genetic Psychology, 13,* 25-60.

Seyforth, R.M., Chaney, D.L., & Hinde, Robert A. (1978). Some principles relating social interactions and social structure among primates. In D.J. Chivers & J. Herbert (Eds.), *Recent Advances in Primatology* (pp. 40-51). New York: Academic.

Smith, E.O., & Fraser, M.D. (1978). Social play in rhesus macaques (macaca mu atta). A cluster analysis. In E.O. Smith (Ed.), *Social Play in Primates* (pp. 79-112). New York: Academic.

Snowden, C.T., Brown, C.H., & Petersen, M.R. (1982). *Primate Communication.* New York: Cambridge University Press.

Spitz, R. (1945). Hospitalism: An inquiry into the genesis of psychiatric conditions in childhood. *The Psychoanalytic Study of the Child, 1,* 53-74.

Symons, D. (1978). The question function: Dominance and play. In E.O. Smith (Ed.), *Social Play in Primates* (pp. 193-230). New York: Academic.

Turnbull, C. (1978). The politics of nonaggression (Zaire). In A. Montague (Ed.), *Learning Nonaggression* (pp. 161-221). New York: Oxford.

Vaitl, E. (1978). Nature and implications of the complexly organized social systems in nonhuman primates. In D.J. Chivers & J. Herbert (Eds.), *Recent Advances in Primatology* (pp. 18-30). New York: Academic.

Van Lawick-Goodall, J. (1971). *In the Shadow of Man.* New York: Dell.

Voland, E. (1977). Social play behavior of the common marmoset (callithrix jaeinus erxl, 1777) in captivity. *Primates, 18,* 883-901.

Walker, S. (1983). *Animal thought.* London: Routledge & Kegan Paul.

Ward, M.C. (1971). *Them Children: A Study in Language Learning.* New York: Holt, Rinehart & Winston.

Washburn, S.L. (1973). Primate field studies and social science. In L. Nader & T. Maretzki (Eds.), *Cultural Illness and Health* (pp. 128-134). Washington, DC: American Anthropological Association.

Whiting, B., & Whiting, J. (1975). *Children of Six Cultures: A Psychocultural Analysis.* Cambridge: Harvard University Press.

Wolcott, H.F. (1982). The anthropology of learning. *Anthropology and Education Quarterly, 13,* 83-108.

PART III

Approaches to the Study of Schools

Preview
8. RICHARD WARREN   *The School and its Community Context*
9. HARRY WOLCOTT   *The Teacher as Enemy*
10. GEORGE and LOUISE SPINDLER   *Ethnography: An Approach to the Study of Education*

PREVIEW

This section provides an introduction to how anthropologists study schools in their community and cultural context. What anthropologists do as they study schools and their contexts in the field is usually called ethnography. Ethnography is one kind of qualitative method. Qualitative approaches to the study of schooling have become very popular among educators during the past decade. This popularity has carried ethnography along with it to the extent that the term "ethnography" is often mistakenly used in education to describe any study that does not use quantitative methods and that has a qualitative flair to it.

This indiscriminate use of the ethnographic label does harm to ethnography, to anthropology (though indirectly), and is misleading to educators. The three chapters of Part III are genuinely anthropological. They use models of social structure and culture that issue from anthropology. And they use methods of research that are clearly those of anthropologists doing fieldwork. Both Harry Wolcott and Richard Warren lived in the study communities for at least one year and were participant observers in their schools. Wolcott was the teacher in the school he writes about. He describes himself as an "enemy", an unusual self-description for a teacher to declare. In making this declaration he focusses on the problem of the intrusive mainstream teacher in a minority community. Teachers in many schools in the United States will recognize his situation and resonate to his problems, if not to his solution of them. Warren is not an "enemy" in his situation in the field. His role is that of the observer representing a friendly and accepted culture, even though he is initially a stranger, and therefore marginal, as all anthropological field workers are at first. He is also a participant in community and school affairs, and is recognized as a fellow professional by school personnel.

The contribution by George and Louise Spindler is of quite a different nature than the preceding two. They are not describing their fieldwork in a specific community; they are providing a brief introduction to the rationale for doing ethnography. They are stating what it is they think they study in schools—a part of the dialogue that defines the national whole—and they

118

describe, albeit briefly, what they do to study it. Space limitations preclude taking the points they raise further in this book, for our concern is less with method than with substance. Interested readers may wish to explore *Doing the Ethnography of Schooling* (ed. G. Spindler, Holt, Rinehart and Winston 1982), and *Interpretive Ethnography of Schooling at Home and Abroad* (ed. G. and L. Spindler, Lawrence Erlbaum Assoc. 1987).

All of the chapters in this volume are in some degree a product of ethnographic fieldwork. The three chapters in part III provide insight into what kind of an approach anthropologists are likely to use when they gather data on educational process. Anthropology as a discipline, however, is so eclectic that the reader should be forewarned that more than ethnography is represented.

The Editor

RICHARD L. WARREN/*California Polytechnic State University, San Luis Obispo*

8 The School and Its Community Context: The Methodology of a Field Study[1]

The educational system of a community constitutes an important vehicle for the transmission of culture. This function may appear to be orderly and stable, if the educational system is viewed primarily as a formal social organization. Goals, curricula, established procedures, hierarchy of authority, formal relationships with community organizations, and other traditional components of the educational process can be identified and described. The result is an assessment of the school as an academically oriented social organization charged with transmitting and mediating the more formal aspects of the culture. The internal organizational requirements of the school, the external expectations of the school's constituency, and the over-all visibility and accessibility of the school's academic program reinforce order and stability in this function.

However, integral to the life of the school are a wide range of activities and functions less subject to organized control and routine. Nuances in disciplinary techniques, teaching styles, faculty and faculty-student interpersonal relationships incorporate and reflect cultural values, norms, and sanctions. They operate often at a less formal, overt level, transmitting aspects of the culture not always clearly defined or articulated but, nevertheless, significantly functional to the life of the school and immediately relevant to assessing the stabilizing and mediating functions the school may perform.

Particular attention was given in this study to the more informal aspects of the educational process and to the role of the teacher in that process. It was assumed that an analysis of these aspects would provide valuable data with regard to the role of the school and the faculty in supporting and maintaining primary cultural directives as well as in effecting a constructive adjustment to change. It was further assumed that the strains and uncertainties created by the process of change would be more manifest in the informal aspects of school life than in the formal, established routine.

---

[1] The study is reported in Richard L. Warren, *Education in Rebhausen: A German Village.* CSEC. New York: Holt, Rinehart and Winston, Inc.

Background for the Selection of a Site

The primary focus of the study was the role of the school in a rural village undergoing rapid cultural changes as a result of industrialization. There were persuasive reasons why a village in West Germany was particularly appropriate.[2] The functional qualities of the educational system have in recent years been the subject of extended debate in West Germany. There exists a growing awareness that the system does not adequately complement the needs of a democratic, industrial society. In the decades since World War II, powerful legacies and developments have tended to converge on German communities, creating different orientations toward the goals and content of the educational system. They include (1) the weight and veneration of historic traditions and loyalties, (2) the reaction to and assessment of the Nazi experience by the younger and older generations, (3) the problem of assimilation involving large numbers of refugees, and (4) the postwar modernization and secularization of German society.

These convergent forces impose on educational institutions problems of cultural maintenance and change. Deeply enmeshed in the relatively isolated, stable folk culture, the schools of the small German community have traditionally operated to maintain and reinforce established cultural patterns— patterns functionally adapted to the local ecology and social system. But the gross and dramatic changes in German society are extending the cultural milieu of the rural community in many directions. Regional differentiations in dialect, religion, and local custom that have traditionally characterized rural Germany are giving way to the leveling influences of an urban way of life. Consequently, the schools are confronted with a perplexing dilemma. The present form and content of education constitute a symbol of cultural stability and continuity, but as a positive force effecting constructive adjustment to change, they are less functional. To sustain a functionally effective role in the community the schools must adjust to the demands of cultural change but at a pace and in a way that will not jeopardize their contribution to cultural maintenance. This kind of adjustment is difficult and fragile. The school which was the object of this study was impressively instrumental in supporting and transmitting the shared community culture, but the response of the school staff to the demands of cultural change was ambivalent.

---

[2] The more mundane, practical ones included knowledge of the language and the availability of a small grant for research in Germany. In addition, I had spent the years 1947–1949 in Germany as a member of the Education Division of the Office of Military Government for Bavaria. Our policy there sought the democratization of the German educational system—not simply through a "denazification" process but through rather drastic changes in the organization of schools, and to a lesser degree, in the content of the curriculum. This rather pretentious, reformist zeal may have been realistic about the centrality of education to the life of a nation, but it was patently naive about how easily an occupying power could effect changes in so basic an institution. On balance little progress was made during the occupation period. If one examines the changes now being considered and effected in West Germany, there is reason to assess the policy as well-conceived.

Selecting a Site

The size of the community was an important consideration in the selection of a site. The community had to be small enough to make possible a relatively comprehensive analysis of the educational system and of the cultural milieu in which it was situated, and it had to be large enough to maintain an educational system of sufficient size to justify such a study. I had envisioned a population of approximately 2000 as being ideal. As it turned out, Rebhausen,[3] the village selected, had a population of approximately 3000, but for other reasons it appeared to be especially suitable. Although it was located only 15 miles from Waldstadt, a city of some 130,000 people, it was one of a group of villages occupying a hilly and traditionally isolated section of southwest Germany—known for the excellent quality of wine produced and the almost primitive character of life. Rebhausen was, however, significantly different because of a chemical factory, established there in 1958, with a work force which had grown in six years from less than 100 to over 900. The village was originally identified, as one among a number of possibilities, through general information provided in part by Stanford colleagues and German acquaintances who either lived in the region or who had conducted research there, and through several weeks of personal investigation.[4]

The problems of establishing residence may or may not impose constraints on the selection of a site purely on the basis of research interests and design. In my case the problems turned out not to be insurmountable, due in part to fortuitous developments. The problems which had to be resolved were that of introducing the idea of the study to local governmental and school officials and ascertaining their attitude toward it, and then locating housing for myself and family (my wife and two children, a boy, 12, and a girl, 14).

The nature of initial contacts with local officials affects not only entree to the community but also the tenor and productivity of interpersonal relations. Such officials are potentially important informants and able to provide introduction to valuable sources of data. Preparation for a study should therefore include attention to those characteristics of community governance, social structure, and the educational system relevant to introducing the study. In this regard two facets of village life in the region where Rebhausen was located were particularly significant. The village school is an integral part of a state-controlled system of education but is autonomous with respect to research intrusions. Consequently I was beholden only to the principal for permission to conduct the research. Second, the mayor's position in the village is preeminent; his power and influence reaches into all aspects of village life, including the school. Hence his reaction to the research proposal had to be antecedent to a final decision about the selection of a site.

---

[3] The pseudonyms employed in the case study will be used here.

[4] If an exploratory trip to select a site and provide for eventual residence is not possible, time and money have to be expended for such purposes in the initial stage of a study. The more of both one can set aside for preliminary investigation the better, even if it means a financial crisis toward the end of the study—which is probably inevitable anyway.

There may be—in this case there were—important historical considerations which make it especially necessary to ascertain the reaction of local officials. In spite of the generally positive tenor of German-American relations, there was no reason to assume that, in the case of individuals, there would not be a legacy of bitterness as a result of World War II and the subsequent occupation and denazification proceedings. It turned out to be an unnecessary precaution but not, I submit, irrelevant given the ubiquitousness of the American "presence" in today's world. The mayor's response was affirmative; he expressed pleasure that his village was being considered for such research. (His interest and support throughout the study was of inestimable value.)

It was my hope that a village, selected solely on the grounds of research interests, would somehow yield up living accommodations for myself and family. Housing facilities were, however, severely limited—another reason for first soliciting the reaction of the mayor whose manifold duties and powers include housing administration. Nothing was immediately available, the one possibility being the apartment development financed by the factory to insure housing for their employees. The personnel executive informed the mayor I would be considered, conditional on a statement describing my research interests. He especially wanted to know my position on the question of an intermediate school for Rebhausen because educational facilities in the village were an important factor in attracting executive personnel. Formal identification with the factory had potential disadvantages. I submitted the statement and was glad for the serendipitous data the exchange was providing, but was relieved when an apartment outside the factory complex became available in two months.

The housing delay aided the study in quite unanticipated ways. For two months we had to temporize, the first month in Waldstadt (after a week in a hotel we found two rooms in a fraternity house, vacated for the summer, where we had cooking privileges). The second month we rented two rooms from a family in Rebhausen who made it a practice of renting to tourists, the more foreign the better. They had children about the ages of our own and the husband and wife were friendly, open individuals. We saw much of each other as families, and the wife became in time one of my most valuable informants.

Developing the Study of the School

From the very beginning my family's interests and experiences extended the purview of the study. More important, theirs was a more natural participation in the life of the community, and some benefits from this relationship presumably accrued to me. My son became—somewhat reluctantly—the first continuing point of contact with the Rebhausen school.

When we arrived in September, schools were in session. My daughter was too old for the Rebhausen school (grades 1–8). She enrolled in a Waldstadt Gymnasium and thereby shared the experience of those very few Rebhausen children who left the elementary school at the end of the fourth grade to begin the preuniversity training which the gymnasium provided. My son was a seventh-grader. When I had settled on Rebhausen as a site, talked to the mayor and located housing, I had not yet met the principal. He was away for two weeks at a conference. I assumed he would cooperate with the study; the mayor assured me he would and the assistant principal appeared interested in the project. My first formal contact with the school was then through my son, who enrolled in the seventh grade and began attending classes. During the first month I made frequent trips to Rebhausen to bring him to school, to become better acquainted with the faculty, and to observe the community at work.

The principal, when he returned, was favorably disposed toward the research. He invited me to spend as much time as I wanted to in the school, offering to make available whatever statistics and pertinent educational material the school had on file. On the day before the fall vacation (almost the entire month of October, during grape harvest) he arranged a meeting with the faculty to give me an opportunity to describe the study. The teachers appeared receptive to the study, although one faculty member openly expressed some reserve and suspicion. Herr Schenke, the seventh-grade teacher, asked if I had come on assignment from a magazine to write a series of typically American exposés of the "awful" German character. Throughout the study he maintained reservations and was generally of a mood to point out things about American schools he thought I ought to study. For this and other reasons he appeared more sensitive than the other teachers to my presence in the classroom, and because, too, my son was in the seventh grade, I did not spend as much time observing in Herr Schenke's class. So far as I could tell, other faculty members had no such reservations.

As soon as vacation ended I started systematic observations in the school, spending at the outset over a week in each class and moving from the first grade through the eighth. After the completion of three months of concentrated observations, I limited classroom visits to specific grades and teachers relative to certain research questions (a fourth month was spent with a first-grade class, in April when the new school year began). While several class periods and a wide range of special school activities and ceremonies were taped and innumerable photographs taken, most of the data about classroom life were acquired through naturalistic observations.

First encounters with classes did not always result in the unobtrusive presence I naïvely hoped I could be. There was always the formal introduction to the class by the teacher, accompanied in some instances by a stern admonition to behave so that "the professor doesn't take back to America a bad picture of German children." In one instance I was peremptorily given the teacher's desk at the front of the room as an observation post—the better to see the children. After one period of this discomfort I demurred and worked my way to an empty seat in the back.

Extensive observational notes were written. They were infrequent during the first day, until, through informal conversations, I felt I had acquainted the teacher with the study and satisfied whatever initial curiosity she had with respect to my interest in her particular class. There were moments when note-taking was judged to be threatening—and was therefore delayed—when, in particular, the teacher was engaged in a heated disciplinary controversy. In recording anecdotal data attention was focussed primarily and almost necessarily on the teacher and on the behavior of those pupils with whom the teacher at any given time was immediately engaged. Random and frequent observations were also made of more inclusive classroom phenomena, such as noise level, pupil attentiveness, generalized responses to teacher behavior, and physical conditions—but these were less systematic.

In preparing to undertake the study, I found myself unable to anticipate clearly how ideally my role as participant-observer ought to evolve, particu-larly in the school. The literature on participant observation is addressed primarily to the benefits of the participant identity within the broader com-munity context—when the identity is so generalized as to preclude being experienced as a threat except perhaps by single individuals or groups. The boundaries of the participant identity within an institution—when one func-tions openly as an observer and when, as in a school, the adult roles are them-selves the subject of extensive "observation" by the community—are not easily delineated. I had originally anticipated the possibility and value of participating actively in the life of the school as, for example, a teacher of English. In the early months of the study I mentioned this interest in ways I hoped were gentle but persuasive. These attempts failed—a failure which I came to count as a blessing after several experiences of supervising classes in the school.

It was not simply that a teaching responsibility would limit the time avail-able for observation; there was also a question of creating an unnecessary ambivalence, personal and social, with respect to my identity as a researcher and a teacher. Within the school my identity had progressed through different phases. I started out as the father of that American boy in the seventh grade. For some first-graders I was simply the man who was always sitting in the back; for some third-graders I was a county school inspector. For most of the pupils (and adults) I was an American who came to learn about German schools. When, however, classes were turned over to me so that I could ad-minister a questionnaire to the fifth grade (it required three periods over as many different days), I quickly became just another teacher. The behavior of the students structured the kind of authority relationship to which they were accustomed, but not to which I was inclined. When the questionnaire was completed, I was glad to return to the sanctity of the observer role.

The few additional opportunities I had to perform as a teacher I re-member now as cases of aborted role-playing. One instance resulted in my having to dry out answers, drenched in beer, to a questionnaire I was giving the eighth grade. It was not easy to find a time and place when I could ad-minister the questionnaire to this class. The pressure of class work made the teacher reluctant to set aside time during school. However, at the end of the year there was a week's lull just before graduation when, for all practical purposes, the class had completed its work. We convened one morning in a local *Gasthaus* (inn)—the most convenient space for the meeting. Herr Kost, the eighth-grade teacher, left me in charge, with the caution that beer and wine were okay but *schnaps* was out. The girls during several breaks stuck to soft drinks; most of the boys had beer to keep them company as they answered questions. The inevitable happened: a bottle was upset. I watched with some consternation as the suds spread slowly over my valuable data.

Questionnaires and essays constituted the two primary sources of systematic data about pupil's perceptions of and attitudes toward various aspects of the life they experienced. The decision about the amount of time and effort to spend eliciting data from pupils was influenced by at least three considerations: (1) Given a study of a school and its sociocultural context, there is a question of achieving an appropriate research balance among three "populations," the community at large, the adults in the school, and the pupils. (2) Given the normal superordinate-subordinate structure of teacher-pupil relationships—emphatically so in this school—there is a question of how extensive an investigation can be made of the subordinate group—with all that implies and requires—without the investigator's appearing to be subverting the relationship to and the research interest in the superordinate group. In this kind of triadic relationship it is difficult for the observer to remain "equidistant" from teachers *and* pupils. (3) Finally, there is a question of how accessible pupils are, that is, what generalized response they exhibit toward, for example, a personal interview, given prevailing norms with respect to adult-child relations.

The considerations are not mutually exclusive. The central question to which the research was addressed was the role of the school in a community experiencing a rural-urban transformation. Conceived, with respect to cultural change, as an agent of stability and potentially of mediation, the instrumental role of the school would appear to be manifest primarily in adult members of the school community. It was the faculty in whom I was most interested; and it was this population and the community at large which I felt required and absorbed most of my research efforts. However, I came to know the students well enough to realize there was an ill-defined but perceptible stirring among the older children—a changing orientation toward urban life to which teachers and parents were beginning to feel they should respond without knowing exactly how. If one is attempting to assess the role of the school in the midst of cultural change, the findings may vary depending on the comparative attention one gives to teachers and students.

In my experience children were not, under any circumstances, very accessible, even for extended informal talks. Their age range and the fact that I was a foreigner may have been factors. Certainly they were not accustomed as pupils to have their attitudes and feelings consulted except generally as part of an academic exercise. Furthermore, it was their nature, teachers insisted, to be reticent to speak up in public, to say what was on their mind.[5] The teachers predicted I would have a difficult time, and I did. Several interviews with small groups of pupils remained stiff and classroomlike; I asked questions and they recited. Interviews with individual pupils, with several exceptions, remained therefore at the level of brief and informal conversations.

Consequently, the most useful sources of data about pupil perceptions of and attitudes toward school, family, and community life were the responses to the questionnaire I administered to the fifth, sixth, and eighth grades and the various essays teachers assigned. The wealth of anecdotal material in the latter had not been anticipated. Beginning with the third grade, pupils are required by the State Ministry of Education to write an essay approximately every three weeks. Over the years, Rebhausen teachers have developed a core of favorite topics for particular grade levels—and, of course, curricular materials from public and private sources are available with limitless suggestions. In most grades there were a wide range of topics covering personal, family, and community life. With certain topics teachers routinely stimulated rather intimate, anecdotal accounts of family life—accounts I would have hesitated to elicit myself. Furthermore, I was at first somewhat surprised that pupils wrote with such apparent ease and openness about personal matters. Admittedly they were in a relatively uncalculating age range, vis-à-vis keeping the teacher at some psychological distance. Nevertheless, the content of the essays violated my expectation as to the inhibitory effect on self-expression and openness which the teacher's authority presumably has. Here it seemed to be simply a question of an assignment that had to be done.

The constraints which teachers imposed on research procedures in which they were involved were minimal but significant. I used a tape recorder quite freely in interviews with most adults in the village, but not with teachers. Assuming the instrument would be intimidating, I waited some months before asking permission to use it. The answer was "No," even by a teacher with whom I felt I had especially good rapport. He had just as soon not, he said; a teacher has to be careful. But I could take notes, and we launched into a series of discussions which totaled more than twenty hours, during which time he spoke freely on what I considered to be for him very controversial and sensitive issues.

It was in this manner that classroom observations of teacher behavior were supplemented. There were formal interviews in which we systematically took up a series of questions to which I wanted all of them to respond. In addition, there were innumerable informal, social occasions involving one teacher or various combinations of teachers and their families, and small

---

[5] *Schwerfällig* was the word widely used to describe this manner of public behavior, not only of pupils, but as a pervasive characteristic of adults in the region.

groups within the faculty, e.g., the younger teachers. The latter had a weekly coffee klatsch—an excuse to socialize and vent their shared feelings about other members of the faculty and school life in general.

There were sources of data beyond the confines of the school itself. 'Archives at a nearby institute of history provided material on Rebhausen's educational facilities and personnel going back almost 200 years. Subject-matter workshops sponsored by the county school office, meetings where issues of educational reform were debated, and interviews with the county vocational training officer, the state assistant superintendent in charge of elementary schools, and with others provided data useful in assessing external conditions and forces which impinged on the life of the school.

Developing the Study of the Community

The publication which identifies village residents is not a phone book (less than 5 percent have phones) but an address listing put out by the mayor's office. On the first page is a listing of primary and auxiliary, public and private agencies and institutions. At the head of this listing is the *Gemeindeverwaltung,* a term which is sometimes used very narrowly to designate the mayor's office and staff and sometimes rather broadly to include what are seen as those agencies and institutions basic to and primarily concerned with the general welfare of the village. Hence the *Gemeindeverwaltung* may also include the offices of the county police stationed in the village (strictly speaking there is no local police), the principal of the school, the Evangelical minister, the Catholic priest, the postmaster, the head of the volunteer fire department, and the railroad functionary in charge of the local station operations. In addition, the first page lists addresses of the various Evangelical and Catholic kindergartens, the Evangelical and Catholic emergency first aid stations, the wine cooperative, the savings bank, the local doctor, the dentist, and the nearest veterinarian.

Organizations and industries are listed on the second page. The former include German Red Cross, German Family Association, Evangelical Church Choir, Football Club, Community Library, Business Association, Bee Keepers Association, Catholic Church Choir, Rural Youth Association, Male Chorus, Community Band, Cattlemen's Association, Horsemen's Association, Riding Club, Chess Club, Tennis Club, Gymnastics Club, Union of War Injured, Dispossessed and Welfare Pensioners, and the Adult Education Association.

Organizational participation is important to the life of the community. For individuals it provides opportunities to pursue avocational and recreational interests; it offers a rich, social context in which the individual can reinforce deep, meaningful friendships and maintain acquaintanceships with an impressive number of residents; it makes possible acting in concert with others as an interest group to affect policy at both local and higher levels.

From the standpoint of the community, organizations are functional in several respects. They are a kind of training ground for village leadership; most members of the village council have been or are officers in one or more organizations. They are as well a training ground for the membership, since important decisions affecting the life of the village are considered, debated, and arrived at through a process and within a social context which mirrors the behavior of organizations. Organizational meetings provide opportunities for the mayor, as the preeminent political and governmental official, to reinforce his own role. He attends many of the meetings, if only to pass his blessing on their work. Finally, through organizations and the selection of officers, the village maintains a vital recognition and reward system for those who in their personal, family, and community activities embody the core values of the native culture.

The organizational life of the community was therefore a good place to begin, and in the early days and months provided the widest possible introduction to my research intents. I attended most meetings. The mayor was usually there and invariably introduced me and described my purpose in being in Rebhausen. The format and setting (people sat at tables, wine was always available, extended hours of talk followed the completion of business) made it possible to become acquainted with a number of members, to fix appointments for interviews, and, of course, to participate in informal conversations with both individuals and groups. Furthermore, there was in the organizational life of the village behavioral characteristics similar to that of the school. The latter was also in one sense a network of interlocking collectivities. Students had to learn under the scrutiny of both teachers and classmates how effectively to manage their behavior in at least one of these collectivities. It was instructive to move back and forth between daytime observations of classrooms and nighttime observations of organizations. Since the study and observation of organizations was central to understanding the life of the community, I will examine in more detail one organization, the men's chorus, to illustrate more specifically the kind of data elicited.

The men's chorus is the oldest and most prestigious organization in Rebhausen (in the summer of 1964 it celebrated its 100th anniversary) and in its organization and operation embodies much that is highly valued in the native culture. There are about fifty active singers in the group who, with the exception of one individual, are natives with long-established roots in the village. Farming, however, is no longer the typical occupation among the members as the younger ones move into skilled trades required by or auxiliary to an industrialized economy. Many of the members hold important offices in other organizations.

The chorus rehearses one evening each week. Throughout the year they are invited to and/or are expected to sing at various events and ceremonies: weddings and funerals of members, birthdays of those in the village over eighty, Christmas programs, and dedications. In addition, they are periodically invited to sing in nearby villages. The director is a professional musician who directs several village choruses.

The chorus presents in Rebhausen at least two formal concerts each year —one semipublic, the other public—as a part of the annual meeting. The semipublic concert is "closed" (as the sign reads on the door to the town auditorium) to all but "active" members, namely, those residents who contribute an amount equivalent to at least twenty-five dollars to the chorus each year. Residents who contribute less are classified as "passive" members. The program for the closed meeting included the following:

1. Songs by the chorus were interspersed throughout the evening.
2. Slides of the 100th anniversary celebration were shown. (The celebration had extended over four days, a songfest involving thirty men's choruses from the region.)
3. A movie of Rebhausen, including shots of the celebration, was shown by the operator of the town cinema.
4. The village band provided music for listening and dancing, the latter continuing until after midnight and talking and drinking for another three hours.

The annual meeting was held on a Sunday afternoon, so that the children's chorus could participate. The meeting was open to the public and more than 300 attended. Business transactions were routine and ended with a unanimous voice vote to retain the present slate of officers. Those who had been members for twenty-five years were presented with medallions which had been struck for the 100th anniversary. A bottle of wine and a wine glass were awarded to the individual who had had perfect attendance at chorus rehearsals and performances; large wine glasses went to the four members who missed only once; a small wine glass to those who missed two to four times.

There were certain questions to be resolved. The president served notice that when the chorus was scheduled to sing for an elderly person's birthday, he was going to let that person know the chorus did not want or expect to be served refreshments (contrary to tradition). "The elderly residents are often poor; we should sing and disappear," he observed. The chorus voted on a two-day singing trip, based on the invitations they had received to which the president said they had to respond. The men were not enthusiastic; he had to urge them to vote, and reminded the minority they had to go along with the majority vote. There was much more enthusiasm for the performance of the children's chorus and for ways of encouraging the group.

The men's chorus is meant to be a social and recreational experience. Men join to sing, to enjoy the comradeship of good friends, to be among people they can trust—people who will conduct themselves properly. Extended interviews with the organization's officers and discussions with other members indicated the kind of social behavior considered unacceptable.

1. Drinking too much. (Where the line is drawn is hard to say, except being "drunk" is too much.)
2. Getting in trouble with the law.

3. Having a negative attitude, constantly complaining, and refusing to go along with the majority.
4. Mismanaging one's business affairs, being delinquent in paying bills.
5. Presenting an unkempt, sloppy appearance.
6. Being selfish and greedy. Under no circumstances should private business interests be pushed during meetings.[6]

Data on the men's chorus consisted of observations of rehearsals, formal meetings, concerts, and special celebrations, interviews with members, statistics on membership correlated with family educational and vocational background, even an analysis of their repertoire (they sang with reluctance the few Italian and French numbers the director introduced and preferred instead songs in praise of their native habitat). Such data provided insight into patterns of interpersonal interaction, the distribution and use of authority, social norms and sanctions, and enduring values of the folk culture. Moving constantly back and forth between the life of the school and the life of the community, one could assess the functional relationships between the socialization experience in the school and the social demands of adulthood.

The male chorus was one of a number of institutions whose activities provided data on the community. The operation of the village government was in this regard central. There were few problems in which the power and influence of the mayor's office were not involved. The office is elective, eight years for the first term and twelve thereafter, and the mayor has both executive and judicial responsibilities. The present mayor had been in office for sixteen years and was largely responsible for bringing the chemical factory to Rebhausen. His native background, his aggressive leadership, and his vision of a more prosperous, industrialized village kept him deeply involved in both the traditional and changing facets of community life. Extensive and periodic interviews with him were useful not only for the basic information they provided but also for the opportunity both to reassess accumulated data and identify new lines of investigation. In addition, systematic observations were made of the various operations of the government.

Religious institutions also reflected the tenor of stability and change in the native culture. Along with the mayor and the principal the clergy occupied the apex of the social structure. Both the Catholic priest and the Evangelical minister were in their thirties, vigorous in their administration of parish life, and themselves "students" of village life—in the sense that they saw the native culture as threatened by industrialization and wanted to help their parishioners effect meaningful adjustments while preserving traditional social and moral values. The priest himself was in the midst of change. The Vatican Council was in session and had sanctioned changes in the mass, par-

---

[6] Two recent cases involved a baker and an auto repair shop owner who berated other members during a meeting for not patronizing them. According to the president, reaction was swift. The men were told openly that that sort of thing was not done and that they therefore were not wanted in the organization. In both cases the men withdrew their memberships.

ticularly with regard to the use by the priest of the native language instead of Latin. The changes the Rebhausen priest chose to make and the reaction of his parishioners were important measures of the rigidity and flexibility of a portion of village life. The Evangelical minister was equally involved in questions of stability and change. He wanted to democratize aspects of church life, including having female representation on the church council, loosening the traditional constraints on age-sex seating arrangements at church services, and persuading members to speak up and participate in church meetings. Every seven years he is expected to make a thorough report to the regional church hierarchy. A report is up to forty pages in length and covers not only church activities but also the social and moral quality of community life. The Rebhausen minister gave me copies dating back to World War I, containing diverse statistics on marriage, divorce, and illegitimate births, as well as descriptions and judgments about political activities and issues and almost every other facet of community life. Both the priest and the minister (supplemented by several of the teachers) conducted religious instruction in the school. Hence in all respects they were important informants.

Questions of Procedure and Data Analysis

Interviews were a basic source of data on the community, as well as the school. They were generally conducted at the respondent's home, in the late afternoon or evening. A rather informal, open-ended interview that had the sense and atmosphere of a social visit proved to be the most efficacious format, primarily because however stiff and formal an interview might be in its inception, the average Rebhausen resident turned it into a social occasion.[7] Consequently, the initiating questions were of a general nature. The talkative propensities of the typical resident made it easy to move informally, through such questions, into the more sensitive areas of community life.

The tape recorder was used extensively with interviews and, depending on the nature of the contact, was introduced at the first or second session. In only two cases was there a preference expressed for its not being used. In the initial interviews the tape recorder was used intermittently with individuals in order to establish a check on its inhibiting influence. An analysis of interview protocols indicated no restrictive influence. The basic procedure followed in the utilization of the material was content analysis. As soon as

---

[7] If a national image has any effect on the kind of rapport a researcher can establish and sustain with respondents, then the year of this study, 1964–1965, was fortuitous. Among Rebhausen residents there remained great admiration for President Kennedy; during the year the flights of Gemini 3 and 4 added to their sense of appreciation for the accomplishments of U.S. society. Individuals in the village and region with whom I have remained in contact indicate that the violent events of the past few years have cast shadows on this somewhat euphoric view of the United States.

possible after each interview the results were written up, or if the tape recorder was used, transcribed.[8] The primary topics developed were in the areas of education, vocations, economics (with particular attention to the impact of the factory on village life), political and governmental institutions, patterns of childhood training, traditions, norms and sanctions with respect to adolescent behavior, courtship and marriage, and the role of the church. Analysis was directed toward establishing interrelationships among the topics and proceeding in subsequent interviews to examine in more depth the substance of such relationships. Individuals selected for interviews represented different age groups, social and organizational affiliations, vocational pursuits, periods of residence, and relationship to the school.

Another instrument used was modeled after the Instrumental Activities Inventory developed by the Spindlers.[9] The establishment of the factory had created numerous job opportunities for natives, and in the course of five years had noticeably affected vocational patterns. The rhythm and atmosphere of work in the factory was in sharp contrast to the life of the farmer. So it seemed useful to elicit attitudes and value judgments about vocations available to natives in Rebhausen. A list of sixteen vocations was prepared, vocations which generally were traditional in Rebhausen and several of which had been added with the establishment of the factory. At the same time my wife made line drawings of each of the vocations (an individual at work). The drawings were useful in stimulating free-flowing, self-revealing statements and were used in interviews with individuals from two groups, (1) nine factory employees representing practically all levels of job classifications and (2) eleven members of the male chorus representing traditional native vocations. In each instance the drawings were spread out in front of the respondent and he was asked to select three vocations which he liked most and three which he disliked most. These choices were then used in the remainder of the interview to explore the background of the preferences, attitudes toward vocations, and changes in village life.

The process of gathering data naturally required adjustments to the personal qualities and work habits of the populace, an experience that was both socially enjoyable and, at times, professionally frustrating. The people were friendly but busy. They were most talkative in informal situations, amenable

---

[8] As a general routine I set aside at least two hours each day for studying and typing notes. Transcriptions of taped interviews were done by a secretary I located in a nearby city—one native to the region and able therefore to understand the heavy dialect which the older natives sometimes lapsed into. This item in the budget became before the end of the study a matter of deficit spending. I underestimated the amount of secretarial help I would need because I had no idea what use I could make of a tape recorder. In retrospect no support service was more important to work in the field and processing the data afterwards than that which made it possible to have typescripts of interviews within two weeks after the interview.

[9] George D. Spindler, and Louise Spindler, 1965, "Researching the Perceptions of Cultural Alternatives," in Melford Spiro ed., *Context and Meaning in Cultural Anthropology.* New York: The Free Press.

to and interested in discussing at length life in Rebhausen. But it was not easy to find time. Farming was, most of the year, a typical dawn-to-dusk operation. Regardless of the occupation of their members, most families owned grape holdings, and the working day was long. Consequently, the best time to capitalize on a developing acquaintance was Sunday afternoon, the traditional visiting time in the village. Visits were arranged, and I was usually urged to bring my family along. Whether I did or not, the host's family was there gathered in the living room for after-dinner talk. It was no simple matter to arrange an interview where the respondent could talk freely, unencumbered by the presence of others.

Sensitivity to social protocol was another quality which created problems. At public meetings the mayor always insisted I occupy a place at the speaker's table, not to participate but simply as a special guest. The gesture was appreciated and had practical advantages in the early part of the study when there was good reason to acquaint the populace with my presence and interest. But the speaker's table was not the best vantage point from which to view or experience a meeting, especially one generating controversy between public officials and the populace. Furthermore, the significant transactions at these meetings often took place after the formalities were concluded. Discussions, lubricated by local wine, continued far into the night. People sat at tables throughout the meeting and seldom moved. Groups gathered together regularly and individuals had their traditional associations. I hoped in the course of the meetings to develop productive contacts with these groups, but it was not easy. Even if I entered the hall unobtrusively, so long as the meeting had not begun, the mayor usually located me in the audience and insisted I come to the speaker's table. I finally evolved a countermeasure that had limited success—a matter of making sure the meeting had begun, spotting a likely table or section of the hall, and then sliding in behind some latecomers.

Conclusions

Chronologically speaking, research on Rebhausen proceeded from a study of the primary educational institution, the elementary school, to a consideration of community life in general and of those economic, social, political, and religious organizations and institutions which appeared to be primary in the structuring and guiding of individual and group behavior. While the school was the central focus of the study, no prior assumption was made as to the significance of education compared with other basic institutions in mediating adjustments to cultural change. However, the highly structured content of the educational program, the authoritarian quality of interpersonal relations in the school, and the emphatic enunciation and reinforcement in the school of values and behavioral patterns common to the total community seemed to indicate that the school was the central, pivotal institution in an assessment of cultural stability and change.

In the course of the research it became apparent that new and changing economic institutions, particularly the factory, assumed a significance almost limitless in its possible implications. In a period of only six years the factory had irrevocably changed the tone and tempo of village life. Its beneficent influence on the appearance of the village and on the basic conveniences the village could offer were everywhere noticeable—paved streets where before 1958 there were dirt roads, a sewer system where once there were primitive outhouses, efficient garbage collection where once there was none at all, and, above all, a 7.2 hectare housing and industrial development (with swimming pool, tennis courts, and eventually a seven-story hotel) where once there was farmland.

Certain historical and cultural phenomena have intensified the significance of the factory. The populace remembers village life as having been characterized almost continually by poverty. Nineteenth-century migrations were forced on the village by a series of crop failures, and primitive working conditions in farming required, as late as the 1930s, exhaustive human effort. The moments of relative prosperity have retained a tentative, illusory quality because of the economic collapses which followed—the inflation of the 1920's and the conditions immediately following World War II. The factory has been the immediate agent of prosperity which the village is now enjoying. There is total employment and a wide latitude of reasonably well-paying jobs is available. But the cost of living is high, a constant reminder that the prosperity may be transitory. Consequently, economic developments have led to a kind of hypersensitive, obsessive ambivalence about wealth. The folk of Rebhausen desire what has long been denied them and what is now accessible, but the goal has a refractory quality that blurs the traditional village portrait with which they strongly identify. In this setting, the school is important to study. Its traditional role reaffirms and sustains the values of the folk culture, but its mediating role in the midst of change is tentative and unstructured for parents, pupils, and teachers.

HARRY F. WOLCOTT/*University of Oregon*

9   The Teacher as an Enemy

I don't like Mr. Wolcott
he always make me work
I hate Mr. Wolcott.

A Kwakiutl Indian boy directed these written words to me while he was attending school in his native village on the coast of British Columbia, Canada. At the time I was the teacher at the village school. My purpose in living in the village and teaching at the school was to study the relationship between village life and the formal education of village pupils. An account of my year as teacher and ethnographer at Blackfish Village is contained in *A Kwakiutl Village and School,* which is a case study of the problems of Western education in a contemporary cross-cultural setting (Wolcott 1967).

As the village teacher I had the responsibility for conducting a one-room school for all the resident village children between the ages of six and sixteen. As ethnographer, I wanted to identify and assess the influence of cultural barriers to classroom performance as a way of studying why Indian pupils have so often seemed refractive to the formal educative efforts of the school.

Although I had taught previously in public schools, I was not prepared for the classroom problems which confronted me at the village school. I found there a firmly entrenched pattern of pupil hostility toward the teacher and toward nearly every nonmaterial aspect of the way of life the teacher represented. In the time that has elapsed since the original fieldwork in 1962–1963, I have had the opportunity to reflect upon the experiences of that year and to return for several brief periods of subsequent study. I have been seeking alternative ways of thinking about the role of the teacher in a cross-cultural setting like Blackfish Village.

In a setting in which critical differences between a teacher and his pupils are rooted in antagonisms of cultural rather than classroom origins, I believe that the teacher might succeed in coping more effectively with conflict and in capitalizing on his instructional efforts if he were to recognize and to analyze his ascribed role as "enemy" rather than attempt to ignore or to deny it. To those educators who insist that a teacher must always present a façade of cheery optimism in the classroom, the notion of the teacher as an enemy may seem unacceptable, overly negative, perhaps even dangerous. One might question, however, whether cheery optimism and a determination to accomplish "good" inevitably serve the best interests of culturally different pupils, especially pupils from socially and economically. depressed or deprived sectors of the population. Any teacher who has faced such pupils in the classroom may have recognized that one alternative for him is to try to do less harm rather than more good. Even with so modest a goal, any strategy that may minimize psychological harm either to pupils or to their teachers merits consideration. The strategy of regarding the teacher as an enemy is explored here as it relates to formal education in antagonistic cross-cultural settings.

Antagonistic Acculturation

Anthropologists refer to the modification of one culture through continuous contact with another as acculturation. Often one of the contact cultures is dominant, regardless of whether such dominance is intended. Not infrequently the situation of dominance leads to a relationship which breeds antagonism on the part of the dominated group.

Antagonism rises rather expectedly out of feelings that one's own cherished ways are being eroded and lost or that one's ethnic group belongs to a have-not class. Antagonistic feelings may be aggravated by the attempts of members of the dominant society to hasten the process of assimilation. Frequently antagonisms are aggravated by a contradiction between the ideal of assimilation and the reality of prejudicial treatment accorded to minority groups within the dominant society. This was the case at Blackfish Village, not because of any problem unique to the village but because there had been a concerted, although not very successful, effort by both the Canadian and U.S. governments to hasten and even to complete the assimilation of North American Indian groups. Indian schools run by the federal governments of both countries consciously directed their efforts toward replacing Indian ways with ways more acceptable to and characteristic of the dominant white middle class, although the respective societies have at the same time responded prejudicially to the Indian who attempted to assimilate.

Contemporary social commentary describing the relation of pupils to their schools among the Sioux Indians, along the Mexican-American border, in Harlem and in Puerto Rican East Harlem, in the Deep South, in Boston, in Washington, D.C., or in the inner city everywhere suggests that cultural barriers to classroom performance are not unique to my confrontation with Blackfish pupils. However, I shall relate my discussion to that specific setting. I will describe how the stresses resulting from "antagonistic acculturation" were manifested in microcosm in the behavior of village children in the classroom. First, I shall describe how I perceived the classroom to be organized to thwart my instructional efforts. A rather different picture of the classroom follows as written accounts from some of the older Blackfish pupils suggest how the classroom looked to them.

Classroom Learning Kwakiutl-Style—as Seen by the Teacher

Here are seven important characteristics of the classroom at the Blackfish Indian Day School as I saw it:

1. The pupils set their own pace, not in the ideal sense of an individualized program with each child working independently at an optimum rate, but rather with doing little in lots of time. My inclination, having found them "behind" in their work, was to get them "caught up." Their inclination was, generally, to let the school day slip by without having expended much—or perhaps any—effort in the direction I was so anxious to push them. Their whole orientation to school, I believe, was one of patiently enduring. What my pupils wanted most to get out of school was to get out of school. Since maturity provided the only means to achieve that goal, the amount of school work accomplished in a day had no meaning unless one's peers wanted to engage in a self-imposed competition or unless one really valued the praise of the teacher. But neither the rewards the teacher had to give nor the manner in which he gave them were likely to warrant the effort necessary to attain them or the risk of incurring the displeasure of one's fellow pupils for having done so.

2. Classroom assignments were frequently perceived as a group task. My worksheets and practice papers were treated as though my class was a secretarial pool—older or brighter pupils did papers for younger or slower ones, sometimes because the assignments were difficult, sometimes because they were fun. My pupils, as a class, were organized to cope with me collectively, while I was trying to cope with them individually. The nature of this mutual classroom help among pupils had several concomitant aspects described below.

3. Almost invariably students collaborated as partners in electing to complete or to ignore classroom assignments, in deciding whether to write long diary entries about their day, in making choices when alternative activities were offered, or in preparing answers to my questions. My "divide and conquer" tactic was constantly subverted. I had great difficulty assessing the progress of any given pupil because pupils so frequently teamed up to write daily entries for each other and to work each other's assignments.

One of the most successful classroom activities of the year was the exchange of a series of letters between the older pupils and a sixth-grade class in a California school. As the exchange of letters progressed, some members of the class began receiving more letters than others. Those who received many letters farmed out the excess and had other pupils write the replies. At another time, I gave eight older pupils a sentence-completion test. I later discovered that instead of eight sets of answers I had received four sets of paired answers in return. Before beginning to complete the sentences each pupil chose a partner with whom he worked out a tentative answer, and then both partners wrote a comparable—or identical—response for each sentence.

4. Teasing and bullying were very disruptive elements in class. Often the teasing was related to inter- or intra-family squabbles which had their origin outside of school. Included in the teasing, however, was a process of pupil socialization in which children learned not to outperform their peers. Particularly, I observed change in the behavior of two children, a fourth-grade girl and a first-grade boy, who came to the village after the school year had begun and who seemed to be particularly capable students. Both underwent continual taunting in class, and both learned to display less overt enthusiasm for school and to restrict their academic prowess to tasks on which they could work alone, while they performed only minimally at those tasks on which greater achievement was apparent to their peers. The boy had come from a provincial school where he was one of few Indian pupils; the girl had been attending a day school in another village, one in which school achievement was more acceptable and school success more frequent. Whether the socialization of these children was due to their ability in school, their being outsiders to the village, or a combination of both, I have never been certain. That the quality and quantity of their academic performance diminished, I am sure. The girl traveled to her parents' village for Christmas and never returned to Blackfish Village; the boy survived the year by learning to perform more like other village boys in school, which meant doing very little on group assignments, although he usually worked well alone. He outperformed all the other pupils in the seclusion of two intelligence tests I administered.

5. At the same time that overperformance was restrained through socialization, there was some tendency to help the slower children of one's age or ability group. Such help differs from the help given to younger pupils, because that assistance seemed to be used to get the tasks completed (if the teacher was going to insist on them) while the helping to which I now refer served to keep a pupil from appearing too inadequate in the eyes of the teacher. For the teacher, this "equalizing" behavior among the pupils made the task of finding suitable material or diagnosing individual learning difficulties almost impossible.

The most glaring instance was that of a fifteen-year-old boy who was almost a nonreader. In September I assigned to him a fourth-grade basal reader which was being read by several other boys. It was some time before I realized that he was so used to having difficult words whispered to him by his reading mates that during my limited opportunity to hear the children read aloud he did not necessarily look at the pages to appear to be reading from them. Eventually I realized he could read independently only at grade-one level, and as late as May I recorded in my notes, "He gets so much help from other kids that I still doubt that I know his own capabilities."

As a social phenomenon, the cooperative efforts of my pupils may appear both remarkable and praiseworthy. In each case, however, the extent of their cooperation and organization inevitably thwarted my efforts in both assessing and instructing them, according to the expectations which I held for myself as a teacher. Further, to whatever extent I was able to see the positive aspects of pupil cooperation rather than to feel threatened by it, I was still unable to mobilize the cooperative potential of the pupils to accomplish *my* purposes. I could not make them help each other, be patient toward each other, or socialize each other toward such teacher-approved purposes as keeping the classroom quiet so pupils could read, working quickly enough to allow time for other activities, or letting younger pupils join in the recess play of the older ones.

6. Antagonistic as they were toward so many aspects of school, my pupils nevertheless held very rigid expectations about the activities they considered appropriate for school work. Insistence on attention to the three R's constituted the only legitimate kind of demand which the pupils both expected and accepted on the part of their teacher. Their notion of an ideal classroom was one in which pupils were busily engaged in highly repetitive but relatively easy assignments for long periods of time, uninterrupted by the teacher. Their notion of an ideal teacher, consistent with this, was of a person who meted out assignments but not explanations, a person who had an infinite supply of worksheets and tasks but who never asked a pupil to engage in an exercise he could not already perform. The only favors or rewards expected of a teacher were in the distribution of coveted materials (crayons, water colors, compasses, scissors, puzzles, athletic equipment), the allocation of prestige positions (attendance monitor, bell ringer), and the rationing of school "fun" ("free" time, art periods, extended recesses, classroom parties).

Given their narrow expectations for proper classroom activities, it is not surprising that the pupils responded most favorably to assignments at the specific tasks required in arithmetic and spelling. Occasionally they requested an assignment to repeat a page of arithmetic drill or requested my validation of a self-imposed assignment to write each spelling word three, five, or ten times.

Weeks passed before the older pupils grew accustomed to my daily assignment—making at least a brief entry in a diarylike notebook. Even when they had grown used to this activity as part of our daily program, they were uneasy that I did not "teach" language arts because I did not often use the language arts texts. Although their basal readers and the accompanying workbooks were difficult, dull, and pedantic, the pupils were never satisfied that they were "having reading" unless these readers were before them. They never completely accepted my progressive idea that reading a book of one's own choice was also a legitimate type of classroom reading. Patiently, and sometimes impatiently, they endured my reading aloud to them, because they had been subjected by their teachers to that dubious pleasure for years, but I could seldom induce them to any kind of classroom discussion subsequent to hearing a story. My attempts to relate social studies to their own lives made them uncomfortable both because they perceived this as prying and because I did not depend on textbooks in my approach. They were generally impatient with instruction in concepts that were not included in their texts (for example, notions from the new math). In short, my pupils had very specific expectations for the formal purposes of school, they generally hated school as defined by these expectations, and they refused to have their expectations modified. They disliked school and that is just how they liked it.

7. Let me conclude this description of the classroom as seen by the teacher with one final pattern of pupil behavior, the attempts of the pupils to socialize their teacher. It is misleading to refer to this socialization as "attempts," for my pupils were good teachers and their techniques were effective. The methods they used to socialize me included giving slow, reluctant responses to my directions, ignoring my comments (by not "hearing" them or occasionally by putting their hands to their ears), mimicking my words or actions, constantly requesting to leave the classroom to go to the toilet, and making me the target of spoken or written expletives. To illustrate, the following note was written to me during the daily writing period by a twelve-year-old boy the day after I took a partially eaten apple away from him and inadvertently forgot to return it:

> We were packing wood yesterday me and Raymond were packing lots of wood. Oh, you little monkey, little asshole you got my apple why don't you mind your own business you think you smart little asshole. Goodbye, that's all I can say now. Goodbye, no more writing because you throw my apple.

The most direct and telling comments were those that identified me as "White man," the outsider, or drew attention to our different cultural origins: "Just like a White man," "That's the trouble with you White guys," or, twice during the year, an angry stare and the comment, "What's the matter; haven't you ever seen an Indian before?" With such a statement as: "We don't have to tell *you* anything," I was at a loss to know whether my distinguishing attribute was that I was white, the teacher, a cranky adult, or all of them.

Classroom Learning Kwakiutl Style — as Seen by the Pupils

Although I have referred frequently to the pupils in the class, the classroom picture presented above is entirely a construct of a teacher's perception. Consequently, it is cast primarily in terms of the teacher's instructional goals and how the subculture of the pupils seemed to be organized to thwart them. Written comments of the older pupils provide some insight into how the class and teacher looked to them.

1. This response was written by a fifteen-year-old girl to an assigned topic, "If I Were the Teacher." Note how she relates her concept of the role of a teacher to perpetuating such middle-class values so revered by teachers as cleanliness, quiet, punctuality, and obedience. Note also the emphasis she

gives to discipline and punishment. The classroom is an orderly, severe, and punishing place.

> If I were the teacher. When I first get here I'd like to meet all the children here. The first day in school I'd tell the pupils what to do. First thing we do is clean the school up then clean the desk and the cupboards. Then straighten the cupboard up for the books. When the school is cleaned up, then I'll give out the books. And ask what grade they're in. Ask how old are they. And give the rules for school. The school starts at 9:00 A.M., recess at 10:30 A.M., dinner at 12:00 P.M., come back in the afternoon at 1:00 P.M., recess at 2:30 P.M. and after school 3:30 P.M. And if anybody's late, they have to write hundred lines.[1] And keep the toilet clean. Their clothes clean and comb hair. First thing they'd do in the morning is Arithmetic, spelling, language, Reading. And the afternoon Science, Social Studies, Health, and free time. And if nobody works they get a strapping. If I had a fourteen year old in my class she or he would take care of grade one and two. And I'd take care of three to eight. If I had a class all in one grade that'll be nice. Then I won't have to bother about other grades except the class I have. And if they get the room dirty they'll sweep the whole classroom. I'd get a monitor for the bath room to be clean and swept. And if anybody talks back. They'd get a strapping. If they get out of their desk they'll have to write lines. If they don't ask permission to sharpen their pencil they'll get strapping. If they wear hats and kerchiefs in class they'll have to stand in the corner for one hour with their hands on their heads. I'd tell the children to draw Indian Design for the room. If they make a noise in class, they all stay in for half an hour. If anybody talks in class they write lines about hundred lines. If anybody's absent they have lots of homework for the next day. And if anybody fights they get a strapping. And I'd have a monitor for the books so nobody touch it except the monitor. Dust the shelves. And on Christmas they'd have to play or sing. And on Halloween they have to dress up for the party.

2. Here is the response of another pupil, a fourteen-year-old girl, to my request for a theme on the same topic, "If I Were the Teacher." Note the contrast she makes between discipline and scholarship. If one of her pupils were to fail to be on time, she would strap him. If he were to fail a comprehensive examination, she would have a talk with him.

> If I were the teacher for Blackfish Village, or someplace else, I'd like my class to be very quiet. If not, they would get a straping from me. They would get a straping if they are late.
>
> They would come to school at nine A.M. No sooner nor later. They would have one recess in the morning and one in the afternoon. In the afternoon they would go home at 3:30 P.M.
>
> The subjects I'd give them in the morning are Math, Spelling, Reading. If they

---

[1] By "write lines" she refers to the practice of repeatedly writing a sentence like "I will not talk out in class" to the satisfaction of a teacher. In my defense I should add that none of the assortment of disciplinary measures she refers to was used in my classroom, although I did have children put their heads down on their desks as a mild disciplinary measure and sent them out of the classroom for a variety of infractions, including that exquisite pupil weapon, sullenness.

do not get it finished they would have it for homework, same in the afternoon. They would have a story, Language, then Library or drawing.

I'd like my class to be very neat, clothes clean, hair neat. In the morning they could sing "God Save the Queen." In the afternoon they would sing "Oh Canada."

I would choose Monitors for toilets, paints and for blackboards, But of course I would do the Attendance myself. I would given them tests before Christmas, Easter, and the final tests at June. After the tests if anyone fails, I would ask them to tell me why. For example if one of my pupils did fail I'd tell that child to write on a paper to tell me why. If that child has a good excuse, I'd tell that child to "smarten up" and pay attention to his or her work more.

I would go to see their parents to see if they have a normal living, like if they go to sleep before nine o'clock, have good meals every day.

Yes sir! If I were the teacher a lot of changes would be made around here at Blackfish Village. The children would have to listen even if I were a girl teacher.

But I didn't plan the future yet. That's for sure I'm not sticking around here in the future.

3. In most cases where the hostility of the children toward the teacher flared up over a specific incident at school the pupils did not record their perceptions of the event in their classroom writing. Typically at such times they refrained from performing any task that might please the teacher, and writing in their notebooks did win teacher approval. The following excerpt reveals one instance where a pupil did record the anger which she shared with several other pupils. I had refused to admit a group of the older pupils into class when they were late in returning from the morning recess, and at least for this fourteen-year-old, trouble at school had precipitated more trouble at home.

Today is a very horrible day for Norma and me. Of course we would be treaten as babies. When we are late in this dump the teacher would [i.e., *did*] tell us to come back in the afternoon. There was Larry, Joseph, Norma, Tommy, Jack, Herman and me. Norma got in trouble too, of course. My brother would tell on me that brat. This is a strict world for some of us. I thought this was a free world. Norma and me can't even go on Larry's boat and for me I'm not aloud to go to their house! My brother said I was in my aunties house. I guess thats why I ain't aloud in their. All the time I was in Sarah's house. The teacher is so lazy to ring the bell I guess he expects us to hear him when he calls us. That's all!!

4. Two final examples suggest the contrast between the pseudowork and satisfaction of the classroom and the real work and real rewards of adult life. Here is a written comment, in the form of a note to the teacher, from a twelve-year-old boy who recognized that although he was required to attend school, he had a more important contribution to make to his family when he could assist with the work of the men:

I am going to go halibut fishing with my father and Raymond. That's why I asked you is there going to be school tomorrow because I want to go with my father. He always has a tough time when he catches halibut [alone]. We got one halibut yesterday.

In a similar vein, the following was written in November by a fifteen-year-old boy. The note mentions only a week's leave, but it was in fact the boy's last classroom assignment forever, because he has never returned to school:

We are going to Gilford Island tomorrow. I'm going to stay there one week. I'm going to dig clams. There is a big tide this week. I'm not coming to school next week.

The Teacher as an Enemy

In the school at Blackfish Village, or for teachers in any number of comparable settings, I believe there would be real utility in having more than one way of perceiving the reciprocal roles of teacher and pupil. In my own case, experience in both roles prior to my year at Blackfish Village had been within the confines of a middle-class setting of which I am very much part and product. Sometimes, in my twenty years as a student, I had experienced antagonism toward teachers and occasionally I had generated antagonism among my students as a public school and university teacher. Such antagonism, however, was a consequence of immediate psychological or personal incompatibility, never an antagonism rooted in social forces outside the classroom. I had never encountered teachers or pupils with whom I did not share relatively similar expectations regarding behaviors, values, and attitudes.

At Blackfish Village my pupils and I shared few mutual expectations regarding our formal role relationship. Those expectations we did share tended to provide pacts that enabled individual survival in a situation beyond our making rather than opening avenues for trust or understanding. No one, teacher or pupils, ever let his guard down very far. If we were not at any one moment actually engaged in a classroom skirmish, it was only because we were recovering from a prior one or preparing for the next. On the last day of school I reflected that I had not won a battle; instead I felt that all year long I had had a tiger by the tail, and we had merely crossed some kind of symbolic finish line together.

I had anticipated that one of my major problems of the year would be to induce my pupils to come regularly to school. Except for the fact that pupils expected to leave school at about age sixteen, however, my pupils and I did not have to do battle regarding school attendance. Economic sanctions could be taken against families who failed to send their children regularly to school, but in fact attendance (other than a perennial problem in getting pupils from certain families to school on time) was not a major concern. Indeed, parents not only sent their children off to school each day but also ritually endorsed the benefits of formal education with such comments as "Education is the only answer."

I had mistakenly assumed that once the pupils were inside the classroom they could be led to a host of new learnings under the guidance of their dedicated teacher. Ever since my year as a teacher at the Blackfish Indian Day School I have been seeking an alternative teaching perspective, one that would have enabled me to present an instructional program without such personal frustration at my lack of success and without nurturing an atmosphere of hostility where I had intended to create an atmosphere of help.

The direction my quest has taken is *not* to ponder how to "outpsych" or outmaneuver my pupils. Training in anthropology had convinced me of the fact that differences exist among groups of human beings and that the differences may touch every facet of human life from household composition to cognition. But I was not assigned to the village to teach villagers their way of life; I was assigned to teach them something about mine.

I think that I might have been a more effective teacher if I had taken the perspective of regarding the *teacher,* me, *as an enemy.* By effective I mean that I would have remained more objective about my lack of success, and I would have been more sensitive to the high cost for each pupil of accepting me or my instructional program. The "enemy" relationship I use here as my analogy does not refer to entering into combat, although on the worst days we may not have been far from it. More appropriate to antagonistic acculturation as manifested in school might be an analogy to a prisoner-of-war camp. Prisoners of war—inmates and captors alike—are faced with the probability that a long period of time may ensue during which their statuses remain unchanged. While great hostility on the part of either group might be present in the relationship, it is not essential to it, because the enmity is not derived from individual or personal antagonism. Nonetheless, the captors, representing one cultural group, are not expected to convert the prisoners to their way of life, and the prisoners are not expected to acculturate the captors.

So far, a teacher in an instructional role has no place in the analogy. Let us extend the analogy one step further. Suppose that along with the usual cadre of overseers the captors have also provided teachers charged with instructing the prisoners in the ways of, and particularly in the merits of, their culture. The purpose of instruction is to recruit new members into their society by encouraging prisoners to defect, and achieving this by giving them the skills so that they can do so effectively. The teachers are expected to provide information about the captors' way of life and about the skills that this way entails. It has been established that prisoners will attend the classes and that they will not be allowed to disrupt classroom proceedings, but beyond these strictures the teacher is not expected to dwell on the negative aspects that have brought his pupils to him. The teacher is not unaware of the probability, however, that since he is perceived as an enemy, his pupils may not see him playing a very functional role in their lives other than as a representative of the enemy culture.

What purposes might be served in cross-cultural education if a teacher were to draw an analogy between himself and an enemy captor in trying to understand his relationship with his pupils? There are several potential advantages one might anticipate.

First, the teacher who can imagine how pupils might feel toward him as a member of a captor society recognizes a distinction between having pupils physically present in class and having them psychologically receptive to instruction. Cognizance of the pervasive hostile and suspicious influence of the enemy relationship helps the teacher maintain realistic expectations for what he can accomplish in the classroom. Despite his most valiant efforts to make his instruction effective, he is never overcome by feelings of personal inadequacy at a lack of response to his lessons. He realizes that under certain conditions the energy and resources of prisoners are utilized in a desperate struggle to survive and to maintain their own identity in the face of overwhelming odds. The teacher recognizes that the antagonism of his pupils may be addressed to the whole cultural milieu in which they find themselves captive rather than to him as an individual. He understands that any attempt on his part to alter or to ameliorate the basis for antagonism may be met with suspicion. He is not personally disappointed when his pupils show tendencies toward recidivism when they feel themselves being seduced by the constant attention and encouragement of their mentor-enemies. If this is how things seem to the prisoners, the teacher realizes that a modification of a lesson plan or an ingenious new teaching technique is not going to make any important difference to them. Taking the point of view of his pupils, the teacher can ask himself, "Just what is it that a prisoner would ever want to learn from an enemy?"

Second, the teacher who can entertain a perspective that regards himself and his pupils as belonging to enemy cultures acknowledges the possibility that there could be important and systematic differences in life styles and in value-orientation characterizing each group. He is not as inclined to share a perception, common among teachers, that if a pupil does not have the same cultural background as the teacher he does not have any cultural heritage at all. Granted, the teacher can be expected to believe that his own life style is right, but he also recognizes that he is not likely to achieve his purposes by insisting that all other life styles are therefore wrong. Anthropologist Ruth Landes has written cogently in this regard, "The educator, or other authority, can advance his inquiries and explanations by taking the position that he represents one culture talking to another. This minimizes personal and emotional involvements by focusing on the grand designs of each tradition. . . ." (Landes 1965:47).

The teacher's instructional objectives are to try to make his own way of life appear sufficiently manageable to his "enemy" pupils that they may choose to explore it further, and, for those pupils who do make this choice, to provide them with a set of survival skills for living in a different culture and having access to its rewards. Children growing up in Blackfish Village, for example, will have to be able to demonstrate the skill aspects of specific middle-class manners and values such as cleanliness, courtesy, responsibility, punctuality, or how to take orders from a white boss in order to survive in the dominant society. They do not, however, need a teacher who insists that such skills are necessary steps on the road to nirvana. They need a teacher who can identify and instruct them in certain specific behaviors which an individual *must* exhibit if he is going to move successfully in a society that heretofore has been regarded as an alien one.

We would hardly expect the teacher to engage in much "correction" of pupils except for what was essential to the maintenance of an orderly classroom. The language or dialect used by prisoners need not be singled out for ridicule, correction, or extermination. What the teacher might do, however, is to teach a standard dialect of his own language to prisoner-pupils who entertained an intellectual curiosity about it or, especially, to those pupils interested in learning the enemy culture well enough to see if they can survive in it.

Most important, the teacher realizes the meaning that accepting his teaching may have for those prisoners who do accept it. It may mean selling out, defecting, turning traitor, ignoring the succorance and values and pressures of one's peers, one's family, one's own people. It can require terrible and anxious decisions for the prisoner, and it may even require him to sever his most deeply-rooted human ties. The teacher needs constantly to review what these costs mean to any human. As a consequence, the teacher interested in his enemy pupils as humans may find himself less inclined to act as a cultural brainwasher and more inclined to weigh both the difficulties of cultural transition and the ultimate consequences of change. In the latter regard a proverb quoted in Robert Ruark's novel *Something of Value* seems particularly appropriate: "If a man does away with his traditional way of living and throws away his good customs, he had better first make certain he has something of value to replace them" (Basuto proverb).

The teacher may feel a greater need to alert his pupils to the fact that he has *not* been able to provide them with all the prerequisite skills for successfully "passing" in the teacher's own society than to fill them with hopes and promises which few may ever realize. His pupils need to know how much information they actually have, what problems they must anticipate, and which vestiges of their earlier heritage may present almost insurmountable handicaps.

Through the exercise of examining his *own* culture as the alien one, the teacher-enemy may be less aggressive about forcing his lessons on his prisoner-pupils. He may not accept so unhesitatingly the belief that what he is doing is necessarily "good" for them. He may be more inclined to think of teaching as an offer of help to members of the dominated group who seek it rather than as an imposition of help from members of the dominant group who insist on giving it. Pausing to consider the possibility of being regarded by his pupils as a member of an enemy culture offers the teacher a perspective for understanding why pupils might sometimes appear able but unwilling to accept his teaching. This perspective also encourages the teacher to give more help to the potential defectors who seek it, rather than to spend his time bemoaning the lack of defection by the prisoner generation of today.

Conclusion

Cultural systems provide us with practical answers to questions of how we should act and what to think about how we act. But no "culture" ever provides its members with a perfect and complete blueprint of how to act in every situation. If cultures accomplished that, they might never change, and we know that change is inherent in human life and human organization. We do not often pause to examine our own behavior, and it can be with a real sense of surprise that in a new role we suddenly discover that we already know exactly how to act; we may even feel we have "known it all the time." Student teachers, as a case in point, provide themselves and observers with remarkable examples of how well they have internalized the teacher behavior associated with the teacher-pupil role relationship even if they have never formally taken the teacher role before.

When circumstances bring us into contact with others who do not share the same cultural orientation, particularly if our "proper" behavior invites inappropriate responses or no response at all, we become more self-consciously aware of our own patterns of behavior. Initially this may result only in our speaking or gesticulating a bit more emphatically, in a manner characteristic of the American tourist abroad. Under conditions of prolonged contact, one might want to do better than simply wave his hands more or talk louder. Regardless of how much effort he makes at understanding those who are different from him, however, it is from his own repertoire of cultural behaviors that the individual most choose. If he has no perfectly appropriate pattern of behavior, then he has to look for relevant analogous situations. The choice of analogies is crucial.

The teacher working with culturally different pupils exhibits a natural inclination to draw upon a single analogy, that of the idealized teacher-pupil relationship suitable for the monolithic transmission of culture. I do not imagine that teachers will ever escape from drawing upon this analogy. Their very identity as teachers requires that they have specific notions about teacher behavior. Teachers should not be asked perfunctorily to discard their own "good customs."

I have suggested here that the teacher seek out alternative behavior analogs rather than depend solely on the not-always-appropriate model of the ideal teacher in the ideal setting. Like the role relationship between teacher and pupil, the relationship between enemies is also a culturally based one. The enemy relationship may actually draw more heavily upon universal aspects of behavior than does the teacher-pupil role which has tended to become so crystallized in Western civilization. In spite of the negative implications of an enemy role, and barring extremes of physical cruelty, there are certain ways in which pupils equated with captive prisoners might get better treatment than pupils regarded as allies. For example, in thinking of antagonistic pupils as prisoners of war, one comes to recognize that the classroom is neither the underlying source of intercultural antagonism nor the site of its critical campaigns. Such a realization may also help the reform-oriented teacher to recognize that the proper target for his efforts at community reform is the adult community rather than young children in school (Hawthorn et al. 1960:303).

One last dimension of the enemy perspective is that few demands are made of enemy prisoners. Demands are made explicitly; they are not based on assumptions of shared values about fair play, individual rights, ultimate purposes, or the dignity of office. In a sense, the behavior between enemies gives more overt evidence of respecting the other person's cultural ways than does that between friendly groups. Based as it is upon the recognition of vital differences rather than on the recognition of underlying similarities, the perspective of thinking about teachers and their culturally different pupils as enemies invites teachers to examine the kinds of differences cherished by enemies just as they have in the past addressed themselves, at least ritually, to what they and their pupils share in common.

References and Further Reading

Goffman, Erving, 1969, "The Characteristics of Total Institutions," In Amitai Etzioni, ed., *A Sociological Reader on Complex Organizations.* 2d ed. New York: Holt, Rinehart and Winston, Inc. Readers interested in exploring the analogy between pupils and prisoners will find a number of strategies which "inmates" pursue suggested in this essay.

Hawthorn, Harry B., C. S. Belshaw, and S. M. Jamieson, 1960, *The Indians of British Columbia: A Study of Contemporary Social Adjustment.* Berkeley: University of California Press, especially Chap. 23, "Schools and Education."

Henry, Jules, 1955, "Docility, or Giving Teacher What She Wants," *Journal of Social Issues* 11:33–41.

King, A. Richard, 1967, *The School at Mopass: A Problem of Identity.* CSEC. New York: Holt, Rinehart and Winston, Inc.

Landes, Ruth, 1965, *Culture in American Education: Anthropological Approaches to Minority and Dominant Groups in the School.* New York: John Wiley & Sons, Inc.

Rohner, Ronald P., 1965, "Factors Influencing the Academic Performance of Kwakiutl Indian Children in Canada," *Comparative Education Review* 9:331–340.

———, 1967, *The People of Gilford, A Contemporary Kwakiutl Village.* National Museum of Canada, Bulletin 225. Ottawa, Ontario: the Queen's Printer.

———, and Evelyn C. Rohner, 1970 (reissued 1986), *The Kwakutl Indians of British Columbia.* Prospect Heights, Illinois: Waveland Press, Inc., especially Chap. 4, "Growing Up Kwakiutl."

Ruark, Robert C., 1955, *Something of Value.* New York: Doubleday & Company, Inc.

Smith, Alfred G., 1968, "Communication and Inter-cultural Conflict." In Carl E. Larson and Frank E. X. Dance, eds., *Perspectives on Communication.* Milwaukee: University of Wisconsin Press.

Wax, Murray L., Rosalie H. Wax, and Robert V. Dumont, Jr., 1964, Formal Education in an American Indian Community. *Social Problems, Monograph #1,* Society for the Study of Social Problems.

Wolcott, Harry F., 1967 (reissued 1984), *A Kwakiutl Village and School.* Prospect Heights, Illinois: Waveland Press, Inc.

GEORGE and LOUISE SPINDLER/*Stanford University*

10 *Ethnography: An Anthropological View*

In the brief compass of these few pages we state what we think ethnography is and what ethnographers study. We are doing so because ethnography has recently become a popular approach to the study of schools, play groups, bars, business establishments — any place where people gather. Anthropologists have "come home" to do their field research more than they did only a few years ago as remote tribesmen and traditional peasants have become less numerous and less accessible.[1] This popularity has been a mixed blessing, for false hopes are raised, particularly in education, partly because many people, who are quite innocent of anthropology as a discipline and who have only vague notions of cultural process, claim to be doing ethnography. We have nothing against anyone doing qualitative, field site evaluation, participant or nonparticipant observation, descriptive journalism, or anything else if it is well done. It will produce some tangible result and may be useful, but it should not be called ethnography unless it is, and it is not ethnography unless it uses some model of cultural process in both the gathering and interpretation of data.[2] This gives us great latitude, but there are boundaries. We will explore these boundaries briefly.

What Do Ethnographers Study?

Culture, cultural process, cultural knowledge, appear in various guises. We need to define what we study when we study culture. As we do so, we will also be talking about how we study it. By "we" we mean the authors in the company of many, but not all, anthropologists.

---

[1]Donald Messerschmidt, ed., *Anthropologists at Home in North America: Methods and Issues in the Study of One's Own Society* (New York: Cambridge Univ. Press, 1981).
[2]Harry Wolcott, "The Anthropology of Learning," in *Anthropology and Education Quarterly* 13 (1982): 83-108.

Reprinted from *Educational Horizons* [63:154-157, 1985] with permission.

151

We often refer to an "American" culture.[3] Objections are immediately raised. America is multicultural. America is too diverse to be called a culture. We say there is an American culture not because we have standardized drug stores, kitchens, cars, and clothing, though uniformities in these things do contribute to some uniformities that are cultural. We certainly do not claim that there is an American culture because we are composed of at least 24 ethnic groups, six social classes, males and females, 14 major religious groupings and countless sects, many degrees of left and right and extreme factions in both contingents, gays and straights, drug users and abstainers, and hillbillies and city slickers. We claim that there is an American culture because since prerevolutionary times we have been dialoguing about freedom and constraint, equality and difference, cooperation and competition, independence and conformity, sociability and individuality, Puritanism and free love, materialism and altruism, hard work and getting by, and achievement and failure. We express the dialogue in great and small institutions, political campaigns, expenditures of billions of dollars, schools and libraries, personnel management, business practices, sales pitches, production goals, foreign policy, etc. It is not because we are all the same, or that we agree on most important matters, that there is an American culture. It is that somehow we agreed to worry, argue, fight, emulate, and agree or disagree about the same pivotal concerns. Call them values, value orientations, cultural foci, themes, whatever. They are pivotal,[4] and they are arranged in oppositional pairs. That is the nature of culture, according to anthropological structuralists.[5] This is the dialogue of American culture. It gives meaning to our lives and actions as Americans. There are other dialogues that give meaning to our personal lives.

Within any social setting and any social scene within a setting, whether great or small, social actors are carrying on a culturally constructed dialogue. This dialogue is expressed in behavior, words, symbols, and in the application of cultural knowledge to make instrumental activities and social situations "work" for one. We learn the dialogue as children and continue learning it all of our lives as our circumstances change. This is the phenomenon we study as ethnographers — the dialogue of action and interaction. We observe behavior and interview, in varying degrees of formality, any "native" (student, teacher, boss, housewife, chief) who will talk with us. When we are in classrooms, we

---

[3]George and Louise Spindler, "Anthropologists View American Culture," in *Annual Review of Anthropology,* edited by B. Siegel, et al. (Palo Alto, CA: Annual Reviews Inc., 1983); Marvin Harris, *America Now: The Anthropology of a Changing Culture* (New York: Simon & Schuster, 1981); and Richard Merelman, *Making Something of Ourselves* (Berkeley: Univ. of California Press, 1984).

[4]George and Louise Spindler, "Anthropologists View American Culture." (*Annual Review of Anthropology,* 72, 49-78, 1983).

[5]Richard Merelman, *Making Something of Ourselves.*

observe the action and talk to students, teachers, principals, counselors, parents, and janitors. We observe, formulate questions, ask them, observe some more, and so on until the patterns of behavior and native explanations for them coalesce into repetitive sequences and configurations. We try to determine how teaching and learning are supported and constrained by understandings, many of them implicit, that govern the interaction of teachers and students.[6] The dialogue of everyday classroom interaction around what is to be taught, how much of it is to be learned, and how the teaching and learning will be conducted is what we try to record and eventually interpret.

In a Nutshell

We think of culture as a continuing dialogue that revolves around pivotal areas of concern in a given community. The dialogue is produced as social actors apply their acquired cultural knowledge so that it works in social situations—they make sense and enhance, or at least maintain, self-esteem. Neither the knowledge nor the situations replicate themselves through time, but both exhibit continuity. The dialogue occurs at several levels simultaneously—from the most explicit and obvious to the tacit and sometimes very hidden.

What Is Education?

We see education as cultural transmission, and of course cultural transmission requires cultural learnings, so learning and transmission are never separated except by convention.[7] Further, we see that aspect of cultural transmission in which we are most interested—education in the broad sense, schooling in the narrower sense (including initiations, rites of passage, apprenticeships, as well as schools)—as a calculated intervention in the learning process. We are not interested in all learning that takes place as children grow into adults, get older, and finally die. We are interested in the learning that takes place as a result of calculated intervention. It is our unique subject matter as educational anthropologists, and without a unique subject matter there is no discipline.

---

[6]Reba Page, "Lower-Track Classes at a College-preparatory High School: A Caricature of Educational Encounters," in *Toward an Interpretive Ethnography of Education,* edited by G. Spindler.

[7]Harry Wolcott, "The Anthropology of Learning," *Anthropology and Education Quarterly* 13 (1982): 83-108; and George and Louise Spindler, "Do Anthropologists Need Learning Theory?," *Anthropology and Education Quarterly* 13 (1982): 109-124.

Within the focus that we think is useful, there are surface phenomena—the manifest, overt, cultural content—and then there are the tacit agreements that make the dialogue of intervention possible. In our long-term study of the Schönhausen Grundschule[8] and in our recent work in the Roseville, Wisconsin, school and community,[9] we find that the implicit, tacit, and hidden levels of culture are most important. They are what explain puzzling persistences that are there over time under a surface level of change, sometimes even apparently dramatic change. And they are what explain, most satisfactorily, some startling differences in classroom management and student-teacher behavior between the German and American schools. Many models for research and analysis used by both social scientists and educators do not permit the study of the very processes we have discovered are the most important—those aspects of the continuing dialogue between students and teachers that are hidden beneath the surface of behavior.

Good Ethnography

We think that *good* ethnography is necessary in order to understand what goes on as education occurs. We have stated what we consider to be the criteria for a good ethnography in *Doing the Ethnography of Schooling*[10] and cannot repeat them here.

We search for clues to the relationship between forms and levels of cultural knowledge and observable behaviors as the dialogue of intervention and response takes place. The search must follow the clues wherever they lead and cannot be predetermined by a schedule of categories of observation or rating scales. Ethnographic study requires direct observation, it requires being immersed in the field situation, and it requires constant interviewing in all degrees of formality and casualness. From this interviewing, backed by observation, one is able to collect and elicit the native view(s) of reality and the native ascription of meaning to events, intentions, and consequences.

---

[8]George D. Spindler, "Schooling in Schoenhausen: A Study of Cultural Transmission and Instrumental Adaptation in an Urbanizing German Village," in *Education and Cultural Process: Toward an Anthropology of Education,* edited by G. Spindler, 230-273 (New York: Holt, Rinehart & Winston, 1974); and George and Louise Spindler, "Roger Harker and Shoenhausen: From the Familiar to the Strange and Back Again," in *Doing the Ethnography of Schooling: Educational Anthropology in Action,* edited by G. Spindler (New York: Holt, Rinehart & Winston, 1982).
[9]George and Louise Spindler, "Schoenhausen Revisited and the Rediscovery of Culture," in *Toward an Interpretive Ethnography of Education.* (New Jersey: Lawrence Erlbaum Assoc. Inc. 1987).
[10]George Spindler, "The Criteria for a Good Ethnography of Schooling," in *Doing the Ethnography of Schooling.*

Eventually we must face the task of interpretation and cultural translation. The native view of reality must be directly represented in this interpretation but it can rarely stand on its own. We must translate it into the vernacular of the readers, natives in another cultural system, caught up in a different dialogue. And we must apply some concepts, models, paradigms, and theories from our professional discipline in order to give our findings wider applicability and, of course, to communicate with our fellow professional natives. As we have said, our persuasion is toward culture and a special canting of it that we have termed *dialogue*.

Our orientation is idiographic and case study oriented. Ideographic research is widely regarded as incapable of producing generalizations. We take issue with this and feel that through grounded, case-oriented, open (that is, not predetermined) ethnographic investigation, generalizations can be formulated most effectively. They may be tested, to be sure, with nomothetic methods employing refined statistical models,[11] and often such methods also produce hypotheses for testing.

There is nothing in what we have said that precludes the use of quantitative data and inferential statistics as a part of an overall research program. We have collected and analyzed such data in every one of our four major research projects.[12] Careful use of statistics defines relationships and parameters in a most valuable way that helps define what must be explored with direct observation and interviewing and, conversely, makes possible the extension of generalizations initially derived idiographically.

Concepts Precede Method

There is much more that should be said about ethnographic methods.[13] Not all anthropologists will agree that what we study is the continuing dialogue that holds a given nation, community, or group together or tears it apart. It is what we believe we study, though we have not always called it that. We feel that

---

[11]George Spindler, ed., *The Making of Psychological Anthropology* (Berkeley: Univ. of California Press, 1978), 31-32; and Weston LaBarre in ibid., 270-275.

[12]Louise Spindler, "Researching the Psychology of Culture Change and Urbanization," in *The Making of Psychological Anthropology.*

[13]See Also Michael H. Agar, *The Professional Stranger: An Informal Introduction to Ethnography* (New York: Academic Press, 1980); Frederick Erickson, "What Makes School Ethnography 'Ethnographic'?" *Anthropology and Education Quarterly* 15 (1984): 51-66; James Spradley, *The Ethnographic Interview* (New York: Holt, Rinehart & Winston, 1979); James Spradley, *Participant Observation (New York:* Holt, Rinehart & Winston, 1980); and Harry Wolcott, ed., "Teaching Fieldwork to Educational Researchers: A Symposium," *Anthropology and Education Quarterly* 14(1983):3.

whether we phrase our object of study as culturally constructed dialogue or simply as culture is relatively unimportant, though to us the former seems less static and more processual than the latter. In any event, what we are after is what the native knows and uses in interaction with others in the situations and instrumental relationships his society provides for him. We want to discover meanings and relationships. The power of this position is great and as yet largely unexploited. Education, business, and government would find it very useful if they employed researchers with the *right stuff*, and the right stuff from our point of view requires training and discipline in cultural interpretation as well as research techniques.

We do not think that this power is going to be exploited quickly in any of its potential sectors of operation. Despite some 35 years of intensive work, five major texts in educational anthropology, and the teaching of more than 3,000 graduate students in professional education at Stanford and Wisconsin, we do not feel that we have made a significant dent in the educationist consciousness. Perhaps the sudden popularity of ethnography as a method will result in consciousness-raising, but it will not unless the conceptual structure is carried along with the method.

PART IV

Education and Cultural Process in the United States

Preview

11. GEORGE SPINDLER *Why Have Minority Groups in North America Been Disadvantaged by their Schools?*
12. R.P. McDERMOTT *Achieving School Failure*
13. JOHN HOSTETLER *Education in Communitarian Societies*
14. GEORGE SPINDLER *Beth Anne: A Case Study of Culturally Defined Adjustment and Teacher Perceptions*
15. HARRY WOLCOTT *The Elementary School Principal*
16. MARGARET GIBSON *Playing by the Rules*
17. SHELLEY V. GOLDMAN and R.P. McDERMOTT *The Culture of Competition in American Schools*

PREVIEW

This part of the book contains 6 chapters. The first, by G. Spindler analyzes a broad topic of great importance - the ways in which our schools disadvantage minority students. This is a reversal of a message the public usually asks "why do minority students fail in our schools"? The issue is not one sided and minority students do fail and drop out of our schools in alarming numbers. But they drop out because they failed in our schools and our schools failed them.

As Ray McDermott's chapter shows, the incompatibility between minority children and schools runs deep. Part of the problem is that children and their communities may be so alienated from the school and the mainstream culture they represent that failing becomes a support of self respect. Margaret Gibson shows us that cultural differences alone, however, are not a sufficient cause for school/student failure. Some of the new immigrants in Australia, Britain and the United States manage to do well in school despite obstacles placed in their way by profound cultural and language differences, prejudice and persecution. The obstacles become hurdles for them, that they will successfully negotiate as long as their motivation to do so is kept at a high level. If they eventually find that success in school bears little relationship to success in life their motivation will die. Their relative success is similar to that of the well established Chinese and Japanese Americans.

John Hostetler demonstrates that minority education can take a different form and succeed. By excluding as much of the mainstream culture and educational input as possible, and by managing their own schools, the Amish and Hutterites maintain their own culture and community successfully.

In the next chapter George Spindler analyzes the adjustment of a "well-adjusted mainstream child who turns out not to be so well-adjusted after all. The costs of successful conformity to high level expectations from teachers and parents are the focus.

In Harry Wolcott's chapter on the elementary school principal we learn something about how the principal is expected to play his role and how he is selected to play it. We also learn something more about the ways in which the ethnographer of education does field research.

In "The Culture of Competition in American Schools" Shelley Goldman and Ray McDermott develop a theme that is a central part of the American dialogue. Competition is pervasive in American business, politics, art, mass media, music, sports and the military. It is more than pervasive, it dominates our social, public and personal lives. Schools are competitive—school against school and within each school. Competitive schools prepare children for lives in a competitive society—so what is wrong with that? What is wrong is that schools select some children for success and some for failure, and the stamp of success or failure is for a lifetime. Given the American academic mania for testing, and testing is a special sanction for competition, the school experience can be very damaging for many children, particularly those who start with learning deficiences, as measured by mainstream criteria. Goldman and McDermott develop the theme in three quite different educational contexts.

The Editor

GEORGE D. SPINDLER/*Stanford University*

11 Why Have Minority Groups in North America Been Disadvantaged by Their Schools?*

In Harlem School?

A description of a first-grade class in a black ghetto in New York City follows. It is not a school in the poorest of the districts. It was considered "typical" for the grade.

> The teacher trainee (student teacher) is attempting to teach "rhyming." It is early afternoon. Even before she can get the first "match" (for example, "book" and "look") a whole series of events is drawn out.
>
> One child plays with the head of a doll, which has broken off from the doll, alternately hitting it and kissing it.
>
> The student teacher tells a boy who has left his seat that he is staying in after school. He begins to cry. Another child teases that his mother will be worried about him if he stays in after school. The boy cries even harder and screams at the teacher: "You can't keep me in until 15 o'clock."
>
> A girl tries to answer a question put to the class but raises her hand with her shoe in it. She is told to put her hand down and to put her shoe on.
>
> Another child keeps switching his pencil from one nostril to another, trying to see if it will remain in his nose if he lets go of it; he is apparently wholly unconcerned with the session in progress.
>
> One child is lying down across his desk, pretending to sleep while seeing if the teacher sees him. Just next to him another child leads an imaginary band. Still a different child, on his side, stands quietly beside his seat, apparently tired of sitting.
>
> While this is all going on the regular teacher of the class is out of the room. When she does return, she makes no effort to assist, or criticize, the student teacher. The student teacher later informed me that the regular teacher was not "just being polite." She rarely directed the student teacher, but simply let her "take over" the class on occasion. The student teacher also remarked that things were no different in the class when the regular teacher held forth.

---

*From *Culture in Process,* second edition, by Alan R. Beals, George D. Spindler, and Louise S. Spindler. Copyright © 1967, 1973, by Holt, Rinehart and Winston, Inc. Reprinted by permission of Holt, Rinehart and Winston, Inc.

Fifteen minutes had gone by, but little "rhyming" had been accomplished. A boy begins to shadow box in the back; another talks to himself in acting out a scene he envisions.

Still another child shakes his fist at the student teacher, mimicking her words: "cat-fat, hop-stop."

Two children turn to each other and exchange "burns" on one another's forearms, while another child arranges and rearranges his desk materials and notebook, seemingly dissatisfied with each succeeding arrangement.

A girl in the back has an empty bag of potato chips but is trying to use her fingers as a "blotter" to get at the remnants. She pretends to be paying attention to the lesson.

Another child asks to go to the bathroom, but is denied.

After a half-hour I left (Rosenfeld 1971:105).

As Gerry Rosenfeld, who taught in a Harlem school and did an anthropological field study there, pointed out, the schooling of these children is already patterned for them at the age of six or seven. "Not much is expected from them," they are from poor families, they are black, and they are "disadvantaged." By high school many of them will be dropouts, or "pushouts," as Rosenfeld terms them. As they get older they become less docile than the children described above, and some teachers in ghetto schools have reason to fear for their own safety. The teachers of this classroom did not have reason to fear their pupils, but they were ignorant about them. Their preparatory work in college or in teacher training had not prepared them for a classroom of children from a poor ghetto area in the city. The student teacher knew nothing about the neighborhood from which the children in her class came. She knew only that she "did not want to work with 'these' children when she became a regular teacher" (Rosenfeld, 1970:105).

As a teacher and observer at Harlem School, Rosenfeld found the teachers held an array of myths about poor children that they used to account for their underachievement and miseducation. At the benign liberal level there are beliefs about the nature of poverty and cultural disadvantage. These conditions become accepted as irrevocable givens. The child comes from such a background, therefore, there is nothing I, as a teacher, can do but try to get minimal results from this misshapen material. Among teachers who are explicitly bigoted in their views of the poor and black, the explanations for failure may be less benign. According to Rosenfeld, and his observations are supported by others, an underlying ethos pervades the slum school which prescribes and accepts failure for the child.

Assistant principals function not as experts on curriculum and instruction but as stock boys and disciplinarians. Boxes are constantly being unpacked and children are being reprimanded and punished. The principal seems more concerned with maintaining a stable staff, irrespective of its quality at times, than with effecting school-community ties and fashioning relevant learning programs. Education appears as a process where children are merely the by-products, not the core of concern. Guidance counselors and reading specialists are preoccupied with norms and averages, not with the enhancement of learning for all the children. Theirs is a remedial task, and where one would not exist, they create it. School directives and bulletins are concerned with bathroom regulations and procedures along stairways, the worth of the children being assessed in terms of their ability to conform to these peripheral demands (Rosenfeld 1970:110).

The new teacher, however idealistic he or she may be at first, will be affected by the environment, and becomes a part of the social structure of the school. A socialization process occurs so that personal commitment and philosophy become ordered around the system. The clique structure among staff personnel also forces the newcomer to choose models and cultivate relationships. Communication must occur. There must be others with whom one can commiserate.

Teachers who keep their idealism, tempered as it is after a time by reality, turn more and more inward toward their own classroom. There one sees the results of the years of educational disenchantment. In the middle grades and beyond, the children are already two or more years behind standard achievement norms. The teacher realizes that for the children the school is an oppressive and meaningless place. He comes to understand also that children have developed counterstrategies for what they have perceived as their teachers' indifference, confusion, despair, and in some cases, outright aggression. But if the teacher persists in the effort to understand his or her pupils, eventually they become individuals. Most are alert and active. They are potentially high learners and achievers. Some are subdued and permanently detached. Some are irrevocably hostile towards schools, teachers, and white people. Others have surface hostilities but are willing to give trust and confidence when it is justified. Some are fast learners with strong curiosity and an eagerness to learn about the world. Others are apathetic or simply dull. Once the children become individuals, with sharp differences, they can no longer be treated as objects or as a collectivity.

The next step for the teacher who is going to become effective as a cultural transmitter and agent of socialization, as all teachers are, is to learn something of the neighborhood and of the homes from which the children come. But this is a step that is rarely taken. Rosenfeld describes the situation at Harlem School.

> Though Harlem School belonged to the neighborhood, it was not psychologically a part of it. On the contrary, teachers felt unwanted, estranged. Perhaps this was why few ventured off the "beaten paths" to the "hinterland" beyond the school, into the side streets and the homes where the children played out their lives. Some teachers at Harlem School had never been to a single child's household, despite the fact that they had been employed at the school for many years. Nothing was known of community self-descriptions, the activity and social calendar in the neighborhood, the focal points for assembly and dispersal, or the feelings of residents toward the "outside world." Teachers could not imagine that they could foster a genuine coming-together of neighborhood persons and

themselves. They hid behind their "professionalism." They failed to realize that the apathy and disparagement they associated with parents were attributed by the latter to them. It is not to be underestimated how "foreign" teachers feel themselves to be at Harlem School, how disliked by the children. Why then do they remain on the job? Part of the answer is in the fact that the rewards of one's work are not always sought on the job itself, but in the private world. Teachers have little stake in the communities in which they work; that is why it may be necessary to link more closely teachers' jobs and children's achievement. It is my guess that all children (except those with proven defects) would achieve if teachers' jobs depended on this (Rosenfeld 1970:103).

It is clear that there are some parallels between the relationship of the school and teachers to the pupils and community in minority populations in the United States and the like relationship that has developed in many of the modernizing nations. Although there are profound differences in the two situations, the similarity is that the educational institutions in both cases are intrusive. These institutions stem from a conceptual and cultural context that is different from that of the people whose children are in the schools. This tends to be true whether "natives" or aliens are utilized as teachers and administrators for the schools. In the modernizing populations, as among the Sisala, the teacher, even though Sisala himself, is alien by virtue of his having been educated, removed from his community, socialized to norms, values, competencies, and purposes that are not a part of his community's culture (Grindal 1972). He is a member of a different class, for which there is as yet no clear place in the Sisala cultural system. He feels isolated from the community, and this isolation is reinforced by the character of the school in which he teaches. In Harlem School, or its prototypes, the teacher tends to be an alien whether he is white or black. Even among black teachers only some can maintain or acquire an identification with the people and community in which the school exists. The same processes of socialization and alienation that have taken place for the Sisala teacher have taken place for the black teacher in the United States. This is particularly true for the black teacher who comes from a middle-class background to begin with, then goes on to the university for advanced training. This teacher may be as far removed from the black community in a slum school as any white teacher. Of course not all black communities are in slums, but the slum school is the one we have been talking about.

At Rosepoint?

The interactions we are describing between school and culture occur elsewhere than in the urban slum. Martha Ward describes a community in what she calls Rosepoint, near New Orleans (1971). Rosepoint is a very small rural community, a former plantation occupied now by some of the people who worked on it, plus others. Rosepoint has its own culture—that of the black South together with a heavy French influence characteristic of the area as a whole, and the unique ecological characteristics of a community built along a levee of the Mississippi River. Martha Ward was particularly concerned with language learning and linguistic features. She found that there were many substantial differences in speech and learning to speak between Rosepoint adults and children and white people. These differences contribute to the separation between community and school, which is the focus of our attention, since the school is taught mostly by whites, although they are by no means the sole cause of this separation.

Rosepoint parents believe that most of the teachers in the schools their children attend—black or white—are authoritarian and punitive. They also see that their children attending white schools for the first time are subjected to discriminatory practices, sometimes subtle, sometimes very obvious. There is little communication between the home and the school, whether primary or high school. Parents have little notion how the school is run, what their children are taught, or how to cooperate with the school or teachers. And the schools show no understanding of the social problems or cultural characteristics of Rosepoint. The conflicts are profound. The irrelevancy of the school for most Rosepoint children is measured by a high dropout rate and low rates of literacy. From about eleven years of age on, states Martha Ward, staying in school is a touch-and-go proposition, especially for males. She describes certain characteristics of the school environment and expectations that are at odds with those of the Rosepoint children.

> The school creates for the Rosepoint child an environment not as much unpleasant as unnatural. For years he has been determining his own schedule for eating, sleeping, and playing. The content of his play is unsupervised and depends on the child's imagination. His yard does not contain sand boxes, swings, clay, paints, nor personnel obliged to supervise his play. At school, however, play is supervised, scheduled, and centers around objects deemed suitable for young minds. There are firm schedules for playing, napping, eating, and "learning and studying" (with the implication that learning will occur only during the time allotted for it). The authority buttressing even minimal schedules is impersonal and inflexible with an origin not in face-to-face social relationships but in an invisible bureaucracy.
>
> Moreover, the Rosepoint home relies on verbal communication rather than on the written word as a medium. Adults do not read to children nor encourage writing. Extraverbal communication such as body movements or verbal communication such as storytelling or gossip are preferred to the printed page. The lack of money to purchase books, magazines, and newpapers partly explains this. . . . [sentence omitted] . . . for children of a culture rich in in-group lore and oral traditions the written word is a pallid substitute.
>
> Another conflict arising out of the home-school discrepancy is language— specifically, "bad" language. Remember, the Rosepoint child is rewarded for linguistic creativity . . . [three sentences omitted]

In the classroom such language has an entirely different interpretation on it. Some educators discretely refer to it as "the M-F problem."[1] [sentence omitted] A nine-year-old girl was given a two-week suspension from classes for saying a four-letter word. This was her first recorded transgression of the language barrier. The second offense may be punished by expulsion . . . [two sentences omitted to end of paragraph] (Ward 1971:91–92).

The problems of Rosepoint and the schools that are intended to serve it are probably less overtly intense than those of Harlem School, its staff, and the community, but they are closely related to each other, and in turn to the problems of education among the Sisala, the Kanuri, and in Malitbog. The school in all of these situations is intrusive and the teachers are aliens. Resentment, conflict, and failures are present in communication from all sides.

We should be very careful here to realize that what we have been describing is not a problem of black minority populations alone. To some extent the disarticulation described between the school and community will be characteristic in any situation where the teachers and school stem from a different culture or subculture than that of the pupils and their parents. There is disarticulation between any formal school and the community, even where the school and community are not culturally divergent. Conflicts ensue when the school and teachers are charged with responsibility for assimilating or acculturating their pupils to a set of norms for behavior and thought that are different from those learned at home and in the community.

Education for minorities in North America is complicated by a variety of hazards. Harlem School operates in a depressing slum environment. No one wants to go there and the people there would like to get out. The conflicts and disarticulation germane to the school-community situation we have described are made more acute and destructive because of this. Rosepoint and its schools have their special circumstances also. The Rosepoint population has inherited the culture and outlook of a former plantation slave population. They are close to the bottom of the social structure. The teachers, particularly if they are white, have inherited attitudes toward black people from the South's past. Let us look for a moment at a quite different place and people, the Indians of the Yukon Territory of Canada and the Mopass Residential School.

In the Mopass Residential School?

The children who come to this school represent several different tribes from quite a wide area of northwestern Canada. Many of these tribal societies adapted quickly to the fur trade economy that developed soon after the first white men arrived and many became heavily acculturated to the other aspects

---

[1] Refers to the use of obscenities in the school, including "Motherfucker."

of European culture. One could not say that on the whole the Native Americans of this area resisted the alien culture. In fact, they welcomed many of its technological and material advantages. As the northern territories have been opened for rapid development during the past decade, however, the Native Americans already there have found it increasingly difficult to find a useful and rewarding place in this expanding economy. The reasons for this are altogether the fault of neither the white Canadians nor the Indians, but certainly prejudice has played a role. One of the serious problems of the Indians, however, has been that, on the whole, they have had neither the skills that could be used in the expanding economy nor the basic education upon which to build these skills. The task of the school would seem to be that of preparing young Native Americans[2] to take a productive and rewarding role in the economy and society now emerging in the Northwest Territories. This is what it is like at Mopass Residential School, according to Richard King, who taught there for a year and did anthropological observations during that period.

> For the children, the residential school constitutes a social enclave almost totally insulated from the community within which it functions; yet Mopass School reflects in a microcosmic, but dismayingly faithful, manner the social processes of the larger society. Two distinct domains of social interaction exist independently: Whiteman society and Indian society. Where these domains overlap, they do so with common purposes shared at the highest level of abstraction — but with minimal congruence of purposes, values, and perceptions, at the operating levels of interaction. The Whiteman maintains his social order according to his own perceptions of reality. The Indian bears the burden of adaptation to a social order that he may perceive more realistically — and surely he perceives it with a different ordering of reality — than does the Whiteman. From his perceptions the Indian finds it impossible to accept the social order and, at the same time, impossible to reject it completely. He therefore creates an artificial self to cope with the unique interactive situations.
>
>   In the residential school, the Whiteman staff and teachers are the end men of huge bureaucratic organizations (church and national government) that are so organized as to provide no reflection of the local communities. These employees derive their social, economic, and psychological identity from the organizations of which they are members. . . . [four sentences omitted]
>   . . . The children of the school are little more than components to be manipulated in the course of the day's work. . . . No job at school is defined in terms of *outcomes,* expected, or observable, in children (King 1970:89–90).

King goes on to describe the factionalism among the adult faculty and staff in the school. He suggests that many of the people who take teaching jobs in the residential school are deviant or marginal personalities, and that the isolation of the school, and its nature as a closed system, tend to create a

---

[2] The term *Native Americans* is preferred by many American Indians. We use Indian and Native American interchangeably in recognition of this preference.

tense interpersonal situation. The children have to adjust to this as well as to the alien character of the institution itself.

> The school children become uniquely adept at personality analysis, since their major task is to cope with the demands of shifting adult personalities. But this analysis is limited to their needs as the children perceive them in specific situations (King 1967:88).

An artificial self is developed by the Indian child to cope with the total situation in which he finds himself. King says that the children sustain themselves with the conviction that their "real self" is not this person in the school at all. Through this, and other processes, the barriers between Whiteman and Indian are firmly developed

> not so much by a conscious rejection on the part of the Whiteman as by a conscious rejection on the part of the Indian child. The sterile shallowness of the adult model presented by the school Whitemen serves only to enhance—and probably to romanticise—memories of attachments in the child's primary family group, and to affirm a conviction prevalent among the present adult Indian generation that Indians must strive to maintain an identity separate from Whitemen (King 1967:88).

There is much more we could say about the social and learning environment that this school provided[3] the Indian children who attended it. King's case study should be read in order to understand it more thoroughly, for it is a startling example of miseducation—and with the best of intentions on the part of the sponsoring organizations and the teaching and administrative personnel of the school itself. All the features of disarticulation, isolation and nonrelatedness we have ascribed to the other schools discussed are present, but in a special and distorted form because the school is a closed residential institution even more removed from the community that it is intended to serve than the other schools. It is also a church school, run by the Episcopalian church for the Canadian government. Its curriculum is even less relevant to the Native American children who attend it than the curriculum of the Sisala school was to the Sisala children, for it is the same curriculum that is used in other Canadian schools at the same grade level. It appears that the Mopass Residential School intends to recruit children into the white culture and a religious faith (since religious observances and education are a regular part of the school life). It fails in these purposes and, in fact, creates new barriers to this recruitment and reinforces old ones. More serious by far is the fact that it does not prepare the children who attend it to cope with the new economy and society emerging in the north. The children leave the

---

[3] The school was closed in 1969. The "ethnographic present" is used in this description to be consistent with the other analyses.

school without necessary basic skills, alienated from what they see as white culture, alienated from themselves, and nonrelated to their own communities. This kind of schooling creates marginal people.[4]

Is There a Way Out of the Dilemma?

In the discussion so far we have dealt only with minority peoples who have had to operate in what some would describe as an essentially colonial situation. That is, they may have the theoretical rights of self-determination and self-regulation, but, in fact, do not and could not exercise these rights. There are now strong movements underway towards self-determination. Some are very militant, separatistic, and nationalistic. Others are more accommodative. But all share in striving for self-determination, and regulation of the schools is an important aspect of this determination. These people recognize, perhaps in different terms, what we have said—that education is a process of recruitment and maintenance for the cultural system. For minority people the schools have been experienced as damaging attempts to recruit their children into an alien culture. Their self-images and identities were ignored, or actively attacked.

There are some minority communities that have successfully resolved the problem. They have done so by creating and maintaining a closed cultural system that maintains a more or less defensive relationship toward the rest of the society. The Old Order Amish and the Hutterites are good examples of this solution. Both are nonaggressive pacifistic peoples, communal in orientation, and socioreligious in ideology and charter.

Amish communities are distributed principally throughout Pennsylvania, Ohio, and Indiana but are also found in several other states. The total Old Order Amish population is estimated at about 60,000. They are agrarian, use horsepower for agricultural work and transportation, and wear rather somber but distinctive dress. They strive to cultivate humility and simple living. Their basic values include the following: separation from the world; voluntary acceptance of high social obligations symbolized by adult baptism; the maintenance of a disciplined church-community; excommunication and shunning as a means of dealing with erring members and of keeping the church pure; and a life of harmony with the soil and nature—it is believed that nature is a garden and man was able to be a caretaker, not an exploiter. The goals of education are to instill the above values in every Amish child and maintain,

---

[4] Mopass Residential School is neither better nor worse than other residential schools for Native Americans because it is Episcopalian, and certainly not because it is Canadian. Most of the same conditions exist in residential schools in both the United States and Canada, in Protestant, Catholic, and non-denominational schools.

therefore, the Amish way of life. John Hostetler and Gertrude Huntington describe the concept of a true education from the Amish point of view.

> True education, according to the Amish, is "the cultivation of humility, simple living, and resignation to the will of God." For generations the group has centered its instruction in reading, writing, arithmetic, and the moral teachings of the Bible. They stress training for life participation (here and for eternity) and warn of the perils of "pagan" philosophy and the intellectual enterprises of "fallen man," as did their forefathers. Historically, the Anabaptist avoided all training associated with self-exaltation, pride of position, enjoyment of power, and the arts of war and violence. Memorization, recitation, and personal relationships between teacher and pupil were part of a system of education that was supremely social and communal (1971:9).

Realizing that state consolidation of schools constituted a severe threat to the continuity of their way of life and basic values, the Amish built the first specifically Amish School in 1925. By 1970 there were over three hundred such schools with an estimated enrollment of ten thousand pupils. When the population of the United States was predominantly rural and the major occupation was farming, the Amish people had no serious objections to public schooling. In the rural school of fifty years ago in most of the United States a curriculum much like that of the present Amish school was followed, the teacher was a part of the community, and the school was governed locally. Consolidation of schools in order to achieve higher educational standards shifted control away from the local area and the educational innovations that followed were unacceptable to the Amish. The Amish insist that their children attend schools near their homes so that they can participate in the life of the community and learn to become farmers. They also want qualified teachers committed to Amish values. Teachers who are merely qualified by state standards may be quite incapable of teaching the Amish way of life or providing an example of this way of life by the way they themselves live. The Amish also want to have their children educated in the basic skills of reading, writing, and arithmetic but training beyond that, they feel, should be related directly to the Amish religion and way of life. They do not agree with what they perceive to be the goals of the public schools, ". . . to impart worldly knowledge, to insure earthly success, and to make good citizens for the state." Ideally, from the Amish point of view, formal schooling should stop at about age fourteen, though learning continues throughout life. They feel that further schooling is not only unnecessary but detrimental to the successful performance of adult Amish work roles. The Amish pay for and manage their own schools in order to attain these goals (Hostetler and Huntington 1971:35–38).

Naturally there have been serious conflicts with state authorities about the schools. Forcible removal of the children from Amish communities has been attempted in some cases, and harassment in legal and interpersonal forms has characterized the relationship of state authority to the Amish in respect to the problem of education. The Amish have doggedly but non-violently resisted all attempts to make them give up their own schools, for they realize that these schools are essential to the continuance of their cultural system. They have made accommodations where they could, as for instance in providing "vocational" schooling beyond elementary school to meet state educational age requirements concerning duration of schooling.

The Amish story is one that anyone interested in the processes and consequences of separatism should know about. Hostetler and Huntington's study is a good up-to-date overview that presents the case for the community-relevant school clearly and objectively and with a sympathetic understanding of the Amish point of view and lifeway.

The Hutterite culture is similar in many ways to that of the Old Order Amish, as seen from the outside, although the Hutterites are more communal in their economic organization and they used advanced agricultural machinery as well as trucks and occasionally cars. Hutterites are Anabaptists, like the Amish and the Mennonites, originating during the Protestant Reformation in the sixteenth century in the Austrian Tyrol and Moravia. They arrived in South Dakota in 1874 and have prospered since. There are about 18,000 Hutterites living on more than 170 colonies in the western United States and Canada. They are noted for their successful large-scale farming, large families, and effective training of the young.

Hutterites are protected from the outside world by an organized belief system which offers a solution to their every need, although they, like the Amish, have been subjected to persecution and harassment from the outside. The community minimizes aggression and dissension of any kind. Colony members strive to lose their self-identity by surrendering themselves to the communal will and attempt to live each day in preparation for death, and, hopefully, heaven. The principle of order is the key concept underlying Hutterite life. Order is synonymous with eternity and godliness; even the orientation of colony buildings conforms to directions measured with the precision of a compass. There is a proper order for every activity, and time is neatly divided into the sacred and the secular. In the divine hierarchy of the community each individual member has a place — male over female, husband over wife, older over younger, and parent over child. The outsider asks, "Why does this order work? How can it be maintained?" The implicit Hutterite answer is that "Hutterite society is a school, and the school is a society." The Hutterites, like the Old Amish, do not value education as a means toward self-improvement but as a means of "planting" in children "the knowledge and fear of God" (Hostetler and Huntington 1967).

We will not go into detail concerning Hutterite schools. Although they differ somewhat from the Amish schools in curriculum and style, particularly in being more strict and "authoritarian," the basic principles are the same. The Hutterites also understand that they must retain control of their schools and teachers if they are to retain their separatistic and particularly their communal and socioreligious way of life. They do this by retaining a "German school" that is in effect superimposed upon the "English school" required by the state or provincial law. The two schools have rather different curricula and teachers and of the two the former is clearly the one that carries the burden of cultural transmission that recruits youngsters into the Hutterite cultural system and helps maintain that system most directly.

The Hutterites serve as another example of how to solve the problem faced by the Sisala, the people of Malitbog, the Kanuri, the children of Harlem School and their parents, the people of Rosepoint, and the children in the Mopass Residential School.

The problem all of these people face is how to relate a culture-transmitting institution that is attempting to recruit their children to a cultural system different from that of the community, class, area, or minority from which the children come. The school and teacher are alien in all of these cases, and they are charged, by governments or the dominant population, with the responsibility of changing the way of life by changing the children. Understandably the consequences are at least disruptive, and at worst tragic.

The Hutterities and Amish have done exactly what is logical according to the anthropologist viewing the relationship between education and culture. Realizing the threat to the continuity of their way of life from the outside world, particularly from schooling and transmission of concepts and views alien to their fundamental principles, they have taken control of their schools to whatever extent they can, given the exigencies of survival in contemporary North America. The schools are so ordered as to recruit and help maintain the traditional cultural system. They are successful. The way of life, beleaguered though it is in both cases, survives, in fact, flourishes.

It is important to understand, however, that, from another point of view, the cost of this success is too great. The result of success is a closed cultural system in a defensive relationship to the rest of society. That there are restrictions on personal behavior, sharp limits on self-expression, and confinement in the very thought processes and world view in both cases, is undeniable. The values of spontaneity, individual creativity, discovery and invention, pursuit of knowledge, and innovation, that are important to men elsewhere, are not values in these or any other closed cultural systems. There is also a kind of self-created disadvantage imposed by the Hutterites and Amish upon themselves. Since they lack higher education, in fact are opposed to it, and control as vigorously as possible the context of primary education, they cannot participate fully in the give and take of our dynamic society. True, they do not want to, but it is a hard choice, and one that could be very disadvantageous to any minority group. Somehow the modernizing peoples of the world emerging from a tribal and then colonial past, and the minority peoples in vast societies like the United States and Canada, must balance the consequences of a closed system and the educational institutions to support it, and an open system and the educational institutions to support it. It is clear, however, that it is necessary for all peoples to exercise and develop the rights of self-determination and self-regulation in education, as well as in other areas of life. It may be that this can be done without creating closed, defensive, and confining cultural systems. It may help for us all to realize that we actually have little control over what happens in our schools, no matter who we are. The educational bureaucracy in a complex urban system functions in some ways like an alien cultural system in relation to the local community, the children in school, and their parents, whether these parents and children are members of minority or majority groups. We all have this problem in common. In this age of cultural pluralism in the United States it is difficult to discern what else we all have in common. Perhaps it is possible to agree that there are some competencies all children should acquire, such as functional literacy, concepts of mathematical processes, and so forth, that are necessary if they are not to be severely handicapped in later life in a complex society. But in the area of specific values, ideologies, and world views we cannot repeat the mistakes of the past, when we assumed that the melting pot would melt all ethnic differences down to the same blendable elements. The cultures of the American Indians, Afro-Americans, Mexican Americans, and Asian-Americans did not disappear as our ideology said they would. The challenge is to recognize and accept the differences without creating disadvantageous separatism or segregation, whether self-imposed or imposed from the dominant group. There are many paradoxes in the relationships we are discussing, and they are not easily resolved.

References

Grindal, Bruce T., 1972, *Growing Up in Two Worlds: Education and Transition among the Sisala of Northern Ghana.* CSEC. New York: Holt, Rinehart and Winston, Inc.

Hostetler, John A., and Gertrude E. Huntington, 1967, *The Hutterites in North America.* CSCA. New York: Holt, Rinehart and Winston, Inc.

Hostetler, John A., and Gertrude E. Huntington, 1971, *Children in Amish Society: Socialization and Community Education.* CSEC. New York: Holt, Rinehart and Winston, Inc.

King, A. Richard, 1967, *The School at Mopass: A Problem of Identity.* CSEC. New York: Holt, Rinehart and Winston, Inc.

Rosenfeld, Gerry, 1971 (reissued 1983), *"Shut Those Thick Lips!" A Study of Slum School Failure.* Prospect Heights, Illinois: Waveland Press, Inc.

Ward, Martha C., 1971 (reissued 1986), *Them Children: A Study in Language Learning.* Prospect Heights, Illinois: Waveland Press, Inc.

RAY McDERMOTT/*Teachers College*

12   *Achieving School Failure: An Anthropological Approach to Illiteracy and Social Stratification*

Abstract

The mixture of intelligent, socially competent children from a low status minority or pariah community and hard working, well-intentioned teachers from a host or dominant community can bring about the same disastrous school records achieved by either neurologically disabled children or socially disabled, prejudiced teachers. Students and teachers in a pariah-host population mix usually produce communicative breakdowns by simply performing routine and practical everyday activities in ways their subcultures define as normal and appropriate. Because behavioral competence is differently defined by different social groups, many children and teachers fail in their attempts to establish rational, trusting and rewarding relationships across ethnic, racial or class boundaries in the classroom. As a result of this miscommunication, school learning is shunned by many minority children, and school failure becomes a peer group goal. The high rate of reading disabilities among minority children can be explained in terms of such miscommunication. The difficulty is usually neither "dumb kids" nor "racist teachers," but cultural conflict.

Introduction

This chapter is divided into four sections. The first defines a problem and asks a question. The problem is that children from minority communities appear to regenerate their parents' pariah status by learning how to act in

Comments on an earlier draft of this chapter were generously offered by Eric Arrow, Jacob Bilmes, Nancie Gonzalez, Robert McDermott, Harry Singer, and Stanley Wanat. I am most heavily indebted to Henry Beck, Harumi Befu, Charles Frake, Karl Pribram, and George Spindler for constant stimulation, encouragement and constructive criticism during the past two years. Even with their excellent counsel, however, the paper may harbor errors for which I am alone responsible.

ways condemned by the larger host community. The question asks where this learning comes from and whether or not it represents a rational adaptation to socialization attempts by host schools.

The second section examines the production of pariah-host social organizations in terms of what both pariah and host members must know about the daily business of treating each other as pariahs and hosts. Early experiences in the politics of everyday life determine the categories children develop for use in deciding how to act in similar situations at future times. In other words, the politics of everyday life socialize the identities, statuses and abilities of children and, as such, are the source of the persistence of social organizations, including pariah groups, across generations.

The third section discusses an example. Specifically, the social organization of learning to read in a host teacher and pariah student classroom is examined in terms of the politics of everyday life. For black American children in white-administered schools, it is argued that competence in reading and competence in classroom politics are inversely proportional. Inability to read is positively condemned by the host population and assures oppression and the assignment of pariah status by the host community. Nevertheless, not learning to read is accompanied by all the social skills essential to a peer-defined political success within the classroom. In peer group terms, it represents more of an achievement than a disability. Accordingly, the hypothesis examined is that a significant number of what are usually described as reading disabilities represent situationally induced inattention patterns which make sense in terms of the politics of the interethnic classroom. Pariah children learn not to read as one way of acquiring high status and strong identity in a host classroom.

The fourth section describes a starting point for culturally induced learning disabilities in terms of cultural or communicative code differences and conflicts. Specifically, it is hypothesized that minor differences in communicative codes can lead to disasters in everyday life. On the basis of communicative code conflicts, teachers classify their students into ability groups. Although in no way related in the first grade to potential reading or social leadership skills, the teacher's classificatory schema has great influence as a self-fulfilling prophecy. Many pariah children adapt to the senseless and degrading relational messages given them by unknowing teachers with different communicative codes by shutting down their attention skills in response to teacher tasks such as reading. Communicative code conflicts between black children and white teachers are discussed in detail, and the high rate of black school failure is tentatively explained.

The Ontogeny of Pariah Minorities

Most modern nations harbor one or more *pariah groups* "actively rejected by the host population because of behavior or characteristics positively condemned" by host group standards (Barth 1969:31). Host standards can be violated by an absurd collection of traits ranging from skin color and occupational specialties to culinary and sexual preferences. What is interesting is the persistence of both host group standards and pariah groups across generations. Even in the face of efforts by modern states to subdue the arbitrary and oppressive standards of host groups and to accommodate minority behavior patterns by programs of rationalization and equalization, pariah groups endure. For example, America has blacks, Native Americans, and Hispanic people; Japan has the Koreans (Mitchell 1967) and the racially indistinct Burakamin (DeVos and Wagatsuma 1966); Norway, the Lapps (Eidheim 1969); Northern Ireland, the Catholics; India, the outcasts; and Israel, the Oriental Jews. In all these groups, each generation of children will renew their parents' life styles, apparently oblivious to the condemnation and oppression that pariah status vis-à-vis the host group will bring down upon their heads.

How does this happen? How is pariah status acquired by each new generation? Despite years of special education, minority American children continue to speak low esteem dialects, fail in school, and attain occupational specialties which run afoul of public morality and legality. Apparently, the acquisition of pariah behavior patterns is a very complex process rooted in everyday life and is not going to be altered by formal training in a classroom for a few hours a week. Indeed, most pariah behavior patterns need not be altered. Black language, for example, bears a pariah label, but it is a perfectly efficient mode of communication with special social functions within the black community (Labov 1969). To treat it as an inferior or deprived language is wrong. To meddle with its use by way of a language arts program in order to homogenize it with the host language is not only wrong, but also naive. It indicates that we understand very little about how people acquire models of and guides to behavior in their own society and how these models are used to generate social structures complete with stratification. This chapter will attempt a better understanding of the acquisition of social structure (Cicourel 1970a)—how children acquire what has to be known in order to act in a culturally or subculturally appropriate way in specific social situations (Frake 1962, 1973).

Two positions are usually taken on the acquisition of pariah social status. To the distant observer and the pariah group member, it seems an obvious case of host populations working to defeat the efforts of each and every pariah child to break the degradation that bonds him without reason from his first day out of the womb. The child is simply tagged as he enters the world in such a way that the tag is available for all to see. Negative differential behavior is then applied to all the tagged regardless of acquired skills. Racial markers can, of course, do this job most efficiently: witness black America. Similar systems have been attempted without racial markers. Tattooing is one possibility. The Japanese of the Tokugawa era attempted another by having all members of the pariah Burakumin wear leather squares on the outside of all their garments (Cornell 1970). The point is that pariah children are made visible to all, defined as deviant because of their visibility, and treated badly as a result.

There is good reason for viewing the ascriptive system just described as too simple a representation of the acquisition of a particular status in a social structure. First, such clear-cut boundaries between host and pariah groups are seldom defined. Racial boundaries are not available in most societies in which there are pariah group problems. In fact, most observers must live in an area for a long time before they can start distinguishing between groups. The codes are subtle. Religion, language, dress and the minutiae of nonverbal communication very often function as markers for ascription. Even where biological boundaries can be drawn, as may be the case for outcastes in India, it takes either a native's eye or an anthropometrist's calipers to do the job (Beteille 1972). In such cases, identification involves much social work on the part of the interactants. The host population must be keyed to spotting certain cues, and the pariah population must in some way send off the cues which will allow them to be identified and abused.

A second problem with viewing status ascription as a simple tagging process is that in most contemporary societies such overt ascription is frowned upon by both legal constitutions and popular ideologies. Formal organizations which operate according to ascriptive criteria are officially prohibited. Japan and America stand out as two countries which have done a great deal to minimize overt ascription with universal schooling and uniform testing procedures for the placement of personnel in both the public and private sectors of their economies (Azumi 1969; Parsons 1959). Yet pariah boundaries remain firm, even within the school systems themselves (Shimahara 1971; Cicourel and Kitsuse 1963). Again it appears that something more than ascription is going on. How else could it be that, even after the demise of formal institutional powers to identify and operate against pariah people, pariah groups survive? The host population does not simply slot a child on the basis of its parentage and then keep a careful eye out for the child so that he never advances a slot. Rather, it seems as if the child must learn how to do it himself; he must learn a way of acting normally which the host population will be able to condemn according to the criteria the hosts have learned for evaluating, albeit arbitrarily, their own normal behavior. Pariah status appears almost as achieved as ascribed.

An alternative to the distant observer's view of the acquisition of pariah social status is the view of a host population native who usually sees in pariahs an obvious case of inferior persons begetting inferior persons. The argument is that pariah children acquire their low status because they are inferior. Unfortunately, each new pariah generation often reaffirms the soundness of the host's classificatory schema by apparently learning the codes of behavior essential to the schema's maintenance. Although there is no evidence that host classifications are accurate assessments of the natural order of people and their abilities, the host perception of pariah group behavior may not always be totally blinded by prejudice. Hosts may merely see what is there for them to see given the standards of evaluation that they use uniformly on all people regardless of race or ethnic identity. The question is, how is it that what is there for them to see is in fact there?

Consider an extreme example. The Burakumin minority in Japan has suffered a long history of political suppression due to its participation in condemned occupational specialties (Ninomiya 1933). Since the formal breakdown of the caste system during the Mejii Restoration a century ago, many Burakumin have attempted unsuccessfully to pass into the mainstream of Japanese life. At present, they are physically, linguistically, religiously, and, for the most part, occupationally indistinct from other Japanese. They can be discovered only on the basis of either their present or past residence in known Burakumin ghettos. Accordingly, most Japanese teachers are unaware of a child's Burakumin status in the early grades (Shimahara 1971). Yet, by puberty, a Burakumin identity will be visible and of increasing importance, as there is an increasing differential in the performances of Burakumin as opposed to non-Burakumin pupils. They lag behind on I.Q. and achievement tests and daily attendance, and they are the first to engage in delinquent activities (DeVos and Wagatsuma 1966; Brameld 1968). How does host group prejudice work against an invisible group? Obviously, it does not. It may be that unconscious host group standards work against Burakumin children in some subtle ways, however, for the children are eventually made visible, sorted out and condemned. But this is not obvious to a liberal and enlightened Japanese teacher, who, through no apparent fault of his own, winds up doing exactly the same job that a prejudiced teacher might do: he winds up failing many more Burakumin than non-Burakumin. The host-group stand appears strong. The teacher has only reacted to what was available for him to see, namely, obviously inferior performances by many Burakumin children. Again, pariah status seems almost as achieved as ascribed.

This Burakumin example sheds great light on this ascription versus inherent acquisition issue. The Burakumin child experiences teachers as prejudiced beings who inflict failing biographies on Burakumin children. The children are perhaps correct given the subtleties of interclass or interethnic communication. They are incorrect in viewing their school records as products of a blind ascription, for their invisibility protects them from such a fate. Host teachers have equally confusing experiences with school failure. They are correct in not assuming complete blame for the high rate of Burakumin school failure. Nevertheless, they are incorrect in viewing school failure as the result of an inherent acquisition, the unfolding of an inferior genetic stock or, at best, the unfolding of an inferior socialization process that leaves the child deprived. First, the Burakumin do not represent a gene pool (Taira 1971). Second, the social disadvantage perspective is almost as simplistic as the ascription stand, for it has never been able to account for how children with failing school records do so well in complex settings outside of school. Learning to talk and learning to behave sensibly in everyday life are far more complex than the tasks learned in school, and most so-called disadvantaged children excel at both, at least to the extent that such children have been carefully studied. Disadvantage is indeed a too simple, and often biased, account of minority school failure. Burakumin children do not come to school disadvantaged; they leave school disadvantaged. The question is, without some ascriptive mechanism working against them, how does this school failure and consequent disadvantage come about? In other words, if neither ascription nor inherent acquisition can completely account for pariah school failure, then how can the acquisition of pariah status be conceived?

A third position is possible. From their respective vantage points, both the pariah and the host groups are correct. To the pariah group, host behavior is indeed oppressive. To the host group, pariah behavior is indeed inadequate. If we understand how the two groups find this out about each other, we will have located the central problem. What is it that pariah people do that has host people react in oppressive ways, even if they do not want to be oppressive? And what is it that host people do that has pariah people react in antithesis to host expectations, even as they struggle to behave adequately according to host standards? If such misunderstandings take place very often in the early grades, the results can be disastrous. Once a host teacher treats a child as inadequate, the child will find the teacher oppressive. Often, once a child finds a teacher oppressive, the child will start behaving inadequately. After such a point, relations between the child and the teacher regress—the objectionable behavior of each will feed back negatively into the objectionable behavior of the other.

It is in this context that a third position makes sense: a child must achieve his pariah status. It is neither ascribed to the child nor naturally acquired by him in the sense that puberty is acquired. First, some form of miscommunication between a child and his teacher must take place. If this is not repaired quickly, a mutually destructive or regressive one-to-one relationship (Scheflen 1960) will be established between the teacher and the child. When teacher-student communication is complicated by interethnic code differences, regressive relations occur with enough frequency to result in the children forming alternatives to the teacher's organization of the classroom. Within the confines of these new social organizations, the children work at becoming visible. As a result, they leave themselves open to even further condemnation. The teacher's role as the administrator in charge of failure becomes dominant. And the children's revolt grows. School work gets caught in this battle, and a high rate of school failure results. A great deal of social work must be performed by both teachers and students in order for so many failures to occur. Whether the records list all passing or all failing grades, student records represent achievements in the sense that many difficult battles in the politics of everyday life had to be fought in their making. Teachers do not simply ascribe minority children to failure. Nor do minority children simply drag failure along, either genetically or socially, from the previous generation. Rather, it must be worked out in every classroom, every day, by every teacher and every child in their own peculiar ways.

Viewing school failure as an achievement implies that school failure can be understood as a rational adaptation by children to human relations in host schools. The rest of this chapter will be aimed at showing just that. The next section will consider, theoretically, how human relations are worked out face-to-face in the classroom. These relations have fantastic implications for the social organization of the classroom—who gets to interact with whom, when, and about what and who gets to learn from whom, when, and about what. In short, face-to-face relations help to organize status and abilities in the classroom. In the last two sections, the interference of interethnic human relations on learning to read is examined for black Americans.

The Social Organization of Status and the Politics of Everyday Life

It is considered a social fact (although actually it is either a native or a professional sociological model, but it is always treated as a fact) that there are different groups in the social organizations of modern states, and some of these are defined as pariah groups. It is this social fact that most social scientists want to explain. Beneath this fact, however, there are many other facts made of the little stuff of everyday life that helps produce larger social facts or patterns available for observation. A social organization is not a thing in itself as Durkheim would have us believe. Rather, it is an accomplishment, the product of great work in the everyday life of innumerable social actors. The term "social organization" is a shorthand term for the organization of social actions performed by social actors (Garfinkel 1956:181; cf. also, Miller, Galanter, and Pribram, 1960:98). The term social organization glosses all the hard work of social actors attempting to deal with each other. It hides all the achievements of everyday life. Social organizations are daily accomplishments, daily products of actors working out rational ways of dealing with each other.

If a social organization shows a division into pariah and host groups, then this is a division produced in everyday life; in their daily dealings, pariah and host people must classify each other into different groups and then treat each other in accordance with the dictates of their classification. Such a division cannot be taken by itself as a topic of our inquiry, for it is a mere gloss of the social acts that make it look like a fact. We must go deeper and ask how this fact is available for seeing and naming by either host or pariah members or the ethnographer. Let us examine, then, not the fact of such pariah-host relationships, the resource, but the fact of that fact, the topic; let us ask how it is that the persons involved in such relationships manage to organize and produce such relationships and to take them as the substance of everyday life (Beck 1972); let us "examine not the factual properties of status hierarchies, but the *fact* of the factual properties of status hierarchies" (Zimmerman and Pollner 1970:83). How is it then that host and pariah people, and the sociologists who study them, come to see their existence as related groups as facts?

The question we started with was how do the children of each generation acquire pariah status. This question has shifted somewhat in our discussion, and we must now ask how children learn to uniformly produce pariah-host statuses in their interactions with each other and their teachers. The designated statuses are not simple, cut and dried slots into which members of different groups are easily placed. *Statuses* do not specify everything that occurs in an interaction; rather they are the labels "used by the observer and actor as practical language games for simplifying the task of summarizing a visual field and complex stimuli that are difficult to describe in some precise, detailed way" (Cicourel 1970b:21). Status labels never reduce the complex stimulus fields so much that social life becomes easy. There is always interaction work to be done; social life is always in process.

One's place in a society is not easily acquired. Even if it is the lowest place on the stratification ladder, it is not simply worn as a piece of clothing. A selective way of seeing oneself in the position and of seeing others in relation to oneself must be developed. As Becker has written, an actor acquires a "symbolic mansion" established and maintained in interaction with other human beings; the symbols develop early in ontogeny and prescribe for the actor what situations he should attend, "what he should do in a particular social situation, and how he should feel about himself as he does it" (Becker 1962:84). Statuses, therefore, must be learned. Depending on how they are learned, a child develops specific identities and abilities for use in specific situations. First they are learned in the home in everyday interaction with family members. Many of these first statuses, identities, and abilities undergo considerable alterations in school on the basis of everyday interaction with class members and especially the teacher. School-specific social and intellectual skills must therefore be understood in terms of the politics of everyday life in the classroom. If the skills developed at home are relevant to what happens in the classroom, or if new skills must be developed, they will be visible, and they will make sense in terms of the politics of the classroom.

The *politics of everyday life* are built on messages of relationship passed between two or more social actors. According to Bateson's classic distinction, communication involves not only the transfer of information, but also the imposition of a relationship (Bateson 1972). A communicative act not only has a content which it reports, it also has command aspects which stipulate the relationship between the communicants. An army sergeant sends out messages of relationship with his uniform and an annoyed wife with her hands on her hips. These relational messages form the context for the transfer of information by classifying its intent (Watzlawick, Beaven, and Jackson 1967: 54). Such a context is read by the interpreter of a communicative act before the content of a message is attended. Thus, with open arms one sets a context which can be interpreted as specifying a love relationship, and everything said after that point will be measured for its value in this context; open arms with a gun in each hand asserts a different context and the information transferred, assuming one does not flee in fear of being shot, is understood differently. In both contexts the host may inform his guest that he has been anxiously awaiting his arrival, but the information transferred would be quite different depending upon the message of relationship sent off before any words were spoken.

Children are extremely well equipped by school age for entrance into the politics of everyday life. Messages of relationship are handled competently by neonates (Caudill and Weinstein 1969) and constitute the only form of communication allowed the child in its early years (Blurton-Jones 1972). Love, hate, support, antagonism, trust and deference are some of the relational messages transferred in daily life. Indeed, apparently few concerted practical activities are possible without the communication of such messages; even a slight eruption in their flow can cause a social breakdown (Garfinkel 1963). Children are especially expert in handling these messages as they have not yet developed competence in the verbal arts of saying what is not meant and interpreting what is not intended. Relational messages are more rooted in nonverbal channels which allow for more leakage and clues to deception than verbal channels (Ekman and Friesan 1969), and children decipher these without hindrance from message content.

At school age, the point at which children start acquiring their institutional biographies, relational messages continue in their dominance over information transfer. This is a decisive and delicate time in a child's life. School success, an essential ingredient in any child's avoidance of pariah status, is dependent upon high levels of information transfer. In these early stages of school, depending upon how the politics of everyday life are handled, the child defines his relations with his classmates and his teachers. These relations, remember, define the context of whatever information is to be transferred by a communicant. If the wrong messages of relationship are communicated, reading, writing, and arithmetic may take on very different meanings than they do for the child who is more successful in getting good feelings from the politics of the classroom. The wrong messages of relationship can result in learning disabilities. More will be said on this issue later. At present it is only essential to realize that children deal seriously in relationships, are profoundly affected by their abilities to do relational work, and acquire a social status and attendant skills on the basis of their successes and failures.

Let us try to describe the setting in which relational work is performed. Its general properties are really well known. Goffman (1963) has described the "primal sociological event" as one in which a person with an obvious stigma, no nose, for example, encounters a person without a stigma; in such a case, a tremendous amount of work must go into unspoken arrangements about how the two are to look at each other, at the nose, around the nose, or at the ground. Looking in this situation carries powerful relational messages. One has the power to induce confusion, embarrassment, anger, fright, trust, or love. The eyes will tell the stigmatized whether he has met a person with a similar stigma, with an acquaintance and understanding of the stigma, or with a fear or hate of the stigma. Goffman's point is that we all suffer from stigma of sorts. Every interaction is marked by some hiding and some probing. How much must be hidden, how much probing can go on, or indeed, whether hiding and probing are necessary at all, is dependent upon the messages of relationship exchanged. A policeman's uniform usually invokes hiding on ego's part and allows for probing on the policeman's part. Sexually suggestive clothing does the opposite. In the first case, ego shuts down, and in the second, an opening up is usually called forth. Situations in which these same cues invoke the opposite reactions can be imagined. The effort is to make as much sense as possible of the person's actions, to infer his intentions, and to then react sensibly given the intentions of both interactants (Schutz 1953).

The cues available in any situation are endless. People can send messages with their ecological setting, e.g., whether they are in a bar or a church (Barker 1968; J. McDermott 1969; Sommer 1969); with their posture (Scheflen 1964); with their spacing vis-à-vis their interpreter (Hall 1966); with their odor (Largey and Watson 1972); with their gaze (Kendon 1967); with their tone of voice (Crystal 1972; Laver 1968); with their sequencing of body and voice rhythms (Condon and Ogston 1966, 1971; Byers 1971; Kendon 1970, 1973); and so on. Everything available to the senses of the actors constitutes a possible contribution to the sense and rationality of an interaction.

More than the success of the interaction rides on how sensibly it can be made. Something important happens to the way in which the stigmatized person is going to interpret his next interaction; if one is treated to understanding and sympathy on one occasion, the next occasion will be attended and scanned for messages in a very different way than if the original interaction resulted in a fight. The selective perception skills that are carried from one situation to another of similar type, following Cicourel (1970b), are called status. In addition to his status, the stigmatized individual's feelings can undergo alteration. In talking about formative experiences during puberty, Erikson has noted that "it is of great relevance to the young individual's identity formation that he be responded to and be given function and status as a person whose gradual transformation makes sense to those who begin to make sense to him" (1968:156). Both status and identity are developed in daily interactions. A great deal is at stake in each and every one of them, for status and identity breakdowns are also developed in daily interactions.

An example of the social organization of status and identity in a classroom may be helpful here. Teachers often break their classes into ability groups in order to simplify their administration of the classroom. Not only the level of work engaged in, but also the people interacted with and the kind of feedback received from the teachers all depend upon the group to which the child is assigned. In this way, the teacher organizes the statuses and identities of the children in the class. What is most interesting is that the children seldom reject their assignment—even if they are assigned the lowest status in the classroom achievement hierarchy, they most often accept it as if it makes sense. If the child does not take his assignment, he may buckle down and work harder to catch the rest of the class. But revolt is seldom attempted. The reason is that the teacher generally assigns children to groups according to the same criteria that the children themselves use in their dealings with each other, and the same criteria that the children's parents and the rest of their community use in their dealings with the children. In short, the teacher handles the children in a way the children are used to being handled. Politically, the teacher, the children and the child's community are in harmony. Even if being placed in a low ability group is not good for the child's ego, the results of grouping, if it makes sense, will not be disastrous. The politics of everyday life in the classroom will be identical to the politics of everyday life outside the classroom, and the children's world will be in order.

The social organization of status and identity sometimes does not go so smoothly. Consider the case of an intense, bright child who arrives in school unable to keep up in reading because of some developmental lag specific to processing printed information. When this child is assigned to the lowest ability group, it makes no sense to him. He is treated as a gifted learner and a sociometric star outside the classroom; anything less than equivalent treatment in the classroom will be inadequate to the child's way of evaluating his place in the world. Of course, he revolts and "a negative motivational cycle" begins to take shape (Singer and Beardsley 1970). Later, the possibilities of a host group teacher successfully grouping minority children into the same ability groups that the minority community might itself perceive will be considered. From the high rate of revolt and "negative motivational cycles" in minority classrooms, the possibilities seem slim. The point here is that the politics of everyday life socially organize a classroom. Ability groupings help a teacher to isolate into accessible units children who are to receive fairly similar messages of relationship from the teacher. If the wrong children are assigned to the low ability groups, they will reject the messages of relationship forwarded from the teacher. They will demand a political reorganization of the classroom, one that is more commensurate with their statuses and identities outside the classroom. In the early weeks of a school year, the politics of the classroom feed the teacher's perception, and the classroom is organized accordingly. Then the children reorganize the class according to their own perceptions. If the teacher is insensitive to their demands, the remainder of the year can be occupied in small battles over each child's status and identity within the classroom. Whether or not anything is ever accomplished in the classroom depends upon how quickly these battles can be resolved. Thus, the development of abilities and disabilities also depends upon the politics of daily classroom life.

The specific division of abilities and disabilities among any pariah and host groups should be understood in terms of the politics of everyday life. It is in the very small political arenas constituted by dyads and only slightly larger groups that social organizations are produced. If we want to understand a large scale organizational division within a social organization, we must start asking how this division is produced. Pariah and host group members acquire different skills and produce the different behavior that makes for the organizational division between pariah and host groups. The division looks so real that we professional social scientists study it, and lay social scientists, or natives, perceive and use it as a model for their dealings with each other. In fact, the division is dependent for its existence on the daily differential use of abilities and disabilities by host and pariah group members. The employment of these abilities and disabilities depends upon man's delightful capacity to attend to, think about, and manipulate only certain selected aspects of his environment. Just what parts of an environment are attended and mastered depends upon the social meaning of the environment as recorded in the experiences of the developing child. For example, reading materials can or cannot be attended depending upon whether looking in a book is an acceptable activity in a particular social milieu and whether books contain information helpful to operating in a particular social environment. The social organization of reading materials will now be considered in more detail.

A Biobehavioral Ethnography of Reading Disabilities

Black children in America have a high rate of learning disabilities. Rates of functional black illiteracy are estimated around 50 percent (Thompson 1966) as compared to 10 percent for white Americans and only 1 percent for Japan (Makita 1968). The high rates of these disabilities do not point to a high rate of genetic inferiority, neurological damage, language deprivation, or any of the other intrapsychic causes suggested in social and behavioral science literature. Rather, the high rates of learning disorders point to learned patterns of selective inattention developed in the politics of everyday life in the classroom. Status and identity work is a dismal failure in early elementary school for many black children with white teachers and, as a result, they turn off, in the sense that they physiologically shut down. As a yoga or Zen master (Kasamatsu and Hirai 1966) may do for an entire environment, black children disattend reading materials and join their peers in the student subculture within the class. Reading disabilities and school failure result.

School failure is an important place to start an inquiry into the acquisition of pariah status, and social science literature on pariah group persistence across generations has often centered on school failure and its causes. Most of the work has centered on the children, independent of the schools they attend, as if there was something naturally wrong with their brains. To paraphrase crudely, the cause of pariah groups is that pariah children do not seem to think too well. This deprivation theme should be fairly offensive to social science; after all, has not a century of anthropology shown that to understand people is to discern difference and not deprivation? Yet the anthropological argument is difficult. Pariah children fail, and fail miserably. How can we claim that they are neither damaged nor deprived? One answer is that we have been measuring achievements with a biased set of standards. Achievements are realized only in particular situations. Rather than attempting to measure the development of absolute capacities that a child uses for all situations through time, perhaps we should center on the situations in which and for which particular skills are acquired. In other words, if we examine the classroom as a set of situations or an "occasion corpus" (Zimmerman and Pollner 1970), a child's failing performance on classroom tests might appear to be something of a situational achievement. Deprivation hypotheses are considerably weakened, if, instead of just looking at the skills stored in children's bodies, we look also at the social contexts in which the skills are turned into achievements.

Medicine, education, and psychology have all produced deprivation hypotheses for social scientists to adopt. Of late, pariah children have been described as genetically inferior (Jensen 1969). Another claim has it that an unspecified number suffer brain damage due to the poverty and ignorance that burdened their mothers in pregnancy and birth (Birch and Gussow 1970). Social science itself has had a hand in claiming that pariah children suffer perceptual handicaps (C. Deutsch 1968; Jensen 1966) and conceptual and linguistic handicaps (M. Deutsch 1963; Bernstein 1964; Entwisle 1971) due to low social class and its associated life-style. All these disciplines assume to discover facts out of context, raw facts about the world and the behavior of its inhabitants. Of course there are no such things. All behavior is context-bound. More important, all behavior is indexical or dependent upon our interpretation of the context in which the behavior is situated (Bar-Hillel 1954; Beck 1972; Cicourel, in press). Yet all assume that facts are available for all to see, and that these facts are invariable. In the case of learning disabilities, each discipline has assumed that whatever is located in the heads of the children studied is invariable. Whether a discipline uses a perceptual, cognitive, or language test, a projective technique or a sociometric status score, each has assumed that it describes the skills the individual has acquired for all occasions and tasks. This is, of course, incorrect. Each of these disciplines assumes too much.

My proposal is that each of these disciplines is describing the same social processes and merely indexing them differently. Scores on perceptual, intelligence, attitude, language competence, and even neurological tests are all remnants of the normal and practical work of persons in a particular situation. Ways of perceiving, thinking, feeling, talking, and the activities of the neural wetware processing our perceiving, thinking, feeling, and talking are all dependent upon the situations in which the person is placed. Testing offers a particular situation which may record little more than the way the subject defines the testing situation in response to the way in which the subject understands the tester's definition of the situation. In short, test scores always have discernible roots in the social world in which they take place (Cicourel, in press). We cannot expect tests to necessarily reveal very much about intra-psychic events and the capabilities of any subject. But tests can, if they are properly read, tell a great deal about interpsychic, social procedures in which a subject is engaged. For example, Cazden (1970) has described black children who do badly on language complexity tests in formal situations, and very well in informal situations; the opposite holds true for white children. What we can learn from such tests has nothing to do with a child's capacity to talk; but there is a great deal of information about social organization stored in this little test. Social organizations are made by people knowing approximately what to do in particular situations; a social organization is a cognitive phenomenon. When we look to tests for information about social organization, about the thinking underlying the social acts to be performed during the test, then they are very revealing.

Reading tests can significantly reveal the dynamics of social organization. Pariah children do very badly at them, almost certainly for social reasons. Reading is an act which apparently aligns the black child with the "wrong" forces in the social universe. In the classroom social organization produced by the politics of everyday life, reading takes its place as part of the teacher's "ecology of games" (Long 1958). To read is to accept these games and all the statuses and identities that accompany them. Not to read is to accept peer group games and their accompanying statuses and identities. In other words, given a particular social organization, reading failure is a social achievement. Conventional testing procedures could never reveal this trend. The battle grounds on which it is determined whether a child learns to read or not are drawn by the statuses and identities made available by the teacher and the peer group, in short, by social relations. If the teacher and the children can play the same games, then reading and all other school materials will be easily absorbed.

The success of educational settings directed by ethnic (Alitto 1969; Hostetler and Huntington 1971) and dialect (Fishman and Leuders-Salmon 1972) minorities for themselves illustrates this point nicely. If the children and the teacher generate their behavior from a shared set of interpretive procedures, efficient classroom learning can almost be assumed. This record contrasts, however, with educational settings designed and administered by outsiders to a community. Such settings often result in school failure. Centuries of failure in the white education of American Indians and blacks and Japanese failures in the education of Korean and Truk natives (Fischer 1961) illustrate this contrasting situation. If the classroom is divided into two separate worlds with teachers and students occupying different ecologies of games, school failure appears to be inevitable. The identities and statuses offered by a school system without roots in the community are apparently not worth seeking or are worth avoiding. For many children in such a situation, a social reorganization of the classroom becomes the main alternative to following the teacher's dictates.

An essential question at this point is how the politics of everyday life get inside a child's body and dictate what shall be perceived. This question can now easily be handled by recent advances in neuropsychology. Not all biology is reductionist, and there is good reason to attempt a view of social life by an examination of the biological foundations of behavior. Geertz alerted us to this possibility in his account of the dynamic, feedback relationship between biology and culture.

> As our central nervous system—and most particularly its crowning curse and glory, the neocortex—grew up in great part in interaction with culture, it is incapable of directing our behavior or organizing our experience without the guidance provided by systems of significant symbols . . . Such symbols are thus not mere expressions, instrumentalities, or correlates of our biological, psychological, and social existence; they are prerequisities of it. Without men, no culture, certainly; but equally, and more significantly, without culture, no men (1965:61).

Attention is the mechanism by which our bodies help us divide the world into significant and insignificant. As Wallace has suggested, man has created a rich and elaborate world for himself "by a process of selective attention to his total environment" (1965:277). Apparently, man suffers tremendous limitations in his ability to process all the information available to him at any one instant. Selection is a ubiquitous and unending process throughout our central nervous systems. Significance is stored not only in the social world, in the symbols out there, but in our equipment for decoding and interpreting the world. As Pribram has indicated, "societies are made up of persons whose brains shape the interactive matrix" (1969:37). What is organized in social organizations are individuals interpreting the world, human brains attending to some aspects of the social world and not to others.

A brief account of the psychophysiological concept of attention will hopefully suggest the importance of attention patterns for social scientists and detail for us how patterns of inattention can result in reading disabilities. The central nervous system has been increasingly conceived as a set of models depicting the world outside the body, in terms of which an organism attends, perceives, thinks, and acts (Sokolov 1969; Pribram 1971; MacKay 1972). Stimuli enter the body and if they are uninformative no attention will be paid to them. If the match is improper, the central nervous system will orient in search of new information which will either restore or redefine the model. In such a case, the organism is said to be "looking to see," and different parts of the brain will be activated in processing the new stimuli until harmony is again established (Pribram 1970). First a decision is made to look for a stimulus and only then is a second decision made as to whether or not the proper stimuli occur (Dewey 1896; N. Mackworth and Bagshaw 1970).

The human system is best discussed in terms of the feedback relations between pertinence, attention, and memory storage. Physiologists are not easily given to talking about pertinence centers in the brain, but they do talk about the efferent control of afferent stimuli on the basis of what central mechanisms deem to be the most pertinent information at any particular time. Central control of the models is called up from memory with plans. Furthermore, there is central control right down at the receptor sites as to what sort of information makes it to the brain for consideration and possible action (Pribram 1970, 1971; Rothblatt and Pribram 1972). The central nervous system is thus intimately involved in the organizational work that goes into the construction of significance in the world. The same symbols that are processed by our bodies are those processed in our social systems. Our bodies are the nodes in the communicative network that is society, and the work of these various nodes produces what has come to be seen as social organization. Statements of this proposition are unfortunately rare, but the trend is apparently changing (Bateson 1972; Beck 1971a,b). Nevertheless, we still have only a few anecdotes interrelating the organization of social events and the organization of neurological events. Pribram has given one delightful example:

> For many years there was an elevated railway line (the "el") on Third Avenue in New York that made a fearful racket: when it was torn down, people who had been living in apartments along the line awakened periodically out of a sound sleep to call the police about some strange occurrence they could not properly define. The calls were made at the times the trains had formerly rumbled past. The strange occurrences were, of course, the deafening silence that had replaced the expected noise (1971:50).

A model of the world for a particular time and place existed in the central nervous systems of many people up and down the Third Avenue El. When the environment did not supply the essential information, the people began orienting and paying attention. In this case, our ecology worked its way into our bodies and told us when to listen, namely at the time when the El had previously roared by; our social system then worked its way into our bodies and told us what to hear when we listened, perhaps a thief or another strange occurrence requiring police assistance. Society and ecology are merely two aspects of the environment with which we communicate. They send us messages about the adequacy of the internalized models of the time and space criteria in terms of which we perceive, think and act. We all live in a world of information which we decode according to the dictates of context. Much of this context is encoded in our memory and evidenced in our attention patterns.

There are many Third Avenue El trains in our lives. In every classroom in America, there is an organization of ecological and social happenings mediated by various neurologies with memory and attention biases wired into the wetware. To study one is to study the other, to study the brain is to study social organization, and vice versa. In this biobehavioral inquiry into reading disabilities, however, both systems are obviously involved. The epidemiological contours of reading disabilities run along ethnic and cultural lines and suggest that they are indeed socially organized. Yet unlike most behavior that we see as socially organized, reading skills or their diminution due to brain insult or socially induced inattention, obviously, rather than implicitly, involve neurological organization. Indeed, the picture we are developing of reading as a "psycholinguistic guessing game" (Goodman 1970; Wanat 1971) fits exactly the picture we have of the structure of the brain's activity in all behavior. In an excellent paper, J. Mackworth has laid the two side by side: reading involves

> a selective process that involves partial use of available language cues selected from the perceptual input on the basis of the reader's expectation, an interaction between thoughts and language. . .; the neuronal model anticipates the future probability and meaning of the next stimulus. A neuronal mechanism checks the meaning and nature of an incoming stimulus against the predictions of the neural model. Thus construction of a neural model is an active process, involving a two-way exchange of messages from environment and brain (1972:704, 708).

Both the environment and the brain are socially constructed. When a child is unable to read, part of the environment is not being processed by the brain. Because the epidemiology of reading disabilities follows a social organization, it is possible to claim that the organization of the proper neurological models for reading also follows a social organization. A brief look at the social organization of classrooms for black children in America will indicate how their brains appear disabled for reading. *In the politics of everyday life, black children in America learn how not to read; they learn how not to attend to printed information and as a result show high rates of reading disabilities.* The implications of this high rate of illiteracy for the acquisition of pariah status is obvious.

Almost a half a century ago, attention was a major focus of classroom research. Primarily this old research attempted to document whether or not children were paying attention to their teachers by noting their gaze direction during lessons. This is not a very efficient method of studying attention, for receptor orientation gives little information about just what a child is attending to during a boring lecture. The literature is significant, however, in documenting contrasting receptor attention patterns between middle American host schools then and minority classrooms now. In their check of gaze direction, it was shown that more than 90 percent of the host children had their eyes fixed on their teachers or their work at any given time (Jackson 1968). This contrasts considerably with estimates obtained from the contemporary classrooms that share in the early century pedagogical style of the teacher directing all attention in the classroom. M. Deutsch (1963) has found that teachers in Harlem elementary schools spent more than half their day calling children to attention. Attention patterns indeed appear to define the "scene of the battle" in pariah group education (Roberts 1970). School does not seem to work for many teachers and pariah children, and formal roles and statuses are not identically defined by teachers and students. The call for attention appears far more often and seems to have far less effect than it did in the twenties when these earlier studies were carried out.

There is much social organization in these attention and inattention patterns. In primate studies, attention patterns have recently been used to delineate the social organization of dominance hierarchies (Chance 1967). The more one baboon visually attends to another baboon, the more responsible it is to the leader's every movement. Similar, in the classroom where teachers and students produce leadership patterns for each other, attention is an issue. To attend to a teacher is to give the teacher a leadership role in the classroom; to attend to the peer group is to subvert the teacher's role. In the older studies, the primary fact is that all the children paid homage to the teacher's leadership role by attending, physically at least, to the teacher's activities. In schools populated by pariah children, this leadership role is much more subject to negotiation: some teachers can pull it off and some cannot; some children give their attention and others do not. It is in the context of this battle for attention that we must consider the nature of pariah reading disabilities. In many pariah classrooms, the politics of everyday life has been escalated into war games; there are teacher games and peer group games, and every student must make his choice. One takes sides by attending or not attending. Those who attend learn to read; those who do not attend do not learn how to read.

Attention patterns increasingly shift from teacher games to peer group games as a pariah child moves through elementary school. In addition to the often reported facts that pariah children learn less and misbehave more often as they get older, data on shifts in the perceptual, language structure and function, and attitude patterns of children in school are now available. The next few years promise to bring us far more information, not only on American blacks, the focus of all the work to be briefly discussed here, but on other pariah groups as well.

Perception

Much of the transmission of social know-how that occurs in the early years of school amounts to perceptual learning. Apparently different cultures learn how to perceive differently. This is especially the case for materials represented in two dimensions which apparently allow for more variability than the three-dimensional world of movement and action (Segall, Campbell. and Herskovits 1966; Forge 1970). Learning how to read involves a great deal of perceptual learning. Many children reverse their letters when first learning how to write, for there really is not much difference betwee p, d, g and b; o and e; u, n, m, v and w. Normals master these subtle differences, and disabled children continue to have difficulty distinguishing these forms after the first grade. Careful attention must be paid to differences in rotation, line-to-line curve, dimension and line-breaking transformations in order to make the proper distinctions between the letters which signal differences in word form and meaning. We develop these skills and store them deep in our nervous system. The more we read, the less work it takes to distinguish the different forms. The eye apparently learns just what to look for and orients only when a drastically misshapen form appears; the difficulties of proofreading illustrate just how well a good reader is programmed to read for meaning and to notice typographic irregularities only when they are given special attention.

Some black children do not permanently develop the essential skills for letter differentiation. In a test designed to analyze a child's competence at handling the perceptual transformations essential to letter discrimination, Gibson (1965) has shown that most children have trouble with rotation and line-to-curve transformations at age five. By age seven most children have mastered these transformations. This is the case for both black and white children. However, black children I tested at twelve years of age showed a mixed range in these skills; those who could read performed well, and those who could not read performed very poorly, scoring below younger black children on the same test. These children had apparently learned how not to see, or, more specifically, learned how not to look in order that they might not see. Reading apparently became a call for inattention, and they submerged the skills essential for a successful attending to reading materials.

Language Structure and Function

This shift in the perceptual properties of many black children is accompanied by subtle but highly significant changes in language structure and function. The brilliant work of Labov and his associates in Harlem has revealed that our language is indeed socially organized. The way in which our vocal chords allow for a passage of air to reverberate into the ears of other social actors depends greatly on just who the interactants are and how they are related. Depending upon who is doing the talking and who is doing the listening, not only will different points of information be passed, but the way of saying it may be remarkably different. Pariah children often learn to use one speech code or register for dealings with pariah people and another for host people; the differences in the code may be subtle lexemic markers as in Japan (Donoghue 1971), subtle phonemic shifts as between social classes and ethnic groups in New York City's Lower East Side (Labov 1964a), gross dialect shifts as between whites and blacks in America, or major language shifts as between French and English speakers in Canada or the Lapps and Norwegians in Norway (Eidheim 1969).

American blacks acquire a nonstandard or dialect English which is most often mutually intelligible with white English. When there is an intelligibility breakdown, the result can be disastrous. Gumperz gives the following example from a postbellum southern teacher's diary:

I asked a group of boys one day the color of the sky. Nobody could tell me. Presently the father of one of them came by, and I told him of their ignorance, repeating my question with the same result as before. He grinned: "Tom, how sky stan'?" "Blue," promptly shouted Tom (1970:4).

This gross level of language interference was, of course, attributed by the teacher to the child's stupidity, and the teacher probably unconsciously related to the child the subordinate status that accompanies being "stupid" in a classroom.

For the most part, however, black and white verbal codes are mutually intelligible in content. Switching does not cause a problem at the structural level; rather the codes function to differentiate the games being played and the meaning attached to the behavior of various other actors in the game. Messages of relationship are differently stored in the codes. Indeed, using one and not the other is itself a powerful relational message. Switching codes causes a problem, then, for an actor's definition of situation. If an actor defines himself in terms of the ecology of games played by the peer group, then taking on the code which demands participation in the ecology of teacher and book games demands an existential leap and is neither easily nor healthily performed.

The differentiation of codes according to grammar alone deals only with what is systemically possible. Learning should not be blocked. Children merely learn new codes. The differentiation of codes on the basis of appropriateness is apparently a much more difficult chasm to bridge. When the social organization of communicative behavior is divided by two definitions of what is culturally appropriate, the one definition belonging to the teacher and the other to the pupils, communication across codes is much more limited than if codes are merely structurally at odds. It is not difficult to learn that "What color is the sky?" and "How sky stan'?" are equivalent, but, when your teacher deems you ignorant for using the one and your peer group shuns you for using the other, then the job of switching codes is difficult indeed.

The ecology of peer group games is well defined by the growth of a highly elaborate linguistic code restricted to peer group members. Labov has performed a masterful task in isolating these games in his delineation of the stages of acquisition of nonstandard English:

1. Up to age 5: basic grammatical rules and lexicon are taken from parents.
2. Age 5 to 12 the reading years: peer group vernacular is established.
3. Adolescence: "The social significance of the dialect characteristics of his friends become gradually apparent."
4. High school age: "The child begins to learn how to modify his speech in the direction of the prestige standard in formal situations or even to some extent in casual speech" (Labov 1964b:91).

The second and third stages are, of course, most important for a consideration of the implications of the school and the peer group registers for learning. The implications are not so obvious; what difference does it make if children use one register for interacting with teachers and reading materials and another for interacting with each other? The importance of these two registers lies in the fact that during the school years the two become mutually exclusive. As children participate more in their peer groups, the less importance is attached to school games. The more children participate in the ecology of games defined by their peers, the more deviant their linguistic registers; it is these linguistic features which help to mark off the peer group from the ecology of the schools.

Labov has documented these trends beautifully. Participation in peer groups, especially those with formal organizations such as street gangs, are accompanied by major phonological and grammatical shifts. One of the many charts presented in his Harlem study is reproduced here (Labov et al. 1968:182):

Percent of Standard Verb Agreement for Club Members, Lames and Whites

Present Tense Forms of Verb	Club Members	Lames	Whites
has (3rd sg.)	19	60	100
doesn't (3rd sg.)	03	36	32
were (2nd sg. + pl.)	14	83	100
does (3rd sg.)	00	13	100
says (3rd sg.)	04	00	100
(No. of subjects	31	10	8)

This illustrates the implications that peer group status has for the speech register employed by black adolescents. Lames do not participate in formally organized peer groups although they are in contact with the gangs and are part of the black speech community. In school, Lames are still open to interpreting favorably some cues from the teacher's ecology. The Inwood whites are of a low social class, but they do not show the extreme alienation patterns which characterize black children in school. Club members show the most extreme deviance from the standard English linguistic code, Inwood whites the least, and Lames fall in between. The same rank ordering can be made for the three groups' participation in school. This is not to say that linguistic difference causes alienation from school; rather it is a standard for nonacceptance of the ecology of games played in white schools. The rise in status of a black child in his peer group, the adoption of the peer group's linguistic register, and alienation from school all develop together.

In terms of this inquiry into reading disabilities, participation in peer group formal organizations and the employment of their linguistic registers are of great importance, for they correlate very well with reading scores. Labov and Robins (1969:57, 167) have shown perfectly the relation between the acquisition of reading skills and the participation in the peer group ecology of games. Not one out of 43 gang members was able to achieve a reading score on grade level and most are more than two years behind the national average. Participation in the peer group ecology of games appears indeed to be exclusive of a participation in the school ecology of games of which reading is a part. Printed materials appear to send few meaningful cues to those interested in improving their status among their peers.

Attitudes

Labov's findings are not limited to classrooms which harbor members of formally organized gangs in Harlem. In two classrooms in suburban New York City, the exact same trends were found. The children were not unaware of the trends, and their significance was readily apparent in the children's attitudes towards each other. This should not surprise us at all. In my high school, I remember that most of us could define others and make very accurate estimates of their grade point averages on the basis of clothes worn, speech patterns, and some postural cues. Our expertise was perhaps not as loaded as that of black children, for their expertise not only defines others but also determines who is to be popular or not. A series of sociometric tests administered in an all black, bottom track, sixth grade were consistent in placing nonreaders at the center of all peer group activities. Similar tests in an all black, nontracked, fifth grade also showed nonreaders at the center of most activities. Reading skills do not recommend an actor for leadership. Indeed, the acquisition of such skills can exclude an actor from the peer group ecology of games.

Ethnographic Summary

Many topics have been briefly touched in this short description of the black classroom, but its thrust can be summarized. Learning disabilities occur at very high rates in the American black population. The distribution of these disabilities overlaps with the distribution of social behavior that leads to the acquisition of nonmarketable and pariah biographies, behavior such as participation in street gangs and classroom subcultures specializing in disruption and failure. This nascent pariah population shows subtle shifts in its perceptual, linguistic, and attitude patterns. What the children are doing is learning to behave in new, culturally appropriate ways in educational settings, new ways which will determine their acquisition of pariah status vis-a-vis the host population. These new ways of behaving involve the development of new cues to be sent out in interaction with other humans, such as new phonemes and morphemes, and the development of new perceptual and evaluative skills, such as the abilities to hear new phonemes and perceive group leaders without confusion. What is being learned are new attention patterns, new ways of seeing, hearing, and construing the meaning of particular items of behavior shared with others in the subculture. When some items are attended, others are disattended, some of them actively so. Learning to behave in a culturally appropriate way in black classrooms in white school systems apparently involves learning to attend to cues produced in the peer group and learning to disattend teacher and school produced cues, such as shouts for attention or the introduction of tasks such as reading. These attention patterns are deeply programmed in the central nervous system. When the child attempts to attend to cues outside his learned competence, he fails. In this way, many black children fail in reading, and they appear neurologically impaired. Obviously, they are usually not impaired at all; they have merely learned to attend to different stimuli in a school situation. Ironically and tragically, for their successful and rational adaptation to the school situation, they are categorized as impaired and treated as inferiors. Thus they acquire pariah status.

Biculturation and the Acquisition of Pariah Status

Now that we have some notion of how a black classroom is organized in American schools and what black children must know in order to act in a subculturally appropriate way in the classroom, we must ask how this know-how is produced. Why is it that the social world of many black children is organized without a place for printed materials? Some observers might point to genes or to various kinds of deprivation leading to cognitive or motivational breakdowns. Others, especially radical educators (Holt 1969; Kohl 1967), black leaders, and P.T.A. groups, point to "underachieving schools" and the failure of teachers to do the job. Implicit in much of this rhetoric is the claim that racism is the primary factor in the failure of whites to educate black children; white teachers expect black children to fail and subtly induce their expectations into the children who indeed do fail.

These are the two alternatives offered by the literature: the children fail because there is something wrong with their heads; or the children fail because the schools are disasters and the teachers are racists. The first argument is far too simple. Gene pools (Montagu 1964) and cognitive and motivational systems are not easily located, and no one has shown why any of these systems fail in school and not in other settings in the social world. The second literature is a little more difficult to dismiss. Obviously, it is not only the schools that fail, for they serve different groups the same product with differential success. When racism is appended to the charge of school underachievement, the argument is intuitively more forceful. However, we have little idea just what racism means of late or, more importantly, how it works especially for the mostly well-meaning, hard-working, and ideologically nonracist teachers that staff our urban schools.

The proposal of this chapter is that reading disabilities are products of the way in which the people in the classroom use their categories for interaction to produce statuses and identities, or ways of attending stimuli, in the classroom setting. Although racist categories work their way into the production of the social organization of black-white relations, a teacher does not have to be a racist for the politics of everyday life to produce a classroom rigidly divided between teacher and peer group games. Any formal differences in the communicative styles of the teacher and the children can introduce havoc to their relations and the messages of relationship they consequently send to each other.

Consider the following important example. Two black Americans attending a Chicago college were introduced to each other. A film, shot at the rate of 24 frames per second, was made of their shaking hands. There was a definite rhythm to their handshake; for three frames their hands went up and for three frames down, and so on. Two Polish Americans at the same college produced a different but also fairly rhythmic interaction. One Pole and one black from each dyad produced a disastrous interaction (Leonard 1972): five up, one down, one up, two down, etc. There was no rhythm to their interaction. There they were, joined together at the hands, but with apparently little idea about what to do with each other. An analysis of the conversational false starts indicates that they also had little idea of what to say to each other. Rational and stigma-free interactions are difficult to make out of such material. Apparently, our communicative codes go into our bodies and establish rhythms and expectations about the rhythms of others. Interacting with a person with a slightly different code or rhythm can be a fatiguing and upsetting experience. On a one-to-one basis, these difficulties can be worked out or negotiated until the two interactants have managed consistent or rational ways of dealing with each other. In a classroom in which a teacher often stands one-to-thirty against a code of difference, negotiations are often not possible and at best limited (Byers, personal communications).

Communicative code differences in a classroom setting can have tremendous effects. A teacher out of phase with his students will undoubtedly fail in the politics of everyday life. Rational interaction with the group will hardly be possible. As a result, the teacher will fall back on his formal authority as a teacher, his so-called "role," to instruct the children in their classroom behavior. The children often reject this authority role and develop an idiosyncratic code, such as the nonstandard peer group code Labov has described. The children's actions make much sense. When rational interaction with a teacher is not possible, that is, when his position of authority makes no sense in terms of his relations with the children, they produce an alternative system and disown the teacher's authority. Reading skills get caught in this battle over which cues are to be attended—peer group cues or teacher cues.

This paper has suggested how a child learns to produce a pariah status in his work in everyday life. It has offered an example of this work in detailing how a large number of black children acquire statuses, identities, and behavioral patterns which produce a pariah biography. The statuses, identities, and behavioral patterns developed by black children in white school systems produce learning disabilities and enable the host population to exclude the black child from participation in the more lucrative institutions of American society. How are these statuses, identities and behavioral patterns produced? Three tasks remain if this question is to be answered.

Communicative Code Differences and the Inhibition of School Learning

First, examples of how minor differences in communicative codes can induce a selective inattention to school material must be given. One of the first reports of such interference was offered by Spindler (1959) in his work on the self-fulfilling prophecies of teachers unconsciously dominating classroom social organization. He showed how middle-class teachers attended to middle-class children and labelled them as the most talented and ambitious of the children in their classes. School success followed along identical lines, but more subtle evaluations of talent divided the populations along different lines. In this case, lower class children gave up trying and acquired failing "institutional biographies" (Goffman, 1963) because of an inability to give evidence of their intelligence in terms of the limited code that the teachers used to evaluate children.

A more specific example has been recently offered for a Boston elementary school with white teachers and black children. The effects of little things were in no way little in this school. Rist offers the following account of the classroom after it had been divided into three "ability groups," the fast, slow and nonlearners at Tables 1, 2, and 3, respectively:

> The organization of the kindergarten classroom according to the expectation of success or failure after the eighth day of school became the basis for the differential treatment of the children for the remainder of the school year. From the day that the class was assigned permanent seats, the activities in the classroom were perceivably different from previously. The fundamental division of the class into those expected to learn and those expected not to permeated the teacher's orientation to the class (1970: 423).

Assignment to each of the tables was based on the teacher's subjective evaluations which, after dissection by Rist, were shown to be rooted in the teacher's evaluation of the children's physical appearance and interactional and verbal behavior. At Table 1 are centered children with newer and cleaner clothes and more of them on cold days, slightly lighter skin, and processed hair. Children with reciprocal traits were positioned at lower tables. Class leaders or direction givers also clustered at Table 1. The children at the low tables spoke less in class, in heavy dialect when they did, and almost never to the teacher. What is most unfortunate is that by the third grade the children at the lower tables were still at the lower tables. Once the child is tracked, it is almost impossible for him to break loose. The lower his table, the less he gets in instructional time. In addition, teacher expectations follow him from year to year. Apparently, the acquisition of a school biography is completed within the first week of school, and all on the basis of a teacher's ethno-centric evaluation of a child's mannerisms.

A similar analysis can probably be carried out for every year of schooling that a child undergoes. Each year, more are sorted out until the "select few" reach college. The word "select" should not be taken in its elitist sense. By the time they enter college, some people may be more select because their enculturation to school equips them to do college work. We should not make the mistake, however, of thinking that the select few were selected for any reason other than that they were most like their teachers. Given Labov's speech data, we can see that the children at Table 3 are not the interactional and verbal dullards that the teacher supposed them to be. By the sixth grade, assuming Labov's data are predictive, the children at Table 3 will talk the most and be the best dressers and the most popular individuals in every class. Their native equipment for leading and learning is in perfect shape, although by the sixth grade it is understandably directed away from school. Why these children are not selected in their early years by teachers has to do with how well prepared both they and their teachers are for working out the conflicting points in their communicative code. The children are often more adaptable than their teachers. They are able and willing to develop new codes; indeed, they do so every day in the playgrounds. However, if the new code is used to degrade the children, as is the case for the children in "lower" ability groups, they will take flight and cut themselves off from whatever rewards the new code has to offer them. If a modus vivendi is not reached in the early grades, the children at the lower tables will create their own subculture defined partly in opposition to the classroom culture attempted by the teacher.

Pariah children invariably share some minor traits which help them to identify each other and to distinguish themselves from the host population. A particular phoneme, lexeme, or body movement can do the job. Invariably, these traits are at most minuscule factors in cognitive development. Even a dialect barrier great enough to produce mutual unintelligibility is not enough to stop German children from speaking and reading High German (Fishman and Leuders-Salmon 1972). Dialect differences between black children and white school officials and books, often claimed as a source of reading failure (Baratz and Shuy 1969), apparently present little formal interference to the reading process (Melmud 1971). It depends on what is done with the differ-ences. In host-pariah teacher-student relations, the differences are used to do a great deal, and are allowed to intervene in interactions to the extent that they cut off the possibility of sense being made between the pair. The child gets stuck in a low ability group for reasons he cannot understand and the teacher finds the child's behavior equally incomprehensible. In such a case the teacher grasps onto a formal definition of the teacher's role in order to make sense of the situation: the teacher develops status or interaction skills in accordance with the definition of the teacher as a person to be listened to and learned from under any circumstances. Faced with this senseless rigidity of the teacher's role, the child develops his status and identity in the alternative source offered by his peer group. Recall the disabled child assigned low status in the classroom despite a high degree of acceptance outside the classroom. The child shut down his learning skills and turned to abnormal behavior (Singer and Beardsley 1970). The same senseless assignment to ability groups is often made in the interethnic classroom. The host teacher has different standards of evaluation than the minority child. Accordingly, the wrong children are often assigned to the low ability groups. Their assignment does not make sense to them, and they understandably shut down their learning skills and revolt. The difference between what happens to the disabled child who perceives a senseless status assignment and a minority child in an identical situation is that the minority child is never alone. The teacher invariably makes mistakes on a number of the children, and the ensuing revolt can develop earlier and more powerfully when a large number of children is involved.

The children in an interethnic classroom have three choices. They can take school as a source of identity; thus, the children at Table 1. They can take the peer group as a source of identity and fight the system; thus, the children at Tables 2 and 3 transformed by late elementary school into the gangs Labov has described. The third and perhaps the worst choice is represented by the children at the lower tables who accept the teacher's definitions and passively fail through school into pariah status. They also fail in their identity work. For the children to dispute the messages of relationship offered by a teacher to the lower ability groups causes havoc in the classroom but solid ego development in the children's own community. For the children to passively accept subordinate status creates classroom calm, but a weak ego. Either way, learning is blocked; in the first case by active selective inattention and misbehavior, in the second case with motivational lag and selective inattention. Neither group learns to read.

Black-White Communicative Code Differences

A second task is to describe possible points of conflict in black and white communicative skills and the difficulties of biculturation or the acquisition of competence in both codes. Work on this topic is just beginning, but already there are indications that the use of time and space in black culture is distinct from the use of time and space in white culture. Regardless of what these codes are an adaptation to, the point is that blacks and whites slice up the world in slightly different ways. When the black child enters a host school, he is asked to alter his codes drastically for spacing his body vis-a-vis (Aiello and Jones 1971; Hall 1971; Scheflen 1971; Johnson 1971) and his timing in conversation (Lewis, 1970; Gumperz and Herasimchuk, 1972; Leonard, 1972). This is very important, for it is in terms of these time and space coordinates that people send each other messages of relationship. If these code differences are not worked out, the teacher and students will tie into or punctuate (Bateson 1972; Watzlawick et al. 1967) each other in all the wrong ways.

Punctuation breakdowns are the stuff of the self-fulfilling prophecies described above. The child moves or speaks in the wrong way at the wrong time according to the teacher's code, and he will be branded hyperactive, out of control, or stupid. The teacher will appear equally disoriented according to the child's code and may well be branded cold and unfair. Slight differences in time and space use do not have to result in such a disaster, but they often do.

In an exciting article, Byers and Byers (1972) have described how black-white code differences can lead to pupil-teacher breakdown. The teacher in question is considered unbiased and talented. Byers and Byers filmed her interaction with four four-year-old girls, two black and two white. In the sequence analyzed, she looks at the black and white children almost an identical number of times. However, the black children look at the teacher more than three times as often as the white children. One might postulate that the children are anxious about their performance, or perhaps they are hyperactive, etc. The Byerses have a much more interesting conclusion to offer, after they add the most important information that the white children established eye contact with the teacher almost twice as often as the black children who are straining three times as hard to catch the teacher's eyes. This is very crucial, for it is during eye contact that the teacher can send the children messages of reassurance and affection, messages such as, "I love you," "You are doing well," "How smart!", or at least, "You are making sense to me." Why do these black and white eyes punctuate each other in all the wrong ways?

Consider what social work is performed by a glance of the eyes. The eyes are engaged in gathering information about the content and report of any interaction that a body is engaged in. Constant surveillance makes people uncomfortable, perhaps because it is a statement of distrust, a sign of one's unwillingness to suspend belief that nothing threatening is about to occur. So the eyes are used in brief spurts only, in passing glances. What is most interesting is that these glances are very well timed to occur at moments of maximum information transfer. Eye glances are paced by conversational rhythms, intonation patterns, and body movements and are sequenced rather neatly to other rhythms between two people. The white girls in the interaction that Byers and Byers have described appear to know just when to look at the white teacher in order to gain access to her eyes and whatever relational messages she is to dispense. The black girls do not appear to have the same information. They appear to be working off a slightly different interaction rhythm. Of course, this is just as Leonard's (1972) analysis of the black-white handshake and Gumperz's and Herasimchuk's (1972) analysis of black-white intonation rhythms predicted. Interaction is indeed an action between people, and if not perfectly timed the interaction will fail. In the case of this teacher and these children, the white-white interaction is successful, and the white-black interaction fails. For all their interactional work, the two black girls receive little relational support, and it is not difficult to predict that they will someday direct their interactional work towards each other. In time, achievement will be located in the peer group, and not in the teacher.

More blatant examples of teacher-student battles over time and space use exist in every American classroom in which teachers generally monopolize 85 percent of class space and 100 percent of class time (Sommer 1969). From the first to the last grade, the teacher attempts to dictate when and where a child should speak or move. In ghetto schools, this often leads to constant and open warfare. Teachers spend an inordinate amount of a child's six years in elementary school fighting with the class about just who is going to say and do what at a particular moment; manuals guiding a new teacher in instructional methods in such a school detail at length exactly how a teacher must rigidly structure time and space (Trubowitz 1968; Board of Education 1966). The children fight this particular structure to the extent that it stifles them; if their function and status in the structure do not make sense to them, that is, if the politics of classroom life do not make sense, they reject the structure and all that comes with it, including literacy.

A large percentage of American blacks are especially adept at making the code shifts essential to smooth interactions with whites. This is no easy task, for enculturation into two cultures, or biculturation (Valentine 1971), can have its drawbacks for ego development. The bicultural child must acquire two sometimes mutually exclusive ways of knowing how to act appropriately, one way for when whites are present and another for when the interaction matrix is all black. Where code shifting is most difficult is apparently in the bureaucratic setting in which the white code, in addition to being the only acceptable medium of information exchange, is also the medium for the expression of host group power and host group access to the essential and even luxurious utilities of the ecosystem that is contemporary America. The police station, the welfare office, the job interview and the classroom are all situations which demand complete subservience to host group codes. In each of these situations, people are being processed rather than negotiated with in an attempt to establish rationality. The rationale is already set. The bureaucrat has it down and the pariah does not. The bureaucrat already has the role defined, and the pariah must fit in if he is to be processed successfully. Even when the bureaucrat attempts to negotiate a rational interaction—to approach his public as he would normal people in everyday life, he is unable to do so because of the sheer numbers of people that must be processed. The teacher, for example, must deal with 30 children at a time, and the give and take that characterizes everyday life become impossible. Consequently, the teacher's code becomes the classroom code, and children are evaluated in its terms.

In the classroom, the teacher has the power; the teacher has the tools to supply the institutional biography that the child needs to escape his pariah origins. Teachers are quick to point this out to children and daily tell them that there is no success without school. If the child attempts biculturation, he adapts to the teacher's code, accepts the teacher's messages of power and dominance, and works hard at school. Many black children do not go this route. They reject the teacher's code and transform their minor differences in time and space use into large differences defining the classroom as the scene of the battle between the races. Code differences do not have to develop in this fashion, but they most often do. It is a measure of the teacher's adaptability in the early grades. The more sensible student-teacher relations can be made in the early grades, the less difference code differences will make. If the teacher fights the children with his formal authority from the early grades on, the children will equate the teacher's code with senseless suppression; it will become a difference that makes a difference. The children will reject the new code and seek the more rewarding alternatives offered by the peer group.

Host group teachers do not produce code differences. Both the teacher and his students partake in long ethnic traditions in their first years of life, and they then bring these traditions to school. The question is, how are ethnic differences made to make a difference? In the earlier grades, teachers make the difference as they are apparently not as adaptable as their students. In later years, as peer group lines solidify and code differences become the focus of most classroom social and political work, the children enforce the distinction between the teacher's code and their own code. In making their code make a difference, they are learning how to produce pariah status vis-a-vis the host group; they are learning to appear like "one-of-those"; they are producing a pariah biography which will haunt them until the next generation again plays the politics of everyday life in the classroom.

Identity and Mobility

The third task cannot be properly dealt with until we have detailed accounts of the politics of everyday life for many pariah groups both here in America and in other cultures. The third task is to explain why blacks do not fare as well as other minorities in classroom politics. All ethnic groups, Jews, Japanese, or Italians, for instance, bring some differences to the classroom. Shouldn't they all lead to communicative breakdowns, degrading relational messages between students and teachers, and, finally, learning disabilities? Yes, and indeed they do. Some groups have worked out ingenious strategies for by-passing host group discriminatory powers. American Catholics, for example, appear to have always understood the complexities of moving through host schools. Accordingly, they have always maintained their own school systems which have functioned not only as socializing agents, but also as protection against the sorting efforts of host group members. Whether or not their diplomas were equivalent in quality to host diplomas, Irish, Italian, and other Catholic Americans have always equipped their children with the institutional biographies required for at least minimally upward mobility.

The strategies of each group for identity work in the face of unacceptable messages of relationship in the classroom are probably deeply rooted in its history. The reasons for its having to develop such strategies exist in the politics of the classroom. If group identity work is necessitated by a breakdown in teacher-student relations, strategies as to what will be attended to and what will be acted upon will be worked out among the students. Learning abilities and disabilities are developed in such a context. School learning is almost always set back; the question is whether the group opts for learning how not to learn, the case described in this paper, whether the group merely opts to learn only about its own materials, as is the case for Hasidic Jews and the Pennsylvania Dutch, or whether the group overcomes the degrading messages and does scholastically better than host children even according to host group standards. The last case is most intriguing because of the records achieved by American Jews and American Japanese. Both groups have soared over mobility barriers and appear to have well escaped pariah status because of their mastery of the American school system. Of course, both groups reached the American shores with tremendous entrepreneurial skills and established traditions of literacy. Nevertheless, the essential question remains unanswered; namely, what did the Jews and the Japanese know that other pariah groups did not know? Alternatively, it can be asked what the host group knew about Jews and Japanese that it apparently does not know about other minorities (Spindler, personal communication). The point is that ethnic identity work defines what is to be learned and how it is to be learned, what is to be read and the strategies used for the reading act. What is different about the ethnic identity work of one group rather than another? Such a question will keep the next generation of scholars busy. If we achieve an answer, we will know a great deal.

Summary

Pariah groups are continually regenerated by host and pariah children learning how to assign *meanings* to particular social acts and how to *act appropriately* on the basis of the meanings assigned. These meanings are programmed into the *central nervous system* as patterns of *selective attention* to the stimuli particular to some acts and not to others. Patterns of selective attention, glossed in everyday language as *abilities, statuses* and *identitites.* shape a child's *institutional biography* and define whether the child, his abilities, statuses and identities, are to be assigned to a pariah or a host group in any situation.

The conclusion of this chapter is that the patterns of selective attention and inattention demonstrated by pariah children in school represent rational adaptations to the politics of everyday life in the classrooms. School failure and delinqency often represent highly motivated and intelligent attempts to develop the abilities, statuses, and identities that will best equip the child to maximize his utilities in the politics of everyday life. If the teacher is going to send degrading messages of relationship regardless of how the game is played, the child's best strategy is to stop playing the game.

The ability to read is taken up in some detail since it is one program which defines the boundary between pariah and host groups. Specifically, it is suggested that the politics of everyday life induce patterns of inattention for the reading task in particular groups. Host teachers and pariah children find each other occasionally unintelligible because of vocal and body language code differences and stereotypes. These differences are escalated into cues for intergroup conflict when degrading messages of relationship are appended by the teacher to the child's use of his own code for interpreting and generating behavior. The child is engaged in identity and status work and often rejects these messages as meaningless. The child then develops patterns of inattention to the teacher, the teacher's tasks such as behaving "properly" and reading, and, eventually, most stimuli generated by the host group. The high rate of black American illiteracy and pariah group membership is explained in this way.

References

Aiello, J., and S. Jones, 1971, "Field Study of the Proxemic Behavior of Young Children in Three Subcultural Groups," *Journal of Personality and Social Psychology* 19(7):351–356.

Allitto, S., 1969, "The Language Issue in Communist Chinese Education." In C. Hu, ed., *Aspects of Chinese Education.* New York: Teachers College Press.

Azumi, K., 1969, *Higher Education and Business Recruitment in Japan.* New York: Teachers College Press.

Baratz, J., and Shuy, R., eds., 1969, *Teaching Black Children To Read.* Washington, D.C. Center for Applied Linguistics.

Bar-Hillel, Y., 1954, "Indexical Expressions," *Mind* (n.s.) 63:359–379.

Barker, R., 1968, *Ecological Psychology.* Stanford, Calif.: Stanford University Press.

Barth, F., 1969, "Introduction." In F. Barth, ed., *Ethnic Groups and Boundaries.* Boston: Little, Brown and Company.

Bateson, G., 1972, *Steps to an Ecology of Mind.* New York: Ballantine Books.

Beck, H., 1971a, "The Rationality of Redundancy," *Comparative Political Studies* 3(4):469–478.

———, 1971b, "Minimal Requirements for a Biobehavioral Paradigm," *Behavioral Science* 16:442–456.

———, 1972, "Everyman Meets the Epistemologist." Paper presented at the 1972 Annual Meeting of the American Political Science Association.

Becker, E., 1962, *The Birth and Death of Meaning.* New York: The Free Press.

Bernstein, B., 1964, "Elaborated and Restricted Codes," *American Anthropologist* 66(6, part 2):55–69.

Beteille, A., 1972, "Race, Class and Ethnic Identity," *International Social Science Journal* 23(4):519–539.

Birch, H., and J. Gussow, 1970, *Disadvantaged Children: Health, Nutrition and School Failure.* New York: Harcourt Brace Jovanovich.

Blurton-Jones, N., 1972, "Nonverbal Communication in Children." In R. Hinde, ed., *Nonverbal Communication.* London: Cambridge University Press.

Board of Education, New York City, 1966, *Getting Started in the Elementary School.*

Brameld, T., 1968, *Japan: Culture, Education and Change in Two Communities.* New York: Holt, Rinehart and Winston, Inc.

Byers, P. 1971, "Sentics, Rhythms, and a New View of Man." Paper presented to the 138th Annual Meeting of the American Association for the Advancement of Science, Philadelphia, December 30, 1971.

———, and H. Byers, 1972, "Nonverbal Communication and the Education of Children." In C. Cazden, et al., eds., *Functions of Language in the Classroom,* New York: Teachers College Press.

Caudill, W., and H. Weinstein, 1969, "Maternal Care and Infant Behavior in Japan and America," *Psychiatry* 32:12–43.

Cazden, C., 1970, "The Situation: A Neglected Source of Social Class Differences in Language Use," *Journal of Social Issues* 26(2):35–60.

Chance, M., 1967, "Attention Structure as the Basis of Primate Rank Orders," *Man* (n.s.) 2(4):503–518.

Cicourel, A., 1970a, "The Acquisition of Social Structure." In J. Douglas, ed., *Understanding Everyday Life.* Chicago: Aldine.

———, 1970b, "Basic and Normative Rules in the Negotiation of Status and Role, *Recent Sociology* 2:4–45.

———, in press, "Ethnomethodology." In T. Sebeok, ed., *Current Trends in Linguistics,* vol. 12. The Hague: Mouton.

———, and J. Kitsuse, 1963, *Educational Decision Makers.* New York: Bobbs-Merrill.

Condon, W., and W. Ogston, 1966, "Sound Film Analysis of Normal and Pathological Behavior Patterns," *Journal of Nervous and Mental Disease* 143(4):338–347.

———, 1971, "Speech and Body Motion Synchrony of the Speaker-Hearer." In D. Horton and J. Jenkins, eds., *The Perception of Language.* Chicago: Charles Merrill.

Cornell, J., 1970, "'Caste' in Japanese Social Structure," *Monumenta Nipponica* 15(1–2):107–135.

Crystal, D., 1972, "Prosodic and Paralinguistic Correlates of Social Categories." In E. Ardener, ed., *Social Anthropology and Language.* London: Tavistock.

Deutsch, C., 1968, "Environment and Perception." In M. Deutsch, et al., eds., *Social Class, Race and Psychological Development.* New York: Holt, Rinehart and Winston, Inc.

Deutsch, M., 1963, "The Disadvantaged Child and the Learning Process." In A. Passow, ed., *Education in Depressed Areas.* New York: Teachers College Press.

DeVos, G., and H. Wagatsuma, eds., 1966, *Japan's Invisible Race.* Berkeley: University of California Press.

Dewey, J., 1896, "The Reflex Arc in Psychology," *Psychological Review* 3(4):357–370.

Donoghue, J., 1971, "An Eta Community in Japan: The Social Persistence of an Outcaste Group." In G. Yamamato and T. Ishida, eds., *Modern Japanese Society.* Berkeley: McCuthchan.

Eidheim, H., 1969, "When Ethnic Identity Is a Social Stigma." In F. Barth, ed., *Ethnic Groups and Boundaries.* Boston: Little, Brown and Company.

Ekman, P., and W. Friesen, 1969, "Nonverbal Leakage and Clues to Deception," *Psychiatry* 32(1):88–106.

Entwistle, D., 1971, "Implications of Language Socialization for Reading Models and for Learning to Read," *Reading Research Quarterly* 7(1):111–167.

Erikson, E., 1968, *Identity: Youth and Crisis.* New York: Norton.

Fischer, J., 1961, "The Japanese Schools for the Natives of Truk." In G. Spindler, ed., *Education and Culture.* 1963. New York: Holt, Rinehart and Winston, Inc.

Fishman, J., and E. Leuders-Salmon, 1972, "What Has Sociology To Say to the Teacher." In C. Cazden, et al., eds., *Functions of Speech in the Classroom.* New York: Teachers College Press.

Forge, A., 1970, "Learning to See in New Guinea." In P. Mayer, ed., *Socialization.* London: Tavistock.

Frake, C. O., 1962, "The Ethnographic Study of Cognitive Systems." In S. Tylor, ed., *Cognitive Anthropology.* New York: Holt, Rinehart and Winston, Inc., 1969.

———, 1973, "How to Enter a Yakan House," unpublished ms.

Garfinkel, H., 1956, "Some Sociological Concepts and Methods for Psychiatrists," *Psychiatric Research Reports* 6:181–196.

———, 1963, "A Conception of, and Experiments with, 'Trust' as a Condition of Stable Concerted Actions." In O. Harvey, ed., *Motivation and Social Interaction.* New York: Roland Press.

Geertz, C., 1965, "The Impact of the Concept of Culture on the Concept of Man." In E. Hammel and W. Simmons, eds., *Man Makes Sense.* Boston: Little, Brown and Company.

Gibson, E., 1965, "Learning To Read," *Science* 148:1066–1072.

Goffman, E., 1963, *Stigma.* Englewood Cliffs, N.J.: Prentice-Hall, Inc.

Goodman, K., 1967, "Reading: A Psycholinguistic Guessing Game." In H. Singer and R. Ruddell, eds., *Theoretical Models and Processes of Reading.* Newark, N.J.: International Reading Association.

Gumperz, J., 1970, "Sociolinguistics and Communication in Small Groups," *Language-Behavior Research Laboratory Working Paper no. 38.* Berkeley, Calif.

———, and E. Herasimchuk, 1973, "The Conversational Analysis of Social Meaning." In R. Shuy, ed., *Sociolinguistics: Current Trends and Prospects.* Washington, D.C.: Georgetown University Press.

Hall, E., 1966, *The Hidden Dimension.* New York: Anchor Books.

———, 1971, "Environmental Communication." In H. Essor, ed., *Behavior and Environment.* New York: Plenum Press.

Holt, J., 1969, *The Underachieving School.* New York: Pitman.

Hostetler, J., and G. Huntington, 1971. *Children in Amish Society: Socialization and Community Education.* CSEC. New York: Holt, Rinehart and Winston, Inc.

Jackson, P., 1968, *Life in the Classroom.* New York: Holt, Rinehart and Winston, Inc.

Jensen, A., 1966, "Social Class and Perceptual Learning," *Mental Hygiene* 50:226–239.

———, 1969, "How Much Can We Boost I.Q. and Scholastic Achievement?" *Harvard Educational Review* 39:1–123.

Johnson, K., 1971, "Black Kinesics," *Florida FL Reporter* 9(1,2):17–20,57.

Kasamatsu, A., and T. Hirai, 1966, "An Electroencephalographic Study on the Zen Meditation," *Folia Psychiat, Neurolog, Japonica* 20:315–336.

Kendon, A., 1967, "Some Functions of Gaze-Direction in Social Interaction," *Acta Psychologica* 26:22–63.

———, 1970, "Movement Coordination in Social Interaction," *Acta Psychologica* 32:100–125.

———, 1973, "The Role of Visible Behavior in the Organization of Social Interaction." In M. von Cranach and I. Vine, eds., *Social Communication and Movement.* London: Academic Press.

Kohl, H., 1967, *36 Children.* New York: New American Library.

Labov, W., 1964a, "Phonological Correlates of Social Stratification," *American Anthropologist* 66(4, part 2):164–176.

———, 1964b, "Stages in the Acquisition of Standard English." In R. Shuy, ed., *Social Dialects and Language Learning.* Champaign, Ill.: National Council of Teachers of English.

———, 1969, "The Logic of Nonstandard English," *Florida FL Reporter* 7(1):60–75, 169.

———, P. Cohen, C. Robins, and J. Lewis, 1968, "A Study of the Nonstandard English of Negro and Puerto Rican speakers in New York City," Cooperative Research Project No. 3288.

———, and C. Robins, 1969, "A Note on the Relation of Reading Failure to Peer-group Status in Urban Ghettos," *Florida FL Reporter* 7(1):54–57, 167.

Largey, G., and D. Watson, 1972, "The Sociology of Odors," *American Journal of Sociology* 77(6):1021–1034.

Laver, J., 1968, "Voice Quality and Indexical Information," *British Journal of Disorders of Communication* 3:43–54.

Leonard, C., 1972, "A Method of Film Analysis of Ethnic Communication Style." Paper presented to the American Ethnological Society Meetings, Montreal, April 6.

Lewis, L., 1970, "Culture and Social Interaction in the Classroom," Language-Behavior Research Laboratory Working Paper no. 38. Berkeley, Calif.

Long, N., 1958, "The Local Community as an Ecology of Games." In N. Polsby, et al., eds., *Politics of Social Life,* 1963. Boston: Houghton Mifflin Company.

MacKay, D., 1972, "Formal Analysis of Communicative Processes," In R. Hinde, ed., *Nonverbal Communication.* London: Cambridge University Press.

Mackworth, J., 1972, "Some Models of Reading Process: Learners and Skilled Readers," *Reading Research Quarterly* 7:701–733.

Mackworth, N., and M. Bagshaw., 1970, "Eye Catching in Adults, Children and Monkeys. Perception and Its Disorders," *ARNMD* 48:201–203.

Makita, K., 1968, "The Rarity of Reading Disability in Japanese Children," *American Journal of Orthopsychiatry* 38:599–614.

McDermott, J., 1969, "Deprivation and Celebration: Suggestions for an Aesthetic Ecology." In J. Edie, ed., *New Essays in Phenomenology*. New York: Ballantine.

McDermott, R., 1974, "The Cultural Context of Learning To Read." In S. Wanat, et al., eds., *Extracting Meaning from Written Language*. Newark, N.J.: International Reading Association.

Melmud, R., 1971, "Black English Phonology: The Question of Reading Interference," Monographs of the Language-Behavior Research Laboratory. Berkeley: University of California.

Miller, G., E. Galanter, and K. Pribram, 1960, *Plans and the Structure of Behavior* New York: Holt, Rinehart and Winston, Inc.

Mitchell, R., 1967, *The Korean Minority in Japan*. Berkeley: University of California Press.

Montague, A., ed., 1964, *The Concept of Race*. New York: Crowell-Collier and Macmillan.

Ninomiya, S., 1933, "An Inquiry Concerning the Origin, Development, and Present Situation of the *Eta* in Relation to the History of Social Classes in Japan," *Transactions of the Asiatic Society of Japan* (second series) 10:47–145.

Parsons, T., 1959, "The School Class as a Social System," *Harvard Educational Review* 29(4):69–90.

Pribram, K., 1969, "Neural Servosystem and the Structure of Personality," *Journal of Nervous and Mental Disease* 149(1):30–39.

———, 1970, "Looking to See. Perception and Disorders," *ARNMD* 48:150–162.

———, 1971, *Languages of the Brain*. Englewood Cliffs, N.J.: Prentice-Hall, Inc.

Rist, R., 1970, "Student Social Class and Teacher Expectations," *Harvard Educational Review* 40:411–451.

Roberts, J., 1970, *Scene of the Battle: Group Behavior in Urban Classrooms*. New York: Doubleday Company.

Rothblat, L., and K. Pribram, 1972, "Selective Attention: Input Filter or Response Selection," *Brain Research* 39:427–436.

Scheflen, A., 1960, Regressive One-to-one Relationships, *Psychiatric Quarterly* 23:692–709.

———, 1964, The Significance of Posture in Communication Systems, *Psychiatry* 27:316–331.

———, 1971, Living Space in an Urban Ghetto, *Family Process* 10(4):429–450.

Schutz, A., 1953, "Common-Sense and Scientific Interpretation of Human Action." In M. Natanson, ed., *The Philosophy of the Social Sciences,* 1963. New York: Random House.

Segall, M., D. Campbell, and M. Herskovits, 1966, *The Influence of Culture on Visual Perception*. Indianapolis: Bobbs-Merrill.

Shimahara, N., 1971, *Burakumin: A Japanese Minority and Education*. The Hague: Martinus Nijhoff.

Singer, H., and B. Beardsley, 1970. *Motivating a Disabled Reader,* Thirty-seventh yearbook of the Claremont College Reading Conference.

Sokolov, E., 1969, "Modeling Properties of the Nervous System." In M. Cole and I. Maltzman, eds., *Handbook of Contemporary Soviet Psychology.* New York: Basic Books.

Sommer, R., 1969, *Personal Space,* Englewood Cliffs, N.J.: Prentice-Hall, Inc.

Spindler, G., 1959, "The Transmission of American Culture." In G. Spindler, ed., *Education and Culture,* 1963. New York: Holt, Rinehart and Winston, Inc.

Taira, K., 1971, "Japan's Invisible Race Made Visible," *Economic Development and Cultural Change* 19(4):663–668.

Thompson, L., 1966, *Reading Disability.* Springfield, Ill.: Charles C Thomas.

Trubowitz, S., 1968, *A Handbook for Teaching in the Ghetto School.* New York: Quadrangle.

Valentine, C., 1971, "Deficit, Difference and Bicultural Models of Afro-American Behavior," *Harvard Educational Review* 41(2):137–158.

Wallace, A., 1965, "Driving to Work." In M. Spiro, ed., *Context and Meaning in Cultural Anthropology.* New York: The Free Press.

Wanat, S., 1971, "Linguistic Structure and Visual Attention in Reading," *Research Reports,* International Reading Association.

Watzlawick, P., J. Beaven, and D. Jackson, 1967, *Pragmatics of Human Communication.* New York: Norton.

Zimmerman, D., and M. Pollner, 1970, The Everyday World as a Phenomenon. In J. Douglas, ed., *Understanding Everyday Life.* Chicago: Aldine.

JOHN A. HOSTETLER/Temple University

13 Education in Communitarian Societies—The Old Order Amish and the Hutterian Brethren

In the United States it is generally assumed that every citizen, regardless of his personal values or ethnic membership, must be educated to the limit, that democracy will prevail when education is made available to all, and that the national goals should become the personal goals of everyone. Education is believed to be important not only for national life but also for personal fulfillment and a wide range of social and economic goals. "Ultimately," says *The Report of the President's Commission on National Goals* (1960:81), "education serves all of our purposes—liberty, justice and all our other aims. . . . The vigor of our free institutions depends upon educated men and women at every level of society. And at this moment in history free institutions are on trial." The goals of education in the United States tend to be in the direction of self-development and fulfillment of individual wants, development of rational powers, and the enhancement of personal freedom. Thus we read in a publication of the National Educational Association (Educational Policies Commission 1961:8) that

> A person with developed rational powers has the means to be aware of all facts of his existence. In this sense he can live to the fullest. He can escape captivity to his emotions and irrational states. He can enrich his emotional life and direct it toward even higher standards of taste and enjoyment. He can enjoy the political and economic freedoms of the democratic society. He can free himself from the democratic society. He can free himself from the bondage of ignorance and unawareness. He can make of himself a free man.

Within the United States there are "little" societies which are threatened by the sweeping effort to educate every citizen. They reject the premise that man "can make of himself a free man." The NEA statement of goals, for example, contrasts sharply with that of the Hutterian Brethren, who say:

> Our children are our noblest, highest, and dearest possession. We teach them from the beginning to know God, to humble and abase oneself before God, to bring the flesh into subjection, and to slay and kill it. We permit them not to go to other schools since they teach only the wisdom, art, and practices of the world and are silent about divine things. (Rideman 1965; 1938 ed.)

In reply to the question: What is a good education? an Amish bishop (Bontreger 1910:77) says:

> A good education does not mean simply book learning, or the acquiring of a great store of information, or a scholarship that has mastered the many branches of learning that are taught in the schools, colleges, and universities of this day. It does mean, however, a store of practical knowledge and skill, a knowledge that can discern between that which is good and useful and ennobling, and that which is a useless accumulation of learning in worldly arts and sciences.

The success of communitarian societies in evading the pervasive educational values of the "great" society, or of integrating some of the insights of public schooling into their indigenous educational system, varies greatly. Many traditional societies have been "swept out by the broom of our industrial and urban civilization," as Everett Hughes (1952:25) has put it. Communitarian societies are faced with the task of not only transmitting their distinctive culture but also maintaining their identity. They engage in what Siegel (1970:11) has aptly called "defensive structuring," defined as "a kind of adaptation that recurs with great regularity among groups that perceive themselves as exposed to environmental stress of long duration with which they cannot cope directly and aggressively."

Over a period of several years the writer has observed differences in the defensive structuring of two communitarian societies, the Amish (Old Order) and the Hutterites (Hutterian Brethren) with respect to education. In this chapter we shall discuss defensive structuring and relate it to community self-realization. At the outset we shall describe the world view and social structure of the two cultures, the areas of tension in relation to education, and then consider the differences in assimilation and disruption patterns. Generalizations dealing with education and the viability of the two cultures will conclude the chapter.

World View and Social Structure

Similarities in World View

Common to both Amish and Hutterites is the dualism of Christianity and of Anabaptism in particular. The doctrine of two kingdoms, the kingdom of God and the kingdom of Satan, light versus darkness, the carnal versus the spiritual, the perishable versus the eternal, and paradise versus wilderness are dominant themes in juxtaposition running through the indoctrination activity and the social structure of the subcultures.

The belief consistently set forth by the Anabaptists (Simons 1956) was that they, like the apostolic community, sought to be the blameless church consisting of those personally awakened and called by God. They believed that those who have been born again, and they alone, are brethren of Christ, because they, like him, have been created in spirit directly by God (Weber 1958:145). Taking the life of the first generations of Christians as a model and "avoiding the world"—in the sense of all unnecessary intercourse with "worldly" people—has been a cardinal principle with the Anabaptists wherever they have lived.

Thus an Amish or Hutterite person must live "unspotted from the world" and separate from the desires, intent, and goals of the outside or outer world. The literalness with which the basic doctrine of separation is practiced is evident in the symbolic systems of dress, in the taboos against forming economic partnerships or alliances with nonmembers, and in forbidding marriage with outsiders. Both groups view themselves—but in different ways, as "a chosen people," "a remnant people," and "a peculiar people." Because they considered infant baptism invalid and began baptizing only adults on confession of faith, they were called rebaptizers or Anabaptists and were greatly harassed by state churches in the sixteenth and seventeenth centuries. Both groups refuse to bear arms or serve in public office, practices which earned them the title of "radicals" during the Protestant Reformation (Williams 1962). Both have strong ascetic tendencies in Max Weber's sense, and in both persecution has been an important element in perpetuating a sense of distinctiveness. Each has an impressive record of martyrs.

The Old Order Amish today number about 60,000 persons. Their Swiss origin and history from the Rhineland to Pennsylvania and to other midwestern states has been well known. (Bachman 1942; Hostetler 1963). The Hutterian Brethren number about 20,000 persons. Like the Amish, they are a Germanic-speaking people but of Tyrol and Moravian origin who have subsequently migrated to Slovakia, Romania, the Ukraine, South Dakota and Montana, and Canada (Peters 1965; Bennett 1967). Hutterite and Amish groups have different dialects, but both use High German in their ceremonial activity. Both societies are communitarian in the sense of having an ideological emphasis on sharing and community, in limiting individual initiative, and in subordinating individual freedom and rationality to community values. The Hutterites are strictly communal, for their basic social unit is a colony, a social entity practicing the community of goods.

The Amish Community

The central integrating institution in Amish society is the ceremonial "preaching service" held every two weeks on Sunday in the home of one of the members. The Amish community consists of a number of farm households in proximity, bonded by a common tradition and faith, articulated in a local church district (congregation), and limited to a few square miles (due to their reliance upon horse-drawn vehicles). Amish and non-Amish farms are interspersed in the same region. The Amish do not own blocks of land as a corporation. Farm machinery, livestock, and individual household units are individually owned. The only property held in common in an Amish church district are the hymn books, and in some districts, the benches used for the church service which are rotated among the households. Sharing and mutual aid in times of fire, sickness, death, or catastrophe are highly characteristic but voluntary.

The authority of the Amish community is vested in the congregation of baptized members, headed by a bishop and several other ordained persons. The basis of all policy is the *Ordnung* (discipline) to which every individual gives assent on his knees when he takes the vow of baptism. The *Ordnung* embodies all that is distinctive of the group and includes common understandings taken for granted. Hence, these rules are unwritten, and most are learned and known only by being a participant member. The *Ordnung* is essentially a list of taboos, reflecting the peculiar problems and encounters of a local congregation. At the basis of any change in the *Ordnung* are the borderline or questionable issues. Any changes are recommended by the ordained and presented orally to the congregation twice each year just prior to the communion service. Each member is asked to approve any changes of the rules. A unanimous expression of unity and "peace" with the *Ordnung* is necessary before the congregation can observe communion. A member can be excommunicated at any time by violating one of the basic rules, but in the case of minor infractions, these must be reconciled before communion. Variations of rules from one congregation to another may be observed, but the most distinguishing rules among all Old Order in the United States are no electricity, telephones, central-heating systems, automobiles, or tractors with pneumatic tires. Required are beards but no moustaches for all married men, long hair (which must be parted in the center if parting is allowed at all), hooks and eyes on dress coats, and the use of horses for farming and transportation in the community. No formal education beyond the elementary grades is a rule of life.

For the Amish farmer who cannot assent to the *Ordnung* there are two means of mobility. Both are difficult and inconvenient. One way is to join a more liberal congregation, but the difficulty is that one may have to be shunned for life by his kin. The other way is to move the household to a community where there is a more compatible *Ordnung*. The *Ordnung* does not prevent a farmer from moving to another community or another state. This degree of freedom is constantly exercised by families who wish to move either because the *Ordnung* is too strict or not strict enough.

The Hutterite Community

A group of married families (from eight to twelve) and their children who live on a Bruderhof or colony constitute a Hutterite community (Hostetler and Huntington 1967). The family is assigned rooms in a long dormitory according to its size and needs. A colony may vary from 70 to 140 persons. With all its dwellings, communal kitchen, schoolhouse and kindergarten, livestock and poultry buildings, storage and machine buildings a colony may have up to a total of 70 buildings. A colony integrates not only religious ceremonialism but an economic enterprise, kinship, socialization processes, and property institutions. This basic community structure is very unlike the nucleated households of the Amish. From their beginning in 1528 the Hutterites equated communal living with the primitive and true expression of Christianity. They rejected as pagan the private ownership of property. Thus, land is owned by the colony corporation. Ownership of farm equipment and the purchase of all goods require the consent of the corporation. The colony is the self-sustaining unit within which the needs of all the members are met.

The authority of the colony is centered in the baptized men of the colony and is headed by a council of five to seven members, one of whom is a preacher. He is ordained by an assembly of preachers and is responsible for the moral leadership of a colony. Although a colony may make its own rules, it must also abide by the rules of a confederation of colones, the *Leut*. All executive functions of the colony are implemented by the council of five to seven men, headed by the preacher. The sale and purchase of goods is the responsibility of the steward who must give an accounting to the colony. From infancy the individual is socialized to be cheerful, to be submissive and obedient to the colony discipline, and never to display anger or hostility or precipitate quarrels. Individual initiative and self-development are de-emphasized. Travel is limited but permitted among colonies, and there are occasional trips to trading centers. Respect for order, for authority, hard work and cooperativeness, and submission of the individual will to that of the colony are dominant in the life style of Hutterite personality. The individual never receives schooling outside of the colony. He attends kindergarten from ages three to five, the colony German school and the English school during the school years, and is baptized at the age of about twenty. Ultimate good is achieved by identification with the colony, its communal work and sharing of goods, and only in this way can God be worshipped and honored properly.

The Areas of Tension and Defensive Structuring

The conflict of the two communitarian groups with the state over educational policy has received widespread publicity. School officials view the problem as one of law enforcement. The Amish and Hutterites view the issue in religious terms and as one of survival. Lawyers interpret the problem in legal categories. Citizens of the community often view the conflict as a "fight" between the old and new sentiments of the community. From the viewpoint of anthropology we are interested in contrasting one culture with another, touching on the significant areas of culture contact, formal and informal, and in defensive structuring as manifested in the socialization process. By concentrating on the areas of greatest tension we may obtain knowledge about the defensive structuring and the consequences for the communities themselves.

Amish Education

Acquiring literacy and skills for their young without subjecting them to a change in world view confronts the Amish community with a fundamental human problem (Hostetler and Huntington 1971). "The Amish as a whole," as one Amish spokesman has pointed out, "are very much interested in teaching their children the three basic parts of learning: reading, writing, and arithmetic" (Kanagy in Stroup 1965:15). The Amish child typically grows up in a large family in a farm environment. His first formal schooling begins when he is six or seven years old. His first major task is to learn the English language. This is not a major problem with brothers or sisters in the same school. While attending school he is expected to assist with farm chores and related family responsibilities at home, as do other members of his family. After completing grade eight, the formal schooling period,—with some exceptions as noted below,—is over.

During the period when the American youngster is in high school, the Amish child is learning to identify with his culture. High school comes at a time in the life of the Amish child when isolation is most important for the development of personality within the culture. During this period he is learning to understand his own individuality within the boundaries of his society. As an adolescent he is learning for the first time to relate to a group of peers beyond his family. As with most adolescents, he is testing his powers against his parents and the rules of the community. It is important for the Amish community that his group of peers include only other Amish persons. If the child should acquire competence in the "English" (non-Amish) culture at this stage, he is likely to be lost to the Amish church. While the parents are loosening their direct control and the community has not yet assumed much control the period is too critical to expose the child to outside influences.

High school would break down this needed period of isolation by taking the youth away from the family farm and by teaching him to identify with non-Amish associates. This is what the Amish mean when they say that high school is "a detriment to both farm and religious life." The public high school also teaches ideas that are foreign to the Amish culture and not appreciated by the community. The "way of life" of the high school is feared perhaps even more than the curriculum itself. If the child is removed from the community for most of the working hours of the day there is virtually no chance that he will learn to enjoy the Amish way of life. The incentive to comprehend his individuality, to master the required attitudes and skills necessary to enjoy life as an Amish person, are achieved during adolescence within the context of family, kinfolk, and church-community.

The Amish family needs the help of its teen-aged children more than the typical American family. The child also feels the family's need of him. To know that the family needs his physical powers and to know that he is an economic asset to the welfare of the family is important to the individual. Quitting school after the elementary grades for greater identification with family and for the rewards of participation in adult society is normative. The typical Amish boy or girl who learns to enjoy his family and his way of life has little regret when leaving school. Rather than relying on authority as a means of controlling the child, the parents now exercise control by showing the adolescent clearly how much the family needs him. The young person who works on the farm can understand and feel the contribution he is making to his family.

The formal objections to public education are based on religious precepts such as "The wisdom of the world is foolishness with God" (I Cor. 3:19). The world is educated, the Amishman would point out, but is plainly corrupt. Education has produced scientists who have invented bombs to destroy the world and through education the world has been degraded. A "high" education is believed to militate against humility and obedience to Christ.

Given the educational goals of "practical knowledge and skills" and avoidance of "that which is a useless accumulation of learning in worldly arts and sciences" the rural elementary public school has from the viewpoint of the Amish been workable in the past. Parents fear a strong, progressive public school. They recognize that its aim is to make the child self-sufficient outside of the Amish community and perhaps moral, although not necessarily Christian. They fear what teachers they do not know are teaching their children. They resent the school for taking too much time away from the family and from the discipline of farm work. Learning, or reading, for purposes other than the goals of the culture are looked upon with suspicion. But in spite of the adverse influences the small public elementary school has had on the Amish child, it helped to make of the child a good Amish person. It provided enough contact with outsiders to enable the child to participate minimally in two worlds, and just enough indoctrination into the outer culture to make the child feel secure in his own family and community.

Until about 1937 the Amish generally accepted most of the legal school requirements. As consolidation became widespread, however, the Amish established private schools as a matter of policy. The intent was not so much to teach religion as to avoid the "way of life" promoted by consolidated school systems. The Amish prevailed upon the school boards to keep the one-room schools open. In the process of consolidation, the public school officials often regarded the strongly populated Amish areas as a "problem" in attaining votes for reorganization (Buchanan 1967). All states with Amish populations have attempted to compel the Amish to meet the minimum standards required by law.

Pennsylvania was the first state to attempt widespread enforcement of the school-attendance law affecting the Amish. The law required children to attend school until their seventeenth birthday, but children engaged in farm work were permitted to apply for a permit which excused them when they reached the age of fifteen. However, many had repeated the eighth grade and were still not old enough to apply for a farm permit. The conflict erupted when schools were no longer willing to tolerate the practice of allowing the Amish children to repeat grade eight. School officials tried withholding the farm permits. When the parents did not send their children to the consolidated high school, the parents were summoned to court and fined. They refused to pay the fines on grounds that this would admit to being guilty and were sent to jail. Anonymous friends and businessmen frequently paid the fines to release the parents from prison. Some were arrested as many as ten times. The Amish fathers and mothers took the position that compulsory attendance beyond the elementary grades interferes with the exercise of their religious liberty, and that the values taught in the public school are contrary to their religion. Attorneys and friends of the Amish who took the case to the courts found no legal solution. After many confrontations and embarrassments, Governor George Leader, in 1955, arranged a reinterpretation of the school code to legitimize a compromise plan, the Amish vocational school (Policy for Operation of Home and Farm Projects in Church-Organized Day Schools 1955). Amish lay leaders took the initiative in developing the vocational schools for those pupils who were not of legal age to obtain a farm permit. Under this plan, known as "The Pennsylvania Plan," the pupils perform farm and household duties under parental guidance, keep a daily journal of their activities, and meet a minimum of three hours per week until they reach their sixteenth birthday. The schools are required to teach certain subjects and to file attendance reports, but teachers are not required to be certified.

The showdown in Iowa between the Amish and the public school officials in 1965–1967 illustrates not only how intense the feelings can become in a rural community but also the social processes when coercion is used (Erickson 1969). In a small Amish settlement centering in Buchanan County, Iowa, school authorities forced their way into an Amish private school to transport the children to a consolidated town school. The press recorded the scene as frightened youngsters ran for cover in nearby corn fields and sobbing mothers and fathers were arrested for noncompliance with an Iowa school law.

A few public school districts have maintained country schools in the more heavily populated Amish areas, thus forestalling the establishment of private schools by the Amish. The boards of these schools seek teachers sympathetic to the Amish way of life, and in keeping with respect for cultural diversity, see that religious values of the pupils and parents are not offended. The few schools that are following such a policy have achieved remarkable results. The arrangement provides for state-certified teachers, more modern curricula and facilities than is possible in the private Amish schools, and for enlightenment that is fitted to the culture. The recent agreement between the Amish and the Department of Education of the State of Indiana (1967) is an attempt to use means other than the courts to solve differences in educational policy.

In summary, defensive structuring in the case of the Amish takes the following forms: The Amish will vote against school consolidation to protect their group solidarity and they establish private schools for the same reason. There is a conspicuous absence of formal dialogue between the Amish and the school officials (Buchanan 1967). The Amish are almost wholly dependent on verbal agreements with school officials which the Amish accept at face value. The turnover of school personnel at local and state levels often operates at a great disadvantage to the Amish. Amish parents will refuse to send their children to school even when it appears to school officials that no religious principle is involved. It seems ironic that the Amish are forming private schools not for teaching religion but for obtaining literacy and practical skills under conditions that enable the culture to survive. Pressure from local residents to make the Amish conform to school-attendance laws is often reinforced by longstanding antagonisms. When negotiations break down on the district level, state officials intervene and usually arbitrate either informally or in the courts. School administrators have, in many cases, not learned the difference between those issues on which the Amishman will "bend" and those on which he will not compromise.

Amish Controls Over the Socialization Process

The Amish have no control over the philosophy of education presented in the elementary public school and their response is to form private schools. In communities where Amish attend public school, the school experience is accepted as necessary but with great reservations. The attitude toward public schooling is defensive. Efforts are made to keep methods and ideology from changing. Schooling beyond the elementary grades is not approved and parents will go to prison if necessary to defend this position. An Amish youth who insists on going to high school or college becomes a deviant. The high school is viewed as a system that prepares the individual for living in the "world," not in the Amish community.

The elementary school experience is considered a normal part of life, but if the school is public, then it is regarded as a part of the domain of the outside world. The public school is outside of the central integrating activity of the Amish community. When the school is private, its activity is also carefully guarded so that in many Amish private schools it is not permitted to teach religion, for this would compete with the roles and function of church officials.

In selecting the curriculum, the Amish have no control over the materials selected by the public school. In the private school some of the older texts discarded by the public school are used. They are less objectionable because they have less emphasis on science, modern technology, and physiology. The need for texts appropriate to the private schools is keenly realized. A few have been written by the Amish and others are in preparation.

Typically the one-room school building is located in the country, somewhat central to the Amish farm community. Whether the school is public or private, the distance to school is essentially the same. Many of the Amish live within walking distance, although some hire buses to transport their children to private schools. The school building is midway between the community and the outside world and is least integrated with other Amish institutions.

Hutterite Education

The constitution of the Hutterian Brethren Church (1950) assures every child of an education in skills and in religious training. The initiative for formal training in school belongs to the colony and not to the nuclear family. At all levels in socialization, the family supports the colony. Hutterite society from its beginning has had a highly institutionalized and effective system of formal education for all the age-sets. The major levels of formal education are kindergarten *(Klein-schul)*, German school *(Gross-schul)*, and Sunday school *(Suntag-schul)*, aside from the English or public school taught by an outside certified teacher (Hostetler and Huntington 1967).

When the group settled in the Dakota territories from 1874 to 1879, schools were formed on each of the three founding colonies and were taught by colony members. After 1889 the Hutterite teachers had to qualify for teaching certificates by written examinations. The first outside teacher was hired in 1909 in the Bon Homme colony (Deets 1939:40). By 1931 all the colonies were staffed by non-Hutterite teachers since few members were able to procure teaching certificates. When the Hutterites moved to Alberta in 1918 the establishment of an ungraded rural school in each of the colonies was acceptable to the province. The Alberta Department of Education appointed an official trustee for each school. When school districts were formed, the Hutterites refused to send their children to schools away from the colony grounds. Three private schools were founded as a result. However, in most of the 140 or more Canadian colonies today, the colony school is not a private school. The teacher is appointed and paid by the Department of Education (in consultation with the colony) and the building, heating, and maintenance is provided by the colony.

The agreement between divisional school boards and colonies in Alberta states that "if the colony insist that they shall have their own school apart from the schools for the division, the other rate payers of the division should not be asked to bear any of the cost of the school in the Hutterite Colony" (Knill 1958:86). Three acres, fenced, with an approved building and a residence for the teacher are to be supplied by the colony. The division appoints and supplies the salary of the teacher, supplies school equipment and books, but permits the building to be used by the colony for church activities. The Alberta School Act does not allow divisional boards the right to impose centralization on any school districts opposed to it. The Department of Education has thus far hesitated to enforce transportation of Hutterite pupils to schools outside their colonies. If this were done, Hutterites would exercise the option of establishing private schools. The Hutterites want and need the benefits of an outside teacher, and the Provincial authorities do not want to force the colonies into a situation where they would form private schools. Hutterites have also resisted forming a centralized school for several of the colonies. When the South Dakota colonies moved to Alberta the several Hutterites who had teacher's certificates were not approved for teaching in Alberta. The colonies permitted four of their young men to attend high school and Calgary Normal School to obtain teacher training. The experiment was considered a failure, for only one boy returned to become a teacher in the colonies. Through such attempts in the past some of their young men in both the Ukraine and in North America deserted the colonies. Although there are presently three college-educated Hutterite men teaching colony English schools, the practice is not favored with unanimity by the leaders. The reason as given by one spokesman is: "It is better to have the worldly school taught by a worldly person so that we can keep the lines straight."

The attitude toward English school is that it is important, especially in the early grades, for all children must know arithmetic and be able to use the language of the country. One leader said: "We expect our children to learn math, reading, and science as required by the Department of Education. We must learn English to understand the people around us." When asked what is most undesirable about the English school, these answers were given: "When the teacher does not cooperate with the German teacher or the preacher; taking pictures and then distributing them to the children or when dancing is held in the school, as it happened once. Learning the worldly ways would lead to their damnation. The old physiology books were all right, but the modern health books contain too much about dating, sex education and anatomy."

Aside from acquiring a good knowledge of arithmetic and reading, the only additional goal for Hutterites is that discipline be maintained in the English school. Teachers are expected and often encouraged to "lay down the law," and if they cannot maintain order, they are considered failures. A German teacher advised a new English teacher to "use the willow, for it's the only language they understand." A common complaint of teachers is that the children lack self-discipline and have less respect for an outside teacher than for the colony's German teacher. Greater respect for colony authority can be maintained if the English school also supports the prevailing authoritarian pattern. The English school on a colony becomes a disruptive force when social distance is not properly maintained. In its place, the school contributes to colony cohesion. Keeping the English school "in its place" is crucial, for here is where the ideology of the world and of the colony compete for the loyalty of the young minds. For the child who has not responded properly to colony indoctrination, the English school can become an important influence leading to possible desertion. In school the child can function as an individual and learn about the world outside his colony from his books and from his teacher. Intimacy between teacher and pupil can lead to defection. Friendships can lead to marriages with outsiders, to changes of denominational loyalties. In some instances, teachers have helped young Hutterites find jobs and leave the colony. Young single teachers, male or female, are greater risks than older teachers who are married and have children of their own.

All children of school age attend the English school of the colony. The colony makes a point of not interfering with the living pattern of the teacher, who may have a radio, a television, and even a separate mailbox. The home of the teacher is a potential source of worldly knowledge to colony people and a source of intrustion if not properly controlled.

The teacher is given moral encouragement in ways that aid the colony pattern, mainly as a strong supporter of discipline. The teacher cannot encroach on the child's colony time pattern by asking a child to stay after school, by staying during the lunch hour, or by homework assignments. A child may not be punished by depriving him of food. Discussion of a teacher's shortcomings in the presence of children limits his influence. Many of the colonies complain about receiving poor teachers. Indeed some are inferior as teachers, but there is evidence that many of the marginally good teachers like to teach in the colonies. Relatively inferior academic teaching is tolerated, and teachers are virtually free from the informal supervision of superiors. There is little pressure from parents for excellence and no parental interference in teaching. Unlike most school teachers, who must participate and relate to the wider activities of the community, the teacher in a colony enjoys a type of privacy and freedom from such demands. The formal relations between colony adults and teacher are cordial. Those with cooperative attitudes, including the poorer teachers, are more readily absorbed into the environment of the colony than teachers who are truly competent by outside standards and demand independent thinking of their pupils. Even then, there is little danger that the teacher will become a model for the children. When the teachers will emulate the colony pattern, in dress or by wearing a beard, disruption patterns are minimized and the children tend to show greater respect for the teacher.

Laws intended to raise the minimum attendance age, requiring children to take formal schooling through the ninth or tenth grades, are now adversely affecting colonies in some states and provinces. A few young Hutterites take correspondence courses from state colleges. Some of the teachers who are assigned to teach in the colony are willing to tutor or to give instruction beyond the elementary grades. Exploratory efforts have been made to establish high schools for Hutterite young people in regions where there are many colonies. All such efforts to take the pupils from the colony grounds have run counter to Hutterite religion. The consequences of having to attend school beyond the time when he is accepted as an adult in his society (age fifteen) adversely affects the pupil himself. At this age young people are given adult work privileges. They serve as apprentices to skilled adults under supervised conditions of learning. There is a tendency for the young Hutterite to feel deprived of his status as a growing person when forced to attend formal schooling beyond the age required by his culture.

The farther the child goes in school the less he is said to learn. From the colony's point of view this is correct, for once a child has mastered the basic skills, much of the rest of the subject matter learned has little relevance to their way of life. The colony German school teaches the children how to live, and the English school teaches facts, many of which are of little use to them. German school teaches proper ritual, the English school teaches worldly knowledge. The schools are clearly different, but both are regarded as necessary. In the ideal colony there is little conflict between the two schools, and the normal child receives an integrated learning experience from the viewpoint of his culture.

Hutterite Control Over the Socialization Process

While Hutterites have no formal control over the educational philosophy of the school, they exercise severe informal controls over the secular educational philosophy. They accept the benefits of the public school system and prefer it to operating their own private school. Leaders want their young to learn enough of the skills of arithmetic, writing, and English to become leaders among themselves in the future. While the "worldly" philosophy is brought into the colony, its influence is carefully guarded in a controlled informal environment.

The Hutterites tolerate the public school experience but reject the elements that are dysfunctional to the colony. Hutterites have a deliberate and well-formalized program of education for all the age-sets. The public school is only one of several "schools" in the life of the pupil and its effects are diminished. From the ages of two to five the child is in kindergarten daily to recite, sing, write, and think as required by the system. When he enters the English school on the colony he is already fortified against a foreign culture. During his school years he attends in the morning and often in the afternoon the colony's German school. This is the "real" school from the viewpoint of the pupil. The noxious effects of the public school are minimized by the German teacher. Instead of sending their children away to the English school as do the Amish, the Hutterites bring the English school into their environs and attempt to control the learning process.

The curriculum is selected by the divisional school boards and the Hutterites have no formal and direct control over text materials. Whether the school is private or public, the curriculum is similar to that in the rural schools. The physical proximity of the school to the colony allows for a great deal of informal visits and a strong degree of informal control over the teacher. This indirectly affects what is taught in the school. Teachers who are assigned to a colony for the first time are typically given a "lecture" by the preacher at the start or with the first offense against the colony. He outlines the colony's expectations of the teacher and sets the limits of practices which are "against our religion." The gifts in kind from the colony to the teacher and his family who reside on the colony may obligate the teacher to comply with the wishes of the preacher. Colonies prohibit the use of a radio, projected films, and the record players in the school rooms. Since the building is used for church in the evening, all art work and visual materials must be removed at the end of the day. Because the role of the teacher in the colonies is a very difficult one for these reasons, some of the most capable teachers by outside standards are not attracted to Hutterite colonies.

The school building is integrated within the colony layout. Its presence in the colony is symbolic of those aspects of schooling that are important to the colony. The colony accepts the English school complex but restrains its influence to serve colony ends. The school and teacherage are on the grounds, but they are oriented to one side of the colony and can function without major interference. The English school remains emotionally outside the colony. The time patterns, schedule, and colony holidays suggest superior loyalties. The first language learned and the first writing skills acquired are in German. German school is held at the start of the day, followed by English school. In effect, the English school is held in the visible presence of the elders, suggested by the council bench in front and the pews in the rear of the school. Thus the English school is encapsulated by the colony pattern, and ideally its influence cannot go beyond the bounds set by the culture.

Assimilation and Disruption Patterns

The type of controls exercised by communitarian societies over the educational offensive of the great society may be a significant variable for explaining why some "little" societies dissolve faster than others. The effectiveness of the controls (and defensive structuring) may be assessed in various ways. We have chosen to examine the extent of assimilation in the two cultures as reflected in the loss of members. A society with the least deserters would be one where we would expect a high degree of solidarity and one whose defensive mechanisms are effective.

Patterns of Mobility in Amish Society

In Amish society there is a constant movement from the orthodox to the more liberal groups of Amish-Mennonites. Individuals, family heads and their children, or entire congregations change their religious affiliation. Thus an Amish farmer who wishes to use a tractor for farming or drive an automobile instead of horses, will usually affiliate with a Mennonite denomination. In virtually all communities where there are Amish people there are also liberalized Amish or Mennonite groups. These groups form a continuum from conservative to liberal positions with respect to the rules of discipline (Fig. 6.1). Thus a deviating person may move from a conservative to a more liberal group without losing his identity as an Anabaptist. Although there are many divisions (as is evident from the different forms of dress and material culture), there is a common value orientation. The most orthodox groups lose the smallest number of members while the more liberal groups lose the most. The gains in the more progressive groups are a consequence of the secularization process and not the result of evangelistic activity. Most defectors from the Amish justify their change in affiliation for religious reasons. To turn against the moral training of early life, against kin, and the severe discipline learned in the formative years is not accomplished in the life of some defectors without cultural and religious shock. Religious revivalism, guilt, and conversion are important stages in the experience of the liberalizing Old Order Amish person.

An intensive study of defection in one Amish church in Pennsylvania revealed that 30 percent of the offspring did not join the church of their parents. Of all those who did not join the church of their parents, 70 percent

Figure 6.1. Cognitive orientation of Amish-Mennonite groups from "low" to "high" church in Mifflin County, Pennsylvania.

joined a Mennonite group and less than 10 percent joined other Protestant groups. In a study of religious mobility in the Mennonite Church, it was found that 24 percent of the converts came from Amish churches, while that denomination lost only 3 percent of its members to the Amish (Hostetler 1954:257). The loss of members varies considerably with affiliation, discipline, and church district.

The problem of land room is generally alleviated by the rather sizable number of persons who leave the orthodox groups. They then join the liberalized groups, who are usually engaged in occupations other than farming. The size of ceremonial affiliations is in many instances kept small by the disagreements over the discipline. Among groups who exercise the rigid form of excommunication and shunning, divisions are an alternative to migration. Migration to other rural areas is another alternative where social distance breaks down between the different groups. The assimilation patterns suggest that the Amish, who make the least use of formal education, whether indigenous or nonindigenous, are most vulnerable in terms of losing members.

Patterns of Mobility in Hutterite Society

In Hutterite society the loss of members is low. Some single boys leave the colony during the summer, but usually return in the fall. Of those who attempt to leave permanently, many return after they have "tried the world." The transition from the communal to individualistic style of living appears to be unnatural for them. Intensive moral indoctrination from kindergarten through adolescence helps to offset attractions in the world. Only 258 men and 11 women left the colony voluntarily from 1880 to 1951 (Eaton and Weil 1955:146), but over half returned.

Our study of Hutterite defection suggests that the communal socialization patterns are so effective that the small number who do abandon the colonies are those who were deprived of the normal communal training usually given a child (Hostetler 1965). The loss of members varies with "declining" versus "cohesive" colonies. A declining colony has chronic problems of internal leadership or dissension that have not been resolved. The rules of mobility do not permit a member to move from one colony to another of his choice. Of 38 defectors interviewed in depth, it was found that half had come from five nuclear families and all were located in declining colonies. In a few cases the school teacher was blamed for leading the young astray, teaching anti-Hutterite doctrine, and for finding jobs for them outside the colony. One colony girl eloped with the school teacher.

In Hutterite society there are no legitimate ways to become a non-Hutterite, not even Mennonite. Mobility is essentially blocked. Most male defectors interviewed tended to be indifferent to religion. They showed little interest in making distinctions between the vast number of denominations that are not Hutterite. The absolutist position of the Hutterite religion continues to structure the thinking patterns of those who defect permanently. The religion taught to them in childhood is basically respected by them in

such statements as: "If I ever want religion, I know where to find it." One
who had abandoned the colony forty years ago said that during the intervening years, "the little faith that you had was right there to sort of guide
you. The guardian angel was always with you, it seemed like."

All colony roles are psychologically marked by strong elements of dependency, especially for women. Any woman who cannot accept the definition of the role given to her will have more difficulty than a man in finding
alternative avenues of expression. Several groups of sisters who abandoned
a colony gave us their reasons that the colony was no longer Christian. An
underlying factor is that these sisters who found company in each other's
misery rejected the submissive Hutterite role assigned to women. Their
conversion to an individualistically oriented fundamentalist denomination
permitted a rational way of escape.

Emphasis on individual self-development constitutes a disruptive influence in a communal society. It is rare that an individual will receive sufficient personal attention to develop adequate personal security to leave
the protective environment of the colony. Parents who show favoritism to
a child or entertain ambitions for a child beyond those sanctioned by the
colony introduce dissident elements and increase the probability of defection. This relationship is understood by Hutterites. They say that if one is
too good to a single child he is more likely to leave. The favored child who
obtains attention and privilege above others in the family or in the colony
acquires self-confidence above his peers. Interests are developed and needs
are felt beyond what the colony can provide. A child that does not experience
the same rejection as his peers will not be frightened by problems that require
imagination and individual solution. A father who wanted his son to become
an engineer (a goal not attained by others in the colony) entertained non-
colony goals for him. A father who wanted his son to become the English
school teacher on the colony entertained a vocation for him that led to
defection. An able leader who exceeds the limits (usually intellectually)
or engages in certain privileges may unwaringly pave the way for subsequent
deviation by his children. When children are treated as separate personalities in the formative years, individualism tends to develop to such an
extent that it constitutes a threat to the colony. The system works best when
the preeminence of the collective welfare over individual welfare is cheer-
fully and unquestionably accepted by all the members. Although the Hutterites recognize real difficulties in maintaining the loyalty of their young,
it will be observed that they have a different pattern of assimilation than
do the Amish.

Conclusions

1. In American society it is assumed that the vigor of national life depends
upon educated men and women at every level of society. The goals of education are directed toward self-development and fulfillment of individual wants,

the enhancement of rational powers and personal freedom. The two communitarian societies we have described emphasize submission of the individual to community goals and the subordination of personal freedom and rationality to community values. Individual fulfillment is realized primarily within the bounds of the culture rather than outside of it. Science, technology, and science-oriented education are held in moderation in order to preserve the social order.

2. While the American young person is in high school, the Amish and Hutterite adolescent is learning to identify with his culture. The task of acquiring the necessary attitudes and skills to enjoy life in the little society are achieved in the context of family, kinship groups, work, and community. Socially it is an age span when greater freedom is permitted. The vows of the church and the commitment to the moral values have not yet been assumed, and during this period the young person is allowed maximal freedom to voluntarily test his beliefs and find his identity. These communitarian societies recognize the danger of exposing their young people to an alien peer group during adolescence. The high school is recognized for what it is: an institution for drilling children in "values, preoccupations, and fears found in the culture as a whole" (Henry 1963:287). The extent to which the communitarian society can control the social patterns of interaction and fulfill the basic needs of personality during the adolescent period is directly related to its viability.

3. The differences in assimilation patterns between the Amish and the Hutterite groups are related to the differences in social structure and defensive structuring. Given the same religious background and values, the communitarian society with the most integrated educational experience has the least amount of assimilation. The individual as well as the family in the Amish society has greater freedom of mobility, where and when he will travel and where he will live, than does the individual in Hutterite society. Amish persons who leave their culture often associate with groups similar to their own in religious orientation. Hutterites often show little inclination for religious affiliation after defection. The Navaho and Zuni adaptations to culture change (Adair and Vogt 1949) appear to have some similarities to these two Anabaptist groups.

4. Hutterites maintain formal education through all ages to maturity. There are "schools" fitted to all ages. The Amish depend entirely on informal education except for the elementary school period. The effect of introducing one more formal system of education (public) in the Hutterite colony is minimal since there is already a great amount of formal instruction. The Hutterites rather than the Amish manifest the least apprehension in accepting certain aspects of public education. The Hutterites integrate certain aspects of public education into their system of total socialization in a manner that maximizes their communal life and neutralizes any noxious effects. Formally they accept the inevitability of public education but informally they "tame" its pagan influences.

5. The management of crises over educational policy in the Amish and Hutterite groups differ significantly. The conflict is felt more directly by the Amish child than by the Hutterite child who may not even know that a "school problem" exists. Amish children often know they are the objects of controversy. When a legal code is enforced against a Hutterite parent the government is faced with religious leaders who are also the school officials and the real defendants. An Amish parent who may be charged with a violation must appraise his own commitment to his church, seek informal support from his church officials, obtain legal counsel at his own expense, or defend his position in court without either legal aid or representation from his church. Social solidarity is thus best maintained in a communitarian society that institutionalizes its contacts with the great society in contrast to one where the individual must represent his own position in an alien culture.

This analysis has not dealt with the products or the personality types developed in the two communitarian societies. These topics are discussed in greater detail in two case studies (Hostetler and Huntington 1967 and 1971). Through internal discipline and community support, often in the face of court action and scant legal protection, the two communitarian societies have transmitted the skills and attitudes required by their culture. Both have been able to mitigate, at least temporarily, the onslaught of the large consolidated school and its associated values.

References

Adair, John, and Vogt, Evon, 1949, "Navaho and Zuni Veterans: A Study of Contrasting Modes of Culture Change," *American Anthropologist* 51 (1947): 547–461.

Bachman, Calvin G., 1942, *The Old Order Amish of Lancaster County, Pennsylvania.* Norristown, Pa.: Pennsylvania German Society. Reprinted 1961.

Bennett, John W., 1967, *The Hutterian Brethren: Agriculture and Social Organization in a Communal Society.* Stanford, Calif.: Stanford University Press.

Bontreger, Eli J., c. 1910, "What Is a Good Education?" In, J. Stoll, ed., *The Challenge of the Child.* Aylmer, Ontario, Pathway Publishing Company, 1967, p. 77.

Buchanan, Frederick R., 1967, *The Old Paths: A Study of the Amish Response to Public Schooling in Ohio.* Ph.D. dissertation, Ohio State University, Columbus, Ohio.

Deets, L. E., 1939, *The Hutterites: A Study of Social Cohesion.* Gettysburg, Pa., privately printed.

Eaton, J. W., and R. J. Weil, 1955, *Culture and Mental Disorders.* New York: The Free Press.

Educational Policies Commissions, 1961, *The Central Purpose of American Education.* Washington, D.C.: National Education Association.

Erickson, Donald A., 1969, *Public Controls for Non-Public Schools.* Chicago: University of Chicago Press.

Goals for Americans. 1960, *The Report of the President's Commission on National Goals.* Englewood Cliffs, N.J.: Prentice-Hall, Inc.

Henry, Jules, 1963, *Culture Against Man.* New York: Random House.

Hostetler, J. A., 1954, *The Sociology of Mennonite Evangelism.* Scottdale, Pa.: Herald Press.

————, 1963, *Amish Society,* revised 1968. Baltimore, Md.: The Johns Hopkins Press.

————, 1965, "Education and Marginality in the Communal Society of the Hutterites." University Park, Pa., mimeographed.

————, and Huntington, G. E., 1967, *The Hutterites in North America.* CSCA. New York: Holt, Rinehart and Winston, Inc.

————, 1971, *Children in Amish Society: Socialization and Community Education.* CSEC. New York: Holt, Rinehart and Winston, Inc.

Hughes, Everett C., 1952, *Where Peoples Meet.* New York: The Free Press.

Hutterian Brethren Church, 1950, *Constitution of the Hutterian Brethren Church and Rules as to Community of Property.* Winnipeg, Manitoba.

Indiana, Department of Public Instruction, 1967, Articles of Agreement Regarding the Indiana Amish Parochial Schools and Department of Public Instruction. Richard D. Wells, Superintendent.

Knill, William, 1958, *Hutterian Education.* M.A. thesis, University of Montana, Missoula, Mont.

Peters, Victor, 1965, *All Things Common, The Hutterian Way of Life.* Minneapolis: University of Minnesota Press.

Redfield, Robert, 1955, *The Little Community.* Chicago, Ill.: University of Chicago Press.

Rideman, Peter, 1965, *Account of Our Religion,* English edition 1950. London: Hodder and Stoughton, Ltd.

Siegel, Bernard J., 1970, "Defensive Structuring and Environmental Stress," *American Journal of Sociology* 76: (July) 11–32.

Simons, Menno, 1956, *The Complete Writings of Menno Simons.* Scottdale, Pa.: Mennonite Publishing House.

Stroup, J. Martin, 1965, *The Amish of the Kishacaquillas Valley.* Lewistown, Pa.: Mifflin County Historical Society.

Weber, Max, 1958, *The Protestant Ethic and the Spirit of Capitalism.* New York: Charles Scribner's Sons.

Williams, George, 1962, *The Radical Reformation.* Philadelphia: Westminster Press.

GEORGE D. SPINDLER/*Stanford University*

14   *Beth Anne—A Case Study of Culturally Defined Adjustment and Teacher Perceptions*

This case study of Beth Anne will demonstrate how culturally unsophisticated perceptions of children by teachers may damage the "successful" middle-class child as well as the academically "unsuccessful" minority child in the school. The situation is in many respects the reverse of those portrayed in the preceding chapters by Raymond McDermott and myself, but in all three chapters the basic theme is the influence of the teacher's culture and the school upon perceptions and interpretations of children's behavior. For this purpose I am using a case study carried out when I was one of three people working in a school system under the aegis of the Stanford Consultation Service, directed by Dr. Robert N. Bush.[1]

Our purpose as a service team was to perform various studies of whole classrooms, teachers, individual children, other groups in the school, and even of whole school systems, as well as top supervisory personnel. Unlike the practice in a usual field study, we shared the data we collected and the analyses of those data with our informants. By so doing we hoped to share any benefits that might result from our research and direct them toward the improvement of the schools and the professional competence of teachers and related staff.

In this particular school, which we will call Washington Elementary School, we had entered to work with the whole staff of twelve teachers and the principal. First, we asked the assembled staff what it was they would like to study. They proposed a study of the "adjusted"—rather than the maladjusted—child in the classroom and in interaction with teachers and peers. We accepted this novel idea enthusiastically and proceeded to set up a mechanism whereby "adjusted" children could be selected for study. After some discussion the teachers helped out by deciding upon several specific children. These children's classes were approached as a whole for volunteers for the study. Among the volunteers were the children picked out by the staff.

---

[1] Details of time and place are left ambiguous, certain minor details of fact are altered, and all personal references are disguised in order to protect all parties involved with the case study.

The studies were cleared with their parents and we proceeded over a period of about three months to collect data and periodically to discuss these data and our interpretations with the assembled staff of the school. Beth Anne, a fifth-grade pupil, is one of the children studied.

The Classroom and Beth Anne's Place in It

The fifth-grade class consisted of 35 children ranging in age from 9 years, 8 months to 11 years, 8 months. The I.Q. range as measured by the California Mental Maturity Test appropriate to this age level was 70–140 with a mean of 106. There were three reading groups in the room, highly correlated with I.Q. scores as well as with reading achievement scores.

The classroom consisted of 20 children who could be described as Anglos whose socioeconomic status ranged from upper lower to upper middle (using the scales drawn from the studies of H. Lloyd Warner and his associates). The other 15 children were from the minority groups represented in the community surrounding the school and included 3 blacks, 2 Filipinos, 3 Japanese-Americans, and 7 Mexican-Americans (the term "Chicanos" was not current at that time).

Beth Anne was 10 years and 3 months old, just 3 months below the average for the whole class. She was in the top reading group and at the 95th percentile with her I.Q. test score of 132.

Excepting for occasional minor illnesses Beth Anne was apparently in good health, according to her parents and to records from the school office. She was dark haired, clear skinned, well developed for her age, had regular features and almond-shaped brown eyes, and wore braces on her front teeth. She always came to school extremely well dressed and was polite and considerate in her relations with her teachers; she appeared to be slightly reserved but equally considerate with her peers. The members of the team as well as the teachers in the school were impressed with her appearance and manners and regarded her as an exceptionally nice-looking child of good background.

Beth Anne was described by the teachers as an "excellent student," one of "the best students in the school," one who is "extremely conscientious," "cooperates well," "never has caused trouble in any of her classes," and who is "well liked by the other children." Further comments from the faculty were elicited in discussions of Beth Anne and the other children selected for study before the studies began.

Her former first-grade teacher said, "She was a very bright little child, perhaps not too friendly. At first she didn't respond too readily to me, but gradually began to work well and by the end of the year appeared to have made an excellent adjustment." Her present fifth-grade teacher said that "Beth Anne has attended very regularly this year. She is very interested in her class work and activities and performs at top level in everything. She even does excellent work in arithmetic and she plays very well with the other members of the class and in general with children of her own age." The principal said, "Her home would certainly be classified in the upper-middle bracket. The parents are middle aged, having married late. They have a very nice home and provide every cultural experience for the children." She went on to say that "one of the things that has concerned me a little, however, is a kind of worried look that Beth Anne has sometimes. It seems that if she doesn't understand the very first explanation in class, she is all concerned about it. She hasn't seemed so much that way this year but I have noticed it a lot in the past." Another teacher said, "Well, the mother has always been very interested in her children and has worked to give them many advantages. Beth Anne and her brothers and her parents go to many things and places together." Another teacher agreed, "Yes, they go to symphonies, I know. And they all went to the football game at Orthodox U."

Several times, and in different ways, we asked the teachers whether they regarded Beth Anne as a "well-adjusted" child. There were no explicit reservations expressed except for the comment by the principal about her "worried look" and the comment by her first-grade teacher that at first "she didn't respond too readily." The teachers all expressed verbal agreement that she was indeed very well adjusted, both academically and socially. Several teachers went out of their way to say that she was not only accepted by her peers but was considered a leader by them.

The Evidence

The study consisted of weekly classroom observations, watching playground activities, interviewing teachers, and administering psychological and sociometric tests. After having established the conditions of our study, our first step was to explain to Beth Anne what we would be doing and why. With her apparent enthusiastic consent, we proceeded then to a first interview followed by administration of the Rorschach projective technique and the Thematic Apperception Test (TAT). Within the following two weeks we also administered a sociometric technique to the classroom group. This technique included the questions, "Whom would you like best to sit next to?" "Whom do you like to pal around with after school?" and "Whom would you invite to a birthday party if you had one?" The sociometric maps of the choices expressed by the children were made up from the results elicited by these questions. They were quite consistent with each other. The sociometric map (sociogram) resulting from the responses to the first question is shown in Figure 7.2. We also administered a status-reputation technique that included thirty-two statements such as, "Here is someone who fights a lot," "Here is someone who never has a good time," "Here is someone who does not play fair," "Here is someone who is good looking," "Here is someone who likes school," "Here is someone who plays fair," and so forth. The children were to·list three names in rank order following every statement.[2] Following are summaries of these categories of data.

Observations

The reports by our three-man team of observers of Beth Anne's behaviors in the classroom and around the playground were monotonously similar. Beth Anne did not cause trouble. She was obedient, pleasant, and hard-working. She responded to questions in a clear voice and was noticeably disturbed when she was unable to provide the answer to a question in the arithmetic section. She read well and easily.

However, she interacted only infrequently with the other children in the classroom, either in the room or on the playground. She seemed quite reserved, almost aloof. Apparently she had a fairly strong relationship with one girl who looked and acted much as she did and who seems to have come from the same general social and cultural background.

Sometimes she chose to stay in the classroom when recess was called and would go out only at the urging of the teacher. She played organized games but not enthusiastically and seemed to find aggressive handling of a ball or other play equipment difficult.

Psychological Test Results

The Rorschach and the TAT were administered the day after the preliminary interview with Beth Anne and before any other observations or other methods of data collection had been implemented. Without becoming involved with the many problematic aspects of their interpretation, I will summarize the results of these psychological techniques. In general we found these projective techniques to be of considerable use in our studies of individuals, though we regarded them with a certain flexibility.

THEMATIC APPERCEPTION TEST ANALYSIS Most of the pictures in the TAT are of people engaged in social interaction and the subject is asked to tell a story about each picture. This story should state what the people are doing and thinking, what probably happened before the situation pictured, and what probably will happen. Beth Anne did not like to tell stories of this kind. Picking up the TAT pictures, she stated perfunctorily who the people were and what they were doing and then laid them down with what appeared to be an impatient air of finality. She was not able to say more upon probing, though

---

[2] With the wisdom of hindsight, I would not administer this technique again. It is potentially destructive to children's self-feelings and stimulates corrosive interpersonal evaluation.

she appeared to be at least superficially eager to comply. The TAT record is consequently rather sparse, though it is revealing.

The resistance to letting her imagination guide her to a creative solution to problems of human relationships as suggested by the pictures seems to be the most important feature of her protocol. She does not seem to like to be in a situation where she has to turn to her own creativity and utilize her emotions for interpretation. She does not seem to be able to empathize freely with the people in the pictures, even when she sees them as children. When asked what they might be feeling or thinking, she answered "I don't know," and if pressed by the interviewer, "How should I know?"

It is hard to pick out the most revealing instance of this aspect of her personality from the large amount of evidence in the TAT protocol. Upon seeing a picture of a little boy sitting in front of a log cabin she said, "It looks like he lives in a log cabin." ("What is he doing there?") "He's probably sitting there thinking about something." ("What is going to happen?") "Probably he is going to do what he is thinking about after a while." ("What is he thinking about?") "I don't know what he's thinking about. He's just thinking about all the things there are to think about!" In my experience with the administration of this technique with children her age, this is an unusual response. Most children as intelligent as Beth Anne seemed to embrace the task of telling the story about each picture with considerable spontaneity and creativity. Not so Beth Anne, who did not seem to be able to let herself go.

In another instance, when she was presented with a blank card and told to put a picture there by telling a story, she said, "There's nothing to make up that I can think of." That appeared to be literally true. She did not seem to be able to dip into any reservoir of imagination.

Beyond this prevailing feature in her TAT protocol, we can say that she shows some overt hostility toward authority. She also shows a certain amount of depression that is fairly rare for children her age, and she is made quite uneasy by symbols of open aggression.

There is no direct evidence of what could be called a pathological character development. What seems to be apparent is a lack of spontaneity and a refusal or inability to use her imagination to interpret the behavior of others.

RORSCHACH   Beth Anne gives evidence in her Rorschach protocol of possessing superior intelligence. She produced forty-eight appropriate responses, a result which is not only well above the average for her age group but higher than most adults achieve. She exhibits a high regard for detail and specification, but does not embark upon any flights of fantasy nor does she often put the details together to form an integrated whole perception.

Both qualitatively and quantitatively her protocol suggests that she is more constricted emotionally and intellectually than her superior productivity would lead one to expect. She has a well-developed perception of the concrete world about her, but these perceptions seem to stop at the level of concrete detail.

There is some evidence that she feels herself to be at times overwhelmed by forces beyond her control. There is also evidence that she has strong feelings that are not channeled into manageable interpersonal relationships or self-development.

It may be misleading to say that she lacks "creativity," but there is little imaginative spontaneity and little use of emotions for interpretive purposes. Beth Anne is what is sometimes known as a "tightrope" walker who sees what it is safe to see. She seems to avoid aspects of the inkblots that may have strong emotional implications for her and does not go deeply within herself for responses that would be emotionally meaningful. She avoids entanglements in emotionally laden material.

Furthermore, she seems to be fairly restricted in her ability to empathize with human motives or feelings. She does not seem to be able to put herself into another person's shoes, possibly because she has suppressed many of her own drives and feelings. At times, this may affect her intellectual performance, since she appears to be led off into inconsequential details and fails to see the larger whole.

Beth Anne is not likely to be a trouble maker. She conforms even at her own personal cost. She says "Thank you" every time a Rorschach card is handed to her and "Oh, pardon me!" when she drops a card an inch onto the desk and it makes a little noise. She seems very concerned about performing adequately and asks continually if she has given enough responses.

There is evidence that there are some definite problems in the handling of emotions. Generally speaking, the emotions seem to be suppressed or avoided, but when they are confronted they seem overwhelming. Given this evidence within the context of a personality adjustment that can be described as constricted and at the same time achievement-oriented, one would predict the probability of some form of hysterical behavior, probably in the form of conversion to somatic disturbances or to chronic invalidism. We shall see later that this prediction was supported.

The Rorschach psychogram is reproduced here (Fig. 7.1). For those familiar with Rorschach interpretation, one can note the heavy emphasis upon the "m" response and upon the "F" category, the absence of textural or shading responses, the absence of controlled color responses, and the presence of several relatively uncontrolled color responses. This psychogram is accompanied by 6 percent whole responses, 51 percent large usual-detail responses, 20 percent small usual-detail responses, and 23 percent unusual-detail or white-space responses. Beth Anne's average reaction time for all responses was 11.5 seconds. As everyone who has worked with the Rorschach knows, not too much faith should be placed upon the formal psychogram. It happens in this particular case that the psychogram relates closely to interpretations that flow from the qualitative nature of the responses. This tends to support the interpretation but does not validate it.

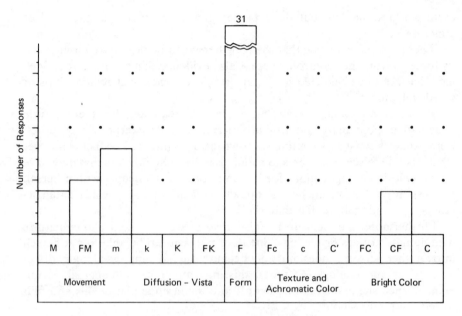

Figure 7.1. Beth Anne's Rorschach profile.

Sociometric Results

The sociogram (Fig. 7.2) maps the results of class responses to the question, "Whom would you like to sit next to?" Without attempting an analysis of the classroom as a whole, I will only say that as is not unusual at this age level, there is a definite separation between boys and girls. While the boys tend to cluster around certain leaders or "stars of attraction," the girls usually relate to each other in smaller cliques or even dyads.

Beth Anne's position in the classroom group insofar as these data show is extremely marginal. She is the second choice of a girl whom she considers (inferred from other data) to be her best friend. She made no choices herself. Her social situation is not significantly altered according to the social mapping of the results of the responses to the other two questions, "Whom would you like to pal around with after school?" and "Whom would you like to invite to a birthday party?"

Responses on the status-reputation test from the classroom group are impressively consistent with the results of the sociometric technique. Beth Anne is rated minimally: once for "Never having a good time" and once each for "liking school" and "Being good looking."

The results from both techniques indicate that Beth Anne is marginal in the classroom group. She is given very little attention—either favorable or unfavorable. It is almost as though she were not there at all. These results are consistent with direct observations made of her behavior and interactions with other children in the classroom and on the playground during recess.

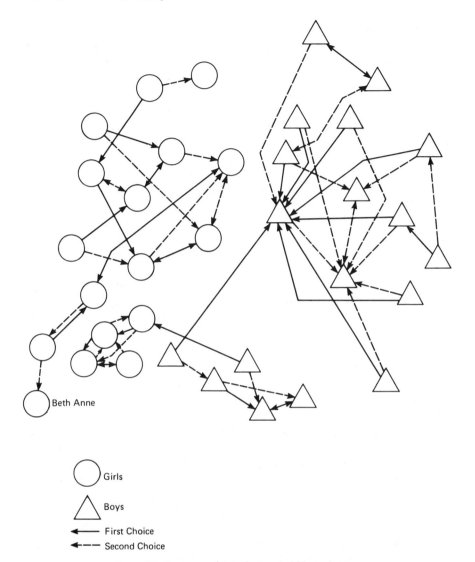

Figure 7.2. Sociogram for Beth Anne's fifth-grade class.

Home Visit and Parent Interview

Her parents were informed that the study of Beth Anne was under way. They had given their enthusiastic permission for the study when they were told, as was true, that Beth Anne was selected as a particularly well-adjusted child for special study. After the data collected above had been discussed within our team, an appointment was made to discuss the material with the parents and I was elected as the team representative. By that time the study had become primarily mine, although all three members of the team had engaged in observations and we had discussed the data as they came in during weekly seminar sessions.

Beth Anne's home was decidedly upper middle class in furnishings and exterior appearance. The interior appointments were luxurious and a two-car garage with a beautifully landscaped lawn completed the picture. Her father's occupation as the manager of a large building materials manufacturing company was appropriate to the socioeconomic status assignment.

When I entered the house Beth Anne's mother was waiting for me and said that her husband would come soon because he was very interested also. We discussed their recent trip to Alaska until Mr. Johnson arrived. Mrs. Johnson's attitude seemed very cooperative, and in fact she appeared pleased that the school had arranged to have a home visit and interview.

As soon as Mr. Johnson arrived we began a cordial discussion over coffee. I wished to make it clear at the very beginning that we were not dealing with Beth Anne as a "problem" case, so I reviewed the circumstances of the selection. We were working with the faculties of several schools in the community in an attempt to improve understanding of the adjustments of children at different grade levels—academically, socially, and emotionally. Having set the stage in this positive manner, I asked what aspects of our results they were particularly interested in. The father, a dynamic doer who wasted no time getting to the point, asked three questions as one, "What did you do, what did you find out, and what are you going to do about it?"

Rather than answer all these questions, I explained the techniques used in our study in some detail, including observations, sociometric materials, and projective tests. I explained why we used these techniques and what each contributed to a rounded picture of the child's adjustment. The parents seemed interested but obviously had some other concerns on their minds.

Mrs. Johnson queried, "Did you find that Beth Anne was temperamental or nervous at all?" I asked her to explain what she meant by that. She went on to explain that Beth Anne was "always complaining about her health. If any little thing is wrong with her, she wants to go to bed and she is always thinking that she is getting sick." She elaborated upon this at some length and then went on further to say, "She used to have a tic. . . . I guess that's what you would call it. When she was reading, and she reads a lot, she would draw her stomach up into a tight little knot and then let it go and the abdominal muscles would jerk back and forth." She continued, "I took her to the doctor, of course, and he said that she was tense and nervous but not to worry about it, that it was just an abdominal tic. He said that she would get over it eventually and as a matter of fact she is better now." This condition had apparently become obvious about a year ago.

Using this as leverage, I asked the parents if she were not rather a perfectionist—if she didn't seem to feel that everything she did, particularly at school, had to be done perfectly. Both parents agreed quickly and rather enthusiastically that this was the case. They appeared to regard my question as somewhat of a compliment. Possibly they could regard the pattern I described as evidence of a high achievement drive. They confirmed the observation implicit in the question with several examples concerning her behavior at home, in her room, her dress, and maintenance of personal possessions. After some minutes of this, I asked them if they thought this perfectionism might not cost her too much in tension and loss of spontaneity. While both parents nodded assent to this, they did not agree as wholeheartedly as they did when I asked them if she were not a perfectionist. They apparently could accept the definition of Beth Anne as an achievement-oriented youngster, but they could not bring themselves to accept the possibility that the standards of achievement could be so high as to make the cost so great. I did not press the point. When a silence in the conversation developed, I did nothing to fill it.

At this point Mr. Johnson said, "There's something else. . . . I'm not so concerned about it but Mary [the mother] is. . . ." And then the mother took up the cue, saying, "There are several junior high schools here [and she named them], now you have had a lot of experience in schools, could you tell us which one is the best?" I replied by asking her what she particularly wanted of the school selected. She said, "Well, we've been wondering whether or not we should move to a different neighborhood when Beth Anne is ready for junior high school. Washington School has been fine and we both appreciate all the things the teachers have done for Beth Anne, but you know there are all kinds of children over there—Mexicans, Italians, Chinese, Japanese, and even Negroes. Now, I believe in being democratic, but I feel that Beth Anne should associate with children that are, well . . . more her *equals!* [emphasis hers]. When she gets into junior high school this will be more important than it is now, but she feels it even now. She came home just the other day and said, 'Oh Mother, do I *have* to dance with them?' I think she should go to a school that doesn't have such a mixed group, where the children are all more her kind . . . don't you think so?"

In response I pointed out that the choice of a school was a decision that should be made by the parents in consultation with the child, and that what was important to one might not be important to another. Furthermore, it seemed to me that two points of equal importance in respect to a child's associates are, first, that the child be given a sense of belonging to a particular group and, second, that he or she should have broad experience with a wide variety of people from different backgrounds. This should enable the child to adjust well in any situation and to respect differences in others. When the parents pointed out that the two seemed contradictory I agreed, stating, however, that both could be accomplished if the parents' attitudes were supportive. To probe their attitudes a bit, I then suggested that they send their daughter to a private boarding school. Mrs. Johnson said that she wanted Beth Anne to be under her supervision, which would not be possible if she went away. However, she said, she wanted Beth Anne to be able to choose her own friends, with no attempt at reconciliation of the contradiction this posed with her other statements. I ended this phase of the discussion by saying that whatever the situation, Beth Anne's attitudes toward her classmates would reflect in significant degree what the parents thought.

I asked if there was any other specific topic they would like to discuss. The father asked how well Beth Anne was liked by her classmates. I replied, "She was not rejected more than a very few times by any other child; apparently they do not dislike her." While this did not tell the whole truth, it was at least in the direction of the truth, and I thought it was about as much as the parents could accept. I then asked if any of Beth Anne's friends were in her class, and Mrs. Johnson named three. My next statement was that Beth Anne was not chosen often either, and that in my opinion some of her classmates may have felt that she was critical of them. However, I told them also that the only negative trait on our status-reputation test was that she was rated as never having a good time. I could not explain the exact meaning of this, but assumed that it represented the children's feeling that she was serious about her school work. Before leaving I reassured them that "Beth Anne is a very excellent student and the teachers all like her a great deal." With reference to the points they had brought up, I told them that it might be important to see that she is encouraged to relax a little more and enjoy life as it comes. I said I thought her school work would keep up since she is very intelligent, even though her parents make this appear less important. I left thanking them for their cooperation and saying that it was a pleasure to talk with parents who were as cooperative as they were. They both uttered the usual pleasantries and said that they very much appreciated my coming to talk with them.

Teachers' Responses to the Evidence

By the end of our study period all of the evidence described above, plus many more details, had been shared with the staff. The teachers' responses could be described as ranging from surface compliance and agreement to deep covert resistance and resentment. I will draw a few representative comments from the tape taken during the final session with the faculty.

"I have her in art for 80 minutes a week where we try to bring out creative ideas, but actually she never offers any ideas. She usually looks at me as if to say, 'Well, what do I do next?'"

"I know Beth Anne and her family quite well and she knows this, but she is aloof with me. Does she impress the rest of you that way?"

"She reads so much. I should think this would aid her imagination. She reads stories about girls, camping, fairy stories, everything that children her age and even older read."

"She belongs to a group that went to camp last summer, but I don't think she went. She does have that little frown or worried look. I remember it bothered you, Mrs. Smith."

"I suppose that when a teacher has thirty-five children she tends to think of normal and adjusted in terms of how well they conform."

"Well they do have a very nice home. The parents just returned from a month's trip to Alaska and they hired a trained nurse to stay with the children. They have always been very thoughtful about their welfare."

"Well she has certainly done outstanding work academically, all the way through since kindergarten right up to the present in this school."

"She was always absent a lot in third grade and she never was particularly friendly. I always felt that she looked down her nose at the other children in the class who weren't quite up to her . . . I don't know whether she just didn't want to enter into things or whether she was fearful of making a mistake or what. Though she did good work, I always had a queer little feeling about her. I don't know just what it was."

"I don't think you have to worry about Beth Anne. She is going to arrive. Her family and their standing will see to that and she represents them very well."

"I agree. She'll be successful! She'll belong to a sorority."

"Well, anyway, she's a great reader!"

Interpretation

This case study virtually tells its own story and in that sense little interpretation is needed. Not all cases are as neat. This one was selected out of a much larger group—not for its representativeness but rather for its ideal-typical characteristics. It pulls together in one configuration dynamic processes that are present in some form in many other cases. It seems to be in part a reversal of the relationship between the teacher and the fifth-grade class and the counselor and his class that I have discussed elsewhere (1959). It is actually only a variation in this relationship. In all of these cases and in many others that we studied during our several years of field research and consultation, it became apparent that teachers, usually quite contrary to their expressed intentions and ideals, were selecting children for the fruits of success in our social system or for the ignominy of defeat and alienation on the basis of undeclared, and probably unknown, cultural biases.

Beth Anne was selected by the teachers by consensus as exceptionally well adjusted. It is difficult to know exactly what "adjusted" means to anyone, though it was a term used very widely in the fifties and sixties in American public schools. These particular teachers said during our preliminary consultations that adjustment meant "conformity to the rules and regulations of the classroom," "success at school work," "the ability to achieve according to the expectations of parents and teachers," "an ability to get along well with one's peers," "a person who is not too conflict-ridden when he or she attempts to get along with their work and play," and "a child who works and plays well with others." The teachers were clearly not all of a single mind concerning what adjustment meant, but their definitions tended toward an adaptation to the situation as defined by teachers, by rules, and, by the culture which the school represented. This is not unreasonable. In every cultural system those who accept the rules and achieve the goals laid down within the system are "adjusted" and those who do not are deviant, maladjusted, or criminal. The teachers' definitions do not pay much attention to what is inside Beth Anne's mind and, in fact, do not have much to do with Beth Anne at all. They have more to do with the school than with the child. This is understandable too.

However, we are faced with the fact that the teachers, even given their own criteria of adjustment, inaccurately perceived Beth Anne's situation. It is true that she achieved well according to the formal standards of academic performance. This achievement, however, was apparently at considerable psychic cost which was almost completely overlooked. Even more startling is the fact that the teachers misread the degree of her social adjustment. She did not "work and play well with others." In fact, she interacted with other children very little and was definitely marginal, really isolated within the classroom group.

Beth Anne's social marginality and isolation within the school was accompanied by severe internal distress in her own psychic system. She was compliant, a high achiever, but fearful of not achieving. She was unable to express her own emotions and had begun to evolve into a very constricted personality—all the more sad because she was such an intelligent girl. These processes had gone so far that a form of hysteric conversion had occurred. The prediction made on the basis of Rorschach evidence that the conversion would take the form of a somatic disturbance or possibly chronic invalidism was strongly supported. She wanted to stay in bed "on the slightest pretext" and suffered an "abdominal tic."

It would be easy to conclude that the teachers misperceived Beth Anne simply because she was academically successful—a high achiever in those areas where the teachers are directly responsible. This is, indeed, part of the cause for the misreading, but it is not a sufficient cause.

As I interpret the whole pattern of Beth Anne's adaptation and the perceptions of others of this adaptation, I see the teachers' perceptions as a self-sustaining cultural belief system. Beth Anne was selected not only because she was a high achiever but because in every other way she represented the image of what is desirable in American middle-class culture as it existed at the time of the study in the fifties and still exists today in slightly modified form. Beth Anne and her family represented success and achievement, the value of hard work, the validity of gratification delayed for future satisfaction, the validity of respectability and cleanliness, of good manners and of good dress as criteria for behavior. Beth Anne fit the criteria by means of which the teachers were selecting behaviors and children for the single channel of success and adaptation for which the school was designed as an institution representing the dominant mainstream culture.

I have characterized the belief in these values and selective criteria as self-sustaining because negative evidence was rationalized out of the system. Despite behaviors and attributes that any alert observer could have picked up in Beth Anne's case without the aid of outside experts or foreign instruments, Beth Anne was seen as one of the best-adjusted children in the school because she fit the belief system about the relationship between certain symbols, certain behaviors, and success as culturally defined.

This belief system, like most, can and does work. When belief systems stop working entirely they cease to exist, but they can continue to work partially for a very long time at great cost. In this case the cost to Beth Anne was profound. The culturally induced blindness of her teachers was in a certain real sense killing her and in ways no less painful than those in which minority children were and are being "killed" in many American schools.

Conclusion

I am not blaming teachers personally for what I have described in this case analysis. The teachers, the children, the administrator, and all of the other actors on the stage are acting out a cultural drama. What I am striving for as an anthropologist of education is an understanding of this drama as a cultural process. As an anthropologist teaching teachers I want to promote *awareness* of this cultural process. None of the teachers that I have described here or elsewhere in my writings in this book are people of bad intent. Most teachers are idealistic, many are quite liberal in their political and social beliefs, but they *are products of their culture* and live within the framework of values and symbols that are a part of that culture. By being made aware of what they are and do they can be freed from the tyranny of their cultures; in turn, they will be able to free children from the damaging effects of premature, inaccurate, or prejudiced estimates and interpretations of their behavior that are culturally induced.

This awareness is not easily gained. Though the teachers were exposed to intimate details of Beth Anne's case as these details developed, and though we exercised responsible skill and sensitivity in the dissemination of this evidence in open and closed discussions, the resistance of the teachers to the implications of the evidence was profound. The educative process had some effect, probably, but I doubt that it was very significant as far as the future behaviors of the teachers is concerned. Nor is a course or two in anthropology the answer. A year's fieldwork in a foreign community where one's assumptions, values, and perceptions are profoundly shocked by raw experience would

.make a significant difference, but not always in a direction that would be useful in the classroom. Matters have improved since the study of Beth Anne, but they have not improved enough. In my opinion a substantial part of the energy and time devoted to training teachers should be devoted to learning how to cope with the kinds of problems that I have been discussing in this and other case studies.

We were somewhat more successful with Beth Anne and her family as individuals than we were with the teachers. We explicitly recommended that the standards of excellence be lowered somewhat for Beth Anne and that she be given to understand that such achievements were not all that was important. Beth Anne seemed considerably improved according to a short follow-up observation the next year. But we cannot be sure of what happened. It may be that doing the study had a positive effect. Beth Anne at least knew that someone else had found out what it was like to be Beth Anne, and her parents discovered that it was possible to face a problem that they intuitively felt to be there because an outside agency had detected the same problem.

HARRY F. WOLCOTT/*University of Oregon*

15 *The Elementary School Principal: Notes from a Field Study**

"Harry, you ought to watch the company you keep," quipped a colleague from the university when he encountered me at lunch one day with a group of five elementary school principals. "He does!" came the immediate retort from the principal sitting next to me.

The principals had just completed an all-morning meeting at the school district central office, where they had been appointed to serve as a Principal Selection Committee for the school district. As such, they were to interview and recommend candidates to fill new positions as elementary school principals for the following school year. I had been present at their morning session in the role of an ethnographer inquiring into the life and work of the elementary school principal from an anthropological perspective.

This chapter draws upon a larger study designed to provide an ethnographic-type account of the elementary school principalship by means of an extensive case study of one principal (Wolcott 1973). In the present chapter, I have selected from the field notes an episode in which attention is drawn to the behavior of a small group of principals rather than to the behavior of an individual. The context of this episode is the proceedings of the Principal Selection Committee. A major portion of the chapter is devoted to a descriptive account of the proceedings of this committee and a discussion and comment based on the data presented. The chapter begins with an overview of the perspective and methods basic to the entire field study.[1]

*The author is professor of education and anthropology and a research associate at the Center for the Advanced Study of Educational Administration (CASEA) at the University of Oregon. The author wishes to acknowledge the support of CASEA during a portion of his time devoted to the preparation of this chapter.

Grateful acknowledgment is expressed to Max Abbott, Norman Delue, Joanne M. Kitchel, and George D. Spindler for critical comment and editorial assistance in the preparation of this material.

[1] A discussion of the methodology employed here has also appeared in *Human Organization* (Wolcott 1970). A more thorough discussion appears as Chapter 1, "A Principal Investigator in Search of a Principal" in the completed monograph (Wolcott 1973).

The Ethnographic Approach

The apparent neglect of attention to the *actual* behavior of school administrators in the literature on educational administration led to the proposal for conducting this research. That literature could well be augmented by a series of detailed ethnographic-type accounts of the actual behavior of people occupying roles in professional education, contextualized not only in terms of the formally organized institution in which they work but also in terms of their lives as human beings interacting within the context of a broader cultural milieu. This study was designed specifically to provide such data about the elementary school principalship.

The ethnographer's task is the recording of human behavior in cultural terms. The standard ethnography provides an account of some cultural process, such as law or divorce, or the way of life of some particular group of people, such as the Tikopia or the Children of Sanchez. This study is ethnographic to the extent that the principal who provides the focus for it is seen as an interacting member of a cultural system. Because the study is social and cultural rather than psychological in orientation, its scope includes not only the behavior of the principal himself but also the behavior of those with whom a principal interacts in the course of his professional life. This includes to some degree his spouse, his family, and his friends, and to a greater degree teachers, other administrators, parents, and pupils. These roles, and the interaction of the people filling them, are the human elements of a cultural system, the school system of one community. To the extent that the cultural system involved in this study is similar to other cultural systems serving the same purpose, this ethnography of a single principal should produce knowledge relevant to the understanding of such roles and cultural systems in general.

There are other ways one might proceed in studying a school administrator, one of which would be for the ethnographer to obtain such a position. In prior fieldwork, however, I had become acutely aware of the limitations on one's ability to observe objectively processes in which he is deeply involved as a participant (Wolcott 1967).

The literature dealing with school administration might have been expected to serve as a source of information about administrative behavior, but that body of writings is susceptible to several of the limitations which characterize the literature of professional education more generally. One such limitation is that much of the literature is hortatory or normative in content. It tells principals (or teachers, or superintendents) how they *ought* to act. It is prescriptive rather than descriptive. Literature of this type can provide a source for inquiring into the *ideal* world of formal education (Lee 1963), but it fails to provide an account of what actually goes on or how the ideals are translated into real behavior. The literature that *is* empirically based, on the other hand, provides factual data which tend to tell too little about too much. Such data prove valuable as a source of census information; for example, we can readily obtain a description of the "average" American elementary school principal (DESP 1968):

a male
married
between the ages of 35 and 49
has had 10 to 19 years total experience in schools
was an elementary classroom teacher just prior to assuming his administrative post.

This description fits the case-study principal perfectly. Yet the data provide little insight into how one becomes a principal, how a principal acts, or what he finds satisfying and perplexing about his role.

The barrage of questionnaires that confront public school personnel to inventory their training, habits, and preferences might also be expected to provide data about the principalship. However, the people who compose these questionnaires have frequently failed to do careful preliminary field-work. The information obtained in answer to questions like "Should a principal attend church regularly?" may reveal little more than the tendency of school administrators to give "expected" responses. Such studies seem to ignore the consequence that if the questions one asks are not crucial, differences in responses are not crucial either.

The nearest approximation we usually get to the actual behavior of administrators is from data based on self-reporting techniques. These techniques have frequently been employed in studies of school principals. Although self-reporting is somewhat comparable to one of the standard methods by which ethnographic accounts have been obtained—intensive interviews with a single or a few selected informants—it is far more subject to problems of informant reliability than is the method of intensive interviewing employed as one of a number of data-gathering techniques in the ethnographer's multi-instrument approach.

The ethnographic approach taken in this study has not been widely employed in conducting research in school settings. To my amazement I have occasionally been asked, "Did the principal know you were making the study?" I spent weeks searching for a suitable and willing subject, and I did not request formal permission from the school district to conduct the study until I had the personal permission and commitment of the selected individual. His family, his faculty and staff, his fellow principals, and many visitors to the school knew something about the research project. The faculty assigned me the nickname "The Shadow" as a way to jokingly acknowledge my presence and purpose at their school, and the name was learned by some of the pupils, too.

In order to learn how it is to be a principal, every aspect of the principal's life had some potential relevance for the study. I was once asked (some-

what facetiously, I suppose) whether I planned to take the principal's temper-
ature each day. I replied, not at all facetiously, that were it readily available
I would have recorded that information, just as it might be interesting to
know what the principal and his family ate at each Sunday dinner, but I would
obviously need priorities in my data gathering. My attention has been drawn
primarily to such aspects of the principal's life as the who, what, where, and
when of his personal encounters, the cultural themes manifested in his
behavior and in his attempts to influence the behavior of those about him, and
the problems and paradoxes inherent in the role of the principal. Although
the behavior of one principal served as the focus of the study, the fieldwork
provided extensive opportunities for observing many principals, ranging
from the rather frequent and often informal contacts of the case study
principal with administrators at nearby schools to his participation in the
official sessions and formal meetings of his school district and his memberships in county, regional, and state organizations of elementary school
principals.

Methods in Fieldwork

An "ethnographic approach" implies commitment to a perspective in both
the methods of field research and the handling of data in subsequent writing,
but it does not explicate the methods for doing either. Whenever it has been
expedient to describe my research methodology by a brief label I have leaned
to the term "field study." Zelditch (1962) has stated a case for the merits of
the participant-observer approach in the field study without going to the
extreme of insisting that participant-observation entails only participating
and observing. He argues, "a field study is not a single method gathering
a single kind of information" (1962:567); rather, the participant-observer em-
ploys three different modes in his research: "enumeration to document
frequency data; participant observation to describe incidents; and informant
interviewing to learn institutionalized norms and statuses" (566). I shall use
these three categories—enumeration, participant-observation, and interviewing—to describe the specific techniques employed during my fieldwork.

Enumeration and Census Data

1. Collecting copies of official notices sent to and from school to pupils, parents,
   or faculty (greatly facilitated by having a faculty mailbox in the office and by
   a school secretary who did not mind making an extra carbon of routine reports
   and correspondence).
2. Collecting copies of records (or, at the end of the year, the records themselves) of enrollments, reports, the principal's personal log of events, and
   daily notices written in a faculty notebook.
3. Collecting "time and motion" data by noting, at 60-second intervals over a

carefully sampled period of two weeks at school, what the principal was doing, where he was, with whom he was interacting, and who was talking.

4. Mapping and photographing the school and neighborhood. [2]

Participant Observation

The primary methodology used at the beginning of the study was that of participant observation. Customarily the principal introduced me by saying, "This is Harry Wolcott. He is from the university and doing some research in which I'm involved." This brief introduction seemed to serve as a sufficient explanation of my presence to all but the most curious, but anyone who asked was welcome to a fuller description. The principal and staff were remarkable in their capacity for allowing me to observe and record without insisting that I become an active participant in their conversations and activities. Although simply "keeping up" with a busy principal precluded the possibility of my ever being a totally passive observer, my active participation at school was limited primarily to engaging in the social banter of the faculty-room during lunch or at coffee breaks.

I made it a practice to carry my notebook with me and to make entries in it almost continuously. My intent was to create a precedent for constant note-taking so that the people would feel it was natural for me to be writing regardless of the topics or events at hand. Notes were taken in longhand in complete and readable form whenever possible. When I could not make complete notes and still remain present as observer, I jotted brief notes in the margins of my notebook and completed the full account later, often before leaving the school building. I never returned to the school until a complete account from a previous period of observation was finished. Nothing was gained by my mere presence as an observer; until the notes from one visit were a matter of record, there was no point in returning to school and reducing the impact of one set of observations by imposing a more recent one. Ultimately the longhand entries were transcribed onto 5 by 8 papers, each entry describing a single event, whether a lengthy transcription such as that containing my notes of the three meetings of the Principal Selection Committee or brief entries such as

> The principal said that when he called his wife to tell her he would be home by 5:30 this evening she replied, "So early! Why—what's wrong?"

> As the principal is trying various keys in the lock [he had just received some duplicates from the central office but did not know which doors they fit] a little

---

[2] This part of the research was conducted by my research assistant, an experienced geographer, who developed a socioeconomic map of the school-attendance area (Olson 1969). Although I carried out the balance of the field research, it was invaluable to have assistance in the analysis of enumeration and interview data by someone less closely connected with the school setting and thus presumably more able to restrict his analysis to the data at hand.

girl from grade two comes up quietly behind him, pokes him gently in the ribs, and says, "Boo." "Oh, my," he says. The little girl continues happily down the hall.

One of the objectives of this research was to see the principal in as many different settings appropriate to an ethnographic study as possible. It was easier, of course, to intrude on his professional life in connection with his work as a school administrator than to intrude into his personal life. At the school I was excluded, by prior arrangement, only from a few "touchy" parent conferences. Although more symbolic than functional, a table and chair were moved into the principal's office for my use. My observation extended to such settings as any school or school district activity or meeting; meetings of local, regional, and state educational organizations; formal and informal staff gatherings; in-service programs; and traveling to meetings with groups of principals.

In reviewing plans for the fieldwork with colleagues, I had been cautioned against becoming "overidentified" with the principal, particularly since he was the formally appointed status leader of the school. I visited often with teachers and staff members, including visits at school on days when I knew the principal was away. "Oh, checking up on us, eh?" someone would inevitably joke, leading me to feel that the caution against being overidentified with "the boss" had been well given.

My apprehension about being overidentified with the principal did not extend to those settings where he was away from his school. However, there are few guidelines for a researcher in accompanying a subject to see about a new battery for his automobile or to attend a service club luncheon. I was able to include within the scope of my observations such settings as the principal's home and family, business meetings at his church and the Sunday School class he teaches, trips to local businesses for school and personal reasons, Kiwanis luncheons, a family wedding and reception, and brief meetings with friends and neighbors.

Informant Interviewing

These interviews were of several types. First were taped interviews of approximately one hour duration, structured but open-ended, which provided excellent data concerning the principal's family life (interviews with his wife and mother) and the perceptions of him as a school administrator (interviews with thirteen faculty and two staff members). The interviews took time to arrange and conduct, and they seemed to take an eternity to transcribe, but they proved extremely valuable for uncovering the range of perceptions and the extent of the affective content expressed by the teachers regarding their work and the people with whom they associated professionally. The fact that I requested each interview as a personal favor and that no interviewing was done until I had spent over half a year at the school undoubtedly contributed to the extensive and useful data gathered via this method.

Another approach was to ask all the pupils in each fifth- and sixth-grade classroom to write briefly (and anonymously) what they thought they would remember about the principal. The phrases which I suggested to them to start their writing were, "What kind of a principal is he?" "Pleasant memories are . . ."; and "One time I won't forget. . . ." The comments I received ran the gamut of opinion, from the succinct response from a boy who wrote that his principal is "a Dam stopit one" to the reflection by a sixth-grade girl that "He is the kind of a principal who helps you figure it out." One boy wrote: "I won't fore get the time when my freind and I were blamed fore bilding a fire in the bath room."

The principal himself served as a primary informant, as he was not only the focus of the research but was to some extent a co-worker as well. I was never too explicit about what data I was gathering, nor did I often share my hunches or tentative analyses with him, but he correctly assumed that a brief recounting of what had occurred at school since my last visit would be helpful to the study. He enjoyed talking and visiting (I found that he did the talking one-third of the total school day during the "time and motion" study), so this self-appointed task came easily to him. At times he reflected on his personal feelings and philosophy and these statements provided valuable insights into his "ideal world." The juxtaposition of actual behavior and ideal behavior provides an excellent means for describing and analyzing a cultural system, and I was fortunate in having an informant who talked easily about aspects of his ideal world.

On a few occasions I emphasized the informant role and asked the principal to relate specific accounts. Plans were always discussed in advance when these sessions were to be taped. Important tapes included a session in which the principal summarized the opening of school and gave a forecast of the coming year, a session in which I asked him to review the wedding list and chat about the people who had been invited to his daughter's marriage and reception, and a session recorded in my automobile as we drove through the school-attendance area while the principal described the neighborhood to three new teachers who accompanied us.

A ten-page questionnaire designed for the study was distributed to all the faculty and staff at the end of the fieldwork. The questionnaire was particularly valuable in enabling me to obtain systematic data about the staff, as I could see no point in holding a long taped interview with each of the twenty-nine members of the regular and part-time staff. This questionnaire provided standard census data and information concerning each teacher's perceptions of the school, community, and classroom. It also provided an opportunity for all staff members to state their feelings about an "ideal" principal.

The use of the questionnaire provided me with a chance to thank the staff for their patience and help during the study. I felt that the questionnaire might also give me an opportunity to elicit staff reaction to the research project, and the last statement of the questionnaire was, "Some things the researcher may never have understood about this school are. . . ." The question did not evoke much response, but it was flattering to read "I think you probably understand more than we may think." I delighted in the humor of one teacher who assumed (correctly) that I did not know "There is no Kotex dispenser in the [women's] restroom."

My presence in the school district throughout the study was, I suppose, viewed as a mixed blessing. The mild but constant surveillance produced little overt strain that could not be alleviated by joking, but I provided so little feedback that there was no "payoff" for the many people who shared their perceptions and feelings with me. Still, a sympathetic and nonevaluative listener can provide an unusual opportunity for emotional catharsis, and I was amazed at how often teachers and principals seemed to appreciate an opportunity to "speak their minds." In this regard I feel that my position as observer and information-getter was considerably enhanced by the fact that, like the teachers and administrators who were the subjects of the study, I spoke the "language" of educators and had been "on the firing line" as a classroom teacher. I believe the case-study principal also found some comfort in having a part-time cohort with whom he could share something of the nature, complexity, and extent of problems which confronted him in the course of his daily work.

From the Field Notes: Proceedings of the Principal Selection Committee

Any number of episodes recorded during the course of the fieldwork could have been drawn upon here to illustrate aspects of a principal's professional life. Many would call attention to the routine of a typical day and to the incessant questions, problems, and meetings that seem to make constant demands on a principal's time and resources. I have chosen instead to draw upon a rather unique set of events, the proceedings of the Principal Selection Committee. This committee met three times during one month in the spring of 1967. These meetings provided a special setting in which the principals appointed to an *ad hoc* screening committee found themselves compelled to review and define—for the purpose of evaluating candidates—the critical attributes and qualifications of their role. This charge to interview and endorse certain candidates to join their ranks, though directed only to the principals appointed to the committee, served as an annual renewal ceremony for all the elementary school principals of the district. The fact of their appointment and task, and the results of their interviews and deliberations, served to reaffirm publicly the standards and responsibilities of their office.

The necessity for adding new members to their ranks occasioned a time when, like the elders among North American Indian tribes, the principals were obliged to "review, analyze, dramatize, and defend their cultural heritage" (Pettitt 1946).

The circumstances underlying the committee's existence — who appointed it, the task it was given, how binding its recommendations would be — provide clues about the formal context in which it worked. As the committee convened, for example, no one explained nor questioned why it had five principals (among the twenty-seven elementary school principals in the district), how or why the four new members had been selected by the director of elementary education and why one member had been retained from the prior year (especially after the director commented, "I tried to eliminate people who had ideas from the past"), how many vacancies or at which schools they would occur ("We will need two people, maybe three. We should pick our best people, not for [specific] positions but for ability, because we don't know where they will go"), or how binding the committee's actions would be on the ultimate recommendation which the superintendent would make to the school board. It was customary in this school district for the director of elementary education to appoint committees of varying sizes and varying purposes, and it was part of her job to "know" when she had sufficient authority to make appointments on her own or when she, in turn, needed the approval of the assistant superintendent or superintendent. The principals seemed to assume that she would be present during their meetings, and she slipped easily into the role of informal chairperson of the group.

For the principals appointed to the committee, to select "two, maybe three" candidates apparently provided sufficient parameters for their task, since in their ultimate decision they ranked the most "controversial" of the acceptable candidates as number four. No one pressed to learn why the number of vacancies was ambiguous. Two new schools were to be opened in the fall. If "maybe three" vacancies were to occur, there was more than mere conjecture about which principals might be in disfavor among the powers in the central office. (The third vacancy proved later to be due to an as yet unannounced plan for administrative reorganization which required the full-time services of one elementary school principal in the central office.)

Although the recommendation of the committee could be ignored by the superintendent, it did not necessarily mean that it would be. The new members checked with the principal who had already served on the committee to reassure themselves that recommendations made the previous year had been honored. The confidence expressed in the superintendent was formal and reciprocal. The committee showed no inclination to test the extent of its power or to threaten the power of the superintendent by making radical or unexpected recommendations. Attention was addressed specifically to assessing each candidate's standing "in the eyes of the superintendent" during discussions prior and subsequent to the interviews. In turn, official recognition was accorded to the committee through brief appearances before and during its sessions by the director of personnel, the assistant superintendent, and the superintendent.

During the total twelve hours of interview and discussion through which members of the Principal Selection Committee sat, fourteen possible candidates were reviewed. A brief profile of the candidates as a group showed them to include male and female applicants from within and outside the district, all holding a master's degree and all experienced elementary school teachers. In age they ranged from thirty-one to sixty-one. Their total experience in professional education varied from eight to thirty-nine years.

The extent of significant variation among the candidates is less than this description implies. One applicant who was not seriously considered and who was not invited for an interview accounted for most of the variation. She was the only female applicant and had served in an administrative capacity for only one year some fourteen years previously. In age and teaching experience she had thirteen more years than the next most senior applicant. The committee shared the feelings of one principal who summarized, "I think she's a wonderful gal and a fine teacher, but I question anyone going into this at 61." While age provided the immediate basis for a decision not to consider her further, it is likely that sex would have been the critical issue had she been younger. Three of the district's twenty-seven elementary schools were administered by women. As one male principal had candidly remarked on a prior occasion, "It's going to be a long time before we put in another woman."

Some candidates were dropped after only a brief comment as the committee sought ways to reduce the number of people who were to be accorded interviews and serious consideration. Regarding a relatively young newcomer in the district who had asked to be considered, for example, no one added any further comment after one principal expressed the opinion, "I see too many people ahead of him." Someone added, "The same with so-and-so." A third principal immediately suggested dropping both their names. Consideration of another applicant, an administrator from outside the district, was summarily ended when the personnel director, during a brief preview of the slate of candidates, recalled that this applicant had "already been hired [i.e., offered a contract] once in this district" and certainly should not have the opportunity to turn them down again. The committee agreed that there was no point in retaining names of people who were not going to be considered among the top eligible candidates, and they expressed concern over the problem of "getting the hopes up" among candidates called in for interviews. Yet any time a candidate's name was about to be dropped permanently, there was some hedging about giving everyone a chance. The frequent statement, "Let's just leave his name on for now" revealed a reluctance to take decisive and final action (eliminating a candidate) when less decisive action (ranking eight "top" candidates for three positions) accomplished the same purpose without requiring the ultimatum.

As the preliminary discussion of the candidates continued, based on the perusal of each candidate's folder of letters and recommendations, two procedural questions were discussed. The first was whether candidates would be selected only from within the district. The assistant superintendent observed that no outsider had been appointed to an elementary school principalship for many years. "We shouldn't overlook good people from outside, but in the past when things have been equal we have given preference for 'in-district.'" The tradition of selecting applicants from within the district was reaffirmed in the final recommendation made by the committee, although two out-of-district candidates were called for interviews. The rationale for interviewing "outsiders" was that the district did not wish to foster the impression that promotions to administrative positions were made only from within the ranks. To reaffirm among themselves that good candidates were always being sought, one principal recounted how an outstanding principal from California had "almost" been hired in a previous year. Another principal reminded the committee that any candidate "might come teach with us first" and work up into a principalship through promotion within the system.

The other procedural question dealt with the manner of conducting the interviews. The alternatives considered were to hold informal interviews, to ask candidates a set of prearranged questions (e.g., "What do you see as the role of the principal?" "How can the principal make the best use of teacher competencies?") or to guide the interview by using either an "in-basket"[3] or a problem approach. The pros and cons of each approach were discussed briefly. When the director of elementary education recalled that in a prior year one of the present applicants had been interviewed by using a structured interview technique, interest in that approach quickly subsided. Though never formally resolved, the actual procedure followed in the interviews was unstructured and was oriented primarily to getting a candidate to talk freely about his experiences, his beliefs about teaching, and his thoughts about the role of the school and the role of the principal.

Excerpts from the interviews and discussions are presented below. I have rearranged the actual order of interviews and have presented the candidates here according to the final rank order decided upon by the committee. The name of each candidate's ordinal position in the final ranking is used as a pseudonym.

Mr. Seventh

Mr. Seventh, age forty-eight, was an out-of-district candidate. Off and on he had been working toward a doctorate in education at the local university. He had served in administrative capacities, first as a principal and more

---

[3] The in-basket approach (cf. Hemphill et al. 1962) presents a series of hypothetical problems typical of those which require the attention of an administrator, presented in the form in which they might come across his desk in notes, memoranda, notices, letters. A whole set of simulated materials has been developed for use in graduate courses in elementary school administration (UCEA 1967, 1971).

recently as an assistant superintendent, for twenty-two of his twenty-five years in education. At the beginning of his brief interview he was asked whether he would plan to stay in the district if he completed his doctorate. He said that even with a doctorate he felt he might be able to advance sufficiently in a district of this size (over 20,000 students) to keep him there. He added that he might not finish his doctorate anyway. One principal joked with him about wanting to "go beyond" the principalship: "Isn't the principal about the best thing you can be?"

One of the interviewing principals had served years before as a teacher in a school where the candidate was principal, and he later said of him, "I think he'd be a pretty good candidate—he's pretty strong." At age forty-eight, however, the committee seemed reluctant to endorse him. Their reservations were reinforced by their suspicion that he wanted to get into their school district only because of its proximity to the university so he could complete his graduate work. When it finally came time to draw the line on candidates, Mr. Seventh's presumed lack of commitment to the principal role and his potential mobility, especially were he to complete his graduate studies, served as the basis for a low ranking. As one principal summarized, "I would have ranked Seventh higher, but I think of the elementary principalship as a career. He's a stronger candidate than some of the others, but I just don't think he's going to stay—he'll stay about four or five years and use us as a stepping stone."

Mr. Fifth

Mr. Fifth, 39, also from outside the district, had been principal of a large elementary school in a growing but still rural community for the previous five of his twelve years in public school work. In spite of his long tenure, his experience, which was confined primarily to rural schools, was regarded as a serious handicap. "Coming from those rural communities, he will be facing a real change if he comes here to be an elementary school principal," noted one committee member. "Would he be willing to come here as a *teacher?*" asked another. At the time they decided to invite him for an interview, members of the committee also tacitly assumed that his age and experience had probably narrowed the range of positions he would accept to that of a principalship. They found themselves in agreement that his rural-conservative school experience had probably failed to provide him with a sufficiently "exciting" background from which he might make a contribution to their own schools (thus rather subtly reinforcing the explicit preference for candidates who have worked in their own district, one they perceive as a school system in which the program *is* exciting).

Committee members were cordial in their greetings and introductions when Mr. Fifth appeared for his interview. He was directed to choose one of the (few) comfortable chairs in the meeting room, prompting the personnel director to joke, "It won't be this comfortable again." After a folksy prelude, the director of elementary education asked, "What things have you been doing and how have you been involved?"

MR. FIFTH: Ma'am?
DIRECTOR OF ELEMENTARY EDUCATION: Well, if you were a principal, what kinds of changes would you want to make?
MR. FIFTH: It would depend on what I found. If I found some needs, I would move in and meet those needs.

INTERVIEWING PRINCIPAL: How do you see the role of the counselor in relation to the principal?
MR. FIFTH: I see the principal as a sort of mediator—right in the middle—if there is a middle.

He described a two-stage role for the principal, first in getting the co-operation of the staff, then in a "selling" role to convince the parents. To illustrate, he elaborated upon an experimental "group counseling situation" recently set up at his school, a topic of immediate interest to the interviewing principals because of district-wide efforts to develop a counseling program at each elementary school.

INTERVIEWING PRINCIPAL: How were the children selected for your group counseling?
MR. FIFTH: Well, being in the school for four years, I pretty well knew which children needed help. Our goals were to help Bill Jones get some subjects so he could do his doctorate. But of course if I was setting up a [real] program, I would identify which kids needed certain things.

INTERVIEWING PRINCIPAL: How have you gotten teacher involvement in curriculum development in your district?
MR. FIFTH: We gave them their choice: "Do you want math or do you want social studies?" You see, they had a choice of what they would do. [There was some laughter at this. One interviewer asked, "No third choice?" Another joked, "Oh, there's a third choice, all right."]
INTERVIEWING PRINCIPAL: Is everyone on one of the two committees?
MR. FIFTH: Yes.
INTERVIEWING PRINCIPAL: Why do you say you like autonomy?
MR. FIFTH: I like to be an individual, just like you do.
INTERVIEWING PRINCIPAL: Do you like your teachers to be individuals, too?
MR. FIFTH: Yes. As a matter of fact, I encourage it.

INTERVIEWING PRINCIPAL: What do you feel is the role of the departmentalized program in the elementary school?
MR. FIFTH: We have "self-contained,"[4] yet I guess there are more exceptions than

---

[4] "Self-contained" refers to the organizational program of a school in which one teacher remains with the same group of pupils throughout the day.

the rule. [He described his reading program, a one-hour uninterrupted period during which the children are regrouped] It's a sort of modified Joplin plan. . . . We have Bible class but we don't let it interfere with reading.

His discussion of the reading program prompted him to comment about the extensive "help" received at his school from a nearby teacher's college:

MR. FIFTH: *So much help* can be a problem. For example, in our building we have fourteen teachers, two aides, nine high school cadet helpers, twenty-eight teacher trainees (ranging from part-time observers to student teachers), plus our own music and special education people, plus five more coming in doing research from the college. After describing how many people are in and out of the building, you could see why I would want to leave.

INTERVIEWING PRINCIPAL: It's not so rare here, either. This morning I had thirteen visitors, four teacher trainees, seven students observing from the university, and three policemen, plus the regular faculty.

The question of salary was introduced as a point of information by one of the interviewing principals, who explained that in the district an administrator's salary is not dependent upon school size but on tenure. The personnel director explained the administrative salary schedule in some detail: "Roughly, a principal gets one-fifth above the teaching schedule. So in your case, the teaching salary of $8,000 for a teacher with a master's degree and ten years of experience [the maximum years of nondistrict experience acceptable in the school district for purposes of salary evaluation] plus one-fifth is about $11,000 for ten months. A total of 205 days; $11,000." Mr. Fifth said that at present he was on an eleven-month contract. "You gain a month there," was the reply. He was informed that many school personnel work for the school district in the summer, writing curriculum or teaching summer school, "but not on the administrative [salary] schedule, of course."

Following the interview, committee members chatted as they watched Mr. Fifth walk out onto the parking lot, get into his pick-up truck, and drive away. "My wife once applied for a teaching position in that district," commented one principal. "It was *very* conservative!!"

In the review of the candidates at the conclusion of all the interviews the following comment of one interviewing principal seemed to summarize the reaction to Mr. Fifth: "We're doing *so much* here for boys and girls. We've gone about as far as we can. These fellows from outside have a real disadvantage, because they're still talking about getting kids in and out of rooms, holding ball games, and so on. I think he'd come along pretty well in a couple of years. He'd know our lingo and he'd be doing a good job. It might just take him a little longer."

A second principal concluded the discussion: "The more he talked, the farther I got from him."

Mr. Fifth, Mr. Seventh, and, in all, the names of ten applicants were excluded from the list of candidates recommended to the superintendent. Slight as the variation was among the original panel of fourteen candidates, the variation among the final four candidates chosen was even less. The four were married males between the ages of thirty-one and thirty-four. They had been in professional education from eight to twelve years, had all taught in the upper elementary grades, and all held degrees received five to ten years earlier at the master's level. Each candidate had been with the district from five to ten years. Although they held somewhat different positions at the moment (administrative intern, teacher on leave to pursue a doctoral program, resource teacher, junior high vice principal), each candidate had managed to alter his status from that of the full-time elementary classroom teacher he had once been; none now had direct teaching responsibilities. With the exception of the resource teacher (an extra teacher assigned full-time to a school to provide instructional assistance to the staff), all had held positions specifically entailing administrative duties. All four were considered eminently qualified to assume a principalship. Each candidate had achieved his present visibility *within* the district. With the exception of Mr. Fourth, each had achieved this visibility without stepping on the wrong toes.

Mr. Fourth's problem, at least in part, was that he had run head-on into a not-unknown obstacle in the path of a young man heading for the elementary principalship—the female administrator. A brief comment here concerning the different roles played by men and by women in the hierarchy of the elementary school, particularly in the professional relationship of the administration-bound male vis-à-vis the authority-holding female, may help put Mr. Fourth's problems as a candidate into perspective.

At the teaching level, the world of the elementary school is a world of women. At the administrative level the ratio of men to women is almost exactly reversed: 85 percent of the elementary school teachers are females (NEA Research Report 1967: 14); 78 percent of the elementary school principals are males (DESP 1968:11). The administration-bound male must obviously be able to survive in a predominantly female setting among his teacher colleagues. In addition, he must be able to survive in such relationships as that of student teacher–master teacher, or teacher–supervisor, where his immediate superior is most frequently a woman. And finally, there is a considerable likelihood that among the principals under whom he serves as a teacher he will be assigned to a "woman principal"[5] at least once—an assignment which probably exceeds random chance because female administrators seem particularly sensitive about securing teachers with whom their male pupils can "identify." Thus while women administrators do not exert a majority influence in the formal organization of their peers (indeed, in that era just

---

[5] In this regard note how the term "principal" is often qualified with the adjective "woman" if the role occupant is female, just as the term "teacher" is usually qualified with the term "man" when the role occupant is male, particularly in referring to teachers at the elementary school level.

prior to Women's Lib, I believe I detected a tendency among male principals to keep their few female colleagues "in their place" in their professional
organizations by relegating to them such assignments as taking charge of
table decorations, sending out invitations and thank-you letters, and performing minor bookkeeping tasks), the women exert a powerful influence
as gatekeepers to the principalship.

Among the fourteen candidates reviewed by the Principal Selection Committee the only two whose current dossiers contained overtly negative statements were two candidates working with female principals. Both had already
achieved nonteaching assignments at their schools as resource teachers, and
both maintained high involvement in the activities of the local teacher association. It was their active participation in the teacher association that
provided the basis for some of the criticism which each candidate received in
his evaluation. One principal noted two complaints in her written evaluation: one, that the candidate was "traditional" in his approach to teaching
(an implied criticism and a somewhat irrelevant one since he was neither serving as a classroom teacher nor being considered for a teaching position); and
two, that he conducted too much of the business of the teacher association
at school, thus detracting from his responsibility as a resource teacher to
assist the teaching faculty. "First things should be first," the principal had
admonished in summary.

"In other words," the personnel director commented after the evaluation
was read aloud to the committee, "the teachers aren't getting the help they
need."

"That's the only man left on her staff," observed one principal. "As I recall, she wasn't satisfied with the only other guy on her staff last year, either."

Mr. Fourth

Mr. Fourth had been highly regarded as a candidate the previous year.
His candidacy was critically reviewed because members of the committee
expressed some hesitation about his present status, particularly concerning
a prevalent rumor that Mr. Fourth and his principal were not getting along
very well. Differences between Mr. Fourth and his woman principal were
more than hinted at, they were openly aired by committee members. The
candidate himself commented of their relationship during his interview,
"She's not too good for a man's ego—especially if you're a little inefficient
like I am."

Unlike the procedure followed with any other candidate, Mr. Fourth's
principal was invited to meet with the committee to share her views about his
candidacy. Her discussion began with these comments:

> I think his one big problem is relating to people, because he tends to want to move
> too fast. . . . One thing he feels inadequate about is making small talk that makes
> people feel comfortable when they come to school. . . . I think he is better with

men than women. I've talked to him about how as an administrator he will be working mostly with women, and he'll have to observe certain amenities.

To the direct question, "Do you think he should be an administrator—say, for example, in a smaller school or some special setting?" she replied, "If I had my druthers, I'd like to have him in a situation where he could get some help—especially in human relations. I think we need to realize he's been in a very difficult position this year, working with a woman. . . . He has told me, 'It hasn't been any morale boost to work *with you.*'"

Immediately after the conference with Mr. Fourth's principal, one principal said, "Well, she hasn't changed my ideas any. We talked last year about his impulsiveness and these other problems." Another principal said, "There's no question of his ability. But I do feel some reservations about him." Another added, "A member of my staff said he walked right by her the other day without speaking. She felt badly about it. Of course, that doesn't pertain here."

Mr. Fourth's position as a former favorite was altered only slightly, but it was sufficient to put him out of the running. One committee member noted that no doubt the outcome would have been different had Mr. Fourth still been assigned to his former school, working with a male principal who had helped both to groom and to sponsor him for the step into administration.

Mr. Third

Mr. Third was less well known among committee members than any other in-district candidate. He had the briefest tenure in the district (five years), and this was his second consecutive year on leave in order to pursue graduate study toward a doctoral degree at the university. He helped reestablish his longevity by remarking to the committee as he entered for his interview, "I sat *here* last year," but the committee had already been reminded by the holdover member that Mr. Third had been "high on our list" the year before.

The search for topics to discuss was more difficult with a candidate who had not been active in the district for the past year and a half. As Mr. Third noted, "I've sort of lost track of some of these different programs." The discussion soon turned to the candidate's observations on the doctoral program at the university. The committee was receptive to his criticism that the "whole question of curriculum and administration at the university is all geared to secondary school." He told them that the set of qualifying examinations he had just written were all of the order, "Imagine yourself the principal of a *secondary school.* What would you do if. . . ."

One interviewing principal asked how Mr. Third's previous school district compared with this one.

MR. THIRD: The principals in this school district have a little more autonomy in the selection of staff.
INTERVIEWING PRINCIPAL: Is this autonomy a good thing?

MR. THIRD: I think this situation is good.
INTERVIEWING PRINCIPAL: Why do you?
MR. THIRD: So a staff can develop its abilities to the maximum. For example, maybe one staff can do more with "flexibility" than another.

Several times during the interview Mr. Third reaffirmed his belief in the importance of the elementary school principalship. In his concluding remarks he summarized, "I think the elementary principalship is a great challenge and quite different from other areas. You are working closely with individuals and different programs. . . . I've been an assistant principal, and now I'd like to try another notch up the ladder."

Mr. Third seemed to have made a good impression among the members of the committee. Their favorable reaction created some dilemmas which they discussed following his interview. One problem was his brief tenure: "He's the least experienced." Although his experience prior to coming to the district included two years as a teaching vice-principal, it was noted that he had held no position other than classroom teacher in his three active years in the district. An earlier bias expressed in the case of Mr. Seventh, who had been suspected of planning to come to the district in order to pursue a doctoral program at the university and then "moving on," was reinterpreted to differentiate between in-district candidates and out-of-district ones. "It's different in using the district if you've come up through the ranks or from outside it," suggested one principal. Mr. Third "might just be willing to stick around," posited another.

Mr. Third's recent efforts as a conscientious and effective supervisor of student teachers, fulfilling a part-time position on the university staff along with his program of studies, were duly noted by principals who had seen him in action: "Often these guys on a degree program don't have time to spend in supervising, but that's not the case here." Another principal added, "We've had some supervisors from the university who have missed a whole term."

Someone questioned, "We don't have anything on the salary schedule for a Ph.D. Couldn't he do better somewhere else?"

"He's told us he likes this district and wants to stay here," assured the assistant superintendent. "He doesn't want to be a professor."

I am quite sure I was the only person at the meeting who did not realize that the candidate was the superintendent's son-in-law.

Mr. Second

Enthusiastic support of Mr. Second's candidacy was expressed before, during, and after his formal interview. His excellent performance as a teacher and resource teacher, that he "dealt with difficult situations very well" as an active member of the local teacher organization, his "energy and interest," his active role in church work, even that his father had been a principal—all were duly reviewed before the interview began. If there was any reservation expressed at all, it was only to suggest that a promotion to the principalship might be a bit premature at present. While comments like "he was highly considered last year" and "I think he has matured greatly" tended to dispel such reservations among committee members, one principal reminded the committee, "He'll be around another year."

Mr. Second's interview began with the suggestion that he describe his "present situation," his experience, and the new programs he was working on. He launched easily into a fifteen-minute description of the educational program in the school where he was presently assigned. The following discussion was precipitated by his account of that program.

INTERVIEWING PRINCIPAL: I think we've heard a lot about the program at your school, and it's been a real good education. Now let's hear about how you think of *yourself* in a program—what do *you* want in a program?

ANOTHER INTERVIEWING PRINCIPAL: Yes, what do you think is the unique role of the elementary school?

MR. SECOND: I think it is to take each child where he is and take him as far as he can go. But that isn't unique to the elementary school. It's also junior high, isn't it? Yet I'm not qualified for the junior high.

ANOTHER INTERVIEWING PRINCIPAL: Who has the responsibility for making improvements in a school's program?

MR. SECOND: That's the principal's job—along with the whole faculty, of course. As an administrator, you should be the last one to take the glory.

To signal the start of the closing ritual during the interviews each candidate was asked if he had questions to address to the members of the committee. No candidate seemed to have a crucial question he wanted to ask, but none forfeited the implicit challenge to be able to ask *something*. The out-of-district candidates wondered which position they were being interviewed for. The in-district candidates already knew that this information was not yet available and that the decision about the annual "administrator shuffle" had not been announced and probably had not been made. Their questions concerned the dates when appointments were to be announced or the types of appointments to be made. The top two candidates expressed their concern about appointments to smaller schools, since the word was out that one of the new appointments might be for a "two-role" person (e.g., principal of two smaller schools, or principal plus some other assignment in one school). Mr. Second's query set off the following series of remarks in this regard.

MR. SECOND: I've been curious as to just how the joint principalships between two schools work out?

INTERVIEWING PRINCIPAL ONE: I've worked with it and it leaves a lot to be desired.

INTERVIEWING PRINCIPAL TWO: I think we took a step backward when we went to it.

INTERVIEWING PRINCIPAL ONE: I think it is better to combine a half-time principal and a half-time resource teacher in *one* school.

INTERVIEWING PRINCIPAL THREE: That looks good on paper, but it never seems to work out.

INTERVIEWING PRINCIPAL TWO: Of course, you know which one will give— just like when we principals have a conflict between supervision and administration.

INTERVIEWING PRINCIPAL ONE: There are no half-time jobs.

INTERVIEWING PRINCIPAL FOUR: How about combining the role of principal and the role of counselor?

INTERVIEWING PRINCIPAL ONE: With the role we're trying to create for the counselor, those two roles are not always compatible. When the axe has to fall, I'm the one who has to do it.

Mr. First

Presently serving in his second year as a full-time junior high school vice-principal, Mr. First had already established himself in an administrative niche. His request to get "back" into the elementary schools was met with a pose of suspicion by members of the committee which masked (but just barely) the significance they attributed to his application as a reaffirmation of the importance of the role of the elementary school.

The discussion prior to Mr. First's interview included the following comments:

ASSISTANT SUPERINTENDENT (reviewing his record): He's been a junior high vice-principal two years, but it only took one year to make him want to come back.

INTERVIEWING PRINCIPAL ONE: He's been so nice to work with over there that for selfish reasons I'd like to see him stay at the junior high level. How did he happen to get put into junior high?

DIRECTOR OF ELEMENTARY EDUCATION: They talked him into it one summer when I was away. They desperately needed a junior high vice-principal. He didn't know what his chances were for an elementary school position, so he took it.

INTERVIEWING PRINCIPAL ONE: Should he stay at junior high? Can he do any good there? Can he move up?

INTERVIEWING PRINCIPAL TWO: I think we should interview him and find out his feelings about junior high, whether he wants to get back into elementary, and if so, why.

INTERVIEWING PRINCIPAL THREE: How often do we ask people to do things in the district because it will be good for the district rather than for them? I'm not sure we're even doing these guys a favor.

ASSISTANT SUPERINTENDENT: Do you think that First's role on the Teacher-School Board Salary Committee has made a difference in how the Board might regard him? When we bring names to the Board, they react.

INTERVIEWING PRINCIPAL ONE: It might, but it shouldn't.

Mr. First's interview got off to a late but jovial beginning—he had thought his appointment was 11:40 A.M. instead of 10:40 A.M. and had to be telephoned at his school. His arrival precipitated the exchange of a few moments of raillery among those present. He knew everyone on the committee.

INTERVIEWING PRINCIPAL: What makes you think you want to be in a gang like this?
MR. FIRST: Are you serious? Do you want me to answer?
INTERVIEWING PRINCIPAL: Yes. That's really why we are all here.
MR. FIRST: Well, this is where I belong. This is where my training and my interest is.

Mr. First described programs and problems at his junior high school. He explained how he had tried to break down the resistance of those parents who "have the attitude that the school only calls once a year and that's when the kid is in trouble." He cited several aspects of secondary school administration which he disliked: "I don't like the sports emphasis in high school, the problems with buses and scheduling, the court cases. Last year I spent one day out of every two weeks in court. I'd rather be working with kids earlier in their lives, not in the kind of conference I sat in recently with a parent when a doctor told the mother her alternatives are either to give the daughter 'The Pill' or lock her up in a cage."

Another question gave him an opportunity to remind the committee of both his prior experience as a school administrator ("When I was an elementary principal in the Midwest," he began, "we had this problem. . .") and of an early encounter he had had with administrative rigidity. He described the attendance area of that school, a predominantly black slum area in a large city, as a "third-generation ADC neighborhood."[6] He discussed the program he had tried to initiate at the school: "It was a very peculiar nongraded program for a very peculiar neighborhood, a program for which the teachers and I were ready but the administration was not. I felt like I'd been kicked real hard when they turned down the program. That was about the time the director of elementary education came through recruiting teachers for this district. That's how I happened to come here."

INTERVIEWING PRINCIPAL: When you went back to the classroom after being an administrator, what were some of the problems?
MR. FIRST: Unwinding!! Not worrying so much about 50-minute programs.

MR. FIRST: One of my goals once was to go into teacher education. I used to think you could do the most good there, but I think now that's too far removed. You can do more good in the public schools—you're closer there. But it has some distasteful parts, too, like worrying over school budget elections or hasseling with the school board over a $100 raise.

---

[6] An ADC, or Aid to Dependent Children, neighborhood, i.e., a neighborhood with many families on welfare.

Final Deliberation

Members of the Principal Selection Committee deliberated for almost an hour after interviewing the last of the candidates before reaching a decision on their recommendation to the superintendent. One principal suggested a straw vote to rank all candidates and "see how near we are to one mind." The director of elementary education proposed that they identify and rank the top five candidates. Selecting a panel of five candidates for a maximum of three positions followed the earlier recommendation of the personnel director who had suggested they rank more candidates than needed because "someone might not take it." When the straw ballot was taken, four "favorite" in-district candidates topped the list. That number was informally adopted as the number of candidates the committee would recommend. Another straw vote was taken which reaffirmed the original ranking of the top candidates but revealed that one committee member was disrupting what was an otherwise highly agreed upon rank order.

INTERVIEWING PRINCIPAL ONE: There's someone who is ranking a top candidate low. I wonder if there is something we should have talked about?
INTERVIEWING PRINCIPAL TWO: I'm the one voting him low. Not because I have anything against him, but I still feel we have an obligation to another candidate. So I'm voting higher for him than I really feel about him. Yet I don't know if that's right, either.

Discussion, without further voting, revealed that all the members were satisfied with the composite results of the ranking and with the specific recommendation of the top candidates, as agreed upon from Mr. First to Mr. Fourth. The director of elementary education summarized: "I'll give these results, and our first vote, to the assistant superintendent. I'll tell him that before we would recommend anyone besides these top four we would want to discuss it."

The meeting, and the Principal Selection Committee itself, disbanded. "I'd much rather interview teachers," commented the case study principal. "So would I," added the director of elementary education.

Discussion and Comments

The proceedings of the Principal Selection Committee were presented here because that event, though well removed from the daily routine of any principal, brought into bold relief several aspects central to the professional life of the case study principal and to the principals with whom he worked. The present discussion is limited to three interrelated dimensions of the principalship which seem to pervade the life and work of a principal and which are substantially reflected in the data presented. These dimensions are (1) the lack of professional knowledge associated with the role, (2) an esteem for personal feelings, and (3) a proclivity toward variety-reducing behavior.

Lack of Professional Knowledge Associated with the Role

Throughout my fieldwork I was struck with the number of occasions in which principals communicated to each other uncertainties about what they "should" be doing and what is their "real" role. To any outsider, whether teacher, pupil, parent, or even researcher, the principals I met were always ready to describe and defend the importance of the elementary school and their contribution to its mission. In their own gatherings, however, free from their usual audiences and oblivious to the observer, they probed constantly for guidelines to answer one common and basic question, "What is the role of the principal?"

The role uncertainty of the principalship seems due in part to the problem of the lack of any professional (i.e., private and/or technical) knowledge or skill which clearly distinguishes the administrator from those administered. This problem is referred to broadly in the field of educational administration as that of working from a "limited knowledge base." Evidence of the limited knowledge base is illustrated in two ways in the proceedings of the Principal Selection Committee. First, in examining dialogue recorded during the committee's proceedings, one becomes aware of the absence of an esoteric technical vocabulary which might have been expected in other settings in the deliberations of such a "board of examiners." Except for Mr. Fifth's use of the terms "self-contained" and "a sort of modifed Joplin plan" the vocabulary evident throughout the proceedings reflects the ambiguous and general terms that characterized the professional language of administrators observed throughout the study: "real challenge," "meeting needs," "good situation," "involvement," "more autonomy," "unique program," "doing so much for boys and girls," and so forth. Indeed, to the extent that there is an esoteric language shared among professional educators (a language sometimes referred to jokingly within their circles as "pedagese"), principals express concern with their own ability to keep up with the latest changes in techniques or terminology. One principal observed, "You hire one or two new teachers and listen to them and you don't even know what they're talking about."

A second example of the problem of a limited knowledge base is suggested by the lack of systematic procedures by which the principals made evaluations necessary for ranking candidates. Having to make judgments which result in identifying one person as superior to another or which distinguish qualified from unqualified personnel can be a difficult and for some people a distasteful business. Nonetheless, the work of the schools is inexorably bound up with evaluating the performance of both staff and pupils. One of the crucial aspects of the principal's job in this school district, as it is elsewhere, is the annual process of preparing evaluative recommendations regarding personnel, particularly for those on probationary status. The lack of special skill or knowledge available to principals in performing this evaluative function was reflected collectively by the Selection Committee in the haphazard approach they took in interviewing and assessing candidates for the principalship. Whatever specific criteria each member of the committee used as a basis for judgment seemed to be assiduously avoided as a topic for mutual discussion and concern. One senses that each principal felt that regardless of the criteria he or his cohorts used, ultimately the group would reach substantially the same decisions regarding the selection and ranking of the candidates at hand. It should be pointed out in this regard that the final decision of the Committee did reflect just such a consensus.

An Esteem for Personal Feelings

The case-study principal and his colleagues seemed to share a distaste for formal evaluative tasks. Their reluctance was particularly apparent in the comments and jokes they made throughout the year about preparing their formal "teacher evaluations" and by the collective anxiety they exhibited as the deadline neared for submitting those reports to the central office. The same distaste was apparent throughout the meetings of the Principal Selection Committee as they spoke of "getting this over with." But their lack of regard for the formality of evaluation *procedures* should not be confused with their regard for the personal feelings of those whom they were evaluating. Their esteem for the feelings of the candidates, for the feelings of each other, and for their own feelings and intuitions as part of the assessment task, are repeatedly revealed in the dialogue. If the role of the principal can be characterized by a lack of professional knowledge, as suggested above, a compensating behavior of those who serve in it may be to give the affective domain considerably more importance than one generally associates with the processes of administration.

All candidates were interviewed graciously under circumstances in which the formalities inherent in the setting, such as meeting by a tight schedule of appointments at the central office, or holding most interviews seated around a large conference table in the formally designated Board Room, were consciously underplayed. The interviewers attempted to engage candidates in light social banter as they arrived for interviews. They asked open-ended questions, starting always with a question intended to put each candidate at ease and let him "tell something about himself." No question addressed to or response of a candidate was treated with the air of a grueling interrogation. Concern was expressed about interviewing any candidate for whom an invitation to appear for an interview might serve inappropriately to arouse his hopes. At the same time, the names of persons whom the committee never intended to consider as serious candidates were gently retained rather than summarily dropped. The only candidate really "rejected," and this primarily at the suggestion of the personnel director, was an out-of-district candidate who had once accepted and then rejected a contract offered him by the school district.

The personal feelings of the interviewing principals also made their way into the discussion of literally every candidate. Some of the statements regarding personal feelings were quite explicit: "I think I know him less well than some of the others, but I have a better feeling about him"; or, "I feel some reservations about how he relates to kids, but there's no question of his ability."

Not only were feelings of the interviewers introduced into the discussions, so also were feelings imputed to the candidates themselves. Most often such descriptions put the candidate in a favorable light or showed concern for his own feelings: "He has as good a feeling about children as anyone I know." "I think it would be a terrible blow to him if he didn't get a principalship."

Under conditions in which most comments are favorable, however, even the least hint of negativism served as a signal of caution: "He may be a bit bitter about education. He's talked to me about changing jobs and about being an administrator." [This comment brought a retort from another principal: "If he's somewhat bitter now, this would be the worst possible thing for him."]

A Proclivity toward "Variety-Reducing" Behavior

The proceedings of the Principal Selection Committee reveal a tendency among the principals to engage in what might be described as "variety-reducing" behavior.[7] This terminology comes from the field of general cybernetic systems. In the present case it draws attention to the fact that when the principals had to express preferences or to exercise choices which might be expected either to generate or to reduce the variation in certain aspects of the schools, their behavior reveals an inclination to reduce and to constrain. Their attention was directed toward keeping things "manageable" by drawing upon and reinforcing the existing system rather than by nurturing or even permitting the introduction of variation. This behavior is exemplified most clearly in the results of the major task confronting them, identifying candidates to receive official sanction. In that gentle but effective culling a panel of fourteen applicants was reduced to a final trio in which the successful members appeared so similar as to be virtually interchangeable. Whatever potential for variation extant among that original panel in terms of age, sex, background, recent experience, type and amount of formal education, marital status — in this instance even height, weight, and manner of speech and

---

[7] I am indebted to anthropologist Alfred G. Smith for suggesting to me the concept of variety-reducing versus variety-generating behavior as a means of analyzing administrative strategies.

dress—was successfully narrowed in the final selection. And while this process was going on, the principals also lent whatever support they could to reducing the potency of other variety-generating agents with whom their work brings them into continual contact, such as local colleges and universities, or central office administrators ready to saddle the principalship with a double role.

That the behavior of the principals in the episode gives such overt evidence of variety-reducing behavior is, in one sense, hardly surprising. The task to which they were assigned was by definition a variety-reducing task: there were almost five times as many aspirants as positions to be filled. Further, the very terms which the concept of "variety-reducing" calls to mind are terms which are descriptive of management processes: organize, systematize, categorize, constrain, control. What may be unusual is the extent to which variation was so thoroughly and systematically reduced, albeit this seemed to be neither an immediate nor a conscious concern of any of the principals on the committee.

Conclusion

I would like to conclude with a note of reflection relating the role of the principal to the emphasis placed on "change" in the public schools. This observation relates particularly to the preceding discussion on the phenomenon of variety-reducing behavior observed during the proceedings of the Principal Selection Committee.

The public schools have a seeming penchant for change. School people write, read, and talk constantly of new programs, new "hardware," new approaches, One can gather the impression from educators that anything "old" is suspect and that "changed" is automatically assumed to be "improved." In the last decade a whole vocabulary of change, including terms particularly familiar to students of cultural dynamics like "change agent," "acculturation," "innovation," and "diffusion," became the vogue in educational circles.

The school principal, charged directly with the role of being the instructional leader of his school, is often described as both instrumental and essential in the continuing process of introducing change into the school. The case study principal and his colleagues recognized this charge and responsibility. They acknowledged not only their formal obligation but their personal commitment to fostering change in the interests of a better education for children.

In looking at the totality of a typical "live" elementary school as the person charged with administering it might do, rather than at what is going on in any particular setting within it, one can appreciate that a school is a very dynamic institution. An elementary school is in a constant state of change without anyone having to do anything to induce or encourage the process. More than 500 people moved constantly into, out of, and within the school in this case study each day. New pupils, parents, teachers, substitutes, specialists, solicitors, sales and servicemen, and visitors arrived constantly to replace former ones or to swell the ranks of those already present. New problems, programs, and personnel are introduced constantly in schools as pupils graduate or move away, teachers "turn over," or interest groups demand and governmental agencies offer to subsidize new curricula and services.

Regardless of what he *says* about the desirability of creating a climate for change, the principal already lives with incessant change as a way of life. If an occasional principal demonstrates such a tolerance of or personal need for change that he actually becomes an innovator who induces significant change into his own school, really creating something new or introducing new degrees of freedom into the setting (rather than simply manipulating or restructuring what was already present) I would think he would be a rare principal indeed. I do not believe I encountered such people among the career administrators with whom I came in contact during my fieldwork. The life of innovative programs for schools, and the tenure of innovative administrators, is frequently short-lived (see Fleming 1967; Miles 1964; Redefer 1950; Rogers 1962; Smith and Keith 1971).

Faced as he is with the inevitability of change as an inherent and major aspect of his task, even though he may not recognize it as such, the school principal is successful in his work as he is able to contain and to constrain the ever-changing group which he is assigned to administer. If his survival in that role necessitates his constant effort at variety reduction, we may have an important clue in helping to explain why certain dimensions of public school education remain so relatively unchanged in spite of the constant attempts to change them both from within and from without. For it may be that the only way one can hope to maintain any control in a system which is inherently so volatile and constantly changing in some dimensions—in this case, its personnel—is to exert all the influence one can in reducing the potential variety which might enter the system via routes more amenable to restraint. Although it presents a curious paradox between their ideal and actual roles as "agents of change" if principals actually serve to constrain rather than to facilitate the dynamic aspects of formal education, that is exactly the paradox which I am suggesting here.

The paradox may be explained by reanalyzing the extent to which managing change is already an inherent and significant part of the principal's role. Change comes in the form of a constantly changing population, both in the local community of parents and children and, perhaps even more, in the day-to-day composition of the adult cadre present at school. How long does it take to orient a new substitute teacher so that her day at school will not be a fiasco? What amenities are required for meeting a parent new to the community or orienting a relief custodian or secretary new to the school? How much more variation might a principal be expected to seek out per day after spending a not-so-unusual two hours orienting "thirteen visitors, four teacher trainees, seven students observing from the university, and three policemen" plus handling the new problems generated by over 500 pupils and staff members already part of the daily complement?

Programmatically the public schools may still warrant the assertion made by Willard Waller years ago that they are "museums of virtue" (Waller 1932:34), but while the air of virtue about them may have remained, the characteristic of "museum-ness" has not. Most urban elementary schools today are large, bustling institutions. The people who manage them live their professional lives among a constantly changing and volatile group of children and adults in which everyone, including themselves, has only relatively temporary status. The irony for the elementary school principal is that the extent of change with which he lives is neither acknowledged by those about him nor even necessarily recognized by himself. Indeed, he listens to the cries for change and often joins ritually with those who attempt to bring it about. Yet ultimately his own actions, in a constant press to keep the institution manageable at all, may tend to reduce the variation with all the ploys and powers characteristic of administrators in general and an elementary school principal in specific: "We'll have to see about that"; "Mrs. X has some good qualities as a teacher, but she and I just aren't seeing eye to eye. I'm going to have to suggest that she either transfer or resign"; "It's a grand idea, but there's no money in the budget for it"; "These fellows from outside have a real disadvantage. . . . I think he'd come along pretty well in a couple of years. He'd know our lingo and be doing a good job."

Could it be that those people who seek to become and are able to survive as principals, through a perhaps inadvertent but apparently critical and essential proclivity toward variety-reducing behavior, have their greatest impact on education not as agents of change but rather as advocates of constraint? If so, we may be better able to account for the remarkable stability and uniformity that has characterized American elementary schools in spite of the forces for change swirling constantly about them.

References and Further Reading

Department of Elementary School Principals, NEA, 1968, *The Elementary School Principalship in 1968*. Washington, D.C.; Department of Elementary School Principals, National Education Association.

Fleming, Emett E., 1967, "Innovation Related to the Tenure, Succession and Orientation of the Elementary Principal," Northwestern University, unpublished doctoral dissertation.

Fuchs, Estelle, 1966; *Pickets at the Gates*. New York: The Free Press.

———, 1969, *Teachers Talk: Views from Inside City Schools*. New York: Anchor Books, Doubleday & Company.

Griffiths, Daniel E., Samuel Goldman, and Wayne J. McFarland, 1965, "Teacher Mobility in New York City," *Educational Administration Quarterly* 1:15–31.

Hemphill, John K., Daniel E. Griffiths, and Norman Frederiksen, 1962, Administrative Performance and Personality. New York: Bureau of Publications, Teachers College, Columbia University.

Lee, Dorothy, 1963, "Discrepancies in the Teaching of American Culture." *In* George D. Spindler, ed., *Education and Culture: Anthropological Approaches.* New York: Holt, Rinehart and Winston, Inc.

Miles, Matthew B., ed., 1964, *Innovation in Education.* New York: Bureau of Publications, Teachers College, Columbia University.

National Education Association Research Report, 1967, "Estimates of School Statistics 1967–1968." *Research Report 1967 R-19.* Washington, D.C.: National Education Association.

Olson, John A., 1969, "Mapping: A Method for Organizing Data about Your School Attendance Area," *Oregon School Study Council Bulletin,* vol. 12, no. 7.

Pettitt, George A., 1946, *"Primitive Education in North America."* Berkeley: University of California Publications in Archaeology and Ethnology 48 (Excerpted in Walter Goldschmidt, ed., *Exploring the Ways of Mankind.* New York: Holt, Rinehart and Winston, Inc., 1960).

Redefer, Frederick L., 1950, "The Eight Year Study . . . After Eight Years," *Progressive Education* 18:33–36.

Rogers, Everett M., 1962, *Diffusion of Innovations.* New York: The Free Press.

Sarason, Seymour B., 1971, *The Culture of the School and the Problem of Change.* Boston: Allyn and Bacon.

Smith, Louis M., and Pat M. Keith, 1971, Anatomy of Educational Innovation: An Organizational Analysis of an Elementary School. New York: John Wiley & Sons, Inc.

Spindler, George D., 1963, "The Role of the School Administrator," in George D. Spindler, ed., *Education and Culture: Anthropological Approaches.* New York: Holt, Rinehart and Winston, Inc.

University Council for Educational Administration. 1967. *The Madison Simulation Materials: Edison Elementary Principalship.* Columbus, O.: University Council for Educational Administration.

———, 1971, *The Monroe City Simulations: Abraham Lincoln Elementary School.* Columbus, O.: University Council for Educational Administration.

Waller, Willard W., 1932, *The Sociology of Teaching.* New York: John Wiley & Sons, Inc. (Science Edition, 1965.)

Wolcott, Harry F., 1967 (reissued 1984), *A Kwakiutl Village and School.* Prospect Heights, Illinois: Waveland Press, Inc.

———, 1970, "An Ethnographic Approach to the Study of School Administrators," *Human Organization* 29:115-122.

———, 1973 (reissued 1984) *The Man in the Principal's Office: An Ethnography.* Prospect Heights, Illinois: Waveland Press, Inc.

Zelditch, Morris, Jr., 1962, "Some Methodological Problems of Field Studies," *American Journal of Sociology* 67:566–576.

MARGARET A. GIBSON/*California State University, Sacramento*

16   *Playing by the Rules*

Immigrant minorities have been found to do well in school in many parts of the world. Examples of Asian immigrant success are well known in the United States, but perhaps less well known are studies of successful immigrant groups in Australia, Canada, and Britain. I will review briefly some of the studies in these countries and then turn to my own study of the Punjabis in California.

In Australia, the children of non-English-speaking immigrants, notably Greeks, Yugoslavs, and Italians, have been found to stay in school longer and to like school more than Anglo-Australian youths of similar class background. Australian research suggests that the educational aspirations of immigrant parents are more important to school persistence than students' IQ or socioeconomic status (Majoribanks 1980; Martin and Meade 1979; Taft and Cahill 1981). Immigrant parents place greater importance on respect for school rules and hard work than on a child's ability.

Canadian studies show language minority immigrants of low socioeconomic background to perform better in school than either the French-Canadian minority, or the English-Canadian majority (Anisef 1975; Masemann 1975; Wolfgang 1975). Canadian-born children of non-English-speaking immigrants tend to be over-represented in college-preparatory classes compared to students whose first language is English (Cummins 1984). Like the Australian studies, the Canadian work indicates that immigrant youth are "more committed to education as the route to a better life" than are indigenous students (Anisef 1975:127). Immigrants also are less likely than indigenous students to relinquish their goals of a university education when their performance in school is poor (ibid., p. 128).

In Britain, where students of working class backgrounds have been found to have far less opportunity to enter universities than is the case in America, again we find a group of immigrants outperforming indigenous students of comparable class background. A higher percentage of Indian-born males entered British universities in 1979 than UK-born males. In addition, significantly more of the Indians were sons of manual workers than were the UK-born (Ballard and Vellins 1985). So striking is the general pattern of success among students of South Asian origin that a government appointed committee in Britain has recently asked the question: What is it that enables

Prepared for *Education and Cultural Process, 2/E.* Printed by permission of the author.

South Asian young people to surmount, to the degree that they do, both the influence of prejudice and discrimination and that of low socioeconomic status? (Swann Committee 1985:86).

All of these studies—British, Canadian, and Australian—reveal considerable success on the part of immigrant youth of non-English-speaking and working-class backgrounds to use formal education as an avenue to middle-class occupational status.

Not all immigrant groups perform well in school, however. In Britain, for example, students of West Indian origin do very poorly (Swann Committee 1985; Taylor 1981; Tomlinson 1983), as do the children of Turkish workers in West Germany (Castles 1984; Skutnabb-Kangas 1981) and Finnish students in Sweden (Paulston 1982:40; Skutnabb-Kangas 1979). Yet my own research in the American Virgin Islands showed West Indian immigrants to be doing quite well academically, and far better, in the case of boys, than the native Crucian West Indian population (Gibson 1982, 1983a). There also are studies indicating that children of Turkish and Finnish origin in Australia appear to be doing better in school than their counterparts in Germany and Sweden (Inglis and Manderson n.d.; Troike 1984:50).

What does all this mean? It means to me that in addition to the social structure of the host society and the cultural background of the minority group, we must attend very carefully to the specific nature of the minority group's relationship to the dominant group.

Most minority students face substantial barriers in school. Those most frequently cited as having an impact on educational performance are low socio-economic status, a home language other than that used in school, unequal employment opportunities, the tracking system of many schools, home-school cultural discontinuities, and the prejudiced attitudes of the dominant group toward the minority. The question I would like to focus on is not *how* these different barriers impede classroom learning, but *why* some groups more readily transcend these barriers than others.

The Punjabi Case

Let us turn now to my study of Punjabi Sikh immigrants in a rural California school district (Gibson 1983b, 1987).[1] Those who settle in "Valleyside" (my name for the research site) differ in a number of essential respects from the urbanized and highly educated Asian Indians, including many Sikh professionals, who have settled since 1965 in metropolitan areas

[1] The fieldwork, upon which the findings reported here are based, was funded by the National Institute of Education (Grant Number 80-0123). I gratefully acknowledge the support of the Institute and the contribution of fellow research team members Amarjit S. Bal, Gurdip K. Dhillon, and Elizabeth McIntosh.

throughout the United States (Gardner, Robey, and Smith 1985; Leonhard-Spark and Saran 1980; Minocha 1984). Most Valleyside Sikhs have few saleable skills, speak little English, if any at all, and, in the case of women in particular, have had little formal education. Most must work, at least initially, in back-breaking and low-paid jobs as farm laborers in Valleyside's fruit orchards. The median family income in 1980 for Valleyside Punjabis was $15,000, just half that of the average white Valleyside family.[2]

The study revealed sharp differences in the performance patterns of Punjabi students who receive *all* their education in America, or English-medium schools, and those who enter the American system after 4th grade. Almost 90 percent of those who arrive in grades five, six, seven, or eight are still limited in English during high school.[3] These later arrivals are an extremely high risk group, with little prospect of achieving their educational and occupational aspirations.

Punjabis who enter the American school system no later than second grade have a distinctly different pattern of school performance. In high school Punjabi girls educated from childhood in this country do as well academically as their white majority-group classmates and Punjabi boys do even better. Not only do these boys receive higher marks, but more significantly they take more of the tough college-preparatory classes in science and math. More Punjabis, proportionately, than white Valleysiders graduate from high school. Although Punjabi immigrants encounter many problems along the way, still they persist with their education.

In school, Punjabi children have to cope with severe prejudice and sharp conflicts between home values and those promoted by the school. Punjabi students are told they stink, directly by white peers and indirectly by their teachers. They are told to go back to India. They are accused of being illegals. They are physically abused by majority-group students, who spit at them, refuse to sit by them in class or on buses, crowd ahead of them in line, stick them with pins, throw food at them, and worse. They are labelled troublemakers if they defend themselves. In one way or another they are told constantly that India and Indian culture are inferior to Western and American ways. They are criticized for their diet, their dress, and their hair style. They are faulted because they place family ahead of individual interests, defer to the authority of elders, accept arranged marriages, and believe in group decision making. They are condemned most especially for not joining in majority-dominated school activities and for resisting as best they can the forces for Anglo conformity.

---

[2]These income statistics are based on family background information gathered from 45 Punjabi seniors and their parents, and a comparable number of white Valleyside seniors and their parents.

[3]This figure is based on an analysis of school records for all 231 Punjabi students attending Valleyside High, grades 9-12, in 1980-81.

While teachers commend Punjabi students for their diligence in the classroom, they are perplexed by their refusal to participate in team sports, clubs, and other non-academic school activities. They don't "fit in socially," which, for many teachers, is the chief criterion for school success.

The more the schools pressure Punjabi children to conform, the more tightly their parents supervise their behavior and advise against contact with non-Punjabi peers. Punjabi parents define "becoming Americanized" as forgetting ones roots and adopting the most disparaged traits of the majority group, such as young people making decisions on their own without parental counsel, leaving their families at age 18 to live independently, dancing, dating, and arranging their own marriages. Punjabi adolescents are warned repeatedly that they will dishonor themselves, their families, and their community if they adopt the values and behaviors of white peers. Such warnings are coupled with community gossip about those whose behavior deviates from Indian village norms. If inappropriate behavior persists the family will likely decide to withdraw the offender from school, first for a period of time and then permanently. A boy is put to work in the peach fields and a girl is kept at home until her marriage can be arranged. The individual who insists on having his or her own way risks being cut off from family and community.

Punjabi teenagers themselves criticize those who socialize at school with non-Punjabis. They say, "He's Anglo, or he thinks he's white. He's not one of us." Punjabi students stick with their own because, as one student put it, "you don't want to be an outcast from your own people." Punjabi young people, in effect, are forced to choose sides. Few find it possible to mix socially in both worlds.

No similar pressure is brought to bear on Punjabi students for accepting the authority of white teachers or doing well in school. Adapting oneself to teachers' expectations, even when their expectations conflict with traditional Indian or Punjabi values, is not viewed as "acting white." Quite the reverse. Students are encouraged to excell academically and teased when grades or behavior are poor. Parents remind their offspring that they have made great sacrifices for them and that the parents' lives will have been wasted if their children are not successful. Young people are also told that those who do well in school can expect to find better marriage partners, that their accomplishments bring credit to their family, and that they set an example for other younger Punjabis to follow. These are powerful messages.

Punjabi parents have high expectations for their children's achievement. If a child does poorly, however, only rarely do they blame the system, or the teachers. "If the child does not wish to study, then what can the teacher do?" parents remark. "Those who wish to learn, will learn," is the general attitude.

Punjabi adolescents, for their part, know first hand the drudgery of manual labor and the precarious nature of orchard farming. They want a better, more secure future. Almost all Punjabi children have direct contact with adults who have overcome substantial obstacles and, in the words of one young Sikh informant, "have been able to beat the system and the whites at their own games" (Gibson and Bhachu, 1986). Academic achievements, in the Punjabi view, represent what can be done even without parental wealth and education. Parents urge their children to become proficient in the ways of the majority culture. They take pride in the fact their children can speak English well and can help them deal with the host society, *providing* they also are maintaining strong roots within the Punjabi community.

Punjabi students conform to their teachers' expectations to the degree possible, but they are nevertheless no bunch of goody-goodies or pushovers. Punjabi Sikhs have a tradition of toughness in the face of abuse. Boys are instructed, for example, that they must protect the honor of family and community. "Turn the other cheek once, twice," Sikhs say, "but the third time defend yourself." The current activist Sikh radicalism in India and abroad, and the Ghadr Party Marxism of Sikh immigrants earlier in the centure (Juergensmeyer 1981; Singh 1966), show Sikhs' readiness to resist their oppressors when they feel no other alternative exists.

Punjabi parents are not unmindful of the difficulties their children face in school. They are especially disturbed by the prejudiced attitudes and actions of white youths, but they choose to downplay the problems. They urge their children to ignore racist remarks and to avoid fights. The parents recognize that they are operating from a position of weakness and that they have little power to turn things around. Their response to prejudice stems from this reality. But it is also a deliberate and conscious strategy of putting education first. The parents I surveyed stated specifically that a situation of response and counter-response would only promote greater ill will between groups and would distract their children from their studies.

Sikh parents advocate a strategy of *accommodation and acculturation without assimilation*. Adapt to the formal demands of the classroom-do what you must to get a high school education-but resist the forces for total cultural assimilation. "Dress to please the people," Punjabis frequently say, "but eat to please yourself."

My study of Punjabi Sikhs, coupled with the general literature on immigrant adaptation patterns, make it quite clear that immigrants perceive their situation very differently and respond to it very differently from many indigenous minority groups. Immigrants bring a comparative perspective: schooling, jobs, and overall chances for getting ahead are far better here than back where they came from. They measure their success not in terms of the white majority, but in terms of other Punjabis settled in this country and back in Punjab. To understand school response patterns we must, as John Ogbu has long argued, attend very carefully to folk theories of success and failure (Ogbu 1974, 1978; Ogbu and Matute-Bianchi 1986). Punjabis, like many immigrants, view formal education as the avenue to a better life. They put up with all kinds of difficulties in school because they believe so strongly that there will be a payoff later. This is true even though many immigrant groups did not pursue education with the same vigor back in their homeland. The context has changed. Their situation has changed. And so too, do their strategies change.

Why do some minority groups have an easier time than others playing the classroom game by the rules? The explanation involves, I believe, a complex and dynamic interaction among three sets of variables: namely, the cultural preferences of the group, the historical context of settlement in the host society, and the group's response to its current situation.[4]

Conclusion

Comparative research worldwide suggests that school performance is directly and strongly affected by, first, minority attitudes about the probable payoff for playing the school game, and, second, minority attitudes about the dominant group and dominant culture. When parents and students do not believe there will be a sufficient return for investing their time and energy in schooling, they turn their energies elsewhere. Likewise, if they feel hostility and suspicion toward the school system and those in authority, it is more difficult for students to accept this authority and to seek to become skilled in the ways of the dominant group.

"Why study immigrants?" I have been asked. There are many reasons, but let me suggest three that are especially pertinent to the field of minority education. First, research on immigrant minorities provides fresh insight into the role of family and community in promoting successful school adaptation patterns. Second, immigrants provide a rich and useful perspective on both the strengths and weaknesses of the American system of schooling. And, thirdly, immigrant studies bring into sharp relief the barriers to equal educational opportunity for minority students.

The Valleyside study and others suggest that non-English-speaking immigrants who enter American schools after fourth grade are an extremely high risk group (cf. Masemann 1975:111,119). They, especially, need a supportive learning environment and good ESL, or bilingual, instruction. With respect to bilingual education, we need to attend carefully to the views of the target population. Many immigrants are strongly opposed to any instruction whatsoever in their mother tongue, and this certainly was the case for the Punjabis whom I studied. They wanted an all-english curriculum. Bilingual education may not be an appropriate instructional strategy for all groups of language minority students, and this is something we need to learn more about.

What the Punjabis do want is a far more rigorous English-as-a-second-

---

[4]I discuss the interaction of these three sets of variables more fully in a forthcoming volume titled "Accommodation without Assimilation: Punjabi Sikh Immigrants in an American High School and Community."

language program taught in such a way that immigrant students are not segregated from the mainstream, nor handed cheap credits and shuffled along through the system with only the pretense of a decent education. Punjabis also want an end to the racial prejudice in school and to the pervasive and intense pressure to conform to the dominant culture. However hard they may work in class, outside of class they are labeled un-American because their behavior deviates from majority norms.

This is what educational programs need to address-this oppression of those who demand the right to be different. Immigrants, too, if beaten down long enough will fight back and will come to view the dominant group with suspicion and hostility. And when they do, they likely will reject the authority of teachers and administrators and resist playing the classroom game by the rules.

References

Anisef, Paul, 1975, "Consequences of Ethnicity for Educational Plans among Grade 12 Students." In *Education of Immigrant Students*. A. Wolfgang, ed., Toronto: Ontario Institute for Studies in Education.

Ballard, Roger and Selma Vellins, 1985, "South Asian Entrants to British Universities: A Comparative Note." *New Community* 12(2): 260-265.

Castles, Stephen, 1984, *Here for Good*. London: Pluto Press.

Cummins, Jim, 1984, *Bilingualism and Special Education*. Clevedon, Avon: Multilingual Matters.

Gardner, Robert W., Bryant Robey, and Peter C. Smith, 1985, "Asian Americans: Growth, Change, and Diversity." *Population Bulletin* 40(4).

Gibson, Margaret A., 1982, "Reputation and Respectability: How Competing Cultural Systems Affect Students' Performance in School." *Anthropology and Education Quarterly* 13(1): 3-27.

_____. 1983a, "Ethnicity and Schooling: West Indian Immigrants in the United States Virgin Islands." *Ethnic Groups* 5(3): 173-198.

_____, 1983b, "Home-School-Community Linkages: A Study of Educational Opportunity for Punjabi Youth." Final Report to the National Institute of Education, Washington, D.C.

_____, 1987, "Punjabi Immigrants in an American High School." In *Interpretive Ethnography of Education at Home and Abroad*. George D. and Louise S. Spindler, eds. Hillsdale, NJ: Lawrence Erlbaum.

_____, n.d. *Accommodation without Assimilation: Punjabi Sikh Immigrants in an American High School and Community*. (Forthcoming)

_____, and Parminder Bhachu, 1986, "Community Forces and School Performance: Punjabi Sikhs in Rural California and Urban Britain." *New Community* 13 (Spring/Summer).

Inglis, Christine and Lenore Manderson, n.d., "Education and Reproduction among Turkish Families in Sydney." Department of Education, The University of Sydney. (Unpublished Manuscript.)

Juergensmeyer, Mark, 1981, "The Gadar Syndrome: Ethnic Anger and Nationalist Pride." *Population Review* 25 (1/2: 48-58.

Leonhard-Spark, Philip J. and Parmatma Saran, 1980, "The Indian Immigrant in America: A Demographic Profile." In *The New Ethnics: Asian Indians in the United States*. P. Saran and E. Eames, eds. New York: Praeger.

Marjoribanks, Kevin, 1980, *Ethnic Families and Children's Achievements*. Sydney: George Allen and Unwin.

Martin, Jean I. and P. Meade, 1979, *The Educational Experience of Sydney High School Students*. (Report No. 1). Canberra: AGPS.

Masemann, Vandra, 1975, "Immigrant Students' Perceptions of Occupational Programs." In *Education of Immigrant Students*. A Wolfgang, ed. Toronto: Ontario Institute for Studies in Education.

Minocha, Urmil, 1984, "Indian Immigrants in the United States: Demographic Trends, Economic Assimilation in the Host Society, and Impact on the Sending Society." Honolulu: East-West Population Institute. (Unpublished Manuscript.)

Ogbu, John U., 1974, *The Next Generation*. New York: Academic Press.

———, 1978, *Minority Education and Caste: The American System in Cross-Cultural Perspective*. New York: Academic Press.

———, and Maria Eugina Matute-Bianchi, 1986, "Understanding Sociocultural Factors: Knowledge, Identity, and School Adjustment." In *Beyond Language: Social and Cultural Factors in Schooling Language Minority Students*. Sacramento, CA: California State Department of Education.

Paulston, Christina Bratt, [1982], "Swedish Research and Debate About Bilingualism." A Report to the National Swedish Board of Education, Stockholm.

Singh, Khushwant, 1966, *A History of the Sikhs: Volume 2, 1839-1964*. Princeton: Princeton University Press.

Skutnabb-Kangas, Tove, 1979, "Language in the Process of Cultural Assimilation and Structural Incorporation of Linguistic Minorities." Rosslyn, VA: National Clearinghouse for Bilingual Education.

———, 1981, "Guest Worker or Immigrant — Different Ways of Reproducing an Underclass." *Journal of Multilingual and Multicultural Development* 2(2): 89-115.

Swann Committee Report, 1985, *Education for All*. The Report of the Committee of Inquiry into the Education of Children from Ethnic Minority Groups. Cmnd. 9453. London: HMSO.

Taft, Ronald and Desmond Cahill, 1981, "Education of Immigrants in Australia." In *Educating Immigrants*. Joti Bhatnagar, ed. New York: St. Martin's Press.

Taylor, Monica J., 1981, *Caught Between*. Windsor: NFER-Nelson.

Tomlinson, Sally, 1983, *Ethnic Minorities in British Schools*. London: Heinemann.

Troike, Rudolph C., 1984, "SCALP: Social and Cultural Aspects of Language Proficiency." In *Language Proficiency and Academic Achievement*. Charlene Rivera, ed. Clevedon, Avon: Multilingual Matters.

Wolfgang, Aaron, ed., 1975, *Education of Immigrant Students*. Toronto: Ontario Institute for Studies in Education.

SHELLEY V. GOLDMAN/*Bank Street College of Education*
RAY McDERMOTT/*Teachers College*

17   *The Culture of Competition in American Schools*

This paper suggests an anthropological alternative to the common-sense talk of teachers, administrators, and psychologists in American schools. Common-sense would have us believe that the problems in any classroom can be stated primarily in terms of student capabilities and secondarily in terms of teacher skills and attitudes. This way of talking offers a cover up for the more comprehensive and demanding understanding of the ways schools and classrooms are organized by and articulated with the demands of their larger communities. This paper points to the cultural and social structural dilemmas that must be confronted in any classroom if we are to deal effectively with the problems that teachers face on a daily basis.

By examining what happens to teachers and learners in school as part of a more inclusive set of cultural dilemmas, we are better able to locate the problems that teachers have to face in trying to be successful. We are only one step towards becoming successful teachers if we embrace the science of individual differences in intelligence, attitude and skill. We can move ahead much more fruitfully when we consider how our notions of individual differences are made possible and constrained in their implications by their life in a series of institutional games that encompass the productive lives of millions of people across the political economy of the nation. In a school system that has all children pitted against each other in the name of celebrating the best, we have become preoccupied with documenting and sorting out the half of our children who do not do as well as their fellow citizens. The sorting function of schools is never far away from any classroom. This makes teaching a most difficult task.

The current focus and reliance on measuring individual student performance on skills and abilities has educators focusing necessarily on intense evaluation and students focusing necessarily on intense competition. An entire science of education spends its time developing tests and analyzing what scores mean; teachers who rarely know what the scores "mean," nonetheless find themselves pressured by state and local school boards to raise

Prepared for *Education and Cultural Process, 2/E.* Printed by permission of the authors.

scores, and hence, to teach for the test; parents and students worry about having to perform better than their neighbors do. In short, school is an intensely competitive place in ways that may cause more harm than good.

Competition can be helpful or destructive depending on how it is linked to outcomes. In our schools, we have a great deal of competition required with little idea of how it connects either our children or our teachers into our culture. Increasing evidence indicates that the connections are invidious. Schools have been left with the unpleasant prospect that they can sort children for their eventual place in life. This is too much to ask of a school system, and it leads to a possibly destructive reliance on face-to-face competition. Schools do not make jobs; they only make some people (at least on paper) differentially ready for whatever jobs are available in the marketplace at any given time. As a result, both competition and incessant evaluation are powerful and thematic forces underlying all aspects of schooling in America without regard to their systematic consequences. At the classroom level, every teacher has to deal with the troubles and embarrassments brought about by differential success. The culture gives us this problem, and few resources with which to produce solutions.

The ways people talk in schools are relentless in the display of competitive themes. The language of schooling rests on the vocabulary of competence and incompetence, and the evaluation of individuals relative to each other is the highlight of the most crucial conversational sequences (Goldman, 1982). Standardized tests, grades and records make competition and evaluation possible, necessary, displayable, and reportable. The very ways we talk about school success and failure are well articulated at many levels of social structure. In this paper, we focus most completely on the role of competition in the interactions between teachers and students during classroom lessons and other school-wide sequences of activity. We do not want to forget, however, that within the largest frame of reference, competition and evaluation make the school well tuned with the more forceful institutions of American life, most particularly the dog-eat-dog world of business. The survival and achievement strategies of corporate executive officers (CEOs) and first graders are hideously similar in that they both must spend their days arranging not getting caught looking incompetent (compare Goldman, 1982 with Jackall, 1983). Whether in school or work, the same cultural themes seem to be visible. How such competitiveness and performance anxiety exist in our schools is the focus of this paper.

Our exploration of the cultural dilemmas encountered by teachers proceeds in three directions. Section I is most extensive and details the importance of competition as an assumed background to all schooling in America. In this line, we follow an established tradition in the anthropological study of American education, and we add to the work of Spindler (1959) and Henry (1963, 1973) only some new examples, based more on the analysis of language performances than on the delineation of modal personalities (Varenne, 1983;

Willis, 1977). We focus almost exclusively on the role of competition in the organization of interaction in one very successful junior high school, and we offer a brief account of the fit between face-to-face competition and the institutional sorting of students into successful and unsuccessful school careers.

In Section II, we consider the workings of the same competitive assumptions in the daily workings of an experimental inner-city junior high school in which the children, despite considerable roadblocks, were offered a pathway to success. The institutional machinations that made that success possible offer us a brief portrait of the social structure that organizes differential success and failure for our children.

Lest any reader be tempted to think that this paper is simply about the schooling of children, in Section III we take a glimpse at a successful program for the enhancement of literacy by a labor union. The similarities in problems and solutions in the organization of learning for adults on their jobs and for children in their schools bring home the point that we are dealing across the board with culturally produced dilemmas well tuned to the alignment of persons to statuses and access to cultural and material resources.

I. The Use of Competition In American Schools

Research on the organization of classroom lessons reveals them to be constituted by strings of face-to-face sequences that have evaluation as a major component. Whenever conversations are organized in classrooms, the possibility of sorting students for differential success is also organized. Many classroom exchanges require a teacher's evaluation of student competencies. Turns to talk are often turns for students to show their competence, and the negotiation of just how and when to seek answers becomes an important element in any teacher's interaction with a class. The meaning of a child's silence or a look away, of a teacher's correction, or of a child's interruption or other misbehavior, is up for interpretation in terms of both local and more classroom-wide conditions: local in the sense of its timing and phrasing in relation to immediately surrounding talk; more classroom-wide in the sense of how it feeds the developing biographies and identities students have put on them in the classroom (e.g., identities such as class clown, class dullard, class baby, class dummy, and other noncomplimentary possibilities).

The role of evaluation as a distinguishing and near omnipresent dimension of all classroom life has been brought home by a number of classroom analysts. Mehan (1979) has made much of the "What time is it?" example. The same question asked in different contexts receives quite different answers, and the different answers offer a useful measure of how the different contexts shape the behavior of their participants. Consider the most obvious form.

1. What time is it? (Question)
   Nine-fifteen. (Answer)
   Thank You. (Appreciation)

This is a quite regular exchange and marks many fast moving interactions among both strangers and compatriots throughout the English speaking world. You can ask almost anyone for the time, you can expect an answer, and you are required only to produce an appreciation. This exchange contrasts with the use of the same question in a second grade classroom:

2, What time is it? (Question)
   Nine-fifteen. (Answer)
   Very Good. (Evaluation)

This second sequence is almost peculiar to classrooms (or homes where there are younger children). The difference is one between Appreciation and Evaluation. Classrooms are about evaluation. The forces that make the "Very good" unremarkable in the classroom are what make classrooms what they are. If you try "Very good" in street encounters in New York City chances are that you will not be well received. Ask an adult stranger for the time, and when they give it to you, say "very good." The question-answer evaluation is a sequence that would have to be followed with a plea for mercy; evaluation is not everywhere welcome.

"What time is it?" is usually a harmless question, but it has to be properly tuned to a wide range of relational circumstances. The same phrase can service different contexts in quite different ways. Consider the negotiation of bedtime in a difficult marriage:

3. What time is it? (Question)
   Going to bed already? (Question)

Neither information, nor skill is at issue here; love and loyalty are. We can go on to the policeman with a college essay due on the use of time in the different groups of people in New York City. He pulls up to a street tough in a police car, and he helps to construct the following exchange:

4. What time is it? (Question)
   Hey, this is my watch, man. (Declaration)

Neither information on the time, nor an evaluation of the time-teller's skill, nor family loyalty is at question here; whether the watch has been stolen takes precedence as the issue among the participants.

The point of these "What time is it?" examples is most generally that the institutional relations between speakers organize how they understand each other. Words cannot do that job on their own. The more specific point is that educational settings seem to require evaluation.

The same focus on competition and the evaluation of student competencies is also evident when almost any segment of interaction in school is analyzed. Life inside school is full of activity and ceremony that culminates in publically announced evaluations of individual student progress. That there are winners and losers at the end of most school events is more than a convenient happening in an institution that must eventually contribute its students to a stratified academic and social order. Competition is a main genre for organizing what happens and what people talk about in schools because it is alive in the children's everyday life outside in their homes and communities as it is in their school lessons.

Let us look more carefully at how competition and evaluation underlie the organization of academic and social life in one school. By illustrating how teaching and learning proceed successfully in a school where competition is both overt and capitalized upon in the organization and structure of activity, we hope to illustrate what all schools are doing, or not doing and thus avoiding, or in rare cases, successfully overcoming.

The Competitive Life at Allwin School

Allwin is a successful middle school (grades 6-8) in a middle-to-upper-middle class suburb near New York City.[1] Competition was an essential feature of school life at Allwin. Interviews with teachers and students revealed their perspectives about why they freely and frequently participated in competitive events. The students were basically uniform in stating that contests made everything more fun and interesting. Win or lose, it was fun to compete. Teachers explained that competitions were an organizing theme for classroom experiences because they so easily mapped onto life in the community.

Teachers shared the student's explanation about how much students responded favorably to competing. They thought that placing competition at the center of activities tended to "motivate" students to participate more vigorously. Their formulations are represented in quotes from a faculty room conversation:

> (On life in the classroom):
> · Gives them an activity to get them to practice word skills, and they moan and groan at you. You make it into a contest, and suddenly everyone wants to be an expert at defining vocabulary words.
>
> (On life in the community):
> Did you ever see the way these kids do sports?... competition drives them, so why shouldn't we capitalize on it?

People in the community made constant reference to how competitive the community was. For example, the priest who is the youth director at the local Catholic Church ran a "relaxed program" because the students had so much

---

[1]The Allwin School and community was studied for 18 months and is described in Goldman (1982). A nearby high school is described in a related study by Varenne (1983).

competition to deal with in the school. Unfortunately, even the church's "relaxed" sports program entered its youth into competitive tournaments. In the priest's words:

> Competition underlies everything they do. If I ran a program with no way to compete, I'd have no program left. They'd all be somewhere else...
> The students compete like crazy, and I mean crazy because they bring so much pressure on them selves by doing it.

These sentiments were confirmed by others in the community. The school principal, teachers and parents contended that the schools were highly competitive, with the most competition centering around academic success. Two high school seniors I travelled with for a day depicted the town as "totally competitive:"

> Mary: There's always something to compete over. Either, it's sports, or grades, or how many Izod shirts you have.

The two went on talking and after a few minutes demonstrated some of the avenues on which competition drives their experiences:

> Mary: By the way, Gerry, did you get any more college acceptances yet?
> Gerry: No, not yet. Just Brown so far.
> Mary: All right! I'm still ahead of you. I got three so far.

The examples are endless. The point is that competition underlies social life within the community. That it filters into school is no surprise. Marrying competition with classroom lessons is a good idea in an institution that keeps children in its grasp for twelve or more years, especially when the institution has the job of producing and maintaining a stratified social order.

In their accounts of the school, teachers and students found it easy to identify the ubiquity of competition. Visitors to the school could amass ample evidence for such assertions. Here we will describe: (a) a classroom game, "Screw Thy Neighbor" (their term!); (b) a school-wide game, "The Brain Bowl"; (c) an arts festival that displays competition; (d) the endless sequence of tests; and (e) formal moments given to the institutional recognition of sorting.

"Screw Thy Neighbor," a question and answer game for reviewing content materials, was a big hit for the eighth grade humanities class. Students, who were placed on two teams, prepared several content questions from their readings and notes on the humanities unit prior to the day of the match. The goal of the game was to stump the students on the opposing team by knowing the correct answers to questions that they couldn't answer. Team members busied themselves thinking up difficult questions during the days prior to the game, and sent spies around in attempts to find out the content being covered in the opposition's questions. Right up to the minute before the match officially opened, a few students from each team were cramming content and facts in an attempt to avoid "being screwed."

The students played the game for the entire class period as the teacher moderated and kept score. During the play, students laughed, raised hands, and even begged to ask or answer another question during the game. When the game was over, the students on the winning team cheered, clapped, whistled, and "gave each other five." Students on the losing team smiled, clapped, booed and asked the teacher when they could have a rematch.

Students enjoyed playing the game and played as if the stakes were high: when they answered correctly, they let out sighs of relief, wiped their brows, and shook each other's hands; when they answered incorrectly, they pouted, cursed, and stomped their feet on the floor. The game, with its competitive theme, rules for play, and question and answer format, organized the flow of activity and the students' participation in it.

The students also practiced mastery of the content materials. In order to prepare for the match each student had to write questions and answers, study the materials, and learn additional content in anticipation of questions that might be asked of them. The game had no consequences for student sorting. Even though the mastery of content was displayed and available for evaluation, the teacher and the students talked about the game as a "learning" event rather than as an occasion for institutional evaluation. Tests, incidentally, were usually discussed as "evaluations," and rarely as "learning events."

Competitions and games were usually the choice genre for school-wide activities. The staff members believed that large scale activities fostered a sense of "school-spirit" and "community." Participation in the activities was always voluntary, although very often highly selective. The activities were spread throughout the school year and included the school play, the "Brain Bowl," the arts festival, the seventh grade camping trip, and the track and field day. A clear picture develops of a competitive genre for interaction and organization of activity as we look at these voluntary activities in terms of student participation in them and their proceedings. The examples also bring into focus how competitive life at the school is both generative of, and adaptive to, its larger community and system that sorts.

The Brain Bowl was a school-wide contest that is modeled after a 1960's television program called "The College Bowl." To play the Brain Bowl, teams of students competed in a tournament by answering general knowledge and trivia questions. Each year, teachers were asked to collect trivia and general knowledge information and to construct questions. The questions were compiled and made into a test which was given to every student wishing to try out for the tournament. Students receive their tournament placements based on their test results. Then the play-offs began and student teams competed in the bowl game as the focus of a school-wide assembly.

Teachers liked the Brain Bowl and so did most of the students. The Bowl was a highly selective and competitive activity and only a few students were chosen for the tournament play. Other students enjoyed the Bowl as spectators, despite Allwin's competitiveness concerning student achievement. Even those students who couldn't play to win could enjoy the spirit of the event since non-participation, elimination, or winning held few implications for sorting. There were no surprise winners in this game and the final round actually offered another formal occasion for recognizing students who were already at the top of the academic hierarchy.

Not all school-wide events were conscious displays of school rankings. Allwin's arts festival was a series of formal events for recognizing student competence in the various arts. Activities included fashion shows, woodworking displays, a gallery show of student art projects, and a music festival which featured band and choral performances. Students generally participated in the festival by choice, choosing a project for display or giving consent to show a project selected by their teacher. Every student was eligible to contribute their work for the enjoyment of all others. The festival became a set of events that highlighted student achievements while minimizing competition around student competence and incompetence.

Even the arts festival, however, made use of competition as an organizing device. The art display was an example. Each art class displayed student work in a designated part of the school gym and organized their display around a theme that highlighted the combined works and applauded the creative talents of the students. The themes that each class chose became instrumental in making the goals of the festival realizable, and students were encouraged to make each display as unique and creative as possible. Encouragement came by way of an award given to the class with the most creative and interesting display.

The competition around the displays was fierce. Some students worried about having a "good enough" display. Other groups kept their ideas secret from others and spent many art classes designing and constructing the displays. The display competition was an organizing device for the students. It was not aimed at generating sorting possibilities, but it was clearly a framework within which students could accomplish their tasks.

Tests were important at Allwin School. Students took classroom tests and quizzes on a regular basis in most subjects, and they punctuated the beginning and end of work on most units of academic study. All students participated in testing occasions. Students usually competed against their own records or the records of their classmates, and test results usually contributed to report card grades. It was not unusual for any student to have two or more tests in one school day, especially on Fridays and near the end of grading periods. Like other kinds of competitions, tests were a genre for social action in classrooms. They provided teachers and students with familiar ways to proceed for both learning lessons and evaluating them. They generated a flow of evaluative moments that were relevant to sorting concerns.

Standardized tests appeared to have the strongest link to sorting work and the construction of individual student biographies. Allwin students took many of them, including diagnostic tests to assess reading and math abilities, national achievement tests, and state-wide competency exams. The tests were considered the ultimate occasions for producing evaluations of students that made sorting decisions possible and fair.

The full round of competitive games and tests were all fodder for each child's biography. Still, there was no one-to-one relationship between any one or even many performances on competitive events and the outcomes for any one child. At the classroom level, test grades were usually averaged together for the purpose of evaluation. When teachers made sorting decisions about students they usually referred to patterns in grades and rarely cited any particular test grade.

More important evaluations in which students were assigned to special programs or selected for next schools, were performed in specially convened meetings of faculty teams. At the meetings, classroom test scores, grades on assigned work, notes on social and classroom behavior, and standardized test results were used to accomplish sorting work. Interestingly enough, standardized test scores did not usually determine placements. Test scores tended to inform decisions in much the same way that teacher opinions did. An equal share was carried by factors having nothing to do with individual performance, such as the availability of programs, special services, and parental pressures.

This loose coupling between competitive performances in the daily school experience an the long-range success or failure of individuals gives school personnel their powers and points to how much individual biographies are keyed to the overall structure of opportunities offered by different school systems. It is in this latter sense that the life of competition in Allwin contrasts so greatly with the nature of competition in schools with a less easily won success rates for their students. Where in Allwin it spurs activities along, in schools with fewer resources, it threatens to crush its participants. We now turn to the other side of the competitive coin.

II. Confronting Competitive Pressures in an Alternative Public School

The competitive pressures that dominate American schools are exaserbated in our inner-city classrooms where the implications for teachers and students are terrifying. Competitive school pressures threaten inner-city children just as they do Allwin students, though chances that they claim our city children for failure are outrageously higher. The results of these pressures are dismaying, and cities like New York, for example, still fight a 50% high school drop-out rate. The children at Allwin end up at the opposite side of the success and failure continuum from our urban charges. When children at Allwin threaten to fall from success, they have a large safety net in their school and community that catches them. When our city children walk the tightrope of competitive pressure, the danger of hitting bottom is much more likely. Children in our cities face the same competitive pressures that our Allwin students do: they take classroom and standardized achievements tests; their classroom lessons are organized around evaluative sequences; their classes are pitted against each other in school-wide and city-wide events. Unfortunately, managing competitive pressures is made doubly difficult for teachers and students who also must contend with working together across racial, ethnic and social class borders, while heaped together at the bottom of large educational bureaucracies where few resources reach them in their classrooms (McDermott and Goldman, 1983). Life outside the school offers no more cause for optimism if teachers and students have no access to practiced parental intervention or a community life that supports their participation in competitive educational markets.

Although inner-city teachers and students must deal daily with unrelenting competitive pressures, they have less access to the political and economic resources inside their schools and outside in their communities than available to those mobilizing the Allwin community. A contrasting set of conditions prevails inside and outside of school. School buildings are old, broken down and grafitti ridden, doors and windows are barred and locked, security guards man all entrances and exits in order to keep children in and perpetrators out. Instructional materials are often at a bare minimum: textbooks predominate, and often there is little else with which children and teachers can work. In the inner-city, the competitive genre is not quite as linked to the life the children experience each day when they leave the confines of their school buildings as it was in Allwin's community. The communities around urban schools are often economically disadvantaged, with poor housing, high unemployment, and rising crime rates. Life outside the school often seems to offer no fix for the lack of resources inside the school. It is no wonder, then, that educators have rarely looked to the strengths of the inner-city when they have prescribed fix-ups for failing urban children; it is more common to bemoan the fact that they are not all living the Allwin life. It is our point, of course, that everyone cannot be expected to do better than everyone else. In our schools, the bottom half must fail, and it is on the backs of our urban failures that Allwin students can make their marks. A small redirection of resources, however, might change the success rates of the inner-city schools and point to the inherent powers of their surrounding communities.

The Promise of Looking To The Inner-City Community

The City and Community School opened its doors to its first class of inner-city seventh graders in 1983.[2] A major premise organizing the school was that

---

[2]The City and Community School was organized and directed by Shelley Goldman, who documented its daily life for almost three years.

education could be more meaningful for students if it was directly tied to their concerns, experiences and community life. The school's model of education was adapted from one developed at a local, non-traditional college that forced a blending of experience at a work setting with the curriculum inside the classroom. When CCS was developed, the program was structured to focus around internships that students would complete throughout the school year in community settings such as day care and seniors centers, hospitals, schools, social agencies, and small local businesses. For two mornings a week, the students were unpaid workers with dual responsibilities: they had to do their jobs well, and once back in school, they had to contribute their work experiences to the collective construction of their junior high curriculum. No one "failed" internship, as the category for evaluation was not measurable or available in school terms. When a student needed to improve his performance at the internship, the school staff used a problem-solving approach for encouraging better work.

The school drew its students primarily from the local neighborhood. The staff was comprised of both experienced teachers from the local district and program development and support staff were taken from the college. Over the three years that the development of City and Community School was documented, the school grew to have 60 students a year and five faculty members. The student population was 100% minority, with 60% Black and 40% Hispanics.

Much daily life at City and Community School resembled life in many other schools. Students went from homeroom to class periods which covered all required subject areas, and they ate lunch in the cafeteria of the larger junior high building in which they were housed. They carried notebooks, textbooks, pens, and pencils while in school, they took quizzes and tests, were assigned homework most nights, and had their parents called at home when they were absent, misbehaving, or falling behind in their work.

Students at CCS took standardized tests each spring and some students were given educational assessments if they seemed far behind the others. In short, for most of their days, CCS students dealt with the same panoply of competitive pressures that their Allwin counterparts did, and there was a close correspondence in both schools around the kinds of competitive events to be encountered (e.g., classroom lessons, school-wide activities, tests, and formal activities for recognizing winners).

There were differences from Allwin, however, in how the CCS students and teachers talked about their competitive pressures. At CCS, students felt very much at the mercy of classroom and standardized test scores. They felt as if their test scores held great power for determining their schooling futures. They knew, for example, that seventh grade was a "holdover" year. The city-wide "holdover" policy meant that students had to score within a year and a half of grade level in order to be promoted into the eighth grade. On the very first day the school opened, several students were already asking about when the tests would be, lamenting the power of the tests over their lives, stating that their elementary school teachers told them the tests don't measure how well they were really doing or what really counts, and complaining that they could do little to change the situation other than try for good test scores. Their wisdom about the competitive dilemmas they faced was astonishing.

The teachers were faced with handling the same competitive demands. They were aware that almost one-half of the first CCS class came into the seventh grade with sixth grade scores that designated them "potential holdovers," and they felt pressure to bring the students' scores in reading and math up high enough for them to make promotion. The "holdover" situation was a great dilemma for the staff. CCS was an alternative school where faith was being placed in the idea that, as students joined in the flow of experiences outside of school in their community internship settings, they would develop reading and math skills because of their daily interaction with them in real workplace situations. This was incredibly difficult for the teachers to handle, and they constantly expressed their desires to spend classroom time with the students to work on needed skills. They felt accountable for the students' success, and often felt as if they were being robbed of time they could control when the students were sent into the community and away from their clutches. Even though the teachers were supported by the local school district's "alternative schools" program in choosing and justifying the internship experience as valid learning time, they felt tied to the demands and powers the tests would have over the students' schooling futures.

The situation that developed at CCS was very real and the teachers' fears translated into the way the program was eventually carried out (e.g., the internship was cut to one day a week during the spring semester, more reading classes were added into the weekly schedule). Even though the school was an alternative to regular junior high, it was still invaded by competitive pressures that were inescapable.

These demands and dilemmas did not hold the school hostage, however, as CCS took an additional and supplemental pathway to minimizing the force of competitive pressures on its students. The internship program gave students learning experiences that fell outside of the definition of school-like tasks and evaluations and provided students with more process, less evaluation, and a sense of independence and success.

The internship program offered a few safeguards to competitive pressures. It offered them non-competitive situations in which to be responsible and in which to learn. It also gave them many adults to protect them from failure. Each can be considered in turn.

The internship opportunities placed the schooling experience in a wider sequence of events and sometimes beyond the pale of contexts in which test scores mattered. Students and teachers became concerned with and addressed problems, issues and events that were being confronted throughout their community. Students interned in settings where they actively dealt with problems of care for children and senior citizens, public housing, local politics, community health, drug abuse and alcoholism prevention, and education. On several occasions, students stayed at their internships because more help was needed on a particular day. Also on several occasions, all students in the school participated as volunteers for large-scale community events. As a group, for example, CCS students registered four year olds for city-wide kindergartens, became marshals for a school district-wide drug prevention picnic, and conducted a voter registration drive. Individually and in small groups they hosted an educational tour of the city schools for Soviet educators, taught computer programming to elementary school students, translated for an English-speaking art teacher with a Spanish speaking class, saved tenants from eviction in local apartment buildings, fed lunch to the chronically ill and elderly, cared for pre-schoolers with working parents, helped police keep records for the adolescent unit of their neighborhood precinct, and addressed the Board of Trustees of a foundation giving development funds to their school.

Because each internship site offered a different experience, students, teachers, and site supervisors became teams that were made responsible for negotiating and defining tasks that students needed to carry out and master. This structured uniqueness and multiple sets of standards for accomplishments involved individual students in the process of planning, reflecting upon and measuring their own learning. Most importantly, the internship focus in the school curriculum exposed students to more comprehensive views of what it means to apply a learned skill, accomplish a task, or solve a problem. The internship experience was part of school, but a part that remained outside the usual structure of competitive demands.

Academically, CCS students had much time on task while at their internships. They were rarely idle, and when they were, they readily complained about wanting more to do. In many ways, they experienced the task environment of their internships in exactly the opposite terms that they experienced their classroom environments where they frequently lamented about how much they were asked to do. The kinds of tasks students completed varied in levels of difficulty and kinds of cognitive demands. The students came to appreciate the up and down demands of adult institutional activities. This was a more serious problem for the staff, since the diversity and setting specificity of their tasks meant they usually did not correspond with typical junior high school curriculum. Curriculum development in the school was oriented towards matching the students real world and school world tasks. That meant: when students worked on percentages in math class, they were asked to help keep and analyze attendance records at a day care setting; when they studied Black history in school, they read aloud an appropriate poem or taught an African dance at a seniors center. When students first started internships, the theme surrounding lessons in every class was establishing and handling relationships in the workplace. The playing back and forth between the internship and classroom both helped to build a curriculum and give individual students a great deal of directions.

The internship program also provided a network of people who could protect students who were in other ways vulnerable to failure. The internships brought many people into the schooling enterprise, including parents, people who worked in community service settings, local business owners, and politicians and community leaders. This was a formidable set of guardians and role models.

The CCS program managed to confront some of the pressures faced by inner-city children and their teachers. It in no way eliminated all of the competitive dilemmas the children faced. It forced all involved in the school to realize that school could be more than an experience aimed at "passing the test." Instead, school could be a place where you learned how to participate in experiences considered useful and important by the entire adult community. Full and responsible participation in the internship was heralded as a virtue and within months of starting, students realized failure was not at issue, but collaboration was. If participation and collaboration are made possible by an institution, learning follows with ease. The same emphasis on sorting instead of participation can arrange for much less learning.

III. Insuring Success Insures Success

Any children who go to school in America can be assured that certain problems will be there to meet them in their classrooms. They will be asked not just to learn to read and write, but to learn to read and write better than their peers. Nationally, there will be only so much success that can be passed around, and an equal amount of failure. By the dictates of the bell curve, an arbitrary cultural device that pits all persons against each other, half the children can pass, and the rest must fail. From the cultural point of view, it is fair to say that school failure will acquire its share of children through competitive means.

Any adults who teach school in America can be assured the same problem. Collectively, they will have to generate as much school failure as success, and they will have to manage, placate, and redirect those who fail, act out and resist. School administrators are never free of these problems either (Wolcott 1973). We can find many victims, but no real villains. It is just that we create these problems when we try to do schooling. It fits our economy and politics well enough. It is possible that it could be different, as schooling in other modern states can be quite different, even in the test driven schools of Japan (Rohlen 1980). But American schools are not different from what they are, nor are they likely to change very easily. We have what we have bargained for, no matter how unconsciously. "You throw your money on the table," warned W.B. Yeats (1934), "and you receive so much change." The problem seems to be endemic. Organize any number of Americans into schools, and they will test, measure, divide, sort and remediate people into piles. Such divisions will develop without regard for the long range potential of the individuals involved and likely, no matter how unconsciously, in line with already well established class and racial borders.

In this paper, we have illustrated how this system works to motivate effort and success in a well-to-do community that had a full compliment of resources for pushing children along, and we have seen how the system had to be reorganized to redirect the resistance of inner-city children into successful school careers. Our next example suggests that the terrors of school failure need to be confronted in all walks of life. Advanced literacy skills, as easy to acquire as they are crucial to participation in a modern society, are seemingly denied to many Americans, at least to the extent that they are faced with classrooms and tests that threaten them with failure and limit their participation. Simpler literacy skills, in the sense of decoding, are well established throughout our own society and massively used in daily life at home and the work place (Varenne and McDermott 1986). That this substantial foundation of knowledge is not systematically expanded into advanced literacies raises questions about the treatment of workers in our marketplace. Why is it that school degrees and literacy tests are the measures of our workers? What ever happened to job performance? Adult literacy is a most unproductive arena in which to have people competing with each other (Street 1985). We need a work force with as many skills as possible, not a work force that hides in fear of failing tests. Our brief example should both illustrate the problem and display a local-level solution.

Exterminating Illiteracy

In New York City, there were ninety men responsible for exterminating pests from thousands of public housing units.[3] Half the men were fully licensed, and half relied on a more conditional license. The latter offered less job security, lower pay, and no access to extra jobs or promotions. What separated the two groups are two tests: the first, in essence, a literacy examination using materials of relevance to the job of a pest exterminator; the second, a test of a person's knowledge of the facts of exterminating. Both tests are written on an eleventh grade reading level, and the word among the workers was that they are most difficult to pass. Some men had been on the job for twenty-five years without even trying to take the test. A few brave souls showed up for the first test, but could not fill out the required forms, which in fact were one of the hardest parts of the test for a person not inside the bureaucracy. The spector of failure loomed where it did not need to exist.

---

[3]David Harmon and Ray McDermott worked on "exterminating illiteracy" with Local 237 of the International Brotherhood of Teamsters. They are preparing a report.

Imagine how much a man with decades of on-the-job experience must know about exterminating. What made the examinations appear so lethal, and how could the men be encouraged to try?

In organizing the instructional program, we relied on two supports: first, the belief that all the men knew more than they needed to know for passing the test, and that we had only to tame their knowledge into a form that would enable them to take and pass the test; second, the knowledge that their union, which organized the classes in the first place, could in the long run insure enough instruction to promise all entrants that they could eventually pass the tests. The first support brought us to an unusual instructional form. We set up peer teaching situations by coupling ten students who needed to pass the exams with two exterminator-instructors taken from among those who had already passed. We assumed that such peer teaching would make greater use of the knowledge the men shared about their jobs.

Knowing that the union would continue to teach all the men until they passed gave us great freedom. We had only to get the men enough time on task, and they could all take aim on passing the test sooner or later. The idea was that we could get success if the classroom was organized for success only. The union could promise eventual success to all, because it had become sufficiently expert at teaching to the test. The field of pest extermination has a limited number of questions that can be asked on an introductory exam, and in a weekend cram course, the union expert can arrange for most of the men to get what they need to pass. In this case, however, the union wanted also for their men to learn as much as possible. Our experimental classroom was designed for a maximal learning experience which was safe from long-term failure because of the union's insurance that all could pass the test eventually.

The classes were successful in a number of ways. Attendance went up during the first two weeks. Most men passed the two exams on the first round, and all passed on the second round. A tremendous spirit and confidence grew among both students and teachers, and the union went to its next bargaining table with the claim that they were all licensed professionals.

From this nice story comes a question: What institutional forces and cultural dispositions would we have to confront in order to start insuring all our children success in school? The strength and staying power of the competitive structures in our schools are testimony to how difficult a major system-wide confrontation with them would be. Even in the workplace, a test is used as the measure of competence. The men understood the test as a measure of their intelligence and school knowledge. They thought themselves short and stayed away from the test. To turn the situation around required a group of educators who believed in the workday knowledge of the men more than they believed in what any "pretest" might have shown, and a sympathetic labor union that made a strong commitment to educate its people.

IV. Conclusion

Competition can be a useful tool for linking individual effort and collective action. Or it can suppress activity by restricting participation. In American society, we have little choice about how to use competition. It seems to have a life of its own. It is everywhere, and it operates without regard for the people it measures and records. We do not do competition. Competition does us.

We have looked at three examples of how the culture of competition organizes schooling in America. All three are success stories. In the Allwin school, competition was a part of the air. All breathed deeply, and most made their way to high academic achievements. In the next two examples, competition was no less thick, but it threatened to choke its participants. There have to be losers, and those with fewer resources gather more than their share. In these situations, competition had to be pushed aside long enough for the students to engage in formal education. Our two examples of how local resources mitigated the damage that competitive dilemmas do to those who would fail are promising. Together they point to the power that educators who are willing to grapple with the pressures of the system have for easing the tragedy of school failure. We will continue to deny many of our students success until we collectively fight to release competition as a handmaiden of our cultural dilemmas.

References

Goldman, Shelley V. 1982. *Sorting Out Sorting: How Stratification is Managed in a Middle School*. Doctoral dissertation, Teachers College, Columbia University.

Henry, Jules. 1963. *Culture Against Man*. New York: Vintage.

_____, 1973. *Sham, Vulnerability, and Other Forms of Self-Deception*. New York: Vintage.

Jackall, Robert. 1983. Moral mazes. *Harvard Business Review* 61: 118-130.

McDermott, R.P. and Shelley Goldman. 1983. Teaching in multicultural settings. In L. v.d. Berg-Eldering, F. de Rijcke, and L. Zuck (eds.), *Multicultural Education*. Dordrecht: Foris.

Mehan, Hugh. 1979. *Learning Lessons*. Cambridge: Harvard University Press.

Rohlen, Thomas. 1980. The juku phenomenon. *Journal of Japanese Studies 6*: 207-242.

Spindler, George. 1959. *The Transmission of American Culture*. Cambridge: Harvard University Press.

Street, Brian. 1985. *Literacy in Theory and Practice*. New York: Cambridge University Press.

Varenne, Herve. 1983. *American School Language*. New York: Irvington Press.

_____, and R. P. McDermott. "Why Sheila can read:" Structure and indeterminacy in the reproduction of familial literacy. In B.Schieffelin and P. Gilmore (eds.), *Acquisition of Literacy*. Norwood: Ablex.

Willis, Paul. 1977. *Learning to Labor.* New York: Columbia University Press.

Wolcott, Harry. 1973 (reissued 1984). *Man in the Principal's Office.* Prospect Heights, Illinois: Waveland Press, Inc.

Yeats, William Butler. 1934. *The Autobiography of William Butler Yeats.* N.Y.: Collier.

PART V

Cultural Process in Education Viewed Transculturally

Preview
18. GEORGE SPINDLER *The Transmission of Culture*
Preview
Part A: Traditional Non-Literate Societies
19. DOROTHY EGGAN *Instruction and Affect in Hopi Cultural Continuity*
20. C.W.M. HART *Contrasts Between Prepubertal and Postpubertal Education*
21. PETER SINDELL *Some Discontinuities in the Enculturation of Mistassini Cree Children*
Preview
Part B: Complex Modern Societies
22. GEORGE and LOUISE SPINDLER *In Prospect for a Controlled Cultural Comparison of Schooling: Schoenhausen and Roseville*
23. MARIDA HOLLAS *Cognition and Learning in Norway and Hungary*
24. JAMES ROBINSON *Social Typing at Hanseong Elementary: A Transcultural Model*
25. THOMAS ROHLEN *Seishin Kyōiku in a Japanese Bank*

PREVIEW

There has been a tendency of late in the writings of educational anthropologists to attend to the problem of education in our own country and neglect the analysis of educational process transculturally. Perhaps our problems at home loom so large it seems unnecessary to go abroad to try to understand the problems of others. Beyond the study of education there has been a marked turn to the study of the culture of the United States as anthropologists have "come home" in increasing numbers to do their work (Messerschmidt 1983, See Chapter 10). Communities abroad in third world countries have become increasingly hostile to study by foreigners unless the study is part of a direct effort to solve their problems, and even then, access to study sites for personnel whom an insecure government may regard as potentially subversive or in some way likely to discredit the national image by reporting "primitive" conditions and practices, is often denied or made very difficult. Nor have foundations from whom support is sought for research in education been oriented toward supporting travel and research overseas.

Nevertheless, a transcultural perspective on education is essential, for education is a cultural process and occurs in a social context. Without attention to cultural differences, and the way education serves those differences, we have no way of achieving perspective on our own culture and the way our educational system serves it nor of building a comprehensive picture of education as affected by culture. The first chapter in Part V samples selected aspects of cultural transmission in fifteen situations emphasizing non-literate, traditional cultures. This chapter serves as an introduction to the more indepth treatment of single cases in sections A and B, following.

Parts A and B of this section examine education in ten quite different cultural contexts: Hopi Indians, the Tiwi of Australia, the Mistassini Cree of Quebec, Germany, Wisconsin, (United States), Norway and Hungary, Korea, and Japan. The chapters in Part A are about education in non-literate, technologically simple cultures, where we might expect the greatest differences from our own. Part B is about education in settings that will be more familiar because they are literate and complex.

The Editor

18   *The Transmission of Culture**

This chapter is about how neonates become talking, thinking, feeling, moral, believing, valuing human beings—members of groups, participants in cultural systems. It is not, as a chapter on child psychology might be, about the growth and development of individuals, but on how young humans come to want to act as they must act if the cultural system is to be maintained. A wide variety of cultures are examined to illustrate both the diversity and unity of ways in which children are educated. The educational functions that are carried out by initiation rites in many cultures are emphasized, and the concepts of cultural compression, continuity, and discontinuity are stressed in this context. Various other techniques of education are demonstrated with selected cases, including reward, modeling and imitation, play, dramatization, verbal admonition, reinforcement, and storytelling. Recruitment and cultural maintenance are analyzed as basic educative functions. The chapter is not about the whole process of education but about certain parts of that process seen in a number of different situations.

What Are Some of the Ways That Culture Is Transmitted?

Psychologists and pediatricians do not agree upon the proper and most effective ways to raise children. Neither do the Dusun of Borneo, the Tewa or Hopi of the Southwest, the Japanese, the Ulithians or the Palauans of Micronesia, the Turkish villagers, the Tiwi of North Australia, the people of Gopalpur, or those of Guadalcanal. Each way of life is distinctive in its outlook, content, the kind of adult personalities favored, and the way children are raised. There are also many respects in which human communities are similar that override cultural differences. All major human cultural systems include magic, religion, moral values, recreation, regulation of mating, education, and so forth. But the *content* of these different categories, and the ways the content and the categories are put together, differ enormously. These differences are reflected in the ways people raise their children. If the object of cultural transmission is to teach young people how to think, act, and feel appropriately this must be the case. To understand this process we must get a sense of this variety.

*Reprinted with minor revisions from *Culture in Process,* second edition, by Alan R. Beals, George D. Spindler, and Louise Spindler. Copyright © 1967, 1973, by Holt, Rinehart and Winston, Inc. Reprinted by permission of Holt, Rinehart and Winston, Inc.

This Is How It Is in Palau

Five-year-old Azu trails after his mother as she walks along the village path, whimpering and tugging at her skirt. He wants to be carried, and he tells her so, loudly and demandingly, "Stop! Stop! Hold me!" His mother shows no sign of attention. She continues her steady barefooted stride, her arms swinging freely at her sides, her heavy hips rolling to smooth the jog of her walk and steady the basket of wet clothes she carries on her head. She has been to the washing pool and her burden keeps her neck stiff, but this is not why she looks impassively ahead and pretends not to notice her son. Often before she has carried him on her back and an even heavier load on her head. But today she has resolved not to submit to his plea, for it is time for him to begin to grow up.

Azu is not aware that the decision has been made. Understandably, he supposes that his mother is just cross, as she often has been in the past, and that his cries will soon take effect. He persists in his demand, but falls behind as his mother firmly marches on. He runs to catch up and angrily yanks at her hand. She shakes him off without speaking to him or looking at him. Enraged, he drops solidly on the ground and begins to scream. He gives a startled look when this produces no response, then rolls over on his stomach and begins to writhe, sob, and yell. He beats the earth with his fists and kicks it with his toes. This hurts and makes him furious, the more so since it has not caused his mother to notice him. He scrambles to his feet and scampers after her, his nose running, tears coursing through the dirt on his cheeks. When almost on her heel he yells and, getting no response, drops to the ground.

By this time his frustration is complete. In a rage he grovels in the red dirt, digging his toes into it, throwing it around him and on himself. He smears it on his face, grinding it in with his clenched fists. He squirms on his side, his feet turning his body through an arc on the pivot of one shoulder.

A man and his wife are approaching, the husband in the lead, he with a short-handled adz resting on his left shoulder, she with a basket of husked coconuts in her head. As they come abreast of Azu's mother the man greets her with "You have been to the washing pool?" It is the Palauan equivalent of the American "How are you?"—a question that is not an inquiry but a token of recognition. The two women scarcely glance up as they pass. They have recognized each other from a distance and it is not necessary to repeat the greeting. Even less notice is called for as the couple pass Azu sprawled on the path a few yards behind his mother. They have to step around his frenzied body, but no other recognition is taken of him, no word is spoken to him or to each other. There is no need to comment. His tantrum is not an unusual sight, especially among boys of his age or a little older. There is nothing to say to him or about him.

In the yard of a house just off the path, two girls, a little older than Azu, stop their play to investigate. Cautiously and silently they venture in Azu's direction. His mother is still in sight, but she disappears suddenly as she turns off the path into her yard without looking back. The girls stand some distance away, observing Azu's gyrations with solemn eyes. Then they turn and go back to their doorway, where they stand, still watching him but saying nothing. Azu is left alone, but it takes several minutes for him to realize that this is the way it is to be. Gradually his fit subsides and he lies sprawled and whimpering on the path.

Finally, he pushes himself to his feet and starts home, still sobbing and wiping his eyes with his fists. As he trudges into the yard he can hear his mother shouting at his sister, telling her not to step over the baby. Another sister is sweeping the earth beneath the floor of the house with a coconut-leaf broom. Glancing up, she calls shrilly to Azu, asking him where he has been. He does not reply, but climbs the two steps to the threshold of the doorway and makes his way to a mat in the corner of the house. There he lies quietly until he falls asleep.

This has been Azu's first painful lesson in growing up. There will be many more unless he soon understands and accepts the Palauan attitude that emotional attachments are cruel and treacherous entanglements, and that it is better not to cultivate them in the first place than to have them disrupted and disclaimed. Usually the lesson has to be repeated in many connections before its general truth sinks in. There will be refusals of pleas to be held, to be carried, to be fed, to be cuddled, and to be amused; and for a time at least there will follow the same violent struggle to maintain control that failed to help Azu. For whatever the means, and regardless of the lapses from the stern code, children must grow away from their parents, not cleave to them. Sooner or later the child must learn not to expect the solicitude, the warm attachment of earlier years and must accept the fact that he is to live in an emotional vacuum, trading friendship for concrete rewards, neither accepting nor giving lasting affection (Barnett 1960:4–6).

Is culture being transmitted here? Azu is learning that people are not to be trusted, that any emotional commitment is shaky business. He is acquiring an emotional attitude. From Professor Barnett's further description of life in Palau (Barnett 1960) we know that this emotional attitude underlies economic, social, political, even religious behavior among adult Palauans. If this happened only to Azu we would probably regard it as a traumatic event. He might then grow up to be a singularly distrustful adult in a trusting world. He would be a deviant. But virtually all Palauan boys experience this sudden rejection (it happens more gradually for girls) — not always in just this particular way — but in somewhat the same way and at about the same time. This is a culturally patterned way of getting a lesson across to the child. This culturally patterned way of treating the child has a more or less consistent result — an emotional attitude — and this emotional attitude is in turn patterned, and fits into various parts of the Palauan cultural system. What is learned by Azu and transmitted by his mother is at once a pattern of child training (the mother had it and applied it), a dimension of Palauan *world view* (Palauans see the world as a place where people do not become emotionally involved with each other), a modal personality trait (most normal adult Palauans distrust others), and a pattern for behavior in the context of the many subsystems (economic, political, religious, and so forth) governing adult life.

Azu's mother did not simply tell him to stop depending upon her and to refrain from lasting emotional involvements with others. She demonstrated to him in a very dramatic way that this is the way it is in this life (in Palau at least). She probably didn't even completely rationalize what she did. She did not say to herself, "Now it is time for Azu to acquire the characteristic Palauan attitude that emotional attachments are not lasting and the best way to teach him this is for me to refuse to carry him." Barnett says that she "resolved not to submit to his plea." We cannot be sure that she even did this, for not even Homer Barnett, as well as he knows the Palauans, can get into Azu's mother's head. We know that she did not, in fact, submit to his plea. She may well have thought that it was about time for Azu to grow up. Growing up in Palau means in part to stop depending on people, even your very own loving mother. But maybe she was just plain tired, feeling a little extra crabby, so she acted in a characteristically Palauan way *without thinking about it* toward her five-year-old. People can transmit culture without knowing they do so. Probably more culture is transmitted this way than with conscious intent.

Discontinuity between early and later childhood is apparent in the Palauan case. Most cultures are patterned in such a way as to provide discontinuities of experience, but the points of time in the life cycle where these occur, and their intensity, differ widely. Azu experienced few restraints before this time. He did pretty much as he pleased, and lolled about on the laps of parents, kin, and friends. He was seldom if ever punished. There was always someone around to serve as protector, provider, and companion, and someone to carry him, usually mother, wherever he might go. Much of this changed for him after this day at the age of five. To be sure, he is not abandoned, and he is still shielded, guided, and provided for in every physical sense, but he finds himself being told more often than asked what he wants, and his confidence in himself and in his parents has been shaken. He no longer knows how to get what he wants. The discontinuity, the break with the ways things were in his fifth year of life, is in itself a technique of cultural transmission. We will observe discontinuities in the treatment of children and their effects in other cultures.

How Is It Done in Ulithi?

The Ulithians, like the Palauans, are Micronesians, but inhabit a much smaller island, in fact a tiny atoll in the vast Pacific, quite out of the way and fairly unchanged when first studied by William Lessa in the late forties (Lessa 1966). The Ulithians educate their children in many of the same ways the Palauans do, but differently enough to merit some special attention.

Like the Palauans, the Ulithians are solicitous and supportive of infants and young children.

> The infant is given the breast whenever he cries to be fed or whenever it is considered time to feed him, but sometimes only as a pacifier. He suckles often, especially during the first three to six months of his life, when he may average around eighteen times during the day and night. The great stress placed by Ulithians on food is once more given eloquent expression in nursing practices. Thus, if both the mother and child should happen to be asleep at any time and it seems to someone who is awake that the baby should be fed, both are aroused in order to nurse the baby. . . .

The care of the baby is marked by much solicitude on the part of everyone. One of the ways in which this is manifested is through great attention to cleanliness. The infant is bathed three times a day, and after each bath the baby is rubbed all over with coconut oil and powdered with tumeric. Ordinarily, bathing is done by the mother, who, as she holds the child, rocks him from side to side in the water and sings:

> Float on the water
> In my arms, my arms
> On the little sea,
> The big sea,
> The rough sea,
> The calm sea,
> On this sea.

[three sentences omitted]

An infant is never left alone. He seems constantly in someone's arms, being passed from person to person in order to allow everyone a chance to fondle him. There is not much danger that if neglected for a moment he will harm himself (Lessa 1966:94–96).

Unlike the Palauans, the Ulithians do not create any special discontinuities for the young child. Even weaning is handled with as little disturbance as possible.

Weaning begins at varying ages. It is never attempted before the child is a year old, and usually he is much older than that. Some children are suckled until they are five, or even as much as seven or eight. Weaning takes about four days, one technique being to put the juice of hot pepper around the mother's nipples. Physical punishment is never employed, though scolding may be deemed necessary. Ridicule, a common recourse in training Ulithian children, is also resorted to. The child's reaction to being deprived of the breast often manifests itself in temper tantrums. The mother tries to mollify the child in a comforting embrace and tries to console him by playing with him and offering him such distraction as a tiny coconut or a flower (Lessa 1966:95).

Apparently this technique, and the emotional atmosphere that surrounds it, is not threatening to Ulithian children. We see nothing of the feelings of deprivation and rejection suffered by Azu.

The reactions to weaning are not extreme; children weather the crisis well. In fact, a playful element may be observed. A child may quickly push his face into his mother's breast and then run away to play. When the mother's attention is elsewhere, the child may make a sudden impish lunge at the breast and try to suckle from it. After the mother has scolded the weanling, he may coyly take the breast and fondle it, toy with the nipple, and rub the breast over his face. A man told me that when he was being weaned at the age of about seven, he would alternate sleeping with his father and mother, who occupied separate beds. On those occasions when he would sleep with his father, the latter would tell him to say goodnight to his mother. The boy would go over to where she was lying and playfully run his nose over her breasts. She would take this gesture good-naturedly and encourage him by telling him he was virtuous, strong, and like other boys. Then he would go back to his father, satisfied with his goodness (Lessa 1966:95).

We also see in the above account of Ulithian behavior that transmission of sexual attitudes and the permissiveness concerning eroticization are markedly different than in our own society. This difference, of course, is not confined to relations between young boys and their mothers, but extends through all heterosexual relationships, and throughout the patterning of adult life.

Given the relaxed and supportive character of child rearing in Ulithi, it is small wonder that children behave in a relaxed, playful manner, and apparently grow into adults that value relaxation. This is in sharp contrast with the Palauans, whom Barnett describes as characterized by a residue of latent hostility in social situations, and as subject to chronic anxiety (Barnett 1960: 11–15).

> Indeed, play is so haphazard and relaxed that it quickly melts from one thing to another, and from one place to another, with little inhibition. There is much laughter and chatter, and often some vigorous singing. One gains the impression that relaxation, for which the natives have a word they use almost constantly, is one of the major values of Ulithian culture (Lessa 1966:101).

Particularly striking in the transmission of Ulithian culture is the disapproval of unusually independent behavior.

> The attitude of society towards unwarranted independence is generally one of disapproval. Normal independence is admired because it leads to later self-reliance in the growing individual, dependence being scorned if it is so strong that it will unfit him for future responsibilities. Ulithians talk a lot about homesickness and do not view this as improper, unless the longing is really for a spouse or sweetheart, the suspicion here being that it is really sexual outlet that a person wants. Longing of this sort is said to make a person inefficient and perhaps even ill. Homesickness is expected of all children and not deprecated. I was greatly touched once when I asked a friend to tell me what a man was muttering about during a visit to my house. He said he felt sad that I was away from my home and friends and wondered how I could endure it. Ulithians do not like people to feel lonely; sociability is a great virtue for them (Lessa 1966:101).

The degree and kinds of dependence and independence that are inculcated in children are significant variables in any transcultural comparison of cultural transmission. Palauan children are taught not to trust others and grow to adulthood in a society where social relationships tend to be exploitative and, behind a facade of pleasantness, hostile. Palauans are not, however, independent, and tend to be quite dependent for direction upon external authority (Barnett 1960:13, 15–16). The picture is confused in Palau by the greater degree of acculturation (than at Ulithi) and the threatening situations that the Palauans have experienced under first German, then Japanese, and now American domination. In American society, middle-class culture calls for independence, particularly in males, and independence training is stressed from virtually the beginning of childhood. But adolescent and adult Americans are among the most sociable, "joiningest" people in the world. Ulithian children are not taught to be independent, and the individual who is too independent is the object of criticism. Palauan children are taught a kind of independence — to be independent of dependency upon other people's affection — by a sudden withdrawal of support at about five years of age. But which is really the more "independent" adult? Palauans are independent of each other in the sense that they can be cruel and callous to each other and exploitive in social relationships, but they are fearful of independent action and responsibility, are never originators or innovators, and are dependent upon authority for direction. Ulithians are dependent upon each other for social and emotional support, but do not exhibit the fearful dependency upon authority that Palauans do.

This does not mean that there is no predictable relationship between the training of children in dependency or independence and the consequences in adulthood. It does mean that the relationship is not simple and must be culturally contextualized if it is to make sense.

Every society creates some discontinuities in the experience of the individual as he or she grows up. It seems impossible to move from the roles appropriate to childhood to the roles appropriate for adulthood without some discontinuity. Societies differ greatly in the timing of discontinuity, and its abruptness. The first major break for Azu, the Palauan boy, was at five years of age. In Ulithi the major break occurs at the beginning of young adulthood.

> The mild concerns of ordinary life begin to catch up with the individual in the early years of adulthood and he can never again revert to the joyful indifference of his childhood.
>
> Attaining adulthood is marked by a ritual for boys and another for girls, neither of which is featured by genital operations. The same term, *kufar,* is used for each of the initiations. . . .
>
> The boy's *kufar* is much less elaborate and important. It comes about when he begins to show secondary sex characteristics and is marked by three elements: a change to adult clothing, the performance of magic, and the giving of a feast. All this occurs on the same day. . . .
>
> The outstanding consequence of the boy's ritual is that he must now sleep in the men's house and scrupulously avoid his postpubertal sisters. Not only must he not sleep in the same house with them, but he and they may not walk together, share the same food, touch one another's personal baskets, wear one another's leis or other ornaments, make or listen to ribald jokes in one another's presence, watch one another doing a solo dance, or listen to one another sing a love song (Lessa 1966:101–102).

Brother-sister avoidances of this kind are very common in human societies. There is a whole body of literature about them and their implications and consequences. The most important thing for us to note is that this is one of the most obvious ways in which restrictions appropriate to the young adult role in Ulithian society are placed on the individual immediately after the kufar. Transitional rites, or "rites of passage," as they are frequently termed, usually involve new restrictions of this sort. So, for that matter, do the events marking important transitions occurring at other times in the life experience. Azu lost the privilege of being carried and treated like an infant, and immediately became subject to being told what to do more often than demanding and getting what he wanted. One way of looking at Azu's experience and the Ulithian kufar is to regard them as periods of sharp discontinuity in the management of cultural transmission. Expressed most simply—what cultural transmitters do to and for an individual after the event is quite different in some ways from what they did before. Another way of looking at these events is to regard them as the beginning of periods of cultural compression. Expressed most simply—cultural compression occurs when the individual's behavior is restricted by the application of new cultural norms. After the kufar, the Ulithian boy and girl cannot interact with their mature opposite-sex siblings except under very special rules. Azu cannot demand to be carried and is told to do many other things he did not have to do before.

In Ulithi the girl's kufar is much more elaborate. When she notices the first flow of blood she knows she must go immediately to the women's house. As she goes, and upon her arrival, there is a great hullabaloo in the village, with the women shouting again and again, "The menstruating one, Ho-o-o!" After her arrival she takes a bath, changes her skirt, has magic spells recited over her to help her find a mate and enjoy a happy married life, and is instructed about the many *etap* (taboos) she must observe—some for days, others for weeks, and yet others for years. Soon she goes to live in a private hut of her own, built near her parent's house, but she still must go to the menstrual house whenever her discharge begins (Lessa 1966:102–104).

The discontinuity and compression that Ulithian young people experience after the kufar are not limited to a few taboos.

> Adolescence and adulthood obviously come rushing together at young Ulithians, and the attitude of the community toward them undergoes a rapid change. The boy and the girl are admitted to a higher status, to be sure, and they are given certain rights and listened to with more respect when they speak. But a good deal is expected of them in return. Young men bear the brunt of the heaviest tasks assigned by the men's council. For their own parents they must help build and repair houses, carry burdens, climb trees for coconuts, fish, make rope, and perform all the other tasks commonly expected of an able-bodied man. Young women are similarly called upon to do much of the harder work of the village and the household. Older people tend to treat these very young adults with a sudden sternness and formality lacking when they were in their childhood. The missteps of young people are carefully watched and readily criticized, so that new adults are constantly aware of the critical gaze of their elders. They may not voice strong objections or opinions, and have no political rights whatsoever, accepting the decisions of the men's and women's councils without murmur. Altogether, they are suddenly cut off from childhood and must undergo a severe transition in their comportment towards others about them. Only in the amatory sphere can they find release from the petty tyranny of their elders (Lessa 1966:104).

What Is It Like To Be Initiated in Hano?

Like the Hopi, with whom they are very close neighbors on the same mesa in Arizona, the Hano Tewa hold an initiation ceremony into the Kachina[1] cult at about nine years of age. In fact, the Tewa and Hopi share the same ceremony. Further examination of this occasion will be instructive. Up until that time Tewa children are treated about the way the Hopi children are. They are kept on a cradleboard at first, weaned late, by middle-class American standards, and on the whole treated very permissively and supportively by mothers, mother's sisters, grandparents, fathers, older siblings, and other people in and about the extended family household, admonished and corrected by the mother's brother, and half scared to death from time to time when they are bad by the Kachinas, or the threat of Kachinas. Of course nowadays the continuity of this early period is somewhat upset because children must start in the government day school at Polacca when they are about seven, and the teachers' ideas of proper behavior are frequently at variance with those maintained by Tewa parents. Excepting for school, though, Tewa children can be said to experience a consistent, continuous educational environment through the early years.

Things change when the initiation takes place at about age nine. A ceremonial father is selected for the boy, and a ceremonial mother for the girl. These ceremonial parents, as well as the real parents and for that matter everyone in the pueblo, build up the coming event for the child so that he or she is in a tremendous state of excitement. Then the day comes. Edward Dozier reports the initiation experience of one of his informants.

> We were told that the Kachina were beings from another world. There were some boys who said that they were not, but we could never be sure, and most of us believed what we were told. Our own parents and elders tried to make us believe that the Kachina were powerful beings, some good and some bad, and that they knew our innermost thoughts and actions. If they did not know about us through their own great power, then probably our own relatives told the Kachina about us. At any rate every time they visited us they seemed to know what we had thought and how we had acted.
>
> As the time for our initiation came closer we became more and more frightened. The ogre Kachina, the Soyoku, came every year and threatened to carry us away; now we were told that we were going to face these awful creatures and many others. Though we were told not to be afraid, we could not help ourselves. If the Kachina are really supernaturals and powerful beings, we might have offended them by some thought or act and they might punish us. They might even take us with them as the Soyoku threatened to do every year.
>
> Four days before Powamu our ceremonial fathers and our ceremonial mothers

---

[1] This word is sometimes spelled Katcina, sometimes Kachina. Voth, used as the source for the description of the Hopi ceremony, spells it Katcina. Dozier, used as the source for the Hano Tewa, spells it Kachina. Either is correct.

took us to Court Kiva. The girls were accompanied by their ceremonial mothers, and we boys by our ceremonial fathers. We stood outside the kiva, and then two whipper Kachina, looking very mean, came out of the kiva. Only a blanket covered the nakedness of the boys; as the Kachina drew near our ceremonial fathers removed the blankets. The girls were permitted to keep on their dresses, however. Our ceremonial parents urged us to offer sacred corn meal to the Kachina; as soon as we did they whipped us with their yucca whips. I was hit so hard that I defecated and urinated and I could feel the welts forming on my back and I knew that I was bleeding too. He whipped me four times, but the last time he hit me on the leg instead, and as the whipper started to strike again, my ceremonial father pulled me back and he took the blow himself. "This is a good boy, my old man," he said to the Kachina. "You have hit him enough."

For many days my back hurt and I had to sleep on my side until the wounds healed.

After the whipping a small sacred feather was tied to our hair and we were told not to eat meat or salt. Four days later we went to see the Powamu ceremony in the kiva. As babies, our mother had taken us to see this event; but as soon as we began to talk, they stopped taking us. I could not remember what had happened on Powamu night and I was afraid that another frightening ordeal awaited us. Those of us who were whipped went with our ceremonial parents. In this dance we saw that the Kachina were really our own fathers, uncles, and brothers. This made me feel strange. I felt somehow that all my relatives were responsible for the whipping we had received. My ceremonial father was kind and gentle during this time and I felt very warm toward him, but I also wondered if he was to blame for our treatment. I felt deceived and ill-treated (Dozier 1967:59–60).

The Hano Tewa children are shocked, angry, chagrined when they find that the supernatural Kachinas they have been scared and disciplined by all their lives up until then, and who during the initiation have whipped them hard, are really men they have known very well in their own community, their clans, their families. To be treated supportively and permissively all of one's life, and then to be whipped publicly (or see others get whipped) would seem quite upsetting by itself. To find out that the awesome Kachinas are men impersonating gods would seem almost too much. But somehow the experience seems to help make good adult Hano Tewa out of little ones.

If the initiate does not accept the spiritual reality of the Kachina, and will not accept his relatives' "cruel" behavior as necessary and good for him (or her), he can stop being a Tewa. But is this a real choice? Not for anyone who is human enough to need friends and family who speak the same language, both literally and figuratively, and whose identity as a Tewa Indian stretches back through all of time. Having then (usually without debate) made the choice of being a Tewa, one is a *good* Tewa. No doubts can be allowed.

There is another factor operating as well. Children who pass through the initiation are no longer outside looking in, they are inside looking out. They are not grown up, and neither they nor anyone else think they are, but they are a lot more grown up than they were before the initiation. Girls take on a more active part in household duties and boys acquire more responsibilities in farming and ranching activities. And it will not be long before the males can take on the role of impersonating the Kachinas and initiating children as they were initiated. The ceremonial whipping, in the context of all the dramatic ceremonies, dancing, and general community uproar, is the symbol of a dramatic shift in status-role. The shift starts with just being "in the know" about what really goes on in the kiva and who the Kachinas are, and continues toward more and more full participation in the secular and sacred life of the community.

Dorothy Eggan sums it up well for the Hopi when she writes:

> Another reorganizing factor . . . was feeling "big." They had shared pain with adults, had learned secrets which forever separated them from the world of children, and now they were included in situations from which they had previously been excluded, as their elders continued to teach intensely what they believed intensely: that for them there was only one alternative—Hopi as against Kahopi.
>
> Consistent repetition is a powerful conditioning agent and, as the youngsters watched each initiation, they relived their own, and by again sharing the experience gradually worked out much of the bitter residue from their own memories of it, while also rationalizing and weaving group emotions ever stronger into their own emotional core—"It takes a while to see how wise the old people really are." An initiated boy, in participating in the kachina dances, learned to identify again with the kachinas whom he now impersonated. To put on a mask is to "become a kachina," and to cooperate actively in bringing about the major goals of Hopi life. And a girl came to know more fully the importance of her clan in its supportive role. These experiences were even more sharply conditioned and directed toward adult life in the adult initiation ceremonies, of which we have as yet only fragmentary knowledge. Of this one man said to me: "I will not discuss this thing with you only to say that no one can forget it. It is the most wonderful thing any man can have to remember. You know then that you are Hopi. It is the one thing Whites cannot have, cannot take away from us. It is our way of life given to us when the world began" (Eggan 1956:364–65).

In many ways the preadolescent and adolescent period that we have been discussing, using the Ulithian kufar and the Hano Tewa initiation ceremonies as representative cases, is the most important of all in cultural transmission. There is a considerable literature on this period, including most notably the classic treatment given by Van Gennep (1960, first published in 1909) and the recent studies by Frank Young (1965), Yehudi Cohen (1964), Gary Schwartz and Don Merten (1968), and Whiting, Kluckhohn, and Albert (1958). Judith Brown provides a cross-cultural study of initiation rights for females (Brown 1963). But these studies do not emphasize the educational aspects of the initiation rites or rites of passage that they analyze.

One of the few studies that does is the remarkable essay by C. W. M. Hart (reprinted in this text in Chapter 16), based upon a single case, the Tiwi of North Australia, but with implications for many other cases. Hart contrasts the attitude of cultural transmitters toward young children among the Tiwi to the rigorous demands of the initiation period.

> The arrival of the strangers to drag the yelling boy out of his mother's arms is just the spectacular beginning of a long period during which the separation of the boy from everything that has gone before is emphasized in every possible way at every minute of the day and night. So far his life has been easy; now it is hard. Up to now he has never necessarily experienced any great pain, but in the initiation period in many tribes pain, sometimes horrible, intense pain, is an obligatory feature. The boy of twelve or thirteen, used to noisy, boisterous, irresponsible play, is expected and required to sit still for hours and days at a time saying nothing whatever but concentrating upon and endeavoring to understand long intricate instructions and "lectures" given him by his hostile and forbidding preceptors. [sentence omitted] Life has suddenly become real and earnest and the initiate is required literally to "put away the things of a child" even the demeanor. The number of tabus and unnatural behaviors enjoined upon the initiate is endless. He mustn't speak unless he is spoken to; he must eat only certain foods, and often only in certain ways, at fixed times, and in certain fixed positions. All contact with females, even speech with them is rigidly forbidden, and this includes mother and sisters (1963:415).

Hart goes on to state that the novices are taught origin myths, the meaning of the sacred ceremonials, in short, theology, ". . . which in primitive society is inextricably mixed up with astronomy, geology, geography, biology (the mysteries of birth and death), philosophy, art, and music — in short the whole cultural heritage of the tribe"; and that the purpose of this teaching is not to make better economic men of the novices, but rather ". . . better citizens, better carriers of the culture through the generations. . ." (Hart 1963:415). In this view Hart agrees (as he points out himself) with George Pettit, who did a thorough study of educational practices among North American Indians, and who writes that the initiation proceedings were ". . . a constant challenge to the elders to review, analyze, dramatize, and defend their cultural heritage" (Pettit 1946:182).

Pettit's words also bring into focus another feature of the initiation rituals implicit in the description of these events for the Ulithians, Hano Tewa, and the Tiwi, which seems very significant. In all these cases dramatization is used as an educational technique. In fact a ceremony of any kind is a dramatization, sometimes indirect and metaphoric, sometimes very direct, of the interplay of crucial forces and events in the life of the community. In the initiation ceremonies dramatization forces the seriousness of growing up into the youngster's mind and mobilizes his emotions around the lessons to be learned and the change in identity to be secured. The role of dramatization in cultural transmission may be difficult for American readers to appreciate, because the pragmatization of American schools and American life in general has gone so far.

These points emphasize the view of initiation proceedings taken in this chapter — that they are dramatic signals for new beginnings and, at various times before and throughout adolescence in many societies, the intensification of discontinuity and compression in cultural transmission. Discontinuity in the management of the youngsters' learning—from supportive and easy to rigorous and harsh; compression in the closing in of culturally patterned demand and restriction as the new status-roles attained by successfully passing through the initiation period are activated. Of course this compression of cultural demand around the individual also opens new channels of development and experience to him. As humans mature they give up the freedom of childhood for the rewards to be gained by observing the rules of the cultural game. The initiation ceremonies are dramatic signals to everyone that the game has begun in earnest.

What Happens in Gopalpur?

In the village of Gopalpur, in South India, described by Alan Beals, social, not physical, mastery is stressed.

> Long before it has begun to walk, the child in Gopalpur has begun to develop a concern about relationships with others. The period of infantile dependency is extended. The child is not encouraged to develop muscular skills, but is carried from place to place on the hip of mother or sister. The child is rarely alone. It is constantly exposed to other people, and learning to talk, to communicate with others, is given priority over anything else that might be learned. When the child does learn to walk, adults begin to treat it differently. Shooed out of the house, its training is largely taken over by the play group. In the streets there are few toys, few things to be manipulated. The play of the child must be social play and the manipulation of others must be accomplished through language and through such nonphysical techniques as crying and withdrawal. In the play group, the child creates a family and the family engages in the production of imaginary food or in the exchange of real food carried in shirt pockets (1962:19).

Children in Gopalpur imitate adults, both in the activities of play and in the attempts to control each other.

> Sidda, four years old, is playing in the front of his house with his cousin, Bugga, aged five. Sidda is sitting on the ground holding a stone and pounding. Bugga is piling the sand up like rice for the pounding. Bugga says, "Sidda, give me the stone, I want to pound." Sidda puts the stone on the ground, "Come and get it." Bugga says, "Don't come with me, I am going to the godhouse to play." Sidda offers, "I will give you the stone." He gives the stone to Bugga, who orders him, "Go into the house and bring some water." Sidda goes and brings water in a brass bowl. Bugga takes it and pours it on the heap of sand. He mixes the water with the sand, using both hands. Then, "Sidda, take the bowl inside." Sidda takes the bowl and returns with his mouth full of peanuts. He puts his hand into his shirt pocket, finds more peanuts and puts them in his mouth. Bugga sees the peanuts and asks, "Where did you get those?" "I got them inside the house." "Where are they?" "In the winnowing basket." Bugga gets up and goes inside the house returning with a bulging shirt pocket. Both sit down near the pile of sand. Bugga says to

Sidda "Don't tell mother." "No, I won't." Sidda eats all of his peanuts and moves toward Bugga holding his hands out. Bugga wants to know, "Did you finish yours?" "I just brought a little, you brought a lot." Bugga refuses to give up any peanuts and Sidda begins to cry. Bugga pats him on the back saying, "I will give you peanuts later on." They get up and go into the house. Because they are considered to be brothers, Sidda and Bugga do not fight. When he is wronged, the older Bugga threatens to desert Sidda. When the situation is reversed, the younger Sidda breaks into tears (Beals 1962:16).

In their play, Bugga and Sidda are faithful to the patterns of adult control over children, as they have both observed them and experienced them. Beals describes children going to their houses when their shirt pockets are empty of the "currency of interaction" (grain, bits of bread, peanuts).

This is the moment of entrapment, the only time during the day when the mother is able to exercise control over her child. This is the time for bargaining, for threatening. The mother scowls at her child, "You must have worked hard to be so hungry." The mother serves food and says, "Eat this. After you have eaten it, you must sit here and rock your little sister." The child eats and says, "I am going outside to play, I will not rock my sister." The child finishes its food and runs out of the house. Later, the child's aunt sees it and asks it to run to the store and buy some cooking oil. When it returns, the aunt says, "If you continue to obey me like this, I will give you something good to eat." When the mother catches the child again, she asks, "Where have you been?" Learning what occurred, she says, "If you bought cooking oil, that is fine; now come play with your sister." The child says, "First give me something to eat, and I will play with my sister." The mother scolds, "You will die of eating, sometimes you are willing to work, sometimes you are not willing to work; may you eat dirt." She gives it food and the child plays with its sister (1962:19).

This is the way the child in Gopalpur learns to control the unreliable world of other people. Children soon learn that they are dependent upon others for the major securities and satisfactions of life. The one with a large number of friends and supporters is secure, and they can be won and controlled, the individual comes to feel, through the use of food, but also by crying, begging, and working.

And among the Eskimo?

Eskimo children are treated supportively and permissively. When a baby cries it is picked up, played with, or nursed. There are a variety of baby tenders about, and after the first two or three months of life older siblings and the mother's unmarried sisters and cousins take a hand in caring for it. There is no set sleeping or eating schedule and weaning is a gradual process that may not be completed until the third or fourth year.

How is it then that, as white visitors to Eskimo villages often remark, the Eskimo have managed to raise their children so well? Observers speak warmly of their good humor, liveliness, resourcefulness, and well-behaved manner.

They appear to exemplify qualities that Western parents would like to see in their own children (Chance 1966:22). American folk belief would lead one to surmise that children who are treated so permissively would be "spoiled." Norman Chance describes the situation for the Alaskan Eskimo.

Certainly, the warmth and affection given infants by parents, siblings, and other relatives provide them with a deep feeling of well-being and security. Young children also feel important because they learn early that they are expected to be useful, working members of the family. This attitude is not instilled by imposing tedious chores, but rather by including children in the round of daily activities, which enhances the feeling of family participation and cohesion. To put it another way, parents rarely deny children their company or exclude them from the adult world.

This pattern reflects the parents' views of child rearing. Adults feel that they have more experience in living and it is their responsibility to share this experience with the children, "to tell them how to live." Children have to be told repeatedly because they tend to forget. Misbehavior is due to a child's forgetfulness, or to improper teaching in the first place. There is rarely any thought that the child is basically nasty, willful, or sinful. Where Anglo-Americans applaud a child for his good behavior, the Eskimo praise him for remembering. . . .

Regardless of the degree of Westernization, more emphasis is placed on equality than on superordination-subordination in parent-child relations. A five year old obeys, not because he fears punishment or loss of love, but because he identifies with his parents and respects their judgment. Thus he finds little to resist or rebel against in his dealing with adults. We will find rebellion more common in adolescents, but it is not necessarily a revolt against parental control.

By the time a child reaches the age of four or five, his parents' initial demonstrativeness has become tempered with an increased interest in his activities and accomplishments. They watch his play with obvious pleasure, and respond warmly to his conversation, make jokes with him and discipline him.

Though a child is given considerable autonomy and his whims and wishes treated with respect, he is nonetheless taught to obey all adults. To an outsider unfamiliar with parent-child relations, the tone of Eskimo commands and admonitions sometimes sounds harsh and angry, yet in few instances does a child respond as if he had been addressed hostilely. . . .

After the age of five a child is less restricted in his activities in and around the village, although theoretically he is not allowed on the beach or ice without an adult. During the dark winter season, he remains indoors or stays close to the house to prevent him from getting lost and to protect him from polar bears which might come into the village. In summer, though, children play at all hours of the day or "night" or as long as their parents are up. . . .

Although not burdened with responsibility, both boys and girls are expected to take an active role in family chores. In the early years responsibilities are shared, depending on who is available. Regardless of sex, it is important for a child to know how to perform a wide variety of tasks and give help when needed. Both sexes collect and chop wood, get water, help carry meat and other supplies, oversee younger siblings, run errands for adults, feed the dogs, and burn trash.

As a child becomes older, more specific responsibilities are allocated to him, according to his sex. Boys as young as seven may be given an opportunity to shoot a .22 rifle, and at least a few boys in every village have killed their first caribou by the time they are ten. A youngster learns techniques of butchering while on hunting trips with older siblings and adults, although he is seldom proficient until he is in his mid-teens. In the past girls learned butchering at an early age, since this knowledge was essential to attracting a good husband. Today, with the availability of large quantities of Western foods, this skill may not be acquired until a girl is married, and not always then.

Although there is a recognized division of labor by sex, it is far from rigid at any age level. Boys, and even men, occasionally sweep the house and cook. Girls and their mothers go on fishing or bird-hunting trips. Members of each sex can usually assume the responsibilities of the other when the need arises, albeit in an auxiliary capacity (1966:22–26).

Apparently the combination that works so well with Eskimo children is support—participation—admonition—support. These children learn to see adults as rewarding and nonthreatening. Children are also not excluded, as they so often are in America, from the affairs of adult life. They do not understand everything they see, but virtually nothing is hidden from them. They are encouraged to assume responsibility appropriate to their age quite early in life. Children are participants in the flow of life. They learn by observing and doing. But Eskimo adults do not leave desired learning up to chance. They admonish, direct, remonstrate, but without hostility.

The Eskimo live with a desperately intemperate climate in what many white men have described as the part of the world that is the most inimical to human life. Perhaps Eskimo children are raised the way they are because a secure, good-humored, resourceful person is the only kind that can survive for long in this environment.

In Sensuron?

The people of Sensuron live in a very different physical and cultural environment than do the Eskimo. The atmosphere of this Dusun village in Borneo (now the Malysian state of Sabah) is communicated in these passages from Thomas Williams' case study.

Sensuron is astir an hour before the dawn of most mornings. It is usually too damp and cold to sleep. Fires are built up and the morning meal cooked while members of the household cluster about the house fire-pit seeking warmth. After eating, containers and utensils are rinsed off with water to "keep the worms off" and replaced in racks on the side of the house porch. Older children are sent to the river to carry water home in bamboo containers, while their mother spends her time gathering together equipment for the day's work, including some cold rice wrapped in leaves for a midday snack. The men and adolescent males go into the yard to sit in the first warmth of the sun and talk with male neighbors. The early morning exchange of plans, news, and recounting of the events of yesterday is considered a "proper way" to begin the day. While the men cluster in the yard center, with old shirts or cloths draped about bare shoulders to ward off the chill, women gather in front of one house or another, also trading news, gossip, and work plans. Many women comb each other's hair, after carefully picking out the lice. It is not unusual to see four or more women sitting in a row down the steps of a house ladder talking, while combing and delousing hair. Babies are nursed while mothers talk and small children run about the clusters of adults, generally being ignored until screams of pain or anger cause a sharp retort of *kAdA!* (do not!) from a parent. Women drape spare skirts about their bare shoulders to ward off the morning chill. About two hours after dawn these groups break up as the members go off to the work of the day. The work tasks of each day are those to be done under the annual cycle of subsistence labor described in the previous chapter. . . .

Vocal music is a common feature of village life; mothers and grandmothers sing a great variety of lullabies and "growth songs" to babies, children sing a wide range of traditional and nonsense songs, while adults sing at work in the fields and gardens during leisure and social occasions and at times of ritual. Drinking songs and wedding songs take elaborate forms, often in the nature of song "debates" with sides chosen and a winner declared by a host or guest of honor on the basis of "beauty" of tone, humor, and general "one-upmanship" in invention of new verse forms. Most group singing is done in harmony. Adolescents, especially girls, spend much of their solitary leisure time singing traditional songs of love and loneliness. Traditional verse forms in ritual, and extensive everyday use of riddles, folktales, and proverbs comprise a substantial body of oral literature. Many persons know much ritual verse, and most can recite dozens of stylized folktales, riddles, and proverbs.

Village headmen, certain older males, and ritual specialists of both sexes are practiced speechmakers. A skill of "speaking beautifully" is much admired and imitated. The style used involves narration, with exhortation, and is emphasized through voice tone and many hand and body gestures and postures. Political debates, court hearings, and personal arguments often become episodes of dramatic representation for onlookers, with a speaker's phrase listened to for its emotional expressive content and undertones of ridicule, tragedy, comedy, and farce at the expense of others involved. The verse forms of major rituals take on dimensions of drama as the specialist delivers the lines with skillful impersonations of voices and mannerisms of disease givers, souls of the dead, and creator beings.

By late afternoon of a leisure day people in the houses begin to drift to the yards, where they again sit and talk. Fires are built to ward off the chill of winds rising off the mountains, and men and women circle the blaze, throwing bits of wood and bamboo into the fire as they talk. This time is termed *mEg-Amut,* after the designation for exchange of small talk between household members. As many as 20 fires can be seen burning in yards through Sensuron at evening on most leisure days and on many evenings after work periods. Men sit and talk until after dark, when they go into houses to take their evening meal. Women leave about an hour before dark to prepare the meal. Smaller children usually eat before the adults. After the evening meal, for an hour or more, the family clusters about the house firepit, talking, with adults often engaged in small tasks of tool repair or manufacture. By 8 or 9 P M most families are asleep; the time of retiring is earlier when the work days are longer, later on rest days (1965:78–79).

Children in Sensuron are, like Eskimo children, always present, always observers. How different this way of life is from that experienced by American children! Gossip, speech-making, folktale telling, grooming, working, and playing are all there, all a part of the stream of life flowing around one and with which each member of the community moves. Under these circumstances much of the culture is transmitted by a kind of osmosis. It would be difficult for a child *not to* learn his culture.

The children of Sensuron do not necessarily grow up into good-humored, secure, trusting, "happy" adults. There are several factors that apparently interact in their growing up to make this unlikely. In the most simple sense, these children do not grow up to be like Eskimo adults because their parents (and other cultural transmitters) are not Eskimo, Dusun cultural transmitters (anybody in the community that the child hears and sees) act like Dusun. But cultural transmitters display certain attitudes and do certain things to children as well as provide them with models. In Sensuron, children are judged to be nonpersons. They are not even provided with personal names until their fifth year. They are also considered to be ". . . naturally noisy, inclined to illness, capable of theft, incurable wanderers, violent, quarrelsome, temperamental, destructive of property, wasteful, easily offended, quick to forget" (Williams 1965:87). They are threatened by parents with being eaten alive, carried off, damaged by disease-givers. Here are two lullabies sung to babies in Sensuron (and heard constantly by older children):

> Sleep, Sleep, baby,
> There comes the *rAgEn* (soul of the dead)
> He carries a big stick,
> He carries a big knife,
> Sleep, Sleep, baby,
> He comes to beat you!

or, as in this verse,

> Bounce, Bounce, baby
> There is a hawk,
> Flying, looking for prey!
> There is the hawk, looking for his prey!
> He searches for something to snatch up in his claws,
> Come here, hawk, and snatch up this baby!
> (Williams 1965:88).

None of the things that the adults of Sensuron do to, with, or around their children is to be judged "bad." Their culture is different from Eskimo culture, and a different kind of individual functions effectively in it. We may for some reason need to make value judgments about a culture, the character of the people who live by it, or the way they raise children—but not for the purpose of understanding it better. It is particularly hard to refrain from making value judgments when the behavior in question occurs in an area of life in our own culture about which there are contradictory rules and considerable anxiety. Take, for instance, the transmission of sexual behavior in the village of Sensuron.

> In Sensuron people usually deal with their sex drives through ideally denying their existence, while often behaving in ways designed to sidestep social and cultural barriers to personal satisfaction. At the ideal level of belief the view is expressed that "men are not like dogs, chasing any bitch in heat," or "sex relations are unclean." Some of the sexuality of Dusun life has been noted earlier. There is a high content of lewd and bawdy behavior in the play of children and adolescents, and in the behavior of adults. For example, the eight-year-old girl in the house across from ours was angrily ordered by her mother to come into the house to help in rice husking. The girl turned to her mother and gave her a slow, undulating thrust of her hips in a sexual sign. More than 12 salacious gestures are known and used regularly by children and adults of both sexes, and there are some 20 equivalents of "four-letter" English terms specifically denoting the sexual anatomy and its possible uses. Late one afternoon 4 girls between 8 and 15 years, and 2 young boys of 4 and 5 years were chasing about our house steps for a half hour, grabbing at each other's genitals, and screaming, *uarE tAle!* which roughly translated means, "there is your mother's vulva!" Adult onlookers were greatly amused at the group and became convulsed with laughter when the four-year-old boy improvised the answer, "my mother has no vulva!" Thus, sexual behavior is supposed to be unclean and disgusting, while in reality it is a source of amusement and constant attention. . . .
>
> Children learn details of sexual behavior early, and sex play is a part of the behavior of four-to-six-year olds, usually in houses or rice stores while parents are away at work. Older children engage in sexual activities in groups and pairs, often at a location outside the village, often in an abandoned field storehouse, or in a temporary shelter in a remote garden (Williams 1965:82–83).

We can, however, make the tentative generalization that in cultures where there is a marked discrepancy between ideal and real, between the "theory" of culture and actual behavior, this conflict will be transmitted and that conflicts of this kind are probably not conducive to trust, confidence in self and in others, or even something we might call "happiness." We are like the people of Sensuron, though probably the conflicts between real and ideal run much deeper and are more damaging in our culture. In any event, the transmission of culture is complicated by discrepancies and conflicts, for both the pattern of idealizations and the patterns of actual behavior must be transmitted, as well as the ways for rationalizing the discrepancy between them.

How Goes It in Guadalcanal?

Many of the comments that have been made about child rearing and the transmission of culture in other communities can be applied to the situation in Guadalcanal, one of the Solomon Islands near New Guinea. Babies are held, fondled, fed, never isolated, and generally given very supportive treatment. Weaning and toilet training both take place without much fuss, and fairly late by American standards. Walking is regarded as a natural accomplishment that will be mastered in time, swimming seems to come as easily. Education is also different in some ways in Guadalcanal. There is no sharp discontinuity at the beginning of middle childhood as in Palau, nor is there any sharp break at puberty as in Ulithi, or at prepuberty as among the Hano Tewa or Hopi. The special character of cultural transmission in Guadalcanal is given by Ian Hogbin:

> Two virtues, generosity and respect for property, are inculcated from the eighteenth month onward—that is to say, from the age when the child can walk about and eat bananas and other things regarded as delicacies. At this stage no explanations are given, and the parents merely insist that food must be shared with any playmate who happens to be present and that goods belonging to other villagers must be left undisturbed. A toddler presented with a piece of fruit is told to give half to "So-and-so," and should the order be resisted, the adult ignores all protests and breaks a piece off to hand to the child's companion. Similarly, although sometimes callers are cautioned to put their baskets on a shelf out of reach, any meddling brings forth the rebuke, "That belongs to your uncle. Put it down." Disobedience is followed by snatching away the item in question from the child and returning it to the owner.
>
> In time, when the child has passed into its fourth or fifth year, it is acknowledged to have at last attained the understanding to be able to take in what the adults say. Therefore, adults now accompany demands with reasoned instruction. One day when I was paying a call on a neighbor, Mwane-Anuta, I heard him warn his second son Mbule, who probably had not reached the age of five, to stop being so greedy. "I saw your mother give you those nuts," Mwane-Anuta reiterated. "Don't pretend she didn't. Running behind the house so that Penggoa wouldn't know! That is bad, very bad. Now then, show me, how many? Five left. Very well, offer three to Penggoa immediately." He then went on to tell me how important it was for children to learn to think of others so that in later life they would win the respect of their fellows.
>
> On another occasion during a meal I found Mwane-Anuta and his wife teaching their three sons how to eat properly. "Now Mbule," said his mother, "you face the rest of us so that we can all see you aren't taking too much. And you, Konana, run outside and ask Misika from next door to join you. His mother's not home yet, and I expect he's hungry. Your belly's not the only one, my boy." "Yes," Mwane-Anuta added. "Give a thought to those you run about with, and they'll give a thought to you." At this point the mother called over the eldest lad, Kure, and placed the basket of yams for me in his hands. "There, you carry that over to our guest and say that it is good to have him with us this evening," she whispered to him. The gesture was characteristic. I noted that always when meals were served to visitors the children acted as waiters. Why was this, I wanted to know. "Teaching, teaching," Mwane-Anuta replied. "This is how we train our young to behave" (1964:33).

It appears that in Guadalcanal direct verbal instruction is stressed as a technique of cultural transmission. Hogbin goes on to describe the constant stream of verbal admonition that is directed at the child by responsible adults in almost every situation. And again and again the prime values, generosity and respect for property, are reinforced by these admonitions.

The amount of direct verbal reinforcement of basic values, and even the amount of direct verbal instruction in less crucial matters, varies greatly from culture to culture. The people of Guadalcanal, like the Hopi, keep telling their children and young people how to behave and when they are behaving badly. In American middle-class culture there is also great emphasis on telling children what they should do, explaining how to do it, and the reasons for doing it, though we are probably less consistent in what we tell them than are the parents of Guadalcanal. Perhaps also in our culture we tend to substitute words for experience more than do the people of Guadalcanal, for the total range of experience relevant to growing up appropriately is more directly observable and available to their children than it is to ours.

> Girls go to the gardens regularly with their mother from about the age of eight. They cannot yet wield the heavy digging stick or bush knife, but they assist in collecting the rubbish before planting begins, in piling up the earth, and weeding. Boys start accompanying their father some two or three years later, when they help with the clearing, fetch lianas to tie up the saplings that form the fence, and cut up the seed yams. The men may also allocate plots to their sons and speak of the growing yams as their own harvest. The services of a youngster are of economic value from the time that he is pubescent, but he is not expected to take gardening really seriously until after he returns from the plantation and is thinking of marriage. By then he is conscious of his rights and privileges as a member of his clan and knows where the clan blocks of land are located. As a rule, he can also explain a little about the varieties of yams and taro and the types of soil best suited to earth.
>
> At about eight a boy begins to go along with his father or uncles when the men set out in the evening with their lines to catch fish from the shore or on the reef. They make a small rod for him, show him how to bait his hook, and tell him about the different species of fish—where they are to be found, which are good to eat, which are poisonous. At the age of ten the boy makes an occasional fishing excursion in a canoe. To start with, he sits in the center of the canoe and watches, perhaps baiting the hooks and removing the catch; but soon he takes part with the rest. In less than a year he is a useful crew member and expert in steering and generally handling the craft. At the same time, I have never seen youths under the age of sixteen out at sea by themselves. Often they are eager to go before this, but the elders are unwilling to give permission lest they endanger themselves or the canoe (Hogbin 1964:39).

The children of Guadalcanal learn by doing as well as learn by hearing. They also learn by imitating adult models, as children do in every human group around the world.

> Children also play at housekeeping. Sometimes they take along their juniors, who, however, do not remain interested for long. They put up a framework of saplings and tie on coconut-leaf mats, which they plait themselves in a rough-and-ready sort of way. Occasionally, they beg some raw food and prepare it; or they catch birds, bats, and rats with bows and arrows. Many times, too, I have seen

them hold weddings, including all the formality of the handing-over of bride price. Various items serve instead of the valuables that the grownups use—tiny pebbles instead of dog's and porpoise teeth, the long flowers of a nut tree for strings of shell discs, and rats or lizards for pigs. When first the youngsters pretend to keep house they make no sexual distinction in the allocation of the tasks. Boys and girls together erect the shelters, plait the mats, cook the food, and fetch the water. But within a year or so, although they continue to play in company, the members of each group restrict themselves to the work appropriate to their sex. The boys leave the cooking and water carrying to the girls, who, in turn, refuse to help with the building (Hogbin 1964:37–38).

Children seem to acquire the culture of their community best when there is consistent reinforcement of the same norms of action and thinking through many different channels of activity and interaction. If a child is told, sees demonstrated, casually observes, imitates, experiments and is corrected, acts appropriately and is rewarded, corrected, and (as in the Tewa-Hopi initiation) is given an extra boost in learning by dramatized announcements of status-role change, all within a consistent framework of belief and value, he or she cannot help but learn, and learn what adult cultural transmitters want him or her to learn.

How Do They Listen in Demirciler?

In Demirciler, an Anatolian village in the arid central plateau of Turkey, a young boy, Mahmud, learns by being allowed in the room when the adult men meet at the Muhtar's (the village headman) home evenings to discuss current affairs.

Each day, after having finished the evening meal, the old Muhtar's wife would put some small earthenware dishes or copper trays filled with nuts or chick-peas about the room, sometimes on small stands or sometimes on the floor, and the old man would build a warm fire in the fireplace. Soon after dark the men would begin to arrive by ones or twos and take their accustomed places in the men's room. This was the largest single room in the village and doubled as a guest house for visitors who came at nightfall and needed some place to sleep before going on their way the next day. It had been a long time since the room had been used for this purpose, however, because the nearby growing city had hotels, and most of the modern travelers stayed there. However, the room still served as a clearing house for all village business, as well as a place for the men to pass the cold winter evenings in warm comfort.

The room was perhaps 30 by 15 feet in size, and along one side a shelf nearly 15 inches above the floor extended about 2 feet from the wall and covered the full 30 feet of the room's length. The old Muhtar sat near the center of the shelf, waiting for his guests to arrive. As the men came in, the oldest in the village would seat themselves in order of age on this raised projection, while the younger ones would sit cross-legged on the floor. No women were ever allowed to come into this room when the men were there. The Muhtar's wife had prepared everything ahead of time, and when additional things were occasionally needed during the evening, one of the boys would be sent out to fetch it. Opposite the long bench was a fireplace, slightly larger than those in the kitchen of the other village homes, in which a fire burned brightly spreading heat throughout the room. The single electric bulb lighted the space dimly and so the shadows caused by the firelight were not prevented from dancing about the walls.

Mahmud would have been happier if the electric bulb had not been there at all, the way it used to be when he had been a very small boy. Electricity had been introduced to the village only a year ago, and he remembered the days when only the glow of the fire lighted these meetings.

As the gatherings grew in size, Mahmud heard many small groups of men talking idly about all sorts of personal problems, but when nearly all of the villagers had arrived, they began to quiet down.

The Hoca posed the first question, "Muhtar Bey, when will next year's money for the mosque be taken up?"

"Hocam, the amount has not been set yet," was the Muhtar's reply.

"All right, let's do it now," the Hoca persisted.

"Let's do it now," the Muhtar agreed.

And Mahmud listened as the Hoca told about the things the mosque would need during the coming year. Then several of the older men told how they had given so much the year before that it had been hard on their families, and finally, the Muhtar talked interminably about the duty of each Moslem to support the Faith and ended by asking the head of each family for just a little more than he knew they could pay.

Following this request there were a series of discussions between the Muhtar and each family head, haggling over what the members of his family could afford to give. Finally, however, agreement was reached with each man, and the Hoca knew how much he could count on for the coming year. The Muhtar would see that the money was collected and turned over to the Hoca.

The business of the evening being out of the way, Mahmud became more interested, as he knew that what he liked most was to come now. He had learned that he was too young to speak at the meetings, because he had been taken out several times the year before by one of the older boys and told that he could not stay with the men unless he could be quiet, so he waited in silence for what would happen next. After a slight pause one of the braver of the teen-aged boys called to an old man.

"*Dedem,* tell us some stories about the olden times."

"Shall I tell about the wars?" the old man nearest the Muhtar asked.

"Yes, about the great war with the Russians," the youth answered.

"Well, I was but a boy then, but my father went with the army of the Sultan that summer, and he told me this story" (Pierce 1964:20–21).

Is there any situation in the culture of the United States where a similar situation exists? When America was more rural than it is now, and commercial entertainments were not readily available for most people, young people learned about adult roles and problems, learned to think like adults and anticipated their own adulthood in somewhat the same way that Mahmud did. Now it is an open question whether young people would want to listen to their elders even if there was nothing else to do. Possibly this is partly because much of what one's elders "know" in our society is not true. The verities change with each generation.

At the end of the "business" session at the Muhtar's home an old man tells a story. The story is offered as entertainment, even though it has been heard countless times before. Young listeners learn from stories as well as from the deliberations of the older men as they decide what to do about somebody's adolescent son who is eyeing the girls too much, or what to do about building a new road. Storytelling has been and still is a way of transmitting information to young people in many cultures without their knowing they are being taught. Any story has either a metaphoric application to real life, provides models for behavior, or has both features. The metaphor or the model may or may not be translated into a moral. The elders in Demirciler do not, it appears, make the moral of the story explicit. In contrast, the Menomini Indians of Wisconsin always required a youngster to extract the moral in a story for himself. "You should never ask for anything to happen unless you mean it." "He who brags bites his own tail." A grandparent would tell the same story every night until the children could state the moral to the elder's satisfaction (Spindler 1971). People in different cultures vary greatly in how much they make of the moral, but stories and mythtellings are used in virtually all cultures to transmit information, values, and attitudes.

What Does Cultural Transmission Do for the System?

So far we have considered cultural transmission in cases where no major interventions from the outside have occurred, or, if they have occurred, we have chosen to ignore them for purposes of description and analysis. There are, however, virtually no cultural systems left in the world that have not experienced massive input from the outside, particularly from the West. This is the age of transformation. Nearly all tribal societies and peasant villages are being affected profoundly by modernization. One of the most important aspects of modernization is the development of schools that will, hopefully, prepare young people to take their places in a very different kind of world than the one their parents grew up in. This implies a kind of discontinuity that is of a different order than the kind we have been discussing.

Discontinuity in cultural transmission among the Dusun, Hopi, Tewa, and Tiwi is a process that produces cultural continuity in the system as a whole. The abrupt and dramatized changes in roles during adolescence, the sudden compression of cultural requirements, and all the techniques used by preceptors, who are nearly always adults from within the cultural system, educate an individual to be committed to the system. The initiation itself encapsulates and dramatizes symbols and meanings that are at the core of the cultural system so that the important things the initiate has learned up to that point, by observation, participation, or instruction, are reinforced. The discontinuity is in the way the initiate is treated during the initiation and the different behaviors expected of him (or her) afterward. The culture is maintained, its credibility validated. As the Hopi man said to Dorothy Eggan, "I will not discuss this thing with you only to say that no one can forget it. It is the most wonderful thing any man can have to remember. You know then that you are Hopi [after the initiation]. It is the one thing Whites cannot have, cannot take from us. It is our way of life given to us when the world began." (See p. 328.) This Hopi individual has been *recruited* as a Hopi.

In all established cultural systems where radical interventions from outside have not occurred, the major functions of education are *recruitment* and *maintenance*. The educational processes we have described for all of the cultures in this chapter have functioned in this manner. Recruitment occurs in two senses: recruitment to membership in the cultural system in general, so that one becomes a Hopi or a Tiwi; and recruitment to specific roles and statuses, to specific castes, or to certain classes. We may even, by stretching the point a little, say that young humans are recruited to being male or female, on the terms with which a given society defines being male or female. This becomes clear in cultures such as our own, where sex roles are becoming blurred so much that many young people grow up without a clear orientation toward either role. The educational system, whether we are talking about societies where there are no schools in the formal sense but where a great deal of education takes place, or about societies where there are many specialized formal schools, is organized to effect recruitment. The educational system is also organized so that the structure of the cultural system will be maintained. This is done by inculcating the specific values, attitudes, and beliefs that make this structure credible and the skills and competencies that make it work. People must believe in their system. If there is a caste or class structure they must believe that such a structure is good, or if not good, at least inevitable. They must also have the skills—vocational and social—that make it possible for goods and services to be exchanged that are necessary for community life to go on. Recruitment and maintenance intergrade, as you can see from the above discussion. The former refers to the process of getting people into the system and into specific roles; the latter refers to the process of keeping the system and roles functioning.

Modernizing Cultures: What Is the Purpose of Education?

In this transforming world, however, educational systems are often charged with responsibility for bringing about change in the culture. They become, or are intended to become, agents of modernization. They become intentional agents of cultural discontinuity, a kind of discontinuity that does not reinforce the traditional values or recruit youngsters into the existing system. The new schools, with their curricula and the concepts behind them, are future oriented. They recruit students into a system that does not yet exist, or is just emerging. They inevitably create conflicts between generations.

Among the Sisala of Northern Ghana, a modernizing African society, for example, there have been profound changes in the principles underlying the father-son relationship. As one man put it:

> This strict obedience, this is mostly on the part of illiterates. With educated people, if you tell your son something, he will have to speak his mind. If you find that the boy is right, you change your mind. With an illiterate, he just tells his son to do something. . . . In the old days, civilization was not so much. We obeyed our fathers whether right or wrong. If you didn't, they would beat you. We respected our fathers with fear. Now we have to talk with our sons when they challenge us (Grindal 1972:80).

Not all of the Sisala have as tolerant and favorable a view of the changes wrought by education, however:

> When my children were young, I used to tell them stories about my village and about our family traditions. But in Tumu there are not so many people from my village and my children never went to visit the family. Now my children are educated and they have no time to sit with the family. A Sisala father usually farms with his son. But with educated people, they don't farm. They run around town with other boys: Soon we will forget our history. The educated man has a different character from his father. So fathers die and never tell their sons about the important traditions. My children don't sit and listen to me anymore. They don't want to know the real things my father told me. They have gone to school, and they are now book men. Boys who are educated run around with other boys rather than sitting and listening to their fathers (Grindal:83).

That these conflicts should flare up into open expressions of hostility toward education, schools, and teachers is not surprising. A headmaster of a primary school among the Sisala related to Bruce Grindal what happened when a man made a trip to a village outside Tumu.

> He parked his car on the road and was away for some time. When he returned, he saw that somebody had defaced his car, beaten it with sticks or something. Now I knew that my school children knew something about this. So I gathered them together and told them that if they were good citizens, they should report to me who did it and God would reward them. So I found out that this was done by some people in the village. When the village people found out their children told me such things, they were very angry. They said that the teachers were teaching their children to disrespect their elders. It is because of things like that that the fathers are taking their children out of school (Grindal: 97–98).

The above implies that the new schools, created for the purposes of aiding and abetting modernization, are quite effective. Without question they do create conflicts between generations and disrupt the transmission of the traditional culture. These effects in themselves are a prelude to change, perhaps a necessary condition. They are not, however, the result of the effectiveness of the schools as educational institutions. Because the curricular content is alien to the existing culture there is little or no reinforcement in the home and family, or in the community as a whole, for what happens in the school. The school is isolated from the cultural system it is intended to serve. As F. Landa Jocano relates concerning the primary school in Malitbog, a barrio in Panay, in the middle Philippines:

> most of what children learn in school is purely verbal imitation and academic memorization, which do not relate with the activities of the children at home. By the time a child reaches the fourth grade he is expected to be competent in reading, writing, arithmetic, and language study. Except for gardening, no other vocational training is taught. The plants that are required to be cultivated, however, are cabbages, lettuce, okra, and other vegetables which are not normally grown and eaten in the barrio. [sentence omitted]
>
> Sanitation is taught in the school, but insofar as my observation went, this is not carried beyond the child's wearing clean clothes. Children may be required to buy toothbrushes, combs, handkerchiefs, and other personal items, and bring these to school for inspection. Because only a few can afford to buy these items, only a few come to school with them. Often these school requirements are the source of troubles at home, a night's crying among the children. . . . [sentence omitted] In the final analysis, such regular school injunctions as "brush your teeth every morning" or "drink milk and eat leafy vegetables" mean nothing to the children. First, none of the families brush their teeth. The toothbrushes the children bring to school are for inspection only. Their parents cannot afford to buy milk. They do not like goats' milk because it is *malangsa* (foul smelling) (Jocano 1969:53).

Nor is it solely a matter of the nonrelatedness of what is taught in the school to what is learned in the home and community. Because the curricular content is alien to the culture as a whole, what is taught tends to become formalized and unrealistic and is taught in a rigid, ritualistic manner. Again, among the Sisala of Northern Ghana, Bruce Grindal describes the classroom environment.

> The classroom environment into which the Sisala child enters is characterized by a mood of rigidity and an almost total absence of spontaneity. A typical school day begins with a fifteen-minute period during which the students talk and play, often running and screaming, while the teacher, who is usually outside talking with his fellow teachers, pays no attention. At 8:30 one of the students rings a bell, and the children immediately take their seats and remove from their desks the materials needed for the first lesson. When the teacher enters the room, everyone falls silent. If the first lesson is English, the teacher begins by reading a passage in the students' readers. He then asks the students to read the section aloud, and if a child makes a mistake, he is told to sit down, after being corrected. Variations of the English lesson consist of having the students write down dictated sentences or spell selected words from a passage on the blackboard. Each lesson lasts exactly forty minutes, at the end of which a bell rings and the students immediately prepare for the next lesson.
>
> Little emphasis is placed upon the content of what is taught; rather, the book

is strictly adhered to, and the students are drilled by being asked the questions which appear at the end of each assignment. The absence of discussion is due partially to the poor training of the teachers, yet even in the middle schools where the educational standards for teachers are better, an unwillingness exists to discuss or explain the content of the lessons. All subjects except mathematics are lessons in literacy which teach the student to spell, read, and write.

Interaction between the teacher and his students is characterized by an authoritarian rigidity. When the teacher enters the classroom, the students are expected to rise as a sign of respect. If the teacher needs anything done in the classroom, one of the students performs the task. During lessons the student is not expected to ask questions, but instead is supposed to give the "correct" answers to questions posed to him by the teacher. The students are less intent upon what the teacher is saying than they are upon the reading materials before them. When the teacher asks a question, most of the students hurriedly examine their books to find the correct answer and then raise their hands. The teacher calls on one of them, who rises, responds (with his eyes lowered), and then sits down. If the answer is wrong or does not make sense, the teacher corrects him and occasionally derides him for his stupidity. In the latter case the child remains standing with his eyes lowered until the teacher finishes and then sits down without making a response (Grindal 1972:85).

The nonrelatedness of the school to the community in both the content being transmitted and the methods used to transmit it is logically carried into the aspirations of students concerning their own futures. These aspirations are often quite unrealistic. As one of the Sisala school boys said:

I have in mind this day being a professor so that I will be able to help my country. . . . As a professor I will visit so many countries such as America, Britain, and Holland. In fact, it will be interesting for me and my wife. . . . When I return, my father will be proud seeing his child like this. Just imagine me having a wife and children in my car moving down the street of my village. And when the people are in need of anything, I will help them (Grindal: 89).

Or as another reported in an essay:

By the time I have attained my graduation certificate from the university, the government will be so happy that they may like to make me president of my beloved country. When I receive my salary, I will divide the money and give part to my father and my wife and children. . . . People say the U.S.A. is a beautiful country. But when they see my village, they will say it is more beautiful. Through my hard studies, my name will rise forever for people to remember (Grindal: 89).

As we have said, the new schools, like the traditional tribal methods of education and schools everywhere, recruit new members of the community into a cultural system and into specific roles and statuses. And they attempt to maintain this system by transmitting the necessary competencies to individuals who are recruited into it via these roles and statuses. The problem with the new schools is that the cultural system they are recruiting for does not exist in its full form. The education the school boys and girls receive is regarded by many as more or less useless, though most people, like the Sisala, agree that at least literacy is necessary if one is to get along in the modern world. However, the experience of the school child goes far beyond training for literacy. The child is removed from the everyday routine of community life and from observation of the work rules of adults. He or she is placed in an artificial, isolated, unrealistic, ritualized environment. Unrealistic aspirations and self-images develop. Harsh reality intrudes abruptly upon graduation. The schoolboy discovers that, except for teaching in the primary schools, few opportunities are open to him. There are some clerical positions in government offices, but they are few. Many graduates migrate in search of jobs concomitant with their expectations, but they usually find that living conditions are more severe than those in the tribal area and end up accepting an occupation and life style similar to that of the illiterate tribesmen who have also migrated to the city. Those who become village teachers are not much better off. One Sisala teacher in his mid-twenties said:

> I am just a small man. I teach and I have a small farm. . . . Maybe someday if I am fortunate, I will buy a tractor and farm for money because there is no future in teaching. When I went to school, I was told that if I got good marks and studied hard, I would be somebody, somebody important. I even thought I would go to America or England. I would still like to go, but I don't think of these things very often because it hurts too much. You see me here drinking and perhaps you think I don't have any sense. I don't know. I don't know why I drink. But I know in two days' time, I must go back and teach school. In X (his home village where he teaches) I am alone; I am nobody (Grindal: 93).

The pessimist will conclude that the new schools, as agents of modernization, are a rank failure. This would be a false conclusion. They are neither failures nor successes. The new schools, like all institutions transforming cultural systems, are not articulated with the other parts of the changing system. The future is not known or knowable. Much of the content taught in the school, as well as the very concept of the school as a place with four walls within which teacher and students are confined for a number of hours each day and regulated by a rigid schedule of "learning" activities, is Western. In many ways the new schools among the Sisala, in Malitbog, and in many other changing cultures are inadequate copies of schools in Europe and in the United States. There is no doubt, however, that formal schooling in all of the developing nations of the world, as disarticulated with the existing cultural context as it is, nevertheless is helping to bring into being a new population of literates, whose aspirations and world view are very different than that of their parents. And of course a whole class of educated elites has been created by colleges and universities in many of the countries. It seems inevitable that eventually the developing cultures will build their own models for schools and education. These new models will not be caricatures of Western schools, although in places, as in the case of the Sisala or the Kanuri of Nigeria described by Alan Peshkin (Peshkin 1972), where the Western influence has been strong for a long time, surely those models will show this influence.

Perhaps one significant part of the problem and the general shape of the solution is implied in the following exchange between two new young teachers in charge of a village school among the Ngoni of Malawi and a senior chief:

> The teachers bent one knee as they gave him the customary greeting, waiting in silence until he spoke.
> "How is your school?"
> "The classes are full and the children are learning well, Inkosi."
> "How do they behave?"
> "Like Ngoni children, Inkosi."
> "What do they learn?"
> "They learn reading, writing, arithmetic, scripture, geography and drill, Inkosi."
> "Is that education?"
> "It is education, Inkosi."
> "No! No! No! Education is *very* broad, *very* deep. It is not only in books, it is learning how to live. I am an old man now. When I was a boy I went with the Ngoni army against the Bemba. Then the mission came and I went to school. I became a teacher. Then I was chief. Then the government came. I have seen our country change, and now there are many schools and many young men go away to work to find money. I tell you that Ngoni children must learn how to live and how to build up our land, not only to work and earn money. Do you hear?"
> "Yebo, Inkosi" (Yes, O Chief) (Read 1968:2–3).

The model of education that will eventually emerge in the modernizing nations will be one that puts the school, in its usual formal sense, in perspective, and emphasizes education in its broadest sense, as a part of life and of the dynamic changing community. It must emerge if these cultures are to avoid the tragic errors of miseducation, as the Western nations have experienced them, particularly in the relationships between the schools and minority groups.

Conclusion

In this chapter we started with the question, What are some of the ways culture is transmitted? We answered this question by examining cultural systems where a wide variety of teaching and learning techniques are utilized. One of the most important processes, we found, was the management of discontinuity. Discontinuity occurs at any point in the life cycle when there is an abrupt transition from one mode of being and behaving to another, as for example at weaning and at adolescence. Many cultural systems manage the latter period of discontinuity with dramatic staging and initiation ceremonies, some of which are painful or emotionally disturbing to the initiates. They are public announcements of changes in status. They are also periods of intense cultural compression during which teaching and learning are accelerated. This managed cultural compression and discontinuity functions to enlist new members in the community and maintains the cultural system. Education, whether characterized by sharp discontinuities and culturally compressive periods, or by a relatively smooth progression of accumulating experience and status change, functions in established cultural systems to recruit new members and maintain the existing system. We then turned to a discussion of situations where alien or future-oriented cultural systems are introduced through formal schooling. Schools among the Sisala of Ghana, a modernizing African nation, and a Philippine barrio were used as examples of this relationship and its consequences. The disarticulation of school and community was emphasized. The point was made that children in these situations are intentionally recruited to a cultural system other than the one they originated from, and that the school does not maintain the existing social order, but, in effect, destroys it. This is a kind of discontinuity very different than the one we discussed previously, and produces severe dislocations in life patterns and interpersonal relations as well as potentially positive change.

References and Further Reading

Barnett, Homer G., 1960, *Being a Paluan*. CSCA. New York: Holt, Rinehart and Winston, Inc.

Beals, Alan R., 1962, *Gopalpur: A South Indian Village*. CSCA. New York: Holt, Rinehart and Winston, Inc.

Brown, Judith K., 1963, "A Cross-cultural Study of Female Initiation Rites," *American Anthropologist* 65:837–853.

Chance, Norman A., 1966, *The Eskimo of North Alaska*. CSCA. New York: Holt, Rinehart and Winston, Inc.

Cohen, Yehudi, 1964, *The Transition from Childhood to Adolescence*. Chicago: Aldine Publishing Company.

Deng, Francis Mading, 1972 (reissued 1984), *The Dinka of the Sudan*. Prospect Heights, Illinois: Waveland Press, Inc.

Dozier, Edward P., 1967, *Hano: A Tewa Indian Community in Arizona*. CSCA. New York: Holt, Rinehart and Winston, Inc.

Eggan, Dorothy, 1956, "Instruction and Affect in Hopi Cultural Continuity," *Southwestern Journal of Anthropology* 12:347–370.

Grindal, Bruce T., 1972, *Growing Up in Two Worlds: Education and Transition among the Sisala of Northern Ghana*. CSCA. New York: Holt, Rinehart and Winston, Inc.

Hart, C. W. M., 1963, "Contrasts Between Prepubertal and Postpubertal Education." In G. Spindler, ed., *Education and Culture*. Holt, Rinehart and Winston, Inc.

Henry, Jules, 1960, "A Cross-cultural Outline of Education," *Current Anthropology* 1, 267–305.

———, 1963, *Culture Against Man*. New York: Random House.

Hogbin, Ian, 1964, *A Guadalcanal Society: The Kaoka Speakers*. CSCA. New York: Holt, Rinehart and Winston, Inc.

Jocano, F. Landa, 1969, *Growing Up in a Philippine Barrio.* CSEC. New York: Holt, Rinehart and Winston, Inc.

Lessa, William A., 1966 (reissued 1986), *Ulithi: A Micronesian Design for Living.* Prospect Heights, IL: Waveland Press, Inc.

Mead, Margaret, 1949, *Coming of Age in Samoa.* New York: Mentor Books (first published in 1928).

——, 1953, *Growing Up in New Guinea.* New York: Mentor Books (first published in 1930).

——, 1964, *Continuities in Cultural Evolution.* New Haven: Yale University Press.

Peshkin, Alan, 1972, *Kanuri Schoolchildren: Education and Social Mobilization in Nigeria.* CSEC. New York: Holt, Rinehart and Winston, Inc.

Pettit, George A., 1946, *Primitive Education in North America.* Publications in American Archeology and Ethnology, vol. 43.

Pierce, Joe E., 1964, *Life in a Turkish Village.* CSCA. New York: Holt, Rinehart and Winston, Inc.

Read, Margaret, 1968 (reissued 1987), *Children of Their Fathers: Growing Up among the Ngoni of Malawi.* Prospect Heights, IL: Waveland Press, Inc.

Schwartz, Gary, and Don Merten, 1968, "Social Identity and Expressive Symbols: The Meaning of an Initiation Ritual," *American Anthropologist* 70:1117–1131. Reprinted as Chapter 8 in this text.

Spindler, George D., and Louise S. Spindler, 1971, *Dreamers without Power: The Menomini Indians of Wisconsin.* CSCA. New York: Holt, Rinehart and Winston, Inc. Reissued (1984), *Dreamers With Power.* Prospect Heights, IL: Waveland Press.

Spiro, Melford, 1958, *Children of the Kibbutz.* Cambridge, Mass.: Harvard University Press.

Van Gennep, Arnold, 1960, *The Rites of Passage.* Chicago: University of Chicago Press.

Whiting, Beatrice B., ed., 1963, *Child Rearing in Six Cultures.* New York: John Wiley & Sons, Inc.

Whiting, John F., R. Kluckhohn, and E. Albert, 1958, "The Function of Male Initiation Ceremonies at Puberty." In E. Maccoby, T. Newcomb, and E. Hartley, eds., *Readings in Social Psychology.* New York: Holt, Rinehart and Winston, Inc.

Williams, Thomas R., 1965, *The Dusun: A North Borneo Society.* CSCA. New York: Holt, Rinehart and Winston, Inc.

Young, Frank, 1965, *Initiation Ceremonies.* Indianapolis: The Bobbs-Merrill Company.

PREVIEW

Part A: Traditional non-literate societies

In both Dorothy Eggan's chapter on the Hopi and Steve (as he is known to friends) Hart's on the Tiwi there is a dominant theme—the transition from childhood to adolescence and later maturity through initiation rituals. This theme appears in many ethnographies of traditional communities and has been a subject of discussion and a focus of theory for much anthropological writing. In both Hopi and Tiwi cultures the initiates experience sharp discontinuity in role relationships. Formerly friendly or aloof adults suddenly become threatening and punitive. The initiate is coerced, cowed, treated as a know-nothing neophyte, and taught esoteric content that must be kept secret. Dissonance is aroused. The childish neophytes are anxious about what is happening to them and experience pain and deprivation. Doubts about one's ability to survive the initiation are raised. Finally, all doubts and fears are resolved by the successful conclusion of the initiation and the transformation of the former child to beginning adulthood. The initiate becomes committed to the very cultural patterns and their symbols that were threatening him, or less frequently, her. Resolution of dissonance appears in many education contexts cross-culturally, not alone in initiation settings. In fact it may be one of several fundamental educational processes that we tend to blur or ignore with our cultural focus on individual development and social and personal "adjustment". This idea is developed in Chapter 3 so we won't dwell on it here. It is worth serious attention for the creation and the resolution of dissonance in the course of education as cultural transmission may be an essential mechanism in the maintenance of cultural systems if it engenders, as we hypothesize it does, commitment to one's culture.

Sindell's report on the educational experience of Mistassini Cree children points to a related process. Discontinuity of culturally patterned experience and social roles is created for Mistassini children, not by a dissonance-resolving initiation ceremony, but by removal from the native community to a residential school run by aliens. The children never learn the culture of their parents and only partially and with ambivalence that is rarely entirely resolved, learn the alien culture. There are parallels in the experience of children from any culturally differentiated ethnic group in America as they adapt, or fail to adapt, to mainstream schools.

The Editor

DOROTHY EGGAN

19   *Instruction and Affect in Hopi Cultural Continuity*[*][1]

Education and anthropology have proved in recent years that each has much of interest to say to the other[2] for both are concerned with the transmission of cultural heritage from one generation to another—and with the means by which that transmission is accomplished. And although anthropology has tended to be preoccupied with the processes of cultural *change,* and the conditions under which it takes place, rather than with cultural continuity, it would seem, as Herskovits has said, that cultural change can be best understood when considered in relation to cultural stability (Herskovits 1950:20).

Both education and anthropology are concerned with learned behavior, and the opinion that early learning is of vital significance for the later development of personality, and that emotional factors are important in the learning process, while sometimes implicit rather than explicit, is often found in anthropological literature, particularly in that dealing with "socialization," "ethos" (Redfield 1953), and "values." From Mead's consistent work, for instance, has come a clearer picture of the socialization process in a wide variety of cultures, including our own, and she examines early "identification" as one of the problems central to all of them (Mead 1953). Hallowell, too, speaking of the learning situation in which an individual must acquire a personality pattern, points out that "there are important affective components involved" (Hallowell 1953:610), and elsewhere he emphasizes a "need for further investigation of relations between learning process and affective experience" (Hallowell 1955:251). Kluckhohn, writing on values and value-orientation, says that "one of the severest limitations of the classical theory

---

*Reprinted from *Southwestern Journal of Anthropology* 12(4) 1956, 347–370, with permission.

[1] The substance of this paper was originally presented to the Society for Social Research of the University of Chicago in 1943, and subsequently enlarged in 1954 at the request of Edward Bruner for his class in Anthropology and Education. Discussion with him has greatly clarified my thinking on the problems examined here. Some elimination and revision has been made in order to include references to recently published work and suggestions from Fred Eggan, David Aberle, Clyde Kluckhohn, David Riesman, and Milton Singer. But intimate association with the Hopi over a period of seventeen years has given me this perception of the Hopi world.

[2] See, for example, Mead 1931:669–687; Mead 1943:663–639; Whiting and Child 1953; Spindler (ed.) 1955.

of learning is its neglect of attachments and attitudes in favor of reward and punishment (Kluckhohn 1951:430). And DuBois states explicitly that, "Institutions which may be invested with high emotional value because of patterns in child training are not ones which can be lightly legislated out of existence" (DuBois 1941:281).

In fact, increasing interaction between anthropology and psychiatry (which has long held as established the connection between emotion, learning, and resistance to change in individuals) has in the last decade introduced a theme into anthropology which reminds one of Sapir's statement that "the more fully one tries to understand a culture, the more it takes on the characteristics of a personality organization" (Sapir 1949:594).

Psychologists, while perhaps more cautious in their approach to these problems, since human emotional commitments—particularly as regards permanency—are difficult if not impossible to examine in the laboratory, emphasize their importance in the learning situation, and frequently express dissatisfaction with many existing methods and formulations in the psychology of personality. The shaping factors of emotion—learned as well as innate —are stressed by Asch (1952:29) in his *Social Psychology,* and focus particularly on man's "need to belong." He feels that the "psychology of man needs basic research and a fresh theoretical approach." Allport speaks of past "addiction to machines, rats, or infants" in experimental psychology, and hopes for a "design for personality and social psychology" which will become "better tempered to our subject matter" as we "cease borrowing false notes— whether squeaks, squeals, or squalls . . ." and "read the score of human personality more accurately" (Allport 1951:168–196). And Murphy, starting with the biological foundations of human learning, particularly the individual form this "energy system" immediately assumes, examines man as psychologically structured by early canalizations in which personality is rooted, to which are added an organized symbol system and deeply ingrained habits of perception, and suggests that the structure thus built is highly resistant to change. He says that, "The task of the psychology of personality today is to apply ruthlessly, and to the limit, every promising suggestion of today, but always with the spice of healthy skepticism," while recognizing "the fundamental limitations of the whole present system of conceptions . . ." as a preparation for "rebirth of knowledge" (1947:926–927).

Anthropologists as well as psychologists are aware that any hypotheses in an area so complex must be regarded as tenuous, but since the situations cannot be taken into the laboratory, there is some value in taking the laboratory to the situation. Progress in these amorphous areas can only come about, as Redfield has said, by the mental instrument which he has called a "controlled conversation" (Redfield 1955:148)—this discussion, then, must be considered a conversation between the writer and others who have brought varied interests and techniques to the problem of resistance to cultural change[3] (DuBois 1955). It begins logically with a recent paper on "Cultural Transmission and Cultural Change" in which Bruner discusses two surveys (SSRC, 1954:973–1002; Keesing 1953; Also Spiro 1955:1240–1251) of the literature on acculturation and adds to the hypotheses presented in them another which he finds relevant to the situation among the Mandan-Hidatsa Indians. As stated in his summary paragraph we find the proposition: "That which is learned and internalized in infancy and early childhood is most resistant to contact situations. The hypothesis directs our attention to the age in the individual life career at which each aspect of culture is transmitted, as well as to the full context of the learning situation and the position of the agents of socialization in the larger social system" (Bruner 1956a:197).

This proposition will be further extended by a consideration of the *emotional* commitment involved in the socialization process among the Hopi Indians; here the "conversation" will be directed to emotion in both teaching and learning, and will center around resistance to cultural change which has been remarkably consistent in Hopi society throughout recorded history *until the Second World War brought enforced and drastic changes.*[4] At that time the young men, although legitimately conscientious objectors, were drafted into the army. Leaving the isolation of the reservation where physical violence between adults was rare, they were rapidly introduced to the stark brutality of modern warfare. In army camps alcoholic intoxication, an experience which was the antithesis of the quiet, controlled behavior normally demanded of adult Hopi on their reservation, frequently brought relief from tension and a sense of comradeship with fellow soldiers. Deprived of the young men's work in the fields, many older people and young women were in turn forced to earn a living in railroad and munition centers off the reservation. Thus the gaps in the Hopi "communal walls" were, for the first time, large enough in numbers and long enough in time — and the experiences to which individuals had to adapt were revolutionary enough in character — so that the sturdy structure was damaged. It is emphasized, therefore, that in this discussion *Hopi* refers to those members of the tribe who had reached *adulthood* and were thoroughly committed to their own world view before 1941. Much of it would not apply as forcefully to the children of these people, and would be even less applicable to their grandchildren.

The major hypotheses suggested here, then, are:

1. That the Hopi, as contrasted with ourselves, were experts in the use of *affect* in their educational system, and that this element continued to oper-

---

[3] Of particular interest in this problem is this paper of DuBois' and the discussion following it. See also Dozier's (1954) analysis of the interaction between the Hopi-Tewa and Hopi; compare Dozier 1955.

[4] An evaluation of these changes has not been reported for the Hopi, although John Connelly is working on the problem; see Adair and Vogt 1949, and Vogt 1951, for discussions of Navajo and Zuñi reactions to the war and postwar situation.

ate throughout the entire life span of each individual as a *reconditioning* factor (Herskovits 1950:325–326, 491, 627); and

2. That this exercise of emotion in teaching and learning was an efficient means of social control which functioned in the absence of other forms of policing and restraint, and also in the maintenance of stability both in the personality structure of the individual and the structure of the society.

These hypotheses may be explored through a consideration of (a) the early and continued conditioning of the individual in the Hopi maternal extended family, which was on every level, an inculcation of *interdependence* as contrasted with our training for *independence;* and (b) an early and continuing emphasis on religious observances and beliefs (also emphasizing interdependence), the most important facet of which—for the purposes of this paper— was the central concept of the Hopi "good heart."[5]

If we examine the educational system by which a Hopi acquired the personal entity which made him so consistently and determinedly Hopi, we find that it was deliberate and systematic (Pettit 1946; Hough 1915:218). Students of Hopi are unanimous on this point but perhaps it can best be illustrated by quoting one of my informants who had spent much time away from the reservation, including many years in a boarding school, and who was considered by herself and other Hopi to be an extremely "acculturated" individual. In 1938 when she made this statement she was about thirty years old and had brought her children back to the reservation to be "educated." Said she:

> It is very hard to know what to do. In the old days I might have had more babies for I should have married early. Probably some of them would have died. But my comfort would have been both in numbers and in knowing that all women lost babies. Now when I let my little son live on top [a conservative village on top of the mesa] with my mothers, I worry all the time. If he dies with dysentery I will feel like I killed him. Yet he *must* stay on top so the old people can teach him the *important* things. It is his only chance of becoming Hopi, for he would never be a *bahana* (white).

The education which she considered so vital included careful, deliberate instruction in kinship and community obligations, and in Hopi history as it is seen in mythology and as remembered by the old people during their own lifetimes. The Hopi taught youngsters fear as a means of personal and social control and for the purposes of personal and group protection; and they were taught techniques for the displacement of anxiety, as well as procedures which the adults believed would prolong life. Children were instructed in religious lore, in how to work and play, in sexual matters, even in how to deal

---

[5] The concept of the Hopi "good heart" as contrasted to a "bad heart," which is *Kahopi,* has been documented by every student of Hopi known to the writer, in references too numerous to mention, beginning with Stephen (written in the 1890s but published in 1940) and Hough in 1915. But the clearest understanding of this and other Hopi concepts may be had in Whorf 1941, especially pp. 30–32.

with a *bahana*. Good manners were emphasized, for they were a part of the controlled, orderly conduct necessary to a Hopi good heart.

Constantly one heard during work or play, running through all activity like a connecting thread: "Listen to the old people—they are wise"; or, "Our old uncles taught us that way—it is the *right* way." Around the communal bowl, in the kiva, everywhere this instruction went on; stories, dream adventures, and actual experiences such as journeys away from the reservation were told and retold. And children, in the warmth and security of this intimate extended family and clan group, with no intruding outside experiences to modify the impact until they were forced to go to an alien school, learned what it meant to be a good Hopi from a wide variety of determined teachers who had very definite—and *mutually consistent*—ideas of what a good Hopi is. And they learned all of this in the Hopi language, which, as Whorf has made so clear, has no words with which to express many of our concepts, but which, working together with "a different set of cultural and environmental influences . . . interacted with Hopi linguistic patterns to mould them, to be moulded again by them, and so little by little to shape the world outlook" (Whorf 1941:92).

Eventually these children disappeared into government schools for a time, and in the youth of most of these older Hopi it was a boarding school off the reservation where Indian children from various reservations were sent, often against their own and their parents' wishes.[6] Here white teachers were given the task of "civilizing" and "Christianizing" these wards of the government, but by that time a Hopi child's view of the world and his place in it was very strong. Moreover, trying to transpose our concepts into their language was often very nearly impossible for them, since only Hopi had been spoken at home. Examining Hopi memory of such a method of education we quote a male informant who said:

> I went to school about four years. . . . We worked like slaves for our meals and keep. . . . We didn't learn much. . . . I didn't understand and it was hard to learn. . . . At that time you do what you are told or you get punished. . . . You just wait till you can go home.

And a woman said:

> Policemen gathered us up like sheep. I was scared to death. My mother tried to hide me. I tried to stay away but the police always won. . . . Then we were sent up to Sherman [in California]. . . . It was far away; we were afraid on the train. . . . I didn't like it when I couldn't learn and neither did the teachers. . . . They never punished me, I always got 100 in Deportment. . . . I was there three years. . . . I was so glad to get home that I cried and cried . . . , glad to have Hopi food again, and fun again.

---

[6] See Simmons, 1942, pp. 88–89, for an excellent description of Don Talayesva of the government's use of force in the educational policy of this period; and pp. 134, 178, 199, and 225 for some of the results of this policy. Cf. Aberle 1951 for an analysis of Talayesva's school years and his later reidentification with his people.

As children, the Hopi usually solved this dilemma of enforced education by means of a surface accommodation to the situation until such time as they were able to return to their own meaningful world. For, as Park has said, man can "make his manners a cloak and his face a mask, behind which he is able to preserve . . . inner freedom . . . and independence of thought, even when unable to maintain independence of action."[7] In other words, because the inner core of Hopi identification was already so strong, these children were able to *stay* in a white world, while still *living* in the Hopi world within themselves.[8] And while for some there was a measure of temptation in many of the things learned in white schools so that they "became friendly with whites and accepted their gifts,"[9] the majority of these older Hopi acquired a white education simply as a "necessary accessory";[10] they incorporated parts of our material culture, and learned to deal with Whites astutely, but their values were largely unaffected.

If we now examine more closely the pattern of integration through which the Hopi erected a communal wall[11] around their children we find in their kinship system the framework of the wall, but interwoven through it and contributing greatly to its strength was a never-ending composition which gave color and form, their religious ceremonies and beliefs.

Let us first contrast briefly the affect implicit in the way a Hopi born into this kinship system experienced relationships and the way in which Western children experience them. In the old days it was rare for a growing primary family to live outside the maternal residence. Normally each lived within it until the birth of several children crowded them out. And in this household each child was eagerly welcomed, for infant mortality was high and the clan was always in need of reinforcement. Thus, in spite of the physical burden on the biological mother, which she sometimes resented, the first strong *clan* sanction which we see in contrast to our own, was the absolute need for and desire for many children. From birth the young of the household were attended, pampered, and disciplined, although very mildly for the first several years, by a wide variety of relatives in addition to the mother. These attentions came both from the household members and from visitors in it. In no way was a baby ever as dependent upon his physical mother as are children in our culture. He was even given the breast of a mother's mother or sister if he cried for food in his mother's absence. True, a Hopi saying states that a

---

[7] Park 1950:361. Cf. Kluckhohn 1951:388–433, who points out that values continue to influence even when they do not function realistically as providers of immediate goal reactions.

[8] Cf. D. Eggan 1955, on the use of the Hopi myth in dreams as a means of "identification."

[9] Simmons 1942:88, and compare pp. 178, 180.

[10] Bruner 1956b:612, indicates that his Mandan-Hidatsa informants were quite conscious of this "lizard-like" quality of protective coloration in white contacts.

[11] Stephen, 1940a:18 says that the Hopi "describe their fundamental organization as a people" by "designating their principal religious ceremonies as the concentric walls of a house." The concept is extended here to include the entire wall of "Hopiness" which they have built around their children.

baby is made "sad" if another baby steals his milk, but it has been my experience that these women may risk making their own babies sad temporarily if another child needs food.

Weaning, of course, when discussed in personality contexts means more than a transition from milk to solid food. It is also a gradual process of achieving independence from the comfort of the mother's body and care, of transferring affection to other persons, and of finding satisfactions within oneself and in the outside world. Most people learn to eat solid food; many of us are never weaned, which has unfortunate consequences in a society where *individual* effort and independence are stressed. The Hopi child, on the other hand, from the day of his birth was being weaned from his biological mother. Many arms gave him comfort, many faces smiled at him, and from a very early age he was given bits of food which were chewed by various members of the family and placed in his mouth. So, for a Hopi, the outside world in which he needed to find satisfaction was never far away. He was not put in a room by himself and told to go to sleep; every room was crowded by sleepers of all ages. He was in no way *forced to find satisfactions within himself;* rather these were provided for him, if possible, by his household and clan group. His weaning, then, was from the breast only, and as he was being weaned from the biological mother, he was at the same time in a situation which *increased* his emotional orientation toward the intimate in-group of the extended family—which was consistent with the interests of Hopi social structure. Thus, considering weaning in its wider implications, a Hopi was never "weaned"; it was not intended that he should be. For these numerous caretakers contributed greatly to a small Hopi's faith in his intimate world—and conversely without question to a feeling of strangeness and *emotional insecurity* as adults in any world outside of this emotional sphere. The Hopi were often successful outside of the reservation, but they have shown a strong tendency to return frequently to the maternal household. Few ever left it permanently.

In addition to his extended family, while a Hopi belonged to one clan only, the clan into which he was born, he was a "child" of his father's clan, and this group took a lively interest in him. There were also numerous ceremonial and adoptive relationships which were close and warm, so that most of the persons in his familiar world had definite reciprocal relations with the child (Eggan 1950:Chap. II; Simmons 1942:Chaps. 3, 4). Since all of these "relatives" lived in his own small village, or in villages nearby, his emotional and physical "boundaries" coincided, were quite definitely delimited, and were explored and perceived at the same time. It cannot be too strongly emphasized that the kinship terms which a Hopi child learned in this intimate atmosphere were not mere verbalizations—as, for instance, where the term "cousin" among ourselves is sometimes applied to someone we have never seen and never will see. On the contrary, each term carried with it definite mutual responsibilities and patterns of behavior, and, through these, definite emotional interaction as well. These affects were taught as proper responses, together with the terms which applied to each individual, as he entered the child's life. This process was deliberately and patiently, but unceasingly, worked at by every older individual in the child's surroundings, so by the time a Hopi was grown kinship reaction patterns were so deeply ingrained in his thinking and feeling, and in his workaday life, that they were as much a part of him as sleeping and eating. He was not merely told that Hopi rules of behavior were right or wise; he lived them as he grew and *in his total environment* (Henry 1955) (as constrasted to our separation of teaching at home, in school, and in Sunday school) until he was simply not conscious that there was any other way to react. Note that I say *conscious!* The unconscious level of feeling, as seen in dreams and life-history materials, and in indirect behavior manifestations (jealousy and gossip), often presents quite a different picture. But while ambivalence toward specific persons among the Hopi— as with mankind everywhere— is a personal burden, the long reinforced conditioned reaction of *interdependence* on both the emotional and overt behavior level was highly uniform and persistent (See Whorf 1941:87, Aberle 1951:93–94, 119–123). Perhaps the strength of kinship conditioning toward interdependence which was conveyed in a large but intimate group, living in close physical contact, can be best illustrated by quoting from an informant:

> My younger sister———was born when I was about four or five, I guess. I used to watch my father's and mother's relatives fuss over her. She didn't look like much to me. I couldn't see why people wanted to go to so much trouble over a wrinkled little thing like that baby. I guess I didn't like babies as well as most girls did. . . . But I had to care for her pretty soon anyway. She got fat and was hard to carry around on my back, for I was pretty little myself. First I had to watch her and joggle the cradle board when she cried. She got too big and wiggled too much and then my mother said to me, "She is *your sister*— take her out in the plaza in your shawl."
>
> She made my back ache. Once I left her and ran off to play with the others for a while. I intended to go right back, but I didn't go so soon, I guess. Someone found her. I got punished for this. My mother's brother said: "You should not have a sister to help you out when you get older. What can a woman do without her sisters?[12] You are not one of us to leave your sister alone to die. If harm had come to her you would never have a clan, no relatives at all. No one would ever help you out or take care of you. Now you have another chance. You owe her more from now on. This is the worst thing that any of my sister's children has ever done. You are going to eat by yourself until you are fit to be one of us." That is what he said. That is the way he talked on and on and on. When meal time came they put a plate of food beside me and said, "Here is your food; eat your food," It was a long time they did this way. It seemed a long time before they looked at me. They were all sad and quiet. They put a pan beside me at meal time and said

---

[12] In a matrilineal household and clan, cooperation with one's "sisters" is a necessity for the maintenance of both the social structure and the communal unit.

nothing—nothing at all, not even to scold me. My older sister carried——now, I didn't try to go near her. But I looked at my sisters and thought, "I need you—I will help you if you will help me." I would rather have been beaten or smoked. I was so ashamed all the time. Wherever I went people got sad [i.e., quiet]. After a while [in about ten days as her mother remembered it] they seemed to forget it and I ate with people again. During those awful days Tuvaye [a mother's sister] sometimes touched my head sadly, while I was being punished, I mean. Once or twice she gave me something to eat. But she didn't say much to me. Even she and my grandfather were ashamed and in sorrow over this awful thing I had done.

Sometimes now I dream I leave my children alone in the fields and I wake up in a cold sweat. Sometimes I dream I am alone in a desert place with no water and no one to help me. Then I think of this punishment when I dream this way. It was the worst thing I ever did. It was the worst thing that ever happened to me. No one ever mentioned it to me afterward but——[older male sibling], the mean one. I would hang my head with shame. Finally my father told him sharply that he would be punished if he ever mentioned this to me again. I was about six when this happened, I think.

This informant was about forty when she related this incident, but she cried, even then, as she talked.

Nor was withdrawal of support the only means of punishment. There were bogey Kachinas who "might kidnap" bad children, and who visited the mesas sometimes when children were uncooperative; thus the "stranger" *joined effectively* with the clan in inducing the "ideal" Hopi behavior. But children *shared* this fear, as they also frequently shared other punishments. Dennis has called attention to the fact that a whole group of children often shared the punishment for the wrong-doing of one (Dennis 1941:263). This method may not endear an individual to his age-mates, but it does reinforce the central theme of Hopi belief that each person in the group is responsible for what happens to all, however angry or jealous one may feel toward siblings.

Before we examine the religious composition of the Hopi "communal walls," we might contrast more explicitly the emotional implications of early Hopi conditioning to those experienced in our society. From the day of *our* birth the training toward *independence* — as contrasted to *interdependence* — starts. We sleep alone; we are immediately and increasingly in a world of comparative strangers. A variety of nurses, doctors, relatives, sitters, and teachers march through our lives in a never-ending procession. A few become friends, but *compared with a Hopi child's experiences,* the impersonality and lack of emotional relatedness to so many kinds of people with such widely different backgrounds is startling. Indeed the disparity of the relationships as such is so great that continuity of emotional response is impossible, and so we learn to look for emotional satisfaction in change, which in itself becomes a value (Kluckhohn and Kluckhohn 1947:109). In addition, we grow up aware that there are many ways of life within the American class system; we know that there are many choices which we must make as to profession, behavior,

moral code, even religion; and we know that the values of our parents' generation are not necessarily ours. If the permissive intimacy in the primary family
in our society—from which both nature and circumstance demand a break in
adulthood—is too strong, the individual cannot mature so that he can function efficiently in response to the always changing personalities in his life, and
the always changing demands of the society (Riesman 1955; Mead 1948:518).
He becomes a dependent neurotic "tentative between extreme polarities
(Erikson 1948:198; Murphy 1947:714–733). But precisely because the permissive intimacy, as well as the punishing agencies, in a Hopi child's life were
so far and so effectively extended in his formative years, he became *interdependent* with a larger but still definitely delimited group, and tended always
to be more comfortable and effective within it. His self-value quickly identified itself with the larger Hopi value (Hallowell 1955:Chap. 4; Erikson 1948:
198n), and to the extent that he could continue throughout his life to identify
with his group and function within it, he was secure in his place in the universe.

We have now sketched the situation which surrounded the young Hopi
child in his first learning situations, and contrasted these with our own. For
descriptive convenience this has been separated from religious instruction,
but in the reality experience of the children—with the exception of formal
initiation rites—no one facet of learning to be Hopi was separated from
others. To understand the meaning his religion had for a Hopi one must first
understand the harsh physical environment into which he was born. While it
is agreed that it would not be possible to predict the character or the social
structure of the Hopi from the circumstances of this physical environment,[13]
it is self-evident that their organized social and ritual activities are largely a
response to it. And such activities are at once a reflection of man's need to
be, and his need to justify his existence to himself and others. If those who
doubt that the forces of nature are powerful in shaping personality and culture were confined for one year on the Hopi reservation—even though their
own economic dependence on "nature" would be negligible—they would still
know by personal experience more convincing than scientific experiments
the relentless pressure of the environment on their own reaction patterns.
They would, for instance, stand, as all Hopis have forever stood, with aching
eyes fastened on a blazing sky where thunderheads piled high in promise and
were snatched away by "evil winds," and thus return to their homes knowing
the tension, the acute bodily need for the "feel" of moisture. When rains do
fall, there is the likelihood of a cloudburst which will ·ruin the fields. And
there is a possibility of early frost which will destroy their crops, as well as
the absolute certainty of sandstorms, rodents, and worms which will ruin

---

[13] Redfield 1955:31–32; cf. Titiev 1944:177–178; Whorf 1941:91; D. Eggan 1948 (first published
in the *American Anthropologist* 1943, vol. 45); Thompson and Joseph 1944:133.

many plants. These things on a less abstract level than "feeling" resolved themselves into a positive threat of famine and thirst which every Hopi knew had repeatedly ravaged his tribe. It is possible that the effects of this silent battle between man and the elements left no mark on successive generations of individuals? It certainly was the reinforced concrete of Hopi social structure, since strongly conditioned interdependence was the only hope of survival.

Thus, the paramount problem for the Hopi was uncertain rain, and the outward expression of their deep need for divine aid was arranged in a cycle of ceremonies, the most impressive of which, at least among the esoteric rituals, were Kachina (Earle and Kennard 1938) dances. These were, for the observer, colorful pageants in which meticulously trained dancers performed from sunrise until sunset, with short intermissions for food and rest. Their bodies were ceremonially painted; brilliant costumes were worn, along with beautifully carved and painted masks which represented the particular gods who were taking part in the ceremony. The color, the singing and the drums which accompanied the dance, the graceful rhythm and intense concentration of the dancers, all combine into superb artistry which is an hypnotic and impressive form of prayer. Ideally, the Hopi preceded every important act with prayer, and with these older Hopi the ideal was apt to be fact. A bag of sacred cornmeal was part of their daily equipment.

In the religious context also, we must remember the intimate atmosphere which surrounded a Hopi child in the learning situation. Here children were taught that if *all* Hopi behaved properly— that is, if they kept good hearts— the Kachinas would send rain. It was easy for the children to believe this because from earliest babyhood these beautiful creatures had danced before them as they lolled comfortably in convenient laps. There was a happy, holiday atmosphere throughout a village on dance days, but while each dance was being performed, the quiet of profound reverence. Lying in the mother's lap, a baby's hands were often struck together in the rhythm of the dance; as soon as he would walk his feet were likewise directed in such rhythm, and everybody praised a child and laughed affectionately and encouragingly as it tried to dance. As the children grew older, carved likenesses of these gods, as well as other presents, were given to them by the gods themselves. And as he grew in understanding, a child could not fail to realize that these dancers were part of a religious ceremony which was of utmost importance in his world— that the dancers were rain-bringing and thus life-giving gods.

When first initiation revealed that the gods were in reality men who danced in their stead, a *reorganization* of these emotions which had been directed toward them began, and there is much evidence in autobiographical materials of resentment, if not actual trauma, at this point. For some of them the initiation was a physical ordeal, but for those who entered this phase of their education by way of Powamu there was no whipping, although all initiates witnessed the whipping of those who were initiated into the Kachina cult (F. Eggan 1950:47–50; Steward 1931:59ff.).[14] However, the physical ordeal seems to be less fixed in adult memories than disillusion.

In Don Talyesva's account of initiation into Kachina we find:

> I had a great surprise. They were not spirits, but human beings. I recognized nearly every one of them and felt very unhappy because I had been told all my life that the Kachinas were Gods. I was especially shocked and angry when I saw my uncles, fathers, and own clanbrothers dancing as Kachinas. . . . [But] my fathers and uncles showed me ancestral masks and explained that long ago the Kachinas had come regularly to Oraibi and danced in the plaza. They explained that since the people had become so wicked . . . the Kachinas had stopped coming and sent their spirits to enter the masks on dance days. . . . I thought of the flogging and the initiation as a turning point in my life, and I felt ready at last to listen to my elders and live right (Simmons 1942:84–87).

One of our informants said in part:

> I cried and cried into my sheepskin that night, feeling I had been made a fool of. How could I ever watch the Kachinas dance again? I hated my parents and thought I could never believe the old folks again, wondering if gods had ever danced for the Hopi as they now said and if people really lived after death. I hated to see the other children fooled and felt mad when they said I was a big girl now and should act like one. But I was afraid to tell the others the truth for they might whip me to death. I know now it was best and the *only way to teach* children, but it took me a long time to know that. I hope my children won't feel like that.

This informant was initiated into Powamu and not whipped. She was about thirty when she made this statement to the writer.

Another woman, from a different mesa, speaking of her initiation into the Kachina society, said to me:

> The Kachinas brought us children presents. I was very little when I remember getting my first Kachina doll. I sat in my mother's lap and was "ashamed" [these people often use ashamed for shy or somewhat fearful], but she held out my hand for the doll. I grabbed it and hid in her lap for a long time because the Kachina looked too big to me and I was partly scared. But my mother told me to say "asqualie" [thank you] and I did. The music put me to sleep. I would wake up. The Kachinas would still be there. . . . I dreamed sometimes that the Kachinas were dancing and brought me lots of presents. . . .
>
> When I was initiated into Kachina society I was scared. I heard people whisper about it. . . . Children shook their heads and said it was hard to keep from crying. . . . My mother always put her shawl over my head when the Kachinas left the plaza. When she took it off they would be gone. So I knew they were gods and had

---

[14] The Powamu society is coordinate with the Kachina society and furnishes the "fathers" to the Kachinas on dance occasions. At first initiation parents may choose either of these societies for their children. It is reported that on First Mesa Powamu initiates were whipped, but my Powamu informants from both Second and Third Mesas were not whipped.

gone back to the San Francisco mountains. . . . My ceremonial mother came for me when it was time to go to the kiva [for initiation] and she looked sad [i.e., serious]. She took most of the whipping on her own legs [a custom widely practiced among the Hopi]. But then I saw my father and my relatives were Kachinas. When they took their masks off this is what I saw. I was all mixed up. I was mad. I began to cry. I wondered how my father became a Kachina and if they [these men, including her father] would all go away when the Kachinas went back to the San Francisco mountains where the dead people live. Then when my father came home I cried again. I was mad at my parents and my ceremonial mother. "These people have made me silly," I said to myself, "and I thought they were supposed to like me so good." I said that to myself. But I was still crying, and the old people told me that only babies cry. They kept saying I would understand better when I got bigger. They said again that the Kachinas had to go away because the Hopi got bad hearts, and they [the Kachinas] couldn't stand quarreling, but they left their heads behind for the Hopis. I said why didn't they rot then like those skulls we found under that house? They said I was being bad and that I should have been whipped more. . . .

When children asked me what happened in the kiva I was afraid to tell them because something would happen to me. Anyway I felt smart because I knew more than those *little* children. It took me a long time to get over this sadness, though. Later I saw that the Kachinas were the most *important thing in life* and that children can't understand these things. . . . It takes a while to see how wise the old people really are. You learn they are always right in the end.

Before we try to find our way with the Hopi to an "understanding of these things" we must examine their concept of the good heart which functions both in their kinship system and religion to maintain the effectiveness of the "wall of Hopiness." Of greatest significance in all activities among these people, and particularly in their religious ceremonies, is the fact that everything of importance is done communally. Thus each individual who has reached maturity is responsible *to* and *for* the whole community. The Hopi speak of this process as "uniting our hearts," which in itself is a form of prayer. A slight mistake in a ceremony can ruin it and thus defeat the community's prayer for rain; so too can a trace of "badness" in one's heart, although it may not be visible to the observer. Thus their religion teaches that *all* distress — from illness to crop failure — is the result of bad hearts, or possibly of witchcraft (here the simple "bad heart" must not be confused with a "Two-heart," *powaka,* witch), an extreme form of personal wickedness in which an individual sacrifices others, particularly his own relatives, to save himself (Titiev 1942; Aberle 1951:94).

This concept of a good heart in *conscious contradistinction* to a bad heart is of greatest importance not only in understanding Hopi philosophy but also in understanding their deep sense of cultural continuity and their resistance to fundamental change. A good heart is a positive thing, something which is never out of a Hopi's mind. It means a heart at peace with itself and one's fellows. There is no worry, unhappiness, envy, malice, nor any other disturbing emotion in a good heart. In this state, cooperation, whether in the extended household or in the fields and ceremonies, was selfless and easy. Unfortunately, such a conception of a good heart is also impossible of attainment. Yet if a Hopi did not keep a good heart he might fall ill and die, or the ceremonies— and thus the vital crops— might fail, for, as has been said, only those with good hearts were effective in prayer. Thus we see that the Hopi concept of a good heart included conformity to all rules of Hopi good conduct, both external and internal. To the extent that it was internalized— and all Hopi biographical material known to the writer suggests strongly that it was effectively internalized— it might reasonably be called a quite universal culturally patterned and culturally consistent Hopi "super-ego."[15]

There was, therefore, a constant probing of one's own heart, well illustrated by the anguished cry of a Hopi friend, "Dorothy, *did* my son die as the old folks said because my heart was not right? Do *you* believe this way, that if parents do not keep good hearts children will die?" And there was a constant examination of one's neighbors' hearts: "Movensie, it is those——— clan people who ruined this ceremony! They have bad hearts and they quarrel too much. That bad wind came up and now we will get no rain." Conversation among the Hopi is rarely censored, and the children heard both of these women's remarks, *feeling,* you may be sure, the *absolute belief* which these "teachers" had in the *danger* which a bad heart carries for everyone in the group.

In such situations, since human beings can bear only a certain amount of guilt,[16] there is a great game of blame-shifting among the Hopi, and this in turn adds a further burden of unconscious guilt, for it is difficult to love properly a neighbor or even a sister who has a bad heart. However, in the absence of political organization, civil and criminal laws, and a formal method of punishment for adults, this consistent "tribal super-ego" has maintained, throughout known history, a record almost devoid of crime and violence within the group,[17] and it has conditioned and ever *reconditioned* a Hopi to feel secure only in being a Hopi.

For through the great strength of the emotional orientation conveyed within the kinship framework and the interwoven religious beliefs, young Hopi learned their world from dedicated teachers whose emotions were involved in teaching what they believed intensely, and this in turn engaged the children's emotions in learning. These experiences early and increasingly

[15] See Piers and Singer 1953:6, where Dr. Piers defines "Super-Ego" as stemming from the internalization of the punishing, restrictive aspects of parental images, real or projected.

[16] See Dr. Piers' definition of guilt and shame (Piers and Singer 1953:5, 16). Hopi reactions are not classified here either in terms of guilt or of shame, since, as Singer points out (p. 52), an attempt to do so can confuse rather than clarify. In my opinion, both shame and guilt are operative in the Hopi "good heart," but it is suggested that the reader compare the material discussed here with the hypotheses in *Shame and Guilt,* particularly with Singer's conclusions in Chap. 5.

[17] Cf. Hallowell 1955, Chap. 4, on the positive role anxiety may play in a society.

made explicit in a very personal way the values implicit in the distinction between a good heart and a bad heart. For public opinion, if intensely felt and openly expressed in a closely knit and mutually dependent group—as in the case of the child who left her baby sister alone—can be more effective potential punishment than the electric chair. It is perhaps easier to die quickly than to live in loneliness in a small community in the face of contempt from one's fellows, and particularly from one's clan from whence, as we have seen, comes most of one's physical and emotional security. Small wonder that the children who experience this constant pressure to conform to clan dictates and needs, and at the same time this constant reinforcement of clan solidarity against outsiders, are reluctant as adults to stray too far from the clan's protective familiarity or to defy its wishes.

There was much bickering and tension within the clan and village, of course, and it was a source of constant uneasiness and ambivalence among the Hopi.[18] But tension and bickering, as I have indicated elsewhere, "are not exclusively Hopi"; the Hopi see it constantly among the whites on and off the reservation. What they do *not* find elsewhere is the *emotional satisfaction* of belonging intensely, to which they have been conditioned and reconditioned. For, as Murphy says, "It is not only the 'desire to be accepted' . . . that presses the ego into line. The basic psychology of perception is involved; the individual has learned to see himself as a member of the group, and the self has true 'membership character,' structurally integrated with the perception of group life" (Murphy 1947:855); Asch 1952:334–335, 605). Actually the Hopi clan, even with its in-group tensions and strife, but with all of the advantages emotional and physical it affords the individual, is one of the most successful and meaningful "boarding schools" ever devised for citizenship training.

In this situation, where belonging was so important, and a good heart so vital to the feeling of belonging, gossip is the potential and actual "social cancer" of the Hopi tribe. It is devastating to individual security and is often senselessly false and cruel, but in a country where cooperation was the only hope of survival, it was the *servant* as well as the policeman of the tribe. Not lightly would any Hopi voluntarily acquire the title Kahopi[19] "*not* Hopi," and therefore not good. Throughout the Hopi life span the word *kahopi,* KAHOPI was heard, until it penetrated to the very core of one's mind. It was said softly and gently at first to tiny offenders, through "Kahopi tiyo"

---

[18] In a short paper it is impossible to discuss both sides of this question adequately, but these tensions, and a Hopi's final acceptance of them, are discussed in D. Eggan 1948, particularly pp. 232–234. Cf. Thompson and Joseph 1944: Chap. 16, where Joseph speaks of fear born of the internally overdisciplined self in Hopi children, and its role both in adult discord and social integration. See also Thompson 1945, for hypotheses regarding the integration of ideal Hopi culture. Aberle (1951) discusses various tensions in Hopi society; see especially p. 94. All authors, however, call attention to the compensations as well as the burdens in Hopi society.

[19] See Brandt 1954. In his study of Hopi ethical concepts, *Kahopi* is discussed on p. 92.

or "Kahopi mana" to older children, still quietly but with stern intent, until the word sometimes assumed a crescendo of feeling as a whole clan or even a whole community might condemn an individual as *Kahopi.*

It it true that we, too, are told we should keep good hearts and love our neighbors as ourselves. But we are not told that, if we do not, our babies will die, *now, this year!* Some children are told that if they do not obey the various "commandments" they learn in different churches they will eventually burn in a lake of hell fire, but they usually know that many of their world doubt this. In contrast, Hopi children constantly *saw* babies die because a parent's heart was not right; they *saw* evil winds come up and crops fail for the same reason; they *saw* adults sicken and die because of bad thoughts or witchcraft (to which bad thoughts rendered a person more vulnerable). Thus they learned to *fear* the results of a bad heart whether it belonged to themselves or to others. There were witches, bogey Kachinas, and in objective reality famine and thirst to fear. Along with these fears were taught mechanisms for the displacement of anxiety, including the services of medicine men, confession and exorcism to get rid of bad thoughts, and cooperative nonaggression with one's fellows, even those who were known to be witches. But the best technique was that which included all the values in the positive process of keeping a good heart, and of "uniting our hearts" in family, clan, and fraternal society—in short, the best protection was to be *Hopi* rather than *Kahopi.*

It is clear throughout the literature on the Hopi, as well as from the quotations given in this discussion, that in finding their way toward the goal of "belonging," Hopi children at first initiation had to deal with religious disenchantment, resentment, and with ever-increasing demands made by their elders for more mature behavior. These factors were undoubtedly important catalyzing agents in Hopi personality formation and should be examined from the standpoint of Benedict's formulations on discontinuity (Benedict 1948:423–424). Here we must remember that shock can operate either to destroy or to mobilize an organism's dormant potentialities. And if a child has been *consistently* conditioned to feel a part of his intimate world, and providing he still lives on in this same world; it seems reasonable to suppose that shock (unless it were so great as to completely disorganize personality, in which case the custom could not have persisted) would reinforce the individual's *need* to belong and thus would tend to reassemble many of his personality resources around this need.

If the world surrounding the Hopi child had changed from warmth to coldness, from all pleasure to all hardship, the discontinuity would have indeed been insupportable. But the new demands made on him, while more insistent, were not unfamiliar in *kind;* all adults, as well as his newly initiated agemates, faced the same ones. He had shared the shock as he had long since learned to share all else; and he now shared the rewards of "feeling big." He had the satisfaction of increased status along with the burden of increasing responsibility, as the adults continued to teach him "the important things," and conformity gradually became a value in itself—even as we value non-conformity and change. It was both the means *and* the goal. Conformity surrounded the Hopi—child or adult—with everything he could hope to have or to be; outside if there was only the feeling tone of rejection. Since there were no bewildering choices presented (as is the case in our socialization process), the "maturation drive"[20] could only function to produce an ego-ideal in accord with the cultural ideal,[21] however wide the discrepancy between ideal and reality on both levels.

And since the Kachinas played such a vital role in Hopi society throughout, we must consider specifically the way in which the altered faith expressed by informants gradually came about after the first initiation (Aberle 1951: 38–41). First, of course, was the need to find it, since in any environment one must have faith and hope. They also wanted to continue to believe in and to enjoy that which from earliest memory had induced a feeling of pleasure, excitement, and of solidarity within the group. A beginning was undoubtedly made in modifying resentment when the Kachinas whipped each other after first initiation; first, it was again sharing punishment, but this time not only with children but *with adults.* They had long known that suffering came from bad hearts implied by disobedience to the rules of Hopi good conduct and then whipped each other for the same reason; thus there was logic in an initiation which was actually an extension of an already established conception of masked gods who rewarded good behavior with presents but withheld rain if hearts were not right, and who sometimes threatened bad children (Goldfrank 1945:516–539).

Another reorganizing factor explicitly stated in the quotations was "feeling big." They had shared pain with adults, had learned secrets which forever separated them from the world of children, and they were now included in situations from which they had previously been excluded, as their elders continued to teach intensely what they believed intensely: that for them there was only one alternative—Hopi as against Kahopi.

Consistent repetition is a powerful conditioning agent and, as the youngsters watched each initiation, they relived their own, and by again sharing the experience gradually worked out much of the bitter residue from their own memories of it, while also rationalizing and weaving the group emotions ever stronger into their own emotional core—"It takes a while to see how wise the old people really are." An initiated boy, in participating in the Kachina dances, learned to identify again with the Kachinas whom he now impersonated. To put on a mask is to "become a Kachina," and to cooperate actively

[20] See Piers (in Piers and Singer 1953;15) for a discussion of the maturation drive.

[21] Erikson 1948:198, fn.: "The child derives a vitalizing sense of reality from the awareness that his individual way of mastering experience (his ego-synthesis) is a successful variant of a group identity and is in accord with its space-time and life plan."

in bringing about the major goals of Hopi life. And a girl came to know more fully the importance of her clan in its supportive role. These experiences were even more sharply conditioned and directed toward adult life in the tribal initiation ceremonies, of which we have as yet only fragmentary knowledge. Of this one man said to me: "I will not discuss this thing with you only to say that no one can forget it. It is the most wonderful thing any man can have to remember. You know then that you are Hopi. It is one thing whites cannot have, cannot take from us. It is our way of life given to us when the world began."

And since children are, for all mankind, a restatement of one's hopes to be, when these Hopi in turn become teachers (and in a sense they had always been teachers of the younger children in the household from an early age), they continued the process of reliving and rationalizing, or "working out" their experiences with an intensity which is rarely known in our society except, perhaps, on the psychoanalytic couch. But the Hopi had no psychiatrists to guide them—no books which, as Riesman says, "like an invisible monitor, helps liberate the reader from his group and its emotions, and allows the contemplation of alternative responses and the trying on of new emotions" (Riesman 1955:13). They had only the internalized "feeling measure" and "group measure" explicit in the concepts of Hopi versus Kahopi.

On the material level, the obvious advantages of, for instance, wagons versus backs were a temptation. And to the extent to which white influences at first penetrated to these older Hopi it was through this form of temptation. But outside experiences usually included some variation of hostility, scorn, or aggression, as well as a radically different moral code, and these were all viewed and reinterpreted through the Hopi-eye view of the world and in the Hopi language, so that a return to the familiarity of the Hopi world with its solidarity of world view and behavior patterns *was experienced as relief,* and increased the need to feel Hopi, *however, great a burden "being Hopi"* implied.

In summary, the hypothesis here developed, that strong emotional conditioning during the learning process was an instrument in cultural continuity among the Hopi, is suggested as supplementary to that of early learning as being resistant to change. It further suggests that this conditioning was *constantly* as well as *consistently* instilled during the entire lifetime of an individual by a circular pattern of integration. For an individual was surrounded by a series of invisible, but none the less solid, barriers between himself and the outside world. To change him, influences had to breach the concentric walls of social process—as conveyed through the human entities which surrounded him and which were strengthened by his obligation to teach others—and then to recondition his early and ever-increasing emotional involvement in Hopi religion, morals, and mutually dependent lineage and clan groups, as well as those attitudes toward white aggression which he shared with all Indians.

In 1938 one old Hopi, who in his youth had been taken away from his wife and children and kept in a boarding school for several years said to me:

> I am full of curiosity; a great *bahana* [white] education would tell me many things I've wondered about like the stars and how a man's insides work. But I am afraid of it because I've seen what it does to folks. . . . If I raise a family, clothe and feed them well, do my ceremonial duties faithfully, I have succeeded—what do you call success? . . . [And again, while discussing fear in connection with a dream, his comment was] Well, yes, we are afraid of *powakas* [witches] but our medicine men can handle them. Neither your doctors nor your gods can control your governments so you have more to fear. Now you are dragging us into your quarrels. I pity you and I don't envy you. You have more goods than we have, but you don't have peace ever; *it is better to die in famine than in war.*

As the old man anticipated, enforced participation in modern warfare soon replaced instruction for Hopi citizenship, and the concentric walls were finally seriously breached. But for these older Hopi the walls still enclose "our way of life given to us when the world began."

References

Aberle, David F., 1951, *The Psychosocial Analysis of a Hopi Life-History.* Comparative Psychology Monographs 21:1-133. Berkeley and Los Angeles: University of California Press.

Adair, John, and Evon Z. Vogt, 1949, "Navaho and Zuni Veterans: A Study of Contrasting Modes of Culture Change," *American Anthropologist* 51:547-561.

Allport, Gordon W., 1951, "The Personality Trait." In Melvin H. Marx, ed., *Psychological Theory: Contemporary Readings.* New York: The Macmillan Company, pp. 503-507.

Asch, Solomon E., 1952, *Social Psychology.* Englewood Cliffs, N.J.: Prentice-Hall, Inc.

Benedict, Ruth, 1948, "Continuities and Discontinuities in Cultural Conditioning." In Clyde Kluckhohn and Henry A. Murray, eds., *Personality in Nature, Society, and Culture.* New York: Alfred A. Knopf, Inc., pp. 414-423.

Brandt, Richard B., 1954, *Hopi Ethics: A Theoretical Analysis.* Chicago: The University of Chicago Press.

Bruner, Edward M., 1956a, "Cultural Transmission and Cultural Change," *Southwestern Journal of Anthropology* 12:191-199.

———, 1956b, "Primary Group Experience and the Process of Acculturation," *American Anthropologist* 58:605-623.

Dennis, Wayne, 1941, "The Socialization of the Hopi Child." In Leslie Spier, A. Irving Hallowell, and Stanley S. Newman, eds., *Language, Culture, and Personality: Essays in Memory of Edward Sapir.* Menasha, Wis.: Sapir Memorial Publication Fund, pp. 259-271.

Dozier, Edward P., 1954, "The Hopi-Tewa of Arizona, *University of California Publications in American Archaeology and Ethnology* 44:259-376. Berkeley and Los Angeles, Calif.: University of California Press.

———, 1955, "Forced and Permissive Acculturation," *American Anthropologist* 56:973-1002.

DuBois, Cora, 1941, "Attitudes toward Food and Hunger in Alor." In Leslie Spier, A. Irving Hallowell, and Stanley S. Newman, eds., *Language, Culture, and Personality: Essays in Memory of Edward Sapir*. Menasha, Wis.: Sapir Memorial Publication Fund, pp. 272–281.

————, 1955, "Some Notions on Learning Intercultural Understanding." In George D. Spindler, ed., *Education and Anthropology*. Stanford, Calif.: Stanford University Press, pp. 89–126.

Earle, Edwin, and Edward A. Kennard, 1938, *Hopi Kachinas*. New York: J. J. Augustin, Publisher.

Eggan, Dorothy, 1948, "The General Problem of Hopi Adjustment." In Clyde Kluckhohn and Henry A. Murray, eds., *Personality in Nature, Society, and Culture*. New York: Alfred A. Knopf, Inc., pp. 220–235.

————, 1955, "The Personal Use of Myth in Dreams." In "Myth: A Symposium," *Journal of American Folklore* 68:445–453.

Eggan, Fred, 1950, *Social Organization of the Western Pueblos*. Chicago: The University of Chicago Press.

Erikson, Erik Homburger, 1948, "Childhood and Tradition in Two American Indian Tribes, with Some Reflections on the Contemporary American Scene." In Clyde Kluckhohn and Henry A. Murray, eds., *Personality in Nature, Society, and Culture*. New York: Alfred A. Knopf, Inc., pp. 176–203.

Goldfrank, Esther, 1945, "Socialization, Personality, and the Structure of Pueblo Society," *American Anthropologist* 47:516–539.

Hallowell, A. Irving, 1953, "Culture, Personality, and Society." In A. Kroeber, et al., *Anthropology Today: An Encyclopedic Inventory*. Chicago: The University of Chicago Press, pp. 597–620.

————, 1955, *Culture and Experience*. Philadelphia: University of Pennsylvania Press.

Henry, Jules, 1955, "Culture, Education, and Communications Theory." In George D. Spindler, ed., *Education and Anthropology*. Stanford, Calif.: Stanford University Press, pp. 188–215.

Herskovits, Melville J., 1950, *Man and His Works: The Science of Cultural Anthropology*. New York: Alfred A. Knopf, Inc.

Hough, Walter, 1915, *The Hopi Indians*. Cedar Rapids, Iowa: The Torch Press.

Keesing, Felix M., 1953, *Culture Change: An Analysis and Bibliography of Anthropological Sources to 1952*, Stanford, Calif.: Stanford University Press.

Kluckhohn, Clyde, 1951, "Values and Value-Orientations in the Theory of Action: An Exploration in Definition and Classification." In Talcott Parsons and Edward A. Shils, eds., *Toward a General Theory of Action*. Cambridge, Mass.: Harvard University Press, pp. 388–433.

————, and Florence R. Kluckhohn, 1947, "American Culture: Generalized Orientations and Class Patterns." In *Conflicts of Power in Modern Culture*, 1947 Symposium of Conference in Science, Philosophy, and Religion, Chap. 9.

Mead, Margaret, 1931, "The Primitive Child." In *A Handbook of Child Psychology*. Worcester, Mass.: Clark University Press, pp. 669–687.

————, 1943, "Our Education Emphases in Primitive Perspective," *American Journal of Sociology* 48:633–639.

————, 1948, "Social Change and Cultural Surrogates." In Clyde Kluckhohn and Henry A. Murray, eds., *Personality in Nature, Society, and Culture*. New York: Alfred A. Knopf, Inc., pp. 511–522.

——, 1953, *Growing Up in New Guinea*. New York: The New American Library. A Mentor Book (First published in 1930, by William Morrow & Company, Inc.)

Murphy, Gardner, 1947, *Personality: A Biosocial Approach to Origins and Structure*. New York: Harper & Row.

Park, Robert Ezra, 1950, *Race and Culture*. New York: The Free Press.

Pettit, George A., 1946, "Primitive Education in North America," *University of California Publications in American Archaeology and Ethnology* 43:1–182. Berkeley and Los Angeles: University of California Press.

Piers, Gerhart, and Milton B. Singer, 1953, *Shame and Guilt: A Psychoanalytic and a Cultural Study*. Springfield, Ill.: Charles C Thomas, Publishers.

Redfield, Robert, 1953, *The Primitive World and Its Transformations*. Ithaca, N.Y.: Cornell University Press.

——, 1955, *The Little Community: Viewpoints for the Study of a Human Whole*. Chicago: The University of Chicago Press.

Riesman, David, 1955, "The Oral Tradition, The Written Word, and the Screen Image," Founders Day Lecture, no. 1, Antioch College, October 5, 1955.

Riesman, David, in collaboration with Reuel Denney and Nathan Glazer, 1950, *The Lonely Crowd: A Study of the Changing American Character*. New Haven, Conn.: Yale University Press.

Sapir, Edward, 1949, "The Emergence of the Concept of Personality in a Study of Cultures." In David G. Mandelbaum, ed., *Selected Writings of Edward Sapir in Language, Culture, and Personality*. Berkeley and Los Angeles, Calif.: University of California Press, pp. 590–597.

Simmons, Leo W., 1942, *Sun Chief: The Autobiography of a Hopi Indian*. Published for The Institute of Human Relations by Yale University Press, New Haven, Conn.

[SSRC] Social Science Research Council Summer Seminar on Acculturation, 1954, "Acculturation: an Exploratory Formulation," *American Anthropologist* 56:973–1002.

Spindler, George D., ed., 1955, *Education and Anthropology*. Stanford, Calif.: Stanford University Press.

Spiro, Melford E., 1955, "The Acculturation of American Ethnic Groups," *American Anthropologist* 57:1240–1252.

Stephen, Alexander MacGregor, 1940, *Hopi Indians of Arizona*. Southwest Museum Leaflets, no. 14. Highland Park, Los Angeles, Calif.: Southwest Museum.

Steward, Julian H., 1931, "Notes on Hopi Ceremonies in Their Initiatory Form in 1927–1928," *American Anthropologist* 33:56–79.

Thompson, Laura, 1945, "Logico-Aesthetic Integration in Hopi Culture," *American Anthropologist* 47:540–553.

Thompson, Laura, and Alice Joseph, 1944, *The Hopi Way*. Indian Education Research Series, no. 1. Lawrence, Kan.: Haskell Institute.

Titiev, Mischa, 1942, "Notes on Hopi Witchcraft." *Papers of the Michigan Academy of Science, Arts, and Letters* 28:549–557.

——, 1944, *Old Oraibi: A Study of the Hopi Indians of Third Mesa*. Papers of the Peabody Museum of American Archaeology and Ethnology, Harvard University, vol. 22, no. 1.

Vogt, Evon Z., 1951, *Navaho Veterans: A Study of Changing Values*. Papers of the Peabody Museum of American Archaeology and Ethnology, Harvard University, vol. 41, no. 1.

Whiting, John W. M., and Irvin L. Child, 1953, *Child Training and Personality: A Cross-Cultural Study*. New Haven, Conn.: Yale University Press.

Whorf, B. L., 1941, "The Relation of Habitual Thought and Behavior to Language." In Leslie Spier, A. Irving Hallowell, and Stanley S. Newman, eds., *Language, Culture, and Personality: Essays in Memory of Edward Sapir*. Menasha, Wis.: Sapir Memorial Publication Fund, pp. 75–93.

20   *Contrasts between Prepubertal and Postpubertal Education**

This chapter represents an attempt to use the body of generally accepted anthropological information as a baseline for considering the educational process. It might be paraphrased as "the educative process, anthropologically considered." I assume that "anthropologically considered" is equivalent to "cross-culturally considered," and I assume that education refers to any process at any stage of life in which new knowledge is acquired or new habits or new attitudes formed. That is, I have taken the question which forms the core problem of this volume and tried to develop a few generalizations about that problem from the general anthropological literature. But it follows that since they are anthropological generalizations their usefulness to education is a matter of opinion. All I claim for them is the old basis upon which anthropology has always justified its preoccupation with the simpler societies, namely that by studying the simpler societies we gain perspective and proportion in really seeing our own society and from that better perspective comes better understanding of common human social processes. I hope that the material contained in this chapter will at least enable the readers interested in education to see our own educative process in better perspective and help them separate what is distinctively American in it from what is general-social and general-human.

My starting point is a distinction that is made by Herskovits. In his chapter on education in the book called *Man and His Works* (1948) he finds it necessary to stress that the training of the young in the simpler societies of the world is carried on through two different vehicles. The child learns a lot of things knocking around underfoot in the home, in the village street, with his brothers and sisters, and in similar environments, and he learns a lot of other things in the rather formidable apparatus of what is usually called in the anthropological literature the initiation ceremonies or the initiation schools.

Herskovits stresses that initiation education takes place outside the home and is worthy to be called schooling, contrasts it with the education the child

---

**Reprinted with minor revision from *Education and Anthropology,* George D. Spindler, Editor, with the permission of the publishers, Stanford University Press; copyright 1955 by the Board of Trustees of the Leland Stanford Junior University.*

receives knocking around the household and the village long before the initiation period begins, and decides that the main feature of the latter is that it
is within the home, and that it should therefore be called education as contrasted with schooling. There he, and many other writers on the subject, tend
to leave the matter.

This tendency, to leave the problem at that point, is rather a pity. Further
exploration of these two contrasting vehicles for training of the young will
pay rich dividends, and it is to such further exploration that the bulk of this
paper is devoted. But before going on, certain unsatisfactory features of Herskovits' treatment must be mentioned. To suggest, as he does, that preinitiation education is "within the home" is misleading to people unacquainted
with the character of primitive society. While initiation education is very
definitely outside the home and—as we shall see later—this remoteness from
home is a very essential feature of it, it does not follow that the other has to
be, or even is likely to be, "within the home." The home in most primitive
societies is very different indeed from the connotation of "home" in America,
and the type of education to which Herskovits is referring takes place in every
conceivable type of primary group. The young child in primitive society
may be subjected to the learning process in his early years in his household
(Eskimo), or in a medley of dozens of households (Samoa); his parents may
ignore him and leave him to drag himself up as best he can (Mundugumor);
he may be corrected or scolded by any passer-by (Zuñi); his male mentor may
not be his father at all but his mother's brother (many Melanesian cultures);
and so on.

I do not intend to explore the social-psychological results of this variety
of primary-group situations; all I mention them for here is to demonstrate
how misleading it is to lump them all together as comprising "education within
the home." About the only things they have in common is that they all take
place in the earlier years of life and they don't take place within the formal
framework of initiation ceremonies. I propose therefore to call all this type of
education by the title "preinitiation" or "prepuberty" education (since most
initiation ceremonial begins at puberty or later), and the problem I am mainly
concerned with is the set of contrasts that exists between what societies do
with their children in the preinitiation period and what is done with them in
the postinitiation period. In other words, Herskovits' distinction between
education and schooling becomes clearer and more useful if they are simply
called prepuberty education and postpuberty education.

One further explanatory comment is necessary. Not all primitive societies
possess initiation ceremonies of the formal standardized type that anthropology has become familiar with in many parts of the world. How "schooling"
or post-puberty education is handled in those primitive societies which lack
initiation ceremonies and what the results of such lack are for the adult culture are interesting questions, but they are outside the scope of the present

paper. What we are concerned with here is the set of contrasts between prepubertal and postpubertal education in those numerous and widespread societies which include formal initiation ceremonies in their set of official institutions.

Prepubertal and Postpubertal Education—How Do They Differ?

If attention is directed to the ways education is carried on in the prepuberty and postpuberty periods in a large number of simple societies—viz., those "with initiation ceremonies"—some very impressive contrasts begin to appear. They can be dealt with under four heads—(1) Regulation, (2) Personnel, (3) Atmosphere, (4) Curriculum; but the nature of the data will require us to jump back and forth between these four divisions, since they are all interwoven.

1. Regulation

Postpuberty education, in such societies, does not begin until at least the age of twelve or thirteen, and in many cases several years later than that. By that age of course, the child has already acquired a great deal of what we call his culture. How has he acquired the things he knows at the age of twelve or thirteen? The traditional anthropological monographs are said to tell us little or nothing about "early education." I suggest that the reason the older literature tells us so little that is definite about the early prepubertal training of the children is basically for the same reason that we know so little about preschool education in our own culture, or did know so little before Gesell. Until the appearance of *The Child from Five to Ten* (Gesell and Ilg 1946), the information on the preschool "enculturation" of the American child was just as barren as the anthropological literature. Whether Gesell has really answered the question for the American child and whether a Gesell-like job has been done or can be done for a primitive society are questions which need not concern us here except to point up the real question: Why is it so rare to find clear information as to what goes on in the learning process during the preschool years, in any culture?

One possible answer is that preschool education is rarely if ever standardized, rarely if ever regulated around known and visible social norms.[1] It is an area of cultural laissez faire, within very wide limits of tolerance, and society at large does not lay down any firm blueprint which all personnel

---

[1] *Editor's note:* Nonanthropologist readers should be aware of the fact that Prof. Hart's statements concerning lack of uniformity in prepubertal child training would be contested by many anthropologists, though the same ones might accept his basic position that in comparison to pubertal and postpubertal training the earlier years of experience are *relatively* less structured and less subject to the pressure of public opinion.

engaged in "raising the young" must follow. If, instead of asking for a "pattern" or "norm," we ask the simpler question, "What happens?" it seems to me that the literature is not nearly so barren of information as has been argued. It tends to suggest that anything and everything happens in the same society. For instance Schapera's account of childhood among the Bakgatla is pretty clear: "The Bakgatla say that thrashing makes a child wise. But they also say a growing child is like a little dog and though it may annoy grownups, it must be taught proper conduct with patience and forbearance" (Schapera 1940). As Herskovits has pointed out, this mixture of strict and permissive techniques is also reported for Lesu in Melanesia by Powdermaker, for the Apache by Opler, and for the Kwoma by Whiting (Herskovits 1948). This list can readily be added to.

There is no point in counting how many cultures use severe punishment and how many do not. The explicit statements of the fieldworkers just cited are at least implicit in dozens of others. Do the natives beat their children? Yes. Do they fondle and make a fuss over their children? Yes. Do they correct them? Yes. Do they let them get away with murder? Also yes. All this in the same culture. I repeat that it is pretty clear what happens in the prepuberty years in the simpler societies. Anything and everything from extreme punishment to extreme permissiveness may occur and does occur in the same culture.

The fieldworkers do not tell us what the pattern of early education is because there is rarely any one clear-cut pattern. What each individual child learns or is taught or is not taught is determined pretty much by a number of individual variables. A few such variables are: interest or lack of interest of individual parents in teaching their children, size of family and each sibling's position in it, whether the next house or camp is close by or far away, whether the neighbors have children of the same age, the amount of interaction and type of interaction of the particular "peer-groups" of any given child. The number of variables of this type is almost infinite; the child is simply dumped in the midst of them to sink or swim, and as a result no two children in the same culture learn the same things in the same way. One, for example, may learn about sex by spying upon his parents, a second by spying upon a couple of comparative strangers, a third by getting some explicit instruction from his father or his mother (or his elder brother or his mother's brother), a fourth by listening to sniggering gossip in the play group, and a fifth by observing a pair of dogs in the sexual act. Which of these ways of learning is the norm? Obviously none of them is, at least not in the same sense as that in which we say that it is the norm for a person to inherit the property of his mother's brother, or to use an intermediary in courtship, or to learn certain important myths at Stage 6B of the initiation ceremonies.

In asking for a uniform cultural pattern in such a laissez faire, anything-goes area, we are asking for the inherently impossible, or at least the non-existent. There are, of course, some cultural limits set in each society to this near-anarchy: there will, for example, be general outrage and widespread social disapproval if one family shamefully neglects its children or some child goes to what is by general consensus regarded as "too far," but such limits of toleration are very wide indeed in every society. The household is almost sovereign in its rights to do as much or as little as it likes—that is, to do what it likes about its offspring in the *preschool* years. The rest of society is extraordinarily reluctant everywhere to interfere with a household's sovereign right to bring up its preschool children as it wishes. And most primitive parents, being busy with other matters and having numerous children anyway, leave the kids to bring each other up or to just grow like Topsy.

There are other strong lines of evidence supporting this judgment that prepuberty education in the simpler societies is relatively so variable as to be virtually normless. One is the self-evident fact which anybody can verify by reading the monographs, that no fieldworker, not even among those who have specifically investigated the matter of child practices, has ever found a tribe where several reliable informants could give him a rounded and unified account of the preschool educational practices of their tribe comparable to the rounded and generalized picture they can give him, readily and easily, of the local religion, or the folklore, or the moral code for the adults, or the local way of getting married, or the right way to build a canoe or plant a garden. This difference can best be conveyed to an anthropologist audience, perhaps, by contrasting the sort of answer fieldworkers get to such questions as "Tell me some of your myths," or "How do you make silver ornaments?" or "How do you treat your mother-in-law?" with the answer they get to a question like "How do you bring up children?" To the former type of question (not asked as crudely as that, of course) the answers will come (usually) in the form of norms—stereotyped and generalized statements that do not differ a great deal from one informant to the next, or, if they do so differ, will always be referred to a "right" way or a "proper" way: the "right" way to build a canoe, the "proper" way to treat one's mother-in-law, the "correct" form of a myth or a ceremony, and so on. Even in the type of sentence structure the answers come in, they will have this official character—"We do it this way" or "It is our custom here to do thus and so"—and often in case of conflicting versions an argument will develop, not over what the informant himself does but over whether what he says is "right" or socially sanctioned as "the right way."

But given the opportunity to perform a similar generalized descriptive job upon "how children are or should be brought up," informants fail dismally to produce anything of this kind. They either look blank and say little or nothing, or come up with a set of empty platitudes—"All boys should be brought up good boys," "They should all respect their elders," etc.—which clearly have no relation to the facts of life going on all around the speaker; or (most common of all) they fall back onto their own life history and do a Sun Chief or Crashing Thunder sort of job. That is, they give in endless and boring detail an account of how they individually were brought up, or how they bring up their own children, but they clearly have no idea of whether their case is typical or atypical of the tribe at large. And the anthropologist equally has no idea of how representative or unrepresentative this case is. This happens so constantly that we are left with only one conclusion, namely, that if there is a cultural tradition for preschool education (comparable with the cultural tradition for religion or for tabu-observance or for technology), then the average native in a simple society is completely unaware of what it is.

This same conclusion is also supported by another line of evidence, namely, the complete change that comes over the picture when we move from prepuberty education to postpuberty education. Postpuberty education is marked in the simpler societies by the utmost degree of standardization and correctness. At puberty the initiation rituals begin, and perhaps the most universal thing about these is their meticulously patterned character. Every line painted on a boy's body, every movement of a performer, every word or phrase uttered, the right person to make every move, is rigidly prescribed as having to be done in one way only—the right way. A wrongly drawn line, a misplaced phrase, an unsanctioned movement, or the right movement made by the wrong person or at the wrong time, and the whole ritual is ruined. They belong to the same general type of social phenomena as the English Coronation ceremony or the Catholic sacrifice of the Mass; there is only one way of doing them, regardless of the individuals involved, namely the "right" way. By contrast that meticulously patterned feature throws into sharp relief the haphazard, permissive, and unstandardized character of the education that *precedes* the time of puberty.

2. Personnel

So far, then, our stress has been on the unregulated character of primitive preschool education. Certain further things become clearer if at this point we switch our attention from the focus of regulation to the focus of personnel —i.e., from the question of whether the education is controlled and standardized to the question of who imparts the education. Anthropologists are coming more and more to realize the importance of the "Who does what?" type of question in fieldwork, and perhaps nowhere is it so important to know who does what than in the area we are discussing. From whom does the child learn in the simpler societies? As far as the preinitiation years are concerned the answer is obvious: He learns from his intimates, whether they be intimates of a senior generation like his parents or intimates of his own generation like his siblings, cousins, playmates, etc. In the preinitiation years he learns nothing or next to nothing from strangers or near-strangers. Strangers and near-strangers are people he rarely sees and even more rarely converses with; and, since learning necessarily involves interaction, it is from the people he interacts with most that he learns most, and from the people he interacts with least that he learns least.

This is so obvious that it needs little comment. But one important point about intimates must be made. In all cultures it appears as if this "learning from intimates" takes two forms. The child learns from his parents or other senior members of his family and he also learns from his play groups. And the interaction processes in these two situations are different in several important respects. The parents are intimates and so are the members of the play group, but there is the important difference that parents, to some extent at least, represent the official culture (are the surrogates of society, in Dollard's phrase), while the play groups do not. All the work upon play groups in Western society has tended to stress what autonomous little subcultures they are, each with its own social organization, its own rules, its own values. The family is a primary group, but one which is tied into the total formal structure of the society and therefore subject to at least some over-all social control. The play group is an autonomous little world of its own, whose rules may be, and often are, directly at variance with the rules of the home or of the wider society.

If, then, as suggested above, it is true that in most societies—simple or modern—each household is allowed a great deal of freedom to bring up its children pretty much as it chooses, and if this wide degree of tolerance leads in turn to a wide variation in the ways in which the culture is presented to different children, then obviously such variation is enormously increased by the role of the play group. Even if we were told of a culture in which all households standardized their child-training practices, it would still fall far short of being convincing evidence of a standardized child-training situation because of the great amount of knowledge which children in all cultures acquire without the household or at least the parents being involved in the transmission process, namely the knowledge which the child "picks up somewhere."

Once we recognize the influence of this second group of intimates on how the child acquires certain aspects of his culture, the case for wide variation in early child training is greatly strengthened. There seems to be no evidence that would suggest that the play group in simple societies functions in any notably different way from the way it functions in modern societies, but unfortunately we have few studies of the "subcultures" of the playworld in other than Western cultures. Among child psychologists dealing with Western cultures, Piaget in particular has some findings that are relevant to the present discussion (Piaget 1929, 1932). These findings tend to show that at least by the age of ten or eleven the child has become empirical and secular in his attitudes toward rules and norms of play behavior, partly because he has learned by that time that each primary group has its own rules, so that there is no "right" way, no over-all norm—at least for children's games such as marbles— for all play groups to conform to. Piaget, of course, is describing European children, but primitive children spend at least as much time in unsupervised play groups as European or American children, and since their preschool period is certainly many years more prolonged, there is no apparent reason why this conclusion of Piaget should not have cross-cultural validity.

However, I am not trying to develop a theory but merely to follow through some of the difficulties that are hidden in the simple statement above that preschool learning is between intimates. There are different sorts of intimacy because of the child's dual relation to his home and to his playmates, and some of his culture is mediated to him by each. We don't know nearly enough about degrees of intimacy, and we may be forced by further research to start making classifications and subdivisions between the different sorts of intimate relationships (different "levels" of primary groups?) to which the child in any culture is exposed in his preschool years. Even if we do, however, the fact still remains that in his preinitiation years the child in primitive society learns nothing from strangers or near-strangers. And this leads to the second comment under the head of Personnel, which is that in his *postpuberty* education in contrast to that of *prepuberty* he *has to* learn from strangers or near-strangers and cannot possibly learn from anybody else. When puberty arrives and the boy is therefore ready for initiation (or the girl for marriage), his family, his siblings, his gangs, his village, all the intimates to whom his training or learning has been left up to now, are roughly pushed aside and a whole new personnel take over his training. Who these new teachers are varies from culture to culture, but a very common feature is that they be nonintimates of the boy, semistrangers drawn from other sections of the tribe (opposite moieties, different districts or villages, hostile or semihostile clans, different age groups, and so on), people with whom he is not at all intimate. Who they are and what they represent is made painfully clear in the ritual. An actual case will help to make clear the nature of the transition.

Among the Tiwi of North Australia, one can see the traumatic nature of the initiation period in very clear form, and part of trauma lies in the sudden switch of personnel with whom the youth has to associate. A boy reaches thirteen or fourteen or so, and the physiological signs of puberty begin to appear. Nothing happens, possibly for many months. Then suddenly one day, toward evening when the people are gathering around their campfires for the main meal of the day after coming in from their day's hunting and food-gathering, a group of three or four heavily armed and taciturn strangers appear in camp. In full war regalia they walk in silence to the camp of the boy and say curtly to the household: "We have come for So-and-So." Immediately pandemonium breaks loose. The mother and the rest of the older women begin to howl and wail. The father rushes for his spears. The boy himself, panic-striken, tries to hide, the younger children begin to cry, and the household dogs begin to bark. It is all terribly similar to the reaction which is provoked by the arrival of the police at an American home to pick up a juvenile delinquent. This similarity extends to the behavior of the neighbors. These carefully abstain from identifying with either the strangers or the stricken household. They watch curiously the goings-on but make no move that can be identified as supporting either side. This is particularly notable in view of the fact that the strangers are strangers to all of them, too, that is, they are men from outside the encampment, or outside the band, who, under any circumstances, would be greeted by a shower of spears. But not under these circumstances (see also Hart and Pilling 1960).

In fact, when we know our way around the culture we realize that the arrival of the strangers is not as unexpected as it appears. The father of the boy and the other adult men of the camp not only knew they were coming but have even agreed with them on a suitable day for them to come. The father's rush for his spears to protect his son and to preserve the sanctity of his household is make-believe. If he puts on too good an act, the older men will intervene and restrain him from interfering with the purposes of the strangers. With the father immobilized the child clings to his mother, but the inexorable strangers soon tear him (literally) from his mother's arms and from the bosom of his bereaved family and, still as grimly as they came, bear him off into the night. No society could symbolize more dramatically that initiation necessitates the forcible taking away of the boy from the bosom of his family, his village, his neighbors, his intimates, his friends. And who are these strangers who forcibly drag the terrified boy off to he knows not what? In Tiwi they are a selected group of his senior male cross-cousins. To people who understand primitive social organization that should convey most of what I want to convey. They are "from the other side of the tribe," men with whom the boy has had little to do and whom he may have never seen before. They belong to the group of men who have married or will marry his sisters, and marriage, it is well to remember, in a primitive society is a semihostile act. As cross-cousins, these men cannot possibly belong to the same clan as the boy, or to the same territorial group, and since only senior and already fully initiated men are eligible for the job they will be men in their thirties or forties, twenty or more years older than he.

By selecting senior cross-cousins to conduct the forcible separation of the boy from the home and thus project him into the postpuberty proceedings, the Tiwi have selected men who are as remote from the boy as possible. The only thing they and he have in common is that they are all members of the same tribe—nothing else. If, then, we have stressed that all training of the child in the prepuberty period is carried on by intimates, we have to stress equally the fact that the postpuberty training has to be in the hands of non-intimates. Anybody who is in any way close to the boy—by blood, by residence, by age, or by any other form of affiliation or association—is *ipso facto* ineligible to have a hand in his postpuberty training.

I selected the Tiwi as my example because the case happens to be rather spectacular in the clarity of its symbolism, but if one examines the literature one finds everywhere or almost everywhere the same emphasis. Those who prefer Freudian symbolism I refer to the initiation ceremonies of the Kiwai Papuans (Landtmann 1927), where during initiation the boy is required to actually step on his mother's stomach; when Landtmann asked the significance of this he was told that it meant the boy was now "finished with the place where he came from" (i.e., his mother's womb). Van Gennep has collected all the older cases in his classic *Rites de passage* (Van Gennep 1909), and no new ones which invalidate his generalizations have been reported since his time.

I therefore suggest two reasonably safe generalizations about initiation rituals: (a) The rituals themselves are designed to emphasize in very clear terms that initiation ceremonies represent a clear break with all home, household, home-town, and friendship-group ties; and (b) as a very basic part of such emphasis the complete handling of all initiation proceedings, and initiation instruction, from their inception at puberty to their final conclusion often more than a decade later, is made the responsibility of men who are comparative strangers to the boy and who are thus as different as possible in their social relationships to him from the teachers, guiders, instructors, and associates he has had up to that time.

3. Atmosphere

It should now be clear what is meant by the third head, Atmosphere. The arrival of the strangers to drag the yelling boy out of his mother's arms is just the spectacular beginning of a long period during which the separation of the boy from everything that has gone before is emphasized in every possible way at every minute of the day and night. So far his life has been easy; now it is hard. Up to now he has never necessarily experienced any great pain, but in the initiation period in many tribes pain, sometimes horrible, intense pain, is an obligatory feature. The boy of twelve or thirteen, used to noisy, boisterous, irresponsible play, is expected and required to sit still for hours and days at a time saying nothing whatever but concentrating upon and endeavoring to understand long intricate instructions and "lectures" given him by his hostile and forbidding preceptors (who are, of course, the men who carried him off to initiation, the "strangers" of the previous section). Life has suddenly become real and earnest, and the initiate is required literally to "put away the things of a child," even the demeanor. The number of tabus and unnatural behaviors enjoined upon the initiate is endless. He mustn't speak unless he is spoken to; he must eat only certain foods, and often only in certain ways, at fixed times, and in certain fixed positions. All contact with females, even speech with them, is rigidly forbidden, and this includes mother and sisters. He cannot even scratch his head with his own hand, but must do it with a special stick and so on, through a long catalogue of special, unnatural, but obligatory behaviors covering practically every daily activity and every hour of the day and night. And during this time he doesn't go home at night or for the week end or on a forty-eight-hour pass, but remains secluded in the bush, almost literally the prisoner of his preceptors, for months and even years at a time. If he is allowed home at rare intervals, he has to carry all his tabus with him, and nothing is more astonishing in Australia than to see some youth who the year before was a noisy, brash, boisterous thirteen-year-old, sitting the following year, after his initiation is begun, in the midst of his family, with downcast head and subdued air, not daring even to smile, still less to speak. He is "home on leave," but he might just as well have stayed in camp for all the freedom from discipline his spell at home is giving him.

The preoccupations of anthropologists with other interests (that of the earlier fieldworkers with the pain-inflicting aspects of the initiations, and the recent preoccupation with early physiological experiences) have directed attention away from what may well be the most important aspect of education in the simpler societies, namely the possibly traumatic aspect of the initiation ceremonies. From whatever aspect we view them their whole tenor is to produce shock, disruption, a sharp break with the past, a violent projection out of the known into the unknown. Perhaps the boys are old enough to take it in their stride and the experience is not really traumatic. If so, it would seem that primitive society goes to an awful lot of trouble and wastes an awful lot of man-hours needlessly. Actually we don't know what the psychological effects of initiation upon the initiates are. All that can be said safely is that judged by the elaboration and the minuteness of detail in the shocking and disruptive features of initiation rituals, they certainly appear to be designed to produce the maximum amount of shock possible for the society to achieve.

This may suggest that our own exaggerated concern with protecting our own adolescents from disturbing experiences is quite unnecessary. If the grueling ordeal of subincision, with all its accompanying disruptive devices, leaves the young Australian psychologically unscathed, we needn't worry that Universal Military Training, for instance, will seriously upset the young American. But perhaps something in the prepuberty training prepares the young Australian and makes him capable of standing the trauma of the initiation period.

4. Curriculum

What is the purpose of all this elaboration of shock ritual? Ask the natives themselves and they will answer vaguely, "to make a child into a man." Occasionally a more specific verb is used and the answer becomes, "to teach a boy to become a man." What is supposed to be learned and what do the preceptors teach in the initiation schools? Perhaps the most surprising thing is what is not taught. It is hard to find in the literature any case where the initiation curriculum contains what might be called "practical subjects," or how to make a basic living. (There appear to be certain exceptions to this generalization, but they are more apparent than real.) The basic food-getting skills of the simpler peoples are never imparted in the initiation schools. Where practical subjects are included (as in Polynesia or in the Poro schools of Liberia and Sierra Leone), they are specialized crafts, not basic food-getting skills. Hunting, gardening, cattle-tending, fishing, are not taught the boy at initiation; he has already learned the rudiments of these at home in his intimate groups before his initiation starts. This is a surprising finding because of the well-known fact that many of these people live pretty close to the starvation point, and none of them manage to extract much more than subsistence from their environment. But despite this, the cultures in question are blissfully oblivious of economic determinism, and blandly leave instruction in basic food production to the laissez-faire, casual, hit-or-miss teaching of parents, friends, play groups, etc. When society itself forcibly takes over the boy in order to make him into a man and teach him the things a man should know, it is not concerned with teaching him to be a better hunter or gardener or tender of cattle or fisherman, even though the economic survival of the tribe clearly depends on all of the adult men being good at one or another of these occupations. The initiation curricula cover instead quite a different series of subjects, which I am tempted to call "cultural subjects"—in either sense of the world "culture."

Of course, there is much variation here from tribe to tribe and region to region, but the imparting of religious knowledge always occupies a prominent place. This (in different cultures) includes such things as the learning of the myths, the tribal accounts of the tribe's own origin and history, and the performance, the meaning, and the sacred connections and connotations of the ceremonials. In brief, novices are taught theology, which in primitive society is inextricably mixed up with astronomy, geology, geography, biology (the mysteries of birth and sex), philosophy, art, and music—in short, the whole cultural heritage of the tribe. As Pettit has pointed out (dealing with North America, but his statement has universal anthropological validity), the instruction in the initiation schools is "a constant challenge to the elders to review, analyze, dramatize, and defend their cultural heritage" (Pettit 1946). That sentence "review, analyze, dramatize, and defend their cultural heritage" is very striking, because you can apply it equally aptly to a group of naked old men in Central Australia sitting talking to a novice in the middle of a treeless desert, and to most lectures in a college of liberal arts in the United States. It serves to draw attention to the fact that, in the simpler societies, the schools run and manned and controlled and financed by the society at large are designed not to make better economic men of the novices, or better food producers, but to produce better citizens, better carriers of the culture through the generations, people better informed about the world they live in and the tribe they belong to. It is here finally, through this sort of curriculum, that each adolescent becomes "enculturated," no matter how haphazard and individualized his learning and his growth may have been up to now. It is through the rigidly disciplined instruction of a common and rigidly prescribed curriculum that he assumes, with all his fellow tribesmen, a common culture. This is where standardization occurs in the educational process of the simpler societies. Everybody who goes through the initiation schools, generation after generation, is presented with the same material, organized and taught in the same way, with no allowances made for individual taste or choice or proclivity, and no substitutions or electives allowed. When we realize how standardized and rigid and uniform this curriculum is, it should help us to realize how variable, how un-uniform, how dictated by chance, accident, and the personal whims of individual parents, individual adult relatives, and the variation in peer and play groups is the "curriculum" on or in which the individual child is trained during the long impressionable period that precedes puberty.

Conclusion

The above discussion has, I hope, provided the basis for some helpful generalizations about education in primitive societies, or at least has opened up some new avenues for further exploration. The main points of this discussion may be summed up as follows:

1. There are typically (though not universally) in primitive societies two sharply contrasting educational vehicles, the preschool process, lasting from birth to puberty, and the initiation procedures, beginning around puberty or a little later and lasting from six months to fifteen years. These two educational vehicles show some highly significant contrasts.

2. From the point of view of regulation, the preschool period is characterized by its loose, vague, unsystematic character. Few primitive societies follow any set standards or rules on how children shall be brought up. It is true that there are frequently, perhaps usually, pretty clear rules (which are actually followed) telling mothers how to hold a baby, correct methods for suckling or weaning, and standardized techniques of toilet training (though I suspect some of these are nothing but copybook maxims), but outside the "physiological areas of child-training" (which therefore have to bear all the weight the Freudians put upon them), it is rare indeed to find in primitive cultures any conformity from family to family or from case to case with regard to anything else in the child's early career. This is not, of course, to deny that there are differences from culture to culture in the degree to which children are loved and fussed over or treated as nuisances or joys. I am not questioning the fact, for example, that the Arapesh love children, whereas the Mundugumor resent them. What I am reiterating is that there is still a wide variation not only possible but inevitable in conditioning and learning between one Mundugumor child and the next.

3. If this view is correct, it raises certain interesting possibilities for theory. Because of the heavy Freudian emphasis in the literature on child training in recent years, there exists a strong and unfortunate tendency to talk of child training as if it were coterminous with swaddling, suckling, weaning and toilet-training practices. But these "physiological" areas or "bodily functions"

areas are only a small part of the preschool education of the primitive child. Even if in primitive cultures the physiological areas of child training are relatively standardized (and this is by no means certain), there is no evidence that the nonphysiological areas are. On the contrary, the evidence points in the other direction. Among adult members of the same society there may be, for example, great variation in apparent strength of the sex drive, or in the overt expression of aggressive or passive personality traits (Hart 1954). Where does such "personality variation" come from? From childhood experiences, say the Freudians. I agree. But in order to demonstrate that personality variation in adult life has its roots in early childhood experiences, it is necessary to show not that childhood experiences are highly standardized in early life and that child training is uniform, but that they are highly variable. How can we account for the self-evident fact of adult personality variation by stressing the uniformity of standardization of childhood training? Surely the more valid hypothesis or the more likely lead is to be found in those aspects of child training which are not uniform and not standardized.

4. So much for the preschool training. But there is also the other vehicle of education and youth training in primitive society, the initiation rituals. The initiation period demonstrates to us what standardization and uniformity of training really mean. When we grasp the meaning of this demonstration we can only conclude that compared with the rigidities of the initiation period, the prepuberty period is a loose, lax period. Social scientists who find it necessary for their theories to stress uniformity and pressures toward conformity in simple societies are badly advised to take the prepuberty period for their examples. The natives themselves know better than this. When they are adults, it is to the happy, unregulated, care-free days of prepuberty that they look back. "Then my initiation began," says the informant, and immediately a grim, guarded "old-man" expression comes over his face, "and I was taken off by the old men." The same old men (and women) who sit around and indulgently watch the vagaries and idiosyncracies of the children without correction become the grim, vigilant, reproving watchers of the initiates, and any departure or attempted departure from tradition is immediately reprimanded.

5. Who are the agents of this discipline? Primitive societies answer in loud and unmistakable tones that discipline cannot be imposed by members of the primary group, that it has to be imposed by "outsiders." The widespread nature of this feature of initiation is, to my mind, very impressive. Making a boy into a man is rarely, anywhere, left to the family, the household, the village, to which he belongs and where he is on intimate terms with people.[2]

---

[2] In the original draft of this paper I mentioned the Arapesh as one of the few exceptions. At the Stanford conference, however, Dr. Mead pointed out that while it is true that initiation in Arapesh is carried out by intimates, they wear masks. To me this correction of my original remark dramatically emphasizes the main point. The Arapesh social structure is such that there are no "strangers" to use for initiation; therefore they invent them by masking some intimates.

The initiation schools are directed at imparting instruction that cannot be given in the home, under conditions as unlike home conditions as possible, by teachers who are the antithesis of the home teachers the boy has hitherto had. The symbolisms involved in the forcible removal from the home atmosphere; the long list of tabus upon homelike acts, homelike speech, homelike demeanor, homelike habits; the selection of the initiators (i.e., the teachers or preceptors) from the semihostile sections of the tribe—all tell the same story, that the turning of boys into men can only be achieved by making everything about the proceedings as different from the home and the prepuberty situation as possible. Everything that happens to the initiate during initiation has to be as different as it can be made by human ingenuity from the things that happened to him before initiation.

6. This becomes pointed up still more when we remember that what is actually being taught in the initiation schools is the whole value system of the culture, its myths, its religion, its philosophy, its justification of its own entity as a culture. Primitive society clearly values these things, values them so much that it cannot leave them to individual families to pass on to the young. It is willing to trust the haphazard, individually varied teaching methods of families and households and peer groups and gossip to teach children to walk and talk, about sex, how to get along with people, or how to be a good boy; it is even willing to leave to the individual families the teaching of how to hunt or to garden or to fish or to tend cattle; but the tribal philosophy, the religion, the citizenship knowledge, too important to leave to such haphazard methods, must be taught by society at large through its appointed and responsible representatives.

In doing this, society is asserting and underlining its right in the child. The fact that, for example, in Australia it is a group of senior cross-cousins, and elsewhere it is men of the opposite moiety or some other specified group of semihostile relatives, who knock on the door and demand the child from his mourning and wailing family, should not be allowed to disguise the fact that these men are the representatives of society at large, the native equivalents of the truant officer, the policeman, and the draft board, asserting the priority of society's rights over the family's rights in the child. Clearly in every society there is always a family and there is always a state, and equally clearly both have rights in every child born into the society. And no society yet—Western or non-Western—has found any perfect way or equal way of adjudicating or harmonizing public rights and private rights. The state's rights must have priority when matters of citizenship are involved, but the assertion of the state's rights is always greeted with wails of anguish from the family. "I didn't raise my boy to go off and get subincised," wails the Australian mother, but he is carried off and subincised just the same. "I didn't raise my boy for the draft board or the school board," says the American mother, but her protests are of no avail either. It is an inevitable conflict, because it arises from the very structure of society, as long as society is an organization of family units, which it is universally. The only solution is to abolish the family or abolish the state, and no human group has been able to do either.

7. The boy is not ruined for life or a mental cripple as a result of the harrowing initiation experience, but is a social being *in a way he never was before*. He has been made aware of his wider social responsibilities and his wider membership in the total society, but more important in the present context, he has been exposed to a series of social situations in which friendship counts for naught, crying or whining gets one no place, whimsy or charm or boyish attractiveness pays no dividends, and friends, pull, and influence are without effect. The tribal tradition, the culture, treats all individuals alike, and skills and wiles that were so valuable during childhood in gaining preferential treatment or in winning approval or avoiding disapproval are all to no avail. He goes into the initiation period a child, which is a social animal of one sort, but he comes out a responsible enculturated citizen, which is a social animal of a different sort.

8. Primitive societies, then, devote a great deal of time and care to training for citizenship. They make no attempt to even start such training until the boy has reached puberty. But once they start, they do it thoroughly. Citizenship training in these societies means a great deal more than knowing the words of "The Star-Spangled Banner" and memorizing the Bill of Rights. It means exposing the boy under particularly stirring and impressive conditions to the continuity of the cultural tradition, to the awe and majesty of the society itself, emphasizing the subordination of the individual to the group at large and hence the mysteriousness, wonder, and sacredness of the whole individual-society relationship. In Australia, the most sacred part of the whole initiation ritual is when the boys are shown the *churinga,* which are at the same time their own souls and the souls of the tribe which came into existence at the creation of the world. Citizenship, being an awesome and mysterious business in any culture, cannot be imparted or taught or instilled in a secular atmosphere; it must be imparted in an atmosphere replete with symbolism and mystery. Whether it can be taught at all without heavy emphasis on its otherworldliness, without heavy sacred emphasis, whether the teaching of citizenship can ever be a warm, friendly, loving, cozy, and undisturbing process, is a question I leave to the educators. Primitive societies obviously do not believe it can be taught that way, as is proved by the fact that they never try.

9. One last point, implied in much of the above but worth special mention, is the rather surprising fact that technological training, training in "getting a living," is absent from the initiation curricula, despite its obvious vital importance to the survival of the individual, of the household, and of the tribe or society. Mastery of the food-obtaining techniques by the children is left to the hit-or-miss, highly individualistic teaching processes of the home, to the peer groups, and to the whimsies of relatives or friends. The reason for this omission from the socially regulated curricula of the initiation schools is, I

think, pretty clear. In the simpler societies there is nothing particularly mysterious, nothing spiritual or otherwordly about getting a living, or hunting or gardening or cattle-herding. It is true that there is apt to be a lot of magical practice mixed up with these things, but even this heavy magical element is conceived in very secular and individualistic terms. That is, it either works or doesn't work in particular cases, and each man or each household or clan has its own garden magic or cattle magic or hunting magic which differs from the next man's or household's or clan's magic. Dobu, for instance, is a culture riddled with garden magic; so is that of the Trobriands, but each group's magic is individually owned and comparisons of magic are even made between group and group. For this reason, garden skills or hunting skills, even though they include magical elements, can still safely be left by society to the private level of transmission and teaching. Public control, public supervision is minimal.

This leads to two further conclusions, or at least suggestions. (1) On this line of analysis, we can conclude the primitive societies, despite their marginal subsistence and the fact that they are frequently close to the starvation point, devote more care and attention, *as societies,* to the production of good citizens, than to the production of good technicians, and therefore they can be said to value good citizenship more highly than they value the production of good food producers. Can this be said for modern societies, including our own? (2) This relative lack of interest in standardizing subsistence-training, while insisting at the same time on standardizing training in the ideological aspects of culture, may go a long way toward enabling us to explain the old sociological problem called cultural lag. Everybody who has taken an introductory course in social science is acquainted with the fact that change in technology is easier to achieve, and takes place with less resistance than change in nontechnological or ideological fields. I do not suggest that what we have been talking about above offers a complete explanation of the culture lag differential, but it may at least be helpful. I would phrase the relation between culture lag and education like this: that because prepuberty education in the simpler societies is loose, unstructured, and left pretty much to individual household choice, and because such laissez faire prepuberty education typically includes food-getting techniques and the use of food-getting tools (spears, harpoons, hoes, etc.), the attitude toward these techniques and tools that the child develops is a secular one and he carries that secular attitude toward them into his adult life. Hence variations from or alternatives to such tools and techniques are not resisted with anything like the intensity of feeling with which variations from or alternatives to ideological elements will be resisted. From his childhood, the boy believes that in trying to get food anything is a good technique or a good tool, provided only that it works, and he is familiar too with the fact that techniques and tools differ at least slightly from household to household or hunter to hunter. Therefore, as an adult he is, in relation to food-getting techniques and tools, both a secularist and an empiricist, and will adopt the white man's gun or the white man's spade when they are offered without any feeling that he is flouting the tribal gods or the society's conscience. The white man's ideology, or foreign importations in ideology, are treated in quite a different way. They are involved with areas of behavior which have been learned not in the secular, empirical atmosphere of the home and the play groups, but in the awesome, sacred atmosphere of the initiation schools, wherein no individual variation is allowed and the very notion of alternatives is anathema.

To avoid misunderstanding, a brief comment must be made about societies like that of Polynesia and the "schools" of Africa such as the Poro, where specialized technical knowledge is imparted to the adolescent males in special training institutions. The significant point is that in such societies ordinary food-gathering techniques (fishing in Polynesia, gardening in West Africa, cattle-tending in East Africa) are still left to the haphazard teaching methods of the individual household, whereas the craft skills (woodcarving in Polynesia, metalworking in the Poro) are entrusted to vehicles of instruction in which apprenticeship, passing of exams, standardized curricula, unfamiliar or nonintimate teachers, heavy emphasis on ritual and the sacred character of the esoteric knowledge which is being imparted, and the dangers of the slightest variation from the traditional techniques of the craft are all prominent. In such societies, despite the inclusion of some technology in the "schools," basic food-getting techniques remain in the common domain of the culture and are picked up by children haphazardly—only the special craft knowledge is sacredly imparted. (Even as late as Henry VIII's England the crafts were called the "mysteries," the two words being apparently interchangeable.)

To conclude then, we may pull most of the above together into one final summary. In primitive society there are two vehicles of education, the prepuberty process and the postpuberty process. No Western writer has ever succeeded in contrasting them as much as they need to be contrasted, because they are in every possible respect the Alpha and Omega of each other. In time of onset, atmosphere, personnel, techniques of instruction, location, curriculum, the two vehicles represent opposite poles. Everything that is done in or through one vehicle is the antithesis of what is done in the other. Standardization of experience and uniformity of training is markedly present in the postinitiation experience: it is markedly absent in the prepuberty experience of the growing child. If this is accepted as a base line, it has very important implications for the whole field of personality studies, especially for those studies which seem to claim that personality is very homogeneous in the simpler societies and for those allied studies which allege that child training and growing up in primitive society are very different from their equivalents in modern Western cultures. It is suggestive also as a base for attempting to answer a question that nobody yet attempted to answer: Why do individuals in simple cultures differ from each other so markedly in personality traits, despite their common cultural conditioning? And it furnishes us finally with another link in the complicated chain of phenomena which exists between the problem of personality formation and the problem of culture change.

All these things are brought together, and indeed the whole of this paper is held together by one single thread—namely, that childhood experience is part of the secular world, postpuberty experience part of the sacred world. What is learned in the secular world is learned haphazardly, and varies greatly from individual to individual. Therefore no society can standardize that part of the child's learning which is acquired under secular circumstances. My only claim for this paper is that the use of this starting point for a discussion of primitive education enables us to obtain some insights into educational and cultural processes which are not provided by any alternative starting point.

References

Gesell, Arnold, and Frances L. Ilg, 1946, *The Child from Five to Ten.* New York: Harper & Row.

Hart, C. W. M., 1954, "The Sons of Turimpi," *American Anthropologist* 56:242–261.

———, and Arnold R. Pilling, 1960, *The Tiwi of North Australia.* CSCA. New York: Holt, Rinehart and Winston, Inc.

Herskovits, Melville J., 1948, *Man and His Works.* New York: Alfred A. Knopf, Inc.

Landtmann, Gunnar, 1927, *The Kiwai Papuans of British New Guinea.* London: The Macmillan Company.

Pettit, George A., 1946, "Primitive Education in North America," *University of California Publications in American Archaeology and Ethnology* 43:182.

Piaget, Jean, 1929, *The Child's Conception of the World.* New York: Harcourt, Brace Jovanovich.

———, 1932, *The Moral Judgment of the Child.* London: Routledge & Kegan Paul.

Schapera, I., 1940, *Married Life in an African Tribe.* London: Sheridan House.

Van Gennep, Arnold, 1909, *Les rites de passage.* Paris: E. Nourry. Translated paperback edition, 1960, Chicago: University of Chicago Press.

PETER S. SINDELL/*McGill University*

21 *Some Discontinuities in the Enculturation of Mistassini Cree Children**

> The establishment of Western schools, especially boarding schools, and curricula in non-Western societies is likely to constitute an extreme type of cultural discontinuity and may do much to force "either-or" choices on their learners (DuBois 1955:102).

Some of the discontinuities which five- or six-year-old Mistassini children experience when they first attend the residential school at La Tuque will be described in this chapter. The world in which these children live before starting school is almost wholly Cree in character. The language spoken at home is Cree, and preschool children have little direct interaction with Euro-Canadians, or "whites." For the small Cree child the most striking figure in the white world is probably the *wabinkiyu,* a form of bogeyman who is thought of as white. When children misbehave parents frequently tell their children that the wabinkiyu is going to take them away.

In the preschool period the children have clear-cut traditional models for identification: parents, grandparents, elder siblings, and other close kin. Most of these kinsmen display behavior and attitudes which conform to traditional Cree values and role expectations.[1] In addition, these kinsmen reward their children, implicitly and explicitly, for conformity to traditional norms.

When the children enter school they must act according to norms which

---

* Printed with permission of the Director of the Canadian Research Center for Anthropology. The author of this paper is a Ph.D. candidate in the Department of Anthropology, Stanford University, Stanford, California, and has been associated with the McGill-Cree Project as a research assistant since July 1966. The research reported on this paper has been supported by the U.S. National Institute of Mental Health grant number MH 13076-01, which is attached to the author's NIMH Pre-Doctoral Fellowship, number 5-F1-MH-24,080-04. This support and the assistance provided by the staff of the McGill-Cree Project are gratefully acknowledged. The author would also like to express his deep appreciation to the Rev. J. E. DeWolf and Mrs. Cynthia Clinton, respectively principal and senior teacher of the LaTuque Indian Residential School.

[1] This is changing now to a certain extent since some of the older children, who have been to school for many years, act in ways which are not traditional. Therefore, they provide their younger siblings with other models for emulation and identification.

contradict a great deal of what they have learned before, master a body of knowledge completely foreign to them, and communicate in an incomprehensible language in a strange environment.

In this chapter I shall discuss self-reliance and dependence, the character of interpersonal relations, cooperation and competition, the expression and inhibition of aggression, and role expectations for children. For each topic the traditional milieu and the first year in the school environment will be compared and contrasted.[2]

As the children attend school, they form ties with their teachers and counselors and learn more about Euro-Canadian culture. Eventually, older students face situations different from those they faced as small children. Upon reaching adolescence, most students experience a conflict in identity which reflects the cultural discontinuities they experience in school, and in alternating between the urban residential school in winter and the trading post during the summer.

The data upon which the following discussion is based were gathered during fieldwork at Mistassini Post and at the La Tuque Indian Residential School from July 1966, to September 1967.[2] The school is operated by the Anglican Church of Canada for the Indian Affairs Branch. It is located in La Tuque, P.Q., which is 180 miles northeast of Montreal and 300 miles south of Mistassini Post by road. Most Mistassini Cree children between the ages of six and sixteen attend the residential school for ten months of each year while their parents go into the bush to hunt and trap. Other children from Mistassini attend the day school at the Post or attend high school in Sault Ste. Marie, Ontario, while living with white families. Only since 1963, when the La Tuque school opened, have the majority of Mistassini children attended school on a regular basis.

In studying the children, interviews were conducted with the children, their parents, teacher, and counselors before, during, and after school. In addition, a series of behavior-rating forms was utilized with the counselors and teacher and hypotheses about the role of imitation and modeling in acculturation were tested in an experiment. Finally, observational protocols were collected on the children's behavior at the Post and in school. The theoretical framework utilized in the study is that of social learning theory as developed by Bandura and Walters (1963). This theory stresses the im-

---

[2] This chapter was written while the author was in the field, therefore many aspects of the shift from the traditional context to the school environment are not dealt with here. Furthermore, many of the ideas expressed must be considered preliminary until further analysis of the data is completed. The usual biographical apparatus is also attenuated for this reason.

I would like to state that my understanding of Cree culture and enculturation has been greatly enriched by reading the works of A. Irving Hallowell on the Ojibwa, George and Louise Spindler on the Menomini, and Edward and Jean Rogers on the Mistassini. The works of Albert Bandura in the field of social learning theory have also influenced my thinking considerably.

portance of such concepts as modeling, imitation, and social reinforcement in the analysis of behavioral and attitudinal change.

The study of the thirteen children who entered school for the first time in September 1966 is that of the first generation of people who will receive extensive formal education. Many of the cultural conflicts discussed below adumbrate those which the children will face as adolescents and adults when they attempt to adapt changing economic and social conditions in the Waswanipi-Mistassini region.

Self-reliance and Dependence

Before Cree children enter school they experience few limits on their behavior. As infants they are fed on demand. When they grow older they eat when they feel hungry and are free to choose from whatever food is available. Usually something—bannock, dried fish, or dried meat—is readily available. Sleeping too is not rigidly scheduled; and the children simply go to sleep when they are tired.

Further, children are free to explore their natural surroundings, either alone or with siblings or playmates. There are no demarcated territorial boundaries which limit their wanderings at the Post. The number of children in any particular hunting group varies, and therefore, a child may spend much or all of the winter without playmates from his own age group. As a result, children learn to depend upon themselves for amusement. They learn to utilize whatever is available—an old tin stove, a few soft drink bottles, a dead bird, sticks, or stones. Anything the child can reach is a legitimate object for play. If the object is dangerous, parents divert the child's attention or take the object away, but do not reprimand the child. For instance, two- or three-year-old children often handle or play with axes. In general, the only limits placed on a child's behavior relate to specific environmental dangers, for example, children are not allowed go out in boats alone.

Whereas at home the children have experienced few limits on their freedom of action, at school there are many. In order to cope with the large number of children (277 at the time the study was made), the school requires them to conform to many routines. They must eat three times a day at specified hours, must wake up and go to sleep at set times, and must learn to obey many other seemingly arbitrary rules. For example, children are not allowed in the front foyer of the dormitory and are not allowed to use the front stairway. Their environment is circumscribed also by the boundary of the school yard. Occasionally the children leave the school property but only in the company of an adult.

The child is dependent upon others to satisfy almost all of his needs. He must depend on the counselor in his living group ("wing") for clean clothes, soap, toothpaste, and even toilet paper when it runs out. Furthermore, he must line up to receive these supplies at the counselor's convenience. Practically the first English phrase which every child learns is "line up!"

The school, then, reinforces the children into submissive, nonexploratory behavioral patterns. These contravene their previous experiences, which led to self-reliant and exploratory behaviors highly adaptive for life in the bush.

Interpersonal Relations

After a child is weaned he is cared for not only by his mother but increasingly by a wide range of other kin, such as older siblings, young uncles and aunts, and grandparents. Consequently, each child forms close ties with several kinsmen. Fairly frequent shifts in residence and in hunting group composition, early death, and the Cree patterns of adoption, mitigate against the development of extreme dependency on only one or two members of the nuclear family. In fact, it seems likely that some frustration of dependency needs results from the disruption of social relationships noted above. Parents and children interact primarily within networks of close kin. Thus, before they go to school, children gain little experience in interacting with people with whom they do not have close affective ties.

As children enter the school at La Tuque, they interact primarily in the context of large groups: the school class, the wings, and the age groups— Junior Girls (age six to eight) and Junior Boys (age six to ten). The children sleep in rooms with siblings of the same sex, but due to differing schedules on most days they see them only at meals and early in the morning. Since practically all activities are segregated by sex, brothers and sisters have few opportunities to talk to each other. Thus, children's social ties begin to shift from warm affective relations with a small multigenerational kin group comprised of both sexes to shallow contacts with a large peer group of the same sex. Preston notes the implications of this shift for the internalization of social controls (1966:6).

While their peer group expands, the number of adults with whom the children interact shrinks. Each beginning pupil is cared for by only two or three adults: teacher, wing counselor, and Junior counselor. Since each wing counselor is also responsible for an age group, one of the wing counselors is the Junior counselor.

With a large number of children competing for a single adult's attention in any given situation, the children learn to beg for nurturance which they could take for granted at home. Dependent behavior, such as crying and yelling, is reinforced as the children discover its effectiveness in eliciting a response from the adult. At home self-reliance and independence are valued and, therefore, crying is ignored from an early age and children learn not to cry. Children learn in school that the smallest scratch will elicit a great deal of concern because the counselors fear that impetigo will develop. Thus, their early training in silently enduring pain is also contradicted.

In summary, the children openly express far more dependence in school than at home, and this dependence is focused on two or three adults rather than upon a multigenerational kin group. At home the children have supportive relationships but these do not involve a high level of overt expression of dependence (see Spindler 1963:384). Furthermore, the children interact with others far more than they did at home and come to need a high degree of social stimulation.

Cooperation and Competition

Most of the tasks which a child performs at home are done cooperatively and contribute to the welfare of the whole group, usually a nuclear or extended family. Children perform these tasks with siblings, parents or other kin. Cooperation in hunting and in household chores is extremely adaptive since it makes the most efficient use of the group's limited labor resources. Sharing food as well as labor is of major importance in traditional Cree culture. Religious values reinforce this since *"mistapeo,"* the soul spirit, "is pleased with generosity, kindness and help to others" (Speck 1935:44).

Children observe this extensive sharing and cooperation within the kin group and participate directly in it. For example, during the summer, young children often are used to carry gifts of fish, bannock, fowl, and so on, between kin. Observations indicate that the children themselves usually share food and toys readily.

Competition rather than cooperation is the keynote of school life. In class the students are encouraged to compete with each other in answering questions, and those who answer most promptly and correctly gain the teacher's attention and win her approval. Both in school and in the dormitory the children must constantly compete for places in line. Those who are first in line get their food or clothing first or get outside to play soonest. Also, because the dormitory is understaffed, each child must compete with many others to ensure that the counselor attends to his individual needs.

Although the teacher finds it difficult to stimulate many children to respond competitively in class, many older children learn to compete aggressively for food and refuse to share their belongings.

Expression and Inhibition of Aggression

Inhibiting the overt expression of aggression is highly valued in Cree culture and serves to maintain positive affective ties among kinsmen, particularly within the hunting-trapping group. Aggression is defined broadly by the Cree and includes not only fighting but also directly contradicting someone else, refusing a direct request, and raising one's voice inappropriately. (These statements apply particularly to relations between kinsmen.) These forms of behavior are unacceptable except if one is drunk and, thus, considered not responsible for his actions. Fighting when drunk is common and appears to arouse anxiety in children observing this. Laughing at people's mistakes or foibles is not usually defined as aggressive behavior. Gossip, teasing, and the threat of witchcraft are covert means of expressing aggression which are prevalent among the Cree. During enculturation fighting and quarreling are punished.

Punishment seems to be infrequent and usually consists of teasing, ridicule, threats of corporal punishment or reprisals by wabinkiyu, and, occasionally, yelling. But corporal punishment is rare and most often is limited to a light slap with an open hand on top of the head or just above the ear.

In contrast to what they have been taught at home, in school, the children learn to express aggression openly. Counselors and teachers disapprove greatly of the children's constant "tattle taling," which serves to express aggression covertly. On the other hand, overtired and frustrated with the demands of controlling large numbers of children, the adults in the school often yell at the children, speak to them sternly, and, occasionally, swat them. Television and observation of white children are other sources of models for openly aggressive behavior. It is apparent from observing the children that these television models, such as Batman and Tarzan, are very important. Mistassini children also learn to express aggression openly because they are forced to defend themselves against some of the more aggressive children from Dore Lake.

Role Expectations for Children

Cree children learn very early in life the basic components of adult roles through observing their parents and elder siblings. As soon as a child is able to walk he is given small tasks to perform such as carrying a little water or a few pieces of wood. If he does not perform these tasks the child is not punished because Cree parents think he is not old enough to "understand" yet. When the child walks out of the tent for the first time on his own, the "Infants' Rite" is held.

> The essence of the baby's rite is the symbolization of the child's future role as an adult. A boy "kills," brings the kill to camp, and distributes the meat; a girl carries in firewood and boughs. (Rogers and Rogers 1963:20)

All but one of the thirteen children in the sample participated in this rite.

At about five or six years of age children begin to perform chores regularly and are punished if they do not obey. Among their new chores are caring for smaller siblings and washing dishes; in addition, they begin to carry significant quantities of wood, water, and boughs. Children also begin to contribute food to the family at this age. They pick berries, snare rabbits, hunt birds, and sometimes accompany their parents into the bush to check traps or to get wood, water, or boughs. At approximately the same time as the child begins playing a more responsible role in performing tasks, the parents believe that his ability to conceptualize develops.

Parents conceive of their children as developing gradually into responsible adults. Much of the children's play imitates the activities of their parents and, thus, rehearses adult roles. For example, little girls make bannock out of mud, make hammocks and baby sacks for their dolls, and pretend to cook. Little boys hunt birds and butterflies, play with toy boats, and pull cardboard boxes and other objects as if they were pulling toboggans. Little boqs and girls sometimes play together in small "play" tents which their parents make for them.

On the other hand, when they go to school, counselors and teachers expect children to live in a world of play unrelated to their future participation in adult society. There are few chores to do and these are peripheral to satisfaction of the basic needs—food, heat, and water—which concerned them at home. Keeping one's room clean and tidy and making one's bed are the principal chores which smaller children are expected to do. Young children are expected to spend most of their time playing and going to school. In school and in the dormitory most play involves large groups of thirty to forty children and consists mainly of organized games such as "Cat and Mouse," "Simon Says," "London Bridge," and relay races. When play is nondirective children frequently resort to imitative play as they did before coming to school, but sometimes with a new content, for example, playing "Batman," "Spaceghost," or "Counselors."

In discussing the child-rearing practices of some societies like the Cree, Benedict says: "The essential point of such child training is that the child is from infancy continuously conditioned to responsible social participation, while at the same time the tasks that are expected of it are adapted to its capacities" (1954:23–24).

Attending school radically disrupts this development. After only one year of school parents report that their children "only want to play" and are not interested in performing their chores. Thus, children have already begun to reject their parents' definitions of proper behavior. This kind of intergenerational conflict increases dramatically with each year of school experience. It is exacerbated because the children are in school all winter and thus, fail to learn the technical skills related to hunting and trapping as they mature. This has serious implications for identity conflicts in adolescence since the children are unable to fulfill their parents' expectations. Children who do not attend school are able to assume adult economic roles at about the onset of puberty. For example, boys begin to trap seriously and girls can contribute significantly to the cleaning and preparation of pelts.

Conclusions

Traditional Cree encultration takes place primarily in the context of multigenerational kin groups and stresses food sharing and cooperative labor, indirect rather than open expression of aggression, and self-reliance. Interpersonal relations within the kin group are supportive, but verbal expression of dependence is discouraged. Children are viewed as "little adults" and contribute labor and food to the kin group commensurate with their level of maturity. Children's self-reliance is placed in the service of the kin group.

During their first year of residential school the beginners experience radical discontinuities in their enculturation. The values, attitudes, and behavioral expectations which motivate the dormitory counselors and teacher in their interaction with the children differ sharply from those of Mistassini Cree parents. In school, children have few tasks and these rarely relate to the welfare of the whole group. Competition and direct expression of aggression are reinforced rather than punished. The children interact primarily in large groups—school class, age group, and wing—and come to need a high rate of social stimulation. Dependence becomes focused on two or three adults, and overt expression of dependence increases since it is effective in eliciting nurturant behavior.

As the data presented in the body of the chapter make clear, during their first year of formal education Mistassini beginners are exposed to great cultural discontinuity. They learn new ways of behaving and thinking and are rewarded for conformity to norms which contradict those which they learned before coming to school. Consequently, after only one year of school they have already begun to change significantly toward acting in ways which are appropriate in Euro-Canadian culture but inappropriate in their own. As they continue their education this process accelerates. After alternating for five or six years between the traditional milieu in the summer and the urban residential school in the winter severe conflicts in identity arise.

In the six years before starting school the children learn behavioral patterns and values which are highly functional for participating as adults in the traditional hunting-trapping life of their parents. Because they must go to school their development into trappers or wives of trappers is arrested. Prolonged residential school experience makes it difficult if not impossible for children to participate effectively in the hunting-trapping life of their parents. Not only do they fail to learn the requisite technical skills, but they acquire new needs and aspirations which cannot be satisfied on the trapline. Yet most Mistassini parents want their children to return to the bush. It remains to be seen how the students will resolve their dilemma.

References

Bandura, Albert, and Richard H. Walters, 1963, *Social Learning and Personality Development.* New York: Holt, Rinehart and Winston, Inc.

Benedict, Ruth, 1954, "Continuities and Discontinuities in Cultural Conditioning." In Margaret Mead and Martha Wolfenstein, eds., *Childhood in Contemporary Cultures.* Chicago: University of Chicago Press.

DuBois, Cora, 1955, "Some Notions on Learning Intercultural Understanding." In G. D. Spindler, ed., *Education and Anthropology.* Stanford, Calif.: Stanford University Press, p. 89–105.

Preston, Richard J., 1966, "Peer Group versus Trapline; Shifting Directions in Cree Socialization." Paper presented at the Annual Meeting of the Pennsylvania Sociological Society, Haverford, Pa., October 15 (mimeographed).

Rogers, Edward S., and Jean H. Rogers, 1963, "The Individual in Mistassini Society from Birth to Death." In *Contributions to Anthropology,* 1960, Part II, pp. 14–36. (Bulletin 190, National Museum of Canada) Ottawa: Roger Duhamel.

Speck, Frank, 1935, *The Savage Hunters of the Labrador Peninsula.* Norman: University of Oklahoma Press.

Spindler, George D., 1963, "Personality, Sociocultural System, and Education among the Menomini." In G. D. Spindler, ed., *Education and Culture.* New York: Holt, Rinehart and Winston, Inc., pp. 351–399.

PREVIEW

Part B: Complex modern societies

Once upon a time, not too long ago, when anthropologists were studying and writing about tribal and peasant cultures in far off places, it seemed apparent that the real business of the anthropologists was certainly not at home and not really any place very "civilized". Now all that has changed and anthropologists are underfoot everywhere—in factories, business offices, welfare agencies, cocktail lounges, religious movements, construction gangs, and schools—at home and abroad.

The four chapters of Part B range through eight modern complex societies, three of them European, two Asiatic, and one in the United States of America. The first chapter by G. & L. Spindler compares two similar elementary schools, one in southern Germany and one in north-central Wisconsin. They find that these schools are structurally similar, occupy similar roles in the region, and even have ethnically similar school populations. The cultures of the classrooms are, however, quite different, in fact, contrastive. We believe that the observed differences reflect the respective national dialogues. We are not trying to recreate national character as a foundational concept, but we do feel that the fit between the themes of classroom action and national preoccupations centering particularly on the relations between the individual and authority, are too obvious to ignore. It is not necessary to posit that the classrooms we studied in Schoenhausen and Roseville represent, respectively, German and American national dialogues, but to us, it makes the comparison more interesting. Even if we disregard such questions we find that the comparison gives us a new perspective on our own process of schooling.

Marida Hollos analyzes the experiences of rural children in Norway and Hungary to see if they are, as often believed, less cognitively able due to being deprived of intensive peer relationships and other experiences possible in urban situations but not in the rural context. She finds that this is not the case and provides explanations that take into account the specific features of family life and home environment.

James Robinson applies a model of social typing and its consequences that has been productive in studies of American schools. He concludes that it works as well when applied to a Korean school. The social typing of children by teachers has much the same consequence as it does in the schools of the United States.

Thomas Rohlen describes how a Japanese bank does some moral education on its employees. The situation and its purposes are very different than anything comparable in the United States. There are parallels between seishin kyoyku and the initiation experience of Hopi and Tiwi pre-adolescents. The initiates in all three situations experience discomfort and anxiety. The resolution of this dissonance, we hypothesize, creates commitment to the cultural and institutional symbols and expectations that produce the initiatory experience.

The chapters of Part B give us some understanding of educational and cultural co-variation transculturally. They also stimulate new insights into the educational process in our own society.

The Editor

GEORGE and LOUISE SPINDLER/*Stanford University*

22   In Prospect for a Controlled Cross-cultural Comparison of Schooling: Schoenhausen and Roseville

Introduction

In "Roots Revisited: Three Decades of Perspective:, presented as the retiring President's talk at the CAE meetings in 1983 (see Chapter 4), four concerns were listed that were pronounced in the 1954 Stanford Education-Anthropology Conference (G. Spindler 1955, 1984). They are: the search for a philosophical as well as theoretical articulation of education and anthropology; the necessity for sociocultural contextualization of the educative process; the relation of education to "culturally phrased" phases of the life cycle; and the nature of intercultural understanding and learning.

We intend to take up an aspect of the latter in this chapter. We are doing a controlled comparison of two elementary schools, one in Germany (Schoenhausen) and one in the United States (Roseville). We will discuss some of the results of this research and the methods employed, focusing on the use of film both as a record of activity and as stimuli for interviews. The argument we wish to promote in this chapter is that a cross-cultural perspective is central to the anthropology of education, in fact that it is the *sine qua non* of our discipline. It has become less central in our work and talk as educational anthropologists during the past decade or so. We believe that it should become central once again.

For support for the contention that concerns with cross-cultural study and understanding have diminished during recent decades we refer you to the review of current ethnographic work on education as a part of qualitative research by Goetz and LeCompte (1984), to David Fetterman's edited volume on evaluative ethnography (1983), to G. Spindler's edited volume on the ethnography of schooling (1982), and to Elizabeth Eddy's review of educational anthropology in the *Anthropology and Education Quarterly* (1985) (see Chapter 1). It seems clear that we educational anthropologists and

A version of this paper was presented at the 84th annual meeting of the American Anthropological Association at Washington, D.C. in the invited session, "Retrospective and Prospective on Education and Anthropology: Four Views," organized by Cathie Jordan for the Council on Anthropology and Education.

ethnographers have shifted decisively to concerns with classrooms, schools and schooling in our own society, that we have lost or blurred our focus on culture, and that a clear cross-cultural or comparative focus is notable for its absence. Of course implicit cross-cultural and comparative dimensions do appear in many current writings when we talk about schooling in multi-cultural America, but they are rarely in sharp, explicit focus. Some of our colleagues such as Marian Dobbert and her associates are including explicit cross-cultural dimensions in their projects (Dobbert 1984). We are speaking of broad trends.

Schoenhausen, Germany and Roseville, USA

Our most recent research in Germany was in the spring of 1985 but we need to say a few words about our previous work there. In previous field trips to Germany we established the sociocultural base line of the Grundschule (elementary school) in the village community of Schoenhausen, and that of Schoenhausen in the Rems Valley region stretching southeast from Stuttgart (G. Spindler 1973, 1974; G. and L. Spindler 1978). A migration and assimilation model guided our earlier work, as we researched the adaptation of children of the migrants to West Germany after World War II and the assimilation of the children in the Rems Valley schools of Schoenhausen and Burgbach. The second phase of our research explored the effects of a massive educational reform over a period of nearly a decade (1968-1977), using both ethnography and the instrumental activities model (see Chapter 3) as sources of methods (G. and L. Spindler 1982 and 1987c). It is relevant to this discussion, particularly because it is an indication of the great staying power of culture, that our results indicate that there were no essential changes in the basic elements of cultural transmission in the school as a result of the very extensive and expensive reform and no significant shift in choices of life styles or instrumentalities leading to them excepting that they tended to become more conservative during the decade in which the reform was implemented (G. and L. Spindler 1987a). The third phase of our work focused on teachers' styles in classrooms and instructional management. We found that though there were as many different styles of teaching as there were teachers the underlying interactions and organization of cultural experience remained quite constant (G. and L. Spindler 1982). The fourth and present phase of research is devoted to a comparative study of the influence of culture on the classroom behavior of teachers and children. To this end we have carried out field research in the Roseville Elementary School in Wisconsin in the autumns of 1983 and 1984 and in the Schoenhausen school in the spring of 1985 (G. and L. Spindler 1987a).

Since we wanted to make a controlled comparison we needed a community and school comparable in size to Schoenhausen—one serving a non-urban district and that was preparing children for both rural and more urban careers. The fact that Roseville's population is predominantly ethnically German was an added bonus.

Schoenhausen is a town of about 3,000 population not far from Stuttgart in the fertile valley of the Rems River (Remstal). It is one of the many *Weinorte*—formerly nucleated villages where the main business of traditional agriculture was the growing of grapes for the making of wine. Today the *Weinberge* (hillside vineyards) still surround the town and the vintners are still living in town and working their holdings. The majority of the population, however, are either natives who no longer work the land or migrants and their descendants from other parts of Germany who settled there after World War II. Most of those who do not work the land commute to work in Remstal offices and factories only a few kilometers distant.

Roseville is a village of about 500 people in a school district in northern Wisconsin that is comparable in size to that of Schoenhausen. The area, like Schoenhausen's, is agricultural, but much less intensively cultivated, and consists of small dairy farms and woodland that still furnishes raw materials for a local lumber mill. About a third of the working population of the district commutes to work in nearby towns, some of them more than forty miles distant.

The elementary schools of Schoenhausen and Roseville have almost exactly the same nmber of students (120) in four grades. Roseville school also has a kindergarten, lacking in the Schoenhausen school. The teaching staff is about the same size (7) but Roseville school has more special staff coming in to work with learning disabled, instruct the band, carry on weekly sessions on self-development, etc. These kinds of functions are either carried out by regular staff at Schoenhausen, or children go to other places in the community for them. The curriculum of the two schools is broadly similar, being mainly engaged with acquiring basic skills. The major difference is that the school day at Schoenhausen starts at 8:30 in the morning and ends at 11:30, when the children go home to eat lunch, for six days a week, including Saturdays. There is a little more time at Roseville for "extras". The Roseville school days starts at 8:30 and lasts until 3:30, five days each week, excluding Saturdays. Most children at Roseville school eat lunch there. Another difference and one of great significance to the children in particular is that there is a large, well-lighted, and modern gymnasium attached to Roseville School. There is nothing like that at Schoenhausen. Children go to the *Turnhalle* (broadly equivalent to a gymnasium) in the community a few blocks from the school. It includes an indoor swimming pool, lacking at Roseville.

The concern with the influence of culture on schooling has, of course, been present from the beginning of our research in Schoenhausen, but until 1983, we lacked a specific site from the United States for cross-cultural comparison. The site at Roseville has afforded us an invaluable perspective. Comparison of the cultural influence in the two schools is carried forward in a chapter by us in

Interpretive Ethnography of Education at Home and Abroad (1987). We will summarize the differences below.

Some Emergent Cultural Differences Between Schoenhausen and Roseville

Schoenhausen behavior patterns: active, teacher centered, frontal focussed. Intensive competition for teacher approval. Intense, high-key and noisy. Chaotic when teacher absent. High, uniform standards collectively attained. Individual brought up to class standard with individual help by teacher.

Roseville behavior patterns: Low-key, small group discussion and individual work occur simultaneously, less overt, "feverish" competition. Teacher approval not the main reward—rather, the chance to work on something one chooses to do, when the required work is finished. Peers teach each other. Less teacher centered than in Schoenhausen. Less noisy. Classroom remains in order and children continue working when teacher absent.

Schoenhausen cultural knowledge: "Katzenjammer Kids" assumption: children are naturally lively and mischievous. When external authority is not present and monitoring activity is not being carried on children will naturally break loose. Teacher is instigator and leader of learning activity. Class hours must be filled with directed activity. Uniform collective achievement is the aim. The individual is given attention so that he or she can be brought up to group standards.

Roseville cultural knowledge: Self-control is to be expected. Authority is (relatively) internalized. Teachers expect classrooms to stay in order when they are absent from the room. Misdemeanors are regarded as a violation of an understanding reached between teacher and child, and as an exhibition of immature behavior. Individuals are the end goal of teaching and learning. The group exists in order to make individual life and achievement possible—as contexts with sufficient order to permit the pursuit of individual goals. Individuals will naturally vary with respect to both quality and quantity of production.

These behavioral and ideational characteristics were established by many hours of classroom observation, the repeated review of films, and interviews with teachers *before* our most recent field research in the spring of 1985. The results of this latter research gave us additional data and an understanding of a somewhat different viewpoint.

Methodology

Our methodology was enhanced in the Schoenhausen school in the 1977 field trip by our first use of film to record key episodes in classroom behavior (G. and L. Spindler 1978). The permanent record of action in these films permitted us to review repeatedly what we had observed, and made it possible to determine whether others noted the same behavior and interpreted it as we did. We have shown these films to groups of students and colleagues for this purpose. A high degree of agreement in noting and interpreting behavior has been consistently exhibited.

Another potential use of these films occurred to us and in the 1981 field research we screened the films of their own classrooms for the Schoenhausen teachers and recorded their reactions. That experiment was a partial success. The individual teachers viewing films of their own classrooms and others' teaching, were very interested but not particularly articulate in explaining what they did or how they felt about various episodes. Group showings were more productive. Teachers commented excitedly about the behavior of individual children and the class as a whole, as well as the teaching methods used in both their own classrooms and those of their colleagues. Intense discussions ensued that gave us a more intimate look into teacher perceptions, understandings, and assumptions—into the knowledge (and we term it cultural knowledge) that they employ in the management of themselves and their classrooms as teachers. Though we had conducted formal interviews with each teacher and repeatedly observed in their classrooms, we derived an inside perspective that was different enough to be significant. We term this usage the use of films as "evocative stimuli" for interviews and discussion.

The Use of Film in Reflective, Crosscultural Interviewing[1]

In our *1985* trip our procedure was different. We had filmed all of the classrooms in the Roseville school (KG through 8) as well as activities in the gym, playground, the Christmas program, and during lunchtime, during our two autumns of field research (1983 and 1984). We had already shown the Schoenhausen films to the Roseville teachers before we left for Germany and recorded their reactions.

When we arrived in Germany in April, 1985, we immediately met with the equivalent of our superintendent of schools for the area *(Regierungschuledirektor)*, two members of his staff, and the principal *(Rektor)* of the Schoenhausen school, to discuss our plans for research and to receive permission to carry it out. The Schuledirektor and his two staff members were so interested in the possibility of viewing films from a small

---

[1] "Reflective interviewing" is not to be confused with "reflexive"—narrative ethnography. Though the two have something in common in that both modes involve reflection on experience, *reflective interviewing* is intended to elicit less personal reactions and "reflections" and is directed at both the reflection of culture in the responses of the informant and the reflections of the informant on behaviors that have pointed cultural implications. (See Ruby, 1982.)

American elementary school that they requested an immediate screening[2]. This was arranged for our third night in Germany. The attending group included all of the five Schoenhausen teachers, the Rektor, ourselves, and the Schuledirektor and his two associates. The proceedings were recorded and constituted in fact our first data gathering session for our 1985 field trip. In the discussion that ensued, that lasted for more than an hour (excluding time for the refreshments of wine, sausage, and various tasty small eatables) the Schuledirektor asked many questions, then launched upon a statement that summed up his reaction. And that reaction was that the Roseville classrooms seemed orderly and the children appeared cooperative but that the dispersion of activity in the room and the relaxed quality of it could only mean that *Leistungsfähigkeit* (productive efficiency) was not being attained. He went further to explain vigorously how classrooms in the German schools were focussed on the attainment of the goals specified in a *Lehrplan* (curriculum plan) for Baden Württemberg (the *Land* of which Schoenhausen is a part), with the overall aim that a common standard for all should be achieved. He asked if Roseville teachers had such a plan, and how it was created if there was one. When he learned that there was, and that the Roseville teachers themselves, together with personnel from the superintendent's office developed it, he expressed surprise. The Lehrerplan for Schoenhausen issues from far above in the hierarchy.

The Schoenhausen teachers and Rektor perceived the Roseville classrooms as self-disciplined, relaxed, *freiwillig* (free-choice oriented), and the children and teachers in them as considerate and friendly with each other. The Rektor in particular was impressed with the relaxed, "conversational", quality of relationships between children and teachers. They also wondered, however, about the goals that were being attained. Both the teachers and the Schuledirektor perceived the same general qualities in the actions filmed in Roseville classrooms but reacted to them somewhat differently.

These perceptions and reactions, produced so quickly in the earliest phase of our work period in Germany, proved to be themes around which all subsequent responses to the Roseville films revolved. The self-discipline, relaxation, cooperation, consideration, dispersion, and free choice of learning activity were seen by every respondent. Teachers said that they would like to

---

[2]We used super 8mm sound-color film throughout our work in both Schoenhausen and Roseville. Video tape would be less expensive and sometimes easier to use, but there are problems in compatibility of equipment overseas. And for use in our own seminars at Stanford and Wisconsin it is much easier to lug around a 25 pound 8mm projector than arrange for video display equipment to be brought in. For public displays it is also true that film offers better resolution than video. The filming itself was usually done with G. Spindler from the outside edges of the classroom group, focussing on the whole group and teacher behavior, and L. Spindler in the inside of the group, focussing on person-to-person interaction.

try *"freiwillig"* (self determined free choice) choices of activities in their classrooms but feared that it would be very difficult for some children to do so, and that disruption and disorientation might occur that would interfere with teaching and learning. With highly specific goals to reach during every hour of instruction, as laid out in the state lesson plan, with instruction limited to 8:30-11:30 a.m. six days a week, they could not afford to lose any time and had to keep instruction on track, they said. They also expressed concerns that if every minute of the class hour was not filled with intensive direct learning activity there would be disruption if not chaos.

These same general perceptions and reactions were shared by the children in grades 1 through 4 who also saw the films and discussed them. The teachers guided discussions with the children after they had viewed the films. Children agreed that the "freiwillig" character of the Roseville classrooms was intriguing but the chances of its working in Schoenhausen were slim. They said that if a person were to walk around the room to go get some materials to work on, on their own, somebody would be sure to stick out their foot and trip them. They also noted many other things, such as black caps on some of the girls (Brownie Day), *Popkorn Tag* (once a week), American Flags and clocks in every room, that adult viewers tended to ignore or overlook. They were enthusiastic about the gym and its use for recesses as well as P.E., and wondered at the school lunch program. It was interesting to see how children's perceptions were both the same as and different than those of adults.

We used the Roseville films, then, as background stimuli for interviews about classroom procedure and rationale, with all of the teachers, the Rektor, and the children of the Schoenhausen school. Our actual interviewing procedure was, however, dependent upon having *both* the Schoenhausen and Roseville experience present in the discussion as a constant frame of reference. We wanted each interview to engage with an active comparison of the two and for the teachers to reflect on the similarities and differences. (We term this procedure "reflective" cross-cultural interviewing). To this end we filmed each class of every teacher. We held one interview before the filming, in which the teacher presented her lesson plan for the hour we were to film, and explained how she would carry it out and how it would fit into the master curriculum guide for Baden Wurttemberg. The plans also included statement of the theme, such as "the significance of water", of a goal "to gain understanding to the process of water circulation in nature", and the *Stunden Verlauf* (course of the hour) — the instructional procedures for the period. These procedures always included: (1) presentation of the problem for the hour; (2) some preliminary demonstration by the teacher; (3) group participation in the activity; (4) written work *(Fixierung* — reinforcement); (5) summation. All activities included all children at the same time and were distinctly teacher managed.

After this interview each period was filmed, following the lesson plans so that each phase of the lesson was recorded.

After the films were developed, usually three days after filming, a second interview was held. We met in the Rektor's apartment where we could view the films in comfort. The interviews centered, in each phase of the lesson, on purposes, rationale, the successes and failures of instruction, and explored the educational philosophy of the teacher. The discussions ranged over many topics, some personal, but mostly professional, but all of them rich.

The major difference between the 1985 interviews and the ones conducted in previous years was the constant comparison between Roseville and Schoenhausen that was explicit in most comments of the teachers about everything. The Schoenhausen teachers saw themselves as goal-directed, and the goals as specifically defined by the general curriculum plan, free to use almost any method to attain those goals, but as centering instruction on teacher leadership and monitoring of all activity. They saw themselves as trying to fill every period right up to the last moment with intense directed activity, preplanned around specific learning goals, and working with the class as a collectivity as well as with individuals, so that all children attain the goal. They did not generally regard this need to fill every class period with teacher-directed activity as an undue imposition of authority but as a necessity imposed by the statement of goals in the Lehrerplan.

There are many other elements that emerged in the interviews. We will mention only the statement in some form common to all, and that is that they would enjoy trying some of the freedom and self-direction obvious in the Roseville films but they would not be able to meet their designated goals if they did and they did not think that some of the children would be able to adjust to such freedom and exercise of free will without disrupting others.

To Sum Up

The following are characteristic of the Schoenhausen school and in the norms maintained by the school director's office as perceived by teachers, the Schuledirektor, and in their own way, by the children: (1) clearly rationalized and specific instructional goals issuing from the upper level of the educational hierarchy; (2) the striving to achieve those goals in the class time allotted; (3) the maintenance of collective achievement standards; (4) the efficient, goal-directed, use of time with no time left over for the exercise of free will and/or disruption; (5) the teachers as constant and active centers of all learning activity; (6) intensive, dynamic activity on the part of children that if uncontrolled, often becomes disruptive and chaotic; (7) the reliance on external, higher authority for goal definition; (8) the wish to experiment with more free choice coupled with the "knowledge" that it won't work.

These perceptions are similar to the observations made by us prior to the 1985 trip but they center more on the goals for teaching and learning and the necessity of constant, directed classroom activity to attain those goals. Our own observations and interpretations focus more on the noisy, to us at times chaotic, behavior that takes place when teacher monitoring ceases or has not yet begun. Our interpretive agenda includes an inference that in Schoenhausen external authority must be imposed to maintain order and that this is assumed to be a "natural" condition (in Schoenhausen), and that in Roseville self control is assumed to be the basis of order and that its development is a major aim of education. There are various levels of manifest and latent, explicit and implicit, in both the statements by the principal actors in these two sites and in our interpretations that need to be worked out as we proceed in our analysis. Nevertheless, taken together they constitute a fairly coherent description of the two situations and the culturally constructed dialogue that takes place within them.

We maintain that these characteristics, both as observed by us through 1985 and as generated by teachers in selective interview, are deeply embedded in German culture and social institutions just as the characteristics described for the Roseville classroom are deeply embedded in American culture and social institutions. They are not amenable to change in the same way that clothing, speech, or even food habits are. They represent long-term stable aspects of German and American cultural tradition, the central features of the persisting national dialogues. They are only partly amenable to manifest, intentional control by the teachers, principals, or higher authority. The school is governed by and transmits these cultural characteristics without their explicit statement as a declared, intentional manifesto.

We do not contend that the Roseville school is typical of American elementary schools, any more than we contend that Schoenhausen is typical of German elementary schools. Both are, however, culturally normative institutions charged with the responsibility for maintaining culturally defined standards and expectations. Dialogue in the classrooms, in administrative direction, and in interaction with the community, is, respectively, an American dialogue and a German dialogue. The features of the American dialogue about which behavior and communication appeared to be centered in the Roseville school are individualism, self-development, self-discipline, and internalized authority. The features of the German national dialogue around which behavior and communication appear to be centered in the Schoenhausen school are collective standards of performance, efficiency in their attainment, and the relationship of individual behavior to external authority. The dialogues and the cultural norms and pivotal concerns that they project vary by region, class, ethnicity, and degree of urbanization, but they revolve around some distinctive commonalities in each cultural framework. That, at least, is our working hypothesis at present.

Work to be Done

We hope to extend the research in both Germany and the United States. In both countries we need to observe, film, and interview teachers in one of the more urbanized schools of the area. Such schools are available in close proximity to both Schoenhausen and Roseville. We can thus keep the general cultural area and its population components constant.

Final Comment

This discussion began with an argument that cross-cultural, comparative research had lagged during the last decade or so and that this was potentially injurious to the state of our discipline. We offered the comments on our research in Schoenhausen and Roseville to give some content to the concept, "cross-cultural, comparative research", as well as to introduce some developments in theory and methodology that we have found intriguing.

While it is true that there is an implicit cross-cultural and comparative perspective in much of the interpretation done by anthropologists in educational settings, wherever they are, including in our own country, there are advantages to be gained by making the cross-cultural and comparative features explicit and as controlled as possible. As stated, we selected the Roseville school and community because it was as close a parallel to the Schoenhausen situation as it was possible to attain in the United States. No attempt at control can be perfect but we agree with Fred Eggan (1954), in his classical article on controlled comparisons, that controls are necessary in order to produce the most useful kinds of comparisons. In our case the controls were exercised over size of school and population of district from which each drew, the rural character of the environment from which the schools draw, the task of the schools, involved as they are in preparation of children for a wide spectrum of careers in the rural-urban sector, and finally even in ethnicity, since many of the children in Roseville are of German descent. It might be more important to control other factors in other studies. But these served our purposes.

The "reflective, cross-cultural interview procedure" stimulated teachers to make many explicit statements that were culturally meaningful without self-consciousness. It isn't that they were self-consciously talking about either German culture or American culture but rather about the things they did and the reasons that they did them that were American or German. We found it difficult under other circumstances to get teachers to talk this way, even though we were on intimate terms, in both situations, with the teachers and administrators. The kinds of talk that we wanted to hear flowed spontaneously and easily and with great involvement on the part of our informants. We feel that this was possible because every statement made was bracketed by observations and images formed from direct, personal exposure to the living documentation of behavior on film.

We found it rewarding not only to collect such stimulating interview material and to further observe the action in both schools, but also to feel that the teachers themselves benefited from the experience. Many teachers in both Schoenhausen and Roseville have commented upon how the cross-cultural exposure (though they didn't phrase it just this way) caused them to look at their own practices with a new perspective. The Roseville teachers began to wonder if they were expecting too much of their children in respect to self-discipline, self-control, and consideration of others. They also began to reflect upon their teaching goals and how they could best attain these goals without diminishing the desirable features of free choice and independent work. The Schoenhausen teachers similarly reflected upon their management of classrooms and instructional materials, and wondered about ways that they might be able to increase independence, free choice, and self-discipline. They also questioned the need for such a tight, goal-oriented curriculum and about the ways in which the goals themselves were formed. This "consciousness-raising" is a by-product of the procedure but could well serve as a major purpose in a more applied research context.

Acknowledgements

The earlier phases of the research in Schoenhausen were supported by the National Science Foundation, the National Institute for Mental Health, the Stanford School of Education Research Fund, and the Wenner-Gren Foundation for Anthropological Research. The latter phases of the research were supported by the Spencer Foundation of Chicago and the Center for Educational Research at the University of Wisconsin, Madison. We gratefully acknowledge this support. We would like also to name the faculty and staff of both the Schoenhausen Grundschule and the Roseville Elementary School but this is impossible since we wish to protect their privacy (the names of the schools are pseudonyms). We do wish, however, to express our deepest gratitude to all of these people who have been so extraordinarily helpful and hospitable. At no time did we experience any feelings of rejection, hostility, or negativism. To the contrary we were welcomed into classrooms, conferences, private conversations, and to homes and public places as friends, colleagues, as well as researchers.

References

Dobbert, Marian L. and Associates, 1983, "Cultural Transmission in Three Societies: Testing a System-Based Field Guide." *Anthropology and Education Quarterly* 15:275-311.

Eddy, Elizabeth H., 1985, "Theory, Research, and Application in Education Anthropology. *Anthropology and Education Quarterly,* (16)2:83-105.

Eggan, Fred, 1954, "Social Anthropology and the Method of Controlled Comparison." *American Anthropologist,* 56:743-763.

Fetterman, David M., 1983, *Educational Ethnographic Evaluation.* Sage Publications.

Goetz, Judith P. and Margaret LeCompte, 1984, *Ethnography and Qualitative Design in Educational Research.* New York: Academic Press, Inc.

Ruby, Jay, ed., 1982, *A Crack in the Mirror: Reflexive Approaches in Anthropology.* Philadelphia: University of Pennsylvania.

Spindler, George D., ed., 1955, *Education and Anthropology.* Stanford University Press.

_____, 1973, *Burgbach: Urbanization and Identity in a German Village.* New York: Holt, Rinehart and Winston.

_____, 1974, "Schooling in Schoenhausen: A Study of Cultural Transmission and Instrumental Adaptation in an Urbanizing German Village." In G. Spindler, ed., *Education and Cultural Process: Toward an Anthropology of Education.* New York: Holt, Rinehart and Winston.

_____, ed., 1982, *Doing the Ethnography of Schooling: Educational Anthropology in Action,* New York: Holt, Rinehart and Winston.

_____, Spindler, George D., 1984, "Roots Revisited: Three Decades of Perspectives." *Anthropology and Education Quarterly,* 15:2-10.

_____, and Louise Spindler, 1978, "Die Vermittlung von Kulturellen Werten und Spezifichen Anpassungmechanismus in eine Dorf mit zunehemend städtischen Gerpräge." In *Rheinsches Jahrbuch für Volkskunde.* Ed. M. Matter. Universität Bonn: 85-96.

_____, and _____, 1982, "Roger Harker and Schoenhausen: From Familiar to Strange and Back Again." In *Doing the Ethnography of Schooling: Educational Anthropology in Action.* George Spindler, ed., New York: Holt, Rinehart and Winston.

_____, and _____, 1987a, "Schoenhausen Revisited and the Rediscovery of Culture." In *Interpretive Ethnography of Education at Home and Abroad.* George and Louise Spindler, editors. New Jersey: Lawrence Erlbaum and Associates, Inc.

_____, and _____, 1987b, "Editorial Introduction to Part I, Ethnography: An Anthropological View." In *Interpretive Ethnography of Education at Home and Abroad. ibid.* (Also in *Educational Horizons,* Summer, 1985).

_____, and _____, 1987c, "The 'Problem' of Women in Four Changing Cultures." In *Festschreft for Melford Spiro.* Marc Swartz and David Jordon, eds. University of Alabama Press.

MARIDA HOLLOS/*Brown University*

23 *Learning in Rural Communities: Cognitive Development in Norway and Hungary*

Introduction

Much of current work directed at investigating cognitive developmental differences between rural and urban children finds that urban children acquire some cognitive skills earlier than their rural counterparts. Instead of attempting to analyze the factors that may be responsible for the rural groups' lower performance, investigators usually resort to explanations in terms of a "lack" in the rural environment and assume that they are dealing with a "deprivation".

It is quite possible that this apparent developmental lag of the rural children is due to a biased view of the rural environment by experimenters who have little understanding of the cognitive demands posed by that environment. This bias results in tasks being presented to rural groups which have little relevance to their experience and to the cognitive skills that they developed in those settings. A related problem is the medium through which the tasks are presented and through which responses are expected. Most cognitive testing strongly relies on verbalization and the rural child's often less developed verbal skills are frequently equated with a lower level of cognitive performance.

The purpose of this paper is to present some studies which compare the cognitive development of rural and urban children, while placing these children into their total learning context. The studies were done in Norway and Hungary and compare the development of different types of intellectual skills in children who come from three social settings: a dispersed farm community, a village and a town. The primary difference between the three communities is the relative isolation of the family dwellings with a consequent variation in the amount and kinds of interaction the children have with peers and adults. The major focus of the research is the cognitive development of children living in the dispersed farming community, who are subjects of a detailed ethnographic study. Their developmental measures are compared to those of the village and

Prepared for *Education and Cultural Process, 2/E.* Printed by permission of the author.

the town children in the same general culture area in Eastern Norway and in Central Hungary.

The performance of the three groups of children is examined on two kinds of cognitive tasks: one involving the growth of role taking ability and a decline in egocentrism, which will be referred to as social cognitions. The other is a group of measures which concern logical operations and physical object concepts, such as classification and conservation.

The basic question which the studies attempt to answer are the following: Is there a difference in the pattern development of these two types of cognitive skills between rural and urban children? And if so, what is the reason for it? What are the channels, methods and situations in which children learn the different kinds of skills? Specifically, how does a child living in a dispersed community spend his time? With whom does he interact and what are the forms of interaction? Are the children consciously taught certain skills or is learning mostly through experience? Given the relatively non-verbal environment, does this effect learning?

After a brief summary of some of the cross-cultural findings on rural-urban differences in cognitive development, I will attempt to answer some of these questions by describing the learning environment of the isolated farm children in Norway and by comparing the test performance of the three groups of children both in Norway and in Hungary.

Cross-Cultural Findings on Rural-Urban Differences in Cognitive Growth

Rural and urban differences in the rate and style of cognitive development have been investigated in a wide variety of cultures, using different kinds of cognitive tasks. The studies include Piagetian developmental measures, classification and sorting tasks, memory tasks, and tests of verbal skills. This brief summary will concentrate on the first group of these studies, in order to provide a background to the research described later. Only those studies that compare children from rural and urban backgrounds within the same culture will be mentioned. Brief mention will also be made of a study of linguistic development which compares rural and urban groups.

Piagetian Research

One of the earliest attempts in comparing rural and urban children on Piagetian measures was done by Peluffo (1962, 1967), who compared 8- and 11-year old Italian boys from various backgrounds on tests of physical causality, conservation and "combinations" and "permutations". He studied children from the following socioeconomic groups: sons of Sardinian peasants newly moved to Genoa, sons of Sardinian immigrants who moved 3 years earlier, sons of native Genoans and rural Sardinians, as well as a sample of illiterate Sardinian peasants. The results showed that the sons of new immigrants to the city lagged behind the other groups on all measures. Peluffo attributed these results to the "low cultural level" of rural Sardinia which "does not stimulate abstract thinking". He claimed that in such an environment relations among the elements are mainly based on perception (as opposed to concepts) and on the positive or negative application of the principles of identity and contiguity.

Vernon (1969) constructed a large battery of tests, tapping a wide range of abilities, including Piagetian concept development tasks, verbal and educational tests, creativity and perceptual/spatial tests. He collected extensive material on the background of his subjects, based on interviews. His subjects were 10-12 year old boys in different countries (Tanzania, Canadian Eskimo, Canadian India, Jamaican and English). The English and West Indian samples included the comparison of rural/urban sub-groups. In England he found the differences between "these sub-groups unexpectedly small." The rural group, however, scored lower on most tests. In the West Indies, the samples included two urban groups, one group from a country town, one from a sugar plantation, and one from isolated rural small holdings. When compared to the English sample, the entire West Indian sample fell behind the English group, with the West Indian rural boys falling most below the urban ones.

Opper (1977) administered a group of seven concrete operational tasks to two samples of Thai 6-11 year old children. The samples came from Bangkok and from a rural farming district. They were matched on average school performance, age and sex. Her findings confirmed the existence of the three concrete operational sub-stages as described by Piaget. There was a significant difference between the performance of the urban and rural children: more rural children were found on the lowest stage on all tasks.

Opper examined a number of factors which may be responsible for producing the differences in the performance of the two groups and found nutrition, heredity, schooling and physical environment to be similar in the two settings. The factors she considered important were the differences in the degree of industrialization (the pace of life is faster) and child-rearing practices: urban parents' awareness of the need for educational achievement and a less competitive rural environment.

Poole (1968) compared three groups of rural Hausa, three groups of urban Hausa, and two groups of Hausa living in large market villages on tests designed to measure "scientific concept attainment". He specifically aimed to show "how scientific concept attainment in Hausa society is affected by degree of urbanization." (1968:57). Poole found significant differences between rural and market village, and between market village and urban Hausa children, favoring the more urban settings. According to the researcher, scientific ideas are "new ideas which rural communities resist", whereas cities have been the focal point of change throughout history.

An extensive investigation of the development of conservation was carried out by Greenfield (1966) among the Wolof in Senegal. Her samples included schooled and unschooled children in rural settings and an urban schooled sample. By the age of 11 to 13 years urban and rural school children gave conservation responses. Only 50% of the nonschooled rural children achieved conservation by this age. Rural and urban children also differed on the reasons for conservation and nonconservation responses. In a follow-up study, Greenfield found that one of the reasons for the rural group's non-conservation was a belief in "action-magic", associated with the investigator, an authority figure.

Kirk (1970, 1977) compared the rate of cognitive development of 5, 8 and 11 year old Ga children from rural, urban and suburban environments. She administered three Piaget-derived tests and also made an extensive analysis of the mothers' teaching and verbal style based on the observation and recording of a controlled teaching session between mothers and their children. Overall, she found that on the composite of the three tests, the suburban children performed best. The rural children lagged behind the other groups on two of the tests but surpassed them on one. Kirk explained these findings on the basis of differential experiences provided by the environments to the children: suburban children have access to better schooling, there is much emphasis on concept manipulation, verbalization and intellectual achievement in their surroundings, their social milieu provides diversity and they have been exposed to situations similar to testing. Moreover, their mothers demonstrated a style of teaching that referred to relationships by the use of specific referents and who most frequently justified and explained concepts. The rural childrens' skills on conservation tasks, on the other hand, was explained on the basis of having more contact with materials such as clay and mud in the process of observing housebuilding and farming.

Piaget, in a comment (1974) on cross-cultural research, reviewed the work on Mohseni in Iran (1956)[1]. Mohseni compared Teheran school children with rural illiterate children on conservation and performance tasks and found a two to three year delay in the development of the rural children on the conservation tasks and a four or five year delay on the performance tasks. According to Piaget, Mohseni attributed the lag to the lack of activity of the country children who do not go to school, have no toys and show a constant passivity and apathy. Thus, Piaget concluded, the rural environment provides a "poor development of the coordinations of individual actions, of interpersonal actions and educational transmissions, which are reduced since these children are illiterate" (Piaget 1974:306).

Since there is little overlap between these studies in terms of tasks, it is difficult to make a direct comparison of the results. It seems, however, that on most Piagetian tasks the rural children were found to lag behind their urban peers by some years.

---

[1]The original study by Mohseni is not available.

Linguistic Development

The only directly comparative study of rural and urban children's language development was done by Entwistle in 1966. She studied the linguistic development of kindergarten, first, third and fifth grade children by administering word association tests based on Brown and Berko's (1960) study. Her subjects were children of blue-collar workers, high-income suburban professionals, rural farmers, and Amish farmers from Pennsylvania. She found no significant difference between the low and high socio-economic urban groups. The high-IQ rural children performed similarly to the urban samples. The low-IQ urban children scored considerably lower. Entwistle concluded that rural residence impedes language development during the pre-school years. Rural children with superior endowment, however, quickly compensate. The handicap of the rural environment consists of less exposure to language: less opportunity for verbal interaction because of the isolation of the dwellings, lack of kindergartens and lower exposure to TV and radio. The Amish group exhibited a pattern of development very similar to the rural Maryland group: The Amish children lagged behind the others in the younger grades.

On the basis of the above evidence Entwistle suggests that "the well-documented IQ differences between rural and urban populations" may be due to other factors than genetic. She suggests that the lack of verbal stimulation at an early age may hinder the development to form class concepts and semantics.

Summary

As the above brief summary indicates, rural children seem to lag behind their urban counterparts on the majority of developmental measures which are used in research. On the Piagetian conservation tasks, there is a difference of several years between the groups in most of the studies, with the rural children persisting in giving more concrete, perceptually bound answers. On a number of classification and sorting tasks, the rural children also base their categories on perceptual attributes rather than on a superordinate category or taxonomic class. They are found to be more "concrete", as opposed to theoretical and abstract. They also often seem to be more passive and less manipulative.

A consistent finding of the studies is the rural children's difficulty to verbalize the results: to give verbal justifications and explanations. They are found to be less talkative in test situations in general.

The researchers attribute the developmental differences between the urban and rural samples to the opportunities provided by the urban environment. The rural environment is perceived as having a "lower cultural level" which does not stimulate abstract thinking. The pace of life is slower in rural communities: the children lack toys and other items and are seen as passive and apathetic. There is also very little verbal stimulation which is also reflected in the mothers' teaching style. Urban mothers explain well: rural ones do not.

Nor are rural parents aware of the need for achievement to the same extent the urban ones are, therefore they do not push the children toward higher intellectual functioning. Rural parents emphasize compliance, urban ones stimulate verbal and analytical skills. By and large, rural environments are conservative where people tend to rely on social explanations and respect authority, whereas "physical" explanations and innovations are more usual in town.

Logical Operations and Social Cognitions

In order to gain a better understanding of the social and environmental correlates of cognitive growth in the rural areas of Norway and Hungary, my methodology was based on extended periods of field observation while living with several farm families in Eastern Norway and Central Hungary. (Hollos 1974, Hollos & Cowan 1973, Hollos 1975). Field methods included the keeping of diaries of daily activities of the children, the taping of conversations, the sampling and description of children's behavior in different settings, the interviewing and observation of mothers on their child rearing methods and in general the following of children through their everyday life.

To gain insight into the importance of the environmental factors, the performance of these isolated farm children on some Piagetian developmental measures was contrasted with that of the other two groups previously mentioned: the children from a village and a town. Two sets of cognitive tasks were employed: one set was aimed at the development of role taking or social skills, the other at the growth of logical operations, involved with object relations. The primary question under investigation was whether different social environmental factors influence different areas of cognitive functioning and if so, in what manner? The assumption was that relatively low frequency of social interaction with others, the absence of a variety of types of people to whom the child has to learn to adjust and the lack of peer groups should probably slow down development in the social cognitive area. The question was then, whether this type of social environment with its relatively low demand for verbal and role-taking skills affects the other areas of cognition which are concerned with relations and concepts in the physical world.

Piaget's theory and description of developmental stages provides an excellent basis for testing for the relationship of these two areas of cognition.

Piaget conceives intellectual development as a continual process of organization and reorganization of structure. Although this process is continuous, its results are discontinuous and are qualitatively different from time to time. In this system, the total course of development is broken down into periods and stages. The sequence of these is invariant, but the age at which a given period or stage appears may vary considerably. *Stage*, therefore, should not be identified with *age*. The age at which the child enters a particular stage is influenced by environmental factors.

The overall development of cognitive structures across the stages is characterized by a progression from overt to covert and internalized actions. In infancy, these actions are overt sensory-motor ones: the infant grasps and sucks objects, makes visual searches. With development, the internalization at first is fragmentary and overliteral; the child replicates in his head simple concrete action sequences he has just performed or is about to perform. As internalization proceeds, cognitive actions become more and more schematic and abstract, broader in range, more reversible and organized into systems which are structurally similar to logico-algebraic systems. Thus, the overt, slow-paced actions of the young child eventually get transformed into quick, highly organized systems of internal operations. A critical shift in this development occurs around the ages of six, seven or eight, when the child advances from the pre-operational to the concrete operational period. In the pre-operational period the child is already capable of manipulating symbols that represent the environment. He has in his repertoire and can differentiate signifiers (words, images) from significates (objects to which these refer). Thinking in this period, however, when compared to the concrete operational period has the following limitations: concreteness, irreversibility, egocentrism, centering, stages vs. transformations and transductive reasoning. (Phillips, 1969). These attributes are applicable both to social and non-social cognitions.

The child, for example, is egocentric both in his social relations and in his representations of objects. He cannot imagine an object from the perspective of another person than his own, nor can he communicate successfully because he is not capable of taking the role of the other and thereby adjusting the content and structure of the message to what the other knows. He is unable to perform the operation of conservation since his thinking is characterized by centering on a single striking feature of an object, by irreversibility and by an immobile, static quality which focuses on momentary conditions of an object but cannot link a set of successive conditions into an integrated set of transformations. When he is given two clay balls of the same size and before his eyes one of them is rolled into a sausage shape, he will say that one now has more clay than the other.

What characterizes the shift in thinking to concrete operations is that operations or actions on the environment that were formerly carried out overtly now become internalized and organized into a network of related acts, or a system. The rigid, static and irreversible structures of the preoperational period become flexible, mobile, decentered and reversible. The child now, instead of centering on the perceptual features of the two clay balls, is able to reverse the operation internally in his head, to decenter from the distorting feature and to take account of other, correcting aspects. (Longer and narrower vs. shorter and wider). In his social relations, he gradually moves from a static and centered egocentrism to multiperspective reversibility. This ability can be seen in non-verbal tasks such as the "three mountains" (Piaget and Inhelder 1936) in which the child facing a three dimensional display of mountains is asked to choose pictures representing what someone else sees from another location. It can also be seen in the child's increased ability to take the role of the other in verbal communication. (Flavell 1968).

The tasks administered in this study attempt to test for the age when this transition between the two periods occurs in the subjects and to examine whether different social environmental factors affect the relative age of transition in the areas of social and non-social cognitions.

Piaget assumes that social and non-social cognitions develop essentially along similar lines and are parallel structures, with the difference that one bears primarily on human relations or persons, the other on objects. The ontogenetic development of social cognitions and the relationship of these two areas of intellectual functioning have been very little investigated.

Nine tasks were used in this study to assess several facets of the child's ability to perform concrete operations. The first six were primarily concerned with logical operations on objects while the last three focussed on the child's ability to adopt a viewpoint other than his own. The logical operations tasks included three tests of classification (class inclusion, multiplication of classes, multiplication of relations) and three tests of conservation (conservation of continuous quantity, conservation of interior volume, conservation of occupied volume). The perspectivism tasks included a test of visual perspectives (the three mountains test), communication accuracy and role taking.

The hypothesis guiding the research was that the effects of the three social settings will be greater for role-taking or social cognitive tasks than for logical operations — given the low degree of social interaction that the farm children are exposed to. If no differences were found among the settings in logical operations performance, or if the farm children were found to perform better, then the results of the study would suggest that some current undifferentiated notions about social deprivation and about the types of environments supposedly favorable to cognitive development should be reexamined.

Learning in Norway

The first study was done in Norway, where I spent 16 months doing anthropological field work in a dispersed rural community. The major focus of the research was on the cognitive development of children living in this farming community. Families here were so geographically separated that there were no peer groups for the children to play with. Prior to school age, with the exception of important holidays and family occasions, they very rarely left the farm. Most of the early learning experiences of these children took place in the context of the isolated homestead, with interaction limited to family members.

The other two groups came from a rural village and a medium-sized town in the same general culture area in Eastern Norway. The village was a densely settled community where peer groups were present and contact with adults outside of the family was frequent. In the town, in addition to these, the social structure was more complex, and the children came into contact with a variety of different kinds of adults in a much larger variety of social situations.

Eastern Norway is quite homogenous culturally. There were no systematic religious, linguistic, or ideological differences among the communities. All of the children who were tested lived in intact nuclear families (two parents and an average of three children). All families were "working class" with relatively low incomes, and the type and amount of schooling received by the parents and children were virtually identical in all three communities.

In the following sections I will first describe the social and learning situation of the isolated children, their daily lives and activities, then give a brief comparison with that of the other two groups and finally present the results of the cognitive developmental measures of all three groups.

The farm child

The farm community, Flathill, is a dispersed area with a population of almost 300. The total land area of the community is about 150 km², most of which consists of pine forest, tundra, bogs or mountain pastures. The farms are located within the forested regions, hidden from view, from each other and from travellers on the road traversing the community. Reaching it from the county seat (our second research site) is via an unpaved, winding country road where the only signs of human settlement are some mailboxes along the side roads or occasional stray cows. No road sign indicates entry into a new district and one could easily drive through it without being aware of its existence until one finally reaches a small centre, consisting of a few houses, a store, a post office, an abandoned school house, a gasoline station and a workshop.

The Flathill area was first used as a summer pasture by the farmers living in the central village, Innbygda. It was first permanently settled about 1800. The settlers utilized the former pasture lands, later groups clearing new forest for pasture and building farms in the midst of these, preferably at higher elevations where the frost danger was least. The settlement pattern today reflects this history, with farms widely scattered, following no regular pattern and with no proximity to the main road or to each other.

The small central settlement is a relatively recent development, originally owing its existence to the erection of the old schoolhouse in 1915. After school centralization was effected in 1964, and the school moved to the central village, the building was abandoned and only occasionally used for voluntary association meetings. In the intervening years, the other facilities were slowly emerging and now form a small service and shopping center for the farms. There are no doctors, nurses or hospitals in the immediate vicinity, nor is there direct transportation to the nearest medical facility. The only public transportation is the school bus that collects the children by the store in the morning and deposits them in the afternoon. Reaching the farms is by dairy truck which transports children and milk twice every day.

The major occupation of the residents is dairy farming with supplementary employment in the forest or in the small local workshop. Women are not employed outside of the home but have a major share of taking care of the animals.

The life of the farm child unfolds in the context of the isolated homestead, with interaction limited to family members. Since the average number of children per family is three and the average age difference between siblings is 2-3 years, interaction takes place with older or younger individuals, almost never with contemporaries.

The birth of a child is eagerly awaited in Flathill. Child raising is considered the primary responsibility of a young woman and women who have no children are pitied and considered either strange, sick or lazy. After returning from the hospital, the mother takes up her full regular load of work, sometimes with the assistance of a country-paid assistant or the mother-in-law. From this day on, until the child is ready to attend school at age 7, he or she is rarely out of the sight or immediate vicinity of the mother.

An infant is never left alone. With a very few exceptions, he is constantly with the mother whether asleep or awake. The baby's crib and later his bed remains in the parents' bedroom until he is about ten years of age. During the first years the child is indulged and nurtured: his crying is immediately responded to, weaning is gradual, feeding is on demand and toilet training is slow and often not complete until 3 or 4 years of age. Mothers do not encourage nor discourage other areas of physical or social maturity but worry about how their child compares to others. They are pleased at the signs of crawling, walking and talking. When the child is ready to move about, he is placed on the kitchen floor and there are no attempts at confining or encouraging him. He is free to explore and investigate while the mother somewhat anxiously watches and stops him from harming himself, but she sets no off-limit areas.

While other family members come and go and basically pay little attention to him, interaction with the mother is constant. This is not manifested in close bodily contact, verbal exchange or conscious attempts at teaching. Rather, while the mother goes about her work and the child is free to occupy himself with whatever he pleases, the mother is continually conscious of his presence, and is immediately responsive to his smallest demand. She is always prepared to shift her interest from what she is doing to him.

After the child has learned to walk and talk, he graduates from the infant (spebarn) stage. He can now move around more freely and leave the immediate vicinity of the mother. The transition is not welcomed by most mothers. Their behavior towards the child is only slowly changing from care nurturance and protection to a minimum of independence training. Mothers do not discourage dependency; on the contrary, signs of independence are not necessarily rewarded.

Depending on the number or presence of older siblings or occasionally of neighbor children, the major change in the life of a two or three year old is freedom to play with others and to do it outside the house, without the mother's immediate supervision. A peer group is lacking in any case since siblings are at least two years older and neighbor children are usually not the same age, either. Moreover, the children are still in the mother's near vicinity. She is at all times aware of their whereabouts and can observe them from the kitchen window. The children generally run in and out of the house and when she leaves on her rounds to the barn, vegetable garden or storage house, they follow her. Consequently, they are also always aware of her movements and destination. Older children occasionally ask and receive permission to go to the edge of the forest to gather berries or flowers or down to the road to watch for the milk truck.

A passage from a recent Norwegian novel, Tarjei Vessaas' *The Great Cycle* seems to describe very well the mother-child relationship as seen through the child's eyes

> Everything glided forward, interlocked as it was supposed to be, so that nobody paid any attention to it. What was to be used appeared, what had been used was hidden away and only brought out again when it had to be used once more and then it was mended and clean. It occurred to Per that Mother did all this. The *days themselves* passed through Mother's hands and were ordered by her before they reached other people.
>
> Then another idea occurred to him, an uncomfortable one: without Mother everything would come to a standstill, grind to a halt, go to pieces. All would be changed into dark night.
>
> But she never came to a standstill. There was no darkness. So there was no need to think about it again for a long time. Mother had always been there. [Author's emphasis.] (1967:88)

As far as discipline is concerned, as long as the child does not wander off or spend much of his time completely out of the mothers's vicinity, he can pretty much do as he pleases. Attempts at obedience training are feeble and consist mostly of a talking to or warning. There is little expected of children this age in the areas of responsibility, obedience, physical self-reliance or achievement.

Mothers do not discipline, nor do they stimulate the child. There are few attempts to teach or to require new achievements or skills. When the children are bored or do not know what to do with themselves the mother does not try to get them interested in particulr activities, to tell them stories, to teach them a new skill, to organize games or play with them, in learning she essentially leaves them alone to find their own way and amuse themselves.

Flathill children have some toys to play with, the majority of which are received as gifts for Christmas or birthdays. Most of these, however, are not much used and stimulate interest only for a while. Instead of toys, most children occupy themselves with playing in the sand or snow, shooting arrows into the barn wall, kicking a ball against the wall or simply by observing the comings and goings of others on the farm. Even when several siblings are together, there is very little cooperative play since the ages generally are quite far apart.

In spite of the almost constant interaction between mother and children, there is relatively little verbal exchange and never any extended conversation or question and answer periods.

Except for important holidays and family occasions, the children rarely leave the farm prior to school age. Apart from the mother and siblings, then, the preschool child has few others to interact with. Although the father and grandparents do enter into his world, they are of relatively minor importance. The father is an occasional source of fun and entertainment. He is not an authority figure since questions of child raising he generally leaves to his wife. The rest of the relatives (with the exception of some grandparents) are far removed from the child's everyday sphere.

The farm child's life drastically changes when at the age of seven he must begin school. Most children and mothers dread this event for different reasons. Mothers are afraid to let their charge out of their sight and into the unknown world. Children's worry is tinged with curiosity and although they fear school and meeting the other children, they look forward to another type of activity.

During the first two grades children go to school only every second day, due to the difficulty of transportation. On school days they are gone all day. They are picked up by the morning milk truck which wends its way through the secondary and side roads to all farms and are taken to the general store from where the mail bus transports them to school. In the afternoon they are returned home by the afternoon milk truck which also carries mail and empty milk cans.

First, and to some extent, second grade teachers try to make school as much like home as possible. They behave towards the child very much as mothers. There is little overt discipline and direct orders. Teaching is through games, songs, acting out letters of the alphabet, much playing and drawing.

The emphasis during the first two years of school is not so much on learning but on socializing the children to a new environment with completely new requirements. The result is that most children come to like their teachers and some of them develop a lasting attachment to them.

Interestingly, however, their relationship to the rest of the children changes very slowly. Their distrust of one another continues well into the second grade and the class does not become a reference group for a long time. This is partially due to the fact that there is no possibility for after-school play groups to develop, nor is there a chance to invite other children home.

Children do not worry too much about doing homework, nor are they embarrassed much if they do not know the day's lesson. They are used to a permissive atmosphere where achievement and task performance are not important. Nor is learning highly valued in the adult society and parents do not try to get them interested in education or in careers outside of farming. There are no grades given out in the first two grades, the parents receive a written evaluation at the end of the school year. Mothers are pleased about positive results but claim that they hope that their child is not a genius which would make him or her a misfit in society.

Apart from being away at school three days a week, the young school child's schedule and life at home does not change much. Unless he is a youngest child, by this time he has one or two younger siblings with whom he continues playing. Much of his time, however, is spent in solitary activities or around the mother. There is no attempt on the part of the mother to encourage "more grown up" or "school appropriate" behaviors.

What generalizations may be made about the activities and the learning environment of the preschool and the young school child living on a Flathill farm?

The following conclusions were reached on the basis of the observation and recording of children's activities from four families over an extended period of time. The ages of the children ranged from 7 to 2.

The first and most strikingly apparent generalization that may be advanced about the actions and interactions of these children is their quietness. With a few exceptions, children speak little and are spoken to only infrequently. When verbal exchange occurs, it is generally limited to brief questions or comments but it is never an extended discussion question and answer period, quarrel or story telling. This is equally true between mother and child and between children. Children do not recount adventures to the others, wonder about some recent occurrence or discuss a newly acquired piece of information. The presence of the rest of the adults in the family does not change the situation since family members do not frequently engage in discussions with one another and extend this behavior to the children. The evenings are spent in quiet eating and TV watching.

A second generalization may be made regarding the fact that although the children interact with a total number of a relatively few people, they are rarely alone. The other person present most frequently is the mother or a sibling. Not being alone in Flathill however, does not necessarily mean interaction; rather it should be thought of as "in the vicinity or immediate region or another person." Moreover, the associate present most frequently is a single person and if interaction does occur it is in dyads, not in triads or groups.

Being with the mother involves mutual observation and awareness of one another. Although the mother does not control or direct the child's behavior, she is always acutely aware of his actions and even in the middle of a conversation with a friend might make a comment relevant to what the child is doing. Mothers also seem to be constantly prepared to step into an action sequence of a child, continue whatever he has started, thereby indicating that they were observing and following his activities. Children tend to play close to the mother and similarly often observe whatever she is doing for long periods of time. Mothers, however, do not directly teach children or instruct them in specific skills, such as reading or writing.

The days of mother and children are filled with short episodes in which they interact briefly, occasionally cooperate but most frequently parallel and non-verbal, non-directive and independent actions in the vicinity of one another.

The most frequent mother-child interactions are of the following type:

1. The mother is washing dishes while Morton (5) plays with a toy truck on the floor, Britt (7) sits by the kitchen table and draws pictures. Britt stands up, stands by the mother who starts taking the silver out of the water. Britt picks up a fork, dries it, puts it in the drawer and goes back to drawing. The mother continues drying the rest of the silver. Britt goes out. Morton starts pushing the truck in and out between the mother's legs. The mother laughs.

2. Kay (7) and Dag (5 1/2) sit at both sides of the kitchen table and copy birds out of a book. The mother cleans vegetables on the other side of the kitchen. She gets up, picks up a bucket and goes out. Dag follows, Kay continues drawing. The mother goes to the barn and gets water from the tap there. Dag helps turn the tap on and off. He remains in the barn after the mother's departure and sits on the steps. Kay remains inside, drawing while the mother rinses the vegetables.

Children's interaction with other children are in many ways similar to that with the mother. These are most often limited to parallel play. There is little activity which requires cooperation, the agreement or setting of rules. Children do most frequently stay in the vicinity of or around a sibling but this does not necessarily involve engagement in cooperative activity. Again, as with the mother, they seem to be aware of the other's presence and frequently brief interation, such as pushing, pulling, giving something to the other, taking something away, shouting at him, making a comment to him, etc. would take place. These incidents, however, are short and both children generally shortly thereafter resume their previous activity.

Similar to the adults, children exhibit remarkably little tendency to control one another. It seems that they tend to mind their own business, relatively little concerned with either co-working with the other child or with bossing him or teaching him. Most fights between children are relatively brief and result in avoidance.

The following types of interaction sequences are common:

1. Bente (6) and Terge (4) are playing outside. Bente is building a sand castle while Terje is picking leaves from a bush which he arranges in a long, straight line about 6 feet from Bente. The end of the line reaches Bente's castle. She pushes Terje's leaves away who shouts at her and resumes building the line at the opposite end.

2. Kay (7) and Dag (5 1/2) are sitting directly across from one another at the table, drawing. Kay reaches over and yanks away the paper Dag is working on and laughs. Dag takes some of Kay's pencils and moves to the opposite end of the table and resumes drawing. Both laugh and continue drawing for a while.

There is some evidence, naturally, of younger children imitating the older ones. But older children do not teach the younger ones or try to train them in skills which would enable them to play with one another.

The third generalization is that, whether in the neighborhood of the mother, other adults or siblings, a great deal of the child's time is spent by having to occupy himself. Children do have toys, but interestingly they only rarely play with them. Most of their activities involve manipulation or observation of items that occur naturally in the environment or observation of other persons.

When outside, the children play in the dirt, pour sand, water, pick and sort flowers and berries, watch hay being brought in and make their own haystack, watch milk being poured into containers, cheese being made, look at a new roof being put on the barn and build their own constructions from leftover materials. Frequently, they spend a great deal of time seemingly doing nothing, especially during the months when there is no snow on the ground and they cannot go skiing. They observe the clouds, the trees and watch for birds. As a result, most six and seven year olds are thoroughly familiar with the kinds of plants, berries, birds and trees of the region and when taken on walks are able to point out the most minute differences between them.

When inside, the children draw, play with clay or building blocks or watch educational TV. The majority of their toys are not educational or challenging, such as puzzles or leggo sets, and none of them occupy them for long.

In summary, the child's activities at home might be characterized as occurring mostly in the vicinity of one or two other persons, all of them younger or older than himself, in spite of which the majority of the activities are non-verbal, non-cooperative, non-directive or directed, which gives the child a great deal of opportunity for self-directive solitary play and observation.

From these observations three points emerge in regard to learning:

1. The child manipulates mostly physical, not social relations. Most of this manipulation is by some kind of activity, visual or manual, as opposed to verbal.

2. There is little pressure on the child, either in terms of time or towards achievement. He has, therefore, plenty of opportunities to explore and experiment, to try out new things and activities on his own without anybody pushing him into these.

3. The adults (mother being most important) do not stimulate or consciously teach the child or try to introduce new things or activities. Learning is initiated by the child. There is, however, always at least one adult present from whom immediate feed-back or confirmation is available.

Village and Town Children

The Village, Innbygda, is a community of about 1400 inhabitants. It is the county seat and a business, industrial, and tourist center. About half of the inhabitants are engaged in dairy farming, the other half is employed in industry or by the county government. Women as a rule do not work, but are not bound to the house full-time as their isolated farm counterparts and have more time and opportunity to devote to other types of activities. There is a great deal of neighborly visiting, trips to the markets, occasional voluntary work, participation in courses and voluntary association.

All Innbygda families live in one-family dwellings surrounded by a yard. The houses are built close together and open on paved or gravel roads. The village is long, built along the main country throughfare. Although there are no special playing fields within the village, there are ample empty spaces where the children can play.

The number of children per family is three, the same as in Flathill. Normally, the major part of the preschoolers' day and the school childrens' afternoon is spent in play with other children. From a relatively early age children are allowed to leave the house alone and to interact freely with others. The children bicycle around the village, go down to the river, play at each others' houses, ski in the winter, or play on the streets in all seasons. Interaction is not limited to peers; children encounter a number of known and unknown adults in a variety of social settings (their friends' houses, shops, etc.). The time spent with the mother is relatively short. In the evenings the entire family assembles and interaction is again, as with peers during the day in a group.

In general, these families seem to be more verbal than the farm families, perhaps because village life provides constant social interaction with others and thus fosters the development of these skills. Family members are apart during most of the day and in different settings. Since their experiences are dissimilar, attempts are made to discuss the days' activities and children are encouraged to participate. However, the children are listened to politely rather than questioned when their accounts are unclear. The major part of the evening is spent as on the farms, watching TV. On weekends visitors or relatives often come to the house.

In summary, the social environment of these children consists of the following components: frequent interaction with peers, relatively little time spent with the mother alone, frequent meeting with a number of known adults outside of the family, occasional meeting with strangers (tourists, shop-keepers), and freedom to range in the social settings that a village of this size offers.

The Town, Elverum, has about 6000 inhabitants. It lies at an important junction of several major highways and to a large extent owes its growth and regional significance to this factor. The town is a county seat and regional commercial and tourist center. It has several small industries and workshops but no major industry as yet. It also houses the offices of the District Court which serves several counties and the District Hospital. Apart from several elementary schools, the town boasts not only a Junior High School, a Teachers' College, and a High School, but also a free adult educational center.

The presence of the educational facilities has given impetus to the broadening of the town's cultural facilities. Elverum has several movie houses and theaters, and concerts are frequently given in the City Hall. Commercially, the town also serves a large region. Residents of several counties consider Elverum their shopping and all-purpose service center. Apart from its midtown section, however, the town creates the impression of a rural village. On both sides of the river, well-spaced, single-family houses with large green yards are connected by winding gravel roads.

The structure of the families is also much like that in the village. The average number of children is again three and there are no extended families. The only difference is that as a result of the higher employment opportunities some mothers work while the grandparents take care of the children during the day. Basically, there are no differences in the children's activities between here and the village. There are large peer groups with whom children spend the majority of their time. In general, they are not required to perform any special chores, and from an early age they are free to roam around inside or outside the town without adult control or interference.

One major difference in the attitude of parents, when compared to the two former groups, is their higher and more pronounced emphasis on achievement in school. The result is that children spend more time on their homework in the evenings.

The major difference between village and town as social settings lies in the fact that town children meet a larger variety of adults; they are used to strangers of all kinds and ages and their activities take place in more settings than those in the village. They receive more stimulus from people and also more pressure towards achievement.

In summary, while the three communities differed in size and structure, the primary difference from the child's point of view lay in the opportunites for social-verbal interaction. The farm children spent a great deal of time with their mothers, without words, imitating them or exploring the physical environment. The village and town children spent much of their time playing with peers, and returning in the evenings to a more talkative family setting. In other major ways the communities, and especially the samples of children chosen to be tested, were very similar.

The Cognitive Tests

In each of the communities 48 children were tested, 16 at each of three age levels: preschool (7 year olds), first graders (8 year olds), and second graders (9 year olds).

As stated earlier, nine tasks were used to assess facets of the child's ability to perform concrete operations. Six of these were logical operations tasks, including the following measures: class inclusion multiplication of classes, multiplication of relations (classification tests), conservation of continuous quantity, conservation of interior volume and conservation of occupied volume (conservation tests). All three classification tasks followed Smedslund's standardized procedures (1964). The conservation tests were based on Piaget's original formulations (1941). Three of the measures focused on social cognitions and included a test of visual perspectives, one of communication accuracy and one of role-taking. The first of these was developed on the basis of a similar one by Piaget and Inhelder (1956), the second was a test used by Piaget in 1926 and the third was developed by Flavell (1969). According to Piaget all of these tasks involve a coordinated system of reversible operations which enables the child to consider simultaneously at least two aspects of transformations of past and present stimuli.

Performance on each test was scored on a four point scale, with four being a response with an explanation definitely indicating a concrete operations developmental level. Because specification of the exact logical skill is still a matter of controversy, it is not possible to determine whether a score of four on each test represents exactly the same level of development.

Results

Table I presents the mean raw scores for logical operations and role taking tasks as a function of age (grade) and social milieu. The means range between 1.97 and 3.44 on a 1-4 scale; ther is, between late preoperations and an inconsistent concrete operations level for the seven-to-nine year olds of the present study.

Table I

Mean raw scores on logical operations and role taking as a function of setting and age (grade).

Norway

	Factor I	Factor II
	Seven year olds (preschool)	
Farm	2.67	2.47
Village	1.97	3.01
Town	2.48	3.22
	Eight year olds (first grade)	
Farm	2.72	2.60
Village	2.56	3.26
Town	2.40	3.26
	Nine year olds (second grade)	
Farm	3.02	2.82
Village	2.60	3.44
Town	2.83	3.44

A principle components rotated factor analysis was performed to examine whether the empirical pattern of interrelationships among tests supported our *a priori* distinction between logical operations and role taking. The criterion for factor extraction of eigenvalues equal or greater than 1.00 resulted in the extraction of three orthogonal factors. One of three, only factors I and II seem directly interpretable, factor III being composed primarily of residuals with the exception of a single high loading on the visual perspective ("three mountains") task. Factors I and II are presented in Table II.

Factor I is quite clearly concerned with logical operations on objects and includes all six measures of classification and conservation. A relatively highly high loading on Communication accuracy was obtained on this factor, but an examination of the scatter plots indicates that the correlation was artifactual and could be disregarded. (See Footnote, Table II). Factor II has its only high positive loadings on all three role taking tests and significant negative loading on Conservation of interior volume and Occupied volume. Interestingly, these are the two tests which extend to formal operations, but why that fact should create negative correlations with role taking is not at all clear.

As part of the original factor analysis, factor scores on the logical operations and role taking factors were obtained for each child. The effects of age and social setting were examined in a two-way analysis of variance, separately for each factor.

Table II

*Factor pattern (Principal components analysis-rotated) and
loadings for each of nine tasks.*

Norway

Tasks	Factor I	Factor II
Class inclusion	.647	.006
Multiplication of classes	.633	.127
Multiplication of relations	.537	.185
Conservation of water	.664	.024
Conservation of interior volume	.421	− .552
Conservation of occupied volume	.541	− .512
Visual perspectives	− .043	.491
Communication accuracy	.523*	.357
Role taking	.186	.595

*Town children tended to have high scores on this measure, while Farm and Village children had low scores; the result is a U-shaped distribution with no scores in the middle range. Since Pearson coeefficients obtained on discontinuous distributions are invalid by definition, this measure was not included in the interpretation of Factor I.

Figure 1a shows the statistically significant interaction of age (grade) and setting in logical operations (F = 3.57; df = 4/128; p<.01). As expected, performance increased markedly with age (F = 20.16; df = 2/128; p<.001). Social setting produced no overall differences, but village seven year olds had significantly lower scores than the other two groups, hence the interaction. It was clear that farm children performed as well or better than their village and town age-mates.

Role taking scores as a function of age and setting are shown in Figure 1b. An analysis of variance yielded a statistically significant effect of setting (F = 30.62; df = 2/128; p<.001) with no significant age or interaction effects. As we had expected, farm children did not perform as well as village and town children on role taking tasks. However, role taking was not, as Kohlberg (1969) suggested, a linear function of *amount* of social interaction: town children had more experiences in social interaction than village children, but their role taking scores were almost identical.

A comparison of figures 1a and 1b indicates that a combination of age and

Norway

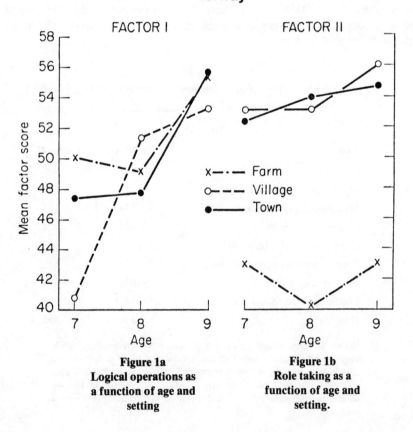

Figure 1a
Logical operations as a function of age and setting

Figure 1b
Role taking as a function of age and setting.

grade maximally affected logical operations while minimally affecting role taking. By contrast, social setting had greater effects on role taking than on logical operations. The form of these results had been predicted, but we had not been able to make specific predictions concerning the relative performance of the farm children. A general deprivation hypothesis, based on the relative isolation of farm children, would have led to the expectation of low scores for them in both logical operations and role taking. The results, however, showed that the low scores of the farm children on role taking were accompanied by logical operations scores equal to or greater than those of village or town children.

Cognitive Development in Three Hungarian Communities

In this study three social settings were selected in Hungary which corresponded closely to the Norwegian communities. This similarly permitted the maintenance of environmental differences while permitting the examination of effects attributable to a different culture. There were two questions of primary concern: first, whether the separation of logical operations and role taking found in the Norwegian study would also be found in another culture with comparable environmental settings and, second, whether the pattern displayed by the different groups of Norwegian children was a unique product of that culture, the particular environmental settings, or a result of the interaction of the setting with a particular culture.

The three samples of children came from three communities on the Central Hungarian Plains: a dispersed farm settlement, a village and a medium-sized town. Again, there were no systematic cultural, linguistic, religious or ideological differences between the communities.

The *dispersed farm area* is situated in the middle on the Hungarian Plains, surrounding the town of Nagykoros. Families of the children I studied live on isolated farms within an area owned and cultivated by one of the local agricultural cooperatives. There are no paved roads in the area and the majority of the non-paved roads are only semi-permanent and become almost completely unusable in the winter and the rainy season. Most of the residents are members of the cooperative and work in groups on assigned tasks which most often take them some distance away from the homestead. Since cooperative members are entitled to a privately owned parcel on the communally owned land which they independently cultivate, the majority of the women also work. The combination of cooperative labor and private cultivation results in adults leaving the home at an early hour and returning late in the evening, when they occupy themselves with the feeding and care of the animals.

Most of the early leaning experiences of the children take place in and around the farm in the company of the mother, the grandmother or an older sibling. Children spend most of their time within the farmyard, or, in colder months, in the kitchen, either in solitary play or observing the others. Most adults are either absent during most of the day or engaged in a variety of tasks in the immediate proximity of the child. Older siblings are also recruited for work at an early age. Siblings therefore rarely interact directly, and when they do, their activities consist mostly of parallel play and involve little cooperation due to the age differential (which is about 3 years on the average). Adults do not play with or entertain younger children but frequently interrupt their work, stop and talk to them or allow them to participate in adult activity. Schoolchildren attend the local district school, but opportunities for the development of play groups are limited since children are required to help contribute to the family's economy by taking care of the animals and must return home immediately after school.

Verbal communication when the family is together is relatively brief and restricted to general observations or brief statements. Children are occasionally joked or bantered with, but most adults are too busy or tired to engage in longer discussions with them. Unlike on the Norwegian farms, there is no television on the Hungarian homesteads because of lack of electricity. Evenings are, therefore, spent by the adults often working and by the children in solitary activities.

The *village* is a medium-sized regional marketing center where the farmers from the surrounding regions sell their wares, shop and attend church. About half of the inhabitants are engaged in agricultural labor for a cooperative or for a state farm: the other half are employed in a variety of service occupations or commute to a nearby factory. The majority of the women are employed.

All families live in one-family dwellings. The houses are built close together and open on nonpaved roads. Within the village and immediately surrounding it there are several empty areas, used as grazing fields. Children take the family's animals there and often spend much of their day with others performing the same task or playing.

From an early age children are allowed to leave the house alone and play with neighbor children. Frequently child care is rotated among a group of working mothers or their older children. Older children are required to help with a variety of chores, but some of these, such as pasturing the animals or taking care of younger siblings, also take them away from the home and are done in small groups. Village children also walk to and from school together. Many of their activities, therefore, occur in groups or at least in the company of one or more children of similar ages. Interaction is not limited to peers; children also encounter a number of known and unknown adults in a variety of social settings. (friends' houses, shops, markets, etc.). Relatively little time is spent at home or alone.

Communication between adult members of the family is somewhat more frequent than on the farms since the adults often work closer to the home and are able to come home for a midday meal. In general, these families seem to be somewhat more verbal than their isolated counterparts, possibly because village life offers more stimulation and provides more opportunities for social interaction which fosters the development of these skills. Children, however, are not often involved in discussions or asked about their experiences by the parents.

The *town* Nagykoros, with a population of 15,000 inhabitants, is the major marketing and administrative center for this area as well as a cultural and administrative center of some importance for this part of the country.

Most of the houses are one-family dwellings surrounded by yards. A major difference between the town and the village is the absence of farmyards and of larger animals in the town. Most of the town families however, also have vegetable gardens or orchards, and many keep chickens behind the houses.

The structure of the families is similar to the village and the farm area. Most of the mothers also work, and the care of young children (over age 3) is entrusted to grandparents, neighbors, or older siblings. Children have large peer groups with whom they spend a large amount of their time. More time is spent with peer groups than in the village since most families do not have animals that need pasturing, thus leaving children with few duties. They are therefore more free to roam around inside or outside of the town without adult control. The major social difference between village and town is that town children meet a larger variety of adults in a large variety of social settings, and their activities take place in more settings than those in the village.

Interaction between family members is also more frequent. Since the adults have few evening tasks around the house, evenings are often spent at home with the others in the family or with neighbors and relatives who often come by. Children are allowed to participate in these activities, but no special attention is focused on them.

In summary, while the communities differed in size and structure, as in Norway, here too, the primary difference from the child's point of view lay in the opportunities for social-verbal interaction. The farm children spent a great deal of time with one adult and without peers and met a limited number of other adults outside of the family. The village and town children spent much time playing or working with peers and were exposed to a number of adults outside of the family. They also participated in a more verbal family setting in the evenings.

In each community 45 children were tested, 15 at each age level: first graders (7 year olds), second graders (8 year olds) and third graders (9 year olds). The ages correspond to that of the Norwegian children.

In comparing the cognitive development of these children 10 tasks were used, including 9 tasks used in Norway and an additional purely verbal measure of egocentrism, which was developed on the basis of the pronoun system of the Hungarian language.

The results closely parallelled those of the Norwegian study as seen in the following tables and figures.

Table III presents the mean raw scores for logical operations and role taking tasks.

Table III

*Mean raw scores on logical operations and role taking
as a function of setting and age (grade)*

Hungary

	Factor I	Factor II
Seven year olds (preschool)		
Farm	2.87	2.32
Village	2.30	2.81
Town	2.07	2.79
Eight year olds (first grade)		
Farm	3.13	2.52
Village	2.58	2.91
Town	2.57	3.32
Nine year olds (second grade)		
Farm	3.36	2.84
Village	3.09	3.52
Town	2.68	3.22

The loadings for factors 1 and 2 are given in Table IV. It is clear that factor 1 is composed of measures of logical operations. Factor 2 has high loadings on only the four role taking measures.

Figure 2a shows the statistically significant interaction of age (grade) and setting in logical operations. As expected, performance improved markedly

Table IV

*Factor pattern (Principal-Components analysis) and
loadings for each of ten tasks.*

Hungary

Tasks	Factor I	Factor II
Class inclusion	.44	.10
Multiplication of classes	.51	− .13
Multiplication of relations	.51	− .19
Conservation of water	.77	− .02
Conservation of interior volume	.64	− .30
Conservation of occupied volume	.50	− .08
Visual perspectives	.04	.27
Communication accuracy	.28	.69
Role taking	.13	.30
Pronouns	.23	.57

with age, F(2,126 = 25.50 p<.001. Social setting also had a marked effect, with farm children performing better than their village and town age-mates, especially at the earliest age levels, F(2,126) = 12.70, p<.001.

Performance on social cognitions as a function of age and setting are shown in figure 2b. The analysis reveals the effect of environmental setting, F(2,216) = 41.56, p<.001, and age F(2,126) = 7.72, p<.01. Tests of main-location effects indicate that the town children were significantly better on measures of social cognitions at all age levels.

When Figure 2a and 2b are compared with figure 1a and 1b, which show results of a similar analysis of the Norwegian children's performance, the striking similarity across cultures is immediately apparent. The patterns of performance on the factorial measures in relation to age and especially to environmental setting are very similar for both Norwegian and Hungarian children. The effect of setting is especially notable—town and village children may change positions relative to each other, but across two different cultures the relationship of the town and village children to the rural farm children remain remarkably consistent.

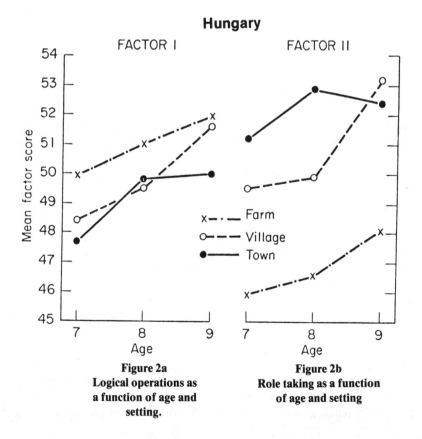

Hungary

Figure 2a
Logical operations as
a function of age and
setting.

Figure 2b
Role taking as a function
of age and setting

Conclusion

The data from the Norwegian and Hungarian communities on the cognitive development of children certainly does not confirm some previous findings that living in the country produces a form of intellectual retardation.

In the original formulation of these studies, the farm children were labeled in terms of their inadequacies. The fact that farm children engage in less social interaction with peers and in less verbal interaction than village and town children was emphasized.

A detailed anthropological study of the farm community in Norway indicated that in many ways the "deprivation" of the children is more apparent than real. The learning environment of these children is far from impoverished. They receive a great deal of social stimulation and support from their mothers, including countless opportunities to observe and imitate. Further, and perhaps more important, they have the freedom to engage in self-initiated play—primarily in manipulating objects and observing their interrelations. In experimental tasks emphasizing logical operations on objects, the farm children performed as well or better than their village and town age-mates. Despite the low-verbal nature of their social environments, they coped well with tasks which required verbal as well as conceptual sophistication. Since the samples were equated on most social variables, the results suggest that relative social-verbal isolation in and of itself does not interfere with the development of logical operations. In fact, the data from the preschool 7 year olds in Norway are consistent with the notion that environments which provide many opportunities for peer interaction may slow down, for a time, the development of logical operations. The data from the Hungarian study indicate that this advantage continues through a longer developmental period. Here the farm children were superior in logical operations to the other two groups at all three age levels, although their advantage diminished at successive ages.

The effects of social setting on role-taking would seem to fit better with a deprivation hypothesis. Clearly, the farm children, who rarely engaged in games with their age-mates, attained lower scores on role-taking tasks. An interpretation in terms of deprivation implies that somehow the children should be doing better if only we could alter their circumstances. We should note again that such an alteration in the 7 year old group in Norway and in all age groups in Hungary might lower the logical operations scores. It would also disregard the possibility that the role-taking skills of farm children are quite adequately developed to cope with the settings in which they live.

The studies strongly suggest that it is an oversimplification to compare the developmental scores of groups from different social milieus on only one kind of cognitive performance. Different settings may produce different patterns of "highs" and "lows." The adequacy of performance in each group should be evaluated in relation to cultural demands. The deprivation approach to the interpretation of cultural comparisons should focus in a more differentiated way on precisely what that deprivation might be.

The research in Norway and Hungary indicates that cognitive development and social environment are closely related and that research on children's cognitive growth should proceed along with a parallel analysis of the social environmental context in which the development takes place. It has been shown that it is necessary to outline and analyze in detail the total social environment of the child in search for correlates of cognitive growth or functioning in the environment. Some factors which seem most obvious might be misleading and produce an effect which, when in combination with other elements in the social environment, is the opposite of what might be expected. In order to learn about as many forces as possible that bear on the child, one should look at his immediate context of learning, including family interaction, the physical and social space occupied by the child and the verbal and non-verbal communication within his milieu.

A description of the social or cultural context of learning should mean more than providing a description of the child-raising practices in a group, or placing the child in a particular "social class," or using variables such as "schooling" or "no-schooling" or "rural" vs. "urban."

Anthropologists and psychologists agree that designation of a child as from a lower or middle class background by itself does not say much. In cross-cultural research this means even less. Similarly, the variables of "schooling" or "no-schooling" which seem to be in vogue in recent Piaget-type developmental studies, are used as summaries of past experience but with no idea what these experiences are. As Goodnow said, "These terms carry their own hazards. It is very easy, for example, to think of 'no schooling' as a state requiring no further specification, as a neutral state, a measure of what might have been if the organism had been left to itself. This is a dangerous assumption likely to lead to the idea that all unschooled children are alike" (1969:456).

Similarly, enumeration of the most obvious elements of another culture without analyzing how that culture functions adds little to our knowledge of the cultural and social forces acting on the child and the kinds of demands made on him. The actual context in which the child grows up and learns should be outlined. "Norwegian" or "Hungarian" culture or even "Norwegian rural" or "Hungarian rural" culture would have been misleading as designating the environmental context of our study unless certain dimensions were enumerated. All three groups of children were "Norwegian" or "Hungarian" and two of them "rural" yet their social environments and the pattern of the development was quite different. In order to understand the demands of these environments the following questions had to be answered. What actually goes on in the everyday life on an isolated farm and what sort of stimulation do children receive from such an environment? Does spatial isolation imply psychological as well? Does the level of noise in the urban environment necessarily mean stimulation? Failure to understand the combination of these factors can lead to a biased expectation and errors in the judgment of intellectual capacities of the rural children who are less familiar to most researchers than their urban counterparts.

The task of the cross-cultural researcher is not an easy one. What is suggested here is that in order to be able to compare groups within cultures (and of course across cultures, to) and to assess their abilities the researchers should: first, search out and identify those features of each environment which foster the development of particular cognitive skills and second, use or devise tasks which accurately tap these skills. Without these efforts, however, no advances can be made in comparative studies and certain groups (rural, lower class, non-Western) will continue to be labeled and treated in terms of their inadequacies and deficiencies.

References

Brown, R.W. and Berko, Jean, 1960, "Word Association and the Acquisition of Grammar. *Child Development* 31:1-14.

Entwistle, D.R., 1966, "Developmental Sociolinguistics: A Comparative Study of Four Sub-Cultural Settings." *Sociometry,* 29: 67-84.

Flavell, John H., 1963, *The Development of Role-Taking and Communication Skills in Children.* New York: J. Wiley & Sons.

Goodnow, J., 1969, "Problems in Research on Culture and Thought." In D. Elkind and J.H. Flavell, eds., *Studies in Cognitive Development.* New York: Oxford University Press.

Greenfield, P., 1966, "On Culture and Conservation." In *Studies in Cognitive Growth.* Bruner, J. Olver, R., and P.M. Greenfield, eds.

Hollos, M., 1974, *Growing Up in Flathill: Social Environment and Cognitive Development.* Oslow and Bergen: Scandinavian Universities Press.

———, 1975, "Logical Operations and Role-Taking Abilities in Two Cultures: Norway and Hungary. *Child Development* 46: 639-649.

———, and P. Cowan, 1973, "Social Isolation and Cognitive Development: Logical Operations and Role-Taking Abilities in Three Norwegian Social Settings. *Child Development,* 44: 630-641.

Kirk (Fitzgerald), Lorraine, 1970, "Cognitive Development Among Ga Children: Environmental Correlates of Cognitive Growth Rate Within the Ga Tribe. Unpublished Ph.D. thesis, University of California, Berkeley.

———, 1977, "Maternal and Sub-Cultural Correlates of Cognitive Growth Rate, the Ga Pattern." In Dasen, P.R., ed., *Piagetian Psychology: Cross-Cultural Contributions.* New York, Gardner Press.

Kohlberg, L., 1969, "Stage and Sequence: The Cognitive-Developmental Approach to Socialization." In Goslin, D.A., ed., *Handbook of Socialization Theory in Research.* Chicago: Rand McNally.

Opper, Sylvia, 1977, "Concept Development in Thai Urban and Rural Children." In Dasen, R.P., ed., *Piagetian Psychology: Cross-Cultural Contribution.* New York: Gardner Press.

Peluffo, N., 1962, "Les Notions de Conservation et de Causalite Chez les Enfants Provenat de Differents Milieux Physiques et Socio-Cultureles." *Archives de Psycholgie* (Geneva) 38: 275-291.

_____, "Culture and Cognitive Problems." *International Journal of Psychology.*

Phillips, John L., 1969 "The Origins of Intellect: Piaget's Theory." San Francisco: Freeman & Co.

Piaget, J., 1926, "The Language and Thought of the Child." Meridan: New York.

_____, 1956, "Need and Significance of Cross-Cultural Studies in Genetic Psychology." In Berry, J.W. and P.R. Dasen, eds., *Culture and Cognition.*

_____, 1974, "Need and Significance of Cross-Cultural Studies in Genetic Psychology." In Berry, J.W. and P.R. Dasen, eds., *Culture and Cognition.* London: Metheun.

_____, and Inhelder, B., 1956, "The Child's Conception of Space." Routledge & Kegan Paul: London (1936).

_____, 1941, Le Developpment des quantites chez l'enfant. Neuchatel, Delachous et Niestle.

Poole, H.E., 1968, "The Effect of Urbanization Upon Scientific Concept Attainment Among Hausa Children." *British Journal of Educational Psychology,* 37:57-63.

Smedslund, Jan, 1964, No. 93, "Concrete Reasoning: A Study of Intellectual Development." *Monographs of the Society for Research in Child Development* 2(29).

Vernon, P.E., 1969, *Intelligence and Cultural Environment.* London: Metheun.

Vesaas, Tarjei, *The Great Cycle.* Madison: University of Wisconsin Press.

Whiting, Beatrice (ed.), 1963, *Six Cultures: Studies of Child Rearing.* Wiley.

Whiting, John W.M., 1966, "Field Guide for the Study of Socialization in 5 Societies. Vol. I. *Six Culture Series.* Wiley.

JAMES H. ROBINSON/Western University

24   Social Typing at Hanseong Elementary: A Transcultural Model of Social Bias in Schooling

This chapter presents the results of a field study that uses a Western model of socialization in schooling applied to a Korean sample. The social typing model used comes from the teacher expectation literature in the U.S.A. It describes the expectations that teachers, students and parents have of each other within school contexts and the consequences of these expectations in teacher and student behavior and in student achievement. In the process, self-fulfilling prophecies elicit differing levels of achievement for students of higher and lower social status groups. The results from these Korean data are similar to those reported in American studies. Even though the cultural contexts of schooling in Korea and in the United States are quite different, the model appears to work effectively in both cultural settings. These results suggest that the process of social typing operates in much the same way in these two different cultural contexts, and possibly in other complex developed and developing societies, particularly but not necessarily limited to societies where the social and economic as well as cultural impact of the west has been significant. In other words, this model works across cultures.

In presenting the data from Hanseong, firstly, the social and educational contexts of the study will be reviewed. Secondly, the statistical relationship between social typing and achievement will be analyzed. Thirdly, the process of social typing will be traced through the ethnographic record from the expectations of teachers, students and parents to their interactions with each other at school. Fourthly, the discussion will review the significance that these results have for building a transcultural model of social typing.

The Cultural Contexts

Throughout Korean history, social status has been a strong determinant of what one could do in life. The traditional society evolved from a caste to a

Prepared for *Education and Cultural Process, 2/E.* Printed by permission of the author.

class society over a two thousand year period. The resulting class system had stratified the society into the following five classes: 1) royalty, 2) yangban, 3) jungin, 4) sangmin and commoners, and 5) chomin, the pariah class (Yi K. T. 1970; Henderson 1969; Lee K. B. 1978). The royalty were composed of the extended royal family, the yangban were the administrative class such as the mandarins in China and the samarai in Japan, the jungin were the illegitimate offspring and desdendants of yangban, the sangmin were farmers, artisans and merchants and the chomin were slaves and people from despised occupations such a butchers, prostitutes, basket weavers and tanners.

Even though this class social structure appeared to be very rigid, evidence existed indicating that social mobility was part of the traditional society. Social mobility was facilitated by the upheavals of the Japanese and Manchu invasions of Korea in the sixteenth and seventeenth centuries. In the nineteenth century, public and private slaves were freed, and the jungin were granted the status of their illegitimate fathers and ancestors, the yangban. In the twentieth century, the Japanese (1910-1945) and American (1945-48) occupations of Korea forced more social change, and the three years of the Korean War devastated the country and leveled the social structure, as Korea became a nation of refugees.

Although the traditional social structure has been leveled, social class or status was still a major factor in determining life outcomes in 1980: what type and what level of schooling one would attain, what kind of job one would get, what level of salary one would be paid, and what kind of family one would ally one's family with in marriage. When asked what remnants of the old class system still survived in Korea, one mother said, "None, except when getting married." One could say that if the socially reproductive institution of marriage was still functioning within the class restraints of the last century, then the effects of that social structure were still strong in this century.

Education and Society

Within both the traditional and the modern social structure, education played a major role in determining social status. Education as a means to success became important with the institutional borrowing of the Chinese examination system about 1,000 years ago. This system became entrenched in Korean society with the proclamation of Confucianism as the state religion at the beginning of tne Yi dynasty in the 15th century (Kang. H. W. 1974). The learning of Chinese characters and the Confucian classics became the road to passing examinations for entrance into the civil and military service.

The emphasis on education as a means to social status was still strong in Korea by the time of the study (Osgood 1951; Barnes 1960; Robinson 1980). A wide variety of examinations guarded the gateways to schooling and to employment in both the private and public sector. The high status knowledge of the past that was tested on civil service examinations had changed. Chinese characters and the Confucian classics were replaced by language arts, mathematics, social studies and science. Mathematics and science had become high status forms of knowledge because of their importance in modernization fields such as engineering, and basic and applied science.

Although the content changed, much of the form of learning did not. The visual learning style of the modern day classroom reminded one of the descriptions of rote memorization from the old Confucian cottage schools (Rutt 1960; Dix 1977). This visual style of learning included copying from textbooks or from the blackboard and repeating after the teacher (Robinson 1982). Primary schoolers held their pens and pencils upright almost perpendicular to the plane of the paper just as the calligraphy brushes of the cottage school students. The singing of the timetables in 2nd and 3rd grade had the same beat and rhythm as the recitations of Chinese characters from Confucian texts. In the modern school system during seatwork or when reading to oneself, all sixty children whispered the words audibly just as their grandfathers might have done when assigned to memorize a page from the Confucian classics. Even with the substitution of a new form of high status knowledge, the traditional forms of learning continued.

Hanseong Elementary School

The neighborhood and school of the Hanseong study were in the capital of South Korea. Seoul means capital, and it has been not only the political but also the economic, educational and social center of Korea for the last 500 years. Seoul's population has increased from an estimated 200,000 at the turn of the century, to about 8 million in 1980. Almost one out of every four Koreans (in South Korea) lives in Seoul, and the other three-fourths probably have relatives there. As in many other capital cities in developing countries, Seoul has become a city of migrants. Unlike other developing countries, migrants to Seoul and other Korean urban centers assimilate into urban life at a rapid pace (Barringer 1980).

With the trend toward urbanization, more than half of the Korean population have become city dwellers. As housing pressures increased, ghetto areas began to appear in Seoul and in other cities. These shantytowns were generally at the outskirts of the city and were called "byondoli" or border area. As more and more migrants came to Seoul, some of the wooded hills within the city were covered by shanties. These shanty areas grew into hill ghettos and came to be called "sandongnei" or hill neighborhoods. Brandt (1971) provided graphic descriptions of the life in the new emerging hill ghettos of Seoul, and described the development of a "culture of poverty" as Oscar Lewis had described in his work.

The neighborhood surrounding Hanseong Elementary was a combination of a hill ghetto and a lower middle SES residential area. The school sat at the base of the hill ghetto and slightly above the lower lying neighborhood. The dirt paths and the shanties that Brandt described in the hill ghettoes of Seoul in 1969 had become concrete paths and cement block, slate-roofed houses. The shantytown had become a permanent lower income housing area. The neighborhood below was marked by the traditional slope of tiled roofs and the intricate woodwork of traditional "hanok" homes that reflected the architectural preferences of Yi dynasty Korea. The homes were beautiful to look at, but a little cramped compared to modern styled homes or the apartments of suburban Seoul. Residents of the area referred to the two neighborhoods as the "arai" and "weai" or the lower and upper neighborhoods. The lower the status of the family, the higher they would live on the hill ghetto. Residents in the upper neighborhood talked about "living at the top of the hill ghetto" in referring to the poorest of families. They talked about moving up and down the hill ghetto as references to downward and upward social mobility. Subtle euphemisms clothed the harsh realities of ghetto life.

Hanseong Elementary was an old school with a history of about 50 years. It was founded during the Japanese occupation of Korea. The school was the pride of the neighborhood in the past. With the hill ghetto springing up right behind, this reputation had somewhat declined. Still, the school was considered a "class A" school. This "class '" rating meant that the school facilities were the best of what one would find in public school education. The school had a science lab, a library, a museum and a radio broadcasting studio. At the beginning of the study, Hanseong had about 5300 children in six grades with 80 teachers. In the typical class, 65 students sat in five columns of double desks with about sixteen students per column in each classroom. One wall of windows provided the major source of light. In the winter, a pot belly stove provided the major source of heat. Even though the classroom was over-crowded, underlighted, poorly ventilated and underheated (in winter), these students were able to learn not only their academic lessons but also how to become good Koreans.

In this school, the researcher made over 200 hours of observations of classroom behavior in six classrooms (two 1st, 3rd and 5th grades) over two semesters. He interviewed 180 students from one set of 1st, 3rd and 5th grades observed, and interviewed their teachers, and also interviewed 40 of their parents. One-half of the parent interviews were conducted in the homes and the other half at the school. At the end of the observational and interview period, a questionnaire of social typing in schooling was developed and given to 58 teachers from the school. These teachers were selected for their positions at the school and rotated every four years by a random process, and so they represented a random sample of teachers from this elementary school district. Within the above cultural contexts, the social typing model was tested through both statistical and ethnographic analyses. The statistical analyses will appear first and be followed by the ethnographic analysis.

The Model of Social Typing

Social typing refers to how teachers stereotype children into groups within the classroom and interact differently with them according to their social group membership. The concept of social typing is similar to that of sex typing (Duncan and Duncan 1978). In social typing, children from different social groups are also given different tasks according to preconceived notions of their proper roles in society. For example, teachers have children from lower SES groups do more cleaning errands in the classroom (e.g. sweep the floor), whereas children from higher SES groups are sent on more errands outside the classroom, to the teacher's room, other classrooms, and the principal's office.

The model of social typing (see figure 1) includes the following six variables: 1) teacher expectations, 2) parent expectations, 3) student expectations, 4) teacher interactional style, 5) student interactional style, and 6) student outcomes. Teachers acquire SES expectations of their students as they stereotype students into social categories and interact differently with them. SES expectations are expectations of achievement based on the SES of the child. Teacher SES expectations trigger self-fulfilling prophecies about the child. They affect teacher behavior (interactional style) toward a child, affect the child's behavior (interactional style) with the teacher and with his or her peers, and affect the child's academic achievement. At the same time, students also have expectations of the teacher, other students and themselves as students in school. These student expectations create peer group pressures in the class and have effects on teacher behavior and SES expectations and on students behavior in the classroom. Parents can also influence the teacher and the behavior of the child in the classroom. Parent visits to the teacher alter or confirm teacher expectations about students. In this study, call on and control behaviors were the variables representing teacher interactional style. A call on is an interactional event where the teacher asks a student to read, to report, to sing or to answer a question in front of the class. A control behavior is an action by the teacher to stop a student from doing something. It could include a look, a word or a swat on the palms. Peer group pressures were measured by quantifying the results of a sociogram that was elicited from the students in the interviews.

This model shares many of the features of models of teacher expectations reviewed in Mittman (1981). Student and parent expectations as well as teacher expectations are taken into consideration: teacher expectations affect teacher and student behavior and student outcomes; and the effect of self-fulfilling prophecies are re-cycled, as the prophesied success or failure confirms teacher expectations. The model of social typing in this study also includes direct effects on teacher expectations by student and parent expectations. This study is unique in its conceptualization of teacher expectations. Most other models focus on teacher expectations of high and low achievers. This model focuses on teacher expectations of a child's achievement based on social background:

SES expectations.

In the Western literature, the evidence supporting the conclusion that social typing influences achievement comes from both quantitative and ethnographic studies. Quantitative studies have provided moderate to weak support for the conclusion (Rosenthal and Jacobson 1968; Elashoff and Snow 1971; Brohpy and Evertson 1981; Mittman 1981). Ethnographic studies have made a stronger argument for the effects of self-fulfilling prophecies on teacher behavior and student achievement (Spindler 1963; Spindler and Spindler 1982; De Vos and Wagatsuma 1966; Rist 1970, 1973).

The Results of the Statistical Analyses

Statistical analyses confirm the significance of the strengths of the relationships between variables in the social typing model. A path analysis of the social typing model provides evidence for the power of the model in one 3rd and one 5th grade of the Hanseong study, and the results of the social typing questionnaire confirm that the trends from the data in the two classrooms used for the path analysis also exist in the classrooms of 58 teachers who were assigned to the school through a random selection process.

The path analysis of the social typing model is given in Figure 1. With the causal theory represented in the model of social typing, path analysis through multiple regression establishes the strength of each linkage between the variables in the model. It does not establish causal relationships between variables, but confirms the hypotheses that these relationships exist (Kim and Kohout 1975). The path between each of the variables in the model is marked by a partial co-efficient. A partial co-efficient delineates the strength of the relationship between the two variables. A partial co-efficient of 0.48 between call ons and achievement would mean that for every standard deviation call ons were increased, one would expect that achievement would increase by 0.48 of a standard deviation. With the assumption that the relationship between the variables in the model is causative in the direction that the arrows indicate, this model represents a causal model of the process of social typing in the classroom. The model explains 53% of the variance in achievement. Most models would be expected to explain between 40 and 70 per cent of the variance of the dependent variable (Roscoe 1975). The greatest part of the remaining variance in this model could be accounted by IQ. The role of IQ was verified for the one 3rd grade where IQ data were available (Robinson 1982b).

Within the model, self-fulfilling prophecies were at work as teacher SES expectations affected teacher and student behaviors in the classroom and eventually influenced student achievement. These effects could be seen in the partial co-efficients given below. The real SES of the child (0.60) and parent visits to the teacher (0.31) affected teacher SES expectations. These expectations affected the peer group membership of students (0.35) and helped

Figure 1: Path Analysis of Social Typing

units: partial coefficients (levels of significance

For effects on achievement: Multiple R = 0.73
R Square = 0.53
f = 20.37 at 0.0001
level of significance

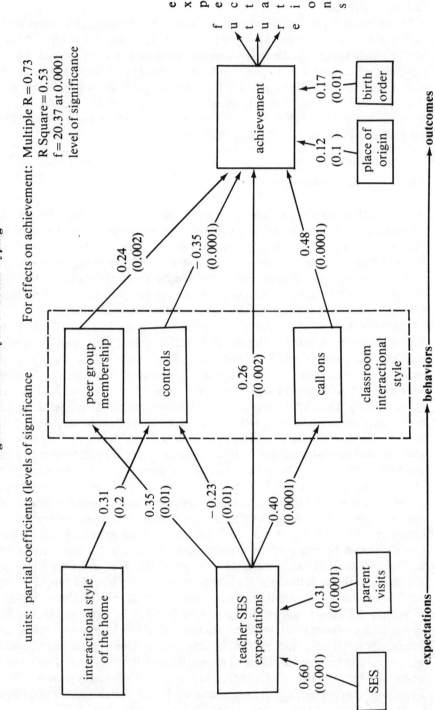

children from the good homes attain a dominant position in the peer social order. They blocked classroom participation by children from the poorer homes (-0.23) with control behaviors and gave the opportunity to learn to children from the better homes (0.40) with call ons. Eventually, teacher SES expectations (0.26), the peer group dominance of higher SES students (0.24), and the differential interactional styles of the teachers in control (-0.35) and call on (0.40) behaviors affected student achievement. Further, the interactional style of the home prepared lower class children to accept their inferior position in the structure of the school and upper class children to seek their position of dominance (0.31). In addition to these influences, birth order (0.12) and place of origin (0.17) had significant effects on the achievement of the children in the Hanseong study.

The generalizability of the Hanseong study was greatly improved with the social typing questionnaire. With the assumption that the teachers completed the questionnaire truthfully, it confirmed that the statistical relationship between the variables of the social typing model for the one 3rd and one 5th grade class also existed in 58 classrooms taught by teachers who were randomly placed at Hanseong. The Pearson correlations in Figure 2 indicated that the correlations between teacher SES expectations and behavioral variables taken from the observational and questionnaire data were almost identical. The similarities between the correlations of SES expectations and behavioral variables in the observational and questionnaire data strongly suggested that the observations made in the one 3rd and one 5th grade classrooms are typical of what one would find in most urban Korean elementary schools.

Next, the ethnographic data will illustrate how the social typing model is acted out within the classroom.

Figure 2

Cross Validity of Observational and Questionnaire Data
[units — correlations with SES expectations]

variable source	call ons	positive feedback	negative feedback	call outs	errands
observational data (level of significance)	0.38 (0.0001)	0.34 (0.0001)	0.25 (0.0001)	0.30 (0.0001)	0.42 (0.0001)
questionnaire data (level of significance)	0.36 (0.0001)	0.39 (0.0001)	0.23 (0.0001)	0.29 (0.002)	0.52 (0.0001)

The Ethnographic Analysis

The process of social typing began with expectations. Even before teachers, parents and students met, they had expectations of each other. From interviews and discussions with teachers, it was apparent that teachers believed that students from better homes did better in school. While the Korean teachers did not refer to a particular student as coming from an upper lower or upper middle social stratum, teachers did talk about students as coming from good, OK and poor homes (loosely translated). The teachers in this study used the educational term "kajung hwankyong" (home environment) for social class or status and classified students as coming from a "jo-eon," a "po-tong," and a "naj-eon' kajung hwankyong. It was also common practice to use the three following Chinese characters to classify students by kajung hwankyong: sang (upper), jung (middle), and ha (lower). After the observational data were collected, the teachers were asked to place each of their students into one of these three categories. In most cases, the teachers were able to come to their decisions relatively quickly. These data were used as the variable, teacher SES expectations: expectations teachers hold about students' achievement based on student SES.

Where did these SES expectations come from and how did teachers form them? It appeared to be the teachers' responsibility to try and understand the home background of every child in the class. After teachers met the students, they would acquire expectations based on their students' SES background from one or more of the following sources: 1) the student's permanent record and the annual home environment survey, 2) collecting student savings accounts, 3) the dress and grooming of the child, 4) conversations with other teachers, and 5) meetings with parents. The first two factors were reflections of the SES of the family (partial co-efficient of 0.60 with SES expectations as the dependent variables in the path analysis), and the last factor was an expression of parent expectations (partial co-efficient of 0.31 with SES expectations as the dependent variable in the path analysis). In considering these sources, they will be grouped into sources from inside and outside the school.

From inside the school, student records and former teachers provided the main source of potential expectations. Each student's permanent record contained biodata on the SES of the family, and remarks on this record also determined some expectations about SES background:

> The child comes from a poor home; the parents are not interested in the education of their children; the father (or mother) has disappeared; the parents are strongly interested in education; the child is from a well educated family.

The annual home environment survey provided a yearly update of the same biodata and was used by the 1st grade teacher to fill in the student's permanent record. Teachers also could get an idea of the family's financial status from the two savings accounts that were collected for students at the school. If school records did not provide the clues to a student's family background, the teacher could discover more about the student's background through solicited or inadvertent comments from other teachers. Teachers sometimes went to the former teachers of a child to ask about the child's problems in the past. Teachers were also constantly meeting over the course of the day, and some students gained reputations from comments made during these breaks.

Another major source of teacher SES expectations came from informal meetings with parents. Through these meetings, parental expectations of their children's future affected the teacher's expectations of the children in the present. Korean parents expected a lot of their children, the society and the institution of education. They expected that if their children did well in school, they would succeed in life. They believed in a "study ethic" or success through study. These beliefs and expectations led parents to put great pressure on their children to succeed in school and to secure any advantage for the betterment of their children's education. Parents tried to influence the teacher through either politeness or gifts and tokens of appreciation. The goal of the parent was more attention for their child in a highly overcrowded and competitive educational marketplace. Because the mother generally met the teacher, this phenomenon of parental influence on the teacher was often considered as part of "chimabaram," loosely translated as petticoat power.

"Chima baram" was one of the means for women to extend their influences outside the home. It could include a wide variety of activities that had both positive and negative effects. One of the effects that Koreans regarded as being more negative came from the visits of mothers to teachers at school. When the mother went to school, she seldom went empty-handed. "Chonji" or a token of appreciation was generally brought along. "Chonji" given to teachers came in all sizes and shapes. The most common was probably a white envelope containing a sum of money—ten or twenty dollars in Korean currency. At Hanseong, one teacher said, "There are a lot of envelopes here." Gifts were also given. They could include a purse, a shawl, cosmetics, and a pocketbook for a female teacher; and, a suit, cigarettes, or alcoholic beverages for a male teacher. Mothers also brought food and drinks. A thermos of hot coffee could provide a very nice touch on a cold, winter day for a teacher and some of her colleagues. Occasionally, a mother would prepare a huge lunch for a dozen or more teachers to show her appreciation.

For most teachers, the thought was more important than the gift. They did not solicit "chonji," but teachers recognized that some of their colleagues consciously favored children whose parents had made visits and given "chonji." Most teachers did not condemn a colleague for receiving an envelope or a gift, but they did state that it was wrong for a teacher to let the token consciously affect teaching. Teachers would admit that at the unconscious level their behaviors were sometimes affected by visits and gifts from parents.

Indications of the power of "chonji" came from the interviews with the parents. One mother explained:

> . . .that when her child started 1st grade, her husband's business was going strong, and they could afford to give tokens to the teacher. When the child entered 2nd grade, her husband's business failed, and they moved into the hill ghetto. They could no longer afford "chonji" for the teacher, and the child's grades declined in both the 2nd and 3rd grades. The parent attributed the decline to her inability to give "chonji."

One teacher once referred to a similar family as having become so poor that they could not give a thing—meaning "chonji." Similar stories were also recounted by other mothers interviewed (Robinson 1982b).

The system of "chonji" was accepted by the society. Typically, the middle class mother saw nothing wrong with giving gifts to teachers. After all, it was for one's child and who would criticize parents for helping their child gain success in life. The mother at the bottom of the social continuum blamed herself and her husband for her child's lack of success in school. She said that she knew nothing about "chonji," for her family was too poor to provide for her children—meaning too poor to give "chonji." With the educational reforms that focused on eliminating the corrupt practices of giving "chonji," many parents from the latter group said naively or politely that they thought such practices had ended.

While teachers did not all necessarily solicit or accept tokens of appreciation, they did appreciate a parent who showed concern for a child and tended to give less attention to children if they saw little concern on the part of the parents. After all, the teacher had 60 or more children to oversee and if the parents did not really care, why should the teacher? One teacher explained to a parent that:

> . . .a bright child whose parents have little concern for his or her education will be just an average student, but the child of average intelligence whose parents show a great deal of concern will become an excellent student.

The underlying message was that visits with the teacher had a direct effect on the teacher's behavior with the child and an indirect effect on their child's achievement: an effect greater than IQ. As we saw in the path analysis of the social typical model, the relationship between parent visits and teacher SES expectations was statistically significant: the more times the parent visited the teacher, the higher on the social continuum the teacher placed the child in their conception of the child's social background and the higher expectations the teacher had of the child's achievement.

When the students came to school, they also had expectations. To examine an element of these expectations, a picture was formed of the styles of praise and punishment used by the mother at home and the teacher at school. The analysis established that the more lenient the mother was with her child at home, the more lenient the teacher was in school, and the stricter the mother was at home, the stricter the teacher was in school. An analysis of differences in the styles of praise and punishment by SES showed that mothers from homes of higher social status were less strict with their children than were mothers from homes of lower social statue (f = 3.062 at 0.05 level of significance). In the classroom, the teacher was not treating children any different from the patterns of praise and punishment that the child received at home, but the students were being treated differently.

This result was important because it suggested the hypothesis that the parent as well as the teacher cooperated in the social typing of the child in school. Data from interviews with parents indicated that lower SES parents had accepted their social roles in the society and were prepared to hand down these roles to their children. Their style of praising and punishing at home might have been preparing their children for the harsh realities of prejudice in the classroom and the society. They might also have reflected the conservative and traditional child practices of the lower SES home. In a sense, the parent might have been preparing the child for a life of being controlled by others. The lower SES child was socialized for the role of follower and so received more punishment and less praise from both parents and teachers. The upper middle SES child was socialized for the role of leader in the society and so received less punishment and more praise in the classroom and at home.

Teacher-Student Interactions

With these sets of expectations, teachers and students interacted with each other in the classroom. Within these interactions, the evidence below demonstrated how teachers gave and withheld the opportunity to learn in the classroom through their call on and control behaviors. Within the model of social typing, call on and control behaviors by the teacher were part of the teacher's interactional style in the classroom. Teacher interactional style acted as an intermediating variable between teacher SES expectations and student achievement. Call on behaviors were directed more at children from the better homes and control behaviors at children from the poorer homes. Call ons and controls were part of an overall interactional pattern in the classroom that favored one group of children over another. The children for whom the teacher had high SES expectations were called on more frequently and controlled less. The children for whom the teacher had lower SES expectations were called on less and controlled more. While only these two behaviors were analyzed here, these patterns of interaction were also found in other teacher behaviors with students: praise, errands, eye contact, touching, and talking privately with the teacher (Robinson 1982b). In the path analysis, the partial co-efficient of 0.26 for SES expectations with achievement as the dependent variable reflected the influence of these other teacher behaviors.

When a teacher "called on" children to read, to report, or to answer a question, the children were being given the opportunity to practice and to learn the forms of "balpyo" (reporting) and to show the teacher and the class how well they had learned their school lessons. With few exceptions from observations in six classrooms, children from the better homes were given more opportunities to report, were given more second chances when they stumbled over an answer, and were given more time to answer. The opposites were true for children from the poorer homes. An analysis of variance of the observational data in three classrooms showed that there was a significant relationship between SES expectations and teacher call on behaviors ($f = 18.164$ at the 0.001 level) and that the relationship was linear ($f = 33.568$ at the 0.001 level) for children from the good, OK and poor homes. Within the path analysis, the partial co-efficient of 0.40 for SES expectations with call ons as the dependent variable and of 0.48 for call ons with achievement as the dependent variable establish that the greater the SES expectations, the more call ons, the higher the achievement. The same relationship was found in the results of the teacher social typing questionnaire given to 58 teachers for both frequency and sequencing of call on behaviors.

One could see teacher prejudice in call on behaviors in all three grades: during the 1st grade, when students were called to come to the front to sing; in 3rd grade, when students were asked questions in their seats; and in 5th grade, when the teacher organized class discussions, to name a few of the classroom contexts. The following discussion of the ethnographic record of these three grades will focus on one of these three contexts taken from a 3rd grade morals class on the Korean War.

In this class, the teacher calls on 14 students. The basic reporting assignment was: to tell the class a story that you had heard from your parents about the Korean War. Of the 14 students chosen to report during this session, four were from good homes, eight from OK homes and two from poor homes. An even distribution by the proportion of students in these three groups would have been two, six, and six. Both children from the good and OK homes were called on more than one would expect for their distribution in the class.

Two of the call ons were with Jinhye and Kongju who were from a good and a poor home respectively. A detailed analysis of these interactions uncovered differential teacher treatment of the two students.

> The teacher calls on Jinhye to report. She is the class monitor and one of the best students in the class. Jinhye starts to answer, but then the teacher stops her and says: "Wait a moment. Speak a little louder." Jinhye continues and after she is finished, the teacher says that it is OK and asks her to think about what she is saying and to state it simply. At a convenient point, the teacher interrupts her story again and says: "OK, that's good. Sit down."

Jinhye was shy even though she was the class monitor. She had trouble both getting started and bringing her report to an end. The teacher interrupted her four times before she finally stopped her.

> The teacher calls on Kongju, and she stands up; but just as she begins, the teacher interrupts and then tells the rest of the class that they must listen to 'kongju.' Kongju then begins and says something to the effect that her mother was born after the Korean War broke out. The teacher rephrases this comment: "Oh, your mother is too young to know about it. That's fine." Kongju sits down.

When Kongju stood and said that her mother was born after the war, the teacher let it go without asking Kongju a backup question about whether she had heard any stories from another source or had any opinions of her own. The teacher simply went on to somebody else. With both Jinhye and Kongju, the teacher and the reporters seemed relieved when the child was allowed to sit down again. Both girls were shy. With Jinhye the teacher went to great lengths to get her to make a good report, but with Kongju the teacher took the first opportunity available to go on to another student. With Jinhye, the teacher was not satisfied with her standing and just simply making a long report, but wanted her to make a good report and gave her second chances to put her thoughts in order. With Kongju, the teacher was satisfied that she could stand up and say anything even if it was that she had nothing to say.

In summary, these interactions showed how the children from the good homes received more opportunities to report in class and within each opportunity, how the teacher had greater expectations of the performance of the children from the good homes. Differences in the treatment these students have received were so great that by 3rd grade two shy girls had differing competences in their reporting skills. The teacher's differing expectations helped elicit these competencies. The competencies of the students matched the expectations of the teacher and indicated that a self-fulfilling prophecy was operating within these interactions. This particular series of interactions occupied 15 of one out of 200 class periods observed. Many similar examples are in the ethnographic record for other classes and grades (Robinson 1982b).

As call on behaviors by the teacher gave the opportunity to learn, control behaviors took it away. Control behaviors included verbal scolding, a pinch of the ear, calling a student's name to quiet him or her, a stern look and a swat on the palms: the teacher controls the students. An analysis of control behaviors in the 3rd and 5th grades observed established that children from the poor homes received more control behaviors than other children and that the trend was greater in 5th than in 3rd grade. In the path analysis, the partial co-efficients were -0.23 for SES expectations with controls as the dependent variable and -0.35 for control with achievement as the dependent variable. These co-efficients confirm that the lower the SES expectation, the more controls, the lower the achievement. An analysis of variance for control behaviors by SES expectations from the social typing questionnaire confirmed the trends of the path analysis for a random sample of 58 teachers. Significant differences existed between the use of control behaviors between the three SES groups (f = 8.644 at 0.0002 level) and the linearity of the relationship (f = 17.202 at 0.0001 level) with the children from the poor homes receiving the largest number of controls. The following interactional analysis of the ethnographic data also showed qualitative differences in control behaviors directed at children from all three groups. In general, the children from OK homes avoided the teacher's ire by being "good little boys and girls," the children from the good homes received a measure of control from the teacher, but the teacher was indirect in his or her control behaviors with these children and the children from the poor homes not only received a greater share of control behaviors, but also the style of control behaviors used for these children was much more direct. With the child from the better homes, the teacher might ask, "How could such a good guy do something like that?" But with the child from the poorer homes, the teacher might ask, "What's the mattter with you?"

The ethnographic record illustrated how teachers are prejudicial in the style of their controlling children from the three social groups.

> In the 1st grade, Unkangie does not even have his notebook. It is behind the teacher's desk. The teacher scolds him for just sitting there like a fool without enough sense to get out of his seat and go get his notebook. Unkangie stands and the teacher catches his arm and lifting him slightly gives him a wallop on the backside.

Just a little earlier the teacher had also spanked Seonki because he was out of his seat again. Neither student was doing his assigned seatwork. Seongki was always out of his seat walking around the classroom. He did it again. Neither of them finished the assignment that day. Both were in the wrong in similar situations and both were spanked. The teacher went through the same motions, but the results were different. With Seongki, the teacher was playful and the spanking was more ritual than painful. With Unkangie the teacher was more severe, the spanking was stronger, and although Unkangie was far from tears after the spanking, he had a far more serious look on his face than the smile that Seongki had.

The ethnographic record was full of other examples of similar differences when teachers scolded children, when children talked in class, and when children were isolated from the class, as well as when corporal punishment was used (Robinson 1982b). Examples similar to the one above were part of a pattern of differential treatment, on the part of the teacher. With children from the better homes, the teacher took on a more affectionate role and with the children from the poorer homes the teacher was more stern. The most important result of the more direct use of controls by teachers with the children from the poorer homes was that through the grades these children were taught to keep quiet and at times were even rewarded for being quiet. After controlling the children from the poor homes, the teacher was then ready to teach. As described above, the teacher generally called on the children from the better homes and gave them the far greater opportunity to learn and to be rewarded for it.

In the ethnographic data from the Hanseong study, the evidence pointed strongly to the teacher using differential interactional styles with students from different social backgrounds. Analyses of class periods also showed that teachers vary their uses of interactional style by class subject (academic vs. non-academic), by class activity (classwork vs. seatwork), and by the academic calendar (before and after tests). Teachers used more egalitarian interactional styles with non-academic subjects, during seatwork and after tests. Conversely, they used more differential interactional style with academic subjects, during classwork, and before examinations (Robinson 1982b). With this picture of the process of social typing within the context of teacher-students interactions, the next section will discuss how peer group behaviors operate within the model.

Peer Interactions

While the teacher was a strong authoritarian figure in the Korean classroom, peer relationships also had a great influence on how students and teachers interacted. Peer group interactions were an element of student interactional style and were influenced by teacher SES expectations and also had a relationship with student achievement. Within the path analysis, the partial co-efficient of 0.35 for SES expectations with peer group membership as the dependent variable and of 0.24 for peer group membership with achievement as the dependent variable indicated that the higher the SES expectations, the more dominant the position in the peer group, the higher the achievement. Behaviorally, positions of dominance and submission were battled for in mock and real fights in 1st grade, in verbal wars in the middle grades and in the verbal exchanges of academic discourse in the latter grades. Teachers supported the dominant position of the higher SES children in the peer social structure by ignoring all but serious fighting in the early grades and, later on, by accepting call outs from students of the better homes and by appointing these children as class leaders. In 1st grade:

> a child hits you on the arm, you hit him, he hits you and back and forth until somebody stops and give up. The one who hits last takes the superior position.

More of these fights were between children from different social backgrounds than from within social groups. In 3rd grade:

> a child from a poor home was called on and answers a question correctly. As soon as the student sits down, a child from a good home who is right behind her calls out: "You think you're so smart!"

The teacher received more call outs from children of the good homes than from any other group and this reinforcement of call outs encouraged the above verbal behavior in 3rd grade. In 5th grade:

> a girl from a poor home gives a report in front of the class, but unlike the previous reports, she receives a mass of questions from children who are from the good homes.

Through physical and verbal battles from the 1st through the 5th grade, a "pecking order" was established in the classroom. Teachers supported this order by their choices of student leaders.

A more detailed look at the ethnographic record illustrated how fighting can control the participation of students in classroom life. In 1st grade:

> Seongki is not finished with his work yet. Over half of the students have already finished and have received the teacher's stamp on their papers. First, Hyounggilie and then Jungokie come to the front and receive their stamps. After each of them receives their stamps, Seongki goes to Hyounggilie's and then Jungokie's desk and hits them. At Hyounggilie's desk he also messes up the papers on his partner's desk. Seongki was not reprimanded for either of these attacks. The teacher apparently neither sees nor hears what has gone on. Seongki is from an OK home and the other children are from poor homes.

In these fights, Seongki was clearly jealous of Hyounggilie and Jungokie because they received the teacher's stamp before he did. In general, Seongki received more teacher attention than any other child in this class, but he saw Hyounggilie and Jungokie as a threat to his position in the class. When other students from backgrounds similar to Seongki's received stamps from the teacher before he did, he did not attack them. When Hyounggilie and Jungokie did, he tried to beat them back into their proper place. Incidents such as this one, established and later maintained a "pecking order" in 1st grde. Teachers reported that they were aware of the fighting but ignored it unless the whole class was disturbed. Attacks were well planned behind the teacher's back or out of her sight or earshot. Retaliation was limited, especially when a teacher's pet was involved in the attack. Consequently, fighting established a small "reign of terror" in the classroom.

The above fight was one of 72 observed in 30 hours of class in one 1st grade. Twice the number of these fights were between children from different SES groups than were between children within the same SES group. More of these fights occurred at boundaries between two groups (good and OK or OK and poor homes) than within groups or between groups at the opposite ends of the social order (good and poor homes). This pattern of fighting in the 1st grade strongly suggested that fighting helped establish the social order in the classroom. As teachers commonly ignored minor altercations between students, they encouraged the establishment of a social order based on fighting. In school at least, the children from the better homes won these battles more often than not.

From the 1st through the middle grades, the battle for the classroom changed from physical to verbal conflict. One expression of the verbal conflict could be seen in call outs. Call outs were defined as a student initiated verbal behavior where the student addresses a comment to the teacher. The teacher might ask a question, and the student would answer by calling out without waiting for the teacher to call on someone. During seatwork, a student might call out "teacher" and ask a question about a problem that was assigned. During a test, a student might "tattle" on someone who cheats. When the teacher wrote something on the blackboard, a student might call out that she could not read the small print. All of these comments by students would be call outs. Call outs were sometimes received or reinforced by the teacher and sometimes ignored.

In general, teachers reinforced more call outs than they ignored although they said that they should not. The home background of a child made a difference in whether a call out was reinforced or not or even if it was attempted. In both 1st and 3rd grade, the teacher reinforced call outs from children of the good homes more than from children of the OK and poor homes. These differences discouraged call out from the children of the poor and OK homes and encouraged them from the children of the good homes. The differences in the call out behaviors of children and the reinforcing behaviors of teachers were important because call outs were one means that children could use to direct the activities of the class towards themselves. As the children from the good homes called out more than the children from the other two groups, the activities of the classroom were being drawn to them as metal to a magnet. The pecking order that was first established in a "hitting match" in 1st grade was maintained and solidified. Teachers gave their sign of approval to the pecking order in the classroom by reinforcing call outs of the children from the good homes at higher levels than the children from the OK and poor homes.

In the 5th grade, formal academic discussions provided examples of how children from the good homes controlled the classroom. During an academic discussion, one student came to the front and made a report and then took questions from the class. During two different discussions, children from the good, OK and poor homes gave reports, but the children from the poor homes received the most questions. When a female student from a poor home held the floor, the children from the good homes either bombarded her with questions or volunteered their answers to questions made by other students, as she became an emcee. The social order of the classroom was upset when a child from a poorer home gave a report. When she gave her report, the boys from the good homes tried to reassert their position in the classroom even though they did not control the podium. When a student from a good home gave a report, there were almost no questions.

Just as the fights in 1st grade and the call outs in the middle grades established and then maintained a social pecking order in the classroom, so the academic exchanges in 5th grade contributed to the maintenance of this social order. This pecking order was established from below by the students and was maintained through the grades with a little physical force first, then with aggressive verbal behaviors, and finally through academic exchanges. The power of the children from the good homes in the classroom became more subtle, as they progressed through the grades and as they became more dominant in the classroom.

The classroom teacher reinforced the social order not only by ignoring fights and reinforcing call outs, but also by conferring the leadership roles of the class on the children from the good homes. In 58 classes surveyed on the social typing questionnaire, 44 said that they had chosen class leaders who they thought were from the good homes. These leaders were extensions of the teacher's authority in the classroom. They were monitors, vice-monitors and group leaders. The class monitor was responsible for discipline in the classroom and might be scholded for allowing the class to become noisy. The other leaders were generally given errands by the teacher and helped take over the classroom when the teacher was out of the room.

Education in Asia and American: toward a transcultural model

From the Hanseong study, one sees a picture of social typing at work in the classroom. Teachers acquire expectations of their students' achievement based on their perception of the families; social status. These SES expectations affect teacher discrimination in the classroom through the differential use of interactional styles with children from differing home backgrounds. Peer group pressures play a role in establishing and maintaining a pecking order in the classroom. Similar models of the process of social typing have been constructed by Western educators to test the effects of teacher expectations on behavior and achievement in the classroom (see Mittman 1981; Bond 1982), but the Hanseong study verifies the existence of the process for a non-Western sample. It provides evidence that social typing is a process that exists across cultures.

This study suggests that within these two different societies the same process of social typing exists. Although in American and Korean cultures students and teachers have different attitudes toward education, different learning and teaching styles, different values for education and different responsibilities (Robinson 1982a), the process of socialization in schooling is similar. In Korean society, social typing focuses on social class differences. As Koreans are one of the most racially, ethnically and linguistically homogeneous people in the world, social typing in the classroom is primarily based on the perceptions a teacher has of the SES of the child. In American society, differences of race, ethnicity, and language affect teacher expectations and behaviors in the classroom. Social typing in both countries is based on social biases rooted in traditional concepts of status and class and are expressed through modern social structure. In spite of the cultural and social differences between classrooms in the East and West, the process of social typing provides a transcultural model of how social bias in schooling orders the classroom in the same image as the society and in turn transmits the biases of the society to children, as they acquire their roles in the class and their future roles in society. The more studies similar to this one that are conducted across cultures, the more we will be able to learn about how society is recreated through social typing in the classroom and how culturally based biases are transmitted to young people in schooling.

References

Barnes, E.M., 1960, "The Schools of Taegu, Kyongsang Pukto Province, Korea in 1954-1955: An Investigation Between Culture and Education." Unpublished Doctoral Dissertation, University of Maryland.

Barringer, Herbert, 1980, "Social Differentiation, Stratification and Mobility in Korea: A Decade of Development," ed. by Y.S. Chang. Seoul, Korea: Seoul University Press.

Bond, George, 1980, "Social Economic Status and Educational Achievement: A Review Article." *Anthropology and Education Quarterly,* Vol. 7 (Winter) No. 4.

Brandt, Vincent, 1971, "Mass Migration and Urbanization in Contemporary Korea. Asia, Vol. 20, pp. 31-47.

Brophy, J. and C. Evertson, 1981, "Student Characteristics and Teaching." New York: Longman.

DeVos, G. and H. Wagatsuma, 1966, "Japan's Invisible Race." Berkeley: University of California Press.

Dix, M.G., 1977, "The East Asian Country of Propriety: Confucianism in a Korean Village." Unpublished Doctoral Dissertation, University of California at San Diego.

Dunca, B. and O. Duncan, 1978, "Sex Typing and Social Roles." New York: Academic Press.

Elashoff, J. and R. Snow, 1971, *Pygmalion Reconsidered.* Worthington, Ohio: Charles A. Jones.

Henderson, Gregory, 1968, *Korea: The Politics of Vortex.* Cambridge, MA: Harvard University Press.

Kang, H.W., 1974, "Institutional Borrowing: The Case of the Chinese Civil Service Examination System in Early Koryo." *Journal of Asian Studies,* Vol. 34, No. 1, pp. 109-125.

Kim, J.O. and F.J. Kohout, 1975, "Multiple Regression Analysis: Subprogram Regression." In *SPSS,* ed. by Nie, et al. New York: McGraw-Hill Book, Inc.

Lee, K.B., 1978, "An Essay on the Social Development of Korea." *Journal of Social Sciences and Humanities.* No. 47, pp. 1-30.

Mittman, A.L., 1981, 'Effects of Teachers' Naturally Occurring Expectations and a Feedback Treatment on Teachers and Students." Unpublished Doctoral Dissertation. Stanford University.

Osgood, Cornelius, 1951, *The Koreans and Their Culture*. New York: Charles E. Tuttle Co.

Rist, R.C., 1970,"Student Social Class and Teacher Self-Fulfilling Prophecies in Ghetto Education. *Harvard Educational Review*. Vol. 40, No. 3, pp. 441-450.

_____, 1973, *The Urban School: A Factory for Failure*. Cambridge, MA: MIT Press.

Robinson, James, 1980, "Spare the Rod and Spoil the Culture." *Korea Quarterly*. Vol. 1, No. 3.

_____, 1982a, "Cultural Differences in the Classroom: Korea and America." *East West Education*. Vol. 3, No. 2, pp. 83-100.

_____, 1982b, "Social Typing in Korean Schools: The Effects of Differential Teacher Interactional Styles." Unpublished Doctoral Dissertation. Stanford University.

Roscoe, J.T., 1975, *Fundamental Research Statistics for the Behavioral Sciences*. New York: Holt, Rinehart and Winston, Inc.

Rosenthal, R. and L. Jacobson, 1968, *Pygmalion in the Classroom*. New York: Holt, Rinehart and Winston.

Rutt, Richard, 1960, "The Chinese Learning and Pleasures of a Country Scholar." *Transactions of the Korea Branch of the Royal Asiatic Society*. Vol. 36.

Spindler, G.D., 1963, "The Transmission of American Culture." In *Education and Culture*. ed. by G. Spindler. New York: Holt, Rinehart and Winston.

_____, and L. Spindler, 1982, "Roger Harker and Schonhausen: From the Familiar to the Strange and Back Again." In *Doing the Ethnography of Schooling*. ed. by G. Spindler. New York: Holt, Rinehart and Winston.

Yi, Kyu-Tae, 1970, *Modern Transformation of Korea*. Seoul, Korea: Sejong Publishing Co.

THOMAS P. ROHLEN/*University of California at Santa Cruz*

25   Seishin Kyōiku in a Japanese Bank:
A Description of Methods and
Consideration of Some Underlying
Concepts*

During the last few years, Japanese newspapers, television, and other media have given considerable attention to the startling increase of company training programs devoted at least in part to *seishin kyōiku,* a manner of training commonly translated as "spiritual education." These accounts have been impressionistic and generally critical of such programs as unwanted and unwarranted echoes of Japan's prewar education, universally condemned until recently as militaristic, nationalistic, and stultifying. The fact that many, perhaps as many as one-third of all medium and large Japanese companies, now conduct some sort of *seishin kyōiku* program may be considered strong evidence of a reaction in business quarters to the "excesses" of Western influenced progressive education and a desire to supplement, at least for their own employees, the education received in the public-school system with some traditional education. The occasional assertion that company *seishin kyōiku* echoes prewar militarism and represents a growing reactionary storm is certainly unwarranted at present, but, it is a sign of the arrest, if not the reversal, of the twenty-year trend in the decline of particularly Japanese forms of education.

In this paper I wish to describe one such company spiritual training program in which I was a participant for its three-month duration in 1969. The patterns underlying the various activities will be summarized since they provide for the non-Japanese something of a definition of the meaning of *seishin* and the educational concepts underlying *seishin kyōiku.*

Training sessions lasted between ten and sixteen hours per day, six days a week. The time devoted to *seishin* education was estimated by the training staff to be about one-third of the entire introductory program. The remaining two-thirds was devoted to training new bank members in the numerous

* Reprinted from the Council on Anthropology, and Education *Newsletter.* Vol. 2, No. 1, February 19, 1971, with permission.

For Harmony and Strength: Japanese White-collar Organization in Anthropological Perspective (Berkeley: University of California Press, in press) by Thomas P. Rohlen contains broad background information for the study reported in this chapter.

technical skills expected of them in their job; however, this estimate of the division of time between spiritual training and technical training ignores the fact that a *seishin* orientation was often given to technical training activities. The atmosphere surrounding the trainees throughout each day was strongly colored by *seishin* concepts. Here and there in the institute, for example, slogans carrying *seishin* messages were posted. Individual performance in the task of learning banking skills was commonly interpreted according to *seishin* concepts and even many aspects of recreation, such as the songs the group sang, were in fact vehicles for *seishin* messages.

While unquestionably this bank's program varies in many details from the *seishin* training of other companies, conceptually the goals and methods are essentially the same according to my experience and inquiry. The underlying similarities among them are the patterns and concepts of *seishin kyōiku*, which this paper will attempt to clarify.

My experience with Japanese who have had no personal contact with company *seishin kyōiku* is that they tend to associate it with the moral education *(shūshin kyōiku)* practiced in the public schools before the war. In a very much altered form, moral education does survive in contemporary *seishin* training programs. The morality is considerably altered in content and presentation. Today, the institution sponsoring the training is the prime focus of morality, whereas before, the nation, in the person of the emperor, was central. Instead of rituals of nationalism the bank today draws attention primarily to its own symbols. Through such daily actions as singing the bank song, reciting its motto, learning of its history, being told of the "company spirit," and hearing inspirational messages from its leaders, the trainees are taught pride and respect for their bank. The nation is not ignored, but rather the company stresses the service given to Japan by the bank and urges its trainees to fulfill their responsibilities to the nation through loyalty to their bank. It is not uncommon that service to the bank even be characterized as service to the entire world and to world peace, so organic is the model of social life taught by the bank. No matter what the ultimate benefit, however, the message is that the moral man is the man who works hard for his own company. The bank and all other institutions, according to this view, serve as intermediaries between individual intentions to aid the greater society and the actual realization of national well-being. The bank, by virtue of this position, regards itself as an interpreter and defender of social morality and when it practices moral education it does so not only for the good of the bank but also for the entire society.

It is an oversimplification, however, to describe the moral education of the bank exclusively in terms of a narrow focus on loyal role fulfillment in the bank. The content of the program includes many quite fascinating elements borrowed from the pool of inspirational stories of other countries. The diary of a missionary's medical work in Vietnam, the pronouncements of President Kennedy, and the opinions of the Ethiopian Olympic marathon champion are among the instructional materials drawn from foreign sources. Such a selection is especially effective for without this contextual sleight of hand, the moral of the story might well be rejected as old-fashioned or militaristic if the example was Japanese. "Foreigners do this," or "abroad the custom is such and such," are common and powerful arguments in the bank's moral instruction program.

In addition to foreign influence, the bank's program utilizes the prestige of scholarship and science, whenever convenient. Writings of famous professors which are consistent with the bank's message are found on the required-reading list for trainees and teachers from the regional university lecture occasionally at the institute.

Yet the overall aim of the moral instruction program is not to "brainwash" or greatly manipulate the thinking of the trainees. This would be an impossibility. What is intended is that the trainees 1. be familiar with the point of view of the bank, its competitive circumstances and its intention to contribute to the social good, and 2. that this moral perspective strengthen their will to perform their work properly in the future. In this way moral education, which is almost exclusively verbal in nature, fits into the overall *seishin* program where the emphasis is primarily on learning taking place through experience.

Keeping in mind that the program included many lectures and assigned readings, we may turn to the activities designed to provide direct lessons in matters of *seishin* for the trainees. These were clearly the heart of the program and provided the most interesting moments during the entire three-month period. The lectures, in contrast, were often sources of boredom for the trainees. What follows is an account of some of the training activities, often in the form of a personal narrative since my experience in taking part in these activities is an important element in my analysis.[1]

Rōtō

For two days during the latter part of the second month of training we stayed at a youth center sponsored by the Japanese government. This center, located on a mountainside, overlooks a large agricultural valley and just below is the market town for the area. Early in the morning after our arrival, we were instructed to go down into that town and there find work from the residents. Our instructions were to go singly from house to house offering to work without pay. We were to do whatever the host wished us to do. It was strongly emphasized that this was not to be a group operation. Each was to go alone and work alone for the entire day. In addition the trainees were

---

[1] *Editor's Note:* Accounts of participation in Zen meditation, visits to military bases, and a weekend outing have been deleted from this presentation because of limitations on space.

disallowed from making any explanation for themselves or their reasons for volunteering to work. They could offer no more than their name and their willingness to work. We dressed for the exercise in white nondescript athletic uniforms common throughout Japan. Without benefit of a social identity or a reasonable explanation for ourselves, we were sent out to make a most unusual request of strangers. Our reliability would not be vouched for by our relationship to a known institution like the bank. We were dependent on the good will of the people we met and on their willingness to disregard their own distrust of strangers.

This form of situation, difficult as it would be anywhere, is of particular difficulty in Japan where as a rule strangers ignore one another and social intercourse between them is unusual and suspicious. Approached by an unknown person with a request like this, the common response would be a hurried and not very polite refusal. People doing *rōtō* in Japanese cities have met refusals perhaps four times out of five. It was with considerable consternation that the trainees left for the town below.

I followed the young men into the town and watched them as they wandered about from house to house. They were very reluctant to leave their friends and go alone to the front gate of some house. In the case of some groups, they walked several blocks together before anyone was able to muster the courage to make his first approach to a house, but gradually the groups dispersed. The common experience was to be refused two or three times before finally finding someone who would allow them in and give them work. All agreed to having been very careful and worried about the first approach, but the second and then the third were easier to make. People who did take them in were regarded as warm and understanding people for whom they were very happy to work hard. The common pattern was to volunteer to do things which even the host would not have thought to ask in order to avoid going out again and seek another accommodating house. Boys who had been raised on farms tended to go to the edge of town seeking familiar work from farming families there. The majority found work in various small shops. One helped sell toys and another assisted a mat maker, a third delivered groceries and another pumped gas, for example. One rather clever young man found work in a small roadhouse by the bus station which served coffee, snacks, and drinks. He quickly established himself as more than just a dishwasher by showing his skill in mixing cocktails. When one of the instructors happened to notice him working there, he was angered by the lack of seriousness with which this trainee regarded the day's exercise. The offender was told he had selected an inappropriate place and instead of doing service for some respectable family, he was busy swapping jokes with the customers and waitresses of a roadhouse. He was sent away from the place and told to find other work. Later he was roundly criticized for taking *rōtō* lightly.

When the group had all returned sometime in mid-afternoon, a general discussion of the day's experience was held in the auditorium. When it was apparent that comments from the floor would not be forthcoming, the instructor in charge had each squad talk over their impressions and then discuss the relevance of the day's experience to the question, "What is the meaning of work?" As usual a variety of opinions emerged. Many trainees seemed to have had such a pleasant time with their hosts that they were unaware of the fact that they had enjoyed doing tasks which they would normally label work. The discussions did often contain the observation that enjoyment of work has less to do with the work performed than it does the attitude the person takes toward it. The bank's major reason for utilizing *rōtō* centers on establishing this lesson.

The original intent of *rōtō*, however, is somewhat different. A Kyoto temple developed it as a method of shocking people out of spiritual lethargy and complacency. The word actually means something like "bewilderment" and refers to the state of insecurity established when the individual is divorced from his comfortable social place and identity. In the course of begging for work, that is, begging for acceptance by others, he learns of the superficial nature of much in his daily life. His reliance on affiliations, titles, ranks, and a circle of those close to him is revealed clearly and, perhaps for the first time, he begins to ask who he really is. *Rōtō* also provides a unique opportunity for a trusting and compassionate interaction between strangers. After a *rōtō* experience, it is very unlikely that a person will continue to disregard the humanity of others no matter how strange they are to him in terms of social relationship. It is hoped that a greater warmth and spontaneity will develop in the individual from this experience.

From the point of view of the bank, there is an additional purpose which they hope this training will fulfill, which helps explain why *rōtō* is included in a training program for new bankers. It has been the experience of many people from the bank who have done this both in Kyoto and under the auspices of the bank itself that "the meaning of work" and "attitudes toward work" have changed after doing *rōtō*. The anxiety of rejection and isolation mounts with each refusal until finally, when some kindly person takes them in and gives them work, there is a cathartic sense of gratitude to being accepted and allowed to help. No matter what it is, even cleaning an outhouse, the sense of relief makes the work seem pleasant and satisfying. Work normally looked down upon is in this circumstance enthusiastically welcomed.

After such an experience, it is difficult to deny the assertion that any form of work is neither intrinsically good nor bad, satisfying or unsatisfying, appropriate or inappropriate to the person, but rather that the result varies according to the subject's attitude and circumstances. Failure to enjoy one's work becomes essentially a question of one's attitude toward it. The experience of *rōtō*, according to the people in the bank, teaches that any work can be enjoyable with a positive attitude. Since it must assign rather dull and methodical tasks to many of its employees, the bank finds this lesson of obvious value. Instead of taking this cynically as evidence of deceit on management's part, we should acknowledge the bank's very great concern that work be enjoyable for all members of the organization.

Endurance Walk

Ever since our first day, we had heard about the twenty-five-mile endurance walk sometime near the end of the training period. Our daily early-morning mile run routine and the many other climbing and hiking activities we had undergone served as preparation for this event. On the morning we were actually to begin our endurance walk, there seemed to be a high level of anticipation and readiness to try it even among the weaker and less athletic trainees.

The program was simple enough. We were to walk the first nine miles together in a single body. The second nine miles were to be covered with each squad walking as a unit. The last seven miles were to be walked alone without conversation. All 25 miles were accomplished by going around and around a large public park in the city. Each lap was approximately one mile, so in total we were to go around the park 25 times. There were a number of rules established by the instructors. We were forbidden to drink water, soda pop, or take any other refreshment. During the second stage, each squad was to stay together for the entire nine miles and competition between squads was not encouraged. Finally, we were strictly forbidden from talking with anyone else when walking alone during the last stage. The training staff also walked the 25 miles but they went in the opposite direction, thus passing each of us each lap. Some dozen or so young men from the bank, recent graduates of previous training programs, were stationed along our route and instructed to offer us cold drinks, which we, of course, had to refuse. This was the program, and there was no emphasis at all placed on one person finishing ahead of another. We were told to take as much time as needed as long as we completed the entire 25 miles. We began around 7:30 a.m. and generally finished around 2 p.m. There was no time limit placed on us.

On the surface, this program was simple enough, but in retrospect it seems to have been skillfully designed to maximize certain lessons related to *seishin*. When we began, the day was fresh and cool, and we felt as though we were beginning a pleasant stroll. Walking together in one large group, we conversed, joked, and paid very little attention to the walk itself. The first 9 miles seemed to pass quickly and pleasantly. The warnings about not drinking water and the severe physical hardship that we had been expecting seemed remote.

As we were forming up in our squad groups at the beginning of the next 9 miles, we were reminded again not to compete with other squads, but discovering squads close before and behind us, we began escalating the pace.

The result was an uproarious competition that involved all but a few squads. Each time a team would come up from the rear, the team about to be overtaken would quicken its pace, and before long we found ourselves walking very fast, so fast that those with shorter legs had to jog occasionally to keep up. There was much yelling back and forth within each squad. The slower and more tired cried out for a reduction in speed, with the others urging them to greater efforts. A common solution was to put the slowest person at the head of the squad. This not only slowed the faster ones down, but forced the slow ones to make greater effort. The competing squads were so fast that within four or five miles they had already begun to lap those squads which chose not to compete. By the end of the second 9 miles, the toll on the fast walkers was obvious. Many, besides suffering from stiff legs and blisters, were beginning to have headaches and show evidence of heat prostration. It was noon by that time, and the full heat of a mid-June sun was baking down on our heads.

Any gratification the leading squad got in their victory was soon forgotten. At the finish line there was no congratulation and no rest. Squads were instructed to break up and continue walking, this time in single file and in silence. Soon a long line of trainees stretched over the entire circumference of the course. Having already covered eighteen miles, the last nine at a grueling pace, we were very tired. Suddenly everything was transformed. The excitement and clamor of competition was gone. Each individual alone in a quiet world was confronted by the sweep of his own thoughts and feelings as he pushed forward.

My own experience was to become acutely aware of every sort of pain. Great blisters had obviously formed on the soles of my feet; my legs, back, and neck ached; and at times I had a sense of delirium. The thirst I had expected to be so severe seemed insignificant compared to these other afflictions. Over and over in my mind I counted the laps still remaining. After accomplishing each lap, instead of feeling encouraged, I plunged into despair over those remaining. My awareness of the world around me, including the spectators in the park and the bank employees tempting us with refreshments, dropped almost to zero. Head down, I trudged forward. Each step was literally more painful than the one before. The image of an old prospector lost on the desert kept recurring in my mind. The temptation to stop and lie down for a while in the lush grass was tremendous and many times near the end I walked for a minute or two and then rested for much longer. The others around me seemed to be doing the same thing. It was so difficult to stand and begin again after one of these rests, however, that I was constantly telling myself not to stop, but just as often giving in to a persistent internal demand that I escape the agony. For some reason, it was heartening to discover that six or eight of the other trainees had fainted and were lying prostrate under a shady tree at the finish line where they were receiving some medical attention. I too wanted to lie there with them and yet I felt encouraged by the fact that

I had not yet fallen. "I was stronger, I could make it" I thought to myself as I passed by. Feverish dreams of somehow sneaking away presented themselves often during the final laps. I reasoned no one would notice if I slipped out of the park and returned just when the event was closing. Bushes became places I could hide behind and rest until the group was ready to go home. I kept going, I suppose, because I feared discovery. Though I was in a feverish state, I was in some sense quite capable of objectively looking at my response to this test of endurance. The content of lectures about *seishin* strength came back to me. I could see that I was spiritually weak, easily tempted, and inclined to quit. Under such stress, some aspects of my thought were obviously not serving my interest in completing the course. Whatever will power I had arose from pride and an emerging almost involuntary belief in the *seishin* approach. If I was to finish, I needed spiritual strength. It angered and amused me to realize how cleverly this exercise had been conceived. I vowed over and over never to get involved in such a situation again, and yet, within days, when the memory of the physical pain had dimmed, I was taking great pride in my accomplishment and viewing my completion of the twenty-five-mile course as proof that I could do anything I set my mind to.

Some Considerations for the Anthropology of Education

First, it might be useful to review some of the characteristics of *seishin* education as they differ from the philosophy of American-inspired contemporary public education in Japan. This is not only an interesting exercise — the comparison is one Japanese educators and their critics are making when they evaluate today's educational system, particularly in the light of student turmoil and popular dissatisfaction with the liberality of youth. Considering the history of Japanese education since the Meiji Restoration, it is not difficult to see official policy make pendulum-like swings back and forth between "Western" progressive and "Japanese" *seishin* approaches.

1. In *seishin* education, emphasis is placed on nonverbal forms of behavior. A well-behaved, but silent class, for example, is not necessarily an indication of lethargy, stupidity, or the failure of the teacher. It is likely to be interpreted as evidence that students are well-disciplined, receptive, and respectful. In some instances, a *seishin* orientation may take a somewhat skeptical view of verbal logic and its forms of understanding, favoring experience as the basis of knowledge instead.

2. Rather than viewing difficulties and hardships the students face as barriers to education and therefore things to be overcome by better facilities or improved methods of instruction, *seishin*-based education is liable to regard problems in the educational situation as valuable assets to the training process itself. They are tests and therefore means of furthering spiritual training.

3. A knowledge of self and reflection on oneself *(jikaku)* will be stressed in *seishin* training. And in the former case, the blame for difficulties or failure, individual or social, will be placed most heavily on spiritual weakness rather than on social organization. This educational approach to social betterment would give precedence to spiritual reform over social reform. Schools are certainly instruments of change and improvement, but their influence should be over individual character rather than over the shape of society.

4. Rather than encouraging students to consider themselves as different from one another and sponsoring individualistic thought and creativity, *seishin* education sponsors outward conformity to teachers' examples and group standards. Conforming behavior reflects not only self-discipline, but it also contributes to the basic unity of the group. Nonconformity, on the other hand, is disruptive of that unity and a sign of character weakness. It is thought that conformity is made from conviction, not dullness, and that to conform to the group is difficult, rather than easy. Consistent with this is the idea that creativity results from long-practicing patterns taught by a teacher. When the patterns are mastered and the barrier of an extended apprenticeship passed, the individual will emerge creative and his art (in the widest sense) will reflect his spiritual development.

5. *Seishin* education aims to allow the individual to achieve contentment based on the development of an ordered and stable psyche free from confusion and frustration. This is to be through the gradual conquest of *waga* or *ga* (one's primitive self, or in freudian terms, id). The phrase expressing this process, *waga o korosu* (literally "kill one's self"), is the extreme opposite of the emphasis in progressive education on teaching a person skills which will advance his career in the external world and intensify his need for gratification of self.

6. Whenever possible, competition will be organized along group rather than individual lines and many events will have no obvious competitive quality. This will not be because competition hurts feelings, but because it disrupts group unity and because the real competition takes place inside each individual.

7. The unchanging nature of spiritual problems and their solutions is another fundamental tenet of the *seishin* approach, rather than emphasis being placed on the changing nature of knowledge as taught in conventional education. Teachers, parents, and senior students are, by virtue of greater experience and training, spiritually more advanced, more knowledgeable, and therefore worthy of respect and authority. Since age is not a sign of outdatedness, intergenerational continuity and concord are more possible.

8. Teachers with a *seishin* point of view, though they know the course of spiritual development in great detail, may often choose not to be explicit about the outcome of their methods when instructing their students, choosing to let them find out directly from the experience itself. They may provide hints and indicate complete understanding by successfully predicting certain

developments, but as a rule they let experience happen, rather than talking overly much about it. The instruction in progressive education (except science) by comparison, seems quite explicit and abstract with the teacher having the role of verbal transmitter rather than that of one who only points the way for students. In some sense the *seishin* teacher conducts experiments in human nature and lets the results speak for themselves.

Turning from questions which focus exclusively on Japanese education, I would like to offer some observations on the significance of this material to the emerging field of the anthropology of education. I have no special expertise in this area and my observations depend on my impression of what are the major directions in the field.

1. The bank example represents a kind of education which to date has received very little attention. It is not centered in a school system, it involves adults, it is not universal for the society, and it is operated by a kind of institution which in other societies may have no direct interest in education at all. Such conditions would hardly attract the attention of anthropologists about to study education, and yet, at least in the case of Japan, such forms of education, training, socialization, or whatever are very significant social forces, and deserve much greater coverage than they have received. It is my impression that relatively far too much attention is devoted to studies of schooling, schools, and school systems and not enough is devoted to religious education, sports training, military indoctrination and the countless other kinds of more subtle and perhaps more effective ways societies improve and integrate their members.

2. The similarity between the bank's program, and processes and methods found in psychiatric therapy of the *Morita* type. Zen training, and religious conversion in Japan illustrates a simple lesson, namely, that educational efforts which seek some kind of character change or improvement are perhaps best studied within a single theoretical framework which will also adequately account for other kinds of psychological transformations. At various points in the *seishin kyōiku* activities, for example, anxiety or deprivation was artificially intensified and then reduced creating a strong sense of relief and catharsis which served to strengthen certain intended directions of change in a trainee's view of himself and of his relationships with the society around him. The parallels between education and such processes as initiation, therapy, and conversion would deserve more attention.

3. Whether the bank's program is education, socialization, or therapy is not a profitable question to ask, but it does raise one important issue. What, in fact, do we mean by education, and how does it differ from or relate to learning and socialization? Again, in my opinion, there is in the West a strong inclination to understand education as verbal instruction leading to (a) the storage, and (b) the manipulation of symbolic information. This is what explicitly happens in schools. Yet, learning, intelligence, knowledge, social-

ization, and other concepts normally related to education progress by many means, not just verbal instruction, and may be grasped and retained without exclusive reliance on symbols. *Seishin kyōiku* emphasizes experience and the development of spiritual strength. There are, no doubt, many other valued avenues of human growth which are as unlike Japanese spiritual education as they are unlike classroom instruction. The use of various halucinogenic drugs to educate religious initiates and train practitioners is one widespread example.

Just as the study of kinship began to make real headway only after considerable skepticism arose about the ethnocentricity of the concerns and impulses which originally gave it momentum, so the anthropology of education could benefit greatly from a reexamination of its implicit understanding of education.

PART VI

The Teaching of Anthropology

Preview

26. GEORGE SPINDLER   *Transcultural Sensitization*
27. PAUL BOHANNAN, MERWYN S. GARBARINO, and EARLE W. CARLSON   *An Experimental Ninth Grade Anthropology Course*
28. GEORGE AND LOUISE SPINDLER   *Teaching and Learning Anthropology: The Case Study Approach*

PREVIEW

So far in this book we have encountered the conceptual structure and history of educational anthropology, non-human antecedents to human culture and education, analyses of minority groups and mainstream relations in schools, the transmission of culture in traditional non-literate societies and complex modern societies, and methods of studying schools and classrooms. Though there have been implications for the teaching of anthropology in much of what has been said there has been no explicit attention to it. This part of the book is devoted to the teaching of anthropology.

Thanks to a number of projects mounted during the 1970's by anthropologists interested in the introduction of anthropological content into the curriculum of both the elementary and secondary schools there is an anthropological component represented in the curriculum of many public schools and perhaps even more private schools. Thomas Dynneson (1981) feels that this implementation reached its apex fairly quickly and already may have begun to decline. In some instances such content has proved to be controversial enough to disturb administrators and school boards. In most cases the decline, if indeed there is one, is probably due to the fact that such content is likely to be regarded as a "frill", just as some departments of anthropology in smaller universities and colleges have proven to be dispensable when budget crunches come. Given the cyclic nature of American affairs we will probably return to a greater level of popularity within the next few years—particularly as our culture deteriorates further at home and we become more aware of our ambivalent and often quite hostile reception abroad. Dynneson's review in the *Anthropology and Education Quarterly* (1981) is helpful.

This section is largely devoted to teaching the introductory course at the university or college level, with the exception of the chapter by Paul Bohannan, Merwyn Garbarino, and Earle Carlson on an experimental ninth grade anthropology course.

The first chapter, on transcultural sensitization, presents a technique that I have used in nearly all of my courses at Stanford or Wisconsin during the last decade. In it I try to describe how the students can be shown through their own responses to visual material how their observations and interpretations of other cultures are likely to be distorted unless they have some special training. The kind of transcultural perceptual distortion that is analyzed operates wherever teachers and students are of different cultures or social classes. It would seem important that some transcultural sensitization experience be built into the teacher training curriculum. I have found it to be essential in preparing Stanford students for fieldwork in German culture at the Stanford University Center in Germany. I also use the technique in the training of graduate students in education and anthropology where objective and sensitized viewing of processes of cultural transmission in other cultural systems is imperative. And we always begin the first phase of our training seminar in ethnographic methodology at both Stanford and Wisconsin with it. The technique can be developed out of a variety of materials and procedures if the principles laid out in the chapter are observed.

In the last chapter Louise Spindler and I discuss the case study method in the teaching of the introductory course in cultural anthropology. We use case materials in all of our courses at all levels wherever and whatever we teach. We would feel lost without them. It is not that we think theory and generalization or conceptual ordering are unimportant. Quite to the contrary. Our experience leads us to the conclusion that students do not learn of such abstractions directly. They must be drawn from exposure to specific, detailed, and interesting culture case material.

The special issue of the teaching of anthropology in the *Anthropology and Education Quarterly* (Rice, 1985) explores a variety of approaches. Case study materials, often implicitly rather than explicitly, are included somewhere in such approaches. The explicit and intentional use of them, however, is not defined and that is what we try to do in our chapter.

Our position is that direct exposure to contrastive ways of life is essential to the teaching of anthropology at every level, but particularly in the introductory course. This position is integral to the experience reported by Bohannan, Garbarino, and Carlson in their chapter on the experimental ninth grade anthropology course. Two of the three authors came into the teaching experiment without experience teaching high school students. They discovered that these students could learn a great deal if they were given a variety of case study material rather than finalized abstractions and generalizations. Even the most lively generalized texts were not very enthusiastically received by these students. The textbooks were "not about anything" they said. There were no cultural cases. (Stanford students are not enthusiastic about generalized texts either.) These three experimenters found that if one uses a considerable amount of good ethnographic material well presented and organized, ninth grade students are very interested and will make connections between the people they read about and their own lives. The teacher can capitalize on the comparative aspects of anthropology, as the authors point out, and students are even willing to help create cultural and social theory.

It should be apparent that nowhere in this Preview or in the chapters selected for this section is anyone arguing for a mindless presentation of "facts", ethnographic or otherwise. What we are saying in different ways is that specific cultural materials, case studies, and ethnographies that are about people living in specific settings are basic starting points for inductive steps to broader generalization and abstraction—even to theory. The generalization, the abstraction, or the theoretical statement *cannot* be taught in and of itself, nor do one or two examples abstracted out of cultural context suffice to make the generalization live. Whether we are teaching in the elementary school, the high school, or university, and whether we are teaching anthropology as a subject or using anthropological materials in a social studies context, it is my conviction that this is the starting point of effective teaching.

In three brief chapters we cannot hope to do justice to the complexities of teaching anthropology at any level. What we have tried to do in this section is to open the topic for discussion and as a focus for further work.

The Editor

References

Dynneson, Thomas, 1981, "The Status of Pre-Collegiate Anthropology: Progress or Peril?" *Anthropology and Education Quarterly* XII 4:304-310.
Rice, Patricia C., ed., 1985, "The Teaching of Anthropology." Special issue of *The Anthropology and Education Quarterly* 16.4 250-317.

26   *Transcultural Sensitization*

This chapter discusses the ways common errors in transcultural observation and interpretation can be anticipated and how sensitivity concerning them can be acquired. The source of data for this discussion is a sensitization technique first administered in the winter of 1968 to Stanford undergraduate students at one of the university's overseas centers, Stanford in Germany. The same technique has been used in advanced education classes at Stanford University on the home campus during most years since 1970. I am not concerned in this chapter with the differences between groups, but rather with the educational purpose of the technique and the kinds of perceptual distortions consistently revealed by it. Whether applied at Stanford in Germany or Stanford in California, the technique has been used in my classes as a way of sensitizing students to the kinds of errors one is likely to make when perceiving and interpreting behavior in cultural contexts other than one's own. Some 800 students have responded to the technique to date. The perceptual/interpretive errors they make are remarkably consistent from group to group.

There is a substantial literature in psychology, and some in anthropology, concerned with cultural variability in perception. Very little, however, has been written about the very complex process of perceiving and interpreting culturally relevant material across cultural boundaries in the manner described here. The interpretive principles applied in this chapter are implicit in much of the reported experience of anthropologists in the field (Spindler 1987), but they have not, to my knowledge, been explicitly stated or applied in the specific ways developed here.

At Stanford in Germany there were usually about eighty students, mostly sophomores, in attendance at any given time. For six months they carried on with their regular academic work while learning the language of and becoming exposed to the history, politics, and economics of their host country. The program was designed to enable nearly all interested Stanford students to have an overseas experience irrespective of their major concentrations or future professional plans. The students live together in the various centers (there are also centers in France, Italy, England, and Austria), but do a great deal of traveling and are in constant contact with the population of the areas in which the centers are located.

Whenever I have been in residence, students at Stanford in Germany have done field research in the Remstal, the area near the study center, on the continuity of the folk culture in the small villages and on the urbanization and industrialization overtaking these villages. This field research has, in turn, been related through classroom discussions and lectures to basic generalizations and interpretive principles in cultural anthropology. The purpose of my courses in anthropology as I taught them at Stanford in Germany has been to help develop a cognitive organization for observation and participation in a culture foreign to the student.[1]

German culture cannot be considered, from the anthropological point of view, to be radically divergent from North American culture. Though there are substantial cultural differences between the various European countries and North America, in the larger sense they must all be seen as versions of the same general culture. There are, however, sufficient differences to make the deeper adjustment and accurate perceptions of the European culture problematic for North Americans unless they have systematic help. Contact, even prolonged, does not necessarily result in adjustment on this deeper level. Learning to speak the language is a major step in this direction but does not guarantee accurate perceptions and understandings. Human beings tend to interpret new experience in the light of past experience unless there is decisive intervention in the interpretive process. The anthropology instruction at Stanford in Germany was designed as such an intervention.

The first step in this intervention, as I came to understand and practice it in my instruction, was to alert students to the types of perceptual distortions to which they would be subject and which could be corrected in some degree by transcultural sensitization. The specific way in which we went about this, and some general conclusions concerning the major types of distortions, are the subject of this chapter.

The Technique and Its Results

The technique consists of the administration of ten 35 mm. color slides selected from several hundred I had taken of the Remstal and its internal cultural variations. During the first week overseas the slides are shown and the students are asked to write their responses to each of the pictures and turn them in to me. I use those responses in a simple inductive content analysis, the results of which I utilize in class discussions. A description of the pictures— several of which are included in this text—and their culturally appropriate interpretation, together with the major categories of student reaction to them follows.

Picture No. 1. The first slide is of a small area of vineyards *(Weinberge)* near the Stanford in Germany center. This area is subdivided into many small plots, most of which are not larger than a tenth of an acre. Each plot is terraced and there are poles and wires for the support of the grape vines.

---

[1] The fieldwork was of such high quality that I was able to utilize it extensively in a Case Study in Cultural Anthropology (G. Spindler and student collaborators 1973).

The picture is very clear and presents no structural or spatial ambiguities. Students are asked to describe what they see in the picture, what it is used for, and what its possible significance might be in the cultural system of the Remstal.

The slide shows very clearly the small, terraced plots of vineyard characteristic of the area. The important point is that the plots are so' small and their distribution so fragmented that mechanized cultivation is impossible. Consequently, traditional labor methods are still used for cultivation of the crop and upkeep of the poles and wires. This is a significant support, though one of several, for the entire traditional complex of viniculture and the way of life associated with it.

Students see a very wide range of possibilities in this picture. The majority see it as connected with agriculture, though usually not as vineyard plots but as an irrigation project, feeding troughs for cattle or pigs, a soil conservation project, erosion control, or cribs for grain storage. A sizable minority (about 35 percent) see it as something entirely unrelated to an agricultural operation, such as Roman ruins, rows of chairs for a mass audience, a religious congregation, a guarded border, fields destroyed by war, or gun emplacements.

The problem in accurate perception seems to be that there is no exact counterpart in the culture of the viewers for what is seen on the screen. Though vineyards are known in California, hilly, small, terraced plots of this kind are unknown. Further, there is no functional complex in the culture of the viewers into which this perception fits, even if the perception is accurate. The small size and fragmented distribution of the plots of vineyard have no meaning. Consequently, students seldom see the plots as vineyards, and only a few perceive their functional relevance. In general, the range of interpretations is wide and the level of inaccuracy high. Only about 10 percent of the students grasp the cultural significance of what is observed.

Picture No. 2. This is a picture of a middle-aged woman in dark clothing bending over and tying grapevines onto a wire trellis on a sunny, early spring day (Figure 1). Students are asked to describe what the subject is doing and why her activity might be functionally significant. They are also asked to indicate what they think the subject is thinking and feeling. The type of labor performed here is skilled labor which frequently is obtained, within the traditional economic framework, from the membership of the extended family. This validates these relationships, thus helping to maintain the family and values associated with it. The necessity of such intensive hand labor in the small distributed plots is one factor that has kept traditional folk-oriented adaptation intact up to the present time in this area of Germany.

Most students see that some form of agricultural activity is involved in this picture. Only a small proportion (5–15 percent) expressed an understanding of the significance of the intensive hand labor. Again, as there is no functional counterpart for this kind of work in North American culture, few students can see its cultural or economic significance.

Figure 1

The interpretations of what the subject is thinking and feeling run through a wide gamut, but the modalities that appear have mostly to do with fairly grim states of mind. "Tired," "old," "tedious," "boring," "aching back," "aching bones," "tired muscles," are the responses that predominate. Though the bones and muscles of German women who work in the Weinberge do ache, the interpretation of this sensation is quite different in the traditional subculture of the Remstal than in middle-class America. Labor and its discomforts are regarded as positive and old women complain about no longer being able to work in the Weinberge.[2] Students project from their own culture the meaning of experience appropriate to the activity as perceived.

Picture No. 3. This is a visually ambiguous picture. It shows an older female teacher helping a child of about nine years of age into an old church tower where they are to examine four very large cast bells about which she had lectured in *Heimatkunde* (homeland) just before the trip to the tower. There are heavy beams in the picture and the surroundings are generally dark and dusty looking. Students are asked to indicate what is "going on" in the picture. Actually, all that is happening is that the teacher is helping the child off the top rung of the ladder into the upper part of the tower where the bells are. Cultural significance is not in question here.

---

[2] Case endings are not observed in the use of German terms in order to avoid confusing the reader who does not know German.

About one third of the students see the teacher as assisting the child in some way, and about one third see her as punishing the child. The other third of the responses are distributed over a wide range. Those who see the teacher as assisting the child refer to help given in going under a fence, coming out of a mine shaft, a cave, an earthquake-stricken building, or a collapsed basement in a deteriorated slum, or out of a bomb shelter; or, in entirely different directions, as assisting her to go to the toilet or even as preventing suicide. Those who see the teacher as punishing the child usually refer to whipping in a woodshed, spanking because the child had gone some place where she should not have, or being caught because she tried to run away. The interpretations in the third category are too variegated to sample adequately. Most of the interpretations in all categories are irrelevant to the actual situation as it occurred.

It seems clear that the range of possible perceptions and interpretations increases as the situation observed becomes more ambiguous. Ambiguity may be either a product of cultural irrelevance or lack of clarity in spatial or structural relations. Both forms of ambiguity enter into the interpretation of this picture, but the latter are probably most important in this case. Spatial and structural relations are not clear, which is why this picture was selected. The act of climbing into an old church tower to examine bells that have been discussed in class is uncommon in both American and German culture, so the spatial and structural ambiguity is compounded. Perceptions and interpretations, therefore, tend to be fanciful and more or less irrelevant to reality. In actual fieldwork, or in ordinary contact within a foreign culture, situations where ambiguity prevails abound.

Picture No. 4. This slide shows a small bake house *(Backhaus)* in which shifts of several village women bake bread and *Kuchen*[3] together at certain hours each week (Figure 2). The small brick building is technically clear, as is the fire in the furnace inside. A woman is standing by the door with the long ash stirrer in her hand. Students are asked to indicate what it is they are seeing and what its significance could be in the culture of the Remstal. The significance of the Backhaus is not only in the fact that women bake their weekly bread there but in that it is a social-gathering and gossip center for the more conservative women of the village. It thus is a contributing element of social control, as there everyone is talked about and judgments passed on their behavior.

About 30 percent of the students see this as a Backhaus, but virtually none have ever perceived the function of this place as a communication and social-control center. The range of interpretations for the other 70 percent of the students is quite wide, including such perceptions as small-town industry, refinery, one-room house with a coal fireplace, fireplace in an inn, a kiln for making pots, an incinerator, and so forth.

---

[3] Various kinds of baked sweet dough usually served with fruit toppings and whipped cream.

Figure 2

Again, there is no exact cultural counterpart to the Backhaus in U.S. culture, though the general form of the structure and even its purpose may not be unknown. The picture is technically clear. The only ambiguity is the cultural one, which seems to produce a wide range of interpretations as to what is in the picture, and the absence of a cultural counterpart in the culture of the viewer leads to interpretations of significance irrelevant to the local situation.

Picture No. 5. This picture shows a man pumping a liquid of some sort into a trough which empties into a long barrellike container laid lengthwise on a trailer hauled by a small tractor. The man is actually pumping liquid from a pit under the manure pile which is found in front of each *Bauernhaus.*[4] The liquid is then taken in the barrel up to the Weinberge and distributed between the rows of grapevines. This is a substantial contribution to the enrichment of the soil, made possible by the total economic-ecological unit represented by the Bauernhaus. The animals live on the ground floor and the

---

[4] The traditional structure, quite large, housing humans, cows, pigs, and chickens, hay, and implements used in maintaining agricultural activity.

people above them. There is a functional interdependence between the Bauernhaus and the Weinberge other than that created by the activities of the people themselves.

Only 5 percent of the students in any of the samples have ever seen this as a pump for liquified manure or anything like it. Interpretations range wide: a cement mixer for fixing broken sidewalks or for building houses, crushed grapes being pumped into a container, water for spraying, loading coal, delivery of a pillar, tar for street repairs, pumping insecticide into barrels, filling old barrels with new wine, washing gravel, loading pipe onto a truck, erecting the base for a monument, rinsing off a grinding stone, locating a plumbing fixture, and so forth.

Again, the picture is very clear technically. There is no visual ambiguity because of structural or spatial relationships. The ambiguity is culturally introduced. There is no counterpart for the pump or for the use of liquid manure in agricultural operations in the experience of the majority of American students. They produce, therefore, a wide variety of interpretations.

Figure 3

Picture No. 6. This is a picture of a small boy helping his father pick black currants (Figure 3). It is a pleasant picture filled with sunshine, green leaves, bursting clusters of currants, and a basket heaped with the fruit. Students were asked to indicate what is going on in the picture and how the boy feels and thinks about it. Children in this area of Germany are not required to work until they are ready to do so because their parents want them to enjoy working in the fields and the Weinberge. Most children enjoy helping their parents and older siblings in this way.

About 90 percent of the students see this as an activity connected with the harvesting of grapes or currants. Most, however, see the boy as wishing he could join his comrades in play, hoping that the work will be finished so he can leave, wondering if he is going to grow up to do a tedious and boring job like his father, restive under his father's hand, wishing the sun were not so hot, resigned to the work, feeling hot and scratchy, wishing there were an easier way to do it, feeling restless, resenting the drudgery, and so forth.

Again, students tend to project their own experience or the stereotype of that experience within American culture into the perception and interpretation of events or situations in another culture. Working in the field under the hot sun, perhaps especially with one's father, is perceived as boring, tiresome, and so on, and one "naturally" wants to escape to play with peers, as a projection, it appears, of attitudes common in U.S. culture. Though it is likely that some Remstal children feel this way, it is doubtful that many do, given the particular cultural antecedents to the event and its interpretation in this culture.

It is clear in responses to this and other pictures that when motivations and feelings are identified, the range of perceptions and interpretations

Figure 4

increases and the potential irrelevancy of these perceptions likewise increases, irrespective of the technical clarity of the stimulus.

Picture No. 7. This slide shows a not atypical Bauernhaus with large double doors through which animals and hay pass through to the ground floor where the animals are kept, the manure pile surrounded by its square concrete retaining wall in front with the pump in the center, and two stories and attic under a heavy tiled roof (Figure 4). The Bauernhaus is the traditional structure housing the extended family and livestock and is an especially significant representation of the traditional agricultural "folk" adaptation.

People live in these houses within the villages and farm the many scattered strips of flatland and small plots of Weinberge from it. The Bauernhäuser, small plots, Weinberge, manure pile, and so forth, constitute a whole functioning culture complex. It is a way of life that is disappearing but still very much in evidence.

Students see the Bauernhaus as a warehouse, a gasoline station, a tavern, combined hotel and restaurant, a shop or general store, a feed store, suburban home with a two-stall garage, factory of some kind, store with a loading platform, cheese factory, a garage where cars are fixed, a house of prostitution, a winery, an apartment house, a bakery and family home combined, and an equipment repair shop. Only about 10 percent of the students in the various groups ever saw this structure as a regular domicile, and only about half of those saw it as a structure sheltering both man and beast within the general complex described.

As in the other cases, the responses to this picture contained a wide variety of culturally ready categories imposed from the perceiver's culture upon the situation presented from another culture. Ambiguity is created not because of lack of clarity in spatial or structural relations (the picture is clear and focused), but rather because there is no specific cultural category in the perceiver's culture for the perceived event, object, or situation. Nor is there any functional complex in which the perceived situation would fit even if it were perceived relevantly.

Picture No. 8. This slide shows a male German teacher of about forty years of age standing before a fourth-grade class in the *Grundschule* (elementary school). He is standing in a more or less relaxed posture with his hands behind his back looking at the class. The children are grouped around the tables facing him. The classroom is entirely ordinary. Specific clues to the effect that this is a German classroom are lacking, so students are told that it is. The students are asked to indicate what kind of a classroom atmosphere probably exists here and what kind of a teacher this man is. The teacher, Herr Steinhardt from the Schönhausen School, is not a "permissive" teacher but certainly is not an authoritarian one. I have observed many American classrooms that were much more strictly run than his. The nature of the school and educational philosophy are described in Chapter 22. The children were allowed considerable freedom of movement and expression. Their grouping at tables rather than in traditional, formal rows of stationary seats is symptomatic of this freedom.

The student respondents saw Herr Steinhardt as formal, strict, and orderly, authoritarian, austere, autocratic, dominating, arrogant, stern, meticulous, demanding, stiff, detailed, traditional, old-fashioned, "uptight," and as a "pompous authoritarian" in about 80 percent of all responses to this picture. The classroom was seen consistently in the same framework, that is, one demanding submission from the children, as having an orderly, "didactic," rigid, "alienating," highly disciplined atmosphere.

It is apparent that students responding to this picture have projected a stereotype that is patterned in their own culture about a situation in another culture. American students have stereotypes about how German classrooms are run and what German teachers are like. These stereotypes are projected. The range of perceptions and interpretations is not broad, but the irrelevancy of those offered is marked.

Picture No. 9. This slide shows the same classroom ten seconds after the slide in Picture No. 8 was taken. The teacher is in a more dynamic posture with hand raised and a lively expression on his face, and the children are raising their hands; some are half risen from their seats. Students are asked to indicate whether this slide causes them to change their interpretation of the first picture of this classroom.

About 50 percent of the respondents say that the second picture does not cause them to modify their first perceptions significantly. The other 50 percent describe the classroom as less autocratic than they had thought, less rigid, more free, and more democratic.

It is significant that approximately one half of the students modify their interpretations in the direction of greater freedom in the classroom. This illustrates the importance of time sampling in any particular sequence of behavior, and is also an important element in transcultural sensitization.

Figure 5

Picture No. 10. This slide shows several boys walking into the *Schönhausen* School with Herr Steinhardt standing out in the school yard with one hand raised pointing toward the door (Figure 5). His posture is rather relaxed and his hand and arm are not in a stiff position. Students are asked to indicate what they think the boys are thinking and feeling as they enter the classroom and school.

About one half of the students in the various groups to which these pictures have been shown see the boys as feeling reluctant, fearful, anxious, resigned, and resentful. About one-third see the boys as eager to enter, excited, anticipatory, wanting to get started, happy, and fascinated. The rest produce a fairly wide range of responses, including "not rushing but o.k," "amenable but not eager," "not thinking or feeling very much," being rewarded for obedience, feeling cheated because the recess break has been cut short, and so forth.

A substantial number of American student respondents appear to draw from their own experience with school. They are probably not only drawing directly from this experience but also from stereotypes about what this experience is like, particularly for boys in U.S. culture. Stereotypes of German classrooms and teachers, and American student responses to these stereotypes, as well as the influence of one's school experience and stereotypes relating to that experience in U.S. culture, are intermingled. This happens frequently in transcultural perception and interpretation.

Conclusions

It should be remembered that the procedures described above are carried out as a part of an instructional program and not primarily for purposes of research on perceptual distortion. With the exception of the groups at Stanford in California, all of the students were at Stanford in Germany and were about to enter or had already entered into fairly intensive contact with German people and German culture.[5] The cultural sensitization procedure was carried out in order to enrich their overseas experience by making them more sensitive and acute observers, and also to increase the probability of success in fieldwork in the Remstal area.

The pictures were all presented on a large screen with a 35 mm. projector. The responses, as stated, were written by each student and collected at the end of the period. The instructor did a content analysis, resulting in the categories of response described above. These results were presented to each class in two fifty-minute discussion periods during which the pictures were again shown and considerable detail presented by the instructor about the content and significance of each slide. Certain general principles of perceptual distortion in transcultural observation and interpretation were derived inductively in these discussions. I will summarize these general principles

---

[5] Two of the Stanford in Germany groups had actually been in Germany for one academic quarter at the time the technique was administered. It is interesting that the same types of perceptual errors were displayed by these groups as by the others. The students had no anthropological training during the first quarter.

briefly, as they have already been anticipated in the discussion of the pictures and student responses to them.

It appears that perceptual distortion in transcultural observation increases when:

1. There is no clear counterpart for the perceived object or event in the observer's culture. Responses to the picture of the Bauernhaus, the liquid manure wagon, and the Weinberge all fall into this category. None of these objects, events, or situations occur in North American culture.

2. There is no functional complex into which the object, event, or situation, even if accurately perceived, fits, so the significance is lost or skewed. This applies clearly to the Weinberge and the Backhaus and, to some degree, to most of the rest of the presented pictures. The Weinberge cannot be understood even if seen as Weinberge unless one understands that the size of the plots and their distribution, as well as their terracing, prevents the application of large-scale mechanical power to their maintenance, and that this in turn is related to the necessity for intensive hand labor, in turn related to the extended family as a source of labor and eventually to the utility of the Bauernhaus and the whole traditional complex. Neither can the Backhaus be understood even if perceived as a house where bread and cakes are baked unless it is seen as a communication and gossip center. This same line of reasoning can be applied to a number of the other pictures and responses.

3. There is a stereotype of experience related to the event, object, or situation patterned in the observer's own culture. This seems clear in the interpretation of the boys' feelings as they leave the school yard to go into the school. Boys would rather play, it is said. The school is confining. This is an image of school in American culture, according to the respondents themselves as they retrospected about their reactions to the pictures and their own experience. The same principle applies to the projection of aching backs and bones, the tediousness of labor, and the desire to escape from it in the interpretation of the picture of the women working in the vineyards and the picture of the small boy helping his father pick currants.

4. There is a stereotype of the experience or meaning of the event, object, or situation as it is presumed to exist in another culture. German teachers and classrooms are believed, in American culture, to be authoritarian, strict, and disciplined. This stereotype is applied to the picture of Herr Steinhardt, with the result that the responses are largely irrelevant to the actual situation portrayed in the picture.

5. There is ambiguity due to lack of clarity in the structural or spatial relations surrounding or involved in the event, object, or situation. This applies particularly to the situation where the teacher is helping a child up the last part of the ladder into the loft of the church to see the bells. The range and irrelevancy of responses is great and seems to be a function of the fact that no one understands exactly what is being seen. Potentially meaningful cues are seized upon, such as the heavy structural beams in the tower, the general dinginess of the surroundings, or the white bandage on the child's

hand. There is not only spatial and structural ambiguity involved here but also cultural ambiguity, because the situation is unfamiliar in American culture.

6. There is projection of emotional states ascribed to subjects in another culture. This applies to all situations in which student respondents were asked to indicate what they thought people in the pictures might be thinking or feeling. The emotional states projected are clearly functions of the patterning of experience and beliefs about experience in North American culture. They tend to be quite irrelevant to the specific situations represented in the pictures.

7. There is a single time sample of the action. This applies most directly to the two pictures of the classroom, but it could apply to any of the situations. In order for interpretations to be relevant (i.e., accurate), they must be based upon a sampling of parts of the whole cycle of activity, whatever it is.

Implications

The processes engaged in by students responding to the pictures described above are similar to those experienced by the field anthropologist. They are also similar to those experienced by the teacher faced with a classroom full of children, particularly when they are from different social classes or ethnic groups than his own. Furthermore, the children also represent a youth subculture different from that of the teacher. Teachers make the same types of errors described in this analysis, and for the same reasons the Stanford students made them. Some of these errors are mainly humorous, others suggest why there is constant, serious, often tragic, misinterpretation and noncommunication in classrooms where cultural differences are sharp.

By applying what we know about culture and about the problems of the anthropologist in the field to the analysis of materials that may be brought into the classroom from another culture, such as the slides I used, we may anticipate the kinds of errors that are likely to occur in transcultural perception and interpretation, control them better, and develop some relevant skills in observation. I have called this a transcultural sensitization process. Something similar, I suggest, should be a part of all teacher-training programs. It is one way that an anthropological perspective may help improve teaching.

References

Spindler, George, ed., 1970 (Reissued 1987), *Being an Anthropologist: Fieldwork in Eleven Cultures.* Prospect Heights, IL: Waveland Press.

Spindler, George D., and student collaboration, 1973, *Burgbach: Urbanization and Identity in a German Village.* CSCA. New York: Holt, Rinehart and Winston, Inc.

PAUL BOHANNAN/*Northwestern University*
MERWYN S. GARBARINO/*University of Illinois at Chicago*
EARLE W. CARLSON/*Northwestern University*

27 An Experimental Ninth-Grade Anthropology Course

In 1965–1966 we initiated a full-year course in anthropology for ninth-graders at the North Shore Country Day School in Winnetka, Illinois. The school, a member of the National Association of Independent Schools, has about twenty students in its kindergarten and in each of its first five grades and about forty in each of its sixth through twelfth grades. It is divided, as most independent schools are, into a lower school, middle school (grades six through eight), and an upper school (grades nine through twelve). It is what is commonly called a progressive school because it emphasizes close personal attention to each student, recognizes human capacities beyond the traditional scholarly ones, and tries to train the visual and aural senses as well as the capacities for reading, writing and computing.

Our students met in two sections, each for forty minutes daily with about eighteen students in each section. These students were "selected" in the sense that their capacities ran from average up. We had a few very bright students but none who were not of at least average capacity and achievement. We think it is an important point that the students of the school are not selected primarily for their scholarly capacities—in fact, that is rather far down the list in the requirements. It is, however, assumed that the students are able to absorb and profit from a good high-school education. Therefore, we had no problems with dropouts or with lack of motivation. We had boys with long hair, and, like the rest of the school, we treated it merely as a hair style.

The course was undertaken when, in a discussion with the headmaster of the school, Nathaniel S. French, Bohannan criticized several new curricula that used anthropology and sociology as decorations on a course that was basically economics and history. He felt the right way to handle the material was to treat the principles of sociology and anthropology as the fundamentals, history and ethnology as the primary sources of data on human existence, and economics and political science as the two disciplines most helpful in evaluating today's newspapers.

*Reproduced by permission of the American Anthropological Association from the *American Anthropologist* 71(3), 1969.

When an opening occurred in the social studies faculty in the upper school, French suggested that if Bohannan would plan such a course, he (French) would appoint whatever teacher of the course the two of them found satisfactory. Bohannan replied that although he needed a co-worker in this program, he would like to teach part of it himself and would prefer a partnership with a second anthropologist rather than to try directing a program taught by someone else. At that time Garbarino had just finished fieldwork among the Seminole Indians and was writing her dissertation. She agreed to become a partner in this project. Throughout the year the two taught more or less alternate units, one for a few days, then the other for a few days; meanwhile keeping in close touch and exchanging "field notes." We did not find this arrangement difficult, and as far as we know, the students did not find it confusing or objectionable.

From the beginning of the program our goal was to teach students in high school the data, methods, theories, and insights of the behavioral sciences. Although we concentrated on anthropology, we also included a good bit of sociology, no inconsiderable amount of psychoanalytic viewpoint and psychological anthropology, some historical and more prehistorical material, and some theory derived ultimately from economics and political science. Our goal was to provide the best available scaffolding for studying history and comprehending the present-day human situation.

We considered ourselves responsible for the first year. We knew that our students would proceed to at least one more year, and some of them to three more years, of social studies in their high-school careers. We wanted to establish a set of viewpoints that would be useful and expandable in the later years with as little as possible to be relearned, unlearned, or jettisoned. We are aware, of course, that ethnographic details will be forgotten. Nevertheless, we are also aware—and our experience proved overwhelmingly—that only good ethnographic factual material can make such a course interesting.

The year was divided into three quarters. In the first quarter we began with American Indians, proceeded to Africa, and included some theoretical material on cultural theory and the structure of society.

The second quarter dealt with human origins. We taught the principles of evolutionary theory (about three quarters of our students had already studied it in their biology course), the evolution of mankind and the development of man's capacity for culture, and prehistory up to the creation of the ancient civilizations, therefore including the acquisition of agriculture, metalworking and the like.

In the third quarter we made a comparative study of civilization. We began with the ancient Near Eastern civilizations and then discussed the history and culture of the civilizations of China and Japan.

What we accomplished could be called a course in non-Western Civilizations. Although it was anthropologically based, it was not limited to anthropology.

Bohannan and Garbarino came into this teaching experiment without experience in teaching high-school students. (Carlson, who took over in subsequent years, had such experience.) Except for our own children and those of our friends, we had not faced or dealt with teenagers since we ourselves had been teenagers. Our basic fear was, How do you teach social science to people who necessarily, because of their age, have limited social experience? We quickly found the answer: You fill them in. And we soon realized that "filling them in" is as good a definition as any other of a liberal education.

First Quarter: Cultural and Social Anthropology

We began with Theodora Kroeber's *Ishi in Two Worlds* (1963). We found this a very good book for ninth graders because they read it with interest, consider it an adult book, and react emotionally as well as intellectually to its contents. On the first day they were assigned the Prologue to Mrs. Kroeber's book. Ishi, the last surviving member of the Yahi tribe of Central California, was driven by hunger and fear to a slaughterhouse outside of Oroville, California, where he was discovered one morning in a corral. Because no communication was possible and because he was naked and on the verge of exhaustion, he was taken to the Oroville jail. The anthropologists at the University of California in Berkeley were notified, and T. T. Waterman went immediately to Oroville to see him.

In spite of the fact that Mrs. Kroeber goes to some pains to point out that the sheriff's action in putting Ishi into jail was neither stupid nor brutal, our ninth graders had a serious reaction to it. On the basis, then, of no more than the Prologue, they started a discussion in which they blamed their own people, and in a sense themselves, for being inept and guilty of mistreatment of Ishi and the Indians. When this attitude became evident, we asked them what they thought would happen if the last wild Indian were to wander today out of the Skokie lagoons into Winnetka; what would we do with him? After a few minutes discussion one boy raised his hand and said, "We would obviously have to put him in jail." We were encouraged by the first session of the class because we were finding the students willing to get involved in both the material we had assigned to them and the discussion of hypothetical situations set in their own community.

The second chapter of *Ishi* gives background material on California Indians. We had the ninth graders make maps, on the basis of the one Mrs. Kroeber gives, and do a little encyclopedia work on the problem of American Indians. Thereafter, we went through this book a chapter a day. The only part of our teaching techniques that might be difficult for someone who is not a professional anthropologist to emulate is that when students asked questions, we answered them with as precise detail and as much theory as we thought necessary to make the details understood.

By the time they had finished *Ishi,* they were well launched into the study of cultural anthropology. It would, perhaps, be possible to write a teacher's guide for this material. It would be vastly preferable, however, for the teacher to have a few good courses in anthropology and to deal with the questions and the material as it comes up. Our two sections brought up different points; yet we think that they were approximately equal in their achievement at the end of the unit. Certainly we could not have achieved so much if *we* had brought up the points and told them what they were to be interested in.

Next we read Alice Marriott's *Ten Grandmothers* (1945). We found this, like *Ishi,* a superb book for teaching ninth-grade social studies. It is an adult book—a factor that cannot be underestimated. With a series of characters running through the story, Dr. Marriott explains the pressures and responses that led the Kiowa Indians to change and develop as they did in the middle nineteenth century. It is fascinating history and superb anthropology and, like all Dr. Marriott's work, well written. On the basis of this material we discussed Plains Indians at length, and some of the students wrote special reports, taking their materials from such standard books as Spencer and Jennings' *The Native Americans* (1965) and Driver's *Indians of North America* (1961).

When we took up our third Indian group, the Iroquois, we made a serious mistake. We considered, and still do, Hazel Hertzberg's *The Great Tree and the Longhouse* (1966), part of the A.A.A.'s Curriculum Development Project, a very fine book. It is, however, written for the sixth grade, and we did not realize that our ninth graders would not be willing to adjust to what was for them easy reading. The attitude was best summed up by a girl who asked, "When are we going to get through with this kid stuff and back to books written for just people?" This judgment is not a considered judgment on Mrs. Hertzberg's book; it is a statement that ninth graders, in our experience, are not able to utilize material that is easy for them nearly so well as they are able to cope with material that is difficult for them. Although we have not tested this proposition further, it is our hunch that it is probably true in all groups of ninth graders. We found that they could not consider the book as just a book from which they should study and get information and perhaps write things that would bring it up to their level. They didn't see it that way. They felt that we were trying to keep them in a junior role. We think that they understood the intellectual aspects of the problem, but emotionally they nevertheless felt that this book was not for them; we also have a hunch that they would not feel that any book that was written for the schools was for them. They need and want well-written material that can be of interest to an adult.

After discussion of these three books, we gave a few short lectures on introductory aspects of the theories of cultural anthropology. We told students how to take notes on lectures, showed them how lectures should be organized and how to judge a good one, and tried to get them to evaluate critically in the structure of lectures. We graded them on the notes they took on our lectures and found that we had to teach them the outline form.

The lecture material covered the prehistory of the American Indians in a very fast sweep, as well as some statements about the culture areas of North America (we used one created by Garbarino on the basis of all the others available; we think that this makes no difference, and the one in Driver can be utilized with no comparative material at all). For a special project that each student was required to do during the quarter, some of our more advanced students made a study of American Indian origins, basing it primarily on Driver and on Spencer and Jennings. We also led a series of discussions in which the ecology and economic adjustment, the political forms, and the family life of the three peoples we had studied were compared, bringing this into line with other material that the students happened to know, with material they had read for their reports, and with their own experiences in families in the middle and upper middle class in the Middle West.

We then attempted to go over the same general ground, but more briefly and in more depth, for the peoples of Africa. We began with Colin Turnbull's *The Forest People* (1961). This book, about the Pygmies of the Congo, is a superb example of what ought to be written to teach anthropology as a basic subject in the social sciences for high-school students. We might add, parenthetically, that the first twelve chapters are, for this purpose, better than the last three, and would suggest that teachers consider skipping the last three chapters unless they plan to use them for considering how a person from one society reacts to geography and social situations that are strange to him. Since we had already explored this idea in *Ishi,* we did not find the last three chapters as useful as the rest of the book.

But *The Forest People* is a hard act to follow. Therefore, rather than try to use material that we thought less suitable, we went directly to a summary position and used Bohannan's *Africa and Africans* (1964). This book (which has fast become obsolete in all except Chapters 7–14, although a new edition, with Philip Curtin as coauthor, is in the works) was not terribly successful in the ninth grade, because it contains too many generalizations, too much summary, and too few ethnographic examples. What we finally did was take a single point from each one of the chapters around which could be built discussions and outside assignments. Our discussions of slavery, of religion, of witchcraft, and of social organization went very well.

We spent about ten days at the end of the quarter on a summary. We gave lectures on basic ideas and fundamentals of social organization, including the family, political structure, and anthropological ideas of economy and religion. We also assigned Douglas Oliver's *Invitation to Anthropology* (1964). We thought, and still think, that it is a very good, short summary of what anthropology is about. Our students did not concur. The reasons that they gave—and this underscores a point we have made above—was that it was not about anything, by which they meant that there were no ethnographic facts or examples in it.

Our conclusions at the end of the quarter were that if you have a lot of good ethnographic fact, well presented and organized, ninth-grade students are extremely interested in it; they do make an association between the people they read about and their own lives so that the teacher can capitalize on the inherent comparative aspects of anthropology; and they are able to learn and are even willing to help to create cultural and social theory.

Second Quarter: Human Origins and Prehistory

Our course took place before the material created by the Anthropology Curriculum Development Project, directed by Dr. Malcolm Collier, was available, but Carlson used that material in the second and third years. The biggest problem in the first year was the plethora of material—highly repetitious, but with comparatively few outstanding books suitable for ninth graders. The irony, or perhaps one should say it is the cause, is that human origins and prehistory have attracted more nonprofessionals and more writers of "books for young people" than all the rest of anthropology put together. Some of the nonprofessional summaries are good. Others are worse than misleading.

This particular topic presents a problem we do not know how to combat: the primary question that both the writers of the books and our ninth graders ask is "what happened in prehistory?" They want to be given a more or less precise history of the development of man and of his culture and civilization. Obviously, with each new discovery, or at least with each major new theoretical development, it becomes necessary to reconstruct prehistory all over again. This means that each of the books contains a reconstruction and that the reconstructions all too often do not jibe. The reason for this is sometimes to be found simply in the dates of the books, but it is often due to special pleading by the authors. Solving this problem means that the teacher must give a great deal of factual and theoretical material on the evolution of the human animal and culture. We gave this material in lecture form because we did not find books that could do the task for us. The "technician's books" were almost all too detailed for this grade level and for our task. The "writer's books" hurried over the technical problems to get to the romance. Highly technical books on evolution, such as those of Dobzhansky, we did not even try at this grade level. Perhaps we were wrong. We used *Early Man,* by F. Clark Howell and the editors of *Life* (1965). It was extremely useful, but it is difficult to use without supplementary material because there is too much material in it for a casual reading and too little to go into any one aspect of the problem.

Because of limitations both in time and in students' backgrounds in biology, our intention was to teach the concepts rather than the actual mechanisms of evolution. On this level, it was expected that there would be little reason for students who had not had biology to suffer any real disability.

In teaching biological evolution we had to combat the tendency of all the students to take a teleological view of natural selection. We had hoped, by presenting cultural anthropology first, to avoid the problem of purpose in evolution. That is to say, by first showing the present day range of human behavior and then adding the time dimension, we would avoid the bugaboo of tribal peoples seen as contemporary ancestors and would demonstrate that nonliterate peoples have histories, although not written, as long as that of Western man. We think it helped, but we still had to counteract the idea that the aim of evolution was to produce Western man.

We stressed in lecture and discussion that biological and cultural evolution were inseparable in man's development and that through the evolution of culture man was able to move into many new environmental zones without gross biological changes. Culture is thus shown as the extension of man's senses and his nonbiological means of adaptation, including adaptation to the social environment. Man then differs from the other primates primarily because of his culture.

To demonstrate the concept of adaptation we first discussed the exploitative potential of various environments at different stages of cultural evolution, but we hoped to avoid the pitfall of geographic determinism by presenting the environment as permitting a range of forms within its limits. Therefore, even in an extreme environment such as the circumpolar regions, while shelter is an essential, we found many forms shelter could take.

In terms of our stated aims of teaching concepts rather than mechanisms, we believe we were successful in the following ways. The students demonstrated reasonable grasp of natural selection and adaptation, and (within the limits of the facts available to them) they understood the positive feedback relationship between culture and biological evolution. They also learned the generally accepted sequence of fossil forms of the hominid line.

Growing out of our study of adaptation to environment, we progressed to post-Pleistocene times and to culture changes arising from the domestication of plants and animals. Domestication in our presentation was only one of many regional adaptations in response to a slowly changing climate. In this fashion we hoped to avoid the mental image of the neolithic or agricultural revolution as a sudden insight on the part of an individual—a point of view many students have. Indeed, for one of our weekly written assignments we got a lively, imaginative story about *the* woman who invented agriculture. It is quite likely that many students tend toward a similar picture of domestication, and we wanted to correct that view. We think we did.

It was easy to generate interest in the changes in behavior caused by a change from hunting and gathering to food production. In fact, the very concept of domestication as opposed to taming resulted in lively class discussion, and some students became so interested that they did independent study projects, which they reported to the class. Among the topics studied were the attributes selected for domestication and a comparison of productive usefulness of children in hunting and gathering as opposed to agricultural societies. There was some class amusement at the realization that children were usually burdens to hunters whereas they could contribute importantly to an agricultural community. Our students had never before considered children as anything but assets by their mere existence.

Here a note on independent research might be injected. The limitations of the school library presented a real difficulty. This is not to be taken as a criticism of the particular school we taught in, for it is highly unlikely that any high school would have adequate resource material in either cultural or physical anthropology unless some recent attempt had been made to obtain it. The fact is that library materials must be expanded if anthropology is to be taught, and from our experience it would appear that most of the expansion must be in the direction of college-level literature, *not* adaptations written for high school students.

Third Quarter: Comparative Civilizations

By the end of the second quarter we had reached the point of talking about civilization as a subset of culture marked by certain specific terms or traits. The students became interested in the "causes" of civilization, a point we could not have started with. To come up with the necessary and sufficient causes of civilization we turned to the data of the archaic civilizations of the Old and New Worlds—Sumer, Egypt, and Mexico. We went to the various works of V. Gordon Childe, taking his criteria for civilization as a place to start. Then, through discussions with the students, we elicited their ideas of the way these various criteria are to be ranked in importance.

From reading and lectures, discussion ensued, and the students decided that although agriculture was necessary to civilization, it was not sufficient "cause"—that, indeed, no one "cause" was sufficient in itself. That conclusion led to the question of why all agriculturists did not achieve civilization and to a discussion of social and ecological limitations to evolutionary potential.

During the whole unit on early civilization we had the students compare *culture* and the *special form* of culture that is called a civilization. The result was happily more than just a list of traits. It came close to being a statement of cultural process and increasing structural complexity. Without using such professional jargon, the students came up with the recognition that civilization has more components and greater specialization of the components than the noncivilized society. Briefly, we discussed the greater complexities and possibilities of food production with differentiation of primary producers and full-time labor specialists versus food collecting or producing with very little specialization.

The students decided—as anthropologists have known for over a century, but we do not think that we precooked their decision—that the presence of writing was one of the two most important of the several criteria of civilization. The only new thing about this idea is that they discovered it in terms that were not available in the nineteenth century when it was discovered —undoubtedly rediscovered—by anthropologists. They pointed out that the capacity to store culture, created by writing, vastly enlarges the choices open to people. At the same time, it reduces the amount of effort it takes to maintain a cultural level. The result is a proliferation of specialist roles and hence the complexification and cultural achievement that civilization exhibits. We had lively discussions about the fact, which they pointed out with no prodding, that the same thing is happening again today because computers provide new kinds of storage mechanisms for culture and that we are only just beginning to feel the effects of them. In our summary we noted that just as speaking means that the demonstrator is not necessary in all situations of learning, and just as writing means that the actively participating teacher is not necessary in all situations of learning, so in the present situation, the written record has been changed out of recognition so that word symbols too are no longer necessary in all situations of learning. It seemed unlikely to our students—and to us—that computers would replace writing any more than writing replaced speaking or speaking replaced demonstration. (We missed, here, an opportunity to explain a Gutmann scale.)

The other item they thought was of fundamental importance was full-time specialization of arts and industries. However, there were many other characteristics of civilization that we discussed, including oral tradition and common expectations as means of social control in homogeneous societies as opposed to the need for a codification of laws in the heterogeneous society that appeared with early urbanization. Urban culture itself, as a new and different set of relationships, was dwelt upon at some length. Without calling it such, we came close to Redfield's rural-urban continuum as a concept useful in describing development over time as well as change in space.

Largely because the class *demanded* some sort of chronology—we think as a result of prior conditioning—we did a time line of invention from 10,000 BC to AD 1500, comparing Old and New World chronologies. The comparison involved not only the invention of technical improvements, such as the wheel and metallurgy, but also the appearance of major structural change, such as the beginnings of complex village life. The visual stimulus of a time line was important to the students. We think now that throughout the year more visual treatment should have been incorporated, perhaps in the form of films.

We ended the unit on early civilization with a few lectures and some discussion of the European Neolithic, the spread of food production into Europe, the Mediterranean influence in the north, and the steppe pastoralists' introduction of the domesticated horse into central Europe. The emphasis here was on the cultural backwardness of Western man during the formative period of civilization and the importance of diffusion and recombination of many ideas from many sources. Once again we tried to avoid the tendency to think of European as the purposive aim of development and tried to stress the importance of interaction in the spread and elaboration of the few very great simplifying inventions and new combinations of old knowledge.

We spent more time on the ideas of civilization than we had originally planned, so we did not have as much time as we had hoped to deal with nonwestern civilizations of the nineteenth and twentieth centuries. The class read two books: Etsu Sugimoto's *Daughter of the Samurai* (1934) and Francis Hsu's *Americans and Chinese* (1955).

The *Daughter of the Samurai* is an excellent book, which ninth graders read with great attention. It contains a great deal of ethnographic material, and Mrs. Sugimoto's coming to America, finding the culture strange, and contrasting it with her own makes this good teaching material. Since Bohannan knew some Japanese ethnography and had been in Japan, he was able to fill in the book with materials on Japanese history, the nature of the Meiji Restoration, and how the social structure led to modern economic development in a way that it did not in most other traditional societies. We also went into such things as how properly to sit, stand, walk, and eat. We tried to conduct one class on the floor, sitting Japanese fashion; we lasted about fifteen minutes.

In the case of China, we had Francis Hsu himself come and discuss further some of the ideas in his book. This was an exciting part of the course. At the end, as a summary, we repeated very quickly the criteria for civilization, drawing on Chinese and Japanese examples.

The Following Two Years

Like many another beginner, we tried to put too much into this course, and in the years following it, Carlson (a doctoral candidate at Northwestern), who took the course over from Bohannan and Garbarino, has not proceeded to the third quarter but rather has spread the original material from the first two quarters over the year, finding that in that way, he could get through it without rushing. New materials have also changed the course, and we now use the experimental units of the Anthropology Curriculum Study Project on "Early Man" and "The Great Transformation" of society and culture from hunting and gathering bands to the beginnings of urban civilization.

The basic strategy was, however, left intact: to introduce the students to as much ethnographic material as they could handle in the first half; then to proceed to human origins and culture history, with a strong emphasis on archeological methods and reasoning by inference, in the second half.

This plan, like any other that a teacher of such a course may produce, necessarily demanded some modifications. Students discovered that they needed evolutionary concepts, geographical orientations, and biological insights to deal with ethnographic and, particularly, historical material. These were reinserted.

The plan for the first half was much the same as that outlined above for the first quarter. The materials were the same with the following exceptions. Hazel Hertzberg's book was replaced by Chapter 9, on the Iroquois, from Wendell H. Oswalt's *This Land Was Theirs* (1962). In the Africa section we followed Turnbull's Pygmies with Elizabeth Marshall Thomas's *The Harmless People* (1965), and we inserted there the material from the A.S.C.P. on the Kalahari Bushmen and the materials from *Early Man* in *Life's* Nature Series, edited by F. Clark Howell (1965). This book proved invaluable in this context and later as an introduction to the idea of man's development through the Pleistocene. In the second year talks and discussions on the Tiv were conducted by Laura Bohannan, and her *Return to Laughter* (1965) was read by the class. This book proved stimulating to advanced students, but it can be more safely recommended for the upper grades of high school than for the ninth.

In the third year no appreciable changes in materials or approach were made, but as the terminal assignment of the first half, each student worked through a monograph approved in advance. The student reported to the class, then, the essence of what he had read and commented on its special value for our studies. Invaluable for this assignment were the paperback volumes in the Spindler series,* Kluckhohn and Leighton's *The Navaho* (1962), and Drucker's *Indians of the Northwest Coast* (1963).

Conclusions

We think we have proved that the three of us can teach anthropology to middle-class ninth graders as readily as we can to freshmen and sophomores in college. In many ways, indeed, it is easier to teach ninth graders. There is less resistance on the part of the students, which may, of course, be a characteristic of this particular group of students, although we are not convinced that that is the case. There is a great eagerness to learn the bases and techniques of social life. At this particular time of their lives, students are struggling with becoming adult members of society. Besides being an important educational period and the time when most students go through the experi-

---

*Editor's note: The reference here is to the Case Studies in Cultural Anthropology (CSCA) edited by George and Louise Spindler and including nearly 100 studies of cultures around the world. The series is published by Holt, Rinehart and Winston, Inc.

ences of puberty and adolescence, high school (and perhaps this continues for the first two or three years of college) is a rehearsal period for adult life; it is something like watching the prepubertal ten- or eleven-year-old boy rehearsing for adolescence. Social science has a great deal to say directly to these people. It tells them about choices in behavior and allows them to ask questions about behavior in their own society and in comparative contexts. Our students, by and large, were not interested in social sciences merely as subject matter or as the basis on which to make reforms and commitments. They were interested in these things, but they were even more interested in creating their own techniques of social living on an adult plane, and for this reason they gave it an attention that goes beyond the specific data, while at the same time the data allow them to compare and contrast their own situations with it. In short, social science is a good way to learn something about life at this time (and perhaps at any other) of one's own life.

On the other side of the coin, there were some problems we did not expect. Statements in class, in texts, in written themes had to be taken *very* seriously in order to convince students that this was not just another assignment but that their communications carried information about themselves and their culture as well as about the subject matter. This care precipitated some crises for students, who thought they were only to say "nice things" about primitive or prehistoric peoples. We found a stubborn sentimentality for the underdog; we did not allow the sentimentality to go unchallenged, but the process of finding that sentimentality can cover prejudice and that they were not as respectful of other human beings as they had thought, or as they tried to make out, was sometimes painful. There was a tendency to turn the world into good guys and bad guys; Ishi and Turnbull's pygmies were good guys, and White civilization was the bad guy. We did our best to make them examine these ideas and go deeper than a good-guy/bad-guy dichotomy into the religion, world view, technology, and history of the groups, and somehow to gain respect for groups and individuals still closer to themselves in experience without the kind of guilt (which is systematically taught to them somewhere) that ultimately will cripple their attempts to make reforms. At the age of fourteen the biases of mature Americans are not yet entirely internalized; the problems our students faced can be compared with those faced by youth anywhere. We think that the possibility of penetrating cultural biases through anthropological studies appears greater at this age than at eighteen. However, we also think that the problem is that teachers have been brainwashed into saying "What 'they' do is good for 'them.'" A teacher once told Bohannan in a workshop, "Their ways are as good as ours." He asked, "Good for what?" Her immediate reply was, "Good for them," and she could not get beyond that.

This leads to our conviction that the difficulty in applying this sort of program lies largely with the fact that teachers are not adequately trained in anthropology. Bohannan and Garbarino have worked at training teachers in a summer institute and in an extension course for Northwestern (also treated as "in-service training" in some of the local high schools). We found the task overwhelming, and for two reasons. First of all, the better the teacher, the more difficult it is to retrain him. We mean this as a compliment, if a rather left-handed one, to successful and good teachers. What such teachers want, and what they should have, is material to add to their already successful courses. They want material to upgrade and enrich their courses, and they often think of using the social sciences from this point of view. We think that such material should be supplied. We would much rather have good teachers using good materials in ways of which we basically disapprove than to have good teachers using bad materials in ways of which we basically disapprove. We would, in fact, much rather have good teachers teaching things of which we disapprove on professional grounds than to have bad teachers teaching materials we think superb. Therefore, we have come to the conclusion that training social-studies teachers should be done in full-blown M.A. programs for teachers who take a year, or even two years, off to take M.A.s in one of the social sciences, or else that it should be done before a teacher goes out and begins to set up his courses and his style of dealing with them. We hope their superintendents and school boards can be brought to concur. We are of the opinion that good teachers are legion in the schools of this country, at least in the areas with which we are acquainted, and that what they need is more and better teaching materials and a much freer hand in using those materials.

The second reason that we think the teacher-training task is overwhelming and must be done in undergraduate and M.A.T. programs, is that for the scholar or the school administrator to insist upon it is to earn the resentment of people who consider themselves successful and have some pretty good bases for their opinions. Our schools today are burgeoning with new curricula in the social sciences. The "new social studies" has become a jargon term— and a pejorative one. When one looks at the wide variety of the curricula being produced, it is not to be wondered that the very best teachers are skeptical.

It cannot be said after these three years that we have found *the* curriculum or *the* program for the proper study of man in the ninth grade. We *can* say that we are unanimous in our rejection of certain materials for this level and only a little less wholeheartedly unanimous in those we accept; incidentally, our unanimity includes our students.

The greatest challenge is working out curricula that integrate objectives, methods, and materials into a series of units. It is easy enough to make lists of objectives and lesson plans to develop them over time, but the unpredictable nature of ninth graders makes any plan highly tentative. The rationale for *making* such plans is, of course, that it gives the teacher adequate command of his material so that changes of plans will not throw him for a loss. Carlson found in teaching the A.C.S.P. materials that he tended to rely too heavily on following the intricate lesson plans and suggestions uncritically, which means, of course, without reference to the particular students in front of him. Teachers not trained as anthropologists usually find them extremely helpful and rich in material. Carlson often found it profitable to abandon the form while retaining the essence of the A.C.S.P. materials; for all that, we all think these are the best prepared materials we know for teaching anthropology in secondary schools.

Our mode of teaching was based on what today's educators are calling "inductive principles" of "discovery." However, we found that ninth graders also have to be filled in; the teacher must allow himself, his information and opinions, and his character to be used as raw material for the discoveries of his students. "Filling in" is best done, in anthropology courses of this sort, by giving facts. The amount of theory that students need can be determined on a "demand" basis. Theoretical presentations should *follow* the facts if the maximum number of students are to gain some appreciation of theory. Stating a theoretical position and then illustrating it is probably poor pedagogy anywhere (except, perhaps, in graduate seminars that are about theory). Certainly it is bad pedagogy in the ninth grade. By the second semester our students had enough sense of theory to apply it to what they were studying and to demand more when they needed it, although certainly, sometimes we sensed the demand before they did. Obviously, the danger of the "inductive method" is that students may discover things that are either wrong or obsolete. This is an especially great risk in social studies.

Finally, we want to emphasize the vast profit that we ourselves got from teaching this course. We were, in a very real sense, daily driven to the wall. Fourteen-year-olds will not be put off with jargon and expertise. We hope that more of our colleagues will try such courses and that they too will discover that the learning that is part of every teaching experience was never more vivid and more fun than with good high-school students. The anthropological point of view is congenial to young people. Young people test the anthropologist's ingenuity and challenge his professional stereotypes.

References

Anthropology Curriculum Study Project, 1967, *Study of Early Man* and *The Great Transformation*. Chicago, Ill.: 5632 S. Kimbark Avenue.

Bohannan, Paul, 1964, *Africa and Africans*. New York: Natural History Press.

Bowen, Elenore Smith (Laura Bohannan), 1964, *Return to Laughter*. New York: Natural History Press.

Driver, Harold E., 1961, *Indians of North America*. Chicago: University of Chicago Press.

Drucker, Philip, 1963, *Indians of the Northwest Coast*. New York: Natural History Press.

Hertzberg, Hazel W., 1966, *The Great Tree and the Longhouse.* New York: The Macmillan Company.

Hoebel, E. Adamson, 1958, *Man in the Primitive World: An Introduction to Anthropology.* New York: McGraw-Hill Book Company.

Howell, F. Clark, and the Editors of *Life,* 1965, *Early Man.* New York: Time-Life Books.

Hsu, Francis L. K., 1953, *American and Chinese: Two Ways of Life.* New York: Schuman.

Kluckhohn, Clyde, and Dorothea Leighton, 1962, *The Navaho.* New York: Doubleday & Company.

Kroeber, Theodora, 1963, *Ishi in Two Worlds.* Berkeley and Los Angeles: University of California Press.

Marriott, Alice, 1945, *Ten Grandmothers.* Norman: University of Oklahoma Press.

Oliver, Douglas, 1964, *Invitation to Anthropology.* New York: Natural History Press.

Oswalt, Wendell H., 1965, *This Land Was Theirs: A Study of the North American Indian.* New York: John Wiley & Sons.

Spencer, Robert F., and Jesse D. Jennings, 1965, *The Native Americans.* New York: Harper & Row.

Spindler, George, and Louise Spindler, n.d., Case studies in cultural anthropology, continuing series. New York: Holt, Rinehart and Winston, Inc.

Sugimoto, Etsu, 1934, *Daughter of the Samurai.* New York: Doubleday & Company.

Thomas, Elizabeth Marshall, 1965, *The Harmless People.* New York: Random House.

Turnbull, Colin, 1961, *The Forest People.* New York: Simon & Schuster (Reprinted by Natural History Library, N 27).

GEORGE and LOUISE SPINDLER/*Stanford University*

28   *Teaching and Learning Anthropology: The Case Study Approach*

At the 84th annual meetings of the American Anthropological Association in Washington, D.C., December 1985, David P. Boynton, for 25 years the anthropology editor for Holt, Rinehart and Winston, was presented a Distinguished Service Award for the publication of the Case Studies in Cultural Anthropology. The award citation described this series as "revolutionizing the teaching of anthropology." As editors of this series since its inception in 1960, we intended that it should make a difference in the teaching of anthropology, but we were surprised and gratified to hear it described as "revolutionary" in its impact.

The series first emerged as an idea in the mid-1950's when we started teaching the introductory course in Cultural Anthropology at Stanford University. Course designs and textbooks available then seemed to us limited and stultifying. We adopted the case study approach in our own teaching before there were good case studies that we could assign to our students.* We made do with what was available, but began working toward the development of a series of relatively short and inexpensive paperbacks written for undergraduate students. We consulted with colleagues at the Center for Advanced Study in the Behavioral Sciences where we were Fellows in 1956-57, and at the Annual Meetings of the American Anthropological Association. Prominent anthropologists such as Alfred Kroeber, George Peter Murdock, A. Irving Hallowell, Margaret Mead, Clyde Kluckhohn, Morris Opler, and many others, helped us formulate our ideas about what the series should include and how it should be presented.

We proceeded to try to interest publishers, but none were stirred by our

---

*George Spindler, in 1978, was presented the Lloyd W. Dinkelspiel Award for Distinguished Contributions to Undergraduate Education at Stanford with a citation for "development of the case study method" in undergraduate instruction.

appeals excepting Dryden Press and a receptive representative, Howard Chandler. We acquired a contract allowing us to solicit and develop ten case studies, which we proceeded to do. Meanwhile Holt, Rinehart and Winston purchased Dryden Press and we began our productive collaboration with David Boynton. The first six case studies were published in 1960 and they are still in print. This relationship survived the purchase of Holt by CBS, Inc. and has produced to date 137 case studies. New ones are still coming out each year.

In 1967 we initiated another series, *Case Studies in Education and Culture*. Altogether this series included seventeen titles, of which several are still in print with Holt, and with Waveland Press, the publisher of this revision of *Education and Cultural Process* (See Hostetler and Huntington 1971, 1980; Rosenfeld 1984; Ward 1971; Wolcott 1967, 1973).

The success of the case studies series suggests that instructors of anthropology, and particularly of introductory anthropology, have accepted the case study principle in their teaching and organization of courses. Case studies may be used in a variety of course contexts and for a variety of purposes.

With this variety in mind, and with respect for it, we will present in this chapter our version of the place of case studies in the teaching of introductory anthropology at the college level. We believe that most of what we say is applicable to the teaching of anthropology in a high school. We use the approach in all of our courses, including the course in Cultural Transmission: Education in Cross-Cultural Perspective, that G. Spindler has taught at Stanford for as long as George and Louise Spindler have collaborated in the teaching of Anthropology 001 — since the mid-1950's — and at the University of Wisconsin since 1978. What we present here therefore can be viewed as a generic model applicable to many course contexts.

The Introductory Course in Sociocultural Anthropology

The beginning course is typically heterogeneous and often includes upper classsmen, but the model student is the proverbial college sophomore. The course is taught for the general education of college students rather than for anthropology majors. The primary goal is to enlarge the horizons of undergraduates, to open and broaden young minds. In this there seems to be widespread agreement. Some of the purposes of the introductory course in most places where it is given are to communicate: (1) a sense of the wide range and variability of human culture, (2) an apprciation of cultures (and societies) as holistic systems, (3) a respect for other ways of life and an understanding of ethnocentrism, (4) a perspective on one's own culture and insights into modern life through the application of anthropological concepts, (5) an awareness of the continuity of human life in long-term evolutionary perspective, (6) and finally, some conception of anthropology as a discipline.[1]

It seems that anthropologists are often more humanistically oriented in their introductory course than in their advanced courses or in their professional research. Even our most tough-minded colleagues turn humanistic in purpose, though not necessarily in method, in the beginning course. The same trend is apparent when anthropologists address themselves to the lay public. Perhaps when the image of anthropology is shaped for non-anthropologists we penetrate to the most fundamental values of our discipline.

While there may be widespread agreement on goals there is a variety of methods used to reach them. If we focus upon that portion of the introductory course concerned with cultural anthropology, we find several different models for the organization of subject matter. We will mention three.[2]

Type 1

The first considers various aspects of culture such as technology, economy, social organization, government, religion, and language. Most of the courses as well as the majority of anthropology textbooks seem to be based upon this form of organization. Ethnographic data are utilized from several cultures to illustrate and document generalizations advanced by the lecturer. For example, the instructor wishes to discuss the relationship between subsistence techniques, size of population aggregate, and systems of social control. He* utilizes segments of illustrative data from nomadic hunting and gathering societies like the Arunta, Eskimo, and Northern Ojibwa, and contrasts these situations with agricultural, sedentary communities, as in traditional East African kingdoms. The procedure is essentially deductive. The conclusions are presented first, then data are found to support them. Most of the data must be decontextualized in order to use it this way.

Type 2

Another form of organization deals with different types of societies in a developmental sequence. The goal of the course is to communicate an understanding of the evolution of culture in general as well as of the growth of particular aspects of culture and their interrelationships. For example, the transition from food-gathering to food-production is a technological change but its full significance emerges only from a consideration of the consequences of the shift for the organization of society. Both archaelogical and

---

[1]Though this list was developed long before the special issue on the teaching of anthropology appeared in the *Anthropology and Education Quarterly* (Rice 1985), it parallels purposes stated by the authors of papers in this volume.

[2]Characterizations of the introductory course as taught elsewhere than Stanford are based upon market research conducted through Holt, Rinehart and Winston as we attempted to find out in what course contexts the case studies were used.

*To avoid the appearance of chauvanism we will alternate "he" and "she."

ethnographic data are utilized, but not usually in the form of whole culture cases. Segments of culture are selected from a variety of areas to illustrate points of general importance in the evolutionary framework.

Type 3

The third type is a course on the nature of culture and may include such topics as cultural relativism, culture as supraorganic, cultural structure, cultural transmission, cultural change, cognition and culture, culture as patterned symbols, and culture as an adaptation to the conditions of survival. Such a course emphasizes theory. Ethnographic data are de-emphasized in favor of the conceptual orientation of the instructor to the nature of culture.

We think that each of these three types of organization can be used to teach successful courses, but that they often contradict and defeat the very goals that anthropologists declare for the introductory course. The problem is that they approach communication directly. Instructors who use them usually assume, it seems, that the systematic understandings they wish to produce in the students' heads can be put there by telling the student what they are. They must also assume that the student does not need to go through the same learning process they, the teachers, went through in order to arrive at the structuring of concepts. The student is conceived of as being emotionally and intellectually passive. He or she is waiting to be told.[3]

And he *is* told. The generalization comes first, then facts are selected to support it. The inductive process through which the generalizations were initially created gets lost. The student does not learn a new way of thinking. She learns how to survive the course.

The organizational type we wish to present we term the *inductive-case-study approach*, though there are both inductive and deductive elements. Culture case studies selected for their representation of cultural types are presented to the student in a variety of way. These culture cases are described in lectures, films are run, records and tapes are used, discussions are held. The goal is to communicate to the student a complex, lively picture of the whole way of life. And this picture cannot be entirely conceptual, because no way of life is wholly conceptual. The material must have some emotional impact. The student must feel as well as think in order to understand any human culture. Vivid dramatized presentations are in order. Films and records or tapes become particularly important. Well-written treatments of whole cultures are very important, and we have tried to supply them in our case study series.

But these case studies must be given significance. Though the information acquired about several culture cases, without generalization or systematic conceptualization, will sometimes cause more or less valid inferences to be produced in the student's mind—he should have some help. But this help proceeds inductively. As the student's exposure to cultural diversity grows he

---

[3]Some very interesting alternative course models are presented in Rice (1985).

can be helped to group the facts and impressions received into a coherent but always tentative cognitive structure. Rather than starting with conclusions both student and teacher start with case data and shared experience. To be sure, the teacher has a structure in mind. She has selected beforehand the culture cases with generalizations in mind that she wishes to reach inductively with the student. But this is the nature of the teacher's role — to withhold and inform: to help the student do what she, the teacher, has already done, to re-create experience; not pre-digest and encapsulate it.

Teachers who elect this organizational approach must be prepared for certain hardships. Confusion grows as the diversity of cases presented increases and the tight conceptual organization usually imposed on subject matter in university and college courses fails to materialize. Students are not accustomed to doing inductive reasoning. They have been presented with the neatly packaged consumer goods of standardized courses too often. Confusion continues until a certain point is reached where the accumulating generalizations and understandings begin to make the still-coming culture cases comprehensible. Then enthusiasm and interest mount rapidly and most students preserve their sense of discovery within a framework of developing analytic powers to the end of the course. We test these powers by requiring a take-home essay in which students analyze two or more cultures, using case studies as primary sources, in response to a problem chosen by them from several possibilities supplied by us. The end-of-course evaluations written about the course over the years by students have been very enthusiastic.

As such an approach must actually be implemented in the classroom discussion group, or lecture hall, the teacher is necessarily eclectic in the use of methods and techniques. Aspects of all of the organizational approaches we have mentioned are combined. But one starts with different assumptions about communication, and the course is centered differently.

The instructor who uses the case study approach assumes that one does not teach a student how to think about behavior and process by simply telling him what he, the teacher, has already decided as the result of his own thinking (or that of his preceptors!). He assumes that a student must learn how to think by experiencing the process of thinking. Therefore he tries to recreate for each new crop of students the vital conditions of learning — new stimuli, guidance to their understanding, and atmosphere of experiment.

The instructor also assumes that learning, at least learning about human cultures, must occur empathetically and emotionally as well as conceptually or cognitively. Actually the two, the so-called emotional and so-called intellectual, are never separate in any learning. Some students, for example, are learning to dislike anthropology at the same time they are learning the encapsulated facts and abstract concepts of anthropology.

Because the instructor makes these assumptions she centers the course structure on case materials and then gropes, or at least seems to grope with the students, towards systematized understandings and generalizations. This groping is inductive because the facts and experience of facts are antecedent to generalization, not subsequent. But the teacher must actually be deductive at times, when he searches back into the accumulated cases for support for an emerging generalization. And his criteria for what it is important to arrive at in the grouping of materials and inferences into generalizations must be derived in part from his own systematized conceptualization of the field, and in part from his own intuitive feel for the facts—for the stuff of culture and human behavior.

The teacher must have a cognitive map of where she is heading if she is going to take her students over circuitous inductive routes to get there.

How this map is drawn will depend upon the individual anthropologist. The ordering should consist of several "master", or "core" ideas around which interpretations, hypotheses, and facts may be grouped. These are not topics with finalized content. They are idea-orientations that make it possible to coordinate diverse facts within a flexible framework.

In our particular order the master ideas are the following:

I. The emergence of human culture in the perspective of non-human primate behavior.

II. The diversity of human cultures and cultural relativism.

III. The common denominators of human cultures and "human nature".

IV. The organization of cultural systems.

V. The transmission of culture to new members of society.

VI. Culture as a system of self-sustaining beliefs and commitments.

VII. The defensive structuring of human communities; ethnocentrism and war.

VIII. The dynamic adaptations of cultures to changing conditions of survival.

IX. The relevance of a cross-cultural perspective for understanding one's own culture.

Any list of idea-orientations is likely to communicate little. One might ask, for example, "where is social organization covered?" The answer is that it is covered inductively under several of these headings. Social organization, for example, can be seen as a significant dimension of the organization of cultural systems but can also be an aspect of every other idea category. Social organization is relevant, for instance, to the transmission of culture to new members of the group, since the roles and statuses provided by the social system determine who transmits what aspects of culture to whom with what sanctions.

Implementation

The implementation of any design for the introductory course must be a process of constant experimentation and adaptation. As any teacher knows, each class is somewhat different and develops a momentum of its own as the quarter or semester proceeds. This is particularly true of groups under fifty, where personal interaction between instructor and students creates a self-sustaining pattern of discovery and reinforcement as ideas and data new to students are presented, and students in turn produce ideas and interpretations, sometimes even data, new to the instructor. In larger groups of 100 and up, the process is less one of interaction than of transmission on a one-way channel. Nevertheless the teacher gets cues from students concerning what is happening with them—through their attitudes and mannerisms in the lecture hall, from personal consultations, and particularly through at least occasional contact with smaller discussion groups. The experiment-minded instructor also approaches his or her own material in somewhat different ways each time the course is given, and new patterns of ideation and communication suggest themselves as the course gains momentum.

When one of the three logico-deductive organizational approaches is used it is usually possible to work out, before the semester starts, a tight schedule of topics to be covered and the specific sequence and times assigned to them. The structure is imposed upon the material from a finalized conceptual framework. The range of possible experimentation is correspondingly narrow.

When an inductive-case-study approach is used, maximum flexibility in scheduling must be preserved. The latitude of possible experimentation is correspondingly of maximum breadth, and predictability is at a minimum. We center our predictive organization on the cases we plan to present. For example, we schedule our films for the whole course beforehand. The possibilities of inductive inference from rich case material seem virtually unlimited. New ideas keep springing up out of the material as the instructor tries to recreate for students the inductive search for generalizations. Under conditions of maximum interaction between teacher and students the former will frequently be surprised at the vitality and worth of inferential thinking by the latter.

With the inductive-case-study approach we have found that use of a regular textbook is destructive. The highly explicit conceptual ordering of most textbooks inhibits the inductive process because the student reads the generalizations before he has had time to infer any from the case materials, so the inductive process simply stops. Why go to all that trouble when the answers are already available? We suspect that most textbooks create problems in most courses, irrespective of the approach used. Most represent the end-results of analysis, and not the *process* of analysis. Some instructors use them because they are insecure about what should be taught. Others use them to cover topics they, the instructors, will not cover. Whatever the reason, textbooks are not, in our opinion, good instructional materials and we have never used one in our more than three decades of teaching introductory anthropology.

The use of films, slides, and tapes—the so-called "audio-visual aids"— is crucial to good communication, irrespective, we think, of the organizational approach employed, but it is particularly germane to the inductive-case-study approach. Students seem to acquire information more quickly, retain it longer and think about it more effectively when they have a sensory and emotional picture as well as a cognitive map of a culture or of any part of a culture. We are fortunate that today we have a wide range of excellent ethnographic films to choose from (Heider, 1983). It was not always so. Each week of the course, we have a film one day. The showings are coordinated with both lectures and culture case readings. In all instances we provide substantial ethnographic and culture area orientation before the film is shown. There are a number of case studies in our series that can be coupled with existing films, such as the Yanomamo (Chagnon), Dani (Heider), Hutterites, and Amish (Hostetler and Huntington), !Kung (Lee), Mardudjara (Tonkinson).

To Summarize

The basic difficulty, as we see it, with the introductory course, is that the instructor often draws from his professional repertoire the generalizations about culturally variant human behavior that he feels are valid on the basis of his training and experience without much regard for the fact that beginning students do not go through any of the experiences he, the instructor, has gone through to arrive at the generalizations or a feeling for their validity. The instructor presents lectures on the family, social organization, ecology, religion, symbolism, etc., drawing illustrations from a variety of unrelated cases that she knows about but the students do not. Everything is formulated for the student. The instructor knows, and the student doesn't. Everything has an air of finality—even with respect to issues current in the field that the instructor mentions but rarely treats in depth. So why should the student get excited? Everything is known, finalized, certain, but the student never finds out how it all got known; nor does he or she find out much about human behavior. What has been presented are abstractions—out of context either in terms of their intellectual or their situational derivation. They are supported by bits and pieces of a number of cultures and students never experience a whole culture.

We have reversed the procedure. Cases are presented in as many different dimensions and in as many different ways as our ingenuity and available materials permit. We try to present the material in a way analogous to learning about a culture in the field—without much abstracted interpretation—at least during the first half of the course. During this period students confess that they are confused, sometimes bewildered. They expect neat topical categories and final conclusions. They "don't know what to take notes on". Sometimes they get angry because they are not being given a highly ordered, systematic overview of anthropology as a discipline.

As the students gain in knowledge of particular cases, we begin to group generalizations out of the case data. When social organization, warfare, or cultural transmission are discussed, for example, the illustrative material comes out of cases they already know in detail. All generalizations are presented as tentative, and an attempt is made to keep them flexible and open-ended, so that sometimes the "generalizations" assume unexpected forms — the instructor actually comes to new conclusions because the case data are being analyzed on the spot. The student is caught up in the analytic process with the instructor. He or she experiences some of what the professional anthropologist experiences in the acquisition of knowledge about human cultures and its interpretation.

Of course the instructor has to have some clear idea of where he or she wants to go. We operate with several "master" or orienting ideas — or conceptual categories. Emerging generalizations concerning culturally patterned and influenced behavior are grouped within these rubrics — but *not in a predetermined order or sequence*. Frequently a particular discussion will engage with aspects of behavior falling in all of these rubrics.

Anthropology is no exception to the generalization that the worst teaching is done at the college and university level. But anthropologists are truly fortunate in that their subject is inherently interesting and colorful as well as important. If they make even fumbling attempts to improve communication they will invoke this rich potential in a significant degree. We think the way to go is to use a case study approach. Our colleagues are quite capable of developing new approaches to the use of case studies that have not occurred to us.

References

Chagnon, Napoleon, 1983, *Yanomamo: The Fierce People.* 3/e New York: Holt, Rinehart and Winston.

Heider, Carl, 1979, *Grand Valley Dani: Peaceful Warriors. ibid.*

———, 1983, "Films for Anthropological Teaching." 7th ed. Special publication of the *American Anthropological Association* #16.

Hostetler, John and Gertrude Huntington, 1980, *The Hutterites of North America,* Fieldwork Edition. New York: Holt, Rinehart and Winston.

———, 1971, *Children in Amish Society, Socialization and Community Education.* ibid.

Lee, Richard B., 1984, *The Dobe !Kung. ibid.*

Rice, Patricia C., 1985, *Anthropology and Education Quarterly,* 16.4 250-317.

Rosenfeld, Gerry, 1971 (Reissued 1984), *"Shut Those Thick Lips": A Study of Slum School Failure.* Prospect Heights, IL: Waveland Press.

Tonkinson, Robert, 1977, *The Mardudjara Aborigines: Society and Spirit in a Desert Culture.* New York: Holt, Rinehart and Winston.

Ward, Martha C., 1977, reissued 1986, *Them Children: A Study in Language Learning.* Prospect Heights, IL: Waveland Press.

Wolcott, Harry, 1967, reissued 1984, *A Kwakiutl Village and School.* Prospect Heights, IL: Waveland Press.

———, 1973, reissued with changes 1984, *Man in the Principal's Office.* ibid.